SILENT WARRIORS
Submarine Wrecks of the United Kingdom

SILENT WARRIORS
Submarine Wrecks of the United Kingdom

VOLUME ONE

RON YOUNG & PAMELA ARMSTRONG

TEMPUS

Frontispiece: Submariners from a 'C' Class boat chatting to local fisher girls on the Tyne, South Shields, 1916. (Courtesy of South Tyneside Metropolitan Borough Council)

First published 2006

Tempus Publishing Limited
The Mill, Brimscombe Port,
Stroud, Gloucestershire, GL5 2QG
www.tempus-publishing.com

British Library Cataloguing in Publication Data.
A catalogue record for this book is available from the British Library.

ISBN 0 7524 3876 X

Typesetting and origination by Tempus Publishing Limited
Printed in Great Britain

CONTENTS

The memorial to the crew of HM S/M E30 in Blyth,
Northumberland carries this inscription:

'They that go down to the sea in ships that do business in great waters,
these see the works of the Lord and his wonders of the deep.'

And it is to these men, the submariners of both nations,
on patrol for eternity, that this book is respectfully dedicated.

INTRODUCTION

For two World Wars German and British navies waged fierce submarine war. British coastal waters were transformed into a pitiless arena where a deadly struggle was played out between U-boats trying to close the sea-lanes, and Allied warships determined to keep them open. This is the story of the submarines that failed to make it home, in both war and peace, but that remain for eternity as the silent warriors of the British coast. It is a story told, wherever possible, in the words of those who were present:

THE SONG OF THE SUBMARINE
I roam the seas from Scapa Flow to the Bight of Heligoland –
In the Dover Strait I lie in wait –
On the edge of the Goodwin Sand
I am here and there and everywhere,
Like the phantom in a dream
And I sing Ho! Ho!
Through the winds that blow
The song of the submarine.

Anon

FOREWORD
BY DR AXEL NIESTLÉ OF DABENDORF, GERMANY

For a long time, recreational divers and naval historians had almost nothing in common. Technical limits from diving gear previously restricted recreational divers to comparatively shallow waters close to the shoreline, which usually had not seen much naval action. Instead, naval history was written at military academies, universities or private offices, using official documents or oral recordings stored at archives or other places. In cases where contemporary records are lacking or incomplete, the precision in the accounts on naval actions or operations often decreased markedly and confirmed truth was replaced by various degrees of guesswork. Of course, it was not ill will on the part of the historians, but a simple lack of information which sometimes led them to dreadful distortions in the narrative of historical events. The operational history of the German U-boat campaign around the British islands during both World Wars in the twentieth century offers a splendid example of this. With a high percentage of U-boats lost with all hands and official records often destroyed or lost to wartime action, documentation of the German part necessarily remained fragmentary. Not surprisingly also, the final fate of many U-boats lost in British coastal waters remained obscure or without proof.

However, in recent times naval history increasingly benefited from the discoveries and information forwarded by the ever-growing number of recreational divers, now perfectly equipped to explore the seabed down to depths that were previously out of reach. Sixty years after the Second World War, many of the wartime wrecks are still preserved in surprisingly good condition. Therefore diving offers a completely new source of additional historic information for naval historians. Taking into account the various problems encountered in reaching a correct assessment of anti-submarine actions, the simple discovery of a U-boat wreck in a certain place can already offer great help in the evaluation of individual attacks. With both divers and historians interested in identifying wrecks, a mutual basis for cooperation is presented. Wreck exploration by experienced divers combined with the expertise of historians has already resulted in numerous wreck identifications over recent years and a more precise understanding of events that would otherwise be left obscured in the shadows of history.

Ron Young and Pamela Armstrong are providing a highly welcome encyclopaedia on charted and recorded U-boat and submarine wrecks around Britain, combining detailed historical information on the individual vessels and their final fate with a fresh account on the present condition of the wreck if it has been located and examined by divers. Meticulously giving the archive sources for the information provided on the subject, readers are entitled to further check or crosscheck the details presented on the subject. With a fair number of recorded submarine wrecks still unlocated today, the book should also be taken as a guide to plan future diving expeditions. The large number of naval sailors who perished or went missing aboard the many submarine vessels now laying strewn on the seabed around Britain, deserve to have their final fates and resting places correctly recorded for their ancestors and history. However, divers should never forget that many of the wrecks are now official war graves and should be treated with decent respect.

FOREWORD

BY MICHAEL LOWREY OF CHARLOTTE, NC, USA

In the First World War, 152 or so German submarines were lost in operations in the North Sea, or around the British Isles, many quite close to the British shore, especially around Dover and Folkestone. While the fate and location of many of these losses were positively established during the war, a substantial number simply disappeared; with today's technology, they can be, and are being, located.

And therein, as several recent cases prove, lies a problem; all too often naval history and wrecks are discussed separately. Attempts are made to identify newly discovered wrecks with an inadequate understanding of First World War submarine operations. At the same time, wreck discoveries, typically, have not made it into history books.

Ron Young and Pamela Armstrong's book on the silent warriors is an attempt to change that. By combining difficult-to-obtain information, including casualty lists, patrol details, and lists of ships sunk – all in one location – it provides the reader with a level of detail that has previously been virtually impossible to obtain in English. Their book also reflects the latest wreck discoveries, both along the English coast and elsewhere, and the very newest theories to explain what happened. At the same time, it contains considerable detail about the state of the wrecks themselves, providing much useful information to divers.

While it is almost certain that our knowledge of First World War U-boats will continue to improve over time, the basic blocks found in this book allow for such discoveries to be easily placed in their proper context.

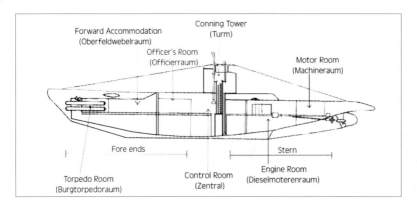

Forward Accommodation
(Oberfeldwebelraum)

Conning Tower
(Turm)

Officer's Room
(Officierraum)

Motor Room
(Machineraum)

Fore ends

Stern

Torpedo Room
(Burgtorpedoraum)

Control Room
(Zentral)

Engine Room
(Dieselmoterenraum)

Diagram of a
basic generic
submarine.

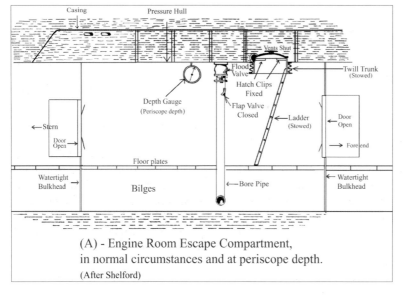

Casing   Pressure Hull

Vents Shut

Flood
Valve

Twill Trunk
(Stowed)

Hatch Clips
Fixed

Depth Gauge
(Periscope depth)

Flap Valve
Closed

Ladder
(Stowed)

Door
Open

← Stern

Door
Open

→ Fore end

Floor plates

Watertight
Bulkhead

Bilges

← Bore Pipe

Watertight
Bulkhead

(A) - Engine Room Escape Compartment,
in normal circumstances and at periscope depth.
(After Shelford)

Diagram
of engine
room escape
compartment,
in normal
circumstances
and at periscope
depth. (After
Shelford)

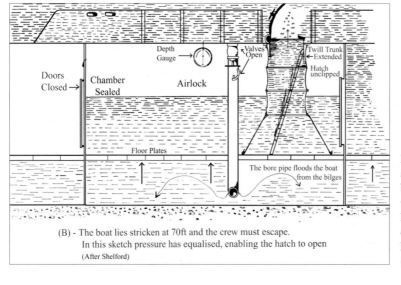

Depth
Gauge

Valves
Open

Twill Trunk
← Extended

Hatch
unclipped

Doors
Closed →

Chamber
Sealed

Airlock

Floor Plates

The bore pipe floods the boat
from the bilges

(B) - The boat lies stricken at 70ft and the crew must escape.
In this sketch pressure has equalised, enabling the hatch to open
(After Shelford)

Diagram showing
a stricken
boat lying at
70ft. Pressure
has equalised,
enabling the
hatch to open.
(After Shelford)

ACKNOWLEDGEMENTS

THE AUTHORS OWE A GREAT DEAL OF THANKS TO THE FOLLOWING
PEOPLE AND ORGANISATIONS:

Nelson McEachan, June Dillon and the staff at the UK Hydrographic Office, Taunton.

Michael Lowrey of Charlotte, North Carolina, USA: lecturer, author, naval historian, researcher and world authority on First World War U-boats.

Dr Axel Niestlé of Dabendorf, Germany; naval historian, author, researcher and world authority on Second World War U-boats.

Brian D. Head, Lt-Cdr, RD★, RNR (Rtd): Submarine Museum Committee chairman and First World War British submarine expert.

Dennis Feary: RN Submarine Museum volunteer. Dennis's father was Petty Officer E.W. Feary, coxswain of HM S/M H49, lost off Holland in 1940. With his mother having already 'passed on', Dennis, aged four years at the time, was then looked after by the Naval Orphanage in Waterlooville and Swanley Naval School until he was fifteen years old. Research on his father later brought him to the Royal Navy Submarine Museum as a volunteer and, with others, he formed a group called 'The Archive Working Party' R.N.S.M. They 'looked up' what the regular staff did not have the time to do. With Brian D. Head as the chairman, the group still helps with archiving material and anything else they are asked to do. Dennis is updating crew names and the Memorial Book in the museum – hence the work is on-going.

John Eade of Perth, Western Australia. John was born in Barking, Essex, in 1946 and spent many years living on the Isle of Wight before moving to Australia. Unfortunately MND forced early retirement from the crane and heavy haulage industry. John spends most of his time researching maritime history, especially in the Royal Navy Submarine Service.

Yves Dufeil of Martigues, France: author and First World War U-boat and maritime researcher.

Paul de Keijzer of Cederlaan, Holland: diver and shipwreck researcher.

Dave Alton: production operator on North Sea Gas Platform, HM S/M D5 information.

Brian Viglietti of Buffalo, New York State: HM S/M D5 information.

Terry Whalebone, Bolton: maritime historian and researcher.

Ian Spokes: author of *The 1901 Great Storm*, maritime historian and shipwreck researcher.

Billy McGee: maritime historian and ship's crew researcher.

Roger Hollywood: maritime historian and researcher.

Andy Mair for the additional information on HM S/M *Truculent* patrols.

Dave Patrick in Australia for 'J' Class boat information.

Bill and Eva Ternström-Lidbetter-Sessions; SS *Ada*'s last voyage in 1917.

Steven Charles for information on U 1063.

Paul Geof Oliver of Whitstable; Channel wreck diver.

Andy Nye; owner and skipper of Taurus Diving at Dover.

Klaus-Peter Pohland; German U-boat researcher.

Jürgen Meyer-Brenkhof; Fregattenkapitän (commander in German Navy with thirty-four years active service), for information about Rudolph Wieser and translating Rudi's letters.

Rudolph Wieser: Matrosenobergefreite and survivor of U 1195.

Ian Smythe, Edmonton, Canada, for his photos of the rescue of crewmen from U 1209 by HMCS *Ribble*. His father was Stoker J.E. Smythe from Edmonton, Alberta, and served on *Ribble* from its commissioning in July 1944 until it was decommissioned in June 1945.

Bruce Barr of Dunstaffnage Marine Laboratory, Oban.

Mr Harold Bennett, The Museum, Chatham Dockyard Historical Society.

Rainer Bruns: U-boat researcher.

Ray of Kirklees Sub Aqua Club 0836.

Colin Armstrong.

Jan-Olof Hendig of Sweden: ship researcher.

Maurice Voss.

Kendall McDonald of *DIVER* magazine and author.

Wayne Acourt.

Paul Sutton.

Gillian Hughes.

Sandra and Peter Gradwell.

Oliver Meise of Marburg, Germany: on-line *Dive* magazine, Taucher.net.

Matt Storey.

Ray and Mary Smith of Sunderland; Ray's brother died on HM S/M *Sidon*.

Dave Howell.

Davie McClymont.

Jöm Jensen.

Pat and Ian Forbes.

René Alloin: French ship researcher.

Theodor Dorgeist of Westfalen Freiberuflicher: maritime historian and researcher.

David Parkinson.

Dave Barlow.

www.wargraves.org.uk

Mr Heinz Thois: chairman of U-boat Memorial Foundation Council.

Herr Karl Schmeink and the Kiel U-boat Comrades Association.

The Bremen U-Boat Comrades Association.

Axel Van Eesbreek from Much, Germany.

Richard Driver from USA.

George Malcolmson and the staff of the RN Submarine Museum.

Klaus-Peter Pohland of Gaillon, France.

Howard Cock and the enthusiastic guys who run http://www.ubootwaffe.net.

Hubertus Weggelar.

Alain Croce.

Captain W.L. Hume, M.N.I. (Retired) Cowes, Isle of Wight.

Newcastle Central Library.

South Shields Library.

Sander Kingsepp.

Jean Michel Forsans of Marseille: ship researcher.

The Mitchell Library, Glasgow.

Tyne Wear Archive.

The Barrow Branch of the Submariners Association.

Siri Holm Lawson of www.warsailors.com

Portree Library.

Bob Baird; Scottish maritime researcher and author.

Special thanks to Bob Jolley for the diving and wreck reports on UB 41 and UB 75.

Also thanks to Steve Old for the wreck GPS co-ordinates for UB 41 and UB 75.

Interviews carried out with the following British veterans by Pamela Armstrong: ex-TI Bill Treble (*Umpire*), ex-Cera Rob Roy McCurrach (*Unity*, *Safari*), ex-CPO Bernard Cranmer (*Sealion*), ex-Cera Ernie Buckingham, ex-CPO Raymond Fry and Signalman Gus Britton (*Truculent*). Stoker Con McCabe (*Sturgeon*), Stoker Taff Harper (*Seal*).

David Asprey: ship researcher.

Volksbund Deutsche Kriegsgräberfürsorge.

Commonwealth War Graves Commission.

Karl-J. Schmeink, Webmaster.

Alan Roberts.

Rolf Kristensen, Åsgårdstrand, Norway.

Mats Karlsson, Köping, Sweden.

Torsten Hagnéus, Vastra Frolunda, Sweden.

Arie Visser, Holland.

Oliver Lörscher: ship and U-boat researcher.

Thanks to Carl Racey and Andy Jackson for help with the wreck details of UB 30.

Adrian Vicary for ship photographs.

Trevor Hallifax, originally from Grimsby, but now resides in Ash Vale, near Aldershot.

Mikael Svensson, Museiassistent/Assistant, Göteborg, Maritime Museum, Sweden.

Rose Young, for proofreading the book.

GLOSSARY

A/S	Anti-Submarine
AA	Anti-Aircraft
Aal	German slang for torpedo (eel)
AB	Able Seaman
AEG	Allgemeine Elektricittäts-Gesellschaft – German electric motors manufacturer
AF	Accumlatoren Fabrik – U-boat battery and parts manufacturers
AFA	Accumlatoren-Fabrik-Aktiengesellshcaft – German battery manufacturers
Aft	Towards the stern of a boat/ship
Agrufront	(*Ausbildungsgruppe für Front-U-Boote*) – training group for Front U-boats, or unit for training submarines to be used operationally
Ahead	In a forward direction
AK	*Ausserste Kraft* – highest speed available
Alberich	Two 2mm layers of a black rubbery anti-sonar substance called Alberich, which was named after the dwarf in Wagner's 'Ring Circle'. The dwarf wore a helmet of invisibility and the substance was meant to do the same for the submarine. As the boat travelled through the water, the stuff oscillated slightly and was meant to shield the boat against ASDIC, by confusing the sound beams.
Amidships/midships	In or towards the centre of the ship/boat
Ammo	Ammunition
Approaching aircraft	Were indicated by interruptions on a line displayed on the cathode ray tubeoscilloscope. From August 1943 the *Wanz* sets replaced *Metox*.
ASCO	Anti-Submarine Control Officer – responsible for working a ship's anti-submarine weapons, usually providing technical advice when required
ASDIC	Anti-Submarine Detection Investigation Committee – a British term for underwater acoustic detection equipment. In effect, an instrument used to detect submarines by transmitting an acoustic pulse in water and measuring distance by recording the time taken for the echo of the pulse to return. The full implications of ASDIC meant that, by 1945, it was a totally automatic killing machine! The American term is SONAR.

The overwhelming majority of Second World War U-boats featured in this book were first detected by ASDIC. ASDIC was housed in a dome, under the hull of an anti-submarine vessel or a submarine. In active mode it transmitted a narrow beam of sound in the form of a series of impulses, which produced a 'ping' or echo from any solid object detected within a maximum range of 3,000 yards from the transmitter. The signal thus produced could enable a skilled operator to deduce the accurate range and bearing of a U-boat. ASDIC could be used passively in hydrophone mode to detect propeller noise. In this mode it could detect bearing but not range.

ASDIC could be baffled by the sound of rushing water (if the hunting ship steamed at more than eighteen knots), differing water densities, by wrecks, a rocky seabed and by shrimps/prawns making their habitual clicking noise.

From August 1944 British warships were fitted with two ASDIC sets: '144-5Q' and '147B'.

144-5Q consisted of:

A range recorder – providing an echo plot,

A bearing recorder – speed and course to be followed,

Automatic control training gear – both the helmsman's gear and the captain's bearing instruments were connected to the ASDIC sets. In effect, the hunting warship was steered automatically by the ASDIC gear.

147B consisted of:

A depth oscillator.

A depth recorder – automatic depth plotter.

144-5Q was used, in general, for obtaining initial contact, determining course to steer, then time to fire. 147B detected the depth of the target. The Depth Charge Pattern Control System delivered the *coup de grace* by means of automatic firing of projectiles.

ASV Air-to-surface radar installed in Allied aircraft from 1942. From 1942 the Germans began fitting *FuMB Metox* R600 radar detector sets in the boats, to warn of approaching aircraft.

ASW Anti-submarine warfare

AUDs Deliberations of the Anti-submarine Assessment Committee which can be found in the National Archive, Kew, London. The AUD Committee would judge the submarine sinking claim on the evidence provided.

Ausbildungsboot Training boat

Auxiliary Patrol In 1914 the commitments faced by the Royal Navy saw it stretched as never before and, on 4 August 1914, British trawlers were barred from the fishing grounds, in order to make them available for naval service in auxiliary duties. The auxiliary patrol bore the brunt of anti-submarine patrols in British coastal waters, thus freeing the RN for more specialised tasks. A total of 5,000 trawlers and drifters were actively engaged, one quarter of them in dangerous minesweeping duties. Trawlers were fitted with surplus naval 6 or 3-pounder guns, but often these guns could not be properly elevated or depressed; the training given to the crews was also as rudimentary as their armament. Nevertheless, what the auxiliary patrolmen lacked in skill, they made up for in enthusiasm, although discipline was a problem: fishermen did not take too kindly to the King's Regulations.

The primary function of the auxiliary anti-submarine patrol was to keep U-boats submerged, driving them into minefields, or alerting escorts or minesweepers to their presence. At the outbreak of war the British coast was divided into twenty-one patrol areas. The essential unit of each patrol was the trawler section, typically four trawlers serving under the command of a retired RN officer on a steam yacht. The yacht officers would be drawn from the RNR, and their expertise was often augmented by a sprinkling of trained RN gunners. Unless involved in a special operation, the trawlers tended to retain their peacetime crews. By the summer of 1918, the availability of potent depth charges, serviceable hydrophones and fast motorboats, all added to the efficiency of the auxiliary patrols. By the end of hostilities this improvised navy had shown its worth: by the end of hostilities, 39,000 of British fishermen (49 per cent) were engaged in naval patrols and 2,000 auxiliary patrolmen had died on active service.

In the Second World War, Sparrow's Nest, Lowestoft, Suffolk, became the central depot of the Royal Naval Patrol Service, which took over where the old Auxiliary Patrol had left off. HMS *Europa* was the administrative headquarters for a force of 70,000 men, crewing 6,000 ships, which ranged from trawlers, drifters, motor fishing vessels and motor launches, to motor minesweepers and requisitioned vessels. Submarine hunting was now largely left to the Escort Groups, but the RNPS carried out the largely unsung, but nevertheless crucial, role of keeping the sea-lanes around Britain free from mines. Interestingly, the badge of the RNPS depicts a shark (symbolising a U-boat) pierced by a javelin.

Baubelehrung	The period before commissioning, when the crew made themselves familiar with their new boat
BBC	Brown, Boveri & Cie – German electric motor manufacturer
B-Dienst	*Beobachtungsdienst* – the German wireless observation service
BdU	*Befehlshaber der U-Boote* – Commander-in-Chief of Submarines, being Karl Dönitz from 19 September 1939
Beam	The greatest width of the boat/ship
BEM	British Empire Medal
Billet	British submarine patrol zone
Binnacle	Compass housing
Blowers	Precious compressed air was used sparingly. Once ballast tanks had been blown and the boat had reached a state of neutral buoyancy, the compressed air was turned off and fans known as blowers were used to rid the boat of excess water
BM	Royal Humane Society's Bronze Medal – for saving life at sea
Bold	An ASDIC decoy ejected by U-boats and known to the British as SBT – Submarine Bubble Target. Each *Bold* canister

contained a mixture of calcium and zinc. The round canister was ejected from a reloadable mechanism adjacent to the stern torpedo (known officially as *Rohr 6*, or more irreverently by the crew as the *Pillenwerfer* or pill-chucker). A hydrostatic valve on the canister controlled the entry of saltwater. Five to ten minutes after ejection, a mass of hydrogen bubbles would be produced. To the ASDIC operator on a British A/S vessel, this mass bore every resemblance to a dived U-boat travelling on a steady course. Thus the hunters would be duped into attacking a mass of bubbles, while their real prey made its escape, see 'Doppler'.

Boot	Boat – the submarine. Submariners of all nations tend to regard calling a submarine a 'ship' or a 'sub' to be deeply offensive. A submarine has one deck. It is therefore a boat.
Bordfliegerstaffel	An aviation squadron that served aboard a ship, because many cruisers and battleships carried seaplanes during the Second World War
Bow	The forward part of the boat/ship
Bridge	The location from which a vessel is steered and its speed controlled
Bugtorpedoraum or *'Bugraum'*	The fore-end torpedo chamber of a U-boat
Bulkhead	A vertical partition separating compartments
Bunting Tosser	Submarine slang for signalman
Camel	Hawser-equipped lifting vessel used in salvage operations
Can Opener	Royal Navy slang describing a routine practice carried out following a submarine 'kill'. Admiralty demanded incontrovertible proof of the destruction of a U-boat. General service responded by targeting a suspected U-boat wreck with a barrage of depth charges, sufficient to shatter the casing with a view to 'liberating' human remains.
Casing	The outer protective skin of a submarine, free-flooding in many places
Cdr	Commander
C-in-C	Commander in Chief
cm	Centimetre
Coaming	A vertical piece around the edge of a cockpit, hatch, etc to prevent water on deck from running below
CO	Commanding Officer
Co.	Company
Control Room	The nerve centre of a submarine corresponding to the German *zentrale*
cyl.	Cylinder
DEMS	Defence Equipped Merchant Ship – army or navy gunners attached to merchant ships
DSEA	Davis Submerged Escape Apparatus – closed circuit breathing set (based on the Fleuss-Davis breathing set) patented in 1929. The set was standard British escape apparatus from 1932 to 1951 (see PP).
DBS	Distressed British Seamen
DC	Depth Charge – the story of the depth charge in the First World War is given on p.265. In the Second World War the

British relied on the old Mark VII depth charge fitted with a pistol to guard against premature detonation. Each canister contained 300lb of amatol. In the early stages of the war, six depth settings were provided between 50ft and 500ft. The depth charge was normally discharged in patterns of five – three from rails at the stern at a spacing of 150ft and two charges being thrown from the beam, to produce this pattern:

```
                  X
        X         X         X
                  X
```

The Mark VII depth charge sank at the rate of 10ft per second in order to allow the hunting vessel to draw clear before detonation. Early in the war it was decided that a faster sinking rate was required to provide a second, deeper layer to the DC pattern. A ballast weight of 140lb was added to one end of the Mark VII depth charge, which gave it a sinking weight of 16ft per second. This was known as the Mark VII heavy. The pattern was altered to provide for the ejection of one heavy DC along with every standard Mark VII. The heavy was provided with depth settings between 140ft and 550ft. Some vessels were fitted to fire depth charges in intermediate positions within the pattern shown above to ensure greater coverage. From January 1943, minol replaced amatol as the DC explosive of choice. By the end of the war depth charges were capable of detonating at 1,500ft. Four patterns could be discharged successively with two-minute reloading delays. Ultimately, the Depth Charge Pattern Control System was introduced. Connected to the ASDIC sets, this system introduced the automatic release of depth charges or Hedgehog projectiles at the most appropriate times.

Allied experiments carried out after the war suggested that a depth charge containing 320lb of minol would have to detonate within 25ft of a U-boat to rupture the pressure hull. A depth charge exploding within 50ft could cause sufficient damage to force the U-boat to surface. Cumulative damage was therefore always a better bet than a direct hit. The Allies estimated that 158 U-boats had been destroyed by depth charge (42.8 per cent), although this figure is now open to question.

DF — Direction Finding

Displacement — The weight of water displaced by a floating vessel, or the vessel's weight

Doppler Effect — The change in frequency of a radio/sound wave, as observer and source shift away or towards each other. *Bold* frustrated many RN A/S hunts. From the late summer of 1944, Royal Navy ships were equipped with ASDIC sets capable of registering 'doppler' effect. Now the hunters could determine the range, bearing and movement of an underwater contact *relative to the ASDIC equipped vessel*. In other words, the Royal Navy could discriminate between a stationary *Bold* canister and the impulse produced by a real U-boat.

Dräger **set**	Oxygen breathing set based, like the British DSEA, upon the Fleuss-Davis closed circuit principle. The KDM ordered the first sets in 1912 and the design remained in use until 1945.
Drop keel	A retractable keel usually positioned in the centre of a boat's hull
Druckkörper	German for the pressure hull
DSM	Distinguished Service Medal
DSO	Distinguished Service Order
DT-Gerat	*Dezimeter Telegraphie – Dezimeter Telegraphie*, or *Teknik*, early series of German radars using 80cm band.
Duck or canoe	Slang name for a small type of U-boat
eB-Dienst	German Navy Signals Intelligence Service
EG	British Escort Group – usually destroyers, corvettes or frigates
Elektra-Sonne	A crude predecessor of the American Loran A (and later C) and the British Decca Radio Navigation System. A master transmitter in Thuringia, supported by several slave transmitters as far apart as Spain and Norway, sent timed signals, which could be received by schnorchelling U-boats at periscope depth. Interpolation of the relative bearing lines enabled navigators to obtain a reasonably accurate fix. U-boats operating submerged for extended periods arrived at the R/V points off their Norwegian ports with navigational errors of less than five miles by relying solely on the *Elektra-Sonne* system.
E/Channel	English Channel
Evasion techniques	These varied significantly but U-boat skippers were able to take advantage of the 'blind time' between depth charges rolling off the deck of a ship and the subsequent explosion. During this time the hunting vessel would inevitably lose ASDIC contact. The U-boat skipper would order '*ausserste kraft*' accompanied by a dramatic alteration in course and depth in the hope of shaking off the hunter at this critical moment.
	Methods of foiling an ASDIC hunt varied but one technique commonly used was to remain at periscope depth, keeping the stern directed towards the hunting vessel, thus providing the smallest possible target. The escaping U-boat would attempt to keep to a straight course wherever possible rather than adopt a zig-zagging course. If certain of having been observed, the U-boat would dive deep but not on its original course. Many U-boat commanders preferred to dive under convoy's track in order to baffle ASDIC operators. The most skilled submarine commanders, British and German, were able to use prevailing conditions to their advantage, such as the varying densities of water or the presence of a rocky seabed, all of which would interfere with the acoustic transmissions of hunters.
FaT	*Federapparat Torpedo*, German torpedo used against convoys, because it ran a wandering course, with regular 180-degree turns
Fathom	Measure of distance – 6ft (1.82m)
FdU	*Führer der U-Boote* – Commander-of-U-boats
Feindfaht	War-cruise
Flak	*Flieger-Abwehr-Kanone* – Anti-aircraft gun

Fessenden equipment A somewhat primitive device enabling submarines to communicate underwater using Morse code. A steel plate was affixed via a tightly coiled spring to the casing of the submarine. When the telegraphist pressed his Morse code keys, an electric current caused the plate to vibrate, thus making the transmission audible to other vessels, including the enemy.

Fliege (fly)   Replaced *Naxos* radar detection sets in April 1944. The *Fliege* system covered a wavelength between 8cm and 20cm. A cross-fertilisation between *FuMB Mucke* (gnat) and *Fliege*: was known as *Tunis* or *FuMB 26*. This arrangement became standard U-boat radar detection equipment in the last two years of the war.

Flottille   Flotilla

Fore-end   The bow section of a submarine

Foxer   Anti-acoustic torpedo gear used by the Allies to combat the Gnat

Freeboard   The distance between the waterline and free-board-deck/gunwale of a boat or ship.

ft   feet/foot

Fuel/Cap   Fuel Capacity

FuMb   *Funkmessbeobachter* – Radar detector set. It was the responsibility of the radio operator to tune his set into a variety of wavelengths by manually turning a dial on the *Metox* set. Approaching aircraft were indicated by interruptions on a line displayed on the cathode ray tube oscilloscope. From August 1943 the *Wanz* sets replaced *Metox*.

FuMo   *Funkmessortungs Geracht* – Radar. Known as GSR to the British. From March 1944 U-boats were fitted with *FuMo 61 Hohentweil-U* (Owl), a large 'mattress' radar antenna which fitted in an extension built into the port side of the conning tower. This radar operated at 54cm. It was effective against aircraft between 15 and 20km. The set was unreliable in detecting low-flying aircraft because the low station of the antenna resulted in the sea causing interference.

Funkpeilrahmen   The circular loop found on the conning tower of U-boats primarily used for taking directional bearings but also for receiving *Goliath* VLF transmissions. This D/F loop was used to receive medium-wave transmissions and to determine the direction of their origins. This loop reinforced the powerful Telefunken E381 S all-band receiver. Local communication between U-boats was carried out on the medium-range band. When not in use the loop retracted into a convenient slot built into the conning tower fairing.

Funker   Radioman or wireless operator

Funkraum   Radio room

Gamma patrol   Aircraft and surface warships used to apply defined search patterns based or Gamma searchon scientific calculation to locate the enemy

F/V   Fishing vessel

GC   George Cross

Gebläse   Super-chargers fitted to some U-boat diesel engines

Gens/General Service   Submariner's term for the surface Royal Navy

GHG   *Gruppen Horch Gerät* – underwater sound detector

GL u. Co.	Garbe, Lohmeyer & Co. – German electric motor manufacturer
GM	George Medal
Gnat	Allied term for the German T5/T5a acoustic torpedo, or *Zaunköning*
Goliath	German scientists discovered that VLF (very low frequency) transmissions could be received by a dived U-boat. Messages sent by the massive *Goliath* transmitter built at Kalbe were capable of being received by the U-boat's Telefunken all-band receiver. Crews described these messages as having been 'sent by Goliath'.
GRT	Gross registered tonnage
GSR	German Search Receiver for RDF transmissions. British term for *FuMo* radar.
Gunwale	The top/upper edge of the side of a vessel
Guz	Naval parlance for the RN establishment at Devonport. The site covers 650 acres.
GW	Germaniawerft – German U-boat shipyard and diesel manufacturers
HA	Howitzer – deck gun – a relatively small cannon that delivers shells at a medium muzzle velocity, usually by a high trajectory
Handelskrieg mit U–Booten	Submarine warfare against merchant shipping, or literally 'trade war with submarines'
Hartmut	German U-boat operations codename during the occupation of Norway
Hawser	Steel cable
HE	Hydrophone effect – the sound of a propeller cutting through water as detected by the hydrophone operator. Fixed shore-based hydrophones designed to monitor minefields were first developed in 1916. Ship-borne hydrophones were introduced in 1915 – the PGS or portable general service hydrophone. The PGS was suspended by a crane over the side of a vessel to a depth of 30ft. The PGS could only be used if the ship's machinery was shut down, otherwise the operator could not distinguish between the sounds of the intruder and the ship's own background noise. The hydrophone operator rotated a wheel until the sound of intruder screws was heard with equal strength in both ears, then the bearing was read off the dial attached to the wheel and plotted. A problem arose with the '180-degree error', in other words the operator was unable to determine from which side of the head the noise was coming. The Mark 1 and Mark 2 portable directional hydrophone (PDH) was introduced in 1917 and largely removed the 180-degree error. In addition it was possible to use the set with the vessel travelling at low speed.
	Passive ASDIC transmissions largely fulfilled the same functions during the Second World War.
Heads	Toilet (RN)
Hedgehog	The A/S Experimental Establishment at Portland had long given consideration to attacking a submerged submarine by means of charges thrown ahead of the ship (see Evasion Techniques). The 'blind time' between losing ASDIC contact, the charges sinking to firing depth and the ultimate explosion, was appreciated by both the British and their German

U-boat opponents. In February 1942, Hedgehog – an ahead-thrown, contact weapon – was developed in earnest. British warships were equipped with two Hedgehog mortar guns. They had a sinking rate of 42ft per second, which cut down significantly on the 'blind time' associated with depth charge attacks. Hedgehog projectiles were fired by fixed elevation, twenty-four spigot mortars, possessing an average range of 275 yards. The missiles produced a circular pattern ahead of the attacking ship. The fuse was armed after travelling 10ft through the water at high speed. A Hedgehog attack was normally carried out with the hunting vessel steaming slowly in such a way that the target bore straight ahead. The hunter would fire at the moment the correct range was reached. Hedgehog was not considered to be effective against deep targets.

HF/DF   High Frequency Direction Finding U-boats made wireless transmissions when sighting or shadowing convoys, reporting weather conditions etc. In this the Germans took a calculated risk. They realised that Allied shore stations would detect these transmissions and that just two shore stations taking cross bearings were capable of locating a U-boat. The dominant assumption in Kriegsmarine circles was that these 'fixes' were inaccurate. By late 1942 the Allies had produced a high frequency ship-borne direction finder (HF/DF or 'huff duff'). Now U-boats could be located with great accuracy. In short, any U-boat transmitting near an Allied convoy could be 'fixed' in more ways than one. Indeed Staff Kapitan Hans Meckel (the staff officer responsible for U-boat signals) warned German intelligence late in 1942 that the Allies had such a device in their armoury. However, no action was taken on his report.

HMCS   His/Her Majesty's Canadian Ship

HMS   His/Her Majesty's Ship

Hohentwiel   A radar device (see *FuMo*)

Horchpeilung   Direction finding or taking a bearing by listening (sound location)

hp   Horsepower

hrs   Hours

HSD   Higher submarine detector – an operative's role, not a machine

HTP   High Test Peroxide

KDB   *Kristalldrehbasis Great* – Rotating 'T'-shaped hydrophone mechanism found just after the foremost bollards on the bow casing of a U-boat. *KDB* produced far superior direction-finding bearings to *GHG,* particularly when the quarry was off the bows; however the operation of KDB required the U-boat to travel at low speeds.

KDM **or** *KM*   *Kaiserliche Deutsche Marine* – Imperial German Navy (1871–1919)

kg   Kilogram – Measure of weight (2.20lb)

km   Measure of distance – 0.621 of a mile

kt   Knot, a measure of speed equal to one nautical mile (6,076ft) per hour

Körting   U-boat paraffin (kerosene)-fuelled engine manufacturer

Kriegsmarine   German Navy of the Second World War

KTB   *Kriegstagebuch* – German war diary, or ship's log

LBD	Length/Beam/Draught
LBDH	Length/Beam/Draught/Height
Leigh Light	A British anti-submarine device used in the Second World War. It was a powerful twenty-two million-candela searchlight of 24in (610mm) fitted to some Coastal Command Bombers and aircraft to help them to spot enemy U-boats at night.
Leitmotif	Recurring theme
Lt	Lieutenant
LTO	Alternative name for the TI. It means Leading Torpedo Operator or Leading Torpedo Instructor or just Torpedo Instructor.
LuT	*Lagenunabhängiger Torpedo* − a type of German torpedo with a 280kg warhead, more sophisticated than the FaT and capable of being shot in any position and bearing.
L/h	Lighthouse
L/v	Light vessel
m	Metre
MAD	Magnetic Airborne Detector. The presence of a U-boat caused variations to the earth's magnetic field. MAD-equipped aircraft at 100ft could detect a submarine up to 300ft below the surface. It was, in effect, a flying indicator loop. MAD was installed in Liberators, Catalinas and Short Sunderlands. In tracking a submerged U-boat, the MAD aircraft flew in circles on each side of the probable course of the submarine, dropping a marker during each circle when a contact was detected. Towards the completion of the fourth circle, the aircraft would automatically (or manually) release a 'retro bomb', rather like a rocket-propelled Hedgehog.
Magnetometer	An instrument for measuring the magnitude and direction of a magnetic field and an instrument used for finding metal/wreckage underwater, by means of an electronic 'fish' towed behind a boat/ship.
MAN	Maschinefabrik-Augsburg-Nürnberg − U-boat diesel engines manufacturer
max-op-depth	Maximum operational depth
MiD	Mentioned in dispatches award
Mixer	Name for torpedo mechanics
ML	Motor launch
mm	Millimetre
MN	Marine Nationale − French navy
Mowt	Ministry of War Transport
MTB	Motor Torpedo Boat
Mucke	'Gnat' or *FuMb* 25 radar detector set (not to be confused with the *Gnat* torpedo)
MWM	Motoren-Werke-Mannheim − U-boat diesel engine manufacturer
Nauen	Code-name for one of the slave transmitters used by the *Elektra-Sonne system*
Nautical mile	Sea mile, approximately 6,076ft or 1,851.96m
Naxos	German radar detector introduced from November 1943 to guard against aircraft equipped with the ASV III radar introduced by the Allies, with its 9.7cm wavelength. *Naxos,* aka *Timor,* was capable of operating on a handy 8–12cm wavelength.
NCO	Non-Commissioned Officer

NELSECO	New London Ship & Engine Co. of Groton, Connecticut, USA
Nordweg	Long-haul route – the route north around Scotland, sometimes via the Fair Isle gap, but the safer route was north of the Shetlands. This route made for a longer travelling time, but was far safer than the shorter, but infinitely more dangerous, run through the Channel.
OOW	Officer-of-the-Watch
O/Sea	Ordinary Seaman
Oggin	Royal Navy slang for sea
Op/R	Operational range
Pairs	Literally 'Lords' – German slang for U-boat seamen
Paravane	First World War British destroyers carried the high-speed paravane, equipped with a 400lb charge, which either exploded on contact, or could be detonated electrically by the operator. Designed by Lt Dennis Burney, paravanes were designed to be towed in pairs, port and starboard at a pre-selected depth. The device resembled a small torpedo with lateral fins. The paravane would remain at its designated depth irrespective of course or speed and it would maintain its set distance from the sides of the ship. The lowest operable depth was 200ft. They were not popular, as this quotation shows: 'We hated the contrivance which was difficult to use and always going wrong. Moreover one had to ease down when getting the device in and out, which was always a risk with a submarine operating in the area. Added to this, no commanding officer feels really happy with two explosive fish towing under his stern. There was always the danger that one might forget them in an emergency and go full speed astern to avoid a collision and find the paravane wires wrapped inextricably around the propellers and the explosive fish themselves bobbing alongside.' Taffrail, *Endless Story* p.267.
Pier Head Jump	British submarine flotillas maintained pools of specialist officers and ratings. Should a regular crew member 'go adrift' or fall sick, a member of 'spare crew' would be given a last minute 'pier head jump' to take his place.
Port	The left side of a boat when looking forward
Pressure hull	The vital inner protective membrane of a submarine. A submarine with a leaking pressure hull was in dire straits.
Props	Propellers
PS	*Pferdestärke*, German standard for horsepower
RAF	Royal Air Force
RDF	Radio Direction Finder – better known as radar. Type 286 M sets were installed in British warships as early as 1941, having previously been used in aircraft. The sets were introduced to submarines in 1942–43. The early British sets transmitted at 214 megahertz or megacycles. At this frequency the transmit/receive aerial was a cumbersome piece of equipment which had to be trained by hand. Not only was there a 'blind' area astern, for instance a target travelling across the stern would involve frantic rotation to recapture it, but coastlines also appeared as arcs rather than as detailed profiles. Small targets did not even register. Centrimetric radar sets known as SJ were gradually

introduced in Allied ships from 1943 onwards. Power driven, they gave an all-round scan and produced superior target definition. Radar operatives, often known as 'wireless mechanics', were highly regarded. Only 50 per cent of entrants passed the initial exams. Training took place at Holyhead, Adrossan, Campbeltown and Glasgow. Submarines temporarily stationed in Loch Foyle performed the role of intruder U-boats for the radar ops to practise upon. Should a crew be taken prisoner, the identity of the radar man was always kept a close secret.

Rev/min   Revolutions per minute

RFR   Royal Fleet Reserve ratings equivalent to RNR

RN   Royal Navy

RNPS   Royal Navy Patrol Service

RNR   Royal Naval Reserve – war diluted the resources of the Royal Navy. The RN had long relied on RNR as a source of personnel in time of war, particularly for experienced officers. Many Merchant Navy officers had served one year in the RN in peacetime and were granted an RNR commission in wartime. Prior to the Second World War, RNR officers were paid an annual retainer of £25 per year. Warships battled with the sea far more often than they confronted U-boats. The skills of RNR personnel were essential.

RNVR   Royal Naval Volunteer Reserve. This force consisted mainly of younger men with shore-based professions but with a love of the sea. A significant proportion were experienced yachtsmen. Many of the ratings were highly educated potential officers, and a commission within the RNVR was highly prized. During the First World War it was said that RNR personnel were sailors trying to become gentlemen and that RNVRs were gentlemen trying to become officers. What is certain is that, in the last two years of the Second World War, the RNVR produced most of the junior officers who were required to specialise in gunnery, navigation, communications and radar. By 1943, RNVR officers began to be awarded their own commands as the escort forces expanded.

Room 40   A top secret department within Admiralty, set up under electronics expert Sir Alfred Ewing (responsibility later passed to Cdr M. James of British Naval Intelligence). The staff of Room 40 comprised naval technology experts and senior academics. The Naval Intelligence Division established a series of wireless direction-finding stations along the British coast, designed to take cross bearings on wireless transmissions from both merchants and U-boats. Lt Hope ran the deciphering section within Room 40. W/T traffic in the Heligoland Bight was particularly useful, as the deciphering team could tell very quickly when the High Seas Fleet had put out from the Jade basin because of the warnings given out to civilian maritime traffic to keep away. Room 40 was thus able to visualise enemy movements at any given time. British movements preceding the encounters at Dogger Bank in 1914, and indeed Jutland in 1916, were both pre-empted by Room 40 intelligence gathering. As files in the National Archive demonstrate,

Lt Tiark of Room 40 had a very accurate picture of where Bauer's U-boat flotillas were at any given time. Tiark routinely tracked U-boats from departure to return and could anticipate a likely operational zone. The Germans responded by changing cypher codes and signals on a regular basis but, by studying the wavelengths, the length of signals and the direction-finding bearing of the senders, Hope and his people were able to send a steady and accurate flow of intelligence to C-in-C Grand Fleet and the Operations Division of Admiralty.

ROV Remote Operated Vehicle, often used to search the seabed and/or shipwrecks

Runddipol Permanent radar detector antenna used by the *Wanz* radar detector sets installed in U-boats after 1943. The *Kriegsmarine* feared that the Allies were able to home in radiation emissions, *Wanz* was believed to radiate less than other versions.

SBT Submarine Bubble Target – the German device used to create false U-boat echoes

Schnorchel Snorkel – a tube device enabling the operation of a dived submarine powered by a fuel-powered engine, using air supplied from the surface. This Dutch design was further developed by the Germans and came into service in February 1944. *Schnorchel*-equipped boats could travel at speeds of up to 8 knots. Higher speeds were often achieved, but a dangerous wake (accompanied by unwelcome vibrations) often resulted. Three hours of *Schnorchelling* could charge the batteries of a Type VII U-boat for a whole day. The standard procedure was to drive the boat on one diesel engine running at 3–4 knots, while the other was used to power the batteries. Hydrophone checks were made every twenty minutes or so. *Schnorchelling* removed the imperative to surface and charge batteries at night, a necessity that had dominated submarine operation up to this point. This was a vital capability in view of the enemy-dominated waters these U-boats were operating in post-'D-Day'. Two types of *Schnorchel* heads were fitted: the ball-float type or *kugelschwimmer*, and the uncommon cylindrical ring float or *ringschwimmer*. This is no mere technical detail: the *Schnorchel* head provides a useful means of identifying wrecks. A *Schnorchelling* school was established in Horten, Norway, to train crews in the handling of this useful device. The 'Snort' mast was designed to work with the exhaust mast ½m underwater. If this depth increased or trim was lost, there was every possibility that the counter-pressure would force the diesels to discharge exhaust gases, including carbon monoxide, back into the boat. The head of the snort was often covered with an anti-radar coating known as *Tarnmatte*. This coating, a combination of synthetic rubber and iron oxide powder, was capable of masking the presence of a raised snort head from the Allied H2S radar.

Seemannstod Literally seaman's death – the ultimate fate of the loyal sailor. Romanticised heroic death in battle with more than a flavour of Wagnerian *Gotterdamerung*.

SM U-boat *Seiner Majestät U-Boot* – His Majesty's Submarine – First World War German submarine

SNO	Senior Naval Officer (Royal Navy)
Sonar buoy	A passive ASDIC device embedded in a buoy dropped by aircraft. When the buoy hit the water, the hydrophone would deploy and the ASDIC would transmit any boat sounds picked up by the hydrophone back to the aircraft.
Spartacists	Leftist subversives who attempted to infiltrate German institutions with a view to fomenting revolution in 1918
Squid	Destroying U-boats became increasingly mechanised, and by the closing stages of the war, the process was largely automatic (see ASDIC). From August 1944 Hedgehog firing mechanisms were connected to the ASDIC gear, enabling the depth to be pre-set at the last possible moment before discharge. In fact the firing process became increasingly automatic. The result was the Squid system, which was fitted to new ships. The weapon consisted of two three-barrelled mortars fitted into a frame, which could be rotated through 90 degrees for loading (which was automatic). This pattern resulted:

X

X   X

	The time-fuse gave detonation settings from 20–900ft. HMS *Loch Killin* is credited with one of the earliest Squid 'kills', using this system in 1944. Squid was arguably the deadliest A/S weapon in the armoury.
Spare Crew	British submarine flotillas maintained a pool of specialist personnel. For example, there were spare crew ERAs, spare crew torpedomen and spare crew officers. Should any crewman fail to turn up on patrol, an appropriate member of the spare crew pool would be given a 'pier head jump' and ordered to join the submarine at harbour stations.
SS	Steamship
SSBN	Ship Submersible Ballistic Nuclear, or Vanguard Class, nukes. They carry Trident II (D5s) and we have five of them.
SSNs	Ship Submersible Nuclear, conventional Swiftsure and Trafalgar Classes. They are armed with cruise missiles and are on their way out.
S/Sp	Submerged Speed
SSW	Siemens Schuckert Werke – electric motor manufacturer
Starboard	The right side of a boat when looking forward
Stick	Slang for periscope, both RN and German
Sub/R	Submerged Range
Subsmash	Code name for submarine lost/sunk
Sur/Sp	Surface Speed
S/v	Sailing vessel
T5	A type of German torpedo with a warhead weighing 274kg, intended to be used as an escort killer, because it locked on to the loudest noise after a run of 400m from its launch, however it could also pick out the U-boat itself as a target. A German acoustic torpedo, or *Zaunkönig*.
Tadpole	Nickname for the small UB 1 class of the First World War

Tauchretter	See *Dräger* set
Thetis	A radar decoy buoy carried by later U-boats. The Thetis 2c buoy was carried in three pieces in the U-boat fore-ends for later assembly on deck. A series of antennae radiated from the assembled buoy, which were capable of foiling the metric frequency of aircraft-borne ASV radar but not the more sophisticated H2s.
TMA	Torpedo-Mine-A – moored German mines, designed for, but never actually used on, U-boats
TMB	Torpedo-Mine-B – small German ground mines with various fuses and an explosive charge of 578.7kg (1,276lb)
TMC	Torpedo-Mine-C – large German ground mines with an explosive charge of 997.9kg (2,200lb)
Torpedominen	Torpedo mines – used by U-boats, delivered through the torpedo tubes
Trim	Fore and aft balance of a boat. If a submarine was in perfect longitudinal and lateral balance it was said to be 'in trim'. Obviously trim changed as torpedoes were fired, stores were loaded or even when personnel moved around the boat. A badly trimmed boat might show its periscope or even its stern to an enemy. Maintenance of trim was of crucial importance and was the responsibility of the First Lieutenant and the Stoker Petty Officer (RN). Using graphs and tables, these men calculated the amount of water to be admitted or expelled from the tanks in order to maintain correct trim.
Trimmed down	State in which a submarine's tanks were flooded until a state of neutral buoyancy was reached. The advantages of a low profile could be combined with the obvious ones of diesel propulsion. Only the conning tower would show above the surface, thus hiding the submarine from view. However, the submarine was vulnerable, should it suddenly enter a patch of denser water.
Trot	Manoeuvre carried out by RN submarine, usually in harbour, when coming alongside or leaving for patrol or exercise
Tunis	The *Tunis* system of radar detection, (a combination of *FuMB* 24 *Fliege* and *FuMB* 25 *Mucke*) required two antennae added to the conning tower. Firstly, a forward-facing *Mucke* cone, and secondly, the aft-facing parabolic antenna of the *Fliege* system. By late 1944 a U-boat conning tower was becoming quite crowded.
Turm	Conning tower of U-boat. One important distinction between the British submarine and the U-boat was that a U-boat commander conventionally made a dived attack from the cramped chamber within the conning tower of his boat. British submarine skippers preferred to make their torpedo attacks from the control room. The design of German conning towers evolved between 1939 and 1945 from the plain cylindrical *Turm 0* to the elaborate *Turm 4* with its dual flak gun platforms known to crews as the *wintergarten*.
Twill trunk	The favoured British submarine escape method during the Second World War. Following the Nasmith Committee recommendations in 1939, escape chambers were removed from submarines as it was felt that their claustrophobic nature had hindered the *Thetis* escape.

Instead of a dedicated escape chamber, new submarines were fitted with a Twill trunk mechanism under designated escape hatches. The Twill trunk was a rubberised cotton concertina, strengthened with metal hoops. When stored, the trunk was designed to collapse under the hatch. When required, the trunk could be extended and tethered to the floor of the chamber. In the highest part of the chamber the flood valve was fitted, backed up by a flap valve. These were used to flood the chamber once the skirt was in place and securely tethered. Water entered the chamber via a bore pipe discharging into the bilges near the floor, thus ensuring that the point of ingress would never be higher than the hatch, so enabling the formation of an airlock. A gauge was fitted near the hatch, giving pressure readings from both inside and outside the submarine. Once pressure had equalised, the escape hatch could be opened. The resultant air lock formed within the Twill trunk enabled a trapped crew to escape to the surface. This method was successfully used by the crews of *Umpire* and *Truculent* (Vol.1), but sadly failed the crew of *Untamed* (Vol.3).

TY	Temporary Lt/PO, etc.
U-boat	*Unterseeboot* – submarine
U/Dt	Underwater displacement
U/Power	Underwater power
Uzo	*Uberwasserzieloptik* – the U-boat torpedo-aiming device mounted on front of conning tower
VC	Victoria Cross
Verschollen	German for 'missing' or 'lost'
W/T	Wireless transmission
Wabo/Wasserbomb	Water bomb – German term for depth charge
Wanz	German radar detector set, replacement for *Metox*. *Wanz* was considered to be more sensitive than *Metox*. Better still, *Wanz* introduced an automatic frequency search, but manual fine-tuning was possible. The *Wanz* set required a permanent antenna known as the *Runddipol*.
Wintergarten	By mid-1944 most Type VII U-boats were armed with one big 3.7cm AA gun on the lower platform and twin C/38 guns mounted on the upper platform. Ready ammunition lockers were built into the *wintergarten* to aid supply of shells. In late 1944 this model was replaced by, either a 1–2cm quadruple 38/43U with armoured shield, or a 1–3cm twin M42 with acoustic detector gear.
IWO	*Erster Wachffizier* – First Watch Officer
IIWO	*Zweiter Wachoffizier* – Second Watch Officer
WRNS	Women's Royal Naval Service
Yaw	To swing or steer off course, as when running with a quartering sea
Zentrale	German term for the central compartment known as the control room in an Allied submarine

FLAG ABBREVIATIONS

BEL	Belgian
BRA	Brazil
DAN	Denmark
FIN	Finland
FRA	France
GBR	Great Britain
GRE	Greece
ITA	Italy
NLD	Nederland
NOR	Norway
POR	Portugal
RUS	Russia/USSR
SPA	Spain
SWE	Sweden
USA	United States of America

AN A–Z OF CREW RANKS

IN VARIOUS BRITISH SUBMARINES BETWEEN 1911 AND 1955

1ST-LT – FIRST LIEUTENANT. A submarine commander in waiting. The 1st-Lt calculated trim, using data collected by the stoker petty officer. The 1st-Lt ordered which tank was to be blown and which valves were to be opened or closed. He dispensed orders and received reports in the control room. Most commanders were content to leave the everyday running of the boat in the hands of the highly experienced first lieutenant. Equivalent German rank was the IWO.

The First Lieutenant (also 'Number One', 'Jimmy the One' or just 'the Jimmy') was the ship's executive officer. In addition to the usual administrative duties he performed the duties of electrical, torpedo, and training officer. As such he was responsible for the carrying out of all drills and for ensuring that the men handled the submarine according to the requirements of the captain. On paper he was also the engineer but these duties were often delegated to the Chief ERAs, while many of the larger boats carried Warrant Engineers. He was the trimming officer being responsible for the trim at all times. The trim was maintained and adjusted under his direct supervision

Successful 'Number Ones' quickly established a good rapport with their senior rates, delegated responsibility to them and relied on their expertise. In handling personnel administration the first lieutenant acted as divisional officer for the entire crew and, through the Skipper, recommended men for promotions, courses and awards, controlled leave and dealt with all but the most serious misdemeanours. Because of the control he exercised over their lives, the sailors always accorded him a subtle extra measure of deference which, in most cases, was well deserved. A good first lieutenant usually meant an efficient and happy lower deck, a strong augury for success.
Note: At the end of the Second World War use of the term 'skipper' when referring to an RN officer would have been derogatory. There was an existing RNR rank of Skipper and it was reserved for temporary officers taken up from the MN and inshore trades who had BoT inshore certificates.

AB – ABLE SEAMAN. From the inception of the Submarine Service to January 1941, men transferred from general service on a voluntary basis. Financial enhancements usually attracted volunteers to British submarines. The old Submarine Service was highly selective. Volunteer able seamen were required to be over twenty-one years of age and the service demanded a far greater level of intellectual ability and competence among its recruits than general service ratings. Sea training in submarines was negligible during the First World War as most skills were learned 'on the job'. During the Second World War, a sea-training course at Blyth lasted just six weeks. The German equivalent to the seaman was the Matrose or Matrosengefreiter.

This does not describe what an AB was. There was no lower age limit for volunteers. They just had to be AB or equivalent. Selectivity went largely by the board with the outbreak of war – both times.

In the Second World War training for men was given at Dolphin until the place was cleared for D-Day preparations. Officer training only was moved to the base at Blyth. After the Normandy invasion, training and drafting returned to the fort. On 23 September 1945 FOSM returned to Dolphin '...where his flag had always flown'.

CERA – CHIEF ENGINE ROOM ARTIFICER. Unlike the U-boat 'LI', the senior engineer on a British submarine was an NCO and, in most cases, the highest-ranked NCO on the boat. The CERA was usually a technician of many years' experience in general service. Large submarines often carried EOs. Often a Warrant Eng., occasionally a Chief Warrant Eng. and sometimes a junior EO. Many boats did rely on the CERA but where an EO was not carried the 1st lieutenant was the official EO. A great many S/M ERAs and CERAs knew little other than submarines. The important criteria was diesel experience and even in the Second World War this was not usual except for those who had done the apprenticeship, either in the navy or in industry. A lot of ERAs were taken up directly from industry.

CPO – CHIEF PETTY OFFICER – COXSWAIN. Usually the most senior, and frequently the oldest, seaman on the boat. The coxswain oversaw the work of the two helmsmen and he took responsibility for maintaining discipline, obtaining and storing supplies. Acting as quartermaster, he liaised with the FL and dished out the daily rum tot. Respected by all rates, a competent and proficient coxswain was the key to maintaining morale and efficiency on the boat. The nearest German rate was that of Oberbootsmann.

The Coxswain was *always* the senior NCO. He was the helmsman at harbour stations, and after-planeman for action and diving stations. Some submarine coxswains were Torpedo Coxswains (CPO) but most were Submarine Coxswains and therefore POs. They were responsible for all escape matters, victualling, rum, leave and discipline. With the 1st Lt they made out and maintained the watches and quarters bill. The cox'n was also the senior man trained in First Aid and acted as the boat's SBA.

One of the senior LSSTs usually acted as the cox'n's understudy and was known as the 2nd Cox'n, or 'Scratcher' (he scratched the Cox'n's back - eh, eh). The 2nd Cox'n was in charge of the upper deck and manned the foreplanes at diving stations. At action stations he was 2i/c of the fore ends.

CPO TEL. – CHIEF PETTY OFFICER TELEGRAPHIST. Very few operational boats had a Chief Tel., usually there was a POTEL who had a staff of two or three Telegraphists.

ERA – ENGINE ROOM ARTIFICER. In general, ERAs, along with stokers, were responsible for propulsion and engineering aspects of the submarine. Watch-keeping experience would be gained in the engine room of a general service warship. The apprentice would be required to sit the Higher Educational test, considered essential for anyone wishing to gain warrant officer status within the RN. Next, the apprentice ERA would be required to study for the 'auxiliary ticket', qualifying him to 'run, start and stop all auxiliary machinery on a warship'. Upon passing this exam, the apprentice was able to discard the 'square rig' of an AB for the blue reefer jacket, trousers and peaked cap of a Petty Officer.

The technological complexity of the submarine demanded a high ratio of ERAs and senior rates in contrast to general service. The number of ERAs varied according to the type of the submarine. The nearest German rate was the Obermaschinistmaat. This bears no resemblance to the training undertaken by an ERA. All navy-trained ERAs started out with a four year apprenticeship then worked their way up through five levels of expertise to become ERA 1st Class. From CERA1 he could be promoted to Chief ERA, which had two levels. Only ERAs 5th and 6th Class were accorded the status of PO, all other ERAs were given the status of CPO but *not* the authority.

All through this period many ERAs were hired off the street, provided they had the technical qualifications. They were given a quick basic training course, a uniform and the staus of a CPO and much more pay than most. They were deliberately segregated from the seamen, and for good reason.

HELMSMEN. (Taxi driver) All seamen were encouraged to take their turn as helmsman, closely following the instructions of the coxswain and FL. During diving stations the coxswain himself would often take over one of the wheels, leaving the other to one of the most experienced L/Seamen or POs. The helmsmen were the only men in the submarine provided with seats at their working stations.

All seamen (gunners and torpedomen) were qualified helmsmen and took their turn on the watch. The Planesmen also had seats as often did the ballast pump operators.

L/SEA. – LEADING SEAMAN. Higher grade of rating than AB and frequently entrusted with high responsibilities on British submarines. The nearest German equivalent was the Mechanikers-maat (though the latter held PO status and the L/Seaman did not).

LSST – LEADING SEAMAN TORPEDOMAN

LS/LTO – LEADING TORPEDOMAN (electrical) rating.

LSGL – LEADING SEAMAN GUN LAYER (only when gun fitted).

L/SIG. – LEADING SIGNALMAN. Trained visual signalman.

L/STO. – LEADING STOKER. Stoker with responsibilities.

L/TEL. – LEADING TELEGRAPHIST. Intermediate level telegraphist, with some supervisory responsibilities.

LT – LIEUTENANT OR SUB-LIEUTENANT (SECOND HAND). Person responsible for the maintenance and operation of all weapons systems on board the boat. The Second Hand worked closely with the TI. Upon passing the medical (and from 1932 the tank exercise) the typical Sub-Lt spent three months training at Blockhouse. The course was partly theoretical, partly based on sea training. It was highly desirable that an officer entrant to the Submarine Service be proficient in hydraulics, engineering and electrics. However these subjects were not introduced to the Blockhouse training course until 1919. General service tended to regard these areas of expertise as the preserve of the NCO. The result was that many young submarine officers were unprepared for the demands of active service during the First World War.

This does not come near describing what a lieutenant was. It does not describe his training, his accomplishment levels or his responsibilities.

The submarine base was HMS *Dolphin* – it was located in Fort Blockhouse. Training was given at 'Dolphin' or in 'Blockhouse' (slang).

LT-CDR – LIEUTENANT COMMANDER. A high percentage of submarine officers emerged from old, established, military families with a tradition of sending a son into the RN. The backgrounds of these men tended to be more homogenous than those of the men they commanded, though a sprinkling of RNR and RNVR men added a touch of variety. The overwhelming majority had been educated at Dartmouth Naval College, or a similar establishment, geared towards preparing cadets for the responsibilities of office. A fee tended to deter all but service or patrician families, so social class, as well as technological merit, was reflected in the submarine officers' uniform. RNVR men were appointed to submarine commands late in both wars. On leaving college a 'Dart' was expected to serve out a term as midshipman in general service. In time he would acquire sufficient 'seniority' to earn the rank of lieutenant. Officer volunteers for the Submarine Service were required to have obtained experience in, and have studied, the disciplines of navigation, weapons, telegraphy and wireless. Most officer candidates had gained the rate of sub-lieutenant before they volunteered for the Submarine Service.

Volunteering for submarines appealed to tough, assertive, technologically-minded young men with a healthy contempt for general service 'bull'. They were gamblers — just volunteering for submarines would constitute the greatest risk they had ever taken. Failure at any stage would see their career in tatters; conversely, success would bring responsibilities unthinkable elsewhere for so young an officer. Appointment to a submarine as a navigator or weapons officer would follow. An average of three years' experience of study, combined with practical experience, was required before the lieutenant could expect an appointment as first lieutenant to a submarine. In peacetime an officer could expect to spend up to four years as a first lieutenant before he could apply to sit the Commanding Officer Qualifying Course (COQC or 'Perisher'). Each candidate was put through a series of simulated attack exercises under the supervision of an experienced submarine captain. Failure resulted in immediate return to 'gens' and there were no second chances. It follows that most peacetime British submarine commanders were in their early thirties. There were limited opportunities for training submarine commanders at Fort Blockhouse, where an 'attack teacher and periscope school' was established before the First World War. The submarine commander was the eyes and mind of his crew. He alone coordinated their actions and took the key decisions.

The success of the mission and the survival of the crew depended upon the skills of the Skipper, arguably the most demanding job in the RN. The prestige compensated for the lack of financial reward. Their crews revered successful captains and he embodied the crew's corporate identity — he personified them.

In wartime there were second chances on the COQC — it all depended on what the screw-up was. Freddy Sherwood (the first VR CO of the Second World War) was given a second go at the Attack Teacher, and there were others.

MATE – PETTY OFFICER. In the First World War there was a rank of mate. The mate was a promoted PO in the process of being commissioned from the ranks. Outwardly a mate was indistinguishable from a sub-lt. After one year as a mate he would be promoted to lieutenant if successful. There were mates in submarines, some even made CO. The rank was discontinued after 1919.

O/ERA – OUTSIDE ENGINE ROOM ARTIFICER. A highly experienced PO technician who was responsible for the efficient functioning of all machinery outside of the engine room; he also serviced systems in the control room, including the periscope mechanism.

Otherwise known as the 'Outside Wrecker'. Usually one of the ERAs, sometimes the Stoker PO. The CR was outside the ER.

O/SEA. – ORDINARY SEAMAN. Lower rank than Able Seaman; usually new entrants. All new entries were Ordinary Seamen, or ODs. They were untrained so not of any value technically.

PO – PETTY OFFICER. A non-commissioned officer.

PO/TEL. – PETTY OFFICER TELEGRAPHIST.

SIG. – SIGNALMAN. Specialised in visual communications.

STO – STOKER. With the exception of 'K' Class boats there were no furnaces on submarines. Stokers carried out watch-keeping over the diesels and motors, carrying out routine maintenance and general labouring tasks within the engines and motor rooms, according to the instructions of the ERAs. The nearest German rate was the Heizer or Maschinist-gefreiter.

Stokers *never* had anything to do with the main motors or the MR. They only ever dealt with the diesel engines and their systems. Many submarine stokers were trained diesel mechanics.

STO/PO – STOKER PETTY OFFICER – SENIOR STOKER NCO, but not senior to a Chief Stoker.

SUB-LT – SUB-LIEUTENANT (THIRD HAND). He was charged with navigating the boat and he also operated the attack computer. The navigator in a British submarine was invariably a commissioned officer, unlike the Kriegsmarine Obersteuermann, who was of CPO rank. In the RN Submarine Service only commissioned officers were allowed to maintain a periscope watch.

TEL. – TELEGRAPHIST. Specialised in radio communications equipment

TI – TORPEDO INSTRUCTOR. A seaman CPO, or highly experienced petty officer, with special responsibility for the weapons, in particular the torpedoes. Answerable to the weapons officer, the TI was authorised to deal with the flooding up and draining down of the torpedo tubes during an attack. The TI routinely subjected torpedoes to sectional examinations, air tests and the application of 'torp oil'. The TI was assisted by a number of petty officers, leading seamen and able seamen. The comparable German rate was Obermechaniker or mechaniker.

The rating of TI is a PO rating and most submarine senior torpedomen were TIs. Some were Chief TIs but not many. The TI was responsible for all to do with the embrkation and disembarkation of torpedoes and the handling of torpedoes inside the submarine. He was also responsible for all small arms, pyrotechnics and demolitions. He was responsible for the operation of torpedo tubes and signal ejectors. Divisional PO for the Torpedo Department.

Torpedoes were seldom parted on board the submarine. It was possible, but the facilities were inadequate for a proper job. Only routine maintenance was performed.

WE – WARRANT ENGINEER (on M2.) As noted above Warrant Engineers were not unusual in submarines.

YOS – YEOMAN OF SIGNALS was a PO signalman. This was unusual as most boats only carried a Signalman or Ldg Sig. Most Second World War boats carried a couple of SDs and often an HSD.

A–Z OF CREW RANKS

IN VARIOUS GERMAN U-BOATS BETWEEN 1914 AND 1945

BTN – *BOOTSMANN* – COXWAIN'S MATE.

D.OB.MASCH – *DIESEL OBERMASCHINIST* – CHIEF DIESEL OPERATOR/MECHANIC AND CPO.

EL.OB.MASCH – *ELEKTRO OBERMASCHINIST* – CHIEF ELECTRICAL OPERATOR/MECHANIC AND CPO. Both artificers of chief petty officer rank, responsible for the smooth running of propulsion systems, reporting directly to the LI. These *obermaschinisten* had authority over the technical rates and the stokers.

F.T.– *GAST* – RADIO OPERATOR. And rank equivalent to a matrose or heizer (seaman/stoker).

FH.Z.S. – *FÄHNRICH ZUR SEE* – MIDSHIPMAN. The midshipman was on board as a trainee, as part of his officer education. This was practical or on-the-job training, together with the guidance of an experienced watch officer to learn the tricks of the trade; so when he was *leutnant zur see* he could start his duties on-board a submarine without the lack of practical experience.

FK.MT – *FUNKMAAT* – RADIO OPERATOR.

FK.OB.GFR. – *FUNKOBERGEFREITER*. Rank just below a *maat*, a fairly low-ranking radio operator.

F.T.MT – *FUNKTELEGRAPHIE* – TELEGRAPH OPERATOR.

GFR. – *GEFREITER* – SEAMAN OR TORPEDO-MAN, ETC., THIRD CLASS.

KORVKPT. – *KORVETTENKAPITÄN* – LIEUTENANT COMMANDER. Generally referred to as 'Herr Kaleu'.

KAP. – *KAPITÄN ZUR SEE* – CAPTAIN.

KPLT. – *KAPITÄNLEUTNANT* – LIEUTENANT. Usually the submarine captain/commander.

KGLTS – *KRIEGSLOTSE* – WAR PILOT. A merchant mariner taken on board to help in navigating along the enemy coast and distinguishing between merchant vessels.

LT.ING. – *LEUTNANT INGENIEUR*. Generally a *leutnant* or *oberleutnant sur zee* on boats where the commander was an *oberleutnant*, this key officer was known as the LI (pronounced 'ell ee'). The LI was responsible for the running of all systems on the boat.

LT.Z.S. – *LEUTNANT ZUR SEE* – SUB LIEUTENANT. The *leutnant zur see* might function as the *zweiter wach offizier*, or IIWO specifically responsible for the deck and flak guns in the Second World War.

MASCH – *MASCHINIST* – A *DECKOFFIZER*, WARRANT OFFICER ENGINEER. An equivalent rank to *steuermann*.

MASCH.ANW. – *MASCHINIST ANWÄRTER*. A candidate for the rank of *maschinist*.

MASCH.GFR. – *MASCHINISTGEFREITER* – ENGINEER SEAMAN.

MASCH.MT – *MASCHINENMAAT* – ENGINE-ROOM DIESEL MAN.

MASCH.STN. – *MASCHINISTEN* – ELECTRIC MOTORMAN.

MECH.GFR. – *MECHANIKERGEFREITER* – TORPEDO-ROOM SEAMAN.

MECH.MT – *MECHANIKERMAAT* – TORPEDO ROOM PETTY OFFICER.

MN.ING. – *MARINE INGENEIUR*.

MN.OB.ING – *MARINE-OBERINGENEIUR* – FIRST WORLD WAR ENGINEERING OFFICER. Equivalent to Oblt.z.S. rank

MN.ING.ASP. – *MARINE INGENIEUR ASPIRANT* – MARINE ENGINEER CANDITATE.

MECH.OB.GFR – *MECHANIKEROBERGEFREITER* – TORPEDO ROOM LEADING SEAMAN.

MT – *MAAT* – PETTY OFFICER THIRD CLASS.

MTS. – *MATROSE*. Seaman who carried out general tasks in the boat.

MTS.GFR. – *MATROSENGEFREITER* – ENGINE ROOM STOKER SECOND CLASS.

MTS.OB.GFR. – *MATROSENOBERGEFREITER* – ABLE SEAMAN.

HZR – *HEIZER* – ENGINE ROOM STOKER.

OB.BTN – *OBERBOOTSMANN* – BOSUN/COXSWAIN. The *oberbootsmann* acted as the senior NCO on the boat, holding responsibility for maintaining discipline in the seamen's branch, often served as fourth watch officer.

OB.BTN.MT. – *OBERBOOTSMANNMAAT* OFTEN REFERRED TO AS *NUMMER ZWO* – CHIEF PETTY OFFICER (NUMBER TWO), ASSISTANT TO THE BOSUN.

OB.FK.MT. – *OBERFUNKMAAT* – CHIEF RADIO OPERATOR.

OB.FK.TEL.MT. – *OBERFUNKENTELEGRAPHIEMAAT* – FIRST WORLD WAR RADIO AND TELEGRAPH OPERATOR PETTY OFFICER.

OB.GFR. – *OBERGEFREITER* – SEAMAN SECOND CLASS.

OB.HZR – *OBERHEIZER* – MORE SENIOR STOKER BELOW PETTY OFFICER RANK.

OB.ING.ASP. – *OBER-INGENIEUR-ASPIRANT* – ENGINEER OFFICER CANDIDATE.

OBLT.Z.S. – *OBERLEUTNANT ZUR SEE* – LIEUTENANT. On boats where the commander was an Oblt.z.S, the Lt.z.S. would function as the IWO (first watch officer). The RN equivalent would be the first lieutenant or FL. The IWO was responsible for the torpedoes and the systems which aimed and fired them.

OB.MASCH.GFR. – *MASCHINENGEFREITEN* – ENGINE-ROOM PETTY OFFICER.

OB.MASCH.MT – *OBERMASCHINISTENMAAT* – ENGINE-ROOM STOKER PETTY OFFICER.

OB.MECH.MT – *OBERMECHANIKERSMAAT* – TORPEDO ROOM PETTY OFFICER.

OB.MT – *OBERMAAT* – PETTY OFFICER FIRST CLASS.

OB.MTS – *OBERMATROSE* – LEADING SEAMAN AND ONCE-PROMOTED SEAMAN. Next rank would be a *bootsmannsmaat* (i.e. petty officer).

OB.STM.MT – *OBERSTEUERMANNSMAAT* – SENIOR HELMSMAN'S MATE AND PETTY OFFICER SECOND CLASS.

OB.STRM – *OBERSTEUERMANN.* The *obersteuermann* functioned as quartermaster and was also responsible for navigation, conning the boat and controlling the helmsmen. The *obersteuermann* helped the commander determine how and when to make attacks. Interestingly the Ob.Strm could also serve as third watch officer. On the command '*UZO zum brucke!*' the Ob.Strm would race out to fit the UZO into the clamp on the pedestal.

SNT.MT – *SANITATSMAAT* – PETTY OFFICER/MEDICAL ORDERLY.

STB.GFR. – *STABSGEFREITER* – SEAMAN FIRST CLASS.

STM. – *STEUERMANN* – HELMSMAN.

Z.MT – *ZENTRALEMAAT* – CONTROL-ROOM MATE, USUALLY A MACHINIST'S MATE.

ORDER OF RANKING

Korvettenkapitän
Kapitänleutnant
Oberleutnant z.S
Leutnant z.S
Marineoberingenieur
Marineoberingenieursaspirant
Marineingenieur
Marineingenieursaspirant
Obersteuermann
Steuermann
Oberbootsmannsmaat
Bootsmannsmaaten
FT-Obergast
FT-Gast

FT-Maat
Obermaat
Maat
Obermatrose
Matrose
Obermaschinist
Maschinist
Obermaschinistenmaat
Maschinistenmaat
Obermaschinistenanwärter
Maschinistenanwärter
Oberheizer
Heizer

CHAPTER ONE

NORTH EAST ENGLAND

INTRODUCTION

The volume of shipping plying up and down the east coast attracted U-boat activity in both World Wars, but especially the First World War of 1914–18. This spectacular coastline has been mute witness to momentous events. Just a little north of Berwick, the cruiser HMS *Pathfinder* was sunk off Dunbar on 5 September 1914 – the first time in naval history that a warship had been sunk by a self-propelled torpedo fired by a submarine in the open sea; HMS *Ascot* sank just south of the Farne Islands with all hands on 10 November 1918 and was almost certainly the last British warship torpedoed in the First World War. Likewise, U 1274 was destined to be one of the very last U-boats destroyed in Home Waters during the Second World War.

Despite being the scene of relentless U-boat attacks, the north-east coast was the last to see the introduction of the convoy system in the First World War ('TM' convoys were only introduced in 1918, though the Admiralty preferred to refer to them as 'controlled sailings'). Although it was late in coming, the introduction of the convoy system north of the Humber was a resounding success. Of 12,122 ships sailing in convoy through these waters during 1918, only forty were sunk. In the Second World War, east coast sailings were coded as 'F/S F/N' convoys. In conjunction with the offshore protective minefield belt, these defences deterred most U-boat skippers from venturing into the swept channel to attack shipping. From May 1940 over 35,000 deep anti-submarine mines were laid in this sector. (ADM 116/6082–ADM 199/2056)

Of the U-boats lost in north-east waters, all but one were destroyed by depth charges, while attacking convoys in the last year of the respective war. The exception was UC 32, sunk in 1917 while mining the Wear roads, and one of several Kaiserliche Marine boats to fall victim to faulty sea-mine design. This coast also preserves proud memories of the Royal Navy Submarine Service.

On 16 December 1914, the day of the infamous bombardment of Hartlepool, the tiny petrol-driven HM S/M C9 (Lt C. Dering) bravely charged after the German High Seas Fleet. Perhaps fortunately for her crew, in diving to escape the shelling, the little boat grounded on the harbour bar. Royal Navy submarines did make more substantial contributions to the two World Wars. Because of their strategically valuable locations relative to the Heligoland Bight/Scandinavian waters, the Tyne, the Tees and the Port of Blyth were selected as submarine bases during the First World War. By the summer of 1916, the 2nd Flotilla (HMS *Bonaventure*) on the Tyne comprised of submarines HMS C7, C8, C9, C10, C12, C13, C14 and C16. A smaller number of 'C' Class submarines clustered

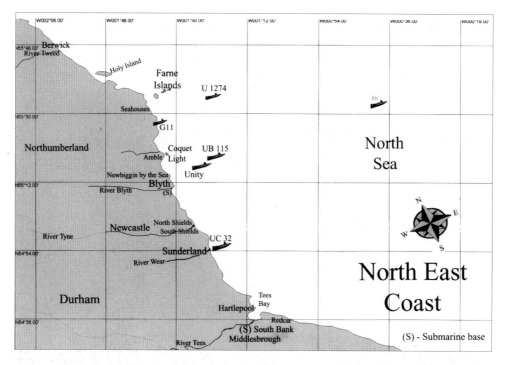

Map of the North East coast.

around HMS *Hebe* on the Wear as the nucleus of the 6th Flotilla. By August 1916, the 10th Flotilla – a far more powerful submarine force – was being developed alongside the depot ship HMS *Lucia* at South Bank on the Tees, made up of the modern boats E39, E44, G7, G8, G9, G11, G12 and G13. The loss of G11 demonstrates the treacherous nature of this wild coastline. The skipper of G11, one of the bravest submariners of all, Richard Sandford VC, is buried at Eston. The 11th Flotilla based on the depot ship *Titania* at the coal-exporting port of Blyth in Northumberland, suffered only two boats lost. One of these, J6 was lost in extraordinary circumstances, as we shall see. The Beach Cemetery contains a superb memorial to men who lost their lives when E30 suffered a battery explosion. By 31 May 1917 the strength of the 11th Flotilla (HMS *Titania*) was; G1, G2, G3, G4, G5, G6, G10, J1, J2, J3, J4, J5 and J6. In the closing stages of the war the 14th Flotilla joined *Vulcan*. By November 1918 her brood included; H8, H11, H12, H23, H24, H25, H26, R1, R9, (plus the huge M1 in September to October 1918). Blyth alone continued as a submarine base in the Second World War, serving operationally between 1939 and 1941 as home to the 6th Flotilla (HMS *Elfin*). HMS *Titania* briefly returned to occupy the same berth she had left back in 1918. The Blyth boats patrolled shallow, mine-infested waters at a time when the enemy had total air superiority. In such impossible conditions, to be detected was to guarantee destruction. The 6th Flotilla suffered appalling losses as a result. At the height of its strength in April 1940 the 6th Flotilla included the following boats; *Sturgeon, Swordfish, Spearfish, Narwhal, Porpoise, Seal, Ursula* and *Unity*. The demise of the latter is inextricably linked with a moving story of self-sacrifice – one which illustrates beyond words, the unique *esprit de corps* of the Submarine Service.

All told, the little port of Blyth exerted an influence far beyond its size when it became the major sea-training station for the Submarine Service from March 1941. An entire generation of wartime submariners trained there. Among the wartime theatres they participated in, these men went on to destroy Rommel's Mediterranean supply lines and played a major role in bringing the North African campaign to a victorious conclusion. A very high percentage of the submariners who trained at Blyth did not survive the war. An annual remembrance service takes place every November in conjunction with the Submariners Association. As for the heritage, the South Harbour remains more or less the same and various buildings of HMS *Elfin* have survived. Links with the Submarine Service remain strong in Blyth, which brings us to that most evocative reminder, a bottle of 'Johnny Walker' whisky kept in the Astley Arms at Seaton Sluice. Won in a sweepstake,

Tyne submarine depot ship *Bonaventure*.

HMS *Lucia*, Tees depot ship.

HMS *Titania*.

Boxing Day 1939, by ERA 'Tug' Wilson, the night before the boat was due out on patrol in the dreaded Heligoland Bight, the landlady, Lydia Jackson, agreed to keep the bottle safe until 'Tug' and the crew of *Seahorse* returned. *Seahorse* was never seen again, but Lydia insisted on keeping the bottle safe, just in case 'Tug' and the boys ever came home. One of Britain's more curious war memorials, the '*Seahorse*' bottle captures the cavalier spirit of these men more succinctly than any tablet of stone. On her retirement Ms Jackson presented the bottle to the Submarine Museum, but a copy can still be seen behind the bar of the Astley Arms.

By the spring of 1945 options were running out for the Norway-based U-boats. Convoy escorts were growing ever more efficient and deadly. Nevertheless, Oblt.z.S. Fitting could not resist attacking the tanker *Athelduke* near the Farne Islands, off Northumberland. What Fitting and his crew lacked in experience, they made up for in courage.

U 1274, KRIEGSMARINE U-BOAT

DATE OF LOSS: 16 April 1945
DEPTH: 63m
REFERENCE: 55 37'.028 N, 001 25'.672 W
ALSO: 55 36'.991 N, 001 25'.830 W
LOCATION: 7½ nautical miles ESE of Longstone and
9½ nautical miles ENE of Seahouses, Northumberland

Type: VIIC/41 ocean-going attack boat   *Builders:* Vulkan Vegesack Werft, Bremen, for Kriegsmarine   *Ordered:* 13 June 1942 within the batch of U 1271–U 1279   *Keel laid:* as Yard No.69 on 21 June 1943   *Launched:* 25 January 1944   *Commissioned:* by Oblt.z.S. Fedor Kuscher on 1 March 1944   *Feldpost:* No.M50 816

TECHNICAL SPECIFICATIONS
See page 339.

U 1274 was assigned to 8.U-Flotilla in Danzig as an *ausbildungsboot* (training boat) on 1 March 1944 with Oblt.z.S. Fedor Kuscher the commander. Fedor Kuscher was born in Trebus on 19 January 1919 and began his naval career in 1939. He served as watch officer with 34th Minesweeping Flotilla, 13th VP-Boat Flotilla and 22nd Minesweeping Flotilla before commencing U-boat training in March 1943. Kuscher was promoted to oberleutnant zur see (R) on 1 January 1944.

In early July 1944, Kuscher and the whole crew transferred on to the new Type XXI boat U 3515 and U 1274 was taken over by a fresh crew under Oblt.z.S. Hans-Hermann Fitting. Fitting was born on 27 May 1920 in Stargard, Pomerania and commenced his naval career in 1939, doing his officer training between September 1939 and August 1940. He served with 23rd and 25th U-Flottilles between May 1941 and March 1943 and was promoted to oberleutnant zur see on 1 October 1943. Having completed training in the Baltic Sea, U 1274 formally joined 5.U-Flottille at Kiel for frontline operations on 1 March 1945.

(1) On her first voyage, U 1274 left Kiel on 24 March 1945 and sailed to Horten (59° 22 29' N, 10° 33 19' E) near Oslo in Norway, arriving there on 27 March.

FINAL VOYAGE
(2) U 1274 left Horten on 1 April 1945 and proceeded to her patrol area off the Firth of Forth. At 17.32 (German time) on 16 April 1945, Fitting attacked the 8,966-ton British motor tanker *Athelduke* (Athel Line Ltd, Liverpool) with two torpedoes, 5¾ miles southeast of Longstone, Outer Farne Islands, off Northumberland. The *Athelduke* was part of convoy FS1784 and on passage from Port Everglades, Florida, for Salt End (Kingston-upon-Hull) via Loch Ewe with 12,600 tons of molasses, when the missiles detonated in the port-quarter, killing twenty-three-year-old William Alexander McKenzie, the fourth engineer officer. The 5,224-ton British steamship *King Neptune* rescued the master, Captain Joseph Errett, forty-one crew, and four DEMS gunners. Following the sinking, however, the ageing 1,325-ton destroyer HMS *Viceroy* relentlessly pursued U 1274. The ex-First World War warship attacked the U-boat with depth charges, 7½ nautical miles east-south-east of Longstone. Narrative of events and log of HMS *Viceroy*:

HMS *Viceroy*.

MT *Athelduke*, sunk by U 1274 off the Farne Islands.

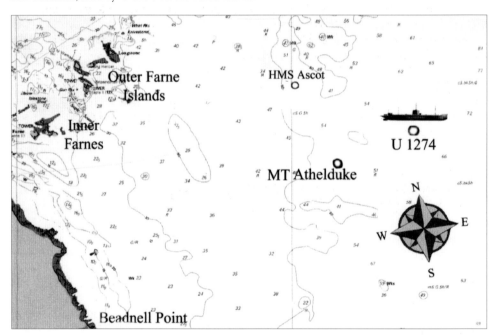

Diagram showing the positions of U 1274 and *Athelduke*.

Convoy FS84 consisted of seven ships formed in two columns, three small ships being in the port column, and four larger ships in the starboard. Course; 1.66 degrees. Speed; 8 knots.

Weather; light wind – Visibility; good, 10 miles.

HMS *Viceroy* was carrying out a broad zig-zag across the front of the convoy at twelve knots, and the other escort, HMS *Woolston*, was zig-zagging on the seaward quarter.

MT *Athelduke*, the second ship in the starboard column was bit aft on the port side by two torpedoes. At this time, *Viceroy* was about one mile ahead of the commodore and on his port bow, steering 126 degrees.

Speed was increased to 18 knots and course altered to port. Three minutes later a good echo was picked up at 2,200 yards, bearing 350 degrees. Speed was reduced. The contact was classified as submarine with moderate-high doppler and, at 1,942½ an attack was carried out using 100ft settings.

Range was opened and a second attack carried out ten minutes later using the same settings. This produced traces of oil.

The third attack was broken off during the later stages of the rim, the operator picking up hydrophone effect from *Woolston* and losing contact and by this time the contact appeared to have no movement and was thought to have bottomed. The third attack was carried out at 20.17, speed 15 knots, using 250ft settings. The first charge of this pattern produced a distinctly prolonged explosion. The attack produced a small, but steady flow of oil, a sample of which has been collected.

Viceroy's fourth and last attack was carried out at 21.13.

SS *Athelduke* sank slowly in position 55° 36' 04" N, 01° 27' 05" W. The bows remained visible, bearing 249 degrees, 3,200 yards from the contact. The bearing was checked each time the ship passed over the contact in the last three attacks.

The 30th Escort Group arrived in the area, and HMS *Launceston Castle* carried out a Squid attack on the contact at about 21.57. *Viceroy* then set course to rejoin the convoy.

On returning to this wreck on 24 April, *Viceroy* again attacked, and evidence, including a bottle of brandy (made in Heilbron), was recovered.

Surface evidence 24 April included a German uniform, jacket, trousers, pulped body parts, one crate of German brandy, German currency notes, one German badge, leather wallet with German notes, leave passes, pages from German books.

Lt Manners was recommended for DSC and ASDIC op PO Mardin was recommended for a decoration.

ADM199/232 – AUD 810/45 – NARA: Series T-1022, Roll 3900, PG31752

The bottle of brandy recovered was later presented to Winston Churchill.

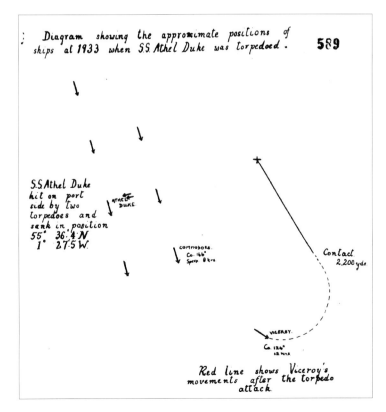

Original sketch drawn by *Viceroy* commander. (Crown Copyright)

THE MEN WHO DIED IN U 1274

Balke, Hans Masch.Mt
Barlowen, von Alexander Lt.z.S.
Barnick, Klaus Oblt.z.S.
Bellman, Werner Masch.Gfr.
Berek Ernst Lt.Ing.
Bier, Gerhardt Mech.Gfr.
Blank, Harry Masch.Mt
Bojar Helmut Bt.Mt
Brehmer, Martin Masch.Mt
Briese, Otto Ob.Masch.Mt
Ebdorn, Friedrich Fk.Ob.Gfr.
Ettinger, Jacob Fk.Ob.Gfr.
Fitting, Hans Oblt.z.S. (Commander)
Fuchs, Werner Mech.Mt
Goldner, Erich Masch.Gfr.
Grube, Ludwig Mts.Gfr.
Gurther, Heinrich Masch.Gfr.
Holz, Bruno Bts.Mt
Kirchenhuber, Rdph Flk.Ob.Gfr.
Kirchmeier, Helmut Flk.Ob.Gfr.
Koppenhagen, Heinz Masch.Gfr.
Langheinrich, Karl-Heinz Masch.Gfr.

Lankamp, Heinz Mts.
Leschke, Walter Mts.
Ludwig, Fritz Ob.Stm.Mt
Lutjen, Heinrich Masch.Gfr.
Miede, Heinrich Lt.z.S.
Persicke, Reinhard Fk.Ob.Gfr.
Pillowski, Rudi Mts.
Potten, Hans Masch.Gfr.
Schneider, Gottfried Mts.Gfr.
Schennegge, Heinz Mts.
Schwarzbach, Martin Masch.Gfr.
Schweiselsen, Fritz Flk.Ob.Gfr.
Stadele, Georg Mts.Gfr.
Stenker, Gottfried Masch.Gfr.
Stroble, Peter Mts.Gfr.
Tanzmann, Richard Ob.Masch.
Tobe, Kurt Masch.Gfr.
Warnicke, Karl Masch.Mt
Weiss, Richard San.Mt
Wende, Waldemar Flk.Mt
Zielke, Fritz Mech.Gfr.

WRECK-SITE

U 1274 is reported to be standing upright on a clean, well-swept, sand and stone seabed in a general depth of 63m (206.7ft). It is still intact, except for the stern end, where, it seems, a number of the depth charges exploded on, or close to, the boat. The hatches are still sealed and the twin steel propellers are there, with the marks of the builder etc. embossed in them. The hull and conning tower have a covering of soft corals, but the conning tower is also draped with a trawl net. Anyone visiting this wreck should remember that it is a war grave and entering the boat would not only be wrong, but would also be a criminal offence.

J6, HM SUBMARINE

DATE OF LOSS: 15 October 1918
DEPTH: 98m–65m
REFERENCE: 55° 37' N, 00° 34' W and 15 knots steering N.73.E
ALSO GIVEN: 55° 34' N, 00° 52' W
LOCATION: 26–30 nautical miles E of Beadnell, Northumberland

By its very nature, war demands decisiveness on the part of those in positions of responsibility. 'The essence of a 'Q' ship attack lay in rapid and overwhelming attack at close range', so wrote Gibson and Prendergast in *The German Submarine War 1914–1918*. Unfortunately the victim of the Q-ship *Cymric* off Beadnell, Northumberland, was the British submarine J6. Even the bravest, most capable, of men can make mistakes.

Type: British 'J' Class Admiralty, fleet patrol, Group I *Pennant No.:* J6 *Builders*: HM Dockyard, Devonport for Royal Navy *Ordered*: J5 and J6 for 1915 Emergency War programme **Keel laid**: 26 April 1915 **Launched**: 9 September 1915 **Commissioned**: 25 January 1916 by Commander Max Horton DSO, who was appointed to supervise her building and remained in command for eighteen months **Completed**: 31 July 1916

TECHNICAL SPECIFICATIONS

Surface displacement: 1,210 tons **U/Dt**: 1,820 tons **LBD**: 83¾m x 7.19m x 4.27m **Props**: 3 bronze (the only triple-screw British submarines ever built) **Machinery**: 3 x 1,200hp 12-cylinder Admiralty Type diesels by Vickers (⅓ of boat's space taken up with two engine-rooms) **S/Sp**: 19 knots **Op/R**: 38 days endurance and 5,000 nautical miles at 12½ knots **Fuel/Cap**: 80 tons and max. 91 tons **Batteries**: Lead/acid **U/Power**: 3 x 675hp General Electric Motors giving 9½ knots **Armament**: 6 x 45.72cm (18in) torpedo tubes (4 x bow and 2 x beam) **Guns**: 1 x 12-pounder HA (5,44kg) and 1 x 2-pounder (0.9kg) **Torpedoes**: 12 **Complement**: 44 (5 officers and 39 ratings)

J6 was part of 11th Flotilla HMS *Titania* and she had two commanders: Cdr Max Horten and Lt-Cdr Geoffrey Warburton from 1 December 1917 to 15 October 1918.

During a patrol in the North Sea on 30 May 1917, J6 fired a torpedo at the Imperial German U-boat U 61, which narrowly missed, (the commander of U 61, Kapitänleutnant Vicktor Dieckmann had been on a patrol from Heligoland around the Orkney Isles, to the south-west coast of Ireland and down to the Western Channel and had returned via the Shetlands. Dieckmann was on the final leg of his voyage home when the incident happened).

FINAL VOYAGE

J6, 15 October 1918 – Friendly Fire: Conditions were clear on that day, there was a slight breeze and the sea was smooth as the Granton (Firth of Forth)-based *Cymric* had proceeded down the swept channel as far as St Abbs Head before pursuing a more south-easterly course, which took her outside of the war channel. Lt Peterson, the commander of *Cymric*, had not been warned to expect any Allied submarine movements, even though his course would bring him close to Blyth, home of the 11th Submarine Flotilla. Evidence of Lt F. Peterson DSO DSC RNR:

> At about 15.30 on the 15th October a submarine was spotted on the surface steaming towards *Cymric*. Visibility at this time was about 6,000 yards and when first spotted the submarine was from two and a half to three miles off. She continued on an opposite course to *Cymric* and I decided she was a friendly submarine...I recognised the bow of the ship as typical of the 'J' Class. When first sighted 'action stations' were sounded, but when I decided this submarine was friendly I told the gun crews, but ordered them to 'stand by'.

There is no obvious evidence that the submarine was hostile: her gun was unmanned and men could be clearly seen on the bridge. But Lt Peterson was disturbed by the position of the gun, as it did not correspond to any of the friendly submarine silhouettes he had been issued with for training purposes. As the lettering on the submarine's conning tower became clearer, suspicion grew that the submarine was an enemy. Some eyewitnesses from *Cymric* claimed that an object was partly obscuring the lettering on the conning tower. Lt Peterson describes what happened next:

> Shortly after this, when the submarine's letter and number could be seen clearly, it appeared to me to be 'U 6'; the submarine at that time was still on the bow: I waited until the submarine was on the beam and still being convinced she was 'U 6', I gave the order for action. The White Ensign was hoisted on the mizzen truck of *Cymric*. There was a pause, but no recognition was shown by the submarine at that time.

J7 leaving the Tyne in
1918.

Lt Peterson (erroneously) believed that it was the responsibility of a British submarine to
make the initial challenge to a surface craft. The failure of J6 to respond convinced him
that the submarine must be German. Enemy submarines regularly struck in the swept
channel and one had been reported just days earlier.

J6 was outward-bound from Blyth on a north-easterly track designed to keep her clear
of the swept channel (where collision with a merchant was an ever present danger). At
15.20 one of the lookouts, AB Luff, reported a sailing ship on the beam without an ensign.
Lt Brierley, the officer on watch, peered at *Cymric*, but saw nothing to give alarm.

Meanwhile, over on *Cymric*, Lt Charles Mutch shared his captain's belief that the
submarine was a U-boat:

> After a short pause, the order was given, 'Drop the bulwarks and open fire!' By this time the
> submarine was well abaft the beam and the range given to the starboard 12-pounder was 1,800
> yards. The first two shots were short, but the third hit the submarine near the after end of the
> conning tower. The order 'independent fire' was made and our guns made several hits.

The result was devastating, as the evidence of Lt-Cdr Geoffrey Warburton DSO, skipper
of J6 testifies:

> As I got out of my bunk, the messenger rushed forward shouting, 'a Q ship firing!' and I heard
> the reports. I shouted out 'full speed on the engines', as I thought from the sound that one engine
> had stopped. When I arrived up on the conning tower we were stern on to the barquentine
> (which was) firing fast. Signalman Field fell down with a rifle in his hand without firing and the
> (recognition) grenade rolled out over the side. Lt Brierley, the officer on watch, had his jaw blown
> off. I fired six grenades which all went off correctly.

Crucially, due to the smoke made by their own guns, the crew of *Cymric* did not spot
these recognition grenades fired by Lt-Cdr Warburton. Lt-Cdr Warburton says:

> During this time we were hit repeatedly, the telegraph being knocked out and a large hole blown in
> the starboard side of the forward engine room. The gun tower was hit abaft the gun and the conning
> tower was also hit but not perforated. The ship was now listing heavily to port, because the external
> main ballast tanks were holed. Lt Robbins having arrived up, I ordered him to get the hands fallen
> in on the disengaged side and to take of his shirt and wave it. The Coxswain was then at the wheel
> and zigzagging. During this time our Ensign was streaming out astern from the W/T mast.

Although several witnesses on *Cymric* observed a flag flying from a mast abaft the conning tower, only one recognised it as a White Ensign. Lt Edward Loly was in his bunk when the first shell hit J6:

> As I turned out a shell hit the port side of the control room forward and blew up the switch board. This must have been the shell which hit the gun tower. At the same time the boat began to list to starboard. I was about to start the blowers when the order came 'go full speed'…the blowing was having no effect. The engine room was reported to be making water very fast and by this stage the engines had stopped. I got the men out and sent up all available woodwork. Leading Tel Wickstead and ERA Robertson remained below.

CERA Robertson was in the engine room:

> I got the order to stop all engines from the captain and called through the voice pipe to the after engine room but received no answer. I stopped the starboard engine and received an order to 'close bulkhead doors'. I went into the motor room to find out if anyone was there. One stoker came out but I was forced away because of the fumes and smoke. I tried once again but there was no answer. I was able to close the forward bulkhead of the motor room.

In fact eight men were missing (two engine room artificers, two stokers and four able seamen), either knocked out by the shelling or trapped within the after engine-room. Either way the closing of the bulkhead door sealed their fate.

When the crew of *Cymric* spotted the white flag, the order was given to cease fire. At this time Lt Mutch observed signal smoke of an indeterminate colour, which convinced him more than ever that this was an enemy submarine, as the Germans were known to copy British signals. Equally damning in the eyes of *Cymric's* crew was the failure of the submarine to stop engines. Unfortunately J6 was unable to stop. The submarine maintained her course and speed. *Cymric's* gunners now brought their howitzer into operation as they pursued the stricken submarine into a bank of haze. By the time *Cymric* caught up with J6, the submarine was clearly sinking. Lt-Cdr Warburton was below:

> I went aft to the engine room. There was about three feet of water above the engine room plates and water was coming in very fast from the starboard group exhaust valve. Chief Stoker Joyner was closing the motor room door and clipped up the beam tube door. I then went forward and closed the foremost door and gave orders to Leading Tel Wickstead to make an urgent morse-code signal for help, which he did. By this time water was coming through the beam tube door. There was no chance of saving the boat and I sent everybody on deck. The Coxswain urged me to come up too and she sank about 20 seconds later.
>
> There were about 20 men in the berthon boat [portable boat] with the rest holding on to the woodwork. I saw Lt Brierley in the water and exchanged waves with him. Shortly afterwards he disappeared. *Cymric* came up in about 20 minutes and lowered boats.

On realising their dreadful mistake, Lieutenants Peterson and Mutch dived off his vessel in order to save the submariners in the water. One of the crew of *Cymric* later wrote:

> The first thing I noticed was the marking 'HM Submarines' on the bands of the men's hats. We had sunk a British submarine by mistaking the 'J' for a 'U'. I can remember a big red headed chap who was badly wounded shouting at us from the boat 'Come on you stupid ***** these are your own ****** side! Give them a hand'.

We pulled over to the sinking men. One man was holding up his commanding officer. He yelled 'come and help me save Mr Warburton'. Others were drowning. We dived in and rescued all that we could. One we took out of the water was too far gone and died on board...We sent a signal to Blyth that we were making for the port with the survivors of J6 aboard. I will never forget entering the port. As we rounded the pier and worked our way into the basin where the depot ship *Titania* and the other submarines were moored, we could see the wives and children of the submarine gazing with anxious eyes to see if those dear to them were among the survivors.

That night *Cymric* anchored in the South Harbour behind the J-boats where there was 'much emotion' from the gathered submariners. Just outside the gates, the wives and dependents of J6's crew had also gathered, drawn to the harbour by the rumours of disaster. T.M. Jones in *Watchdogs of the Deep* claimed that some of the crew of J6 had felt a premonition of disaster prior to the boat's departure. Jones knew the crew of J6 personally and was present when the survivors were landed at Blyth.

Sadly nothing could be done for Artificer Engineer Bright, despite frantic attempts at resuscitation. Artificer Engineer Bright died of shock and was buried at the Beach Cemetery, Blyth, where his grave may still be seen. Of the fifteen men who were lost, his was the only body recovered. The remainder are commemorated on the Portsmouth and Plymouth Naval Memorials.

The Inquiry into the loss of J6 was held at Blyth on the submarine depot ship *Titania* on 16 October 1918. The officers presiding decided that it would be inappropriate to take any further action against Lt Peterson.

In a hand-written note to Admiral David Beatty (First Sea Lord) after the war, Commodore S.S. Hall (Senior Officer in Command of the Submarine Service) made the following observations:

> It does not appear reasonable that an officer whose particular business it was, should be capable of mistaking the silhouette of J6 for 'U 6' even if he did not know that U 6 had been sunk 3 years ago...The C/O of *Cymric* seems to have expected J6 to challenge and to be unaware that it is clearly laid down that the surface craft should challenge and submarines only to reply. To expect a German submarine in this position to have mast up and colours flying, gun unmanned and men on deck in low visibility shows a further want in judgement – particularly in an area where he must have known that British submarines are constantly on passage...it is not known what other action could have been taken by J6.

(U 6 was sunk in the Arctic off Stavanger by the British submarine E16, under the command of Lt-Com E. Talbot DSO, on 15 September 1915.)

It was not the opinion of the group that one might expect to have been Lt Peterson's harshest critics, the crew of J6. So impressed were they by Lieutenant Peterson that, as he turned to leave the courtroom, the survivors stood smartly to attention, saluted and cheered him. Surely the supreme accolade hardened submariners could bestow, and perhaps implicit recognition between submariner and Q-ship sailor of a shared knife-edge existence.

The loss of HM S/M J6 and the Court of Inquiry was classified for seventy-five years, following the hearing and it makes fascinating reading:

ADM. 156/131, Court of Enquiry into sinking of HM S/M J6 by Special Service Vessel *Cymric* under Lt F.H. Peterson DSO DSC RN, 156/147 and 131 156/172 were only opened in 1997, presumably to protect the reputation and identity of Lt Peterson.

J6 was fired upon because the crew did not get their flares away in time to signal that the boat was friendly so subsequently, following her loss, the flare pistol was mounted next to the periscope for speed of access.

Grave (left) of Artificer Engineer C.T. Bright in Blyth Cemetery.

THE FIFTEEN MEN LOST WITH HM S/M J6

Armstrong, Ernest William, E.R. Artificer.3rd
Brierley, James Roger Ingham, Sub-Lieutenant
Bright, C.T. Artificer Engineer
Burwell, Herbert Edward Philip, E.R.Artificer.4th
Hill, Arthur Herbert, Able Seaman
Lamont, Athol Davaar, E.R. Artificer.3rd
Rayner, Edward George, Leading Seaman
Russell, William Thomas, Able Seaman
Savidge, Albert Edward, Stoker.1st
Stevenson, Percival James, L/Stoker
Tachon, Philip, Stoker 1st Class
Thompson, William Piper, Stoker.1st
Tyler, Frank Andrew, Able Seaman
White, Henry Thomas, Able Seaman
Wickstead, George Herbert, Leading Telegraphist

Sexton, Henry Percy Boy Telegraphist, was born in Portsmouth on 8 March 1901. He joined HM S/M G2 on 23 October 1917 and then, on 1 July 1918, reported to J4 before moving to J6, but that date is unknown, his previous occupation being an errand boy – ship messenger.

Cymric (Official No.101751) was an iron-hulled 228-ton auxiliary-engined, topsail schooner or barquentine, that had dimensions of 37.49m in length, 7.32m beam and 3¼m draught. William Thomas shipyard built and launched *Cymric* at Amlwch in 1893, just six days before Captain William Thomas, the owner, died. She was powered by sail, but fitted with a 52hp three-cylinder triple expansion auxiliary steam engine that used one boiler. The vessel was used in the Thomas fleet and, within three months of her launch on 25 June 1893, she sailed the Atlantic, visiting Porto Alegre in Brazil. The vessel was later bought by the Admiralty and visited Boston, USA, in 1912. In 1914 she was converted into one of the cloak-and-dagger Q-ships.

Mrs Sarah L. Hall of Arklow owned her in 1920 and she was registered at Beaumaris (the Halls and the Tyrrells were the two leading Arklow schooner owners). Old *Cymric* survived the First World War but, while carrying coal to Lisbon on 24 February 1944, she sank in the Bay of Biscay during heavy weather. All of her crew of eleven were lost.)

WRECK-SITE

The wreck of HM S/M J6 has never been located and the original position offered by *Cymric's* crew was never swept in an attempt to locate it. The original coordinates at the time of the sinking are: 55° 37' N, 00 34' W and 55° 34' N, 00 52' W. The nearest wrecks to these positions are at: 55 37'.782 N, 000 55'.862 W and 55 34'.093 N, 000 34'.217 W, but there is another possible candidate at 55 32'.120 N, 000 54'.539 W.

Left: 'J' Class boat in dry dock.

HMS J6 and M1 at Blyth, September 1918. (Courtesy of RN Submarine Museum)

Right: 'J' Class boat send-off.

Below: J7.

HMS *Titania* with submarines at Blythe, 1919. (Courtesy of Mr Dave Perkins)

G11, HM SUBMARINE

DATE OF LOSS: 22 November 1918
DEPTH: 1–5 m
REFERENCE: 55 27'.002 N, 001 35'.005 W
LOCATION: Close inshore at Howick, Northumberland

Legends abound on the haunted Northumbrian seaboard. One of the most intriguing concerns the crew of a British submarine who, according to the story, had all got blind drunk on Armistice night and driven their submarine on to rocks near Howick. The reality behind this particular folk myth, however, is infinitely more terrifying and tragic.

Type: 'G' Class British 'Overseas' submarine *Builders:* Vickers Armstrong Ltd at Barrow-in-Furness for the Royal Navy *Ordered:* for the 1914 Emergency War programme *Keel laid:* as Yard No.466 on 28 March 1915 *Launched:* 22 February 1916 *Completed:* 13 May 1916

TECHNICAL SPECIFICATIONS
Hull: Double *Surface displacement:* 693 tons *U/Dt:* 964 tons *LBD:* 57m x 6.86m x 4.11m *Props:* 2 bronze *Machinery:* 2 x Vickers Admiralty 800hp diesels *S/Sp:* 9 knots *Op/R:* 2,400 nautical miles at 12 knots *Fuel/Cap:* 44 tons *U/Power:* 2 x 420hp electric motors at 10 knots *Batteries:* Exide lead/acid *Armament:* 5 (2 x 45.72cm (18in) bow torpedo tubes, 2 x 45.72cm (18in) beam tubes and 1 x 53.34cm (21in) stern tube) *Torpedoes:* 10 *Guns:* 1 x 76mm (3in) Quick Firing HA gun on disappearing mount *Complement:* 3 officers and 27 ratings

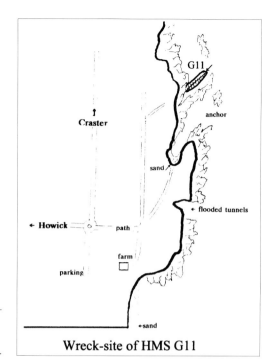

Right: Map showing wreck site of G11.

Below: G11.

The 'G' Class boats were equipped with Fessenden Underwater Sound Telegraphy and were built as 'Bight & North Sea Patrols', as the bow section was raised during the war to improve sea-keeping abilities. These boats were based on the 'E' class, adopting the double hull design concept favoured by the Italian, Laurenti, but in practice they showed no improvement on the 'E' Class. Her commanding officers were:

Lt Andrew Wilmot-Smith from 10 February 1916.
Lt Charles Manners Sutton Chapman from 1 March 1917.
Lt Richard D. Sandford VC, hero of the Zeebrugge raid, was appointed commander of G11 on 1 November 1918 (Nominal List). However, he later became gravely ill and was admitted to the local hospital, suffering from typhoid. Lt-Cdr George F. Bradshaw DSO took over as temporary commander of G11 on 19 November (on 15 September 1909, Lieutenant George F. Bradshaw had begun a submarine course on HMS *Mercury*). Prior to his service on G11, he was posted to HMS *Onyx* on 1 January 1910 (additional to the crew) and then to HMS *Forth* on 1 February 1911 (additional). On 28 February 1913, Lt Bradshaw assumed command of HM S/M A9 (*Onyx*) and on 20 February 1914, he served on HMS *Bonaventure* (additional). He assumed command of HM S/M C7 on 4 February 1915 and became CO (additional) with HMS *Dolphin* on 29 August 1916.

Lt Richard Sandford. VC

In command of HM S/M G13, he successfully torpedoed and sunk an enemy submarine on 10 March 1917, showing skill and determination: 'their Lords consider great credit due to Lt Bradshaw, officers and men for this successful attack.' He was recommended the DSO by *Grand Fleet Gazette* 12 May 1917.

Lt Bradshaw was (additional) CO on HMS *Lucia* from 21 October 1916 until June 1918. In 1921, he was also CO of HM S/M K15, which sank at its moorings at Blockhouse, due to oil getting into ballast tanks. However Lt Bradshaw was on leave at the time.

(Lt Sandford VC was also present on K6 during the Battle of May Island.)

FINAL VOYAGE

G11 left South Bank, home of the 10th S/M Flotilla at 16.30 on 19 November 1918. The war had been over for eight days when Lt-Cdr George Bradshaw DSO left the Tees for a billet over the Dogger Bank. At the time HM S/M L11, Bradshaw's own command was undergoing a refit on Tyne and this much-respected skipper was unfamiliar with both G11 and her crew.

At 20.00 on 20 November G11 was ordered home following an unremarkable patrol. Navigating Officer Lt Maclure RNR was able to fix G11's position by the Dogger Bank Light Vessel, but from that point onwards until the Coquet Light was spotted, navigation would be down to dead reckoning. The weather was overcast, the boat's compass appeared to be faulty and the fixes given by ACW (wireless direction) were wildly inaccurate. To add to the crew's discomfort the Logan log used to record distances had ceased to function. Bradshaw proposed to pass 10 miles north of the mined area, then to alter course to 228 degrees, once Coquet Light was passed. Lt-Cdr Bradshaw intended altering course so as to pass between 7 and 10 miles to eastward of the coast and outside the war channel, thus avoiding the danger of a collision. Both skipper and navigating officer estimated that, with a speed of 9–11 knots, Coquet Light should be spotted at 19.00 on 22 November.

On 22 November, the skipper took over from the officer on watch at 17.00, with the experienced Coxswain Palmer as lookout. At 17.50 Bradshaw altered course for Coquet Island. The tide was practically slack and the wind and tide had gone down. The submarine was reckoned to be 14 miles from Coquet at 19.00. Although visibility was otherwise clear, a curtain of fog screened the land. Lt-Cdr Bradshaw:

> About 1840 I observed what I took to be a fog bank ahead. On entering the fog I sensed something ahead. I asked the Coxswain if he saw anything ahead, he replied 'No Sir'. Sighting land straight ahead I immediately gave the order, 'Hard-a-starboard, stop both'.
>
> Immediately after the engines stopped we struck a rocky shore at a speed of 9 knots. The boat ran up the shelving rock until her bows were nearly clear of water and immediately began bumping very heavily.
>
> On grounding she was holed somewhere on the port quarter, either in the motor room or the engine room. Subsequently the port hydroplane-shaft was snapped off and the shaft forced into the boat…she was badly holed in the port engine room bilges and after flat. Most of the keel was torn away from the pressure hull…all moveable gear fell into the port bilges, water was seen entering the motor room and the First Lieutenant reported that he could hear the electric battery cell containers cracking.
>
> The boat began to take a dangerous roll to port, which increased with each roller breaking over her. I concluded that the boat was hopelessly aground and in imminent danger of capsizing and sinking. I therefore gave the order 'All hands on deck' I spotted low-lying land ahead at about 12–20 yards from the bow. The boat was now lying over at an angle of 50 degrees and bumping so heavily that I considered she would be holed and flooded at any second and that the only possible course was to try and save the Crew.
>
> I ordered the men on deck and lined them along the starboard side of the casing. I then ordered First Lieutenant Smith to go forward to the bows and endeavour to get ashore with a heaving line and then to haul a hemp rope ashore. According to PO Palmer, Stoker Foster was thrown overboard from the port side of the bridge by the tower hatch following a heavy bump made by the boat just after he had emerged from the conning tower hatch. The deck at this time was nearly vertical. While the crew were coming up by the conning tower and working their way forward I heard someone say 'There is a man overboard!' I switched on the aldis lamp and eventually saw a man swimming towards the rocks about 20-yards on the port beam and about 20-yards from the rocks. The surf was so bad that I did not allow anyone to go in after him but gave an order to throw a heaving line. I regret that owing to the almost vertical position of the upper deck, it was impossible to get the casing flaps open for some time and long before this the man was swept out of sight and I fear killed on the rocks.

In pitch darkness and at great personal risk Lt Smith and AB Birch had succeeded in clambering over the slippery rocks to secure a line. Lt-Cdr Bradshaw ordered his men to line up on the starboard casing. One by one they used the line, initially to hang on to, and then to guide them to the safety of the shore while the skipper trained the aldis lamp on the rope, thus providing as much light as he could. Holding the rope was, in itself, a hazardous undertaking and Tel. Back slipped to his death in the cold November sea.

As soon as Lt Smith discovered that two men were missing, the crew volunteered to go back to the shoreline and mount a search. The freezing and bedraggled men were given sustenance at a nearby shepherd's house and by the kindly fisher folk of Craster. The indefatigable Bradshaw walked along the cliffs to the Craster coastguard station where he telephoned the SNO of Blyth and Tees to inform them of the catastrophe. Throughout their ordeal the crew of G11 had behaved in an exemplary manner.

Telegraphist George Philip Back's grave in the far south-west corner of the peaceful little churchyard of St Peter's at Longhoughton, close to where he was washed ashore. Near to the grave, on the right-hand side, is a badger sett.

G11 wrecked at Howick, November 1918.

The inevitable inquiry held that Bradshaw, having been more used to the performance of L11, miscalculated the loss of speed on encountering heavy seas – a reduction of speed which would have been greater in his old submarine than in G11. It was this miscalculation coupled with the fog curtaining the shore, which had proved fatal to G11. Bradshaw had a highly distinguished record and none had the stomach for a court martial. The Inquiry Conclusion:

> We are of the opinion that the accident was primarily caused by overestimating the loss of speed due to the sea running at the time... Soundings were not taken prior to grounding owing to the conviction of the CLO that he was at least 16 miles from shore at the time... The fog was a severe one...it was not possible to take any immediate action to salve the ship and that all possible steps were taken for the essential and expeditious removal of the crew from the boat...while the sextant may have been read incorrectly...we are of the opinion that no blame be attributed... FL Smith and AB Birch (AB helmsman) singled out for praise for their work in the rescue.

The body of Stoker Foster was never recovered and he is now remembered on the Plymouth Naval Memorial, however Telegraphist George Philip Back's corpse was later recovered and buried in the south-west corner of the sleepy little churchyard of St Peter's at Longhoughton, Northumberland, and near to where he was washed ashore. Telegraphist Back's father lived in Chelsea, London.

There is perhaps one final casualty to mention – Lt Richard D. Sandford VC, who died of his illness the day after his submarine, G11 was lost. He is now buried in Eston cemetery, near Middlesbrough, in Plot JU 79. (ADM 137/3807 – *The Loss of HM Submarine* G11)

Extensive salvage work took place on the wreck of G11 during 1919 and then again in 1938, at the outbreak of the Second World War.

WRECK-SITE

Nowadays, there is little left of G11 and the shoreline has been abandoned to the screaming seabirds and ghosts. The submariners would surely have had no argument with that?

Reaching the wreck-site entails a considerable hike from the bend in the coastal road, near to Howick village, then down along a track by the hedgerow to the rocky cliff tops, just to the north of a small house, often referred to as the 'Bath-house', which is said to belong to a local doctor. What remains of the wreck lies in a submerged gully that runs seaward from the shore at the low water line and out for about 80m. You can literally step into the water at low tide and find parts of the wreck dispersed amongst the rocks and weed. There is a solid brass escape hatch visible, albeit well concreted into the nearby rocks, submarine air tanks, rusting air-ducts and bent steel hull plates, part of the keel and the remains of the engines that lie at the deepest point – around 5m on a low spring tide.

UB 115, SM IMPERIAL U-BOAT

DATE OF LOSS: 29 September 1918
DEPTH: 49m
REFERENCE: 55 14'.468 N, 001 22'.440 W
LOCATION: 4½ nautical miles NE of Beacon Point,
Newbiggin-by-the-Sea, Northumberland

Parallels can be drawn between the loss of UB 115 in 1918 and the destruction of U 1274 off the north-east coast some twenty-seven years later. In the last year of the First World War both submarines made desperate attacks against convoys guarded by a Royal Navy that was able to benefit from technological superiority – in this case, aerial surveillance provided by an RNAS balloon.

Type: UB III torpedo attack boat *Builders*: Blohm & Voss, Hamburg for Kaiserliche Deutsche Marine *Ordered*: 23 September 1916, within the batch of UB 103–UB 117 *Keel laid*: as Yard No.321 *Launched*: 4 November 1917 *Commissioned*: 28 May 1918 by Oberleutnant zur See Reinhold Thomsen

TECHNICAL SPECIFICATIONS

Hull: Double *Surface displacement*: 519 tons *U/Dt*: 65 tons *LBDH*: 55.30m x 5.80m x 3.68m x 8¼m *Props*: 2 bronze *Machinery*: 550ps MAN/Vulcan diesels *S/Sp*: 13.3 knots *Op/R*: 7,420 nautical miles at 6 knots *Sub/R*: 55 nautical miles at 4 knots *U/Power*: 394ps electric motors giving 7½ knots *Batteries*: Lead/acid/accumulators *Fuel/Cap*: 35–36 tons *Armament*: 4 bow and 1 stern 50.04cm torpedo tubes *Torpedoes*: 10 x 50.04cm (19.7in) *Guns*: 1 x 105mm forward-facing deck gun *Ammo*: 160 rounds of 105mm *Mines*: None *Diving*: Max-op-depth 50m (164ft) and 30 seconds to crash-dive *Complement*: 3 officers and 31 ratings

UB 115 was formally assigned to Flandern I.U-Flottille, Zeebrugge, on 3 September 1918, with Reinhold Thomsen the commander from 28 May 1918.

(1) UB 115 left Hamburg on 31 August 1918 and transferred to Zeebrugge, where she arrived on 3 September.

FINAL VOYAGE

(2) UB 115 departed Zeebrugge for her first operational patrol on 18 September 1918, being the last boat to do so. She arrived off Sunderland on 21 September and, one mile south-south-east from Roker lighthouse, sank the 336-ton British steamer *Staithes*, which was en-route from Port Mulgrave, near Whitby for the Tyne, loaded with iron ore. Three men were lost.

THE MEN WHO DIED

Jonson, Otto, 37, mate
Radford, L.H., 48, master
Worrell, A., 35, able seaman (cook)
Wyatt, Charles Victor, 52, engineer

Nemesis was then to appear in an unexpected form, however. Thomsen cruised off the Tyne, then moved up the Northumberland coast, reaching Newbiggin-by-the-Sea by 29 September. Here, the crew must have been experiencing some problems with the tanks because, as she lay submerged, 4½ miles offshore, the crew of the British airship R29 – fortuitously engaged on convoy protection duties nearby – observed oil bubbling to the surface. The convoy system had just been introduced to east coast convoys the previous month, but the use of airships in convoy defence was an even more recent innovation. The East Fortune-based R29, proved her worth. The suspicious oil slick was reported and two 230lb bombs and a calcium flare were released over the position. Destroyer HMS *Ouse* raced to the scene and was soon joined by the 1896 vintage destroyer HMS *Star*. The two warships then dropped seven depth charges, set at 50, 100 and 200ft respectively. Three RN trawlers also joined in and ten more depth charges were dropped. The Royal Navy vessels were fitted with hydrophones and heard the U-boat start her engines at 14.00, resulting in a further twelve depth charges being sent down. An hour later the engine noises were heard again, resulting in two more depth charges being dropped. From 16.00, the sound became intermittent but continued until 18.25, by which time it was assumed the U-boat crew must have been, mercifully, dead. Oil poured up to the surface continually all night and for the following two days – minesweepers reported that the source of the oil was an obstruction. UB 115 was lost with her entire crew of thirty-nine. The odds had tipped decisively against the Flanders U-boats. Log of HMS *Star*:

Sun 29 Sept –	Berthed alongside collier *Ryhope* at Jarrow (am)
12.00 –	Cruising stations starboard quarter of convoy escorting TM convoy. Proceeding up war channel – zig-zagging.
1.50 –	Rigid airship observed to drop bomb to eastward.
1.51 –	Full speed closed spot.
1.54 –	Commenced dropping depth charge – dropped 5 in quick succession.
2.32 –	Full speed. Dropped 6th depth charge on spot indicated by airship. Oil seen coming to surface, also air bubbles.
2.50 –	Full speed.
2.51 –	Dropped 7th depth charge on oil patch. Stopped to collect oil and examine vicinity.
4.50 –	Rejoined convoy.

ADM 53/61347 – NARA: Series T-1022, Roll 42, PG61870

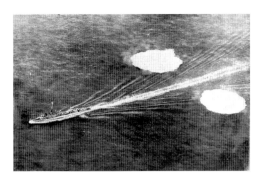 

Above left: Depth charge attack on UB 115 off Northumberland, 29 September 1918. (Courtesy Imperial War Museum, London)

Above right: The end of S/M UB 115. This aerial photograph is part of a unique montage taken from an East Fortune-based RNAS balloon. One destroyer is off the picture listening in, while the RN trawlers are cutting off any line of escape for the U-boat. A second destroyer has just raced in to drop a depth charge over the contact. The picture was taken on 29 September 1918 from a height of 1,000ft. (Courtesy of Imperial War Museum, London, Reg. Q 63907)

THE MEN WHO DIED IN UB 115

Bansemer, Mts.

Becker, Masch.Mt

Benz, Mts.

Bonn, Lt.z.S.

Bonningsen, Hzr

Buddenhagen, Ob. Mts.

Börner, Masch.Mt

Dmock, Ob.Hzr

Eckert, Ob.Masch.Mt

Eisermann, Ob. Masch.Mt

Grünau, Masch.Mt

Hansel, F.T.Mt

Hausich, Mts.

Heinze, Hzr

Hösel, Mts.

Knörr, Mt

Kratzius, St.Mn

Krauthausen, Hzr

Köllmann, Kap.

Köppe, Mts.

Lob, Mts.

Mebus, Masch.Mt

Mehne, F.T.

Moss, Hzr

Müller, Hzr

Nuss, Masch.Mt

Peters, Ob.Mt

Post, Masch.Mt

Preising, Bt.Mn

Ronkel, Hzr

Rosenbusch, Hzr

Rück, Mts.

Schauber, Ob.Hzr

Schieweg, Ob.Masch.Anw

Schoth, Mts.

Tegge, Masch.Anw

Thomsen, Reinhold Ob.z.S.

Trumpfheller, Ob.Mts.

Wilkens, Mn.Ing.

WRECK-SITE

The wreck lies on a seabed of fine-sand and broken shells in a general depth of 49m (167.7ft), being the lowest astronomical depth. In 1973, it was reported as sitting upright and still intact on the seabed, with the hatches closed and the hull covered in deadman's fingers. It is also alleged to attract a lot of small fish around the conning tower (probably pout-whiting (bib)). It is now reported as being broken into two parts, each standing around 2–3m high, probably destroyed by trawlers. A 1m-scour surrounds the wreck and both sections are covered in an array of soft corals. A couple of miles south of the wreck,

67

is a spoil-ground that was used by the old power station, where huge quantities of fly-ash have been tipped over many years, so it is quite possible that some of that may have been swept north on the ebb tide and on to the wreck-site.

UNITY, HM SUBMARINE

DATE OF LOSS: **29 April 1940**
DEPTH: **50m**
REFERENCE: **55 13'.963 N, 001 19'.733 E**
LOCATION: **6½ nautical miles ENE of Newbiggin-by-the-Sea, Northumberland**

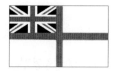

Type: Unity Class (U-Class Prototype), British small-patrol submarine **Pennant No.:** 66C (1939 – 66D). **Builders:** Vickers-Armstrong at Barrow-in-Furness for the Royal Navy **Keel laid:** 19 February 1937 **Launched:** 16 February 1938 **Commissioned:** 15 October 1938

TECHNICAL SPECIFICATIONS
Hull: Double **Surface displacement:** 540 tons **U/Dt:** 740 tons **LBD:** 58.22m x 4.88m x 4.22m **Machinery:** 2 x 400hp running at 600rpm max. Paxman diesels (diesel-electric-drive), constant rating was 380hp at 530rpm **Props:** 2 bronze **S/Sp:** 11¼ knots **Op/R:** 4,010 nautical miles at 10 knots **Sub/R:** 120 nautical miles at 2 knots **U/Power:** 2 x 412ps General Electric motors giving 9 knots **Batteries:** Lead/acid **Fuel/Cap:** 41 tons **Armament:** 6 x 53.34cm (21in) torpedo tubes (4 internal and 2 external) **Torpedoes:** 10 x 53.34cm (21in) torpedoes **Guns:** 1 x 105mm (4.13in) forward deck gun **Ammunition:** 160 rounds of 105mm **Mines:** None **Diving:** Max-op-depth 60.96m (200ft) **Complement:** Peacetime: 4 officers and 23 ratings; Wartime: 4 officers and 27 ratings

COMMANDERS
Lt-Cdr S.H. Pinchin – 15 November 1937.
Lt Norris Edwin Cutler – 7 January 1939.
Lt J.F.B. Brown – 15 June 1939. Lt Brown served in the boat for two months when the Second World War commenced and took her on eight active service patrols.
Lt Francis J. Brooks assumed command on 20 April 1940, but his command was short-lived, when his boat was lost after just eight days.
The 'U' Class boat was a simply designed training submarine that was built to replace the 'H' Class. However, the boats were built, not to train submariners, but operators of ASDIC, who were based on surface warships, learning the art of submarine detection. *Unity, Undine* and *Ursula* were 'clockwork mice' and were designed to have no armament whatsoever. After 1933 and the rise of Hitler, tubes were added. In order to bring them in line with the firepower of the 'S' Class, two extra tubes were added in the form of the bulbous addition to the bow. The original design of the 'U' Class boat had six bow torpedo tubes (four internal and two external), but the external tubes were removed on all but the first three vessels built.

A second generation of boats – *Upholder, Upright, Usk* and *Utmost* – also had the raised bow, but no external torpedo tubes as they were too advanced in construction to change. *Una* and *Umpire* were built at Chatham and all the rest were built by Vickers at Barrow. The majority of 'U' Class boats were deployed in the North Sea and Mediterranean. All together, nineteen of these boats were lost during the Second World War.

HMS *Unity* in all her splendour. (Crown copyright)

Unity served in the 6th Flotilla based at Blyth, Northumberland. *Unity* did not sink any enemy vessels but her eight wartime patrols were carried out mainly in the shallow, mine-strewn waters of the Heligoland Bight and Kattegat, at a time when the enemy had total superiority. During this phase the Submarine Service suffered the worst losses in its history and the 6th lost more boats than any other flotilla. In the course of one patrol, on 5 April, during the German invasion of Norway, *Unity* made an attack on U 2. On 9 April a Q-ship pinned down *Unity* for several hours.

FINAL VOYAGE

The 29 April saw a thick fog descend on the north-east coast. The CO of the 6th Flotilla was in London. Although a staff officer (Ops) was on hand to advise a skipper in case he had any queries prior to sailing, no one at Blyth would take the responsibility of postponing the patrol in such impossible conditions. In the hope that the weather might improve, *Unity*'s departure was delayed until 17.30 but, in fact, visibility only deteriorated further. As usual, the Signals Distribution Office was buzzing with activity. Teleprinters rattled out minefield information updates (QZHs) and last-minute communications relayed from Horton's HQ. Each boat had its own 'pigeon hole' and, should a message arrive late, a WRNS messenger (Women's Royal Navy Service) sat poised on a motorbike ready to take it down to the harbour, before the boat sailed.

The duty petty officer was usually given the responsibility of 'letting go' a submarine from harbour. On 29 April, this duty fell to Petty Officer Telegraphist Norman Drury of *Sturgeon*. Unable to see from one side of the harbour to the other, Norman was appalled to learn the boat was to sail as planned. With visibility down to a matter of yards, this decision smacked of official madness. No sooner had *Unity* cleared the wall, than she disappeared into the murk beyond.

Lieutenant Brooks had been ordered to 'Proceed with Dispatch', which was generally interpreted to mean the submarine must travel on the surface to take advantage of the greater speed offered by the engines.

Lt Trickey:

> At 17.50 *Unity* rounded the fairway buoy and a course of 070 was set to make a position in the centre of the main swept channel By 18.30 the marker coded '20R' was located, signifying the boat had now entered the main East coast Swept channel and a course of 345 degrees was set.

Despite the dreadful visibility, Brooks did not see fit to use the boat's siren to warn other vessels – after all, he did not expect to encounter any. Estimating it would take another four hours before the boat reached 'Gap B' through the minefield, the skipper was keen to maintain a steady 8 knots. At 19.00, Third Hand Lt George Hunt stepped onto the bridge to relieve Lt Trickey as officer of the watch (OOW). He found the skipper, Lt Trickey and the lookouts straining their eyes trying to spot the next buoy, '20F'. Lt Hunt came to the bridge at 19.00 to relieve the OOW. At 19.07 the silence was pierced by a loud, mournful wail and the men on the bridge knew its significance only too well.

More wails signified that *Unity* was sharing the channel with a convoy. Should that convoy happen to be steaming south, there was every possibility of a collision. Lt Brooks acted quickly, ordering the helm to be put hard over, sounding *Unity's* own feeble siren in the process. The lookouts stared through the mist to locate the ship, then another wail boomed out, this time so near, it was deafening. At 19.09, looming out of the fog like some monstrous apparition, reared the huge bows of a merchantman. The men on the bridge were momentarily transfixed with disbelief but collected enough to call out: 'Collision stations, prepare to abandon ship'. Lt Trickey:

> At 19.09 I saw a merchant ship about 25 degrees on the port bow about 30 yards distant which seemed to be steering across the bow. The engines were put full astern and three short blasts were made. At 19.10 the merchant struck the port bow about the bulkhead in the fore-ends. The speed of the other ship appeared to be about 4 knots. The impact was gentle. I estimate our position to have been 55° 13.5 N, 1° 19 W.

Engine Room Artificer Rob Roy McCurrach was enjoying a cigarette down in the mess when the order to abandon ship came. Concluding it was an exercise, a collective groan broke out, for the sailors resented any interruptions of their otherwise ordered lives. Rob Roy:

> I felt a bump up for'rard, no worse than coming alongside with an inexperienced boat handler. Telegraphs clanged 'Full Astern' Chiefy Potter galvanised into action. He shot through the Control Room to grab the Engine Room bulkhead just before a young seaman was about to shut it.

Had the door been shut against them, the engine room staff would have been asphyxiated by the diesels before they had the opportunity of shutting them down.

> 'Abandon ship!'

The submarine went astern on her motors. Already taking on a bows-down angle, Brooks realised it was now a case of keeping her afloat for as long as possible to allow the crew to escape. Rob Roy slowly became aware that the emergency was for real:

> Still sitting in the Mess, watching all this activity and fearful of being in someone's way, I heard Nat ask, 'You staying Bob?'
> I heard the engines being stopped and shut down. Charlie Foster and 'Dusty' Miller came into the Control Room from aft. The First Lt stood at the foot of the ladder.

The engine room artificer's mess and some crewmen in the closing stages of *Unity*'s penultimate patrol. (Courtesy of Rob Roy)

'Can we take a D.S.E.A set?'

'Take anything you like', replied First Lt John Low.

'Anything?' I looked round quickly. 'I'd like a sextant, pair of binoculars and a telescope. I wouldn't mind the engine room clock. After all it had governed my life, night and day, awake or asleep.'

The crew made their way up the ladder and crowded on to the bridge. As they climbed, Lieutenant Low called out reassuringly: 'No hurry lads, there's only 3 feet on the depth gauge.'

As Rob Roy dithered over his choice of souvenirs, he became aware of the wardroom steward urging him up the ladder:

'Up you go Bob.'

'Oh, no up you go. You were here first.'

'Six feet of water showing on the gauge', called out John Low.

I glanced round quickly. Nothing looked wrong. All lights on, the mess neat and tidy. Curtains a bit off-centre and we were slightly bows-down. I went up to the bridge and heard the captain shout, 'Some of you down to the casing'.

With the submarine assuming an angle of 25 degrees, it dawned on the crew that *Unity* was finished. A short distance away they could just discern the bulk of *Atle Jarl*.

The Norwegian freighter which had accidentally rammed them, was now hove to with its lifeboat lowered. Already submariners were entering the freezing water and swimming towards it. Catching sight of the heads bobbing about in the swell, Lt Brooks ordered: 'I must have the main motors stopped'. Rob Roy knew why immediately:

But of course, those propellers would mince us. Knowing how to stop them, I shouted 'Right Sir, I'll go', and turned to re-enter the boat, nearly treading on 'Dusty' Miller's head. Having heard the last order he said, 'I'll go Bob, I'm better placed'.

As 'Dusty' clambered back down the ladder to join F.L. Low, Rob Roy made his way down from the bridge to the casing:

> Water filled my shoes so I kicked them off. Through stockinged feet I felt the propeller vibrations stop. I knew I could now swim away to safety. The sea was bitterly, cold – so cold it took my breath away. Silly thoughts ran through my head such as 'I bet I catch a chill' or 'what I really need is a piece of my mother's blackberry and apple pie'. I wanted company. I didn't want to die alone. On spotting a head at the top of a wave, I swam in that direction. 'Pusser' Hill was lying on his back, ears underwater, so I reached out and pulled his hair.
>
> 'Pusser have you a lifebelt?'
> 'No.'
> 'A D.S.E.A set?'
> 'No, not a thing, you okay?'
> We trod water and saved our breath. The bow was well underwater now and lacking the restraining force of the motors on full astern.

At 19.29, and without warning, the stern swung up to a near vertical position, hung motionless for a few seconds, then, with her Ensign still flying proudly, HM S/M *Unity* plunged to the bottom of the North Sea, taking John Low and 'Dusty' Miller with her. Rob Roy and 'Pusser' had no time to dwell on it:

> There was no break in the waves, just a strong oily swell. At the top of one I saw a lifeboat and a good dozen swimmers. I grabbed 'Pusser' and gasped 'Come on…swim'. We headed in the direction of the lifeboat and were making progress when it altered course. This was quite demoralising.

Rob Roy and 'Pusser' had drifted away from the main knot of swimmers. All around them miniature acts of courage and endurance were being played out. A man was drowning, his hands raised in a final gesture of resignation when Stoker Burville swam over to support him, risking his own life the process. As the last man jumped from the bridge, the submarine had lurched over, trapping Charlie Foster against the bridge telegraphs. 'Chiefy' Potter spotted his predicament, refusing to leave him even though *Unity* was really gathering speed in her plunge to the bottom. Potter pulled Foster's DSEA set over his head as he frantically set about freeing him. Both were dragged down some distance when the formation of an air bubble allowed Potter to unhook Charlie from the repeater bar.

The two men surfaced together but Charlie had not followed DSEA drill, having failed to open the exhaust valve on his set. Potter turned to find his lifeless body, but still he refused to abandon his 'sprog' to the deep. Meanwhile Burville and the drowning man had reached the lifeboat when Alf spotted another swimmer in difficulty. Without hesitation, Burville turned his back on safety to return to the perishing water. He swam over to the man and hauled him to safety. Lieutenant's Hunt and Trickey chose to remain in the water, a particularly courageous decision on the part of Trickey, who could not swim. Eventually Rob Roy and 'Pusser' caught up with the rest:

> At last we made it and hung from the gunwales. Whacked. To my right, in an equally sorry state bobbed the Capt. 'Give us a hand', shouted 'Pusser', as loud as he could, they just sat like numbed, frozen effigies. 'I can't hang on much longer Mac. Can you pull me up?' I shook my head, 'No'. 'Look, push my left foot up and hook my heel over gunwale'. 'Pusser' did this and with a great effort, I managed to scramble into the boat, then I turned and pulled him. Between us we did the same for the Captain.

HM S/M *Unity* painted in watercolour by submariner ERA William Fry DSM in accordance to the description of events given by his friend, Rob Roy McCurrach. William Fry died in *Trooper* in 1943. (Rob Roy and Pam Armstrong)

They found themselves opposite Alf Potter and Charlie Foster, who although not dead, appeared to be in a very bad way.

> Charlie Foster lay in front of me, slumped in a heap, was out cold, unconscious, a flat DSEA set strapped his chest. A green slime was oozing from his opened mouth He looked near to death. Suddenly a brand new tin of Grey's cigarettes was thrust under my nose and someone asked me 'Smoke?' I took one gratefully. Now that was clever. How did he keep them dry? The matches too! I puffed away luxuriously.

The submariners were helped onboard *Atle Jarl* by the anxious Norwegian crew. The ship had left Methil in Fife earlier that day in convoy, bound for the Tyne with a cargo of coal and coke. It had been estimated that the F/S convoy should have been off Blyth by 19.30. Tragically, Lt Brooks was unaware of this and *Unity* had blundered directly into the course of the oncoming ships. Each survivor was treated to a large glass of whisky while a scratch roll call was made. The drink was sufficient to revive Charlie Foster, who was now observed to be 'full of beans and grinning sheepishly'.

Apart from Low and Miller, two other men were missing – Stoker Shelton and AB Hare, last seen in the water making their way towards the lifeboat. Much earlier these men were known to have purchased some heavy boots sold off by Blyth Fire Station at a bargain price. They were known to have been wearing them at the time of the collision. The survivors solemnly concluded that these boots must have dragged them to their deaths. Indeed Chief Engine Room Artificer Potter declared that his decision to kick them off before he entered the water saved his life. When *Atle Jarl* anchored off the mouth of the Tyne, Rob Roy volunteered for lookout duties wrapped in the Norwegian skipper's greatcoat. Next morning a motor launch picked up the survivors, landing them at North Shields Fish Quay.

Transport arrived in the form of some ancient fish lorries. For Lt Brooks, already at the end of his tether, this was all a little too much. He telephoned HMS *Elfin* to demand more suitable transport. A short time afterwards, a brand new coach arrived to take the weary matelots back to Blyth, but Alf Potter did not remain with the rest. He left in a fast hydrophone-equipped launch for the last known position of *Unity*. The launch stopped off Cresswell where, more in hope than expectation, Potter listened in for any sounds which might indicate that Lt Low and Miller were trapped but alive. There was just the chance that they had been able to shut the hatch before *Unity* sank. In these circumstances they would have reverted to their DSEA sets and attempted to escape, but in his heart, Potter knew that even if they had been able to escape and reach the surface, they would not have survived for very long. CERA Potter remained at sea until darkness and intense cold forced him to abandon his vigil.

Lt Francis Brooks personally broke the bad news to Mrs Marjorie Low, then serving as a Wren Officer at *Elfin*. Simultaneously a telegram was sent to the home of Mrs Miller, informing her that the Submarine Service had claimed yet another of her sons – his caul having failed to protect him. The next day Rob Roy attended a compulsory medical with the base doctor.

> The M.O. asked me 'How do you feel?' I was tempted to say, tired, jubilant, sad, cross…that I had become enormously attached to that little boat, that I had lost a significant part of that which made me tick. That I had a brush with death and there's nothing like it for making you realise how good it feels to be alive. As it was, knowing that survivors automatically get fourteen days leave, I replied, 'Fine Sir', I was in two minds to add, 'Ask me when I get back'.

As experienced submariners, both Lt Low and Henry Miller would have been aware of the risks when they volunteered to return inside the boat. In so doing, they sacrificed their own lives to save those of their mates. Their courage was initially recognised with the award of the British Empire Medal, but this was later exchanged for the George Cross.

On 23 May an Admiralty Inquiry was held at *Elfin* into the loss *of Unity*. Each witness was carefully examined and cross-examined and it rapidly became obvious that Lt Brooks had been totally unaware of the southbound convoy. This was odd because there was little doubt that an Admiralty signal warning of its approach had been received at the Signals Distribution Office (SD) in *Elfin*, well before *Unity* was due to sail. The key questions were; why had Brooks not been informed of Signal 1428/29/4? And if the skipper had not known about its contents, had anyone else?

Chief Yeoman of Signals Christopher Reading remembered seeing this message come tapping through the teleprinter, and he made sure of placing it in the appropriate pigeon hole ready for collection by Tom Moon, *Unity*'s signalman. Signalman Walter Warren corroborated this evidence. He too had seen the signal still awaiting collection when he came off duty at 16.00 but interestingly, his relief, Tel. Percy Marks had no recollection of this message whatsoever. It was a submarine signalman's responsibility to collect all available information from the SD Office before handing it over to the first lieutenant prior to sailing. The evidence of Thomas Moon was therefore of crucial importance. Moon's career to date had been exemplary. 'Shiner' Moon was insistent he had no knowledge whatsoever of Signal 1428/29/4. He was certain it had not been among the bundle of 'Q.7' messages he had collected from the SD Office. In keeping with routine practice, Moon assured the Inquiry, everything in the *Unity* pigeon hole had been handed to Lt Low. Obviously the Inquiry was at a major disadvantage in that virtually all of the hard evidence had gone down with the boat, and so had Lt Low. Without his evidence, Moon's account could neither be disproved nor corroborated. Yet not all the available evidence was considered: only officers and selected ratings were called to give evidence.

The court did not hear the disturbing tales of signals regularly ending up in the wrong pigeon holes, or of messages spasmodically appearing on the wrong submarines. In fact the Inquiry was remarkably selective with regard to the material it wished to consider. A civil court would have doubtless reached an open verdict but this was not a civil court. Max Horton added the following conclusion:

> It appears most probable that the signal was in fact read by Leading Signalman Moon, who failed to show it to the Commanding Officer. I consider however that the probability of obtaining sufficient evidence to secure conviction of this rating for the offence is remote and that the assembly of a court martial is not justified under present conditions.
>
> Max Horton 567/SM172

Francis Brooks was censured for his failure to discuss last-minute developments with the intelligence officer. It was also noted that *Unity* had been travelling at high speed in bad visibility. The court did not see fit to question why the boat had ever been allowed to sail in such adverse conditions in the first place. While there was glowing praise for the way in which the crew of *Unity* had conducted themselves, the proceedings did little to dispel a lingering suspicion that the verdict was a whitewash. By deflecting the lion's share of the blame onto a rating, Admiralty had deftly sidestepped some embarrassing questions.

Submarine ace Cdr 'Dead Eye Dick' Cayley demonstrated his view of the proceedings by selecting 'Shiner' Moon for his signalman, first on the crack submarine *Utmost*, then on P311. Both men died when P311 batted in early January 1943. As for Rob Roy, he was handed a draft-chit for Blockhouse. Blyth had been his home for the past six traumatic months; now it was time to say farewell to the people who had shown him such kindness:

> I packed my kit then joined Cookem for one last run ashore in Blyth. We went to Seghini's for coffee and then, just like the old days, took all six girls to the cinema, walked them back home and then stepped out to the Watsons for a very special supper. Mr and Mrs Watson were in tears when I left. They admonished me to be careful and come back soon. This to my eternal regret, I never managed to do.
>
> Extracts from *In Fear and Affection,* reproduced by kind permission of Rob Roy McCurrach DSM

The crew of *Unity* was broken up; the submariners were given a choice between joining two of the new 'U'-class boats currently under construction, *Upright* and *Utmost*. Lt Commander Francis J. Brooks transferred to the Admiralty's Operations Division Staff. He was later killed in an air crash.

Friendly fire incidents were common during the Second World War and convoys opened fire and frequently tried to unwittingly run down the British submarines. Coastal Command also attempted to bomb the boats, particularly when they were off Sunderland, for some unknown reason. *Umpire* (see Chapter Three – East Anglia) was lost in similar circumstances.

THE MEN WHO DIED IN *UNITY*

Hare, James, 25, Able Seaman
Low, John, 29, Lieutenant GC
Miller, Henry, 39, GC
Stoker Cecil Shelton, 21, Stoker

WRECK-SITE

The wreck is in a half-metre scour and is orientated in a north–north-east to south, south-west direction. It lies on a seabed of sand, mud and shells, in a general depth of 50m, being the lowest astronomical depth. The wreck is upright, reasonably intact, broken open, but still fairly complete with the twin propellers attached and covered in a profusion of plumose anemones and soft corals. A large ball of trawl net and some monofilament fishing lines are snared up and floating above the conning tower. However, except for a small shoal of bib, very few other fish have been reported around or over the wreck-site. It is now classified as a war grave, in honour of the two brave men who lie within.

UC 32, SM IMPERIAL U-BOAT

DATE OF LOSS: 23 February 1917
DEPTH: 12–13m
REFERENCE: 54 54'.521 N, 001 19'.320 W
ALSO: 54 54'.510 N, 001 19'.621 W
LOCATION: ¼ mile NE from north pier light, Sunderland

During the First World War, Kaiserliche Marine submarines regularly mined the busy roadsteads of Tyne, Wear and Tees. The soluble chemical plugs within the mine mechanism designed to give the 'UC' submarine time to clear the area were frequently unstable. The 'UC' crews were thus under threat not just from British A/S forces, but also from their own deadly cargoes.

Type: UCII coastal mine-laying boat *Builders*: Vulcan AG, for Kaiserliche Deutsche Marine *Ordered*: 29 August 1915, within the batch of UC 25–UC 33 *Keel laid*: as Yard No.71 *Launched*: 12 August 1916 *Commissioned*: by Oberleutnant zur See Herbert Breyer on 13 September 1916 *Combat ready*: 27 November 1916

TECHNICAL SPECIFICATIONS

Hull: Double *Surface displacement*: 400 tons *U/Dt*: 480 tons *LBDH*: 49.45m x 5.22m x 3.68m x 7.46m *Machinery*: 2 x 250ps MAN diesels *Props*: 2 bronze *S/Sp*: 11.6 knots *Op/R*: 10,040 nautical miles at 7 knots *Sub/R*: 55 nautical miles at 4 knots *U/Power*: 2 x 230ps electric motors giving 6.6 knots *Batteries*: lead/acid *Fuel/Cap*: 41 + 14 *Armament*: 2 external 50.04cm torpedo tubes at the bow, one either side of the mine chutes and 1 stern-internal tube *Torpedoes*: 7 x 50.04cm (19.7in) maximum *Guns*: 1 x 88mm (3.46in) forward deck gun *Ammo*: 133 rounds of 88mm. *Mine tubes*: 6 *Mines*: 18 x UC 200 *Diving*: max-op-depth 50m (164ft) and 33 seconds to crash-dive *Complement*: 3 officers and 23 ratings

Torpedo load as designed: 4 – a torpedo in each tube plus a reload for the stern tube. Storing an additional torpedo in pieces internally for the stern tube later augmented this, although this was optional. Two extra torpedoes (total) for the external bow tubes could be carried as well – these were lashed to the deck. So up to a total of seven torpedoes were carried, although not all boats sailed with that many.

With Herbert Breyer the commander from 13 September, UC 32 was formally assigned to the Germany-based I.U-Flottille at Brunsbüttel on 27 November 1916. Breyer conducted three war patrols:

(1) UC 32 left Germany on 11 December 1916 and cruised along the English east coast to lay mines. On 14 December, the SS *Burnhope* (Captain William C. Saddler) detonated one of the mines laid that same day. The steamer had just set out on a voyage from Hartlepool to London with a 2,600-ton cargo of coal and was swinging to starboard

Camouflaged UCII coastal mine-laying boat, UC 59, following her surrender in 1918/1919. (RN Submarine Museum)

before altering course in Hartlepool Bay. The pressure and blast from the enormous explosion that followed smashed the ship's wheelhouse windows and even the glass in the compass binnacles. A second explosion beneath the port bow followed seconds later, which so seriously damaged the vessel that she began to sink by the bows. The captain immediately ordered the starboard lifeboat made ready and swung the ship to portside in order to reach shallow water. After twenty minutes, her bows touched ground and a minesweeper towed her stern-end round, into the shallower water. However at 09.00, the *Burnhope* (Burnett SS Co. Ltd, Newcastle) took on a big list to port and her crew, except for the captain, abandoned ship. Gradually the list got so bad that by 10.15 she went over onto her side and Captain Saddler had to be picked up out of the sea by the crew of the minesweeper, unfortunately only to suffer a heart attack and die soon afterwards.

The *Ida Duncan* (C. Duncan & Sons Ltd) carried a crew of six, working in and around the mouth of the river Tees. On 31 January 1917, the tug was en-route from Middlesbrough to Tees Bay when she struck one of the mines and sank, half a mile off the river mouth, near to the South Gare Lighthouse. The explosion killed all of the crew and actually lifted the boat out of the water. Her stern-end went straight under the water, but the vessel's bows remained bobbing on the surface for a further fifteen minutes before she finally sank altogether. The wreck was later dispersed, using explosives.

THE MEN WHO DIED
Duncan, Charles Crystal, 30, Engineer
Duncan, Lional, 29, Master
Gibson, James, 16, Deck Boy
Scott, Harry Charles, Fireman
Tinmouth, Robert, 56, Mate
Walker, Thomas, 47, Fireman

A mine from UC 32 also probably sunk the 2,494-ton SS *Hildawell* (T.W. Willis, West Hartlepool) bound from Bilbao for Middlesbrough with iron ore. All her crew was lost. The mine was laid on 14 December. Having dropped her pilot off at Yarmouth in Norfolk on 19 December 1916, the ship was never seen again.

THE MEN WHO DIED

Capsey, J., 46, Able Seaman
Clarke, John Stephen Lloyd, 26, Donkeyman
Hansell, Robert Ernest, 26, First Mate
Helland, M., 30, Able Seaman
Henderson, Benjamin, 32, Fireman
Ingram, Henry, 56, Master
Kohn, Ole, 24, Fireman and Trimmer
Lee, Thomas Wallis, 27, Steward
Patterson, Robert Masters, 26, Ship's Cook
Peterson, Alexander, 33, Able Seaman
Prentice, Robert, 33, Second Engineer
Pulli, Jacob, 22, Sailor
Rowlands, Harold, 33, Boatswain (Bosun)
Screeton, George Robert, 21, Second Mate
Small, F., 39, Fireman
Stubbernd, H.C., 21, Sailor
Warren, David Stewart, 17, Mess Room Boy
Wheeler, George William, 42, Fireman
Wilmhurst, Walter, 20, Third Engineer
Witten, Richard Arthur, 44, First Engineer

UC 32 arrived home on 27 December 1916.

On 17–18 January 1917 two signals, which were intercepted by the Admiralty from UC 32 north of Heligoland, suggested that she was at sea at the time. The submarine in question later captured the drifter *Mayfly* and put a petty officer on board. However, an Allied Q-ship drove the submarine off and the German officer was taken prisoner. During the interrogation the man informed his captors that he was from UC 32, but this proved false, because his boat was in fact UC 31.

(2) UC 32 left her Brunsbüttel on 28 January 1917 and sailed for mining operations off the English east coast. The Norwegian SS *Jerv* (Aktieselskapet 'Jerv'), which was carrying a crew of sixteen and in ballast, travelling from Rouen to Middlesbrough, suddenly blew up and sank at 14.00 on 1 February; she was under the command of Captain Adolf Bernhard Sørensen from Lyngør. According to eyewitnesses, she probably detonated a mine, but it was later revealed that UC 32 had torpedoed her; sailor Thorleif Tjøstolfsen, drowned. UC 32 returned to Heligoland on 5 February 1917.

Another mine accounted for the Italian SS *Apollonia* (Sicilia Società di Navigazione, Palermo) off Flamborough Head on 1 March 1917. The ship was carrying munitions from Middlesbrough for Lagos and the local lifeboat rescued seven crewmen, the rest having perished. No crew names are available.

Allegedly, during one of her voyages, one submariner was washed off the deck casing and drowned, when UC 32 was caught by surprise off Sunderland and was forced to crash dive, in order to escape.

FINAL VOYAGE

(3) On 17 February 1917, UC 32 left Heligoland to operate and lay mines off the English east coast. The Heligoland U-boat base intercepted radio messages from British merchantmen, which showed that Breyer was attacking Allied shipping five days after he left port. At 18.30 and in darkness on 23 February, Breyer was on the surface at the entrance to the river Wear and had just laid his first mine when there was a violent

explosion under the boat's hull. (It is believed that a plug holding the mine to the sinker had dissolved prematurely, releasing the mine under her stern-end; the mine was the one at the bottom of the fifth chute.) Oblt.z.S. Breyer and Ob.Stm.Mt Skau, who were in the conning tower when the vessel blew up, quickly found themselves in the water. As UC 32 sank, a rush of air pushed the only other survivor, Ob.Hzr Schirm, to the surface. An examination vessel, which happened to be close to the scene, rescued the three men.

UC 32 was 328 yards from the breakwater, according to navigating officer, Oberstauermansmaat Skau. Breyer had ordered the laying of the last mine when the boat suddenly keeled over, the stern seemed to break away from the rest of the boat.

Extract from PRO records

This account of the sinking and incident was found in a letter addressed to the mother of survivor, Reinhard Schirm:

Friday 6.15
I was in the Control Room. The explosion extinguished the lights immediately and I was hurled forward owing to the pressure of the water flooding in [for the boat had been torn in half].

I was driven upward. I held my breath. At the same moment the bottles containing compressed air burst and I was thrown into the conning tower. As for the moment the pressure was greater from inside than outside, I could take breath again. The boat in the meantime had sunk to the bottom. I let go and was at last thrown out. I swam on the surface 200 metres from the boat. I shouted for help and found my strength failing me (I had not slept for some 28 hours) and had swallowed a good deal of oil. I also had my heavy leather clothing and sea boots on. I took my boots off and managed to pull one leg out of my leather breeches but swallowed a great quantity of oil in the process. Now for the other leg. Because my hands were quite numb I could not get my knife out but somehow I managed to get my remaining leg out of the leather breeches with great difficulty. I felt my limbs stiffening with the cold. I shouted for help again. At last I saw a light and soon after a second one. The first was the Sunderland [sic] lighthouse, the second the light of an English patrol boat. I swam towards it and when I was about 20 yards off someone threw me a lifebelt. An English sailor handed me an oar and pulled me into his boat. I heard a voice 'Hullo Schirm, you here too?' I recognised the captain. There were only three of us.

We were very well looked after on the steamer and the English sailors were kind to us. They must have felt sorry for us because they kept giving us their cigarettes. My English helped a bit. We were given dry clothes and in the evening taken off to hospital. Again we were kindly treated and well fed, but we were strictly guarded. On Sunday we were taken to the station. We were not exactly looking at our best, but you should have seen the curiosity of the crowd, particularly the women.

The following day (24 February) the wreck was located by a chain sweep and divers were sent down. However, 'soup-like' visibility from the river Wear prevented them from examining the U-boat. On 27 February iron gratings covering the mine-chutes were found by a diver and he managed to retrieve a fraction of the shattered pressure hull. The 88mm forward-deck gun and its mountings were also reported as intact. Next day the divers found the conning tower and two intact periscopes and noticed that the conning tower hatch was open. However, the entrance was too small to accommodate a fully-suited diver. Although the forward section of the U-boat was undamaged, the hull near the engine room was severely shattered and about 30ft of the stern, with the propellers and rudders attached, was missing; divers came across this portion on 1 March. 'Small trawling nets were towed continuously round the wreck for books, loose gear etc.', but nothing was found. Over the next few days all operations were halted when gale-force winds and heavy seas developed and the wreck markers/buoys were torn free and lost. Lt-Cdr Guybon C.C. Damant, who was previously Inspector of Diving and primarily responsible for salvaging gold from the sunken liner *Laurentic* off Lough Swilly for the 1917 dive season, was called away to Sunderland to oversee the diving on UC 32.

On 18 March a diver located the rear door of the starboard bow tube and twelve hours later Lt-Cdr Damant had one of the torpedoes, complete with its warhead and pistol intact, retrieved for examination. By the end of March it was decided to end further salvage operations because they didn't expect to find anything new; plus, the wreck still harboured fourteen unexploded mines in the fore section and these posed a serious hazard to both vessels and salvage crews. It was at first proposed to detonate the mines by charge, but in the end the Admiralty decided not to blow the wreck up.

THE MEN WHO DIED IN UC 32
Adler, Ob.Hzr
Beyes, Masch.Mt
Dreyer, Masch.Mt
Ebenkamp, Hzr
Eckloff, Btn.Mt
Eissler, Hzr
Falcke, Lt.z.S.der Reserve
Gabriel, Hzr
Handreck, Ob.Masch.Mt
Hansen, Mn.Ing.Asp.
Hein, Hzr
Hoffmann, Mts.
Kasch, Ob.Mts.
Klöden, Ob.Mts.
Lachmund, F.T.
Reidhardt, Mts.
Schmidt, Masch.Mt
Schulzke, Hzr
Ungenannt, Masch.Mt
Vollert, Mn.Ing.
Wind, Mts.
Zahn, Ob.Btn.Mt der Reserve

CREWMEN WHO SURVIVED
Breyer, Herbert, Oblt.z.S.
Schirm, Ob.Hzr (Head Stoker)
Skau, Ob.Stm.Mt

ADM 137/3897, 137/3918, 137/3875 – NARA: T-1022, Roll 85, PG61944
NARA: Roll T-102, Roll 81 Abschriften aus Fragebogen series.

Mr R. Mitchinson, a resident of Hendon, Sunderland, at the time, stated:

> As a young boy of nine years old, I can remember living in a house that overlooked the quayside and docks and I remember watching as three U-boat sailors, one of whom was the commander or captain, were brought ashore under armed escort. I can still see the hatred against the Germans on the faces of those local Hendon people, who lined the quay, they must have really despised them.

The three men were jeered and spat on when they were helped ashore from the boat and onto the quayside, before some armed policemen led them away. The captain, however, did show his gratitude at being rescued because he gave one of his rescuers a memento from his pocket, I think it may have been a cigarette lighter or case, they certainly seemed happy to still be alive, because the North Sea around here is very cold at the best of times.

UC 32 was credited with sinking four Allied vessels and possibly the SS *Hildawell*:

AREA	VESSEL'S NAME	FLAG	TONS	D	M	YEAR	LOCATION
North Sea	*Burnhope*	GBR	1,941	14	Dec	1916	Mined off Hartlepool
North Sea	*Hildawell*	GBR	2,494	20	Dec	1916	Mined English east coast (possibly)
North Sea	*Ida Duncan* (tug)	GBR	139	31	Dec	1916	Mined 1½ miles E of South Gare Middlesbrough
North Sea	*Jerv*	NOR	1,112	1	Feb	1917	Mined 7 ¼ miles E of Scarborough
North Sea	*Apollonia*	ITA	2,891	1	Mar	1917	Mined 1 mile off Flamborough Head

WRECK-SITE

Up until about 1980, a substantial amount of the U-boat's wreck was still intact, including the twin bronze propellers, which were inscribed '*Vulcanwerke, Volcad Werke, Rubel Bronze, 29/7/1916*' and '*Durchmess, Steigung*'. When it was found, the complete periscope and about five whole telegraphs were also there, as well as the two propellers. However, they are now long-since gone, plundered when the wreck was first discovered by accident.

In the early 1990s, a diver from a Sunderland Sub Aqua Club 'rediscovered' the wreck and told the media about what he had found. From that day on, lots of officialdom, including the German Embassy, became involved and it was designated as a war grave. Because it was close to the shipping channel and there were still live mines and torpedoes on board, the Royal Navy brought in divers to examine the remains and decided to disperse it. Now, the police launch from the river Wear usually appears and warns off any diving boats moored anywhere near the wreck-site. It lies approximately 400m north-north-east from the north pier lighthouse at Sunderland, in 12–13m of water. There is still a substantial amount of it left, in three main sections, and lots of copper and brass can be seen, along with dozens of giant lead batteries, standing in rows. One torpedo tube also still contains a live torpedo too, just ready for firing.

UB 110, SM IMPERIAL U-BOAT

DATE OF LOSS: 9 July 1918
DEPTH: 47½m but salvaged
REFERENCE: 54° 39' N, 00° 55' E
LOCATION: 4½ nautical miles NE from
Hunt Cliff, Saltburn (later salvaged)

Type: UB III torpedo attack boat   *Builders*: Blohm & Voss, Hamburg for Kaiserliche Deutsche Marine   *Ordered*: 23 September 1916, within the batch of UB 103–UB 117   *Keel laid*: as Yard No.316   *Launched*: 1 September 1917   *Commissioned*: by Kapitänleutnant Werner Fürbringer on 23 March 1918

TECHNICAL SPECIFICATIONS
Hull: Double   *Surface displacement*: 519 tons   *U/Dt*: 651 tons   *LBDH*: 55.30m x 5.80m x 3.68m x 8¼m   *Machinery*: 2 x 550ps MAN/Vulcan diesels   *Props*: 2 bronze

S/Sp: 13.3 knots *Op/R*: 7,420 nautical miles at 6 knots *Sub/R*: 55 nautical miles at 4 knots *U/Power*: 394ps electric motors giving 7½ knots *Batteries*: lead/acid *Fuel/Cap*: 35 + 36 tons *Armament*: 4 bow and 1 stern 50.04cm torpedo tubes *Torpedoes*: 10 x 50.04cm (19.7in) *Guns*: 1 x 105mm (4.13in) forward deck gun *Ammo*: 160 rounds of 105mm *Mines*: None *Diving*: Max-op-depth 50m (164ft) and 30 seconds to crash-dive *Complement*: 3 officers and 31 ratings

Kplt Werner Fürbringer was the boat's only commander. One fascinating dimension of the last patrol of UB 110 is that both main protagonists committed their recollections to print. His autobiography *Alarm! Tauchen!!*, published in 1933 (re-published in 1999 by Leo Cooper as *FIPS − Legendary U-boat Commander*), is a First World War classic and cannot be recommended highly enough − not just because it features several of the boats featured in this book, but for the insight it provides into the life (and death) of the First World War U-boat man.

On 12 July 1916, Fürbringer was commander of UB 39 and he took the boat right inshore at Seaham Harbour and fired thirty-nine shells. The number of shells fired was in honour of his boat's number. Sadly one of the shells killed Mary Slaughter from Hebburn-on-Tyne, who was visiting Seaham. The lady was out walking with her friend at the time. Fürbringer and his crew were supposedly aiming at the ironworks, which the Germans believed was producing armaments. However when the skipper observed the proximity to the town of Seaham and became aware of the devastation such an attack would cause, there is convincing evidence that the humane 'Fips' Fürbringer deliberately fired his symbolic barrage over, rather than at the town. The submarine then escaped on the surface. Fürbringer was also the former commander of UB 58, but was admitted to hospital and, during his illness the boat was taken over by Oblt.z.S. Werner Löwe and then lost with the entire crew on 10 March 1918, leaving Fürbringer devastated. He said that he felt that somebody had stolen his boat and kidnapped the crew. At least half of the men had been with him from previous boats and he felt responsible for them. His steward, Mts. Tiede, had been with the skipper since the very beginning and had even got married on the same day as Fürbringer. After leaving hospital, Fürbringer was assigned to the new UB III boat, UB 110. He took her on two voyages.

(1) After completion of trials and working-up, UB 110 left Hamburg on 19 June 1918 and sailed around the Dutch coast for the transfer to Bruges and Flandern II.Flotilla. However, during the voyage, the boat's port diesel broke down and Fürbringer was instructed to proceed to Ostend for repairs, as Bruges yard had no capacity.

UB 110 was standing about 2km offshore after leaving Zeebrugge for the one-hour journey to Ostend, when two aircraft approached from the sea. At first Fürbringer thought they were German, but the planes swooped in for an attack. Fortunately the skipper had taken measures for such an event by installing a machine gun on the upper casing and having the quick-loading anti-aircraft gun manned and ready. The gun crews were ordered to open fire and the boat was put at maximum speed with the helm hard over to starboard. The first plane made two bombing runs, dropping a large dustbin type bomb each time, with the last one exploding just 10m away; the iron deck casing was also spattered with machine-gun bullets. The second plane also dropped two 'dustbin' bombs, one exploding near to the boat, and then it peppered UB 110 with machine-gun fire. Just as the planes began heading away, anti-aircraft shore batteries opened fire. UB 110 arrived at Ostend on 27 June 1918.

FINAL VOYAGE
(2) UB 110 departed Bruges on 4 July 1918, with orders to proceed to the English east coast for operations in the area off Hartlepool and to return to Flanders after twelve days. Having

negotiated the Bruges–Ostend canal and nearing Zeebrugge, Fürbringer was informed that the catering petty officer and cook had forgotten the boat's entire cutlery. Fortunately the loch-keeper at Zeebrugge was persuaded to let them have the entire stock of reserve cutlery – enough for half of the crew. (UB 110 also left Zeebrugge following the famous raid.) The boat was subjected to daily depth charge attacks from 7 to 18 July, as she cruised along the swept channel looking for TM convoys. On one occasion, UB 110 attacked a tanker and suffered twenty-six depth charges for the privilege. On 16 July, Fürbringer torpedoed and sunk the steamship *Southborough* (Hazelwood Shipping Co. Ltd), 5 miles off Scarborough. She was in convoy and on passage from La Goulette via Dover for Middlesbrough with a cargo of iron ore. The torpedo detonated in her forward bunker on the starboard side at 13.43. The ship immediately took on a severe starboard list, before turning turtle and going down to the bottom in a matter of minutes. Thirty people on-board the steamer, which included Captain W.H. Eade and a pilot, were lost; eight survivors who went into the sea were picked up by an escort vessel and landed at Middlesbrough later that day.

TWENTY-SIX OF THOSE WHO DIED
Bayliss, William, Fireman
Bonny, William, 29, Steward
Buytaert, T., Able Seaman
Cameron, James, Second Mate
Carroll, John Joseph, 28, Boatswain (Bosun)
Carse, James, First Mate
Cocks, Charles William, Pilot
Eade, W. H., Master
Gigg, Percy Harold Oliber, 27, Trimmer
Hankins, J., Sailor
Hayes, Walter, 25, Chief Cook
Heazlewood, Charles Thomas, 22, Fourth Engineer Officer
Hollywood, James, Fireman
Hood, Alfred Robert, Sailor
Lawson, John, 28, Donkeyman
Ledan, George Perry, Third Engineer
Lind, Charles Frederick, 39, Fireman
McKeon, Andrew, 49, Fireman
McMaster, Donald, 49, Sailor
Pearce, Hy John, Second Engineer
Power, Ernest, 21, Third Mate
Richard, Lazarus, Assistant Cook
Smart, Henry Thomas, 33, Fireman
Thomas, Thomas Charles, Chief Engineer
White, J., Fireman
Yeoman, Philip Randolph, 27, Able Seaman

The four people missing from the list were probably DEMS gunners.

On 18 July Fürbringer met up with Oblt.z.S. Dobberstein in UC 70 and, at 10.01 the following morning, exchanged recognition signals with UB 77. After the meeting with UB 77 Fürbringer moved to the north and was allegedly spotted on the surface, north-east of Whitby by an American aircraft and, as UB 110 dived, she was bombed – this was according to a letter from the Pilot Ensign J.J. Schieffelin, which was written on 9 January 1966.

From there, Fürbringer continued north, submerged for three hours and sighted a huge, southbound convoy off Hartlepool, consisting of about forty ships and protected by four destroyers, six RN motor launches, six armed trawlers, one Convoy Leader, a barrage balloon and three aircraft. Fürbringer took up position to launch a torpedo at the French coaster *Yolande*, but the periscope had been spotted:

Lt Chick RNR on ML263 one of the convoy escorts, slightly astern of the convoy on the port beam sighted a periscope 50 yards on the starboard bow. ML263 dropped two depth charges set for 100'. ML49 dropped 1 depth charge. 15 seconds later the submarine surfaced, her forward hydroplanes were possibly jammed. ML49 opened fire with machine gun and 3 pounder scoring hits on the conning tower and on the waterline, forward.

The escort destroyer HMS *Garry* then rushed to the scene. It is fascinating to note that the captain of *Garry* was none other than famed *Titanic* survivor, Lt-Cdr Lightoller RNR.

The British view – Log extract of HMS *Garry* 19/7/1918 – Lt-Cdr Lightolller

10.45	Sighted periscope on port side. Dropped 4 depth charges.
13.37	Heard ML[263] sound 6 blasts
	Full ahead, dropped 2 DC one at 150ft the other at 50ft.
	Submarine broke surface 100 yards away off port bow.
	Rammed sub at right angles and passed over him.
	Sub again broke surface.
	Turned, guns firing, 12 pounder and port. Waist gun hitting sub and rammed again, tearing all superstructure open. Sub heeled over and sank.
	Proceeded in direction of beach until damage was ascertained.
	Down by the head, but not sinking.

The position was given as 54° 39.20' N, 00° 54.40' E. Thirteen of the U-boat crew survived but twenty-three men perished.

The German perspective - Werner Fürbringer's account:

I had already decided to remain on patrol for three more days. We were three miles south of Hartlepool when we sighted a large southbound convoy, which included a 3000-ton steamer. I was sizing up an attack position at periscope depth when to my utter dismay there was a patrol vessel speeding in to ram. I gave orders to dive to 17m but a depth charge exploded very near our bow causing serious damage. The fore hydroplane was not only jammed, forcing us upwards but the port motor shorted and fuel pumps ceased to work. No.2 fuel tank on the starboard side was ruptured. At any rate I had to stop our ascent to the surface so I ordered my men to rush into the fore-ends. This was beginning to have some effect when a destroyer rammed into us, hurling me into the well. Immediately afterwards a second charge exploded, again causing us damage where we could least afford it – the hydroplanes and the pressure hull. The submarine would not dive. Now it was a case of saving my crew. The order was passed to blow all our tanks and surface the boat. Already the enemy shells were striking us. I gave the order 'Abandon Ship', but we had sustained so much damage that we had the greatest difficulty in opening the conning tower and torpedo loading hatches. At last we got them open but as the crew were evacuating the boat, the destroyer rammed us a second time. Over I went, into the water. The water was frigid and I felt as if my heart was stopping when suddenly I was roughly pulled from the sea by a British sailor and thrown into a whaler. Four officers, our war pilot and 9 ratings were picked up.

In this contemporary account recorded by a British naval intelligence officer in the days following his capture, Fürbringer made no reference to the atrocities he later claimed had been meted out to his crew. On the other hand it could be argued that the intelligence officer was unlikely to either investigate or even record such hugely embarrassing allegations. In his autobiography, published in 1933, 'Fips' Fürbringer described how all his crew, having succeeded in evacuating the boat, now floated helplessly in the water. The U-boat men were beyond resistance, trapped between fear of the sea and a terror of what the British might do to them. He describes how Forster, one of the engine room hands, was brutally struck by a British PO as he attempted to scramble up the side of the destroyer. Worse was to come:

> …my crew were in the water waiting to be rescued. But there was indiscipline aboard the British ship. Men from the destroyer fired on the survivors, while others hurled lumps of coal at the heads in the water. The smaller craft had closed and were also exercising their machine gunners…I saw my steward…he looked towards me imploringly…I had started to swim towards him when his skull was split open by a large lump of coal. He was dead before I got to him. Oberleutnant Loebell who was swimming nearby had no lifejacket, said that he had been shot in the thigh. I gave him support. 'Let me die in peace,' he said, 'they are just going to murder us all in any case.' I made no reply and merely held on to him…

Werner Fürbringer *Alarm ! Tauchen!!,* 1933

While the timing of these claims may elicit some scepticism, there is overwhelming evidence that something very unpleasant took place here. Records reveal that several of the survivors were evacuated to hospital suffering from gunshot wounds – though some of these wounds may have been inflicted as the crew was abandoning the U-boat. Charles Lightoller briefly described the destruction of UB 110 in his autobiography, *Titanic and other Vessels.* This is all he has to say of the German crew: '…I left the rescue work to the others, who picked up fifteen out of the water and then took stock of the damage we had sustained…'

As the British did not investigate the affair, readers must decide for themselves whether an atrocity took place. The authors conclude that friend and foe alike regarded Fürbringer as a patriotic and highly professional naval officer: he was an honourable and humane man, not given to lying. Nor was Fürbringer the only captured U-boat man to claim that atrocities had been committed by the British (see Chapter Four).

On 2 August news was passed to the German authorities via the Red Cross, reporting that the boat had been sunk and her captain, watch officer and some of the crew were being held as prisoners.

After Fürbringer was made prisoner, he was taken to HMS *Satellite* at Jarrow and the local fisher-folk gave him a hard time on the way to the train station.

THE MEN WHO DIED IN UB 110
Brenzel, Mts.
Burkhard, F.T.
Eskerski, Mts.
Freifinger, Ob.Mts.
Ibele, F.T.Ob.Anw
Ingenhaag, Masch.Mt
Iserhardt, Hzr
Jessberger, Hzr
Klein, Masch.Mt
Lüdtke, Mts.

Masuhr, Mts.
Merkle, Masch.Mt
Neuhäuser, Masch.Mt
Ollegott, Mts.
Oswald, Mts.
Ploen, Mn.Ing.
Roosen, Hzr
Rosenblüh, Mts.
Santer, Hzr
Schmidt, Masch.Mt
Stein, Hzr
Strauss, Mts.
Träger, Hzr

SALVAGE

The wreck of UB 110 was not difficult to find because a continuous flow of oil was rising to the surface and Cdr Wheeler located her on 29 July 1918, lying on the seabed in 26 fathoms, north-east of Saltburn Pier. When divers descended to her they attached a buoy to the bow and reported that the boat's bottom was painted a dirty green in colour. One of the divers who landed on her deck casing described how the gun must have been 'carried away'. He described how a circular hatchway, 2ft in diameter, was already open and the conning tower was smashed. This was evidence of the U-boat being rammed on the port side, just forward of the conning tower and abreast of where the deck gun should have been. The impact of the submarine being rammed would have knocked the gun from its mounting. Incidentally the boat had been rammed twice, the second time aft on the starboard side.

Once examined, all diving operations were then suspended by Cdr Wheeler until it was decided what they were going to do with the U-boat. Wheeler and his divers returned to the wreck on 10 August and again on 15 August and decisions were taken to salvage UB 110. By 19 September, she was raised to the surface and the long tow to Swan Hunters Shipyard on the Tyne began. On arrival at Swans on 4 October, the Admiralty wasted no time in opening her up. A valuable haul of codebooks, ciphers, documents and radio logs was recovered on 9 October. However, one of the most important finds was the General Message/Radio Book, or *Allgemeines Funkspruchbuch*, the substitution tables for Gamma Alpha (conversion tables for the ciphers etc.). A journalist later claimed that material found during the salvage of UB 110 was responsible for the capture and destruction of about six more U-boats – in particular, charts giving the location of safe bottoming-out zones off Flamborough Head in Yorkshire and Souter Point, just south of the Tyne. However, this was strongly denied by the Germans. The authors however, have combed through ADM 137/3900 and found no supporting evidence, other than speed tables and photographs.
ADM 53/4245, HMS Garry – ADM 186/394-408 – NARA: Series T-1022, Roll 42, PG 6186

CHAPTER TWO

THE YORKSHIRE AND LINCOLNSHIRE COAST

INTRODUCTION

This is a coastline of infinite contrast: from the offshore reefs of Redcar, through dramatically situated towns and villages, past the chalky cliffs of Flamborough to lonely Spurn, where the county of Yorkshire dies away in an anticlimax. Beyond lies Lincolnshire, an equally delightful melange of sand dune and salt marsh, curving down to Gibraltar Point. Every settlement has its maritime tale to tell. A casual visitor strolling past Scarborough Lighthouse may be forgiven for not recognising the significance of the old 'Hornsund Gun', which overlooks the harbour. *Hornsund* was an Admiralty collier torpedoed a couple of miles off the coast by UC 71 on 23 September 1917. The Admiralty and the Board of Trade hoped that equipping merchantmen with guns such as this would deter marauding U-boats. In this they were cruelly mistaken. The gun is a reminder that *Hornsund* and hundreds like her paid the price for the myopic policy pursued by Admiralty and the Board of Trade, in terms of their adherence to a system of individual sailings, rather than introducing the convoy system to the vulnerable east coast until very late in the war – and long after it had been introduced elsewhere.

If coal was the very lifeblood of the war effort, then for two World Wars the east coast swept channel, or 'war channel', has been its artery. By the winter of 1914 a mine-swept channel, guarded by a protective minefield of questionable value, ran from Kirkwall in the Orkneys down to the Thames. Disrupt or even sever this supply line and the British war machine would rapidly grind to a shuddering halt, a point not lost on German naval planners. During the First World War – and all the lost submarines in this chapter date from the First World War – this long, vulnerable coastline witnessed a titanic struggle between British A/S forces fighting to keep this sea-lane open and German U-boat crews equally determined to send vital tonnage to the bottom. Following the second phase of unrestricted submarine warfare (declared February 1917) the slaughter of merchantmen unleashed off this coast intensified. Those seeking more information are recommended to read *Shipwrecks of the North East Coast* (two volumes) and *Shipwrecks of the East Coast* (two volumes), both written by Ron Young and published by Tempus Publishing Ltd.

Why was such maritime carnage tolerated? Although ships, particularly those in the coal trade, had been convoyed on the east coast since the eighteenth century, there was a

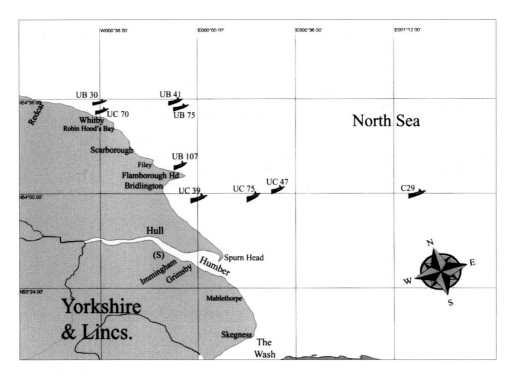

Map of the Yorkshire and Lincolnshire coast.

profound commercial aversion to this system. After all, a convoy can only proceed at the speed of the slowest unit. Ship owners much preferred their vessels to sail individually and rely on their speed. Admiralty equally doubted the practicality of the measure, owing to the fear that escort units would be overstretched and it would be impossible to impose any form of organisation on notoriously independent-minded shipmasters. Unescorted east coast sailings continued throughout 1917. The armed trawlers guarding areas 8 and 9 based at Scarborough, Whitby, Bridlington and the Humber did their best but, by April 1917, one in every four merchant ships was not coming home. The battles of Somme and Arras counted for nothing: the U-boats were winning the war, all on their own.

The confidence of the U-boat crews during this period has passed into legend. In *Shipwrecks of the Yorkshire Coast*, Godfrey and Lassey relate how, after the war, one U-boat skipper claimed to have landed at a remote place on this coast and even visited a local cinema. He produced his dated ticket as proof! What is known is that on 27 July 1917, Steuermann Gallus and Bootsmanmaat Sohlmann waded ashore at Ness Point, much to the astonishment of the Bay folk. Following their arrest, the U-boatmen claimed that their boat UB 21 (Franz Walther) had been surfaced and observing sea traffic when a patrol vessel suddenly appeared. The boat dived, leaving them stranded in the water. They had, they maintained, been left with no option but to inflate their lifebelts and swim towards land. British Naval Intelligence believed their story. However, an appendix to UB 21's KTB in PG61764 provides a more sinister explanation for the presence of these two German sailors in Yorkshire waters. They had been landed as a sabotage party in Hayburn Wyck Bay on 19 July and ordered to destroy an 'industrial railway' close to the shore. It is possible that German intelligence had mistaken the coastal line for Port Mulgrave iron ore railway. The would-be saboteurs failed to rendezvous with the boat and UB 21 returned without them. Where the two men had been and what they had been doing for the past nine days between landing and capture must remain yet another mystery of the Yorkshire coast. We can add with more certainty that on 4 September 1917 UB 21 returned to this coast to fire thirty shells at Scarborough.

UC 47 and UC 39 were both surprised and sunk by patrol vessels in 1917, but in the main, U-boat attacks were pressed home with consummate ease. Something was eventually done to ease the crisis however. A large, deep minefield of questionable efficiency had been laid between Filey and the Tyne as early as July 1916. This minefield, between 7 to 12 miles offshore, was further strengthened by a series of moored nets attached to 'EC' mines. Now, with the establishment of HMS *Vernon* in Portsmouth (December 1916), Admiralty began to look seriously into the science of combating U-boats with sea-mines. By May 1917, some 486 mines were laid off the Humber. On 1 September a new deep (Mark H2) field, consisting of 1,200 mines, was laid 6 miles off Robin Hood's Bay, followed by another off Flamborough Head in December, comprising 1,500 mines. These mines soon bore fruit. UB 41 was destroyed in October 1917, while UB 75 was blown up with all hands in December. It was the introduction of 'controlled sailings' between the Thames and Methil in Fife in 1918 that saw the initiative pass gradually to the British. In June 1918 the following sailings were introduced: TM – Tyne to Methil, UT – Humber to Tyne. These convoys were large, averaging fifty ships, but UT18 was the largest of all, numbering seventy-three, making it the largest single convoy of the First World War. From June to November 1918, 23,000 ships sailed on east coast convoys for the loss of thirty-five ('Admiralty Technical History Section TH8 Scandinavian and East Coast Convoys'). Rosyth destroyers, reinforced by anti-submarine (A/S) patrol vessels, usually escorted these convoys. Often, RNAS balloons and aeroplanes provided aerial surveillance. UB 30 was depth-charged off Whitby, while observing a convoy on 6 August 1918. UC 70 was both bombed and depth-charged by an aircraft as she awaited an oncoming convoy. The destruction of UC 75 by one of the oldest ships in the Royal Navy demonstrates that, even when a U-boat succeeded in penetrating a convoy screen, the most unlikely of escorts could effectively destroy it. Yet single unescorted sailings continued throughout 1918, and the strange fate of UB 107 off Flamborough Head will intrigue all of us who love mysteries.

Tees submarine depot ship with flotilla.

HMS C11. (Crown copyright)

A 13-pounder gun from SS *Hornsund* on display at Scarborough. *Hornsund* was sunk by UC 71 on 23 September 1917. (Pam Armstrong)

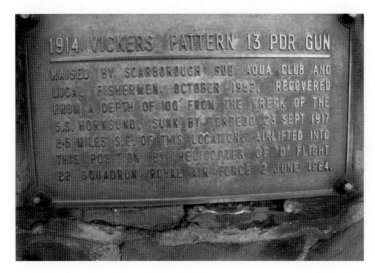

The plaque explaining where the gun came from. (Pam Armstrong)

British submarines also operated off this coast, and one will remain here for eternity. The 6th Submarine Flotilla, comprising C9, C11, C13, C10, C7, C8 and C12 was formed at Immingham in the autumn of 1914 around the depot ship *Bonaventure*. (*Bonaventure* subsequently moved to the Tyne, and *Forth* took her place at Immingham.) HMS *Vulcan* followed it and the 3rd Flotilla, made up of D1, D3, D4, D6, D7 and D8 in 1916. The use of trawler/C-Class submarine combinations had met with success elsewhere, but the accidental destruction of C29 brought this experiment to an unfortunate close although the idea was briefly resurrected using 'H' Class boats in the south-west approaches in 1940. The Bridlington Harbour Museum in Harbour Road contains relics of UC 39, including her stamped propeller.

UB 30, SM IMPERIAL U-BOAT

DATE OF LOSS: 13 August 1918
DEPTH: 45m
REFERENCE: 54 32'.351 N, 00 35'.671 W
LOCATION: 2.92 nautical miles NNE of Whitby north pier

Type: UB II coastal torpedo attack boat   *Builders*: Blohm & Voss, Hamburg for Kaiserliche Deutsche Marine *Ordered*: 22 July 1915, within the batch of SM UB 30–UB 41 *Keel laid*: as Yard No.254 *Launched*: 16 November 1916 *Delivered*: 16 March 1916 *Commissioned*: by Oberleutnant zur See Kurt Schapler on 16 March 1916

TECHNICAL SPECIFICATIONS

Hull: Single *Surface displacement*: 274 tons *U/Dt*: 303 tons *LBDH*: 36.90m x 4.37m x 3.70m x 7.34m *Machinery*: 2 x 142ps Benz diesels *Props*: 2 bronze *S/Sp*: 9.06 knots *Op/R*: 7,030 nautical miles at 5 knots *Sub/R*: 45 nautical miles at 5 knots *U/Power*: 2 x 140ps electric motors gave 5.71 knots *Batteries*: AFA lead/acid *Fuel/Cap*: 21 + 7 tons *Armament*: 2 bow 50.04cm torpedo tubes *Torpedoes*: 4 x 50.04cm (19.7in) *Guns*: 1 x 88mm (3.46in) forward deck gun *Ammo*: 120 rounds of 88mm *Mines*: None *Diving*: Max-op-depth 50m (164ft) and 30 seconds to crash-dive *Complement*: 2 officers and 21 ratings

UB 30 was assigned to the Baltic U-Flottille at Kurland (now Courland, the chief port being Libau) on 8 May 1916, with Oblt.z.S. Kurt Schapler assuming command on 18 March 1916.

UB 30 made seven patrols in the Baltic Sea, the last of which was under the boat's second commander, Oblt.z.S. Cassius von Montigny; he assumed command on 2 October 1916 and sank six small Russian and Swedish boats during October of that year.

On 16 February 1917, UB 30 left the Kurland and sailed for a new base in Flanders. However, on 23 February the compass failed and in heavy fog she went aground on Walcheren. After some manoeuvring the submarine managed to pull free, but Dutch torpedo boats arrived and forced her to proceed to Vlissingen. She was released on 8 August 1917. On 23 February UB 30 formally transferred to the Flandern U-Flottille. (Not all German submarines that went aground in Holland were released. Both UB 6 and UC 8 grounded in Dutch waters and UC 8 was sold to the Dutch. However, UB 6 was interned for the duration. The difference may have been that UB 30 got free on her own, while UB 6 and UC 8 had to be towed off by the Dutch.)

Oblt.z.S. Wilhelm Rhein assumed command when the boat was released on 8 August 1917 and Rhein took her on the following patrols:

(9) UB 30 left port on 26 August 1917 and patrolled the English east coast, where Rhein torpedoed the British coaster *Vernon* (Cory Colliers Ltd) on 31 August; she was bound from Seaham Harbour to London with coal, and the fifty-one-year-old master, Captain J. Snowling, was killed in the explosion. The SS *Ragnhild* (Pelton SS Co. Ltd) was torpedoed on a voyage with coal from Jarrow-on-Tyne to Rouen. The chief engineer was in his bunk when the torpedo struck and said later:

> Seawater poured rapidly into the ship and she looked in danger of going down quickly. All the crew then rushed to the starboard lifeboat, clambered in and lowered it down, the port one having been totally smashed in the explosion...unfortunately the boat then capsized, drowning Captain Schulz and fourteen of the men, but him and three other survivors clung on to the upturned lifeboat. The ship, although half full of water, was still afloat, so one of the men courageously swam back to her, managed to launch the jollyboat and rescued the others.

Two hours later, at 10.00, a torpedo boat-destroyer arrived at the scene and picked up the survivors. The warship took *Ragnhild* in-tow, but had no sooner got underway when it sank. The four crewmen were landed at Grimsby. UB 30 returned to Flanders on 4 September 1917.

(10) On 17 September 1917, UB 30 left Flanders and sailed for operations in the Flamborough Head area. The French steamer *SNA 3* (Soc. Nationale d'Affrètements, Havre) was torpedoed 10 miles off Hornsea, while on passage from Newcastle for Rouen with coal. UB 30 returned to Zeebrugge on 29 September 1917.

(11) UB 30 sailed from Zeebrugge on 7 November and patrolled the English Channel. Rhein sank the 129-ton *Morning Star* with gunfire on 12 November and returned to port on 22 November.

(12) Between 8 and 18 December 1917, UB 30 made a fruitless patrol in the English Channel.

(13) UB 30 left Flanders on 30 December 1917 for a war-cruise in the English Channel. Rhein torpedoed and sank three large British steamships during this sortie: two men were killed in the explosion on the *Gartland* (Gart SS Co. Ltd, Glasgow), which was hit with a torpedo on the port side abreast the engine room at 03.15 on 1 January, while voyaging from the Tyne to Gibraltar with coal. The survivors got away in the boats and watched their ship sink at 03.25; they were all picked up by the SS *Numina* and landed at St Helen's, Isle of Wight. The *Glenarm Head* (Ulster Steamship Co. Ltd (G. Heyn & Sons), Belfast) was hit aft at midnight by a torpedo, on 4 January 1918, while travelling from Southampton to Boulogne with ammunition; the ship sank in five minutes with the loss of Captain R. McCaulay and seventeen-year-old Deck Boy James Brookman. The *Whorlton* (Furness, Withy & Co. Ltd, West Hartlepool) sank while on passage from the Downs for Southampton. UB 30 arrived back at her Flanders port on 14 January 1918.

(14) Leaving Zeebrugge on 31 January 1918, UB 30 sailed for operations in the English Channel. Rhein torpedoed the SS *Jaffa* (Ellerman's Wilson Lines Ltd, Hull), which was bound for Southampton from Boulogne in ballast and ten crewmen were lost on 2 February. She was hit below the bridge on the port side at 12.10 and sank by the head in three minutes; the starboard boat was launched with the second mate and three men in it and they managed to pick up the survivors, but ten were missing. Ten minutes after the ship sank UB 30 surfaced and closed on the lifeboat to question the master. After searching for their colleagues, the boat made for shore and reached Littlehampton at 08.00.

THE MEN WHO DIED
Biggadike, William, 28, Able Seaman
Friel, John, 50, Fireman.
Hawkins, George, 37, Fireman
Hooley, Albert, 50, Fireman
Major, Henry William, 33, Carpenter
MacLachlan, Allen, 47, Able Seaman
Richardson, Thomas, 31, Fireman
Webb, William, 36, Mess Room Steward
Webber, Abel, 66, Able Seaman
Winn, William, 26, Fireman

The US steamship *Armenia* (US Shipping Board, New York) was hit by a torpedo off St Catherine's Point, while voyaging from Dartmouth to West Hartlepool. The ship was towed to Stokes Bay and beached, but the damage was so bad it was scrapped. (Just two months earlier on 5 December, the *Armenia* was also damaged off Start Point and beached in Dartmouth Harbour, but re-floated later.) UB 30 returned to base on 11 February 1918.

(15) Rhein left the Flanders with UB 30 on 28 February 1918 and patrolled the English Channel, where the Norwegian SS *Braatt II* (Skibs Aktieselskapet Braatt, Sarpsborg) was sunk on 7 March; she was on passage from Newport for Rouen with coal. A single torpedo was fired while she was surfaced and the wake of it was spotted long before it struck home. All the crew abandoned ship and were picked up and landed at Portsmouth.

On 16 March the SS *Lightfoot* (Wandsworth, Wimbledon & Epsom District Gas Co., Newcastle) was hit by a torpedo on the port side of the No.3 hold at 01.30 and sank in three minutes, while voyaging from London to Barry Roads in ballast; all of the crew got away in their own boats and were picked up by patrol boats and landed at Portsmouth.

On 5 March UB 30 damaged the British steamer *Clan Mackenzie* (The Clan Line Steamers Ltd, Glasgow), which was bound for Plymouth from London with chalk, but she reached Southampton water safely. UB 30 arrived in Bruges on 18 March 1918.

On 24 March 1918, UB 30 was bombed while in the port at Bruges; serious repairs were undertaken, but she frustratingly continued to leak oil. Oblt.z.S. Rudolf Stier assumed command of the U-boat on 22 April 1918.

(16) UB 30 left port on 29 April 1918, but after two days, the oil leakage forced Stier to return.

(17) UB 30 sailed to the areas between Flamborough Head and Sunderland for operations, between 20 and 31 May 1918, but no ships were sunk.

(18) On 15 June the boat left Zeebrugge for a war-cruise off the English east coast. At 18.23 Stier torpedoed the British, steamer *Norfolk Coast* (Coast Lines Ltd, Liverpool) on 18 June. The weapon detonated under the bridge leaving eight of her crew of fifteen dead and one seriously injured. When the ship immediately started to sink, the survivors abandoned ship by leaping into the sea. They were picked up by convoy escorts and landed at Middlesbrough and the Tyne. Captain HRE Thomas managed to save the confidential papers, but the Wartime Codebooks were lost with the ship. She was voyaging from Rouen to the Tyne in ballast.

SEVEN OF THE MEN WHO DIED
Higgitt, Charles, 52, Fireman
Hoole, Frederick Spooner Wallis, 25, Fireman
Livingstone, Ernest Llewellyn, Mate
McKenty, Patrick, 20, Able Seaman
Munson, Edwin, 56, Seaman

Shimmin, William Raymond, 26, Second Engineer
Williams, William, 32, Fireman

UB 30 returned to Flanders on 30 June.

(19) On 16 July, UB 30 left port and travelled to the English east coast for operations, but during the patrol she was depth-charged and oil began to leak out again; on 24 July 1918, UB 30 arrived back at Zeebrugge.

FINAL VOYAGE

(20) On 6 August 1918 UB 30 departed Zeebrugge. Area 8 anti-submarine patrols first became aware that there was a U-boat heading their way at 04.10, when Rudolf Stier transmitted the following message while voyaging on Route 3: 'Have started journey to the north.' 'Room 40' was thus able to warn Immingham that a U-boat could be arriving off Flamborough Head that night ('Room 40' was a top secret office within the Admiralty building at Whitehall). Confirmation came on 10 August when Stier destroyed the 509-ton coaster SS *Madam Renee* (Becker & Co. Ltd), travelling from London to the Tyne with copper pyrites. The torpedo detonated amidships on her port side at 08.37 and the ship sank almost at once; the crew had to jump into the sea where ten of them drowned. Local boats from Scarborough picked up seven survivors clinging to floating wreckage.

SEVEN OF THE MEN WHO DIED

Austwick, Charles Robert, 33, Second Engineer
Balmain, Robert Dunn, 32, First Mate
Douglas, Robert, 22, Able Seaman and Lamps
House, John Evans Peel, 22, Able Seaman
Manley, William, 56, Steward
Sutoe, Iwai, 26, Donkeyman
Woodward, Harold, 24, Second Officer

At 12.08 on 13 August, Stier was observing a distant 'MT' (southbound) convoy at periscope depth, when the armed trawler *John Gillman* (Admiralty No.3502) spotted the periscope mirror reflection at a range of 300 yards. The trawler made full speed across and attempted to ram the U-boat, but Stier saw it coming and commenced an emergency dive. This resulted in *John Gillman* scraping noisily over the casing. Two depth charges set at 100ft were dropped and another two at 80ft, which brought an oil slick and air to the surface. A Dan-buoy was placed over the spot and the trawler called for reinforcements and waited in anticipation.

Two hours later, UB 30 attempted to surface, but the Tyne-based requisitioned anti-submarine trawlers *John Brooker* (Admiralty No.3605) and *Viola II* (Admiralty No.6) were listening in to her motors on hydrophones. When the submarine broke surface they were lying ready to pounce and fired two shells each before UB 30 dived again. The two boats then dropped five depth charges between them set at 100ft. It seems likely that this depth charge barrage caused the fatal damage as the trawler crews could clearly see oil pouring out of the submarine's pressure hull (UB II boats were fitted with external saddle tanks, which carried water ballast amidships and oil fuel toward the ends). Ten minutes later Stier made an attempt to surface but the RN yacht *Miranda II* together with requisitioned minesweeping trawler *Florio* (Admiralty No.1653) and HMT *Sparrow* (Admiralty No.58) joined in, dropping four more depth charges set at 100ft and two more at 150ft.

UB 30 did not move again. Provided with adequate equipment, the auxiliary patrol had carried out a highly efficient attack. Evidence of just how efficient came at 20.30, when wire sweeps revealed an obstruction. Four days later Royal Navy divers, under

Cdr Wheeler, inspected the wreck. A telegram sent by Admiralty Salvage states: 'Submarine sunk on 13th August near L Buoy was today, Saturday, located by divers in 27½ fathoms LWOS. Unable to obtain number?' Salvage work on UB 30 was called off in favour of lifting the all-important UB 110, which sank on 9 July off Saltburn, North Yorkshire.

UB 30 carried a crew of twenty-six at the time of her loss (her normal complement was twenty-two). <u>NARA: T-1022. Roll 56, PG61777</u>

THE MEN WHO DIED IN UB 30

Beuckert, Mts.
Biller, Mts.
Boesen, Masch.   Müller, Ob.Hzr
Breitfeld, Ob.Hzr   Pohl, Masch.Mt
Daut, Hzr   Prescher, Masch.Mt
Dieterich, Hzr   Prinz, Lt.z.S.
Feit, Ob.Masch.Mt   Schneider. Mts.
Franke, Mts.   Schreiber, Hzr
Kirchhoff, Mts.   Schwartz, Ob.Mts.
Kraeft, Ob.Btn.Mt   Stier, Rudolf, Oblt.z.S.
Kruczeck, Ob.Hzr   Tielke, Masch.Mt
Kusche, F.T.Ober Gast   Voget, Mts.
Lettau, Masch.Mt Möller, Masch.Mt   Wiatzka, Mts.
                                        Wohlers, Ob.Bts.Mt

UB 30 sank twenty-two vessels, totalling 36,277 tons, and the following is a list of the known vessels believed sunk or damaged:

AREA	VESSEL'S NAME	FLAG	TONS	D	M	YEAR	LOCATION
Baltic	Augusta (barque)	SWE	346	21	10	1916	Sunk off the Finngrundet Light Vessel
Baltic	Elly	SWE	88	23	10	1916	Sunk NW of Mäntyluoto
Baltic	Elin (sailing vessel)	RUS	127	24	10	1916	Sunk in the Rauma area
Baltic	Ingersoll (sailing vessel)	RUS	239	24	10	1916	Sunk in the Rauma area
Baltic	Jenny Lind (sailing vessel)	RUS	53	24	10	1916	Sunk in the Rauma area
Baltic	Urpo (sailing vessel)	RUS	111	24	10	1916	Sunk in the Rauma area
North Sea	Vernon	GBR	982	31	8	1917	22 miles SE by S of Spurn Point
North Sea	Ragnhild	GBR	1495	3	9	1917	14 miles SSE of Flamborough Head
North Sea	S.N.A. III	FRA	1709	26	9	1917	7 miles E of Horsea
English Channel	Morning Star	GBR	129	12	11	1917	10 miles ESE of Barfleur
English Channel	Gartland	GBR	2613	3	1	1918	5 miles ESE of the Owers Light Vessel
English Channel	Glenarm Head	GBR	3908	5	1	1918	5 miles SW by S of the Brighton Light Vessel
English Channel	Whorlton	GBR	1469	12	1	1918	Near the Owers Light Vessel
English Channel	Jaffa	GBR	1383	2	2	1918	3 miles E by S of the Owers Light Vessel
English Channel	Armenia	USA	5463	9	2	1918	St Catherine's Pt (2nd time torpedoed & beached)
English Channel	Clan Mackenzie	GBR	6544	5	3	1918	Damaged S of the Isle of Wight

English Channel	Braatt II		1834	7	3	1918	4 miles SW of St. Catherine's Point
English Channel	Lightfoot	GBR	1873	16	3	1918	2 miles S of the Owers Light Vessel
North Sea	Norfolk Coast	GBR	782	18	6	1918	23 miles SE of Flamborough Head
North Sea	Madame Renee	GBR	509	10	8	1918	1 mile NNE of Scarborough

WRECK-SITE

The wreck leans over to port at about 45 degrees and lies on a dirty seabed of sand and mud, just outside of the Whitby spoil-ground, in a general depth of 45m. Sport divers from Scarborough Sub Aqua Club – Carl Racey, Andy Jackson and a comparatively novice diver – first located the wreck in June 1993. Carl stated:

> The conning tower hatch, which must have being blown off by Royal Navy divers soon after it sank, was the first thing we found. It was alone on the seabed, well off on the port side, the dive boat's anchor having slipped off the wreck before we got down. …all I saw was the hatch, then, as my eyes adjusted in the gloom, I could make out the bow area of my first submarine. There was some damage and decay in places, mostly in the bow area, but the pressure hull was largely intact. One of the torpedo tubes was in place with the remains of a torpedo still inside. The other tube, which was badly damaged and had broken off, was found on the seabed, shrouded in lost fishing nets. The twin screws, which have thick encased prop shafts attached, were still in place. The small conning tower was still intact, but the hatch cover was missing; this was found on the seabed well clear of the wreck. The forward and rear hatches are also both open, with high levels of silt inside them. Both periscopes are mostly retracted with the rear one bent forward. One of the exhausts was laid on seabed, aft of conning tower on the port side, along with some other wreckage. The deck gun that used to be in place on the fore deck has now fallen onto the seabed on the port side and is also entwined with lost nets. When the wreck was first located, it was absolutely enveloped with gill and trawl nets, plus numerous lost crab/lobster pots that had accumulated and these were tangled up with the wreckage and nets. Divers however, have patiently removed many of these since it was found.

Sadly, while diving the wreck on 25 August 1994, a Whitby diver died after his air ran out. The find has been reported to the German Embassy and the Archives, at Cuxhaven. Apart from being dangerous, no attempt should be made to try and enter the wreck because it is a war grave.

Before August was out, the Royal Navy was to destroy another U-boat in these waters. For UC 70, destruction came quite literally out of the blue.

UC 70, SM IMPERIAL U-BOAT

DATE OF LOSS: 28 August 1918
DEPTH: 25m
REFERENCE: 54 31'.599 N, 000 40'.131 W
LOCATION: 1½ nautical miles N of Sandsend
and 2.78 nautical miles NW of Whitby

Sketch of wreck of SM UC 70. (Pam Armstrong)

Type: UCII coastal mine-laying boat *Builders*: Blohm & Voss, Hamburg for Kaiserliche Deutsche Marine *Ordered*: 12 January 1916, within the batch SM UC 65–UC 73 *Keel laid*: as Yard No.286 *Launched*: 7 August 1916 *Commissioned*: by Oberleutnant zur See Werner Fürbringer on 20 November 1916

TECHNICAL SPECIFICATIONS

Hull: Double *Surface displacement*: 427 tons *U/Dt*: 508 tons *LBDH*: 50.35m x 5.22m x 3.68m x 7.46m *Machinery*: 2 x 250ps MAN diesels *Props*: 2 bronze *S/Sp*: 12 knots *Op/R*: 10,420 nautical miles at 7 knots *Sub/R*: 55 nautical miles at 4 knots *U/Power*: 2 x 230ps electric motors giving 7.4 knots *Batteries*: Lead/acid *Fuel/Cap*: 41 + 15 tons *Armament*: 2 external 50.04cm torpedo tubes at the bow, one either side of the mine chutes and 1 stern internal tube *Torpedoes*: 7 x 50.04cm (19.7in) maximum *Guns*: 1 x 88mm (3.46in) forward deck gun *Ammo*: 133 rounds of 88mm *Mine tubes*: 6 *Mines*: 18 x UC 200 *Diving*: Max-op-depth 50m (164ft) and 33 seconds to crash-dive *Complement*: 3 officers and 23 ratings

Torpedo load as designed: 4 – a torpedo in each tube plus a reload for the stern tube. Storing an additional torpedo in pieces internally for the stern tube later augmented this, although this was optional. Two extra torpedoes (total) for the external bow tubes could be carried as well – these were lashed to the deck. So up to a total of seven torpedoes were carried, although not all boats sailed with that many.

On 22 February 1917, UC 70 was formally assigned to Flanders/Flandern II Flottille with Werner Fürbringer as her first commander. Fürbringer had previously commanded UB 39. He sank Allied vessels totalling 27,323 tons and was later promoted to Kapitänleutnant. In the Second World War he was promoted to Konteradmiral. He was also awarded, among others, the Prussian Royal Hohenzollern House Order (a significant award although it went to only about 8,300 officers during the war), the Knight's Cross-with-Swords, the Iron Cross Second Class and Iron Cross First Class and the First World War U-boat Badge. Fürbringer was born on 2 October 1888 and died in Braunschweig on 8 February 1982 at the age of ninety-three, but not before writing a highly readable book about his time in U-boat service *Alarm! Tauchen!* (See Chapter One), republished as *FIPS – Legendary U-boat Commander*, translated and edited by Geoffrey Brooks. Much of the material concerns the time Fürbringer spent in command of this boat. His vivid yet unassuming book conveys to the reader the human dimension behind the statistics of First World War U-boat patrols.

With UC 70, Fürbringer made the following patrols:

(1) UC 70's first patrol was the transfer from Germany to Flanders, leaving Hamburg on 19 February 1917 and arriving at Bruges on 22 February.

(2) On 27 February UC 70 left Bruges and patrolled in the Hoofden, but sank no vessels before returning to port on 2 March 1917.

(3) UC 70 left Flanders on 10 March and sailed to the Bay of Biscay. Fürbringer's mission was to lay a mine barrage off Île de Groix, Le Four, and Point de Chassiron, and attack Allied shipping, with troop-transports from the United States the priority targets. On 14 February Fürbringer sank a pilot cutter just off the Gironde Estuary; her crew of two were allowed to row back to the shore. Fürbringer decided to move northwards and was off the island of Oléby by daybreak. No troop-transports were located, but he sank the 28-ton fishing ketch *Corduouan* with explosive on 16 February. The next morning he found himself in the middle of a fleet of twelve French fishing boats and sank all of them with explosive charges, in ninety minutes. However just as the last ketch was being disposed of, a French naval vessel approached from the Gironde Estuary and opened fire. Fürbringer completed the job, before heading out to sea on the surface at 12 knots.

A short while later two more fishing boats came into view. Fürbringer ordered the gun crew to fire a shot across the bows of the leading boat when it was about 500m away, but the two vessels sailed on until they were within 150m of UC 70. Then there was feverish activity on-board the forward boat as a canvas came down amidships and a large gun, that had been hidden opened fire. The vessel was *Hyacinthe Yvonne*, a French Q-ship. A violent gun battle ensued, with both vessels being severely battered. UC 70 was hit in six places and many of the submarine's crewmen were badly injured, when someone in the control room shouted that the boat was taking in water. Fürbringer ordered a fast dive down to 30m. Apart from other damage, UC 70 had lost two-thirds of her reserve compressed air. The piping of six compressed air bottles was split open, and five of the crew, including Telegraphist Lindemann, were seriously injured. UC 70 travelled submerged away from the scene until the skipper deemed it safe to come up to periscope depth, but so much water had entered the boat only the conning tower was above the water. For two days the U-boat drifted, during which time the injured were treated and much of the damage was made good, before Fürbringer was able to take her back to Flanders, arriving at Bruges on 22 March 1917. Fürbringer was also unaware that his brave little French adversary, *Hyacinthe Yvonne*, had sunk.

Mines laid by UC 70 during the war-cruise sank three steamships. The SS *Tasso* (Bolivian General Enterprise Ltd) sank on the 17 March, she was transporting war materials from Manchester to La Pallice and nineteen crewmen, including the master were lost. Two days later the French steamer *Michel* (Worms & Cie) sank while en-route from Newport to Bordeaux. Later that same day, the SS *Bergsli* (Aktieselskapet Dampskipsselskapet Bergsli, Bergen), a Norwegian ship on passage from Penarth for Blaye with coal, also struck a mine and sank, the mine having been laid on 15 March.

(4) After leaving Bruges on 15 April 1917, UC 70 travelled down the Channel as far as the Bay of Biscay and laid mines. In his book, Fürbringer describes the nerve-wracking

experience of laying mines in shallow road-steads with UC 70, caught between the fear of being spotted by warships on the one hand and the ever present danger of grounding in shallow water on the other. The reader must add to this cocktail of peril the very real menace of premature mine detonation (see UC 32 in Chapter One). On the voyage to Biscay, Fürbringer sank the 476-ton barque *Eduard* on 16 April – it was sailing in ballast to Port Talbot from London. The next day, a mine damaged the SS *Nirvana* (British India Steam Navigation Co. Ltd, Glasgow) off the Nab Light Vessel; she was carrying Government stores from Havre to Southampton, but reached St Helen's Roads safely. The Norwegian SS *Eden* (H.S. Horgen) was torpedoed and sank on 30 April, bound for Rouen with coal from the Tyne.

The SS *Lowmount* (Capel & Co., Leith) detonated a mine beneath No.2 hold at 10.25 on 7 May, while carrying iron ore from Bibao to Stockton; five of her crewmen were killed outright in the explosion, or blown overboard and drowned. The ship sank immediately. The remaining crew got away in the boats and were rescued by torpedo boats and landed at Portsmouth.

THE MEN WHO DIED
Callan, James, 33, Fireman
Garcia, Raphael, 26, Fireman
Harrison, Joseph, 20, Mess Room Steward
Jensen, 24, Able Seaman
Monk, Fred Alfred, 24, Able Seaman

UC 70 had already arrived in Bruges by 2 May.

(5) UC 70 sailed from Flanders on 16 May 1917 and Fürbringer laid a small minefield off Le Havre. After leaving the relatively calm water off Le Havre, UC 70 steered a low-speed course for Ushant, in search of convoys. Off Brest a heavy sea mist developed and the boat just drifted for two days, the crew listening for approaching ships. Eventually, the shadow of a suspicious-looking steamer was observed and Fürbringer took the boat down to 20m and set course for the French coast. She hadn't gone far when a continuous bumping prevented the boat from going forward. The order was given to surface and UC 70 was found to be well off-course; she had, in fact, run aground in a horseshoe bay near Île de Seine. Heavy surf crashed over the conning tower as Fürbringer attempted to go full astern, but to make matters worse, shells from five old field guns began exploding close-by. Once clear, UC 70 submerged and made off at full speed.

Six vessels were sunk and two damaged during this patrol and another was damaged later.

Off Guernsey, the steam coaster *Dromore* was voyaging from St Malo to Swansea in ballast when Fürbringer sent her to the bottom on 18 May. On 23 May the Spanish SS *Begoña No.3* (Cia. De Nav. Begona) was sunk while carrying iron ore from Almeria, Spain to Barrow. The 2,195-ton French sailing vessel *General de Boisdeffre* was bound for Brest with nitrate when it struck a mine laid by UC 70 and disappeared with all hands.

While on a voyage with general cargo from Falmouth to Lisbon and Spanish ports, the 1,245-ton *Ancona* (J. Hall, Jun. & Co., London), which was built in 1883, was reported missing on 27 May, however, the ship was known to have passed the Lizard earlier that day. On the evening of 28 May, UC 70 torpedoed what was described in her KTB as an 'unknown, zigzagging, armed steamer of about 1,500 tons, with three masts and one funnel', 110 miles west, and south-west of Ouessant. The ship sank in half a minute from a single torpedo hit, so there is a strong probability that the ship in question was the *Ancona* (it had already been torpedoed on 6 September 1916, but reached its destination).

UC 70 put into Ostend on 1 June 1917 where she was signed over to the shipyard repairers, leaving the chief engineer and four men as watch-keepers (the rest of the crew being given shore-leave at Bruges).

While UC 70 was under repair, British Monitors, stationed offshore, bombarded the coast at 04.00 and at least one 38cm shell exploded in the harbour basin, sinking UC 70, two auxiliary naval steam trawlers, and two lighters. The Flottille commander and Fürbringer were called to the scene and found just the U-boat's conning tower protruding from the water. The boat was raised on 22 June, but it was many months before she was ready for sea again. The crew was assigned to other boats and Fürbringer, as a veteran commander, assumed command of UC 17, whose skipper had taken ill. When he returned, Fürbringer was sent back to Germany to take over the command of UB 58, a UB III boat.

UC 70 was seaworthy again by April 1918 and Oblt.z.S. Kurt Loch took over the command on 8 April and made the following two patrols:

(6) UC 70 sailed for operations off the English east coast on 24 April 1918, but Loch failed to sink anything and returned to port on 6 May.

(7) On 26 May 1918 UC 70 sailed from Flanders and returned to hunt off the English east coast where Loch damaged the British steamer *Cento* (Corinthian Shipping Co. Ltd, Liverpool) with a torpedo on 4 June; she was sailing from Hull to Narvik in Norway and was towed into Middlesbrough for repair (*Cento* had also been damaged on 11 September 1917, while en-route from Cardiff to Queenstown, but she managed to reach Queenstown, Ireland). Two smaller vessels were also destroyed during the patrol.

The U-boat arrived back in port on 8 June 1918. Oblt.z.S. Karl Dobberstein assumed command of the boat on 9 June 1918 and made the following war patrols:

(8) Leaving Zeebrugge on 9 July 1918, Dobberstein searched for ships in the Hoofden before returning on 14 July 1918; just one small Dutch sailing vessel was captured and sunk on 9 July.

(9) UC 70 left port on 16 July 1918 and laid mines in the Hoofden, then proceeded to the English east coast. Torpedoes fired by UC 70 damaged three steamers and sunk two more; the SS *Genesee* was hit off Flamborough Light and was taken into Hull for repair. The steamship *Mongolian* (Indian & Peninsular Steam Navigation Co. Ltd, Glasgow, Bombay) was torpedoed on passage from the Tees for London. The ship was carrying a crew of eighty-nine and a general cargo, consisting of stores destined for the Italian Government. Two torpedoes struck the vessel almost simultaneously and she sank very quickly. Her port boats were lowered and some of the crew managed to get clear of the ship before she went down. The remainder, including Captain W.A. Milne, went into the sea and an escort vessel picked them up. Unfortunately five Europeans and thirty Lascar seamen were lost in the incident.

While transporting a general cargo from Southampton to the Tyne, a torpedo struck the steamer *Boorara* 12 miles off the Tees, and she had to be towed to the Tyne. Also hit by a torpedo, the Greek SS *Kilkis* (T. Bistis & Hadzikyriakos, Argostoli) sank off Hartlepool; she was travelling from Almeria to the Tyne with 6,800 tons of iron ore. Before returning to Flanders, Dobberstein badly damaged the French steamer *Ango*, travelling from Falmouth to Hartlepool; she was towed into West Hartlepool (on 26 November 1917, this ship was also damaged on passage from Havre for Santos, beached and later re-floated). UC 70 arrived home on 29 July 1918.

FINAL VOYAGE

(10) On 21 August 1918, Dobberstein left Zeebrugge for a mine-laying operation in the Hoofden and to attack ships off the English east coast. However, at 15.30 on 28 August 1918, a Blackburn Kangaroo bomber (Serial No.B9983) of 246 Squadron, on anti-submarine patrol, piloted by Pilot Officer Waring RAF, spotted an oil slick apparently

emanating from an elongated shape beneath the surface. (At the time, 246 Squadron was based at Seaton Carew near Hartlepool.) Suspicious that a U-boat might be lurking below, P/O Waring followed the trail of the oil slick and dropped a single 250lb bomb over the top of the boat. P/O Waring noted that large quantities of oil and air bubbled to the surface. The destroyer HMS *Ouse* witnessed the explosion and made full speed for the scene, guided by P/O Waring's pistol flares. *Ouse* made several runs and dropped ten depth charges set at 50ft (15m), aimed in the centre of a big oil patch bubbling to the surface. More oil and bits of debris came up in the maelstrom. It is not clear whether the aircraft, the destroyer or a combination of both destroyed the submarine. It is possible that the U-boat had previously been damaged in the new British minefield off Yorkshire and was lying on the bottom effecting repairs when the slick was spotted.

On 14 September Lt-Cdr Damant's 'tin openers' arrived and the celebrated Dusty Miller was sent down. He confirmed the wreck of a U-boat and entered her through a massive hole in the hull. Pushing his way through the devastation and dead inside, Dusty entered the control room and very quickly located the waterproof metal box containing the logs and codebooks. Thus the boat was identified as UC 70. Contained in the box were some papers charting the minefields she had laid since leaving Flanders.

As for Pilot Officer Waring, he survived the war only to die in a crash in 1919.
NARA: Series T-1022, Roll 109, PG61991

THE MEN WHO DIED IN UC 70

Baethke, Masch.Mt
Bau, Mts.
Bürger, F.T.Ober Gast
Baalmann, Ob.Mts.
Christensen, Ob.Mts.
Dames, Masch.Mt
Dienst, Ob.Masch.Mt
Dobberstein, Oblt.z.S.
Drees, Hzr
Eckert, Ob.Masch.
Engelhard, Masch.Mt
Fischer, Ob.Hzr
Hartmann, Ob.Mts.
Heinrich, Lt.z.S.d.Res
Michelsen, Mts.
Paffen, Hzr

Peters, Hzr
Rabe, Masch.Mt
Rochna, Ob.Masch.
Rosenbaum, Mts
Schaller, Ob.Hzr
Schattschneider, Bts.Mt
Scheibner, Ob.Masch.Mt
Schmidt, Mts.
Schröter, Hzr
Seidel, Mts.
Siedhoff, Hzr
Stolze, Stm.
Thomale, F.T.
Tillmann, Ob.Masch.Mt
Wörmann, Hzr

The following is a list of the known vessels believed sunk or damaged by UC 70:

AREA	VESSEL'S NAME	FLAG	TONS	D	M	YEAR	LOCATION
Bay of Biscay	*Marthe Yvonne* (pilot cutter)	FRA	30	14	3	1917	15 miles WSW of La Coubre Point
Bay of Biscay	*Corduouan* (sailing vessel)	FRA	28	16	3	1917	Sunk off Gironde
Bay of Biscay	*Louis XIV* (fishing-vessel)	FRA	44	17	3	1917	Sunk off Gironde
Bay of Biscay	*Renee Islander* (fishing-vessel)	FRA	25	17	3	1917	Sunk off Gironde
Bay of Biscay	*Notre Dame du Perpetuel Seceurs* (fishing-vessel)	FRA	29	17	3	1917	Sunk off Gironde
Bay of Biscay	*Nozal* (fishing-vessel)	FRA	34	17	3	1917	Sunk off Gironde
Bay of Biscay	*Juliette* (fishing-vessel)	FRA	29	17	3	1917	Sunk off Gironde

Bay of Biscay	Dieu te Garde (fishing-vessel)	FRA	30	17	3	1917	Sunk off Gironde
Bay of Biscay	Camillie Amelie (fishing-vessel)	FRA	20	17	3	1917	Sunk off Gironde
Bay of Biscay	Alcide Maria (fishing-vessel)	FRA	26	17	3	1917	Sunk off Gironde
Bay of Biscay	Rupella (fishing-vessel)	FRA	38	17	3	1917	Sunk off Gironde
Bay of Biscay	Madone (fishing-vessel)	FRA	31	18	3	1917	Sunk off Gironde
Bay of Biscay	Tasso	GBR	1859	17	3	1917	Mined 5 miles S of Île de Groix
Bay of Biscay	Entente Cordiale (fishing-vessel)	FRA	22	18	3	1917	Sunk off Gironde
Bay of Biscay	Felicite Albert (fishing-vessel)	FRA	32	18	3	1917	Sunk off Gironde
Bay of Biscay	Hyacinthe Yvonne (s/v Q-ship)	FRA	43	18	3	1917	Sunk off Gironde
Bay of Biscay	Michel	FRA	1773	19	3	1917	Mined in the Bay of Biscay
Bay of Biscay	Bergsli	NOR	2370	19	3	1917	Mined 3 miles off Chassiron light
English Channel	Eduard (barque)	GBR	476	16	4	1917	Sunk SW of Beachy Head
English Channel	Nirvana	GBR	6021	17	4	1917	Mined & damaged off Nab Light Vessel
English Channel	Eden	NOR	1304	30	4	1917	10 miles S of Worthing Pier
English Channel	Lowmount	GBR	2070	7	5	1917	Mined 4 miles N of Owers Light Vessel
English Channel	Dromore	GBR	268	18	5	1917	6 miles S of St Martin's Point.
English Channel	C.E.C.G. (fishing-vessel)	GBR	47	18	5	1917	30 miles SSE of Start Point
English Channel	Bergona No.3	SPA	2699	23	5	1917	Sunk off Penzance
English Channel	Madora	GBR	4484	24	5	1917	Damaged in the English Channel
English Channel	General de Boisdeffre (sail-vessel)	FRA	2195	26	5	1917	Sunk in the English Channel
English Channel	Ancona	GBR	1245	27	5	1917	Missing in the English Channel
North Sea	Elin (mot)	NOR	139	27	5	1917	Damaged 15 miles SSE of Flamborough Hd
North Sea	Wayside Flower (mot)	GBR	21	27	5	1917	20 miles NE by N of the Humber
North Sea	Coronation (mot)	GBR	19	28	5	1917	13 miles ESE of Flamborough Head
North Sea	Cento	GBR	3708	4	6	1918	Damaged at 54° 22.30' N. 00° 13' E
North Sea	Freder (sailing-vessel)	NLD	91	9	7	1918	20 miles off Maas Light Vessel
North Sea	Genesse	GBR	2830	21	7	1918	Damaged 4 miles NNW of Flamborough L/h
North Sea	Mongolian	GBR	4909	21	7	1918	5 miles SE of Filey Brigg
North Sea	Boorara	GBR	6570	23	7	1918	Damaged 12 miles S of Tees
North Sea	Kilkis	GRE	4302	24	7	1918	Sunk off Hartlepool
North Sea	Ango	FRA	7393	26	7	1918	Damaged 2 miles E of Flamborough Head

WRECK-SITE

The wreck stands 3m high and has a slight list to starboard. It sits in a small scour, on a flat sand and gravel seabed, in a general depth of 25m, being the lowest astronomical depth. The wreck shows up well on an echo sounder and is in fact still intact, with some areas of plate, where the seams have blown. Don Foster asserts that the two deck hatches are open, as are five of the mine-chutes, which can be clearly seen, and the deck gun is still mounted and intact. The conning tower hatch is open, but the inside is festooned with cables and is very silted, just waiting to claim its first careless diver. Divers removed one of the propellers in 1992, and when this was brought to the attention of the German Embassy in London, they wanted the wreck declared as a war grave. However, in the end, all parties agreed that diving would be allowed, but only on a 'look but don't touch' basis and the wreck should be treated with all due respect.

UB 41, SM IMPERIAL U-BOAT

DATE OF LOSS: 5 October 1917
DEPTH: 54m
REFERENCE: 54 27'.845 N, 000 17'.723 W
LOCATION: 8.01 nautical miles ENE of
North Cheek at Robin Hood's Bay

Type: UBII coastal torpedo attack boat *Builders:* Blohm & Voss, Hamburg, for Kaiserliche Deutsche Marine *Ordered:* on 22 July 1915, within the batch of UB 30–UB 41 *Keel laid:* as Yard No.265 *Launched:* 6 May 1916 *Commissioned:* by Oberleutnant zur See Friedrich Karl Sichart von Sichartshofen on 25 August 1916

TECHNICAL SPECIFICATIONS

Hull: Single, saddle tank design *Surface displacement:* 274 tons *U/Dt:* 303 tons *LBDH:* 36.90m x 4.37m x 3.70m x 7.34m *Machinery:* 2 x 142ps Körting diesels *Props:* 2 bronze *S/Sp:* 9.06 knots *Op/R:* 7,030 nautical miles at 5 knots *Sub/R:* 45 nautical miles at 5 knots *U/Power:* 2 x 140ps electric motors giving 5.71 knots *Batteries:* AFA lead/acid *Fuel/Cap:* 21 + 7 tons *Armament:* 2 x bow 50.04cm torpedo tubes, plus two external tubes *Torpedoes:* 4 x 50.04cm (19.7in) *Guns:* 1 x 88mm (3.46in) forward deck gun *Mines:* None *Ammo:* 120 rounds of 88mm *Diving:* Max-op-depth 50m (164ft) and 30 seconds to crash-dive *Complement:* 2 officers and 21 ratings

UB 41 was consigned to the II.U-Flottille at Heligoland on 2 November 1916 until 13 September 1917. Von Sichartshofen made the following six patrols:

(1) UB 41 went on anti-English submarine patrol off the Horn Riff between 5 and 7 November 1916.

(2) On 12 November 1916, UB 41 sailed to the English east coast for operations and captured the Norwegian steamer *Thyholm* (Aktieselskapet Skiens Motor, Skien) in the North Sea on 21 November. She was en-route from Holmestrand to West Hartlepool with pit props; a prize court then condemned the ship (in 1920 she became *Aldebaran* in the German Navy). UB 41 arrived back at Heligoland on 23 November 1916.

(3) UB 41 patrolled off Horns Reef between 26 December 1916 and 1 January 1917, but sank no ships.

(4) UB 41 left port on 16 January 1917 and patrolled off the Scottish east coast. On 18 January von Sichartshofen damaged the 139-ton fishing boat *Cetus* with gunfire at position 56° 21'N, 00° 21'E, but she was towed into Aberdeen. UB 41 arrived home on 22 January.

(5–6) On patrols 5 and 6, between 1 and 16 February 1917, UB 41 made war-patrols off the English east coast, but in two patrols von Sichartshofen failed to sink anything. Oblt.z.S. Gunther Krause assumed command on 21 March 1917 and carried out six patrols:

(7) UB 41 departed Germany on 15 April 1917 and patrolled along the English east coast. While voyaging from Caen to the Tyne in ballast, the Norwegian SS *Ellida*

(Aktieselskapet Dampskipsselskapet Ellida) was torpedoed and sunk off Whitby, none of her crew was lost. Krause arrived home with the boat on 23 April.

(8) Leaving Heligoland on 17 May 1917, UB 41 made a war-cruise along the English east coast.

On 22 May, UB 41 was some 1½ miles astern of the *Lanthorn* (Captain Shewan), when it was shelled with the deck gun. The steamer was in ballast and on passage from London for the Tyne. Captain Shewan altered course and increased speed to bring his vessel inshore, but the U-boat kept on firing, scoring at least five direct hits over the next half hour. To save the lives of his men, the captain stopped the engines and ordered 'abandon ship' at 09.00. The eighteen crewmen got away in the boats and motor fishing boats rescued them soon after. They were put ashore at Whitby. Some of the crew from UB 41 boarded the steamer and placed explosive scuttling charges below her decks; at 11.20 the ship exploded and went down to the bottom. The Norwegian SS *Monarch* (Aktieselskapet Dampskipsselskapet 'Monarch', O.M. Larsen, Kristiania) was taking pitch from the Tees to St Nazaire when she was torpedoed and sunk by UB 41 off Seaham Harbour; the following ten of her crew of seventeen were lost, including one woman:

Andersen, Stoker (Kristiania)
Costa, Silva 22, Stoker (Brazil)
Daasvand, Olaf, Sailor (Kristiania)
Edvardsen, Nils, Sailor (Tronheim)
Ivano, Oreka, 20, (Riga/Russia)
Johansen, Sigurd A., 42, Second Engineer (Kristiania)
Johansen.Olaf, Sailor (Kristiania)
Johanson, Kristine, Cook (Kristiania)
Nilsen, N.O., 30, Master (Arendal)
Peterson, Peter, Sailor (Gøteborg, Sweden)

UB 41 arrived back in Heligoland on 27 May.

(9) On 9 June 1917 UB 41 left Heligoland and patrolled off the Scottish east coast where two steamers and a small sailing vessel were sunk: the British coaster *Silverburn* (Rose Bros, Sunderland) was transporting coal from Sunderland to Peterhead when she was stopped and sunk by gunfire on 13 June and the Danish SS *Angantyr* (Aktieselskabet Dampskibsselskabet Gefion, Copenhagen) was torpedoed and lost on 14 June, while on passage from Göteborg, Sweden, for Rouen with general cargo and 2,000 tons of iron. UB 41 returned to Germany on 21 June.

(10) Krause failed to sink anything on the tenth patrol off the English east coast, between 4 and 16 July 1917.

(11) UB 41 departed Heligoland on 2 August 1917 and patrolled off the river Tees, where Krause captured and scuttled the little coaster *Talisman* (W. McLachlin & Co.) with explosive charges; she was bound for Grimsby from Greenock in ballast. The boat arrived at her base on 12 August.

(12) On 1 September 1917, UB 41 left Heligoland to operate off the Yorkshire coast. Krause torpedoed the steamship *Harrow* (Cory Colliers Ltd, London) off Whitby on the crossing from Granton to London with coal. The torpedo detonated on the ship's port-quarter at 18.45, instantly killing the sixty-two-year-old first mate, George Albert Bailey and one gunner (name unknown) as well as leaving another gunner seriously injured. Captain B.R. Davison was injured when the force of the blast threw him out of his cabin. The ship's stern end was shattered and her propeller and rudder were blown completely off the ship. The surviving crewmen abandoned ship at 19.00 and were picked up by an escort vessel and

taken to Whitby, about the same time as the *Harrow* went down to the bottom. UB 41 then returned to Germany and reported to the newly established V.U-Flottille base at Bremerhaven on 13 September 1917; Oblt.z.S. Max Ploen then took over command the next day.

FINAL VOYAGE

(13) UB 41 departed Bremerhaven with a crew of twenty-four on 30 September 1917 and sailed to the stretch of English coastline between Flamborough Head and Whitby; this being the thirteenth and unluckiest patrol of all. On 3 October 1917 and 5 nautical miles off Scarborough, Ploen torpedoed and heavily damaged the 502-ton SS *Clydebrae* (Albert Chester, Glasgow–Middlesbrough), which was journeying from Calais to Middlesbrough; she was beached at Scarborough, but re-floated and the engine was later replaced.

On 5 October, a British steamship reported the sighting of a German submarine, only 2 nautical miles east from Scarborough. Then two hours later the Scarborough signal station watchers reported a massive detonation, bearing east-north-east in the estimated position 54° 18' N, 00° 21' W. Rescue vessels raced through heavy seas to the scene and found debris, but no sign of any survivors or human remains.

The U-boat was reported as missing on 5 October 1917. German post-war studies concluded that as UB 41 had been the only U-boat operating in that area at the time, she must have caused the explosion. The study also pointed to the fact that UB 41 may have detonated a mine laid by UC 55 on 9 July, in that approximate position. However, recent research suggests that UB 41 had blundered into the extensive British minefield laid in September by the 4,298-ton Admiralty-requisitioned steamer HMS *Angora* and the 1,687-ton Marksman Type Flotilla leader, HMS *Abdiel*. No fewer than twelve lines of deep mines had been laid at depths between 94ft and 126ft off Robin Hood's Bay, as part of the east coast mine barrage. <u>NARA: T-1022, Roll 12, PG61800</u>

THE MEN WHO DIED IN UB 41

Baer, Mn.Ing.Asp.
Buresch, Ob.Hzr
Eder, Mts.
Findel, Mts.
Grall, Ob.Mts.
Görlich, Masch.Mt
Harbauer, Hzr
Hasse, Ob.Masch.Mt
Hundeshagen, Masch.Mt
Hüschen, Masch.Mt
Häfner, F.T.
Janitschke, Stm.
Jessat, Hzr

Kühl, Ob.Hzr
Külper, Btn.Mt
Langheinrich, Masch.Mt
Leuchter, Ob.Hzr
Maas, Hzr
Ploen, Max, Oblt.z.S.
Schlecht, Hzr
Sobczynski, Mts.
Stolle, Btn.Mt.d.Res
Weikart, Btn.Mt
Weisbach, Lt.z.S.d.Res
Wettenmann, Mts.

UB 41 is recorded as having sunk eight vessels totalling 8,387 tons and the following is a list of the known vessels believed sunk or damaged:

AREA	VESSEL'S NAME	FLAG	TONS	D	M	YEAR	LOCATION
North Sea	*Thyholm*	NOR	259	21	11	1916	Captured as prize near Blyth
North Sea	*Cetus*	GBR	139	18	1	1917	Damaged off the E coast off Scotland
North Sea	*Ellida*	NOR	1124	19	4	1917	2 miles NW of Whitby
North Sea	*Lanthorn*	GBR	2299	22	5	1917	3 miles E of Whitby

North Sea	Monarch	NOR	1318	23	5	1917	2 miles E of Seaham
North Sea	Alwyn (s/v)	GBR	73	12	6	1917	5 miles SE of Girdleness
North Sea	Silverburn	GBR	284	13	6	1917	4 miles SE of Cove Bay
North Sea	Angantyr	DAN	1359	14	6	1917	Sunk SE of Cove Bay
North Sea	Talisman	GBR	153	6	8	1917	7 miles ESE of Hartlepool
North Sea	Harrow	GBR	1777	8	9	1917	4 miles SE of Whitby
North Sea	Clydebrae	GBR	502	3	10	1917	Damaged 5 miles N of Scarborough

Scarborough Sub Aqua Club sport/wreck divers first discovered the wreck of S/M UB 41, on 2 September 2002 10 miles north of where it was supposed to have been lost. This position is consistent with her loss having been caused by the September 1917 British minefield, probably mine lines E, F, G or H. The same divers had also discovered the long-lost UB 75 that lies just 1½ miles from UB 41 and 28½ miles north–west from the position where it was thought to lie.

WRECK-SITE
Experienced wreck diver and underwater photographer Bob Jolley, also from Scarborough, filmed the wrecks of both UB 41 and UB 75 during 2003 and 2005. Bob kindly supplied the authors with the following wreck description of UB 41:

The wreck is broken into two sections and lies on a seabed of sand, stones, gravel and shells, in a general depth of 54m, being the lowest astronomical depth. The main section is lying over on its starboard side at an angle of about 45 degrees. The two bow tubes also lie on the starboard side, off the main part of the wreck and are still facing forward. Starting at the rather small conning tower, the rear periscope is mounted on the outside and is bent over towards the bows; the glass in the eye is also broken; the forward periscope must have been extended, because it is actually snapped off. Moving across the top of the conning tower, the remains of a steering connection comes into view. Not far from the conning tower on top of the hull, there is some kind of valve unit. Forward of this is the 88mm deck gun, most of which is totally engulfed in heavy trawl net, with the gun barrel sticking out and pointing skyward. Proceed forward again and you arrive at the 'open' bow, which appears to have twisted even more to starboard. Peering into the open bow area, some switch gear and other items can be seen hanging down, while twisted, broken battery plates that would have normally been located under the floor, can be observed towards the right–hand side. Glancing to the left, it is obvious that this is where the hull imploded after striking the mine. Proceeding over a bit of open seabed to your left, you come to the two bow torpedo tubes, the first thing you see is the heavy outer doors; moving across the doors and down the bottom tube, you arrive at the open hull. By peering up inside, the gears for the forward hydroplane are visible. Swimming to port you can observe where the rear door of the top torpedo tube is broken, which has exposed the propeller of a live torpedo inside. Masses of lost or discarded fishing gear, ropes, trawl doors and lobster pots are strewn between the main hull and the torpedo tubes. Returning to the main hull and to the rear of the conning tower, the small opening to the engine room comes into view and by shining a lamp down it, a generator can be seen and what looks like a compressor, located on the front of the diesel engines. On the top of the engines, open rockers are evident on the port engine and the engine telegraph is still in place, with the indicator showing either full ahead or full astern. However, heavy silt covers much of the mechanism inside. Down on the seabed, is what appears to be a torpedo, lying partially buried in the sand, with the nose facing towards the U-boat's hull. The starboard side of the wreck, including the starboard propeller is engulfed in abandoned nets and trawling gear. With the wreck leaning well over on its starboard side, the port propeller, which has its blade-ends badly damaged, can be clearly seen, along with the centre cone. Moving back onto the hull, the first thing that you pass is a rudder quadrant and then

A G-torpedo book cover, incredibly, still readable, taken from the wreck of S/M UB 41, eighty-five years after she was lost to a mine off Robin Hood's Bay, Yorkshire.

a large 'lifting-eye' and the 'parrot-nose' mooring, or 'hebehaken', a type of lifting hook (specially fitted directly onto the pressure hull to allow the lifting vessel SMS *Vulkan* to operate her lifting device; for that purpose the two hooks should be 12m apart).

Then after passing the engine room opening, it brings you back to the conning tower; looking across and down onto the seabed (on a good day), you can see the forward 'hebehaken' level with the seabed, on the broken-off bow section. A profusion of colourful soft corals are now well established all over the remains of this 'iron coffin'. Shoals of bib can also be found all around it, especially the conning tower area. The wreck-site is a war grave and should be respected as such.

UB 75, SM IMPERIAL U-BOAT

DATE OF LOSS: Around 13 December 1917
DEPTH: 56m
REFERENCE: 54 27'.147 N, 000 15'.715 E
LOCATION: 9.10 nautical miles E from
North Cheek, Robin Hood's Bay

Type: Type UBIII coastal torpedo attack boat **Builders:** Blohm & Voss, Hamburg for Kaiserliche Deutsche Marine **Ordered:** 23 September 1916, within the batch of UB 75–UB 79 **Keel laid:** as Yard No.304 **Launched:** 5 May 1917 **Commissioned:** by Oberleutnant zur See Franz Walther on 11 September 1917

TECHNICAL SPECIFICATIONS

Hull: Double **Surface displacement**: 516 tons **U/Dt**: 648 tons **LBDH**: 55.30m x 5.82m x 3.68m x 8¼m **Machinery**: 2 x 550ps MAN diesels **Props**: 2 bronze **S/Sp**: 13.6 knots **Op/R**: 8,680 nautical miles at 6 knots **Sub/R**: 55 nautical miles at 4 knots **U/Power**: 2 x 394ps electric motors giving 7½ knots **Batteries**: AFA lead/acid **Fuel/Cap**: 34 + 39 tons **Armament**: 4 bow and 1 stern 50.04cm torpedo tubes **Torpedoes**: 10 x 50.04cm (19.7in) **Guns**: 1 x 88mm (3.46in) forward deck gun **Ammo**: 160 rounds of 88mm **Mines**: None **Diving**: Max-op-depth 50m (164ft) and 30 seconds to crash-dive **Complement**: 3 officers and 31 ratings

UB 75 was formally assigned to the Germany-based V.U-Flottille at Bremerhaven on 24 October 1917, with Oblt.z.S. Franz Walther the only commander. Walther made two war patrols:

(1) UB 75 left Germany on 2 November 1917 and operated along the English east coast. Walther damaged the SS *Lucida* (Admiralty requisition, London) off Scarborough and the ship was beached, but re-floated later; she was on passage from the Tyne for London with steam-coal. The Norwegian SS *Frithjof Eide* (Aktieselskapet Dampskipsselskapet Frithjof Eide, Haugesund) was also torpedoed and sunk on 11 November, while transporting saltpetre from Skien via Bergen to the Tyne. At 10.00 on Friday 9 November, they passed the Tyne Pier and at 19.00 a loud explosion was heard, close to hatch No.3. The master, Anton Austad from Haugesund, asserted that a torpedo had probably caused it. The ship, which was carrying a crew of sixteen and a pilot, sank after a couple of minutes, approximately 3½ nautical miles east-north-east of Flamborough Head. Eleven men, including the pilot, were lost.

THE MEN WHO DIED

Andersen, Karl, First Engineer, Bergen
Anesett, John, Stoker, Tjøme (Tønsberg)
Christfromfersen, John, First Mate, HaugesundDahl, Paul, Second Mate, Porsgrunn
Hansen, Carl, Sailor, Haugesund
Kvam, Arthur, Sailor, Bergen
Norbotten, Peder, Sailor, Haugesund
Olsen, Oscar, Steward, Kragerø
Svensson, Abel, Donkeyman, Karlskrona, Sweden
Ve, Tørres, Sailor, Haugesund
The pilot, name unknown

UB 75 returned to the port of Borkum on 11 November.

FINAL VOYAGE

(2) Escorted by two minesweepers, UB 75 left the German island base of Borkum on 29 November 1917, in company with UB 61, UB 64 and UC 49. However, UB 61 was lost on her way out, after she detonated a British-laid mine (the wreck of UB 61 was located in 1980 and photographed by divers).

With Franz Walther in command and carrying a crew of thirty-four, UB 75 returned to the Yorkshire coast for operations. Having arrived off Whitby in early December 1917, UB 75 created mayhem in the first few days. On 5 December the SS *Aigburth* (West Lancashire SS Co. Ltd) was torpedoed off North Cheek at Robin Hood's Bay. The steamer was on passage from the Tyne for Treport with coal when the missile detonated amidships, killing Captain Geddes and ten of her crew of fourteen. The second engineer and second mate found themselves in the sea, clinging to floating wreckage, and were picked up by a patrol vessel. The only other survivor, a DEMS gunner, managed to swim to the patrol boat and the three men were landed at North Shields later that day.

TEN OF THE MEN WHO DIED
Burge, William George, 60, Engineer
Burns, Robert, 17, Ordinary Seaman
Geddes, W.B., Master
Griffiths, Hugh, 19, Able Seaman
Horswell, Albert Edward, 26, Stoker
Hughes, Hugh, 45, Mate
Johnston, John James Swan, 48, Stoker
Jones, Owen, 18, Able Seaman
Keefe, James, 20, Able Seaman
Taggart, Patrick John, 56, Stoker

On 6 December the Dutch steamer, *Leda* (N.V. Koninkl Nederland. Stoomboot Mij., Amsterdam) was torpedoed and sunk while en-route from Methil to Amsterdam with a cargo of coal. Six of her crew were killed. That U-boat was probably UB 75.

The 1,780-ton SS *Highgate* (Cory Colliers Ltd, London) was torpedoed and sunk by the submerged UB 75 at 15.15 on 7 December. She was under the command of Captain A. Wanless and travelling at a steady 8 knots when the torpedo detonated just in front of the bridge. However, the crew – three of whom were injured in the blast – managed to get away in one of the boats, then they watched as their ship went down, just three minutes later. Almost at once, two motor-launches picked up the crew and landed them at nearby Whitby. The steamer was carrying 2,400 tons of coal and a crew of twenty, on passage from the Tyne for London. Five men were lost with the SS *Lampada* (Gas Light & Coke Co.), on a voyage from the Tyne to London with coal; she was torpedoed off Whitby at 15.15 on 8 December. The crew got away in two boats, but a heavy sea was running and a huge wave swamped one of the boats, drowning two of the occupants. The other boat picked up the three others, either dead or dying. A steamship rescued the survivors and transferred them to a motorboat that took them to Whitby.

THE MEN WHO DIED
Johansen, Gustave, Fireman.
McColl, Michael, 27, Steward
Pazzal, Ralph Nathaniel, 14, Mess Room Steward
Ringholdsten, A., Fireman
Smith, John Edward, 40, Fireman

On 10 December, Walther torpedoed the steamer *Venetia* (Venetia SS Co. Ltd, Glasgow) which was travelling on sealed orders from Newcastle with coal. The master ran for shallow water and beached her close to Whitby west pier. Part of the crew left the ship and were picked up by a patrol vessel, the rest of the crew however remained on board until she was firmly aground before being taken off by Whitby No.2 lifeboat. The U-boat was never observed at any time. From that day on, nothing more was ever heard from UB 75. It failed to answer all signals and when the boat was due back at her base on 13 December 1917, it was listed as missing, presumed lost with all hands, in an area off Flamborough Head, with extensive British minefields. Walther however, must have moved north before his boat detonated a mine 10 miles off Robin Hood's Bay. NARA: T-1022, Roll 80, PG61835

THE MEN WHO DIED

Bach, Masch.Mt.d.S.I
Bay, Hzr
Becker, Hzr
Binnebös, F.T.
Böhm, Mts.
Büxten, Btn.Mt
Dippel, Masch.Mt
Geisler, Hzr
Greul, Masch.Mt
Hochkeppler, Mts.
Hühn, Masch.Mt.d.Res
Jendroszek, Obe.Mts.
Jung, Ob.Masch.Mt.d.Res
Keller, F.T.
Koopmann, Ob.Mts.
Krause, Mts.
Lindner, Btn.Mt

Meissel, Mts.
Pierags, Ob.Mts.
Pierson, Hzr
Pupps, Mts.
Radojewski, Ob.Mts.
Schernowski, Ob.Btn.Mt
Schidzig, Mts.
Schiek, Masch.Anw
Schier, Masch.Mt
Schneider, Ob.Hzr
Schulz, Mn.Ing.d.Res
Sick, Masch.Mt
Straubing, Ob.Masch.Mt
Stürtz, Stm.
Utpadel, Lt.z.S.d.Res
Walther, Franz, Oblt.z.S.
Zabel, Ob.Hzr

The following is a list of the known vessels believed sunk or damaged by UB 75:

AREA	VESSEL'S NAME	FLAG	TONS	D	M	YEAR	LOCATION
North Sea	*Lucida*	GBR	1477	4	11	1917	Damaged 2½ miles N of Scarborough area
North Sea	*Frithjof Eide*	NOR	1207	9	11	1917	2½ miles ENE of Flamborough Head
North Sea	*Aigburth*	GBR	824	5	12	1917	2 miles ENE of South Cheek, Robin Hood's Bay
North Sea	*Highgate*	GBR	1780	7	12	1917	2½ miles E of South Cheek, Robin Hood's Ba
North Sea	*Lampada*	GBR	2230	8	12	1917	3 miles N of Whitby
North Sea	*Venetia*	GBR	3596	9	12	1917	3 miles NNW of Whitby
North Sea	*Leda*	NED	1157	6	12	1917	Sank off Flamborough Head 54° 12' N, 00° 08' W

WRECK-SITE

Scarborough Sub Aqua Club sport/wreck divers brought history to life on 1 September 2002, when they successfully located UB 75. The following day, they also discovered the long-lost UB 41. Experienced Scarborough wreck diver and underwater photographer Bob Jolley supplied the following visual account of the wreck:

The main body of the wreck is leaning at an angle of about 20 degrees to port and lies on a seabed of sand, stones, mud and gravel, in a general depth of 56m, being the lowest astronomical depth. The 88mm gun is still in place on the deck, just in front of the conning tower. Most of the gun is engulfed in lost fishing nets, but the barrel is exposed and points skywards. Moving from the gun onto the starboard hull, some unexploded 88mm shells can be seen and a number of the heads appear to have pushed into the shell casings. Proceeding forward along the side of the hull towards the bows, parts of the outer casing are missing and the round inner pressure hull can be clearly observed. However the main hull section comes to a sudden halt, because the bows are missing. The only thing obvious is a bulkhead with four broken torpedo tubes. In the bottom port tube, the head of a 50cm torpedo still protrudes from it and the broken tubes run down into the seabed. A large shoal of whiting, pout whiting, poor cod and codling are all massed around this area. By moving forward across the rather desolate seabed you come upon the 'saw-tooth' net cutter, which was once attached on the top at the bows; wires still run away from the net cutter and by following these, you arrive back at the broken torpedo tubes. Moving around these, one of the large external torpedo tube doors is visible. Off to the right, more debris from the wreck can be seen. Continue down the port side of the outer hull, sections of the pressure hull also come into view. Lots of colourful soft corals (deadman's fingers) and small clumps of seaweed are well established all over the wreck. On the port side below the deck gun, huge numbers of unexploded 88mm shells can be seen, this apparently being the area of the main ammunition store. The live brass detonators are also still visible in the shell heads, along with the carrying handle at the base of the shells. On the top of the hull, two large air tanks are draped in fishing nets. Move towards the stern and the wreck comes to an abrupt end again, with no hydroplanes or propellers; in fact the stern end, similar to the bows, has vanished. (Maybe the U-boat struck two mines?) A large 'flywheel' valve protrudes from the aft bulkhead. The wreck is absolutely covered in lost trawl nets, ropes and gill nets, yet uncharacteristically, local fishermen and nearby residents refer to this wreck as 'No Snags'. Moving over to the starboard side and back towards the top of the hull, there is a hole leading part-way into the submarine, which is full of debris. Further on, the engine room hatch cover can be seen, but this is firmly closed and is draped in nets. Towards the conning tower, the bulge of the hull sides is obvious and on the top of the hull, there are two more large air tanks, sitting directly opposite the other two. Standing off the deck and about 1m high, is a tripod steel/iron object, just to the rear of the conning tower. This is possibly a binnacle. On the starboard side of the conning tower, a pile of alloy cases can be seen, ensnared under lost fishing nets; these contain 88mm shells and appear to have been carried round at the base of the conning tower in ready use as ammunition lockers; the unexploded shells are also quite close. Moving up the front of the conning tower, the first thing that comes into view is a broken brass tube, which is the remainder of the outer steering mechanism. The conning tower hatch is firmly closed and a little further back is the fully retracted attack periscope, then the second periscope, which protrudes slightly from its housing.

Michael Lowrey affirms that: 'the "bulkhead with four broken torpedo tubes" would be the forward end of the pressure hull. Although you cannot judge distances based on the description accurately, in an UB III there was about 10m from the forward pressure hull bulkhead to the extreme bow, where the forward point of the net cutter was attached. The thinner steel outside the pressure hull always rots away much faster, so it is doubtful that a mine caused this damage. I suspect a single mine hit aft, therefore there is the probability of a separate small stern section somewhere nearby, with at least the stern torpedo tube.'

This wreck is a war grave and should be respected as such.

The next U-boat wreck injects a sense of lingering mystery, one that the passing years have done little to dispel. Whatever happened to UB 107?

UB 107, SM IMPERIAL U-BOAT

DATE OF LOSS: 27 July 1918
DEPTH: 26m
REFERENCE: 54 08'.350 N, 000 04'.742 W
ALSO: 54 08'.338 N, 001 04'.730 W
LOCATION: 1.20 nautical miles N from Flamborough Head

Type: UB III torpedo attack boat **Builders**: Blohm & Voss, Hamburg for Kaiserliche Deutsche Marine **Ordered**: 23 September 1916, within the batch of UB 103–UB 117 **Keel laid**: as Yard No.313 **Launched**: 21 July 1917 **Commissioned**: by Oberleutnant zur See Hans Howaldt on 16 February 1918

TECHNICAL SPECIFICATIONS

Hull: Double **Surface displacement**: 519 tons **U/Dt**: 649 tons **LBDH**: 55.30m x 5.80m x 3.60m x 8¼m **Machinery**: 2 x 550ps MAN-Vulcan diesels **Props**: 2 bronze **S/Sp**: 13.3 knots **Op/R**: 7,420 nautical miles at 6 knots **Sub/R**: 55 nautical miles at 4 knots **U/Power**: 2 x 394ps electric motors giving 7½ knots **Batteries**: AFA lead/acid **Fuel/Cap**: 35 + 36 tons **Armament**: 4 bow and 1 stern 50.04cm torpedo tubes **Torpedoes**: 10 x 50.04cm (19.7in) **Guns**: 1 x 105mm (4.13in) forward deck gun **Mines**: None **Ammo**: 160 rounds of 105mm **Diving**: Max-op-depth 50m (164ft) and 30 seconds to crash-dive **Complement**: 3 officers and 31 ratings

UB 107 was assigned to the Flandern II U-Flottille on 16 May 1918, with Hans Howaldt the CO from 16 February 1918 until 16 May 1918. Howaldt, who was born on 12 November 1889, also served as commander on UC 4, UB 40 and UC 90 and died on 6 September 1970. On his last patrol on UB 40, the boat's second commander, Howaldt, was promoted to Kapitänleutnant and awarded the distinguished *Pour Le Mérite* (Blue Max) on 23 December 1917.

(1) On 2 May 1918, UB 107 left Germany and sailed to the English east coast for torpedo operations. At 00.15 on 10 May, Howaldt attacked a convoy with torpedoes and hit the Swedish steamer *Naparima* (Captain E.A. Carlsson) off Blea Wyke, near Robin Hood's Bay. Owned by Axel Ingmanson, the 1,649-ton ship was on passage from Göteborg, Sweden for Grimsby with 122 postsacks and wood. One seaman, A.W. Johannson, was injured in the explosion, but all of her nineteen crew abandoned ship safely. Local fishermen then bravely launched their Yorkshire fishing cobles in pitch darkness and steered the men back to shore. *Naparima* stayed afloat, and the next day the Grimsby salvage vessel *Recovery* towed her to Scarborough, where the cargo was unloaded. Temporary repairs were made and *Naparima* left Scarborough on 21 May and sailed to West Hartlepool under her own steam, where full repairs were carried out.

One of the torpedoes Howaldt fired at the convoy also struck the 1,630-ton Norwegian SS *Erich Lea* (Bergen Lloyd Aktierederi & Bjornstad & Broekhus) which was voyaging from the Tyne to Rouen with 2,493 tons of coal. None of the crew was lost.

UB 107 arrived at Zeebrugge on 16 May and formally joined the Flandern II.U-Flottille.Kplt. Eberhard von Prittwitz und Gaffron assumed command of the boat on 17 May 1918.

Von Prittwitz, who was born on 21 September 1889, had been a kapitänleutnant since 16 November 1917, but was seriously injured in December 1917. He had previously been kommandant on torpedo-boat destroyers T92, S138, S141, V57, S167, S66, before taking the appropriate course at the U-Schule. However, until then he had never commanded a submarine. Von Prittwitz made three war patrols with UB 107:

(2) UB 107 left Zeebrugge on 5 June 1918 and patrolled along the English east coast. Just south of the Farne Islands, von Prittwitz torpedoed the SS *Hogarth* (Aberdeen Steam Navigation Co.), 10 miles south-east from the Longstone light. The steamer, commanded by Captain David Stephen, had sailed from London for Aberdeen with 650 tons of general cargo, but was hit amidships at midnight and sank almost at once; with the loss of twenty-five crewmen. The sole survivor was the senior DEMS gunner, who happened to be in his cabin at the time; the next thing he could remember was being in the freezing water and clinging to some of the ship's floating wreckage. It was two days before a passing patrol boat picked

him up and took him to Newcastle-upon-Tyne, where he was treated for hypothermia. On 27 June 1917 the *Hogarth* rescued the fourteen-man crew of the coaster SS *Longbenton*, which had been torpedoed by UC 63, 12 miles south of Flamborough Head.

Moving down to Flamborough Head area, von Prittwitz torpedoed the SS *Kalo* (The Shipping Controller) at 04.45 on 13 June; she was under the command of Captain P. Winckler and on passage from the Tyne for Pauillac with coal. Three of her crew of eighteen were killed when the vessel was hit at position 53° 51' N, 00° 12' E. An armed trawler took the steamer in tow and tried to reach shallow water, but it foundered before the task was accomplished. The rest of the crew were taken on board the trawler.

According to ADM 137/3917, at 07.00 UB 107 was 'bombed' or depth-charged in position 53° 55' N, 02° E.

The 1,334-ton Swedish steamer *Agnes* (Rederiaktieb Agnes, Landskrona) was in ballast and carrying a crew of nineteen, comprising eighteen men and one woman, on a voyage between Hull and Blyth on 13 June, when UB 107 hit her with a torpedo at 22.45. She sank with the loss of two crewmen: Pontus Valdemar Norrman and Mauritz Engelhard Hansson. UB 107 reported to U-boat Command at 04.00 on 15 June.

At 21.30 on 15 June, Von Prittwitz torpedoed the SS *Kieldrecht* (The Shipping Controller). The torpedo detonated on the port side in her No.2 hold, sending her to the bottom in less than five minutes. Commanded by Captain T. Visser, she was on passage from the Humber for the Tyne; an escort vessel picked the crew of twenty-one up soon after they abandoned ship. UB 107 returned to Zeebrugge on 17 June.

(3) On 6 July 1918 UB 107 departed Flanders and sailed back to the English east coast for operations. In the early hours of 8 July, the SS *War Crocus* (The Shipping Controller) was in convoy, travelling from Hartlepool to Southend-on-Sea with 6,620 tons of coal, when a torpedo from UB 107 sank her. The brand new ship had just left William Gray's shipyard at 15.30 the day before and sailed from Hartlepool that evening, on her maiden voyage. The torpedo detonated in the No.2 hold at 01.45, but none of her crew of forty-four were lost and they abandoned ship in the boats at 01.55. An escort vessel landed them at Grimsby.

Later that same day, the SS *Chicago III* (Ellerman's Wilson Line Ltd) was also torpedoed off Flamborough Head, while on passage from North Shields for Gibraltar, with 7,811 tons of coal. The torpedo detonated level with the No.2 hatch and the ship immediately started to sink by the stern. The fifty crewmen and a pilot abandoned ship in the boats, but the third officer and two seamen were lost. The crew had no sooner cleared the ship than she plunged to the bottom. An escort vessel picked up the survivors within ten minutes and landed them at Grimsby.

On 9 July, von Prittwitz torpedoed the Swedish SS *Fryken* (Ångbåts A/B Ferm, Kristinehamn) off the Humber. The ship, commanded by Captain A. Borjesson, was on passage from Göteborg, Sweden for London with general cargo; the crew abandoned ship in the boats just before she sank. UB 107 returned to Zeebrugge on 11 July.

FINAL VOYAGE

(4) All that is known for certain about UB 107 on her last patrol is that she left Zeebrugge on 26 July 1918 for operations off the English east coast, with Kplt. Eberhard von Prittwitz und Graffron and a crew of thirty-eight (three officers and thirty-five crew). The U-boat never returned. In order to investigate this tortuous tale, we must now examine the traditional British account, based upon documents in ADM 137/3900 and ADM 137 4019, the contemporary account of the destruction of UB 107 – 27 July 1918:

> This encounter took place many miles north of Scarborough in position 54° 23' N, 00° 24' W and in very heavy seas. At 20.30 UB 107 surfaced in full view of the requisitioned trawler *Calvia* (Admiralty No.852) (Lt W. Croucher RNR), which radioed for immediate assistance. The

356-ton steam yacht HMY *Vanessa II* and two additional anti-submarine requisitioned trawlers, HMT *Warter Priory* (Admiralty No.653) and *Commander Nasmith* (Admiralty No.1968), commenced a concentrated depth charge attack. A mass of oil, bubbles and wreckage rose to the surface. The three little warships stayed in position overnight and the following morning the crew of *Vanessa II* spotted the headless body of a man in 'German naval uniform'.

At any rate the Admiralty accepted this version of events – and a number of more recent authors also went along with it.

So far so good… on closer analysis, however, the story begins to unravel. A widespread sweep of the position in the days that followed failed to reveal a submarine.

Moreover at 23.25 on 27 July, a submarine torpedoed the 984-ton British steamer *Chloris* (J&P Hutchinson Ltd), 17 miles south by east from Flamborough Head. The torpedo detonated on the starboard side under No.2 hold; sixteen crewmen took to the boats and were picked up by a trawler and landed at Grimsby, but the master and two seamen were found to be missing. *Chloris*, which was in convoy and armed with a 13-pounder, sank at 00.30 on 28 July, in position 53 52'.058 N, 000 10'.175 E (WGS84). She was on passage from Christiania for Hull, with rough wood pulp and timber.

About the same time as the *Chloris* was hit, the Swedish steamer *John Rettig* (Angfartygs Aktieb, Gelfe) was also struck by a torpedo. She was sailing in the same convoy, on passage from Göteborg, Sweden, for Hull with general cargo and escorted by British warships. At 23.30, crewmen saw a white trail in the water coming towards them on the starboard side. The torpedo struck the vessel close the stern. The crew abandoned ship and were picked up by a trawler from the convoy, but two men stayed on the stricken steamer. The men prepared a wire, ready for towing, but let it go when she began quickly going down by the stern. The trawler remained by the wreck until 03.00 in the morning. Parts of the wreck were rising 6ft above the surface. The only submarine that could have sunk these vessels was UB 107.

What of the 'headless body' and the evidence of UB 107's destruction? Close examination of the original anti-submarine group war diary provides a number of interesting details. This corpse was found several miles from the site of the encounter, though this is not in itself remarkable, as it could have come from anywhere. What is noteworthy is that local staff officers did not immediately link the discovery with the submarine incident until some time later. This body was considered 'too far gone to merit recovery', and therefore the conventional search for documents and identification was not made.

Just as interesting is the evolution in language, from a sighting of 'a headless body in a frock coat that resembled a northern or German uniform' in the initial dispatches, to 'a headless body in a German naval uniform' in the A/S Division Monthly reports. This is far from unusual in cases of U-boat encounters. Admiralty intelligence officers, for press consumption, routinely embroidered sparse logbook contents. Faced with this evidence, the claim that *Calvia* and her consorts sank UB 107 looks questionable. In 1985 proof emerged that *Calvia* and her 'sisters' could not possibly have destroyed UB 107.

A mystery solved? In the summer of 1985, divers clearing lobster pots discovered the wreck of a steamship, in a poor condition. Lying at right angles with the ship and actually underneath it, but apparently intermingled with her cruiser stern, was a First World War German submarine. The propellers identified the boat as the lost UB 107. After nearly seventy years, the last resting place of Kplt. Eberhard von Prittwitz und Graffron and his crew had been found. This begs the question as to how UB 107 came to be embedded under the wreck of a steamship. A clue may lie in the identity of the ship…

A steel plate under the bows of the ship bore the letters 'MAL'. Extensive detective work by diver/historians Peter Lassey and Arthur Godfrey identified the ship as the 1,244-ton London & Edinburgh Shipping Co. steamship *Malvina*. Commanded by Captain T. Harris and armed with a 12-pounder, the ship had left London on 31 July, on passage for Leith, carrying a crew of twenty-eight and 750 tons of general cargo, including bagged cement. On 2 August 1918, the *Malvina* was off Flamborough Head and travelling at 12 knots, in a light easterly swell, when a torpedo struck her at 04.35. Lookouts in the forecastle never saw the submarine. The torpedo detonated amidships on the starboard side, level with the boiler room, and the ship buckled in two at once. The port lifeboat was lowered, but capsized at once and the men in it were thrown into the water. Those men still on the sinking ship were forced to jump overboard and tried to swim clear to avoid being sucked down. Many grabbed hold of floating wreckage. The patrol boat *Gaul*, a trawler, which was ½ mile northward at the time of the explosion, rescued fourteen survivors and landed them at Scarborough. However, the fourteen men who were thrown into the water were not picked up, including Captain Harris.

Post-war analysis ascribes the sinking of *Malvina* to UB 104. However, U-boat historian Michael Lowrey made a fascinating discovery when he examined the original KTB (war diary/ship's log) of UB 104 in 2004. The KTB reveals that at 00.35 (German Time) on 3 August 1918, UB 104 spotted a steamer of about 1,000 tons, heading north in ballast. At 00.45, 3 miles east of Flamborough Head, she fired a single torpedo. It found its mark and the steamer disintegrated and sank immediately. The log also notes there were light winds and slight seas, cloudy with intermittent rain, and limited visibility.

There are no other sinking claims, or even attacks on this day, or the previous day, in this area by UB 104. The complication is that there were *two* vessels lost off Flamborough Head on 2 and 3 August 1918, not one. Arno Spindler, in his writings, credits UB 104 with sinking *Malvina*, but he does not assign credit to any U-boat for sinking *Cambrai*. ADM 137 4019 (★Old 675) states: 'at Lat.54.8.20.N Long.0.2.50.E at BST 11.40am (35am) on Aug.3rd *Cambrai* was hit and sank in five minutes. Crew all French. Quartermaster first, then Chief Officer were picked up by HMS *Scomer* about two hours later and landed at Bridlington. *Cambrai*, a 963-ton French steamer, left Rouen on 31 July 1918 for Sunderland in ballast, on government service (for City of Paris)'.

There is every possibility that UB 104 was responsible for torpedoing *Cambrai* rather than *Malvina*. If UB 104 is now removed from the equation, then the fates of *Malvina* and UB 107 may well be intertwined in more ways than one.

It is possible to assume that UB 107 torpedoed *Malvina* and then suffered some overwhelming calamity, which resulted in her own destruction. It is also feasible that UB 107 struck a mine. Certainly mines breaking free due to heavy weather had fouled the War Channel and the Flamborough sector had required a temporary cessation of traffic the previous day, while the lane was swept. UB 104 even destroyed a floating mine at 06.30 on 3 August, thirty minutes before sighting Flamborough Head. The hulls of both vessels have deteriorated too far to provide evidence, but mining must remain a plausible cause of the submarine's loss. Nor can a diving accident, or torpedo detonation be ruled out.

Shipping reports comment on poor visibility off Bridlington and Flamborough that week. UB 104 reported heavy rain and a sea fret on 3 August, although the sea was not particularly rough. There may be valid grounds for the intriguing theory that UB 107 attacked *Malvina*, which had broken in two and sank on top of the U-boat, thus suffering mortal damage to her pressure hull. This is supported by evidence at the wreck-site. Divers report that the cement cargo has collapsed onto to the U-boat casing below the stern torpedo tubes. In the final analysis these theories are mere speculation. We know she cannot have been sunk by *Calvia*, but equally we are unable to prove what destroyed UB 107.

In a final analysis of the mystery, the US/Canada-based 'Deep Sea Detectives' TV company made a documentary about the two wrecks in 2004, in an attempt to solve the riddle. The divers, which included local Scarborough sport/wreck divers and American diver John Chatterton, made inspections of the wrecks. Carl Racey, one of the Yorkshire divers, noticed that the base of the forward radio mast seemed to be stuck in the 'up' position. If that is correct, it argues very strongly that UB 107 was actually at the surface when whatever occurred happened and the boat was not planning to conduct offensive operations at the time. This leads to the speculation that the U-boat possibly detonated a loose mine, or she was taken by surprise, dived and met her end in an accident. However, because the wrecks are breaking up very quickly now, it appears that *Malvina* and UB 107 will remain locked in mysterious eternal embrace at the bottom of the North Sea.

There was also some confusion as to what type of vessel the *Vanessa* actually was. Authors Kemp and Bendert refer to her as a destroyer, but Groner says she was a steam yacht. The *Vanessa* in question was almost certainly a 356-ton steam yacht, built in 1899 as *Golden Eagle* and hired to the Admiralty as *Vanessa* on 15 October 1914. Her name was changed to *Vanessa II* in February 1917. She was returned to her original owners on 5 March 1919 and hired again in the Second World War as *Carina* from January 1940 to 1946.

THE MEN WHO DIED IN UB 107:

Ackermann, Ob.Mts.
Alt, Hzr
Anlauf, Ob.Hzr
Böhm, Hzr
Brix, Ob.Masch.Mt
Carstensen, Masch.Mt
Damann, Masch.Mt
Diehl, Btn.Mt
Diehn, Ob.Hzr
Engel, Ob.Hzr
Ewald, Mts.
Fenkner, Oblt.z.S.
Filaferra, Ob.Hzr
Folprecht, Masch.Mt
Franz, Mn.Ing.
Fröhlich, Ob.Mts.
Gäthje, Mts.
Grüneberg, Masch.Mt
Hartwich, Hzr
Hilscher, Ob.Masch.Mt

Kiessling, Mts.
Krug, Hzr
Kullenberg, Hzr
Maas, Mts.
Müller, Hzr
Pagel, Ob.Mts.
Pollednick, Ob.Mts.
Prittwitz und Gaffron, von
Kapitänleutnant
Richter, Oblt.z.S.
Schneider, F.T.
Schrader, Masch.Mt
Schütze, Masch.
Sippel, Ob.Masch.Mt
Sperling, F.T.Ober Gast
Thumann, Hzr
Übel, Ob.Btn.Mt
Viehweger, Ob.Mts.
Wünsche, Mts.

The following is a list of the known vessels believed sunk or damaged by UB 107:

AREA	VESSEL'S NAME	FLAG	TONS	D	M	YEAR	LOCATION
North Sea	*Erich Lea*	NOR	1630	10	5	1918	6 miles SE of Whitby
North Sea	*Naparima*	SWE	1685	10	5	1918	Damaged near Hartlepool
North Sea	*Hogarth*	GBR	1231	7	6	1918	10 miles S ½ E of the Longstone, Farne Islands
North Sea	*Agnes*	SWE	1334	13	6	1918	12 miles E of Flamborough Head
North Sea	*Kalo*	GBR	1957	13	6	1918	18 miles S by E ½ E Flamborough Head
North Sea	*Kieldrecht*	GBR	1284	15	6	1918	21 miles E by S of Flamborough Head
North Sea	*Chicago*	GBR	7709	8	7	1918	4 miles NE of Flamborough Head
North Sea	*War Crocus*	GBR	5296	8	7	1918	2½ miles E by N of Flamborough Head
North Sea	*Fryken*	SWE	943	9	7	1918	Sunk off the Humber Estuary
North Sea	*Chloris*	GBR	984	27	7	1918	17 miles S by E of Flamborough Head
North Sea	*John Rettig*	SWE	1809	27	7	1918	18 miles S of Flamborough Head

WRECK-SITE

The engraving on the propeller identified the wreck as UB 107. It is lying on a hard seabed of sand, stone and rock, in a general depth of 26m, being the lowest astronomical depth. The remains are also mixed up with the broken two halves of the 1,244-ton steamship *Malvina* that sank shortly after. The submarine is at right angles to the *Malvina* and is actually embedded into it, with part of her disappearing under the engine area of the steamer, which lies broken in two. Solid bags of cement have fallen onto the deck casing of UB 107 and divers say it appears that the U-boat struck the prop shaft of the steamship, knocking the propeller off the bracket. Both wrecks are badly collapsed and broken up and most, if not all of the interesting artefacts have since been removed as souvenirs by visiting divers. The periscope is believed to be in one of the local dive clubs. This wreck is classified as a war grave, because the crew was lost with the boat.

UC 75, SM IMPERIAL U-BOAT

DATE OF LOSS: 31 May 1918
DEPTH: 31m
REFERENCE: 53 56'.478 N, 000 09'.036 E
ALSO GIVEN: 52 56'.467 N, 000 09'.067 E
LOCATION: 11.17 nautical miles E by N from Hornsea
and 13.20 nautical miles SSE from Flamborough Head

Type: UCII coastal mine-laying boat   *Builders:* AG Vulcan, Hamburg for Kaiserliche Deutsche Marine   *Ordered:* 12 January 1916, within the batch of UC 74–UC 76   *Keel laid:* Yard No.80 *Launched:* 6 November 1916 *Commissioned:* by Kapitänleutnant Georg Paech on 6 December 1916

TECHNICAL SPECIFICATIONS

Hull: Double   *Surface displacement:* 410 tons   *U/Dt:* 493 tons   *LBDH:* 50.45m x 5.22m x 3.68m x 7.46m *Machinery:* 2 x 250ps MAN diesels   *Props:* 2 bronze   *S/Sp:* 11.8 knots   *Op/ R:* 10,420 nautical miles at 7 knots   *Sub/R:* 52 nautical miles at 4 knots   *U/Power:* 2 x 230ps electric motors giving 7.3 knots   *Batteries:* Lead/acid   *Fuel/Cap:* 41 + 14 tons   *Armament:* 2 external 50.04cm torpedo tubes at the bow, one either side of the mine chutes and 1 stern internal tube   *Torpedoes:* 7 × 50.04cm (19.7in) maximum   *Guns:* 1 x 88mm (3.46in) forward deck gun   *Ammo:* 133 rounds of 88mm   *Mine tubes:* 6   *Mines:* 18 x UC 200   *Diving:* Max-op-depth 50m (164ft) and 33 seconds to crash-dive   *Complement:* 3 officers and 23 ratings

Torpedo load as designed: 4 – a torpedo in each tube plus a reload for the stern tube. Storing an additional torpedo in pieces internally for the stern tube later augmented this, although this was optional. Two extra torpedoes (total) for the external bow tubes could be carried as well – these were lashed to the deck. So up to a total of seven torpedoes were carried, although not all boats sailed with that many.

UC 75 was formally assigned to the Germany-based I.U-Flottille at Heligoland on 10 February 1917 with Kplt. Georg Paech the CO until 16 March 1917, when Oblt.z.S. Johannes Lohs assumed command. Johannes Lohs, who was born on 24 June 1889, later went on to command UB 57. He was lost with his crew in that boat when she ran into a minefield off Zeebrugge. Lohs sank seventy-six Allied vessels, totalling 148,677 tons. On 4 April 1918, he was awarded the *Orden Pour Le Mérite* for outstanding service against enemy shipping. Johannes Lohs made the following nine patrols with the boat:

(1) On 22 March 1917 UC 75 left Heligoland for operations off the English and Scottish east coasts. On 25 March Lohs sank three trawlers and captured, shelled and sunk the Norwegian SS *Marshall* (Bernhard Schattenstein, Narvik) off Peterhead; the steamer was bound for Tromsø from the Tyne with coal. Off Whitby on 29 March, the Belgian steamer *Schaldis* (Van Hemelrijck & Geurts) commanded by Captain B. Peelman, was torpedoed and sunk, while en-route from Dunston-on-Tyne to Calais with a cargo of coke. UC 75 arrived back at Heligoland on 4 April.

(2) On 28 April UC 75 left Heligoland and sailed for operations off the Irish south coast. Lohs sank ten small vessels with gunfire or explosives on this patrol and torpedoed and sunk the SS *Polymnia* (Crown Nominees: Kaye, Son & Co. Ltd, London) without warning; she was transporting iron ore and fruit from Huelva and Lisbon to Falmouth when the missile detonated just abaft the engine room and eight men were lost. The survivors got away in the two boats, but were stopped and questioned by the U-boat crew, until a torpedo boat destroyer approached and it was forced to dive. The survivors were picked up by a drifter at 09.00 and landed at Falmouth.

However, in the English Channel on 5 May, Lohs torpedoed the 1,250-ton British sloop HMS *Lavender*, on which ninety-three men were lost when she sank. This made Lohs into something of a hero when he returned to Germany on 18 May 1917.

(3) On 3 June 1917 UC 75 departed Heligoland and made a sortie in the western end of the English Channel, where Lohs sank five vessels and damaged the British steamer *Kathlamba* (Bucknall Steamship Lines Ltd, North Shields). The vessel was on passage from Melbourne for London with general cargo, and was beached 1 mile south of Crow Point; she re-floated next day. Three of the vessels were small, but one man was lost when the SS *Anglian* (F. Leyland & Co. Ltd, West Hartlepool (Liverpool)) was torpedoed and sunk, while on a voyage from Boston, USA, to London with general cargo.

The SS *Kelso* (T. Wilson, Sons & Co. Ltd, Hull) was also carrying general cargo from Oporto to London when Lohs sunk her with a torpedo, 33 miles off Bishop Rock. UC 75 returned to Germany on 23 June.

(4) Departing Heligoland on 22 July 1917, UC 75 sailed for mine-laying operations in the English Channel and as far as the Irish Sea. On 29 July the French SS *Saint Marcouf* (Soc. des Forges et Aciéries de la Marine et d'Homécourt, Havre) was sent to the bottom by a torpedo, while en-route from Glasgow for Rouen. Eleven men were lost with the SS *Karina* (African Steamship Co., London), which was transporting passengers, palm oil and kernels from Sierra Leone, West Africa to Liverpool when a torpedo sunk her. The SS *Beechpark* (J&J Denholm, Greenock) was torpedoed and sunk, voyaging from the Tyne to Port Said with coal and coke. Lohs took UC 75 into Zeebrugge on 5 August 1917, instead of Heligoland, where she formally transferred to the Flandern/Flandern II U-Flottille.

(5) Leaving Flanders on 20 August 1917, UC 75 travelled to the Irish Sea to lay mines. Ten men were lost on the SS *Cymrian* (Golden Cross Line Ltd, London) after a torpedo strike, while transporting a general cargo from Newport, Monmouth to Dublin. She was steaming at 8 knots when the missile detonated amidships on the port side at 10.20 and went down at once. When the survivors were clear of the area they were stopped and questioned by Oblt.z.S. Lohs; later the men were rescued by the Russian steamer *Odessa* and landed at Larne.

The full-rigged ship *Cooroy* was en-route from Tocapilla, Chile to Liverpool with nitrate and went down on 29 August.

The SS *Lynburn* (Stainburn SS Co. Ltd, Workington) detonated a mine at 14.30 on 29 August and sank in three minutes, while voyaging from Cork to Whitehaven with pit-wood and eight men were lost, the mine having been laid on 29 July. Although the boats were lowered, they were all sucked down by the sinking ship; only the master, chief engineer and mate, who were wearing lifejackets, were left, and the Wicklow lifeboat rescued them later.

Lohs returned to Zeebrugge on 3 September 1917. However on 28 September, the British steamer *William Middleton* was transporting hay from Dublin to Falmouth when she detonated a mine, but she reached Rosslare Harbour (a mine had also previously damaged the same ship on 23 December 1916; it was beached at Tenby the next day, was patched up and re-floated, then taken to Port Talbot).

(6) On 30 September the U-boat left Flanders and returned to the Irish Sea for operations. On this patrol, four steamers were sunk. The *Maine* (Maine Colliery Co. Ltd, Cardiff) was shelled and sunk in Luce Bay on 9 October 1917; she was en-route from Belfast to Liverpool in ballast (the ship was re-floated on 7 August 1920, repaired and returned to service in 1922).

The *W. M. Barkley* (Arthur Guinness & Sons Co. Ltd, Belfast (Dublin)) was taking stout from Dublin to Liverpool when it was torpedoed and the master and three crewmen were lost. The arched deck steamer *Eskmere* (The Bromport SS Co. Ltd, Liverpool) sank with the loss of twenty crewmen, including the master, while in ballast on passage from Belfast to Barry.

Twenty-two men (all hands) also went down with the SS *Britannia* (Leith, Hull & Hamburg Steam Packet Co., Leith), en-route from Middlesbrough to St Malo with pig iron (it was missing since landing pilot at Deal on 18 October 1917, and was presumed torpedoed by UC 75). Lohs arrived at Zeebrugge on 20 October 1917.

(7) Leaving Flanders on 28 October 1917, UC 75 once again returned to the Irish Sea for operations. South of the Isle of Man on 3 November, Lohs damaged the SS *Atlantian* (Fred Leyland & Co. (1900) Ltd, Liverpool) with a torpedo, when she was on passage from Galveston, Texas for Liverpool with general cargo (the ship was eventually torpedoed and sunk by U 86 on 25 June 1918, 110 miles off Eagle Island). Next day the French steamer *Longwi* (Soc. Anon des Chargeurs de l'Quest, Nantes) was hit with a torpedo and went down with all hands, en-route from Bilbao for the Clyde with ammunition.

The British coaster *The Marquis* (J. Hay & Sons, Glasgow) was stopped 16 miles east-south-east from Rockabill and sunk by gunfire on 8 November, voyaging from Abergele, North Wales to Ayr with limestone. UC 75 arrived back at Zeebrugge on 12 November 1917.

(8) On 30 November 1917, UC 75 departed Flanders on a mine-laying operation in the Irish Sea. Lohs sank three large steamships with torpedoes. The *Euphorbia* (Stag Line Ltd, North Shields) was transporting 4,500 tons of rice and 150 bales of hides from Bassein, Burma, to London and fourteen men were lost (all hands). The *Rydal Hall* (Hall Line Ltd) was sunk and twenty-three men (all hands) were lost, taking a general cargo from Calcutta to Dunkerque. The SS *Earl of Elgin* (Anglo–American Oil Co. Ltd, Glasgow) was lost, along with eighteen men, including the master, while voyaging in ballast from London via Milford Haven to Dublin.

A torpedo also damaged the SS *Milton* (Shakespear Shipping Co. Ltd, London) on 3 December and she was towed to Dublin; she was voyaging from Manchester to Barry. UC 75 returned to Zeebrugge on 10 December 1917.

(9) Leaving Flanders on 22 December 1917, UC 75 sailed to the Irish Sea, where Lohs sank three small fishing boats and six steamers. The SS *Alfred H. Read* (Mersey Docks & Harbour Board, Liverpool) was engaged in examining incoming neutral ships for contraband cargo and was carrying sixteen pilots in addition to her crew of twenty-three when she struck a mine laid on 26 December off Black Can Gas Buoy in Queen's Channel, Liverpool. She sank at 07.00 with the loss of the captain, twenty-three crewmen and the sixteen pilots – just two men were picked up alive and landed at Liverpool, along with several bodies.

The *Chirripo* (Elders & Fyffes Ltd, Manchester (Liverpool)) was requisitioned from the owners when she detonated a mine and sank while on passage from Liverpool for Kingston, Jamaica, with general cargo. The Norwegian steamship *Asborg* (Aktieselskapet

To, Kristiansand) was sunk without warning following a torpedo attack by Lohs, while carrying steel plates and coal from Newcastle to Livorno, Italy. After sinking the SS *Asborg*, UC 75 had lain in wait off the Isle of Wight and hit the *Leon* on the starboard side, level with the No.2 hold, on 3 January. At first the crew thought they had struck a contact mine and panic broke out; a lifeboat was launched before the ship had slowed or stopped and as soon as it touched the water it capsized, and the four occupants were drowned. Patrol boats rescued the remaining thirty crewmen and landed them at Portsmouth. The *Iolanthe* (London Maritime Steamship Co. Ltd, London) was transporting trucks and hay from the Clyde to St Helen's Roads when a torpedo sunk her off Portland Bill. The missile was fired without warning and detonated level with the No.3 hold at 23.05 on 4 January; attempts were made to tow the ship, but the crew had to abandon her as it began to sink. A patrol vessel rescued them and took them to Weymouth.

The SS *Arca* was badly damaged by a torpedo off Start Point and put into Devonport for repairs; she was transporting coal from Cardiff & Brest for St Nazaire (however, on 2 October 1918 she was lost with all hands).

The SS *Gascony* (David MacIver, Sons & Co. Ltd, Liverpool) was voyaging from Southampton to Calais with Government stores when a torpedo detonated amidships on her port side at 23.17 on 7 January 1918. All of her thirty-nine crew abandoned ship and boarded a patrol boat. Two tugs tried to take her in tow, but she sank at 14.00 the following day.

Finally, the French armed steamer *Leon* (Delmas Frères, La Rochelle) was torpedoed and sunk in the Channel, while voyaging from the Tyne and London to Tunis. UC 75 arrived back at Flanders on 8 January 1918.

Johannes Lohs finally moved on to command a UB III attack-boat on 30 January 1918 and the following day Oblt.z.S. Walter Schmitz took over as commander, UC 75 being his first U-boat command. Schmitz was born on 1 February 1891, became a crewman in April 1909, and served on SMS *Rostock*, *Elbing* and *Kolberg* as W/O and FT Officer; for a while he served at the headquarters of Baltic U-boats and joined the U-boat school in April 1917. Schmitz made the following four patrols:

(10) Leaving Flanders base on 2 February 1918, the U-boat sailed to the English east coast, but Schmitz failed to sink anything and returned to port on 13 February.

(11) On 2 March 1918, UC 75 left Flanders for mine-laying operations in the Irish Sea. During that war-cruise Schmitz sank four small vessels and two steamers and his mines left another two steamships seriously damaged. The Spanish steamer *Arno Mendi* (Compania Naviera Sota y Aznar) went down with all hands off Stack Light, following a torpedo attack while en-route from Agua Amarga, Spain to Ayr with a cargo of copper ore. The next day a torpedo fired by Schmitz sank the SS *Tweed* (John George Hill Steam Shipping Co. Ltd, Newcastle), carrying coal from the Clyde to Devonport; no-one was lost on the ship. A torpedo struck the SS *Navigator*, on passage from Middlesbrough for South Africa with general cargo and she put into Weymouth.

A torpedo also damaged the SS *Dryden* (Liverpool, Brazil & River Plate Steam Navigation Co. Ltd, Liverpool), bound from Buenos Aires and Sierra Leone to Liverpool with wheat and general cargo, but she reached her destination. UC 75 arrived at Zeebrugge on 21 March 1918.

(12) Between 11 and 30 April 1918, UC 75 patrolled along the English Channel and two steamships were sunk with torpedoes off the Owers Light Vessel. The SS *Hungerford* (Government requisition, London), which was sailing in ballast from Havre to New York via St Helen's Roads, was hit with a torpedo from UC 75. The missile detonated on the port side of the engine room at 04.35 on 16 April, with four of the men being killed outright. The crew abandoned ship in the boats, but it appeared that the ship was not going to sink immediately, so the master went back on board. However, a second torpedo

struck her on the starboard side, so the master quickly left. Ten minutes later, at 07.20, the ship sank. At day-break a body was seen floating on the surface and, by then, three of the men in the open boat had died from exposure. A patrol vessel rescued the forty-six survivors and landed them at Portsmouth. The *War Helmet* (The Shipping Controller, London) was in ballast from London to Barry when a torpedo detonated on the port side and in the aft part of No.4 hold at 05.45. After abandoning ship, the crew of eighty-five and one passenger were picked up by two Royal Navy ships and landed at Portsmouth.

FINAL VOYAGE

(13) At 19.00 on 22 May 1918, UC 75 left her Flanders base with a crew of thirty-three for mine-laying operations off the English east coast. Having delivered his mines, Schmitz then made his way north and cruised around. By studying the situation, he was able to ascertain that convoys could usually be expected off Flamborough Head about 02.00 or 03.00. This was the sort of valuable information required for a U–boat commander and usually made his voyage of destruction more worthwhile. At 03.00 on 28 May, Schmitz attacked the leading steamship in a southbound convoy, but the British escort destroyer HMS *Ouse* caught sight of the boat. Schmitz crash-dived, but *Ouse* dropped a series of depth charges around the submarine, leaving her leaking oil and slightly damaged. UC 75 managed to escape from the destroyer but, for almost two days, the boat's crew were kept busy, repairing what damage they could, before recommencing their mission. On 29 May HMT *Dirk*, a 181-ton RN trawler and ex-Oban-Coll-Tiree-Bunessan mail-service ferry detonated a mine laid by UC 75 off Flamborough Head and sank with all hands.

At 01.55 (GT) on 31 May, Schmitz again spotted a 'MT' convoy, some thirty ships-strong and about 12 miles south of Flamborough Head. It was a calm, dark night with a very smooth sea. Overcast, with no moon or stars. Visibility was also reasonable. By 03.00 UC 75 had manoeuvred into the classic attack position, one that would orientate her at 90 degrees, bows-on to the convoy and lying at periscope depth. Penetrating an escort screen and then taking up a firing position required great skill on the part of the submarine crew. In such a large, concentrated convoy, the danger came not only from the warships, but also from the closely stationed merchantmen. It would appear from the post-war report offered by Schmitz that UC 75 dived under the escort screen only to arrive at periscope depth amid a line of merchant ships, too close for comfort. The steamer *Blaydonian* rammed the submarine then ran over her. ADM 137/3898 provides interrogation accounts gleaned from German survivors:

> 31st May 12 miles south of Flambro' Head. Weather fine, visibility low. UC 75 was coming to the surface when she was rammed by *Blaydonian*. The submarine's stem was bent by the force. The conning tower was struck and the hatch was damaged. A large quantity of water was seen to enter the boat. The SS *Tronda* and *Peter Pan* also bumped the submarine. The tanks were blown and the submarine surfaced.

As UC 75 broke surface, lookouts on the merchant ships raised the alarm. Abaft of the beam of the rear ship in the convoy, was the 1896 vintage 'C' Class destroyer HMS *Fairy*. Lt Geoffrey Barnish takes up the story:

> The convoy was steaming in darkness. After rounding Flamborough Head, I left our small bridge in order to have a walk on the after deck. It was generally considered that a German submarine was not likely to attack south of Flamborough Head, because of the proximity of rocky shoals. At 02.05 I heard a heavy crash from the direction of the convoy like the detonation of a torpedo. The officer of the watch, Lt Bennett, had sounded the alarm. We increased speed and headed for source of the noise. The men poured up on deck, and a few seconds later a surfaced submarine

was sighted off the port bow at a distance of 300 yards. Initially there was some doubt as to the identity of this submarine, the proximity of the Tees, Tyne and Blyth, being contributory factors to initial indecision. We made a series of signal grenade challenges but to no avail. I decided to damage rather than sink her – in the increasingly unlikely event that she was a returning British submarine. I ordered Coxswain Spinner to steer for her stern torpedo tubes. As we drew closer German voices calling 'Kamerad! Kamerad!' were clearly audible. I ordered the coxswain to port the helm in order to hit her in a more vital spot. We were too close for the helm to have any effect, and quickly passed over the stern of our enemy. There was no obvious force of impact at this time, and I fear we probably damaged ourselves more than we did him. However, on passing over him, I determined to renew the attack by ram, and sending the gunner aft to open fire with our after gun, proceeded to turn the *Fairy* round. The submarine fired her gun but we shelled her from point blank range with the after 6-pounder. In all, forty direct hits were made. The Germans on the submarine's bridge now jumped into the water as we came on again with our ram. The destroyer's bows struck the U-boat close beside the gun. How far our stem buckled in is uncertain but within seconds our foredeck was under water and the submarine had disappeared leaving two Germans calmly standing on our submerged fo'castle with their hands held up.

The German account continues:

HMS *Fairy* swung round and rammed her (UC 75) again. Because of the serious inrush of water, the C/O gave the order to abandon ship. He flooded the tanks sinking the boat. 14 officers and men were rescued by *Fairy* and the trawler.

ADM 137/3898, NARA Roll T-102, Roll 81 Abschriften aus Fragebogen series

Obersteuermannsmaat Stengel described how the crew of UC 75 flung open the hatches and vents and then slid down into the water. He claimed that British sailors continued firing rifles at the men floundering in the water. Stengel also maintained that some U-boat men had manned the deck gun in a courageous effort to return fire at the destroyer. In the context of alleged atrocity, it is worth noting that in the version of his post-war report held in NARA, Schmitz claimed that *Fairy* had deliberately speeded up just as the swimmers reached her, resulting in needless deaths amongst his crew.

Fourteen German survivors, including Schmitz, were taken aboard *Fairy*, but there was no time for triumph, as her bows were 'opened up like tinfoil' as far as the bridge. Lt Barnish again:

Signals were sent reporting our damage. Boats were put over the side, and the prisoners were taken charge of and searched. The artificer engineer, Lt Palmer, reported extensive damage to the hull, and it was decided to steam very slowly towards the beach. However, this was too much strain for the bulkhead forward, and efforts were then made to steam her stern first. This was very soon useless, as both propellers were out of water. Engines were then stopped, the crew embarked into the boats and ordered to lie off at a safe distance. A last message was sent to Captain (D) by wireless informing him we were about to abandon the Fairy, and then, as we could do no more and the ship had taken a very dangerous angle, I told the two signal ratings, who had remained with me, to swim across to one of the boats. I then hitched my binoculars, to the bridge rail, took off my coat, stepped off the bridge, and swam to the nearest Carley float. Reaching the float, I watched the Fairy's screws getting higher and higher out of the water until she disappeared at 0305.

Less than an hour after being plucked from the sea, the German survivors were back in the water again. Not all it seems survived to be rescued by the 7th Flotilla destroyer HMS *Greyhound*. There were no British casualties and all were landed at Immingham by 08.00.

For this action Lt Barnish received the DSO and Mr Palmer, ERA, the DSC. Five of the *Fairy* crew were awarded the DSM and nine officers and men were mentioned in despatches.

Walter Schmitz died of influenza in Skipton POW camp, Yorkshire on 7 March 1919; he is buried in Cannock Chase, Grave Ref., Block 14, Grave 259.

THE MEN WHO DIED IN UC 75

Bauer, Masch.Mt

Benker, Mts.

Böttcher, Masch.Mt

Bröderdorp, Hzr

Dreher, Ob.Mts.

Fischer, Masch.Mt

Fischer, Mts.

Kürschner, Mts.

Lauenstein, Ob.Hzr

Lehrke, Mts.

Lötte, Masch.Mt

Melchin, Ob.Masch.Mt

Meyer, Hermann Hzr

Meyer, Otto, Mts.

Meyer, Stm.

Patzke, Masch.Mt

Prokscha, Ob.Mts.

Springer, Hzr

Ullrich, Masch.Anw

Wagner, Hzr

Wüst, Ob.Masch.Mt

The following is a list of the known vessels believed sunk or damaged by UC 75:

AREA	VESSEL'S NAME	FLAG	TONS	D	M	YEAR	LOCATION
North Sea	*Industria* (trawler)	GBR	113	25	3	1917	Sunk off Scotland
North Sea	*Marshall*	NOR	1123	25	3	1917	17 miles E of Peterhead
North Sea	*Median* (trawler)	GBR	214	25	3	1917	30 miles ESE of Aberdeen
North Sea	*Rosslyn* (trawler)	GBR	113	25	3	1917	54 miles ESE of Girdleness
North Sea	*Schaldis*	BEL	1241	29	3	1917	6 miles N of Whitby
English Channel	*Alide* (sailing–vessel)	RUS	175	1	5	1917	Sunk off Lands End
Irish Sea	*Carberry King* (fish–vessel)	GBR	31	3	5	1917	14 miles S of Stags
Irish Sea	*Eleanor* (fishing–vessel)	GBR	31	3	5	1917	13 miles S of Stags
Irish Sea	*Fastnet* (fishing–vessel)	GBR	31	3	5	1917	13 miles S of Stags
Irish Sea	*Hibernia* (fishing–vessel)	GBR	21	3	5	1917	14 miles SE of Baltimore, Ireland
Irish Sea	*Lucky Lass* (fishing–vessel)	GBR	10	3	5	1917	15 miles S of Stags
Irish Sea	*North Star* (fishing–vessel)	GBR	15	3	5	1917	13 miles S of Stags
Irish Sea	*Sir Edward Birkbeck* (f/v)	GBR	23	3	5	1917	16 miles SE of STAGS
Irish Sea	*Marie* (sailing–vessel)	FRA	772	4	5	1917	Sank in position 58 30N 14W
English Channel	*Lavender* (HMS)	GBR	1250	5	5	1917	Sunk S of Mine Head, Ireland
English Channel	*President* (barque)	FRA	354	6	5	1917	12 miles W of Trevose Head
English Channel	*Polymnia*	GBR	2426	15	5	1917	15 miles W of the Lizard
English Channel	*Wilhelm* (sailing–vessel)	GBR	187	7	6	1917	20 miles SE of the Lizard
English Channel	*Anglian*	GBR	5532	11	6	1917	43 miles WSW of Bishop Rock
English Channel	*Kathlamba*	GBR	6382	18	6	1917	Damaged in position 40N 0830W
English Channel	*Kelso*	GBR	1292	19	6	1917	33 miles WSW of Bishop Rock
English Channel	*Benita* (sailing–vessel)	GBR	130	20	6	1917	15 miles S of Portland
English Channel	*Bidartaise*	FRA	123	20	6	1917	15 miles SSW of Portland
Irish Sea	*Saint Marcouf*	FRA	1117	29	7	1917	Sunk in St Georges Channel

Atlantic	*Karina*	GBR	4222	1	8	1917	17 miles SSW ½ W Hook Point
English Channel	*Beechpark*	GBR	4763	3	8	1917	4 miles S of St Mary's Scilly Isles
Irish Sea	*Cymrian*	GBR	1014	25	8	1917	134 miles SE by S of Tuskar Rock
Irish Sea	*Cooroy* (sailing ship)	GBR	2470	29	8	1917	16 miles SSE of Ballycotton
Irish Sea	*Lynburn*	GBR	587	29	8	1917	Mined ½ mile SE of North Arklow L/v
Irish Sea	*William Middleton*	GBR	2543	28	9	1917	Mined & damaged WSW of Breakwater L/v
North Channel	*Main*	GBR	715	9	10	1917	1½ miles E of Drummore, Luce Bay
Irish Sea	*W.M. Barkley*	GBR	569	12	10	1917	7 miles E of Kish L/v
Irish Sea	*Eskmere*	GBR	2293	13	10	1917	15 miles WNW of South Stack Rock
English Channel	*Britannia*	GBR	765	19	10	1917	Sunk off Portland
Irish Sea	*Atlantian*	GBR	9399	3	11	1917	Damaged S of Isle of Man
Irish Sea	*Longwi*	FRA	2315	4	11	1917	Sunk in St George's Channel
Irish Sea	*The Marquis*	GBR	373	8	11	1917	16 miles ESE of Rochabill Light
English Channel	*Euphorbia*	GBR	3109	1	12	1917	14 miles E by S of Royal Sovereign L/v
English Channel	*Rydal Hall*	GBR	3314	1	12	1917	14 miles E by S of Royal Sovereign L/v
Irish Sea	*Milton*	GBR	3267	3	13	1917	Damaged in St George's Channel
Irish Sea	*Earl of Elgin*	GBR	4448	7	12	1917	10 miles W ½ S of Caernarvon Bay L/v
North Sea	*Alfred H. Read*	GBR	457	28	12	1917	Mined at the entrance to the River Mersey
Irish Sea	*Chirripo*	GBR	4050	28	12	1917	Mined ½ mile off Black Head, Belfast Lough
English Channel	*Asborg*	NOR	2750	3	1	1918	3 miles SE ½ E of St Catherine's Point
English Channel	*Day Spring* (fishing-vessel)	GBR	39	4	1	1918	8 miles SE of Berry Head
English Channel	*Gratitude* (fishing-vessel)	GBR	40	4	1	1918	8 miles SE of Berry Head
English Channel	*Varuna* (fishing-vessel)	GBR	40	4	1	1918	15 miles ESE of Berry Head
English Channel	*Iolanthe*	GBR	3081	5	1	1918	10 miles SE by E of Portland Bill
English Channel	*Arca*	GBR	4839	6	1	1918	Damaged 7 miles SW of Start Point
English Channel	*Gascony*	GBR	3133	7	1	1918	10 miles SSE of the Owers Light Vessel
English Channel	*Leon*	FRA	2401	7	1	1918	13 miles NNE of Triagoz
English Channel	*Edourd Marie* (fish-vessel)	BEL	32	5	3	1918	Sunk SW of the Lizard
Irish Sea	*Marguerite* (sailing-vessel)	GBR	10	9	3	1918	20 miles NE of Scarborough
Irish Sea	*Wave* (fishing-vessel)	GBR	47	10	3	1918	10 miles SW by W of St. Bess Head
Irish Sea	*Arno Mendi*	SPA	2827	12	3	1918	14 miles S of Stack Light
Irish Sea	*Tweed*	GBR	1777	14	3	1918	15 miles SSE of Tuskar Rock

English Channel	*Eliza Anne* (sailing-vessel)	GBR	36	17	3	1918	33 miles SSW of Scilly Isles
English Channel	*Navigator*	GBR	2808	18	3	1918	Damaged 10 miles N 66 W of Portland Bill
Irish Sea	*Dryden*	GBR	5839	28	3	1918	Damaged near Trinity Light Vessel
English Channel	*Hungerford*	GBR	5811	16	4	1918	9 miles SSE of the Owers Light Vessel
English Channel	*War Helmet*	GBR	8184	19	4	1918	3 miles ENE of Owers Light Vessel
North Sea	*Dirk* (HMT)	GBR	181	29	5	1918	Mined off Flamborough Head
North Sea	*Fairy* (HMS)	GBR	355	31	5	1918	Sunk SE of Flamborough Head (UC 75 sunk)

WRECK-SITE

The wreck is orientated in an east–north–east to west–south–west direction and lies on a seabed of sand, mud, gravel, small pebbles and broken shells, in a general depth of 31m (101.7ft), being the lowest astronomical depth. It is largely intact, sitting upright, with the bows to the east–north–east and has a big sand peak built up on the starboard side, while the port side and stern are clear of it. The wreck of the submarine was found in 1989 and even though it is a war grave, considerable salvage has taken place. It has been reported that the 88mm deck-gun, torpedo tubes and propellers have all been recovered. As for HMS *Fairy*, she avoided an ignominious end in a breakers yard. The old tub died gamely off Bridlington and lies in 34m (see *Shipwrecks of the East Coast, Volume 2* by Ron Young).

UC 47, SM IMPERIAL U-BOAT

DATE OF LOSS: 18 November 1917
DEPTH: 52m
REFERENCE: 54 00'.633 N, 000 23'.300 E
LOCATION: 17.82 nautical miles SE from Flamborough Head

Type: UCII coastal mine-laying boat   *Builders*: A.G. Weser, Bremen for Kaiserliche Deutsche Marine   *Ordered*: 20 November 1915, within the batch of UC 46–UC 48   *Keel laid*: as Yard No.257 on 1 February 1916   *Launched*: 30 August 1916   *Commissioned*: by Kapitänleutnant Paul Hundius on 13 October 1916

TECHNICAL SPECIFICATIONS

Hull: Double   *Surface displacement*: 420 tons   *U/Dt*: 520 tons   *LBDH*: 51.85m x 5.22m x 3.6m x 7.46m   *Machinery*: 2 x 250ps MAN diesels   *Props*: 2 bronze   *S/Sp*: 11.7 knots *Op/R*: 7,280 nautical miles at 7 knots   *Sub/R*: 54 nautical miles at 4 knots   *U/Power*: 2 x 230ps electric motors gave 6.9 knots   *Batteries*: Lead/acid   *Fuel/Cap*: 41 + 14.5 tons *Armament*: 2 external 50.04cm torpedo tubes at the bow, one either side of the mine chutes and 1 stern internal tube   *Torpedoes*: 7 x 50.04cm (19.7in) maximum   *Guns*: 1 x 88mm (3.46in) forward deck gun   *Ammo*: 133 rounds of 88mm   *Mine tubes*: 6 *Mines*: 18 x UC 200   *Diving*: Max-op-depth 50m (164ft) and 33 seconds to crash-dive *Complement*: 3 officers and 23 ratings

Torpedo load as designed: 4 – a torpedo in each tube plus a reload for the stern tube. Storing an additional torpedo in pieces internally for the stern tube later augmented this, although this was optional. Two extra torpedoes (total) for the external bow tubes could be carried as well – these were lashed to the deck. So up to a total of seven torpedoes carried, although not all boats sailed with that many.

UC 47 was formally assigned to the Flandern/Flandern II Flottille from 23 January 1917 with Kplt. Paul Hundius assuming command from the commissioning. Hundius made the following ten patrols:

(1) On 21 January 1917, UC 47 left Bremen and sailed to Flanders, arriving there on 23 January 1917.

(2) UC 47 departed Flanders on 27 January 1917 to lay mines off the English east coast. The Norwegian SS *Modiva* (Aktieselskapet Ivar An. Christensens Rederi, Christiania), commanded by Captain F. Arentz, was on passage from Hartlepool to Rouen with coal, when she detonated a mine and sank on 31 January, the mine having been laid on 28 January.

The SS *Portia* (Aktieselskapet Portia, Bergen) also sank after striking a mine laid by UC 47 on 28 January, while taking coal from Sunderland to Bilbao in Spain. UC 47 arrived back in port on 30 January.

(3) UC 47 left port on 2 February 1917 for mine-laying operations in the English and Bristol Channels. HMS *Ghurka*, an 870-ton destroyer built by Hawthorns in 1907, detonated one of the mines and sank off Dungeness on 8 February at 19.45. The armed trawler *Highlander* heard the explosion and went to assist, only to find the extreme bow of *Ghurka* showing above the surface; rough seas prevented boats being lowered and just five bedraggled, oil-covered men were dragged from the water. Cdr F.H.L. Lewin RN, the destroyer flotilla gunnery officer, was on board *Ghurka* when she sank and refused to be rescued until the four ratings with him were picked up (he was later awarded the Stanhope Gold Medal for the bravest deed of the year).

On 8 February the SS *Lullington* (Southdown SS Co. Ltd, London) struck a mine on the port side near No.2 hold at 18.00. The crew of twenty-six immediately abandoned ship in two boats and the ship sank at 18.10; the ship was en-route from Blyth for Rouen with coal (UC 47 had laid both of these mines the previous day).

The SS *Japanese Prince* (Prince Line Ltd) was en-route from Newport News to Southampton with a general cargo when a single torpedo from UC 47 struck her at 12.20 on 10 February. The helm was put over when the wake of a torpedo was sighted, but it detonated on the starboard side just abaft the engine room and she sank eighteen minutes later. A Royal Navy warship rescued the crew of seventy-five after they had abandoned ship in the lifeboats.

The Greek steamer *Aghios Spyridon* (John Roussos & Sons) went down on 12 February, while voyaging from Swansea to Naples with coal. Also sunk on that day were two small fishing boats. Then, at 22.00 on 13 February, the steamer *F.D. Lambert* (Westoll Line, Sunderland) detonated one of the mines laid on 7 February, while transporting gas-coal from Newcastle to Savona, Italy. The crew abandoned ship in two boats immediately and the ship sank soon after. Eastbourne lifeboat found the smaller boat with four men in it, while the trawler *Fuji* rescued the master, Captain W.C. Lamb and the remaining crew and landed them at Dover. UC 47 returned to Zeebrugge on 16 February 1917.

(4) UC 47 left Flanders on 6 March 1917 for operations in the Bristol and St George's Channel. UC 47 sank ten small fishing boats with gunfire or explosive charges, a large French sailing ship and six steamships of different nationalities during the patrol. The French steamer *Charles le Cour* (Soc. Anon. des Chargeurs de l'Ouest, Nantes) was destroyed with her crew in a torpedo attack, while sailing from Cardiff to Nantes, France with coal.

The *G.A. Savage* (Zillah Shipping & Carrying Co. Ltd, Troon), a small coaster, was sent to a watery grave while carrying pitch from Workington to Swansea. Two seamen were killed when SS *Brika* (English & American Shipping Co. Ltd, London) was sunk by torpedo at 23.55 on 13 March; she was transporting 5,000 tons of sugar from Santiago de Cuba to Bristol. Twenty minutes after abandoning ship in the boats, at 01.30, the crew of the steamer sighted the U-boat, which went alongside and questioned the master before diving. The thirty-one survivors were rescued by the Norwegian steamer *Stavn* and landed at Liverpool.

The SS *Solferino* (Dampskipsselskapet Aktieselskapet Otto Thoresen's Linie, Christiania), a Norwegian steamer, was captured in the channel and scuttled with explosive charges, while sailing from Oporto to Stavanger with general cargo and passengers. Another Norwegian ship, the SS *Wilfred* (Aktieselskapet Det Selmerske Rederi, Trondheim), was captured and scuttled with explosive charges, 18 miles N ½ W from Ouessant, while taking general cargo from Newport, Monmouth to Gibraltar. UC 47 returned home on 19 March 1917.

(5) Leaving Zeebrugge on 14 April 1917, the U-boat laid mines in the Bristol and St George's Channels. During that patrol Hundius sank three steamships, five sailing vessels, a fishing boat and the requisitioned trawler *Star of Freedom* (Admiralty No.955), as well as damaging the Q-ship, *Gaelic* (HMS Q22).

The steamer *Goldcoast* (Elder Line Ltd, Liverpool (crown nominees), was torpedoed while transporting a general cargo from Dakar, West Africa, to Liverpool. The ship was originally German, but was captured in Cameroon River and put into service under the British flag; at 20.50 on 19 April she was struck amidships and her crew abandoned ship, then two U-boats appeared and circled around the lifeboats. Someone from one of the submarines enquired about the master, but was told he had perished in the explosion. The SS *Inniscarra*, SS *Dallington*, and an unknown warship, rescued Captain E.E. Allen and his crew of fifty-two.

At 00.45 on 23 April, the steamer *Imataka* (Imataka SS Co. Ltd, Liverpool) was hit on No.2 hold by a torpedo, while carrying sugar, rum and frozen meat/meal from Demerara and Le Havre to Liverpool. Four passengers (probably DEMS gunners) and the crew of thirty-six abandoned ship in three boats at 01.15, with just Captain C. Hendry remaining on board until it sank at 03.30. The boat with the master in was picked up by warships and landed at Queenstown, the others went to other ports.

The second engineer was killed when the SS *Plutus* (J&P Hutchinson Ltd, Glasgow) en-route from Rouen to Barry Roads in ballast, was attacked with a single torpedo at 04.30 on 24 April. The ship was hit on its starboard quarter and sank in ten minutes and the master was injured by wreckage in the sea. An RN patrol vessel picked up the sixteen survivors and took them to Penzance. The 842-ton Norwegian sailing vessel *John Lockett* had just crossed the Atlantic from Philadelphia with a cargo of oil for Liverpool when Hundius sent her to the bottom, off the Lizard. UC 47 arrived in port on 28 April. However, the British steamship *Mary Baird* (Page Shipping Co. Ltd, West Hartlepool (Cardiff)) detonated one of the mines beneath the No.1 hold at 22.55 and sank on 18 May, the mine having been laid the previous day. The ship's engine was stopped, but she was still under way and going down by the head when a lifeboat was lowered with difficulty. A second boat was then lowered but falling debris struck the boat and seven men in it were killed. She was on passage from Rouen for Newport in ballast. A patrol vessel landed the survivors at Penzance.

(6) UC 47 left port on 8 June to lay mines in the Bristol Channel and off the south coast of Ireland. One of the mines sank the RN trawler *Carew Castle* on 12 June; she was requisitioned in May 1915 and converted as minesweeper Admiralty No.6271.

The steamer *Dart* (Mercantile Steam Ship Co. Ltd, London) was torpedoed and sunk on 14 June, while transporting 4,700 tons of pyrites from Huelva, Spain, to Garston. The torpedo detonated in the engine room at 16.00, killing four men instantly and seriously injuring four more; the twenty-four survivors abandoned ship at 16.10 and the ship sank ten minutes later. A patrol vessel landed them at Queenstown.

The large steamer *Great City* (Great City SS Co. Ltd, Bideford) was damaged by a mine and beached at St Mary's in the Scilly Isles; she was voyaging from Newport News, south-east Virginia, for London with steel roots and was re-floated. UC 47 arrived back in port on 23 June.

(7) UC 47 sailed from Zeebrugge on 14 July and laid mines at the western entrance to the English Channel. The Norwegian coaster SS *Ruth* was left damaged on 18 July, but made it safely to port. Two steamships were torpedoed and sunk on 20 July. The *Beatrice* (Cleeve's Western Valleys Anthracite Colliers Ltd) was attacked at 03.45, while on passage from Penarth, Wales, for Honfleur, France, with coal. The missile detonated between the engine room and the boilers and she sank in one minute. Eleven crewmen were lost. Captain R.W. Hopper, a steward, an able seaman and a donkeyman were rescued by the steamer *Skelwith Force* and landed at Plymouth while the SS *Aalesund* saved two others and took them to Falmouth. The *Bramham* (James Mitchell & Son, London (Dundee)) was taking coal from Barry to Rouen when she was struck at 00.15 and one man died in the explosion. The ship sank at 01.49, Captain Tweedle and the surviving crew of twenty-two took to the boats and were rescued later. UC 47 returned to port on 22 July.

(8) With a quick turnaround, Hundius returned for operations at the western entrance to the English Channel between 25 July and 2 August 1917. Eleven crewmen went down with the British SS *Fremona* (Cairn Line of Steamships Ltd), which was hit by torpedo on 31 July, while bound from Montreal to Leith with grain and lumber. That same day, the US tanker *Motano* (Standard Oil Co.) was carrying fuel oil from New York to Liverpool when she sank following a torpedo hit.

(9) On 20 August UC 47 left Zeebrugge and laid mines in the Bristol Channel. During this patrol, three steamships were sunk and another one damaged by torpedoes. The Norwegian steamship *Gro* (Dampskipsselskapet Aktieselskapet Avenir, Christiania) was torpedoed and sunk, probably with all hands, transporting coal from Glasgow to Rouen. The Norwegian SS *Peer Gynt* (Dampsk. Selsk. Peer Gynt, Bergen) was carrying coal from Port Talbot to Rouen when she was torpedoed and sunk in the Bristol Channel. Six men were lost.

The SS *Veghtstroom* (Lawrence D. Holt, Liverpool) was torpedoed and sunk off Godrevy Light Vessel, while voyaging with coal from Penarth to Le Havre. The missile detonated on the starboard side level with the bridge at 04.05 on 23 August. The entire crew of twenty-nine got into the two boats, but when the ship sank seven minutes later, one of the boats was pulled under and the chief engineer, chief, second steward, a donkeyman and ship's carpenter all drowned.

Finally, the Belgian SS *Seresia* was hit off Trevose Head, while transporting coal from Barry to Bordeaux, but the ship put back to Swansea on 27 August. UC 47 arrived back at Flanders on 28 August.

10) UC 47 sailed from Zeebrugge on 22 September 1917 to patrol, and laid mines off the Cornish and south coast of Ireland. One sailing vessel was sunk and the British steamer *Boynton* (Morgan & Cadogen Ltd, London), which was on passage to France from Manchester with a general cargo, was torpedoed and sunk. Twenty-three crewmen, including her master, were lost (all hands). The U-boat arrived back in Flanders on 6 October.

Oblt.z.S. Günther von Wigankow assumed command of UC 47 on 9 October 1917, while Paul Hundius returned to Germany to take command of UB 103; he was awarded the *Pour Le Mérite* on 18 August 1918. Von Wigankow made three war patrols with UC 47:

(11) On 16 October UC 47 sailed to the English east coast for operations, where two steamships were torpedoed and sunk; the *Cadmus* (Christian Salvesen & Co., Leith)

was returning a 900-ton cargo of empty shell cases from Dunkerque to Blyth when she was hit. The crew immediately abandoned ship and *Cadmus* sank in ten minutes. UC 47 surfaced and stayed in the vicinity of the boats for twenty-five minutes, but von Wigankow made no attempt to harass the survivors. Not far away, the survivors from the *Cadmus* saw the submarine make off in the direction of another steamer and then watched as the SS *Togston* (South Metropolitan Gas Co., London) was also hit. The torpedo slammed into her port side near the engine room, at 19.15 on 18 October. The surviving crew of *Togston* were forced to jump into the sea as the ship started to sink, and one man drowned. Some men clung to an upturned lifeboat and were amazed as the U-boat surfaced close-by and then someone on the boat asked for details of their ship; five out of eighteen of her crewmen were lost in total. Survivors from *Togston*, which was en-route from the Tyne for London with 1,700 tons of coal, were later picked up by the SS *John Siem* and landed at Middlesbrough. UC 47 put into Zeebrugge on 22 October 1917.

(12) Von Wigankow operated off the English east coast between 6 and 13 November 1917 and sank three steamships and a fishing boat. Thirteen crewmen, including the master, Captain G. Cook, were lost when the SS *Ballogie* (J&A Davison Ltd, Aberdeen) was torpedoed at 16.10 on 9 November. She sank immediately, on a voyage from Middlesbrough to Dunkerque with slag; a patrol boat picked up six men alive and recovered the bodies of the master and steward and landed them at Grimsby. Six men died when the French SS *Isabelle* (Cie. Auxiliaire de Navigation, Nantes) was torpedoed at 20.05 on 9 November, en-route from the Tyne for Rouen with 3,700 tons of coal. Six men were killed on the ship, but she stayed afloat, then HMS *Swallow* rescued twenty-seven survivors and took the vessel in tow. However she sank at 01.20 the following morning. At 11.30 on 11 November, the Swedish SS *Dana* (R. Göhle) was hit by a torpedo on the port side, while on passage from Göteborg, Sweden, for Hull via Kirkwall with 688 tons of iron, paper-pulp and a deck-cargo of 563 standards of (sawn) timber. The ship was blown to pieces amidships and eight crewmen were lost, including: Captain Anders Rasmusson, Chief Engineer Efraim Jansson, Erik Valfrid Olsson-Nordqvist the donkeyman, and Karl Alfred Larsson the steward, who were all amidships and were sucked down deep, and drowned as the ship broke in two and sank. Other crewmen lost were: Albin Jonsson, second mate, Able Seaman Anders Olsson-Blogren, Stoker Axel Viktor Lundall and Erik August Nathanuel Johnsson the first mate. Before UC 47 returned to Flanders on 13 November, von Wigankow also sunk a 68-ton Dutch fishing boat.

FINAL VOYAGE

(13) Commanded by the experienced von Wigankow, UC 47 departed Zeebrugge on 17 November 1917 with orders to sink Allied shipping off the English east coast. For what happened next we must look at British records. The purpose-built patrol boat HMS P57 (Lt-Cdr H.C. Birnie RNR) was on a converging course with the U-boat by 06.00 on 18 November just off Flamborough Head. It was still quite dark at around 06.00 that morning and P57 had just finished challenging a vessel, using her searchlight, when a lookout reported sighting a buoy on the port bow.

Log of P57 18 November 1917:

6.19 –   Spotted unidentified object
6.20 –   Came to 'action stations'

As there was no known buoy in that locality, P57 altered course towards it. Lt-Cdr Birnie and Lt Isdale, RNR, Officer of the Watch, immediately realised that the object, now just 200 yards away, was the conning tower of a U-boat. P57 turned hard-to-port to ram the submarine and full speed rang out on the telegraphs. Fifteen seconds later the armoured stem of P57 ripped into U-boat's hull, just before the conning tower, and almost at right angles. The force of the impact pushed UC 47 forward and down.

P57's log continues:

6.23 –   Rammed and sunk hostile submarine – Violent shock – 2 depth charges released
9.30 –   Placed buoy in vicinity of submarine
10.20 –   Dropped third depth charge

A dan-buoy was placed over the spot. Birnie established the exact position and half an hour later, oil and bubbles were seen rising to the surface within 50 yards of the buoy.

All day and the following night HMS P57 patrolled around the area, but none of the U-boat's crew of twenty-eight came to the surface. Later that day, a minesweeper arrived on the scene and located the wreck in 30 fathoms, hooked the wreck with an explosive chain-bottom-sweep and destroyed it with an explosive charge. Royal Navy divers in standard hard-hat gear then explored the wreck later that day. They entered the submarine and recovered publications and papers. Even more importantly, they also discovered valuable charts, listing minefields laid by UC 47 off Guernsey on 16 July and off Cherbourg on 24 September.

Lt-Cdr Birnie, one of his officers, and two crewmen, received the usual rewards.
ADM 53/56626

THE MEN WHO DIED IN UC 47

Appel, Ob.Hzr
Arndt, Hzr
Creutzfeldt, Btn.Mt
Deichsel, Masch.Mt
Dohrmann, Mts.
Finke, Ob.Mts.Artl
Garbers, Mts.
Gathmann, Hzr
Glöckner, F.T.Mt
Gohla, Ob.Mts.
Grobel, Mts.
Hilger, Masch.Mt
Klees, Ob.Masch.
Koch, Hzr

Krull, Masch.Mt
Lass, Ob.Mts.Artl
Liebs, Masch.Mt
Matthies, Masch.Mt
Müller, OB.Hzr
Panse, Mts.
Schneider, Masch.Anw
Scholz, Hzr
Schumann, Btn.Mt
Siegel, Lt.z.S.d.Res
Stracke, F.T.
Wigankow, Günther von, Oblt.z.S.
Zessler, Masch.Mt.d.Res
Zocher, Stm.

UC 47 accounted for fifty-two Allied vessels, totalling 65,884 tons.

The following is a list of the known vessels believed sunk or damaged by UC 47:

AREA	VESSEL'S NAME	FLAG	TONS	D	M	YEAR	LOCATION
North Sea	Modiva	NOR	1160	31	1	1917	Mined 17m off Flamborough Head
North Sea	Portia	NOR	1127	1	2	1917	Mined off Flamborough Head
English Channel	Ghurka (HMS)	GBR	880	8	2	1917	Mined 4m SE of Dungeness
English Channel	Lullington	GBR	2816	8	2	1917	3 miles E of the Royal Sovereign Light Vessel
English Channel	Japanese Prince	GBR	4876	10	2	1917	24 miles SW of Bishop Rock

Irish Sea	*Aghios Spyridon*	GRE	1618	12	2	1917	5 miles off Pendeen Lighthouse
Irish Sea	*Brissons*	GBR	60	12	2	1917	Sunk W of Tintagel Head
English Channel	*Brissons* (trawler)	GBR	60	12	2	1917	9 miles W of Trevose Head
English Channel	*F.D. Lambert*	GBR	2214	13	2	1917	Mined 1 mile E of the Royal Sovereign Light Vessel
Irish Sea	*Carles le Cour*	FRA	2472	11	3	1917	7 miles NNE of Pendeen Lighthouse
English Channel	*G.A. Savage*	GBR	357	11	3	1917	Sunk off Cornwall
English Channel	*C.A.S.* (fishing-vessel)	GBR	60	12	3	1917	12 m N by W of Trevose Head
English Channel	*Ena* (fishing-vessel)	GBR	56	12	3	1917	10 miles N by W of Trevose Head
English Channel	*Gratia* (fishing-vessel)	GBR	37	12	3	1917	12 miles NNW of Trevose Head
English Channel	*Hyacinth* (fishing-vessel)	GBR	56	12	3	1917	15 miles N by W of Trevose Head
English Channel	*Internos* (fishing-vessel)	GBR	59	12	3	1917	12 miles NNW of Trevose Head
English Channel	*Jessamine* (fishing-vessel)	GBR	56	12	3	1917	14 miles NNW of Trevose Head
English Channel	*Lent Lilly* (fishing-vessel)	GBR	23	12	3	1917	13 miles NNW of Trevose Head
English Channel	*Nellie* (fishing-vessel)	GBR	61	12	3	1917	13 miles NNW of Trevose Head
English Channel	*Proverb* (fishing-vessel)	GBR	37	12	3	1917	25 miles NW of Trevose Head
English Channel	*Rivina* (fishing-vessel)	GBR	22	12	3	1917	15 miles NNW of Trevose Head
Irish Sea	*Brika*	GBR	3549	14	3	1917	13 miles SE by S of Coningbeg Light Vessel
Atlantic	*Solferino*	NOR	1155	15	3	1917	Sunk off Ushant
English Channel	*Wilfred*	NOR	1121	15	3	1917	18 miles N ½ W from Ouessant
English Channel	*Medusa*	ITA	1274	16	3	1917	Sunk off Ushant
English Channel	*Sully* (sailing-vessel)	FRA	3455	16	3	1917	15 miles W of Ushant
English Channel	*Dantzic* (sailing-vessel)	GBR	108	17	4	1917	30 miles S by W of St. Ann's Head
English Channel	*William Shephard* (s/v)	GBR	143	17	4	1917	30 miles S by W of St. Ann's Head
Atlantic	*Gold Coast*	GBR	4255	19	4	1917	14 miles S of Mine Head. Ireland
Irish Sea	*Jewel* (sailing-vessel)	GBR	195	19	4	1917	20 miles SE of Coningbeg Light Vessel
English Channel	*Star of Freedom* (HMT)	GBR	258	19	4	1917	Mined off Trevose Head
Atlantic	*Gaelic* (HMS Q22)	GBR	224	22	4	1917	Damaged off Mine Head, Ireland
Atlantic	*Imataka*	GBR	1776	23	4	1917	15 miles SSW of Daunts Rocks, Cork
English Channel	*Heather*	GBR	58	24	4	1917	14 miles W of Bishop Rock
English Channel	*Plutus*	GBR	1189	24	4	1917	9 miles NNW of Trevose Head
English Channel	*Aigle* (sailing-vessel)	FRA	172	26	4	1917	11 miles SW of Start Point
English Channel	*John Lockett* (sail-vessel)	NOR	842	26	4	1917	25 miles S of Lizard
English Channel	*Mary Baird*	GBR	1830	18	5	1917	Mined 2½ miles W ½ N of Pendeen Lighthouse
Irish Sea	*Carew Castle* (HMT)	GBR	256	12	6	1917	Mined off Hartland Point
Atlantic	*Dart*	GBR	3207	14	6	1917	6 miles SSW of Ballycottin Lighthouse
English Channel	*Great City*	GBR	5525	19	6	1917	Damaged 30 miles W of Bishops Rock
English Channel	*Ruth*	NOR	549	18	7	1917	Damaged west end of Channel
English Channel	*Beatrice*	GBR	712	20	7	1917	10 miles E by S of the Lizard
English Channel	*Bramham*	GBR	1978	20	7	1917	10 miles E by S of the Lizard Point
English Channel	*Fremona*	GBR	3028	31	7	1917	10 miles N by W of Ile de Batz
English Channel	*Motano*	USA	2730	31	7	1917	20 miles SE of Start Point
English Channel	*Gro*	NOR	2667	22	8	1917	6 miles S of of Start Point
Irish Sea	*Peer Gynt*	NOR	1144	23	8	1917	8–9 miles NE of Godrevy Light Vessel

English Channel	*Veghtstroom*	GBR	1339	23	8	1917	7 miles NW of Godrevy Lighthouse
English Channel	*Seresia*	BEL	2342	26	8	1917	Damaged 6 miles NE of Trevose Head
English Channel	*Perseverance* (s/v)	GBR	118	23	9	1917	14 miles NW by N of St.Valery
English Channel	*Boynton*	GBR	2578	25	9	1917	4 miles N of Land's End
North Sea	*Cadmus*	GBR	1879	18	10	1917	20 miles SSE of Flamborough Head
North Sea	*Togston*	GBR	1057	18	10	1917	20 miles SSE of Flamborough Head
North Sea	*Ballogie*	GBR	1214	9	11	1917	1½ miles NE of Filey
North Sea	*Isabelle*	FRA	2466	9	11	1917	3 miles NW of Flamborough Head
North Sea	*Dana*	SWE	1620	11	11	1917	1 mile SE from 'R' buoy, War Channel
North Sea	*Huibertje* (fishing-vessel)	NLD	68	12	11	1917	25 miles off the Dutch coast

AUTHOR'S COMMENTS

It has always been something of a mystery as to how such an experienced commander as Günther von Wigankow was caught on the surface by a patrol boat. The headquarters of UC 47, being part of the Flanders Flottille, was at Bruges. When U-boats were operating in the North Sea, communication with headquarters was always difficult. The wireless mast positioned on the low hull of a U-boat, only had a range of some 30 miles. Without the use of a telescopic extension, the captain would have had to rely on passing messages via other boats closer to home. The mast could be fully extended by use of small electric motors inside the boat, which increased her wireless range up to about 100 miles. It is almost certain now that von Wigankow was using the fully extended mast, when HMS P57 caught him on the surface. When using the mast, the majority of submarine commanders would have run out to sea, rather than remain inshore. The overconfidence of von Wigankow may well have contributed to the destruction of his command.

WRECK-SITE

The remains of UC 47 were discovered in the summer of 2001 and are said to be difficult to locate amongst the sand peaks. It is orientated in a south-south-east to north-north-east direction and lies on an undulating seabed of sand peaks/dunes, consisting of fine sand, broken black shells and small pebbles, in a general depth of 52m, being the lowest astronomical depth. In 2001 it was reported lying with the bows buried deep down into the sand with only the conning tower, deck gun and a telescopic wireless/radio mast, rising above it. The stern however, was 6m clear, with the twin three-bladed bronze propellers still *in situ*. In 2004, divers reported that the propellers had both been removed and the gun, which was hanging off in 2002, had also disappeared. A live torpedo that was lying on the seabed close-by has also gone. Together with the gun, it may have been swept away by beam-trawlers (live torpedo! Nice little find for some trawler skipper?). The stern torpedo tube, which is empty, lies on the sand and completely clear of the wreck on its starboard side (it is believed that this was blown clean out of the submarine, by a depth charge from HMS P57). Near to the stern on the port side, there is a large hole in the hull, also probably caused by one of the depth charges. The aft-hatch near to the engine room is still closed and a little way forward there is extensive damage to the casing, running all the way to the bow. The conning tower and control room periscopes are lying on the seabed, pointing aft on the starboard side. The conning tower hatch is open, probably where the Royal Navy divers entered the boat to retrieve the valuable documents. Live and spent shell cases did lie scattered round, but these will almost certainly have been lifted by now. The hatch covers on the six mine chutes are just clear of the sand. The outer hull casing and twin torpedo tubes at the bow are all torn off the

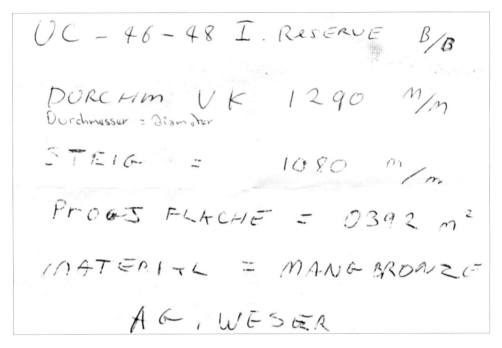

A piece of paper recording notes about propellers. Found on the wreck of UC 47 after eighty-seven years. (Courtesy of Steve Old)

wreck, but the pressure casing inside is still intact. The starboard side air ballast tank has also been badly ruptured and has a large hole in it. The wreck is very badly silted up, with sand coming to within 1½m of the hatch cover. It is, of course, officially classed as a war grave. Significantly, the extended telescopic wireless/radio mast towered 7m above the hull casing.

UC 39, SM IMPERIAL U-BOAT

DATE OF LOSS: 8 February 1917
DEPTH: 24m
REFERENCE: 53 55'.523 N, 000 04'.562 E
LOCATION: 8.43 nautical miles E from Hornsea

Type: UCII coastal mine-laying boat   *Builders:* Blohm & Voss, Hamburg for Kaiserliche Deutsche Marine   *Ordered:* 20 November 1915, within the batch of UC 34–UC 39   *Keel laid:* as Yard No.280   *Launched:* 25 June 1916   *Commissioned:* by Kapitänleutnant Otto Heinrich Tornow on 29 October 1916

TECHNICAL SPECIFICATIONS
Hull: Double   *Surface displacement:* 427 tons   *U/Dt:* 509 tons   *LBDH:* 50.35m x 5.22m x 3.68m x 7.46m   *Machinery:* 2 x 250ps MAN diesels   *Props:* 2 bronze   *S/Sp:* 11.9 knots   *Op/R:* 10,180 nautical miles at 7 knots   *Sub/R:* 54 nautical miles at 4 knots   *U/Power:* 2 x 230ps electric motors gave 6.8 knots   *Batteries:* Lead/acid   *Fuel/Cap:* 40 + 15 tons   *Armament:* 2 external 50.04cm torpedo tubes at the bow, one either side of the mine chutes and 1 stern internal tube   *Torpedoes:* 7 x 50.04cm (19.7in) maximum   *Guns:* 1 x 88mm

(3.46in) forward deck gun **Ammo**: 133 rounds of 88mm *Mine tubes*: 6 **Mines**: 18 x UC 200 **Diving**: Max-op-depth 50m (164ft) and 33 seconds to crash-dive **Complement**: 3 officers and 23 ratings

Torpedo load as designed: 4 – a torpedo in each tube plus a reload for the stern tube. Storing an additional torpedo in pieces internally for the stern tube later augmented this, although this was optional. Two extra torpedoes (total) for the external bow tubes could be carried as well – these were lashed to the deck. So up to seven total torpedoes carried, although not all boats sailed with that many.

UC 39 was formally assigned to Flandern Flottille on 3 February 1917 with Kapitänleutnant Otto Heinrich Tornow the CO from 29 October 1916 until 31 January 1917.

(1) Oblt.z.S. Otto Ehrentraut assumed command on 1 February 1917 and then, later that day, transferred UC 39 from Kiel to Zeebrugge, where she arrived on 3 February.

FINAL VOYAGE

(2) UC 39 departed Zeebrugge for her second patrol on 7 February 1917; Ehrentraut's mission was to lay mines off Flamborough Head. Significantly, the renewed policy of unrestricted submarine warfare had only just been declared. The patrol had a promising start. Ehrentraut captured, shelled and sank the Norwegian steamer *Hans Kinck* (Aktieselskapet Dampskipsselskapet Hans Kinck, Bergen) off the Noord-Hinder Light Vessel on 7 February; the steamer was en-route from Rotterdam to the Tyne in ballast. On the following day, the Swedish steamer *Hanna Larsen* (The Admiralty) was captured after UC 39 fired four shells at her at 23.20 on 7 February. She was in ballast on passage from London for the Tyne to load up with coal. Captain Thomas Reid stopped the ship's engines, but fifteen minutes later re-started them and ordered full-steam ahead in an attempt to get clear of the submarine. However when another shell was fired, the engines were stopped again. This time he instructed the men to abandon ship, but four of them were injured when more shells rained down; one man was so badly injured that he died later. At just before midnight, UC 39 drew alongside the lifeboats and took the master and chief engineer prisoner; the U-boat crew then pillaged the steamer before attempting to sink her with explosive scuttling charges. UC 39 stood off for a while, but the charges failed to sink her so they returned to finish the looting and placed more explosives on board. The *Hanna Larsen* blew up and sank early in the morning of 8 February. (Ehrentraut also took a fireman and a navigator prisoner from one of the other ships, according to Heizer August Sauer of UC 39.) Later that day, Ehrentraut captured the Norwegian steamer *Ida* (H. Skougaard), which was in ballast on passage from Leith for London; Captain C. Nilsson of the *Ida* and his crew were forced to abandon ship in the boats, while explosive scuttling charges were placed in their vessel and she sank soon after.

Ehrentraut was unafraid to advertise his presence, because he also attacked a number of fishing vessels in the same vicinity. The 7th Flotilla destroyer HMS *Thrasher* (Lt E. Hawkins RNR) was soon on UC 39's trail.

At 13.18 lookouts sighted UC 39 in the process of trying to sink the British steam collier *Hornsey* with gunfire. Among the German eyewitnesses, FT-Obergast Richard Lassig claimed that *Thrasher* charged in from astern, taking the submarine by surprise. Bootsmann Carl Stolte said in his interrogation report that the destroyer appeared out of the fog and, as they tried to crash-dive to 15m, *Thrasher* fired a volley of shells. Ehrentraut made an emergency dive but left a large swirl on the surface. The destroyer ran over this position and dropped a single depth charge just ahead of the disturbance. Steuermann Max Eschenbach of UC 39 described how, shortly after reaching 17m, the boat was rocked by a heavy explosion and shook violently. This explosion was so powerful that Eschenbach witnessed the engine room hatch lid fall to the floor, while water surged through in an uncontrollable torrent. Another eye-witness, Heizer August Sauer, maintained that the depth charge explosion shattered a deadlight in the conning tower, causing serious flooding in the control room, as well as blowing open the deck hatches and destroying most of the depth gauges. August Sauer asserted two smaller explosions followed that one heavy explosion, forcing the captain to blow all tanks. The boat came to the surface with a 20-degree list to starboard. Contradicting this statement, FT-Obergast Richard Lassig was adamant that the captain had not given the order to blow the tanks and believed it was either the first lieutenant in the control room, or the chief engineer who gave this order. Max Eschenbach stated that the British warship immediately opened fire on UC 39 as soon as she surfaced and only ceased after sighting the two British prisoners on board. On surfacing, the submarine rolled steadily to starboard and water poured through all the open hatches. One of the men, who appeared at the conning tower bravely waving a white flag, was Captain Thomas Reid, master of the Swedish steamship *Hanna Larsen*, apparently endeavouring to prevent any further bloodshed.

Oberleutnant zur See Ehrentraut climbed onto the bridge only to be killed by a shell splinter, according to Sauer, who watched the destroyer, some 150m away and bearing down fast, continue firing, even though the entire submarine crew was on deck. Finally the destroyer ordered the boat to stop (at this time she was still under way with her rudder hard over and the electric motors forcing the boat to turn in a circle). When she stopped, the British dispatched a lifeboat. Richard Lassig claimed he was the last man to emerge from the U-boat. Lassig saw Lt.z.S. Lauterbach and Arthur Gerlach standing in the conning tower, both already stripped to the waist while the rest of the men were still all wearing their oilskins. Lauterbach and Gerlach then dived overboard he said, leaving the rest of the crew to their own fate. This was an act which disgusted the surviving crew. The British lifeboat then came alongside, removing two badly wounded ratings. The ship's boat returned and the remaining crewmen were removed. Although the stern casing was dry, the submarine was well down by the bow with the screws out of the water. Sauer also mentioned that a British officer boarded the U-boat and lifted a pair of binoculars from the conning tower.

The log of HMS *Thrasher* Thursday 8 February 1917:

13.18	Gunfire on the starboard beam ESE
	Opened fire on enemy sub, dropped depth charge 1,2,3
	Opened up broadside 6 and 12 pounders.
	Sub surrendered. Took prisoners
	Itchen and Quail standing by
14.40	Prisoners searched and carefully attended to
16.40	Secured to Albion at East Boom

There is a postscript: UC 39 remained afloat and HMS *Itchen* attempted to tow her away as a prize but the battered submarine was having none of it and sank soon afterwards. In all, seven of the U-boat's crew were killed.

ADM137/3897 notes that, of the five survivors, two were taken to hospital in Lincoln. Naval intelligence regarded all the prisoners as being of above average intelligence. One of them, Aspirant Ingenier Gerlach was surly, violent towards the ratings and singled out for 'special watching'. Lt Hawkins of *Thrasher* was awarded a DSO.

Extract from a report by Rear Admiral commanding the East Coast

The following members of the crew of SS *Hannah Larsen* were found onboard:
Thomas Reid, Master, Walter Scott, Chief Engineer.
They appeared to be steady respectable men and quite unaffected by the strain to which they had been subjected. They reported as follows.

'The Hannah Larsen left London AM Tuesday 6th Feb in ballast for the Tyne. She left Yarmouth PM 7th Feb and at about 23.20 when off Spurn Head, they heard a shot fired. It was hazy at the time and nothing could be seen. Four more shots were fired in quick succession and the master stopped the ship. A few minutes later he went ahead again when 3 more shots were fired. He stopped, lowered the boats and abandoned ship. The submarine continued firing and demolished the chart house. The master burned all his papers before leaving the ship. The master and five others were then ordered on board the submarine but only the master and chief engineer were kept on board. The practice of taking prisoner the master and chief engineer was to spread panic and discontent among seafarers, thus to cripple the British Merchant Service.

At about 0800 on the 8th Feb shots were fired [presumably sinking the SS *Ida*]. The submarine remained on the surface for most of the forenoon, diving once. Submarine stopped every hour to take soundings. At about noon, 9 shots were fired by the submarine, when it was surprised by *Thrasher*. Consternation and confusion ensued and they dived hurriedly but a depth charge shook them badly and almost at once caused water to spurt through the sides of the submarine and brought her to the surface where she was rapidly disabled by shell fire. Ehrentraut the CO went up the hatchway first and was killed by a shell splinter. The two British prisoners went up last. The two British prisoners and the German wounded were taken off first. The body of Ehrentraut was taken off by Thrasher. He has since been buried at Hull.'

In May, later that year, another destroyer located the wreck of UC 39 and sent divers down to inspect it. Interestingly the divers found the submarine was already covered in barnacles, after just four months. On 7 June 1918, the destroyer HMS *Quail* spotted small bubbles of oil rising to the surface and, believing it could be a U-boat, dropped a depth charge over the position which brought up large quantities of oil. The following day, divers found they had just re-discovered the wreck of UC 39.
ADM 137/63010 – ADM 137/ 3897 – ADM137/3897 – NARA: T-1022, Roll 86, PG619

THE SEVEN MEN WHO DIED IN UC 39
Albert, Masch.Mt.d.Res
Bickel, Hzr
Böttcher, Ob.Masch.Mt
Döring, Masch.Anw.
Ehrentraut, Otto, Oblt.z.S.
Ricke, Masch.Mt.d.Res
Roszgowski, Mts.

Otto Ehrentraut is buried in Cannock Chase, block 13 row 5 plot 113.

The following is a list of some of the vessels believed sunk or damaged by UC 39:

AREA	VESSEL'S NAME	FLAG	TONS	D	M	YEAR	LOCATION
North Sea	*Hans Kinck*	NOR	2667	7	2	1917	5 miles NW of the Nord Hinder Light Vessel
North Sea	*Hanna Larsen*	GBR	1311	8	2	1917	20 miles E ¾ N of Spurn Point
North Sea	*Ida*	ITA	1172	8	2	1917	About 15 miles SE of Flamborough Head

WRECK-SITE
The wreck is orientated in an east to west direction and lies on a seabed of sand, gravel, pebbles and small broken black shells, in a general depth of 22m, being the lowest

The grave of Otto Ehrentraut, commander of SM UC 39, at Cannock Chase. (Paul Sutton)

astronomical depth. Graham Garner, a Leeds diver, reported that, in early 2001, the wreck was sitting upright, and as you swam along the casing you could look down inside where the mines came out (probably the mine-chutes). He said he never saw the conning tower, but the forward hatch was open and shells were visible inside, although everything was covered in silt. One of the hatches was lying on the seabed, on the port side, and all of the brass mechanism was missing. Brass taps, wheels and bits and bobs of various pieces of the submarine's machinery were also lying on the seabed. Inside the boat is what appears to be one of the telegraphs but, after further inspection by one of his buddies, it turned out to be part of the brass mechanism that operated the hydroplanes, and was well bolted to the hull. Unfortunately, another report says the wreck has recently been blown apart using explosives, making it partially buried and very difficult to find. Most of the interesting artefacts have been removed. In 2000, divers removed a number of small copper boxes, the contents of which are not known. The two bronze propellers have also been recovered and one of them is on display in Bridlington Harbour Museum, along with a large brass shell casing. The steering wheel is in the Ship Inn, Sewerby.

C29, HM SUBMARINE

DATE OF LOSS: 29 August 1915
DEPTH: 36m
REFERENCE: 53 58'.750 N, 001 23'.786 E (Hydrographic position)
ALSO GIVEN: 53 48 790 N, 001 06'.030 E
LOCATION: 37 nautical miles ENE from Spurn Head

British submarines C28 and C29 at Dundee Naval Base, 1912. (Courtesy of Richard Driver, USA)

Type: 'C' Class British coastal patrol boat of Group-II *Pennant No.:* I.59 *Builders:* Vickers Yard, Barrow-in-Furness for Royal Navy *Keel laid:* as Yard No.383 on 4 June 1908 *Launched:* 19 June 1909 *Completed:* 17 September 1909

TECHNICAL SPECIFICATIONS
Hull: Single *Surface displacement:* 290 tons *U/Dt:* 321 tons *LBD:* 43.28m x 4.11m x 3.51m *Machinery:* 1 x Vickers 600hp, 16-cylinder petrol engine *Props:* 1 bronze x 3 blades of 1.70m (5ft 7in) *S/Sp:* 11½ knots *Op/R:* 740 nautical miles at 12 knots, or 910 nautical miles at 8 knots *Sub/R:* 16 nautical miles at 8 knots *U/Power:* 1 x 200bhp electric motors giving 8 knots *Batteries:* Exide lead/acid of 68½ tons (20 per cent of boats submerged displacement) *Fuel/Cap:* 15½ tons *Armament:* 2 x 45.72cm (18in) bow torpedo tubes *Torpedoes:* 4 x 45.72cm (18in) *Guns:* None *Diving:* 30.48m (100ft) max-depth *Complement:* 2 officers and 14 ratings *Cost:* To build: £47,000

The 'C' Class submarine represented the final development of the original Holland Class of boat and was the last class to be equipped with petrol engines, which proved unreliable, as well as the risk of petrol vapour explosion making them quite dangerous. They were also the first British submarines to be built in any quantity. The 'C' boats were very uncomfortable, having no accommodation for the crew, who had to either sleep on the deck/floor, or in hammocks. The Group II design, there were twenty built in all, incorporated forward hydroplanes and were the first British submarines to be designed in this way. Group II boats were built at two yards: Vickers at Barrow-in-Furness between 1908 and 1910 and His Majesty's Naval Dockyard at Chatham between 1908 and 1909. 'C' boats operated from Devonport, Portsmouth, three were in the Baltic and three from Hong Kong, throughout the First World War.

The endurance range of the class was rather limited and they were used mainly as harbour and coastal defence. Out of the total of thirty-eight 'C' Class boats built, thirteen were lost. HM S/M C29 was part of the 8th Flotilla, based at Harwich. She was one of a trawler-submarine team set up to trick U-boats into thinking the trawler was by herself and an easy target – a kind of Q-ship duet. The submarine was trimmed down so that her deck casing was awash, while being towed by a disguised trawler. Then when an enemy vessel was sighted, the tow was slipped and the submarine would go in for the kill, catching the German U-boat or any other enemy vessel by surprise.

COMMANDERS OF C29
Lt A.B. Prowse – May 1909
Lt E.C. Boyle – March 1910
Lt D.I. McGillewie – November 1911
Lt W.R. Schofield RN assumed command of C29 in March 1913.

FINAL VOYAGE

On 29 August 1915, the hired, but disguised, steam trawler *Ariadne II* (Admiralty No.349) was towing HM S/M C29, when she inadvertently strayed into a minefield. Unfortunately the submarine, which was in telephone contact with the trawler at the time, detonated one of the mines. She blew up and was lost with all hands in seconds, sixteen crewmen, including Lieutenant W.R. Schofield RN died. This system of trawler-submarine ploy was discontinued soon after this accident.

The crewmen of HMS C29 are commemorated on the Plymouth Naval Memorial, but Sub-Lt Evans has a memorial window in his parish church of Holy Trinity Church, Northwood, Middlesex.

THE MEN WHO DIED IN C29

Ahern, Andrew, Able Seaman
Bignell, Frederick Walter, Stoker Petty Officer
Chambers, Frederick Gordon, Leading Stoker
Darby, Edward James J., Able Seaman
Evans, Tim Evelyn, Sub Lieutenant, First Lieutenant
Faux, William Henry, Leading Stoker
Gibson, Robert Christopher ERA, Second Class
Hobbs, Charles Ernest J., Able Seaman
Johnston, John K., Stoker First Class
Lane, George Ernest J., Able Seaman
Moore, Frederick George M. ERA, Fourth Class
Mullins, Thomas Reginald, Able Seaman
Norris, Lewis George Norris, PO and Coxswain
Schofield, William Richard, Lieutenant CO
Sinclair, Archibald McVicar ERA, Second Class
Smith, Arthur Henry, Leading Seaman
Watson, Harold Frederick J., Boy Telegraphist

WRECK-SITE

The wreck lies on seabed of sand, gravel and small pebbles, in a general depth of 36m. It is largely intact, but the casing is beginning to corrode, allowing the engine cylinders to be observed through holes which have appeared in it. The bronze propeller was still in place and the rear hydroplanes were reported to be like a 1950s 'Dan Dare' space-rocket. The conning tower, which has been pulled off to starboard – probably by a trawler for all the world – makes the hull look like a rocket. The bow section brings home the reality of what happened on that fateful day, when the submarine detonated a mine which blew her to bits. The upper side of the fore-ends casing (just behind the hydroplanes) has been blown open. Some complex bronze machinery remains on the upper side of the hull. The function of this machinery on the upper side of the vessel confused the diving party until they looked at a sectional line drawing of this class of boat. This was in fact the remains of the hydroplane mechanism, although the hydroplanes themselves are missing. All gears were stamped with the broad arrow. At the time of writing, the forward torpedoes are exposed beneath the hydroplane gearing. Two torpedo tubes still contain corroded weapons.

CHAPTER THREE

EAST ANGLIA

INTRODUCTION

The great arc of East Anglia stretches from the Wash – past sandy, estuarine Norfolk – to the marshy, tortuous creeks of Suffolk and Essex to Shoebury Ness and the mouth of the Thames. The Nelson heritage is much discussed on this coast, but what is not so well known is the intense wartime activity and, in particular, the loss of nineteen submarines off this coast, more than half of them British. Indeed more British submarines were lost off this coast than any other sector.

The proximity of East Anglia to the Flanders bases brought the U-boats to this coast during the First World War. There were other attractions, notably the imperative to obtain a navigational fix. Numerous lightships and buoys such as Smiths Knoll and Shipwash drew U-boats like moths to a flame. Dousing the lights made little difference, the U-boat skippers still sought them out. Anti-submarine patrols learned from experience and several U-boats were destroyed while patrolling around these navigational aids. East coast traffic and intense activity around the mouth of the Thames provided further incentive to mount patrols in this sector (the southern area known to Germans as the 'Hoofden' (Dutch for, 'the heads'), but to the British it was 'the Nore Command'). The Admiralty reciprocated by stepping up patrols and installing listening stations with a view to detecting U-boat wireless transmissions. 'Room 40' took a close interest in the Hunstanton Station. Following the introduction of the 'Beef trip' convoys to Rotterdam in 1917, the outbound traffic assembled at Harwich. In response, mine-laying submarines regularly fouled the Harwich and Yarmouth roadsteads. The intact capture of UC 5, engaged on such a mission, provided useful information for British anti-submarine forces. As will shortly be explained, only a handful of the submarines lost in this section were destroyed as a result of direct enemy action. UB 4 was apparently sunk in an engagement with a diminutive decoy vessel off Smiths Knoll. Similarly, UB 27 may have been destroyed by HMS *Halcyon* in the same vicinity, though conclusive proof is missing. However, more certainty surrounds the loss of UB 16, surprised by the Harwich submarine E34 off Aldeburgh. The fortuitous ramming of little UC 2 in the summer of 1915 by the steamer *Cottingham*, witnessed the first experimental diving expedition by 'Dusty' Miller and his team.

Of course Harwich was a major British submarine base in both World Wars. Submarine flotillas based here held a certain strategic advantage in operations against enemy forces in force on the Belgian coast and Dogger Bank. In August 1914 HMS *Maidstone* and *Adamant* anchored at the west end of Parkeston Quay with the submarines of the 8th Flotilla. On 23 August units included: E4, E1, E3, E2, E6, E8, D8, E9, E5, E7, D4, E11, D7,

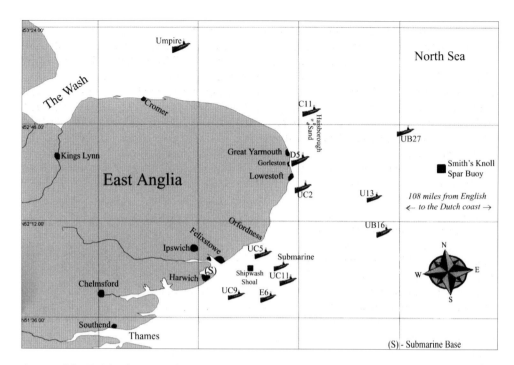

A map of the East Anglian coast. (Ron Young)

A busy day at Parkeston Quay, Harwich. (RN Submarine Museum)

D1. By 29 July 1916, the depot ship HMS *Forth* moved from Immingham to Harwich. The 9th Submarine Flotilla, was henceforward constituted at Harwich with the following submarines on its strength; E23, E29, E30, E31, E35, E37, E38, E42, E43, E45, E53 E54 E55, E56, E32, E33, E46, E47, together with destroyers *Firedrake, Lurcher* and *Melampus*. The depot ship HMS *Pandora* provided accommodation. Given the presence of the 1st and 3rd Destroyer Flotillas, all elbowing for space, Harwich Harbour must have been crowded. HMS *Alecto* took up position at Great Yarmouth and her flotilla was now designated the 8th Submarine Flotilla. The 8th shared the harbour and Gorleston anchorage with the local herring fleet.

The London North East Railway (LNER) owned a railhead at Parkeston Quay and had no objection to the submariners taking over a couple of large transit sheds, though for the most part *Maidstone* was self-sufficient. In the event of more extensive repairs being required, apart from the Ipswich port facilities, the Royal Dockyards of Sheerness and Chatham were conveniently close.

One striking aspect of this section is the number of British submarines lost in accidents, ranging from C11 in the high summer of 1909 to the ramming of *Umpire* in 1941. Most incidents, however, date from the First World War. Escape from a submarine demands skill, presence of mind and, above all, luck. The crew of C16 evidently possessed the first two but were tragically lacking in the last. On the other hand, Stoker PO William Brown was able to make a truly astonishing single-handed escape from the sunken E41 following an accidental collision off Harwich in the summer of 1916. The crew of the other submarine, E4, were not so fortunate – as their graves in Shotley, testify.

Yet the greatest cause of submarine loss off this coast, was neither enemy action nor accident, but mining. Submariners learned to fear mines above all else. A skipper could use his skill to escape ramming and depth charges, but sea-mines were different; like some terrible mysterious ancient god, all-powerful and merciless. Between 23 and 24 April 1918 the submarine E41 laid a large minefield designed to protect Harwich and the war channel, east of the Shipwash Bank. This field may well have claimed UC 11 – and probably many others stamped as 'verschollen' (missing) in German naval archives – but mines also took the crews of C33, D5, E6, E30 and E37. Both sides liberally mined East Anglian waters in the First World War and there seems little doubt that submarines of both nations were destroyed on their own mines, loose or otherwise. All it took was for the compass to wander (as it inevitably would) as the submarine approached land. The ubiquitous east coast fret would do the rest and under these circumstances charts would be useless. In the middle of a minefield, courage and seamanship count for little; a crew could only pray. A few men on watch sometimes escaped from the conning tower of a submarine mined on the surface but, almost invariably, a boat mined while submerged will be a submarine lost with all hands.

In the Second World War, the Kriegsmarine tended to leave East Anglia to 'E' boats, mines and aircraft. However, U 15 of the Weddigen Flotilla mined the Lowestoft roads in November 1939. The early loss of U 13 while taking up position to attack a convoy, may well have reinforced this tendency to avoid deploying submarines against the FS/FN route. Initially, Blyth and Rosyth were the only designated east coast submarine stations during the Second World War – Harwich was an afterthought triggered by all too accurate fears of a German invasion of the Netherlands. On 28 September the 'S' Class submarines of the 3rd Flotilla were summoned from Malta to Harwich (HMS *Badger*). The LNER sheds were once again occupied. Pink lists for the 7 April 1940 reveal the following unit strength: HMS *Cyclops* (depot ship), *Sealion, Seawolf, Shark, Snapper, Sterlet, Sunfish* and *Salmon*. Elements of the French 10th Flotilla: *Amazone, Orphee, Circe, Calypso, Antiope, La Sibylle* and *Doris* are also listed (though they soon moved to Rosyth). Operating off the Netherlands, Heligoland Bight, Kattegat and Skaggerak, the 3rd Flotilla faced the same impossible odds

Submarines E33 and L17 in the floating dry dock, Harwich. (Courtesy of Richard Driver, USA)

'C' Class boats in port. (Courtesy of Richard Driver, USA)

HMS *Camperdown* (right) and HMS *Ganges II* with 'C' Class at Harwich. (Courtesy of Richard Driver, USA)

as the Blyth and Rosyth flotillas. Indeed, of the British submarines previously mentioned, only *Sealion* was destined to survive the war (see Volume 3). By the summer of 1940 the 'S' Class boats were gradually dispersed, leaving only a core of 'H' boats on anti-invasion watch. Operational patrols ceased in the autumn of 1940. All that remained were four wooden dummy submarines riding on buoys alongside Parkeston Quay.

Given the operational dangers, it is therefore surprising that the only British Second World War submarine lost in these waters was *Umpire*, victim of an incident off Blakeney Point in 1941, reminiscent of the collision which sank *Unity* (see Chapter One). As with the *Unity* catastrophe, the courage and selflessness with which the submariners conducted their escape bid is profoundly moving. So what remains of East Anglia's submarine heritage?

The RN Patrol Service Museum, Sparrows Nest, Lowestoft commemorates the vital anti-submarine work carried out on the east coast during the Second World War. This little museum is a *must* for anyone interested in the desperate fight to keep the east coast sea-lane clear of mines and submarines. The collection includes a mock-up of a trawler bridge as well as photographs, models, artefacts, displays and documents describing the evolution of the anti-submarine vessel. The museum manages to celebrate the courage of these brave men while simultaneously conjuring up something of the atmosphere of those heady days when the FS/FN convoy route was the very artery of the nation (Tel: 01502 586250).

Parkeston Quay, Harwich, is now the departure point for Continental ferries – ironically given its history – to Zeebrugge and Hamburg. At the time of writing a few forlorn sheds and structures that formerly housed HMS *Badger*, the shore base, can still be seen.

Across the estuary from Harwich at Shotley Gate, on a marshy peninsula dividing rivers Orwell and Stour, stands the former training base HMS *Ganges*, deserted since 1976. No fewer than 200,000 boy sailors trained here between 1906 and 1976. James Magennis was one of them:

> …I was just 15, a pale faced Belfast boy when I was introduced to life at *Ganges*…my head was shaved. My first lesson was in sewing my name in chain stitch onto my clothes. Any fear of heights was soon overcome by acrobatic drill on high mast and yard arm: my pay 8 shillings per week. For becoming a member of the 'draggers union' – stealing a smoke – I got 14 days jankers, plus the punishment of marching with a stick above my head during recreation time. 'Below Moderate', that was my assessment on leaving *Ganges*.

James Magennis would graduate from HMS *Ganges* to win the Victoria Cross in an 'X' craft. At night its walls must echo to the laughter of a thousand boyish ghosts: 'If it moves, salute it, if it doesn't, blanco it'. Not far away lies the Church of St Mary, Shotley. Within a larger Commonwealth War Graves Commission naval cemetery can be found the 'Submarine Enclosure'. A memorial reminds us that 'Harwich was once an important submarine base'. One of those buried here is L/S W. Barge. His frantic efforts to beat off a German seaplane attack with a machine gun when C25 was attacked off this coast on 5 July 1918 were captured on a series of much reproduced German photographs. C25 was towed back to Harwich with L/S Barge dying of his wounds. Nearby lay Julian Tenison and several of E4's crew. The authors believe that Boy Tel. Denison, aged sixteen years, of E4, was the youngest British submariner to die in any war. A few graves further along can be found the tragic Harold Boase and the men of C16. Nearby, one inscription reads 'Sleep after toyle. Port after stormie seas'. German and Briton, veteran and novice, their voyages ended here, at this tranquil maritime Valhalla beside the Suffolk marshes.

Right: The Royal Navy Patrol Services Memorial in Bellvue Park, Lowesoft. (CWGC)

Far right above: Shotley Naval Cemetery, often referred to as a 'tranquil maritime Valhalla beside the Suffolk marshes', is located on a river peninsula across the Orwell from Harwich, very close to the site of HMS *Ganges*. (G.J. Anderson)

Far right below: The memorial at Shotley Naval Cemetery. (G.J. Anderson)

UMPIRE, HM SUBMARINE

DATE OF LOSS: 19 July 1941
DEPTH 14.8m
REFERENCE: 53 09'.909 N, 001 06'.021 E
LOCATION: 11.96 nautical miles NNE from Blakeney Point

Type: 'U' Class British patrol submarine of Group 1★ *Pennant No.:* No.82 *Builders:* His Majesty's Dockyard at Chatham for the British Navy *Keel laid:* as Slip-7 on 1 January 1940 *Launched:* 30 December 1940 *Commissioned:* by Lt Mervyn R.G. Wingfield RN on 10 July 1941

TECHNICAL SPECIFICATIONS

Hull: Double *Surface displacement:* 540 tons *U/Dt:* 740 tons *LBD:* 59.99m (196ft 10in) x 4.87m (16ft) x 4.41m (14.4ft) *Machinery:* 2 x 615bhp 6-cylinder Admiralty Diesels (diesel-electric-drive) *Props:* 2 bronze *S/Sp:* 11¾ knots *Op/R:* 4,050 nautical miles at 10 knots *Sub/R:* 120 nautical miles at 2 knots *U/Power:* 2 x General Electric motors developing 825bhp gave 8.9 knots *Batteries:* Exide lead/acid *Fuel/Cap:* 41 tons *Armament:* 4 x 53.34cm internal torpedo tubes forward *Torpedoes:* 8 x 53.34cm (21in) *Guns:* 1 x 5.44kg (12-pounder) HA deck gun *Ammo:* 160 rounds of 5.44k *Mines:* None *Diving:* Max-op-depth 60.96m (200ft) *Complement:* 4 officers and 29 ratings

Umpire and *Una*, both built at Chatham, were fitted with a flush bow. The majority of 'U' Class boats were deployed in the North Sea and Mediterranean. Altogether, nineteen of these boats were lost during the Second World War.

Commanded by Lt (later Captain) Mervyn R.G. Wingfield RN, HM S/M *Umpire* had moved down the river Medway towards the end of July 1941, prior to setting course northbound for the Clyde where she was to carry out sea-trials and commence training with the Dunoon-based 3rd Submarine Flotilla, before taking her place in North Sea operational patrols. She briefly stopped overnight at Sheerness to await the convoy of merchant ships leaving the Thames the following day.

FINAL VOYAGE

Umpire found the FN convoy (East Coast Convoy EC.4), which was escorted by Royal Navy motor launches and trawlers off Southend and took up her station astern. As they moved around the great curving coastline, a low-flying German bomber attacked the lead ships. Lt Edward Young RNVR, as officer of the watch, gave the instructions to crash-dive. *Umpire* then successfully completed her first actual dive and surfaced a few minutes later, once the Heinkel bomber had disappeared. Unfortunately a faulty diesel engine had to shut down, forcing *Umpire* to reduce speed. Mervyn Wingfield, in receipt of QZH transmissions, realised that a southbound convoy (FS44) was on converging course within the same narrow buoyed channel. At this rate it would be due about midnight. On 19 July 1941 things were about to go badly wrong.

According to international rules of the sea, ships must keep to the starboard side and pass each other port-to-port. However, when Lt Wingfield was called to the bridge, he was amazed to discover the southbound convoy was actually ahead of him and spread across his starboard bow. Being a wartime situation and under constant threat from German E-boats, none of the ships showed any lights. Suddenly Wingfield was aware of a dark shape looming up ahead on *Umpire's* starboard bow and recognised it as a trawler. If it had kept to its present heading, the vessel would have passed dangerously close. The trawler had the right of way and Lt Wingfield considered altering course to starboard, but such a

HMS *Umpire*, June 1941. (RN Submarine Museum)

move would certainly have placed *Umpire* in the path of an endless line of dark shapes, as far as the eye could see. Wingfield ordered 'Hard-a-port', but simultaneously the Harwich-based requisitioned trawler *Peter Hendriks* (FY260), also turned to starboard. Realising the serious dilemma, Lt Wingfield called down the voice-pipe, 'Full-astern-together', but it was too late; the *Peter Hendriks* smashed into *Umpire* with a sickening crunch, about 6–9m abaft the starboard bow. The submarine heeled over to port and the two vessels stayed locked together for a few seconds in a steel embrace. Lt Mervyn Wingfield:

There was a shower of sparks – The bow went down a bit, the submarine slid round to port until I on the bridge was abreast the bridge of the trawler near enough to touch it; about ten or fifteen seconds after the impact of the collision the submarine's bows suddenly dropped and I and the others on the bridge were washed off...I shouted 'You stupid bastards, you have sunk a British submarine!'

All four of us shouted to the trawler 'THROW-A-LIFEBUOY' and they shouted back. I remember my binoculars floating in front of me, chin high. I was wearing a 'Kapok' coat, and found myself supported to some extent by the buoyancy of my Burberry. The others, who were wearing heavy sea boots, held onto me at first, but after a very short time one of them let go and I did not see him again. A little later the second seaman let go, leaving Godden (Lt. Tony Godden) and I...he held onto me. We remained like this for some time, but Godden's leather sea-boots were keeping him down. Godden let go. I remember nothing more except the conviction that I was drowning. It wasn't even painful, just a quiet drifting into unconsciousness. There's nothing difficult about dying. Your past does not come before you; it's all rather prosaic. During this time the trawler moved away and appeared to us (I thought I may be mistaken) to make a circle to starboard. Eventually a searchlight was turned on to us, but just about this time I heard a boat approaching.

The boat picked me up, they placed me face down in the bottom of the boat and took me back to the Peter Hendricks. The first thing I remember was someone reading out from the gold bracelet I wore, 'MRG Wingfield, HM Submarines'.

'At least we've got that bugger's name' said one of my rescuers. I protested that I wasn't dead and asked if there were any other survivors.

'None so far', they said.

'I'm the Captain', I said, 'you had better throw me back!'

'U' Class engine room. (Author's collection)

What of the men down below? Just before the collision, CERA George Killan had been tending to the troublesome port motor bearing. The bearing had become too hot through loss of lubricating oil pressure and a piston to seize. George Killan felt the impact and heard a bang, and could see a pink atmosphere, which he imagined was a fire of some description, but he felt no blast. He was just about to shout 'stop-the-engines', when someone else in the engine room stopped them. CERA George Killan:

> I don't think it would be very long before the lights went out except for a police light. It was reported to me that somebody was lying in the control room. I went into the control room but could not find anybody, so I returned to the engine-room and shut the watertight door; by means of tackle, because of the list of the ship. The boat had hit the bottom. I did not realise that at once, probably because the submarine sank so quickly.

LTO Arthur Band:

> I was making my way to the fore-ends. A terrible flash tore through the boat from the control room to the fore-ends. I shut off the battery ventilation forward. I recall other crew members were evacuating the fore-ends. Then the bulkhead door was shut and clipped from within by the men left inside. I came back to the control room and checked the battery ventilator. The Tel was still in his office transmitting a distress signal. I left him and made my way back to the engine room escape lockers. By this stage the boat was taking on a bad bow-down angle.

Lt Edward Young RNVR:

> I was in the corridor outside the ward room and there was an explosion forward and a flash. I cannot say exactly where it was. Somebody, I think the First Lieutenant, Lt Bannister gave the order 'SHUT-WATERTIGHT-DOORS' and I stood by the wardroom bulkhead door and let four or five men go through before shutting the door. There was nobody else there attempting to go through; there was a lot of smoke so I shut the door. The ship listed quite heavily to starboard with a slight bow-down inclination and there seemed to be a lot of water coming into the control room. Most of the lights had gone out... only a dim light left in the control room, so I went into the Wardroom (which was in darkness) to collect torches and went back into the control room and remember shutting off the voice pipe valve. The depth gauges were reading 25-feet. The First Lieutenant tried blowing No.1 main ballast, but it seemed to have no effect.

HM S/M *Umpire* lay on the bottom in 18m, listing to starboard and sloping forward at an angle of 10 degrees, with water pouring in through the ventilation shafts. In the years that followed, Lt Young would blame himself for failing to close the bulkhead door valve. George Killan later testified that the ingress came from a large hole torn through casing and pressure hull, leaving the torpedo stowage compartment totally flooded. Fortunately the dive had forced the conning tower hatch shut so the control room was saved from flooding. The source hardly mattered. Contaminated batteries were already producing chlorine gas. The only hope for the crew lay in immediate escape. Six would attempt to escape from the conning tower, and the rest would exit from the engine room. Lt Young takes up the story:

> Eventually one of the ratings went into the engine room and shut the door, and four of us, the First Lieutenant, Able Seaman Meikle, and ERA Foster and myself, went up into the conning tower. I was last in the conning tower and when I left there was nobody left in the control room. We shut the lower lid and I discussed what we should do. We decided to escape from the conning tower. The First lieutenant tried to open the upper lid, but the outside pressure was too great, so we eased the lower lid to equalize the pressure, which was building up in the Control room, and we did that until we smelt chlorine gas. We shut the lid then and the First Lieutenant opened the top lid and we went out.

As the hatch lifted Lt Bannister called out: 'Come on lads. Here we go for fourteen days survivor's leave!' None of the men were wearing any DSEA gear for the 45ft (13m) journey from the conning tower to the surface. All four made it safely to the surface, but they became separated and, by the time an RN launch rescued Edward Young, the first lieutenant and Able Seaman Meikle had drifted away. Young could only listen to their pitiful shouts for help. The reader may be interested to know that twenty-eight-year-old ERA Charlie Foster had only barely survived the loss of *Unity* in April 1940 (Chapter One). Lt Young had earlier found him in a nauseous condition due to carbon dioxide poisoning. Although ERA Foster made the ascent, Lt Young could not find him on the surface and he almost certainly died as a result of faulty DSEA technique. Of this group of escapees, only two men survived.

Seventeen men (some accounts say twenty) were trapped in the engine room where George Killan, as senior rating, took command of the escape attempt, assisted by PO Trebble. When he broke open the boxes he was dismayed to find only fourteen DSEA sets. Three men volunteered to escape without them:

> Shortly after the door was shut, we set about getting the trunking down and the T.I. set about getting the chaps acquainted with the sets. And when we had the trunking in place, I suggested that the chaps who had no sets went up one at a time with those who had. I was confident that there were ships above us I heard their screws overhead clearly. I talked to the men who had no

sets, and I tried to get them to suggest, if possible, what they should do. I discovered that they wanted to go up as quickly as possible, and I suggested that they should go up one at a time with the fellows who had a set.

LTO Arthur Band:

The CERA started to flood the compartment. I can still see Inspector Bardoe's face. He was very worried but he did have a DSEA set. When the water was waist high he managed to get over to me and asked what he had to do. I explained and he said he understood. The crew without sets kept above water hoping to stay in the airlock when fully flooded.

George Killan:

We started to flood up with water... The lads were magnificent, absolutely one hundred percent. No panic at all. When it covered the bottom of the twill trunking I went inside the trunk with Telegraphist Beddie and opened the vent until there was a small airlock only at the top. I eased the wheel, left Beddie there, and returned to the engine-room. LTO Band then went into the trunk and escaped with Beddie. The two men without sets went up behind Band and Beddie. After that I went through the twill trunk onto the casing to make sure that they had got clear and then returned to the boat...I was very anxious to find out whether the men who had already left for the surface had got clear of the escape hatch and that there were no obstructions barring the way to further escapes. So, wearing my DSEA I dipped under the trunk and made my way up through the escape hatch. By reaching out as far as I could, I was able to reassure myself that there was nothing in the vicinity of the hatch that would prevent further ascents. I then climbed back into the engine room to the remaining men.

LTO Band:

John Beddie who had no set agreed to escape with me. I dipped under the twill trunk and he came into the air lock beside me. He was young and so very brave. I started to take the clips off. John said, 'Don't forget the air release valve'. I cracked this, removed the last clips and went up. John never made it. I will never forget him. His mother later sent me a photo. On November 11th each year I look at it and think of all the other young submariners who never made it home.

The men escaped at five-minute intervals until only five remained. As Chief Petty Officer William Trebble recalls, Mr Bardoe, the dockyard electrical inspector, was having problems with his DSEA set:

...for some reason or other he used up the oxygen in his bottle. He was told to come to me to put him right. I gave him instruction in his set, gave him some oxygen from the manifold, and impressed on him not to do anything until I told him. Here again was another instance where I did not know whether the dockyard official should come up first or anywhere in between. I finally decided that the best thing to do would be to send him up in between the remainder, so he was left until he was about the fourth from the last. In the meantime, the ratings were making their escape one by one, but on two more occasions the dockyard official had lost the oxygen that he had had supplied to him from the manifold. When it came to his turn to go up I gave him explicit instructions, re-charged his bag with oxygen and my last words before he went up were 'Do as I say and you will be alright mate, good luck'. There were three left in the compartment, and we took turns to go up until only I was left. There I was alone sitting on the port engine in the darkness. To keep up my spirits I shone the torch around the deserted engine room. The greasy oily water reflected in the light. To assure myself it was not some horrible dream I called out, 'Is anybody there?' The sound of my voice was more nerve racking than the silence. I said to myself aloud, 'The best thing you can do is to get out of here before you go crackers'. I got my set ready, wondering if I would remember the drill I had drummed into the others. I took a final look round, gripped the mouthpiece then dipped under the twill trunk. I was shooting through the water. It was dark but little bubbles passed me. Then suddenly I was on the surface looking at the dark sky. I saw a light and swam towards an MTB.

It is sad to relate, the three men who volunteered to escape without DSEA sets all perished. In all, two officers and twenty-two men were lost with the boat, including the dockyard electrical inspector, Mr Bardoe. Sixteen men survived and most of them owed their lives to George Killan and William Trebble.

The Court of Inquiry discovered that HMT *Peter Hendriks* had previously been involved in another unfortunate incident on 21 June 1941, when she was towing the steamship *Gasfire*. The *Gasfire* was accidentally towed into a mine and sank in position 52 20'.126 N, 001 53'.818 E (WGS84). The Inquiry also made the following critical observations:

(a) The convoy proceeded on the wrong side of the searched channel because of faulty navigation.

(b) The failure (of Lt Wingfield) to switch on navigation lights on the submarine on sighting *Peter Hendriks* and to make sound signals. In these circumstances the s/m commander should have made the alteration to port even though this would have taken him outside the swept channel. The risk would have been justified.

However no good purpose would be gained in taking disciplinary action of a severe nature. It is therefore proposed that action in respect of Lt Wingfield should be confined to informing him in that the sense of responsibility rests upon him for the collision.

ADM178/270
Memoirs of Lt Mervyn Wingfield and Arthur Band, reproduced by kind permission of the RN Submarine Museum.

This may seem a harsh judgement in retrospect, but Lt Wingfield was appointed to *Sturgeon* soon afterwards. He later commanded *Taurus* with distinction, having been awarded the DSO and DSC★. Lt Edward Young became the first RNVR officer to command a submarine in the Second World War (*Storm*) and ended the war as Commander Edward Young DSO DSC RNVR. Later he wrote the acclaimed *One of Our Submarines* and entered the publishing business with considerable success (he died in 2005).

CERA Killan was awarded the British Empire Medal for his bravery. Many thought he deserved a higher award. Here there is an interesting postscript. Upon inspection by divers, the torpedo stowage-room watertight door was found secured, just as LTO Band had testified, from the inside. By virtue of self-sacrifice some anonymous heroes had saved the lives of their boat-mates. There was bravery in the air that night, off Blakeney Point.

THE MEN WHO DIED IN *UMPIRE*
Baker, Victor Edward, Able Seaman
Banister, Peter Charles McConnel, Lieutenant
Beddie, Charles, Leading Telegraphist
Duffy, Joseph Angus, Leading Seaman
Foster, Charles Henry, E.R. Artificer Third
Godden, Stephen Anthony Golder, Sub Lieutenant
Henson, Henry William, Telegraphist

A sketch of the remains of HMS *Umpire*. (Pam Armstrong)

Hoey, Patrick John, Leading Seaman
Houston, William John, Stoker First
Jennings, Harold, Leading Signalman
Lewin, Walter William, Stoker First
Phillips, Victor George, Stoker First
Roberts, Robert, Able Seaman
Sumner, Frank, Able Seaman
Town, Ronald Thomas, Leading Stoker
Welham, Frederick, Able Seaman

WRECK-SITE

The wreck lies on its starboard side, on a seabed of gravel, silty sand, mud and shells, in a general depth of 14.8m (48½ft), being the lowest astronomical depth. Looking forward, the keel is to the left and the deck to the right. What remains of the hull is covered in a dense carpet of hydroids and the exposed ribs have large clusters of beautiful plumose anemones. The wreck is now quite broken and has been opened up by commercial salvage teams, for access to the non-ferrous metal, i.e. the electric motors, periscopes, control-room instruments and the four bow torpedo tubes, which are all gone. The hull forward has collapsed around the control room position beneath the conning tower, where Lieutenants Bannister and Young made their escape. The remains of the conning tower can be found just slightly away from the wreck and showing as a section of curved metal, almost buried in sand and gravel and quite close to the base of the gun-mount. The 3in gun is lying on one side and partially buried in the seabed a little further aft and away from the main hull section. Peering through openings in the pressure hull, one can see batteries strewn about the whole length of the hull. A small anchor-winch sits on the intact section of the bow deck and forward of this; the wreck is broken almost completely across this section. While almost level with the little winch, a bow hydroplane can be seen in the sand and standing upright. The bow forward of this point has collapsed with just a few flanges, valves and steel plating sticking out of the sand. Colourful anemones cover sections of bent pipe on the outside of the hull. A fair amount of wreckage has fallen away from the deck casing.

At the stern end, the port propeller has obviously been salvaged, but the propeller-shaft protrudes out of the wreck. The starboard shaft and possibly the propeller appear to be buried. The gearboxes are still in place and attached to the propeller shafts, but the electric motors have been detached and removed. A section of steel hull shelters one of the two diesel engines that seems to have rolled out of the wreck, while the other one is still inside, but somewhat obscured by debris. James Holt of Norfolk Dive Charters, based at Lowestoft, says: 'live torpedoes are still in place and large edible crabs can be seen munching away on explosive substances. Trawl nets are also tangled up with the bow section'.

C11, HM SUBMARINE

DATE OF LOSS: 14 July 1909
DEPTH: 21m
REFERENCE: 52 59'.433 N, 001 34'.649 E
ALSO SUGGESTED: 52 53'.347 N, 001 42'.431 E
LOCATION: 10½ nautical miles NE from Cromer

Type: 'C' Class British coastal patrol boat of Group I *Pennant No.:* I.59 *Builders:* Vickers Yard, Barrow-in-Furness for Royal Navy *Ordered:* for 1905–1906 programme (C1–C11) *Keel laid:* as Yard No.346 on 6 April 1906 *Launched:* 27 May 1907 *Completed:* 3 September 1907

TECHNICAL SPECIFICATIONS
Hull: Single *Surface displacement:* 287 tons *U/Dt:* 316 tons *LBD:* 43.28m x 4.11m x 3.51m *Machinery:* 1 x 600hp Vickers 16-cylinder petrol engine *Props:* 1 bronze x 4 blade 1.3m (4ft 4in diameter *S/Sp:* 12 knots *Op/R:* 740 nautical miles at 12 knots, or 1,000 nautical miles at 8.7 knots and 10-day endurance *Sub/R:* 14 nautical miles at 7 knots *U/Power:* 1 x 200hp electric motors gave 7½ knots max. and 7 knots service speed *Batteries:* Exide lead/acid of 68.6 tons (20% of submerged displacement) *Fuel/Cap:* 15½ tons *Armament:* 2 x 45.72cm bow torpedo tubes *Torpedoes:* 4 x 45.72cm (18in) *Guns:* None *Diving:* Max-op-depth 30.48m (100ft) *Complement:* 2 officers and 14 ratings *Cost to build:* £47,000 (more 'C' Class details with C34)

Lt Charles Gordon Brodie took command of the boat on 23 September 1907 and was the only commander.

FINAL VOYAGE
On the afternoon of Wednesday 14 July 1909, HMS *Bonaventure*'s brood of eight torpedo boats and nine 'C' Class submarines left Grimsby on exercise. At 23.45 the flotilla was steaming south at 10 knots towards Lowestoft, 4½ miles north-west of Haisborough Light. The vessels were well illuminated and the flotilla actually looked like 'a floating small town'. It was a clear night. Submarine C11 was leading slightly and the torpedo boats were steaming in line astern. Heading in the opposite direction towards Hull was the 3,850-ton steamship *Eddystone*. *Eddystone* (Captain T.B. Pritchard) was homeward bound from the Sea of Azov with a full cargo of wheat. Eyewitnesses on the torpedo boats

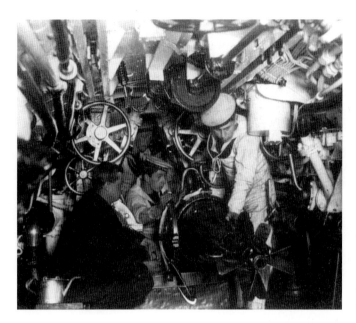

Left: Fore end of 'C' boat. (Author's collection)

Below: C15 portside underway in 1910. (Author's collection)

watched with professional interest as the steamship attempted to pass between the lines of submarines. The sight of *Eddystone* (Messrs Farrar, Groves & Co.) heading towards them, caused mayhem among the boats as they hastily altered course; the inevitable collision occurred, however.

At this time Lt Brodie and the majority of the crew were down below. Lt Watkins was on the bridge, as officer of the watch. The force of the impact hurled Lt Watkins into the sea and jolted Lt Brodie from his slumber. The boat was fatally damaged. Water was pouring in from the missing stern, Brodie rushed around in an attempt to rouse his crew. The water reached his chest leaving Brodie with no option, other than clambering up the ladder behind AB Stripes. C11 sank in forty seconds, leaving Watkins, Brodie and Stripes fighting for their lives on the dark surface. Lt Watkins in particular had difficulty remaining afloat because of his heavy waterlogged duffel coat and sea boots. Brodie helped support him. Fortunately HMS *Bonaventure*'s searchlight was already playing on the water against a background cry of 'man overboard'. A lifeboat from HM S/M C12 then picked up the three gasping survivors. In the frenzy of activity following the appearance of *Eddystone*'s bows, C16 and C17 careered into each other without causing major damage (C17 had to be towed back to Sheerness by the tug *Herculanean*). However, C11 was struck aft, her stern sheered off with the impact, and she sank like a stone.

Divers investigated the wreck and this report was made:

> The wreck was found in 17½ fathoms, lying with her starboard bilge and conning tower on the bottom, upside down. A hole about 3ft long was found on the upper side aft, between the superstructure and the rudder. Another hole, 12in in diameter was found between the bilge heads.
> One plate was found bulged in with rivets loose. It was positioned close to the bow on the starboard side. The wreck was lying with the stem to the southwards…two bodies were discovered in the conning tower.

The report ends with this recommendation:

> …The Admiralty should have a special salvage officer in charge of their salvage operations. His duties may be light and occasionally expensive, but when an accident does occur, he would save waste and anxiety as to whether a submarine can be raised in the hope of saving life.

It is sobering to consider that these words were written thirty years before the *Thetis* disaster.

THE MEN WHO DIED IN C11
Charge, William Henry, Able Seaman
Coles, Herbert, Able Seaman
Goodall, Edward John, Stoker
Kissick, Thomas, Stoker Petty Officer
McGowran, James, Stoker
Potter, Henry Albert, Able Seaman
Pym, Harold Richard, Engine Room Artificer
Reaney, Fred, Able Seaman
Robertson, George, Able Seaman
Smith, Henry Worth, Able Seaman
Stainer, Richard William George, Stoker
Taylor, Ernest, Engine Room Artificer
Winstanley, Albert John, PO and Coxswain

THOSE WHO SURVIVED
Brodie, Charles Goschen, Lieutenant and Commanding Officer
Stripes, Able Seaman
Watkins, Geoffrey Robert Sladen, Lieutenant and First Officer

Lt Brodie survived the First World War and served through the Second World War, finally retiring as a Rear Admiral. He was also appointed an ADC to King George VI. His twin brother, Lt-Cdr Theodore Stuart Brodie, was lost in HM S/M E15 when she was sunk in the Dardanelles on 15 April 1915.

The crew of C11.

A spate of pre-war incidents similar to the loss of C11 only served to confirm the worst suspicions lingering in the more inelastic Admiralty minds with regard to the worth of investing resources in the Submarine Service.

WRECK-SITE

The wreck lies on a seabed of sand and shingle, in a general depth of 21m (68.9ft), being the lowest astronomical depth. It is now partially buried, very broken up, and standing no more than 2m (6½ft) high.

On 7 September 1914 navigational aids likely to be of use to U-boats were either removed or moved. Thus the Inner and Outer Dowsing, Sandiette and Smiths Knoll lights were extinguished, as were all east coast lights between Orford Ness and Wick. The North Hinder light was shifted. Smiths Knoll in particular attracted U-boats like a magnet, providing them with a useful positional fix.

UB 27, SM IMPERIAL U-BOAT

DATE OF LOSS: 29 July 1917
DEPTH: 47m
REFERENCE: 52 47'.020 N, 02 23'.884 E
LOCATION: 25½ nautical miles ENE of
Winterton-on-Sea off Smith's Knoll Spar Buoy

Type: UB II coastal torpedo attack boat   **Builders**: AG Weser, Bremen for Kaiserliche Deutsche Marine   **Ordered**: 30 April 1915, within the batch of UB 24–UB 29   **Keel laid**: as Yard No.241 on 8 July 1915   **Launched**: on 20 December 1915   **Commissioned**: by Oberleutnant zur See Viktor Dieckmann on 23 February 1916

TECHNICAL SPECIFICATIONS

Hull: Single, saddle tank design   **Surface displacement**: 265 tons   **U/Dt**: 291 tons   **LBDH**: 36.13m x 4.36m x 3.70m x 7.34m   **Machinery**: 2 x 142ps Benz diesels   **Props**: 2 bronze   **S/Sp**: 8.90 knots   **Op/R**: 8,150 nautical miles at 5 knots   **Sub/R**: 45 nautical miles at 5 knots   **U/Power**: 2 x 140ps electric motors gave 5.72 knots   **Batteries**: Lead/acid   **Fuel/Cap**: 22 + 6 tons   **Armament**: 2 bow 50.04cm torpedo tubes   **Torpedoes**: 4 x 50.04cm (19.7in)   **Guns**: 1 x 88mm (3.46in) forward facing deck gun   **Ammo**: 120 rounds of 50.8mm   **Mines**: None   **Diving**: Max-op-depth 50m and 22 seconds to crash-dive   **Complement**: 2 officers and 21 ratings

UB 27 was originally assigned to the I.U-Halbflottille, operating from German ports. (Originally, the Kaiserliche Deutsche Marine organised their North Sea-based submarines into four 'Halbflottille', or half flotillas. Later these were upgraded to full flotilla status. I and II.Halbflottille were originally part of the old, original I.Flottille, while III and IV.Halbflottille were part of the original II.Flottille. With the upgrade, the four Haldflottille became U-Flottille and an extra command level was removed.)

Oblt.z.S.Viktor Dieckmann assumed command on 23 February 1916 and on 14 April 1916, UB 27 was formally assigned to I.U-Flottille at Brunsbüttel, Germany.

(1) On 23 April 1916, UB 27 left Germany and sailed to the Firth of Forth area. During the patrol Dieckmann sank five small vessels and torpedoed four steamships, one of which was only damaged. The SS *Teal* (General Steam Navigation Co. Ltd) was on passage from Leith for London with a general cargo when a torpedo was fired at her, but missed. UB 27 then began shelling the steamer and the ship was captured and explosive charges placed on board. However she refused to sink and Dieckmann eventually sank her with another torpedo. On 29 April 1916, the SS *Wandle* (Wandsworth, Wimbledon & Epsom Gas Co., London) was on passage from South Shields for London when she sighted a German submarine on the surface, rigged up with a sail as a deception, 15 miles ESE of Souter Point. The *Wandle* steamed straight at the U-boat in an attempt to ram it but, realising the steamer's intention, Dieckmann shelled it before crash-diving. *Wandle* went so close to the U-boat that the crew thought they had struck her a fatal blow as it went down. Everyone on board was elated, especially the fuss that was made when they arrived in the Thames. However, at the end of the First World War, records showed that in fact the submarine, which turned out to be UB 27, was not even damaged in the incident and had actually only dived because other British ships were approaching the scene.

The Norwegian SS *Mod* (Aktieselskapet Ivarans Rederi) was transporting pitprops from Gothenburg to Blyth when Dieckmann sent her to the bottom on 30 April. Fifty miles off Longstone in the Outer Farne Islands, the Brazilian steamer *Rio Blanco* (Nisario Gurgel, Rio de Janeiro) was sunk by a torpedo, while carrying a general cargo from Christiania to Hull. UB 27 arrived back in Germany on 5 May 1916.

(2) Departing Brunsbüttel on 20 May 1916, UB 27 proceeded to the Firth of Forth area for operations. Following an unsuccessful war patrol, UB 27 returned to port on the 30 May.

(3) On 15 August 1916, UB 27 left Germany and sailed to the Pentland Forth in support of High Seas Fleet sortie. Twenty miles east of the Skerries, the *Duke of Albany* (The Admiralty) was torpedoed and sunk; the ship was employed on Government service as an armed boarding steamer and carried a complement of thirteen officers and ninety-

HMS *Halcyon*. (Author's collection)

eight ratings, of which Cdr George N. Ramage RNR, Eng-Lt Maskell and twenty-two ratings were drowned. The Norwegian steamer *Skjaereg* was captured in the North Sea on 27 August. UB 27 returned to Germany, arriving on 29 August.

(4) Dieckmann's left Germany for his last patrol in UB 27 on 30 September 1916 crossed the North Sea and proceeded to the Scottish east coast. A torpedo fired from UB 27 on 7 October damaged the 2,124-ton SS *Jupiter* (W.C. Bradley & Sons, West Hartlepool (Hull),; she was taking timber from Arkhangelsk, Russia, for Hull and was towed into the Firth of Forth (on 21 May 1918, the *Jupiter* was torpedoed and sunk by UB 40 off Beachy Head, while en-route from Dieppe to Manchester in ballast, and nineteen crewmen including the master were lost). A small fishing vessel was also sunk on this patrol. UB 27 put into Brunsbüttel on 14 October 1916. Oblt.z.S. Hans Georg Lübbe assumed command of the boat on 1 November 1916.

(5) Lübbe sailed from port with UB 27 on 13 November 1916 and searched the North Sea for ships, but after a fruitless voyage, returned to Germany on 27 November.

(6) Between 5 and 10 January 1917, UB 27 patrolled the North Sea but found no ships.

(7) UB 27 sailed from Brunsbüttel on 16 January 1917 and made fruitless patrol around the North Sea, before returning to port on 26 January. On 1 February 1917, UB 27 formally transferred to II Flottille at Heligoland.

(8) Lübbe departed Heligoland with UB 27 on 3 February 1917 and patrolled off the Scottish east coast, before returning to base on 14 February.

(9) UB 27 sailed from Heligoland on 5 March 1917 and patrolled the waters between Rotterdam, Harwich and the Thames, sinking two steamers. The Norwegain *Thode Fagellund* (Wilhelmsen's Dampskipsselskapet Aktieselskapet) was captured and scuttled with explosives, while voyaging from Shanghai for Rotterdam with sesame-seed. On 14 March and 40 miles off the Dutch coast, the SS *Davanger* (H. Westfal-Larsen, Bergen) was captured and scuttled with explosives. She was on passage from New York for Rotterdam with barley. UB 27 returned to Germany on 18 March.

On 21 April 1917, UB 27 formally transferred to the Baltic U-Flottille at Kurland and Oblt.z.S. Heinz Freiherr von Stein zu Lausnitz took over the command on 24 April 1917. ('Kurland' is German for Courland, which was a former duchy on the Baltic. It later became a province of Russia and in 1918, was incorporated into Latvia. The chief port was Libau (now Liepaja, in modern day Latvia) where the U-boat base was situated.)

(10) The boat left Heligoland on 14 June 1917 and sailed for Libau, but the voyage was aborted and she returned to base on 17 June.

(11) On 20 June UB 27 left Heligoland and sailed to Libau, where she arrived on 22 June.

(12) UB 27 left harbour on 30 June 1917 for a short patrol in the Baltic and put into Kiel on 3 July.

(13) On 14 July UB 27 left Kiel and arrived at Zeebrugge on 19 July, where she formally transferred to the Flandern U-Flottille.

FINAL VOYAGE

14) UB 27 departed Zeebrugge on 22 July 1917 with von Stein to patrol in the Hoofden, but did not return. On 21 July 1917, UB 27, along with UB 18 and UB 35, were ordered to sail and attack the Holland to England convoys, based upon sighting reports radioed from aircraft (or re-sent via Brugges from aircraft). The three boats were instructed to remain in defined areas from dawn until 08.30 (continental time) listening for these radio messages. The order sheet went on to list these assigned KTB (war diary) grid reference locations as: UB 18: 125 alpha, UB 27: 126 alpha, to 133 alpha, UB 35: 134 alpha.

During the other parts of the day, the boats could operate at the CO's discretion. The boats were to return according to their munitions expenditure, but no later than eight days. Following eight days spent on patrol, the boats were permitted to return according to their munitions and fuel expenditure.

UB 27 was at Brugge on 21 July and first had to sail to Zeebrugge before heading to sea. She reached Zeebrugge that evening and cleared the port at 00.45 on 22 July (Continental time).

A U-boat was allegedly running at periscope depth off the Smith's Knoll Spar Buoy on 29 July 1917 when the old torpedo-gunboat HMS *Halcyon*, on a routine patrol, sighted it in the approximate position of 52° 47' N, 02° 24' E. *Halcyon* immediately increased speed, turned quickly and rammed the U-boat. Log of HMS *Halcyon, 29* July 1917:

10.57 Attacked German submarine lat. 52 47 N Long. 02 23 E

11.00 Dropped first depth charge

11.10 Dropped second depth charge. Buoyed site and hoisted out seaplane

ADM 53/43660 – KTB of UB 18, NARA: T 1022, Roll 67, PG 61759.

Two 228.80kg (500-lb) depth charges were dropped on the U-boat as she passed over. *Halcyon* stood by and a large oil slick and bubbles rose to the surface. Later that day, Royal Navy vessels swept the position with bottom-lines and found a large object lying on the seabed. Divers were sent down to inspect it, but underwater visibility was so poor they could not find the target.

While it has traditionally been accepted that *Halcyon* sank UB 27, the specifics of the U-boat's orders call this into question. The location of *Halcyon*'s attack is some 30 miles north of UB 27's assigned morning station. The attack came on the day the submarine was due back in port, at a location sufficiently far from home that she could not have managed to cover the distance during the remainder of that day.

It is possible that *Halcyon* did sink UB 27 but, with no wreck to be found, there are equal grounds for suspecting that the submarine may have fallen foul of one of the many minefields in this particular sector or was lost through accidental causes.

THE MEN WHO DIED IN UB 27

Beeck, Lt.z.S.d.Res.

Bock, Masch.Mt

Boldt, Btn

Büscher, Ob.Hzr

Ehlert, Mts.
Franke, Mn.Ing.Asp.
Franke, F.T.Obergast
Gotter, Masch.Mt
Heitmann, Stm.d.Res.
Hinzmann, Ob.Mts.
Kirchner, Ob.Masch.Mt
Klinkusch, Mts.
Kühlig, Masch.Mt
Ludwig, Ob.Btn
Przesdzink, Mts.d.Res.
Püsche, Masch.Anw.
Rudolph, Hzr
Schilling, Masch.
Schultz, Ob.Hzr
Schwehr, Ob.Mts.d.Res.
Stein zu Lausnitz, v. Heinz, Oblt.z.S.
Thien, Masch.Mt

The following is a list of the known vessels believed sunk or damaged by UB 27:

AREA	VESSEL'S NAME	FLAG	TONS	D	M	YEAR	LOCATION
North Sea	Blessing (fishing boat)	GBR	19	28	4	1916	Sunk near the Tyne Estuary
North sea	Christian (sailing boat)	DEN	180	28	4	1916	Sunk near the Tyne Estuary, but refloated
North Sea	Teal	GBR	766	29	4	1916	2-miles E of Seaham Harbour
North Sea	Wandle	GBR	889	29	4	1916	Damaged 15 miles SE of Souter Point
North Sea	Mod	NOR	664	30	4	1916	Sunk in the Firth of Forth
North Sea	Rio Blanco	BRA	2269	1	5	1916	Sunk in the Firth of Forth
North Sea	Mars (lighter)	NOR	777	2	5	1916	Sunk N of the Dogger Bank
North Sea	Memento (sailing vessel)	NOR	654	2	5	1916	Sunk N of the Dogger Bank
North Sea	Superb (lighter)	NOR	721	2	5	1916	Sunk N of the Dogger Bank
North Sea	Duke of Albany	GBR	2184	25	8	1916	20 miles E of the Pentland Skerries
North Sea	Skjaereg	NOR	1019	27	8	1916	Captured in the North Sea
North Sea	Jupiter	GBR	2124	7	10	1916	Damaged in the Firth of Forth
North Sea	Magnus (fishing boat)	GBR	154	8	10	1916	40 miles NE of Longstone, Farne Islands
North Sea	Thode Fagellund	NOR	4352	12	3	1917	Sunk in the North Sea
North Sea	Davanger	NOR	5876	14	3	1917	Sunk in the North Sea

WRECK-SITE
The wreck of this U-boat was never found during any surveys. It is, however, still possible that UB 27 is still there in the position offered, but collapsed and buried beneath the sand.

UB 4, SM IMPERIAL U-BOAT

DATE OF LOSS: 15 August 1915
DEPTH: 30m
REFERENCE: 52 43'.027 N, 002 17'.885E
LOCATION: Near Smith's Knoll Spar Buoy

Type: UB I coastal torpedo attack boat **Builders:** Germaniawerft, Kiel for Kaiserliche Deutsche Marine **Ordered:** 15 November 1914, within the batch of UB 2–UB 8 **Keel laid:** 3 November 1914 as Yard No.242 **Launched:** March 1915 **Commissioned:** by Oberleutnant zur See C. Groß on 23 March 1915

TECHNICAL SPECIFICATIONS

Hull: Single **Surface displacement:** 127 tons **U/Dt:** 142 tons **LBDH:** 28.10m x 3.15m x 3.03m x 7.30m **Machinery:** 2 x 30ps Daimler diesels **Props:** 2 bronze **S/Sp:** 6.47 knots **Op/R:** 1,650 nautical miles at 5 knots, or 1,900 nautical miles and 13 knots **Sub/R:** 45 nautical miles at 4 knots **U/Power:** 2 x 60ps electric motors gave 5.51 knots **Batteries:** Lead/acid/accumulators **Fuel/Cap:** 3½ tons **Armament:** 2 bow 45cm torpedo tubes **Torpedoes:** 2 x 45cm (17.72in) torpedo tubes **Guns:** 1 machine gun (no deck gun) **Ammo:** 300 rounds **Mines:** None **Diving:** Max-op-depth 50m (164ft) and 20–33 seconds to crash-dive **Complement:** 1 officer and 13 ratings

After commissioning, UB 4 was transported to Antwerp by rail, where she formally joined Flandern U-Flottille on 12 April 1915, with Oblt.z.S. C. Groß as the boat's commander from 23 March 1915.

UB 4 made fourteen short patrols with Groß, all about three days long, with the first ten taking her to the Noord Hinder or Maas Light Vessel regions; during April 1915, Groß sank two steamships in those areas. The first victim of Flandern U-Flottille and UB 4 was the British steamer *Harpalyce*, which was torpedoed and sunk by UB 4 on 10 April 1915, 7 miles off the North Hinder lightship. The SS *Harpalyce* (J&C Harrison Ltd, London) was on passage from Rotterdam for Norfolk, Virginia in ballast and engaged in Belgian Relief Service. She was also well embellished with the words 'Belgian Relief'. Very large black letters were written on large white patches along both sides of her hull and she was flying a big white flag that was similarly marked. Groß had no hesitation in sinking this relief ship, on which fifteen of her crew of forty-four, including the master, were lost. The second victim was the Greek SS *Ellispontos* (Embiricos Bros), en-route from Amsterdam to Montevideo, which sank from a torpedo attack on 17 April.

(11) Between 9 and 10 July 1915, Groß patrolled off Great Yarmouth, but sank no ships.

(12) Leaving Zeebrugge on 27 July 1915, UB 4 returned to the Great Yarmouth area to hunt for ships. Groß torpedoed and sank the Belgian steamer *Princesse Marie José* (Ocean Soc. Anon. Belge d'Armement & de Navigation, Antwerp), near the Shipwash Light Vessel on 29 July; she was on passage from Dunston-on-Tyne for Bordeaux with coal. The U-boat arrived back in Flanders on 30 July.

(13) Departing Zeebrugge on 5 August 1915, UB 4 operated around the Lowestoft area without sinking any vessels and returned to Flanders on 7 August.

FINAL VOYAGE

(14) UB 4 left Flanders on 13 August 1915 for operations off the Yarmouth area. She reached her intended destination, Smiths Knoll Buoy, on 15 August, which is an area just to the north-east of where she had sunk the *Harpalyce* earlier. At around 18.20 on Sunday, Groß sighted a typical group of British fishing boats going about their normal business. What Groß was totally unaware of was that four Lowestoft fishing smacks had been converted into armed decoy vessels, complete with RN crews – in effect, miniature Q-ships.

The fishing boat in question was *Inverlyon*. She had no engine, was flush decked and possessed a bluff-bow, two masts with a stubby bowsprit. She was also armed with a 47mm (3-pounder) quick-firing gun under the expert eye of Mr Ernest Jehan RN, commander of the boat. The remainder of the crew comprised three RN reservists and Mr Phillips, her peacetime skipper. His Majesty's Armed Smack had been assigned to 'fishing', about

20 nautical miles east of Great Yarmouth with her trawl streamed out to maintain the deception. The weather was quite hazy in the fading light off Smith's Knoll Spar Buoy and Groß was oblivious that his intended victim was a decoy. The U-boat surfaced close-by and slowly approached on *Inverlyon*'s starboard side. Mr Jehan took up position beside the concealed gun while two other crewmen armed themselves with rifles and hid behind the bulwarks.

When the range had closed to 30m, Mr Jehan noted that Groß was standing alone, abaft the open conning tower hatch, guiding his boat. The U-boat's machine gun had not been mounted on its tripod. Groß shouted something that sounded as if they were being ordered to abandon ship, or heave-to. His intention was probably to place explosive charges on-board to sink the smack rather than waste a torpedo on her. Ernest Jehan's handwritten account of the UB 4 action, written on a scrap of notebook, in RN Library, Portsmouth:

Sunday 16th. Smack Inverlyon Submitted

I have the honour to report 2010, position N by E 3 miles Spar Buoy, Smiths Knoll, 820.

Submarine sighted steering NNE. Smacks crew at once manned ship side with rifles and lying under cover, two men at gun, one below to pass up ammunition. When within 30 yards I observed German Ensign and heard shouting. All I could understand was 'boat'. Sub stopped. I at once gave the order to 'Up Ensign' and 'Stand by to Fire'. I then fired my revolver at officer steering, which was signal to open fire. First and third shots pierced centre of conning tower and exploded inside. Second shot cleared aft. Part of conning tower and ensign flew off. The officer steering falling over starboard side. Sub coming round our stern with tide 10 yards from smack. The wounded shouting 'Stop', 'Stop'.

Sub sinking with two men lying with part of body down hatch and head hanging over side. Then she was brought to bear on starboard quarter, 1st, 2nd 3rd and 4th shots striking conning tower, 6 and 7 over. 6, 8 and 9 hitting hull. Sub sinking at angle of 80 degrees head down. 3 bodies appearing, one shouting. Skipper Phillips undressed and swam with lifebuoy but could not reach man before he sank. A large volume of water and oil was thrown up.

Smack having trawl down drifted over sub and brought up. We are lying by trawl, which is foul of submarine. There were no casualties on board as they only fired 6 rounds.

I emptied 4 revolvers and 1 repeater. All rifles were emptied. No. of casualties on board sub before sinking were 6. The smack crew behaved splendidly, also the *Dryad*'s men, particularly the gunlayer. The greatest distance between ships was 30 yards, nearest 10 yards. Pigeons were sent out at 0500 also smack *Arthur Williams* with verbal message to nearest drifter.

Respectfully
EM JEHAN Gr HMS *Dryad*

(Courtesy of Portsmouth Naval Museum archive)

The submarine was observed to settle quickly by the bow and then her stern rose up almost vertically and she plunged to the bottom. Oily debris welled to the surface and amid it lay three bodies. When Skipper Philips heard one of the 'bodies' cry for help, without a thought for his own safety he pulled off his jacket and sea-boots, grabbed a lifebuoy and dived over the side. The vortex caused by the sinking U-boat, however, pulled both men down, and the skipper alone was hauled safely back on deck. All the crew of fifteen were killed. *Inverlyon*'s net had snared the submarine wreck, anchoring her to the spot. A steam drifter was used to relay the news to shore, followed by two pigeons at dawn.

The crew of *Inverlyon* all shared in an immediate cash gratuity and Gunner Jehan RN was awarded the Distinguished Service Cross. He ended his career in the Navy as a lieutenant commander. He died in the early 1930s. Three weeks after the encounter with UB 4, *Inverlyon* attacked another U-boat, but this time her quarry escaped.

ADM 131/85 Special service vessels and 'Q' ships: engagements with enemy submarines
NARA: T-1022, Roll 39, PG61727

THE MEN WHO DIED IN UB 4

Beil, Masch.Anw
Bethke, Btn
Both, Ob.Stm.Mt.d.S.I
Gross, Oblt.z.S.
Herwig, Hzr
Hinze, Ob.Masch.Mt. der Reserve
Kahrau, Mn.Ing.Asp
Kunkel, Hzr
Lerch, Stm.d.S.II
Nieme, F.T.Obergast
Rohde, Mts. Ers.Res.
Schleif, Obe.Mts. Ers.Res.
Steinbrecher, Masch.Mt.d.S.I
Werdermann, Mn.Ing.Ob.Asp.
Wollrab, Ob.Masch.Mt

UB 4 sank the following three vessels, totalling 10,883-tons:

AREA	VESSEL'S NAME	FLAG	TONS	D	M	YEAR	LOCATION
North Sea	*Harpalyce*	GBR	5940	10	4	1915	7 miles ESE of Noord Hinder Light Vessel
North Sea	*Ellispontos*	GRE	2989	17	4	1915	Sunk in Noord Hinder Light Vessel area
North Sea	*Princesse Marie José*	BEL	1954	29	7	1915	1½ miles E of Shipwash Light Vessel

WRECK-SITE

The wreck believed to be that of UB 4 lies on a seabed of silty sand and fine gravel, in a general depth of 30m, being the lowest astronomical depth. The latest report says that it was partially salvaged in recent years and what remains is also buried to a degree, well broken up and collapsed, with just loose plates and steel debris strewn around. Very little marine life has been reported and tidal streams are quite brisk. This site is also a war grave.

D5, HM SUBMARINE

DATE OF LOSS: 3 November 1914
DEPTH: 25m
REFERENCE: 52 32'.071 N, 001 50'.854 E
LOCATION: 2 miles SSE of South Cross Sand,
off Gorleston-on-Sea, Norfolk

HMS D5.

Crew of D5 on the conning tower. The commander, Godfrey Herbert, is in the centre.

Type: 'D' Class British overseas patrol submarine *Pennant No:* I.75 *Builders:* Vickers Yard, Barrow-in-Furness for Royal Navy *Ordered:* for 1909–1910 programme (D2–D8) *Keel laid:* as Yard No.405 on 22 February 1910 *Launched:* 28 August 1911 *Completed:* 19 January 1912

TECHNICAL SPECIFICATIONS

Hull: Saddle tanks and full deck casing *Surface displacement:* 495 tons *U/Dt:* 620 tons *LBD:* 50.2m x 6.24m x 3.35m *Machinery:* 2 x 6-cylinder Vickers diesels that developed 1,200bhp *Props:* 2 bronze x 3 blade of 1.60m (5¼ft) diameter *S/Sp:* 14 knots *Op/R:* 2,500 nautical miles at 10 knots and 24-day endurance *Sub/R:* 65 nautical miles at 5 knots *U/Power:* 2 x 550shp electric motors giving 9 knots *Batteries:* 220-cell Exide accumulators of 87 tons *Armament:* 3 x 45.72cm bow torpedo tubes, 2 bow tubes, arranged vertically and 1 stern *Torpedoes:* 6 x 45.72cm (18in) *Guns:* none *Diving:* Max-op-depth 30.48m (100ft) *Complement:* 3 officers and 22 ratings

The boats of this class were the last British ones built without transverse watertight compartments.

Displacement of the 'D' Class can be divided into three sections, D1 – 483 tons, D2 – 489 tons, and the rest were 495 tons. Also, D4, although the same size as others in that group, had a different ballast system and tankage. A certain amount of ballast was kept in the tanks for good sea-keeping and, depending on the amount, this made a difference in surface displacement. With all internal and external main ballast tanks 'empty' and carrying the normal load of fuel, the displacement would be different. D4 was the only 'D' Class to carry a deck gun.

The 'D' Class were the first British submarines to be fitted with diesel engines, designed for overseas patrol work and to have twin propellers, which made them much safer and more reliable than the petrol-driven ones. Major improvements in the design of the 'D' Class, included the fitting of ballast tanks external to the pressure hull – the first saddle tank design, giving more room inside the hull for the crew and increasing the reserve buoyancy. The larger conning tower was also a break from previous designs, and they had full deck casing. The 'D' Class boat was able to transmit and receive radio messages, which was a further new innovation. However, signals could not be received when submerged, and the tip of the transmitter aerial had to be clear of the water in order to work. The aerial also had to be erected manually – previous boats only had receivers. Homing pigeons were still used when the boat was out of wireless range.

Reference: Admiralty Monograph BR 3043 'The Development of HM Submarines from Holland No.1 [1901] to Porpoise [1930] by A.N. Harrison CB CVO OBE, Director of Naval Construction 1961 to 1966'.

D5 had two commanders: Lieutenant T.F.P. Calvert from 26 October 1911 to 19 November 1913, and Lieutenant Godfrey Herbert from 19 November 1913 to 3 November 1914. Both were promoted to lieutenant commander while in command of the boat.

D5, one of the Gorleston-based boats, operated in the Heligoland Bight. On 21 August 1914 the boat made a difficult attack on the cruiser SMA *Rostock*. The periscope was spotted and shelled by the escorts. Herbert closed to 200 yards before firing, but inexplicably, the torpedoes missed. German records suggest that the torpedoes passed under the ship. In fact, a design fault caused a depth-keeping anomaly in British torpedoes but this was improperly understood at the time. As a result of this failure, Herbert received a reprimand from Commodore Keyes and his career was widely considered to be 'under a cloud'. His superstitious crew were convinced their teddy bear mascot was 'hexed'. Herbert found a sailor ripping up the teddy bear with the words 'That'll teach you to be a poxy joss'. In view of what was about to happen, this action was perhaps unwise. It was later realised that pre-war practice torpedo heads were lighter than warheads, so depth settings were different. Also, it was discovered there was a design fault which affected a torpedo's depth keeping. Other boats suffered similarly before these faults were ironed out.

FINAL VOYAGE

During 1914 Harwich played host to the 8th Submarine Flotilla. On 3 November 1914 the hit and run raid by the German High Seas Fleet was to witness a pursuit that would lead to the destruction of D5.

On this day, ships of His Imperial German Majesty's Navy (the Kaiserliche Deutsche Marine) bombarded the British coast around Yarmouth. The enemy warships were from the First and Second Scouting Group and included the battle cruisers SMS *Von der Tann* (Kapitän zur See Han, Flag of KA Tapken), SMS *Moltke* (Kptn.z.S. von Levetzow), SMS *Blucher* (Freggattenkäpitan Erdmann), and *Seydlitz*, (Kapitän zur See von Egidy, Flag of Konteradmiral Franz Hipper) in the First Group. The Second Scouting Group comprised the SMS *Stralsund* (Kptn.z.S. Harder), *Strassburg* (F.k. Retzman), *Graudenz* (F.k. Pullen), and SMS *Kolberg* (Kplt.z.S. Widenmann). The *Stralsund* also laid a line of 100 mines, 5 miles long, off Smith's Knoll Passage. The bombardment, which was very heavy and aimed at the civilian population, was rather ineffective due to the misty weather – only a few shells landed on the beaches at Gorleston. The German warships approached and fired on our old friend, the torpedo gun boat *Halcyon* (see UB 27). In response, the submarines D3, E10 and D5 – the latter being under the command of Lt-Cdr Godfrey Herbert – were ordered out into the roadstead to intercept the enemy fleet (Herbert had previously been the skipper of A4 when she narrowly escaped destruction during underwater signalling experiments). Cdr Turner DSO in D3 witnessed events as they unfolded:

> I was woken at daylight by gunfire and found on arrival at the conning tower, that a German squadron was bombarding Yarmouth. We were ordered out to our patrol areas, E18 to the Skagerrak, D5 and D3 to the Bight. The D Class had no lining inside the hull and moisture condensed on the hull and made things pretty damp. I used to sleep under an umbrella, which prevented the drips falling on my head! There was no comfort and little facility for cooking beyond electric kettles and hot plates. The only navigation facility was a magnetic compass with a reflector tube for the helmsman below. On deck we used a boat's compass, which had to be passed down when diving, and was rarely used away from the English coast. Anyway on leaving harbour, E18 steered a northerly course, while D3 and D5 proceeded eastwards. On clearing the shoals, I was leading D5 half a mile astern of me. We met the returning fishing fleet. They were waving and sounding their horns and calling out 'Mines, Mines Everywhere'. I altered course to northward and I watched D5 put her helm over to follow suit. As she did so, a mine exploded aft. There was a cloud of black smoke and the boat had simply disappeared. The explosion was bad enough to unseat the master Kingston-valve on my port side. The saddle tanks flooded and D3 took on a dangerous list. As a drifter had immediately closed the position where D5 had gone down, I got all my crew on deck – less the minimum needed to operate the boat – and proceeded to clear the minefield.

The explosion had occurred 2 miles south of South Cross Sand Buoy, off Yarmouth, possibly the result of striking a loose British mine.

> On returning to harbour and going alongside, to my surprise there was 'Bertie' Herbert in a fisherman's gansey. He and five others had been picked up, his coxswain having been shot out of the tower and, although insensible, kept afloat by the air trapped in his oilskin coat.

Lt–Cdr Godfey Herbert asserted:

> I remember being able to kick off my seaboots, which were always 4 sizes too big, just in case of emergencies. Realising that I was to have a long swim I managed to get rid of my coat and trousers and finally had to jettison a pair of good Zeiss glasses.

> Memoirs of Cdr Turner reproduced by kind permission of the RN Submarine Museum

The crew of the drifter *Faithful* (Skipper James Collin) had bravely moved in and picked up four survivors: Lt.Cdr Godfrey Herbert, Sub-Lt Ian Macintyre, CPO Robert Speirs and AB Charles Sexton. AB Suttill, who was from Leeds, was picked up by a local fishing smack later. For his display of gallantry, the master of *Faithful* was awarded £97, which he shared with his crew. Sadly, twenty-one of D5's crew went down with the boat. This was destined to be the second of many brushes with danger for Godfrey Herbert in the course of his astonishing wartime career (see Volume 3).
ADM 1/8401/405

Above: Type IIB boats at Kiel. (Courtesy of Oliver Meise of Taucher.net

Right: Two IIB Type Kriegsmarine U-boats, U 7 and U 4, tied up along the quay in a small Baltic port.

THE MEN WHO DIED IN D5
Blunsdon, Frederick Drury, Petty Officer
Boardman, Wright, Leading Seaman
Bradley, Frederick, Leading Stoker
Brodie, Donald Francis O'Callaghan, Lieutenant
Copeland, William John, Engine Room Artificer
Crimp, George, Leading Seaman
Dowsett, William Richard Cass, Signalman
Simmons, Sidney Charles Stanley, 1975 Stoker
Smith, Arthur Cecil, Chief E.R Artificer.2
Smith, Timothy, Stoker Petty Officer

Tilley, John Thomas Percival, E.R Artificer 3
Dunne, Joseph, Able Seaman
Houlcroft, Edward, Engine Room Artificer.3
Ingham, Thomas, Stoker
King, George Clarence, Telegraphist
Leake, John Robert, Leading Stoker
Norris, Albert, Leading Seaman
Penhaligon, Richard Charles, Stoker
Whiting, Harry, Stoker.1
Wilcox, Ernest, Able Seaman
Worth, Ernest, Stoker.1

WRECK-SITE
The wreck thought to be that of HM S/M D5, lies on a seabed of sand and shingle in a general depth of 25m (82ft), being the lowest astronomical depth. The wreck is marked on the Admiralty chart as a 'foul', which means the remains stand no more than 2m high, so everything will now be totally collapsed and well broken up, with a lot of scattered steel debris. The site needs to be dived to establish what the wreck actually was, but the location is certainly where D5 sank, all those years ago. If it is the submarine, the site will also be classed as a war grave.

U 13, KRIEGSMARINE U-BOAT

DATE OF LOSS: 30 May 1940
DEPTH: 28m
REFERENCE: 52 27'.311 N, 002'.01'.506 E
LOCATION: 11 nautical miles SE of Lowestoft

Type: IIB coastal torpedo patrol submarine **Builders:** Deutsche Werft AG, Kiel-Gaarden for Kriegsmarine **Ordered:** 2 February 1935, within the batch of U 13–U 16 **Keel laid:** as Yard No.248 on 20 June 1935 **Launched:** 9 November 1935 **Commissioned:** 30 November 1935 by Kplt. Hans-Gerrit Adalbert Karl Theodor von Stockhausen **Feldpost No.:** M 15 421

TECHNICAL SPECIFICATIONS
Surface displacement: 279 tons **U/Dt:** 329 tons **LBD:** 42.7m x 4.1m x 3.8m x 8.60m **Machinery:** 2 x 6-cylinder, 4 stroke, 350ps Motoren Werke Mannheim diesels **S/Sp:** 13 knots **Props:** 2 bronze **U/Power:** 2 x 180ps electric motors by SSW gave 7 knots **Battery:** 1 x 62-cell lead/acid by Accumulatoren Fabrik Aktiengesellshcaft, Berlin **Op/R:** 1,800 nautical miles at 12 knot, or 3,900 nautical miles at 8 knots **Sub/R:** 43 nautical miles at 4 knots **Fuel/cap:** 21 tons **Armament:** 3 bow torpedo tubes (no stern) **Torpedoes:** 5 **Gun:** 1 x 20mm (0.79in) AA **Ammo:** 220 rounds of 20mm **Mines:** Only carried on special order and in exchange for torpedoes **Diving:** Max-op-depth 100m (328ft) and 30 seconds to crash-dive (apparently this type was later restricted to 45m (150ft)) **Complement:** About 25

Kplt. von Stockhausen (Knight's Cross), her first commander, was born in Kassel on 11 August 1907 and commenced his naval career in 1926. He spent time as a student at Kiel Anti-Submarine School and with U-Flottille 'Weddigen' in 1935. Von Stockhausen was promoted to Korvettenkapitän on 1 November 1940 (he died in a road accident in Berlin on 15 January 1943).

U 13 was assigned to U-Flottille '*Weddigen*' at Kiel as a *schulboot* (training boat) and then front line boat from November 1935 until the end of December 1939, when she transferred to 1.U-Flottille at Kiel on 1 January 1940. Here, she was again initially used as a *schulboot* for training, then for front line duties.

Kplt. Karl Daublebsky von Eichhain assumed command from von Stockhausen on 10 October 1937 and was CO until 5 November 1939. Daublebsky von Eichhain was born in Pola on 9 July 1909 and commenced his naval career in 1929. He served as watch officer on U 7 in 1935 and 1936. On 1 April 1943 he was promoted to Korvettenkapitän. U 13 carried out the following ten operational patrols:

(1) With Daublebsky von Eichhain in command, the boat left Wilhelmshaven on 25 August 1939 and patrolled the southern part of the North Sea. She returned to Germany on 31 August.

(2) On 2 September 1939, U 13 left Wilhelmshaven for a mine-laying operation off Orfordness and laid a field of TMB mines on 4 September. At 17.25 (Continental time) on 10 September, one of those mines sank the 8,641-ton British steamer *Magdapur* (Thomas & John Brocklebank, Liverpool) and killed six of her crew, at position 52° 11' N, 01° 43' E; she was on passage from South Shields for Southampton in ballast. Aldeburgh lifeboat and coasters rescued the master, Captain Arthur George Dixon, and seventy-four crewmen. Harry Atherton (master mariner) second officer and Radio Officer Ralph Grierson Bell, were two of the crewmen killed and registered with CWGC.

On 10 September, another mine damaged the 10,902-ton freighter *City of Paris* (City Line Ltd) at position 52° 14' N, 01° 43' E. She was on passage from Beira and London for Hull and the Tees with a general cargo; her master, Adam Niven Hogg, was killed.

At 01.00 (Continental time) on 24 September, the 2,660-ton French SS *Phryné* (Soc. Navale Caënnaise, Caën) was transporting coal from Immingham to Bayonne when she detonated a mine laid by U 13 on 4 September. The ship sank 3½ miles east of Aldeburgh Light Vessel, but Alderburgh lifeboat rescued all of the crew. Two empty lifeboats were later recovered. U 13 arrived back to Germany on 6 September.

(3) On 11 September 1939 the boat left port and proceeded to the Firth of Forth for operations against Allied ships. En-route she rescued the crew of a ditched German aircraft, before patrolling the Scottish north-east coast, arriving at Kiel on 3 October.

(4) U 13 sailed from Wilhemlshaven on 25 October 1939 for operations off Kinnaird Head. At 22.50 (Continental time) and 15 miles north by east of Peterhead on 30 October, Daublebsky von Eichhain attacked the 4,666-ton steamer *Cairnmona* (Cairn Line of Steamships Ltd) with a torpedo. The ship had dispersed from Convoy HX 5B (comprising sixteen vessels) and sunk at position 57° 38' N, 01° 45' W; she was on passage from Montreal and Halifax, Nova Scotia, for Newcastle and Leith with a general cargo, including copper and wheat. The 203-ton RN drifter *River Lossie* (Skipper J.C. Spence RNR) rescued the master, Captain Frederick William Fairley, and forty-one crewmen, but the following three men were lost: George Barrette, Richard Lynch and Frank Thomas, all firemen and trimmers. U 13 arrived back at Kiel on 3 November.

Kplt. Heinz Scheringer assumed command of U 13 on 6 November 1939. Scheringer was born in Buenos Aires on 29 August 1907 and commenced his naval career in 1927. He studied at anti-submarine school from July to September 1935 and assumed command of U 10 on 11 September 1935 for three months. Scheringer was promoted to Korvettenkapitän, on 1 January 1942.

(5) On 15 November 1939, U 13 left Germany and sailed to an area north of the river Tyne for operations. At 23.28 (Continental time) on 19 November, the 793-ton British steam tanker *Bowling* (George Gibson & Co. Ltd) was torpedoed and sunk at U-boat grid position AN 5183 (55° 45' N, 01° 35' W), about 6¼ nautical miles NNE of Longstone, Outer Farne Islands; there were no survivors from the crew of thirteen. The vessel had

left Leith earlier that day, en-route to Antwerp and was never seen again. Kplt. Scheringer reported hitting a darkened tanker, carrying a full cargo of about 2,000 tons, with one torpedo, and there was a massive explosion in the fore-section; the ship then broke in two and sank within forty seconds. The Commonwealth War Graves Commission lists the following thirteen crewmen as lost on 20 November 1939:

Cameron, Alexander, Second Officer
Gilfallan, Peter Fireman
Hutchison, James Second Engineer
McDiarmid, Alexander, Ordinary Seaman
McTaggart, Walter, Donkeyman
Moran, W., Ordinary Seaman
O'Brien, John, Able Seaman
Scott, James, Master
Short, James Ian Swanney, Ordinary Seaman
Stark, Donald, Chief Engineer
Watson, William, Chief Officer
Young, Alfred, Fireman
Young, Thomas Fisher, Steward

U 13 returned to Kiel on 25 November.

(6) U 13 left port on 9 December 1939 and proceeded to the Firth of Tay, where she laid mines between positions: 56° 27.5, 56° 24.4N and 02° 35.8, 02° 38.5W. On 6 January 1940, the 8,317-ton SS *City of Marseilles*, which was on passage from Calcutta and London for Dundee and the Clyde with 4,000 tons of jute and 1,450 tons of pig-iron. She was damaged after detonating a mine, some 8 cables and 120 degrees from Tay Fairway Buoy. The ship arrived safely at Dundee on 7 January 1940. That mine was almost certainly attributed to U 13.

The 1,421-ton Estonian steamer *Anu* (ex-*Excelsior*) struck a mine and sank in that same area off the river Tay on 6 February 1940, between No.1 and 2 Buoys; she was voyaging from Gothenburg and Aberdeen to Dundee with a general cargo.

THE SEVEN PEOPLE WHO DIED
Aavik, Johannes, Third Engineer
Kongas, Eduard, Fireman
Meius, Aarne, Second Officer
Raudsoo, Johannes, Master
Raudsoo, Liis, Mrs and Master's wife
Viitong, Oskar, Able Seaman

Jürisson, Elna Mrs, the cook, died in Dundee Hospital of burns received during the explosion.

U 13 returned to Wilhelmshaven on 14 December. Oblt.z.S. Wolfgang Lüth assumed temporary command between 16 and 28 December 1939.

Oblt.z.S. Max Schulte took command of the boat on 3 January 1940. Max Schulte was born on 24 September 1915 in Wuppertal-Barmen and commenced his naval career in 1933. He served as watch officer on board U 9 between October 1938 and September 1939, before becoming commander of U 9 on 19 September 1939. He was promoted to Kapitänleutnant on 1 October 1940.

(7) U 13 left Wilmhelshaven on 24 January 1940 and sailed for operations off Kinnaird Head.

U 13 torpedoed the 1,168-ton Norwegian steamer *Start* (Aktieselskapet Start, Christiania), on 31 January; she had left Sunderland on 29 January and sailed for Oslo with 1,478 tons of coal and was never seen again.

THE MEN WHO DIED

Andersen, Jens Kristian Berg, Mate
Bartmann, Jacob, Master
Bjørkback, Arvid, Deck boy
Bratlid, Johannes, Seaman
Christensen, Erling, Ordinary Seaman
Fossberg, Oskar Kristian, Seaman
Hansen, Hans Johan, Stoker
Johansen, Guttorm Rørnes, Trimmer
Johansen, Ove Jermund, Able Seaman
Klæboe, Bjarne Schultz, Stoker
Lønne, Johan Arnt Olsen, First Mate
Olsen, Oluf Martin, Engineer
Østensen, Olaf Olai, Steward
Pedersen, Klaus Edvard, Stoker
Thoresen, Sverre Oistein, First Engineer

At 01.43 (continental time) on 1 February 1940 Schulte torpedoed the Swedish steamer *Fram* (Ångfartygs A/B Kjell, Kalmar) off Rosehearty Bay, in Aberdour Bay, west of the Orkney Isles, in position 57° 43' N, 02° 06'W. The 2,458-ton *Fram* (ex-*Russ*) was in ballast and bound for Hartlepool from Stockholm. Nine of her crew of nineteen were lost:

Hansson, Svea Antoinetta, Female Purser
Jansson, Sture Vitalis
Johansson, Ivar Napoleon
Johansson, Sven Emanuel
Lövlimo, Oskar (Norwegian)
Nilsson, Erik Gunnar Herbert
Norbäck, Olof Edvard
Norman, Karl Fredrik Ragnar
Rane, Sven Erik, Captain

U 13 arrived back at Wilhelmshaven on 5 February 1940.

(8) U 13 sailed from Germany on 16 February 1940 for a two-week patrol, before returning on 29 February. Though several vessels were attacked with torpedoes, no hits were achieved.

(9) Schulte had sealed orders when he left Wilhemshaven on 31 March 1940, to take part in Operation *Hartmut*. The orders took U 13 to the Norwegian coast to support German transports and try and protect them from British warships. During her deployment to the Pentland Firth area and east of the Orkneys on 16 April, Schulte claimed a destroyer damaged in a torpedo attack. The 4,935-ton British steamer *Swainby* (Ropner Shipping Co. Ltd, Stockton) was sailing independently from Maaloysund, Vaargo Island, Norway, to Kirkwall in ballast when U 13 torpedoed and sunk her at 17.33 (Continental time) on 17 April, 25 miles north of Muckle Flugga, Shetland Isles. The ship sank in position:

The sloop HMS *Weston* hunted down and sank U 13. (Author's collection)

U 14, sister boat to U 13. (Author's collection)

61° 00' N, 05° 00' W, but her master, Captain Hugh Thompson, and his crew of thirty-seven, took to the boats and landed safely at Nor Wick Bay, Shetland.

At 01.17 (Continental time) on 25 April, Schulte also claimed responsibility for sinking the 1,281-ton Danish steamer *Lily* (Dampskibsselskab aktieselskab Progress) with a torpedo off the mouth of Loch Eriboll. She had left Fowey on 2 April, bound for Aarhus, Denmark via Kirkwall with a cargo of china clay and nothing more was heard from her (lost with all hands).

North-east of Kinnaird's Head on 28 April, the 6,999-ton Sutton & Co. steam tanker *Scottish American* (E.J. Tankers Ltd) was badly damaged in a torpedo attack by U 13 at position 58° 41' N, 04° 40' W. The ship was carrying 9,491 tons of fuel/oil from Trinidad for Scapa Flow when the projectile detonated at 01.29 (Continental time). She was towed to Loch Eriboll, the cargo discharged and the ship repaired. U 13 returned safely to Kiel on 2 May 1940.

FINAL VOYAGE

(10) Schulte left Kiel with U 13 on 26 May 1940 for operations in the southern North Sea. The boat was sent to Cross Sand in order to operate against the traffic voyaging to the river Thames. On 19 May, during the fights of Dünkirchen, heavy traffic with refugees was seen at North Goodwin, so U 13 was ordered to go southwards. On 31 May the U-boat was off Lowestoft and was near convoy FN 184. Unfortunately for twenty-four-year-old Max Schulte, the Falmouth Class sloop HMS *Weston* (Lt-Cdr S.C. Tuke) sighted the boat on the surface. *Weston* report: 30 May 14' SE of Lowestoft – 52, 23' N 02, 01' E – 17 fathoms:

HMS *Weston* in situation ahead of a convoy sighted, beam on against the afterglow of sunset, a U-boat, which she challenged. The U-boat did not reply, but turned towards and crash-dived to about 100ft. *Weston* attacked at once with a pattern of six depth charges (s150ft), three of which exploded fairly close, putting the submarine's depth gauge out of action and causing some other damage. A second pattern of six depth charges was dropped (same settings), smashing numerous instrument glasses and starting minor leaks. *Weston* then sighted HMS *Foresight* on passage to the northward to meet two liners. One of these passed directly over the U-boat and owing to the numerous heavy wakes; contact was lost for about ten minutes. When it was regained *Weston* made a third attack with another pattern of dcs (s 250ft) one of which exploded very close to the conning tower and did considerable damage inside the U-boat. *Weston* lost contact after this attack and began a sweep up and down the tide. The U-boat moved slowly keeping as close to the bottom as possible and touching bottom several times. *Weston* regained contact after half an hour about 4 miles NE of the original position and made two attacks with patterns of d/cs. (same settings).

The fourth attack put all the lights out in the U-boat and caused leaking to become serious; as *Weston* turned to pass over the position after the fifth attack, it surfaced right ahead 400 yards away. *Weston* was not moving fast enough to ram; she opened fire but the crew were seen to be gathering abaft the conning tower, shouting with their hands up. The U-boat sank within two minutes.

ADM 199/1974 - M.011171/40.

The entire crew of three officers, eleven rates, and twelve junior ratings, was picked up, and British divers salvaged the boat, saving some Enigma rotors and the operating manual. However, a set of Admiral Dönitz's 'standing orders' was also recovered, and were later used against him at the Nuremburg Trials. The 'orders' stated: 'Do not rescue any men; do not take them along; and do not take care of any boats of the ship.' Dönitz claimed that he was forced to issue such a notice, because too many of his skippers were wont to carry out humane rescues, which was 'suicide for the U-boat' in the heavily-patrolled waters around Britain.

THE CREWMEN CAPTURED
Bau, Willi, Btn
Binder, Willy, Ob.Gfr.
Demeter, Franz, Masch.
Esterer, Rainer, Oblt.z.S. (IWO)
Fehlbeck, Ernst, Ob.Fk.Mt
Goletz, Heinz, Masch.
Grandjean, Hans-Hugo, Oblt.Ing.
Haloschan, Franz, Gfr.
Herzog, Willi, Ob.Gfr.
Hornschuh, Ernst, Masch.
Kania, Heinz, Mech.Gfr.
Kuppers, Heinrich, Ob.Masch.

Leis, Herbert, Ob.Fk.Mt
Jahnke, Fritz, Masch.Gfr.
Joswig, Herbert, Gfr.
Mayer, Karl, Ob.Masch.
Mohr, Karl, Ob.Gfr.
Reinel, Herbert, Btn
Riese. Heinz, Masch.Gfr.
Schekatz, Ernst, Masch.Gfr
Schrepper, Helmut, Mech.Mt.
Schulze, Fritz, Stb.Gfr
Schulte, Max, Oblt.z.S.
Surm, Herbert, Ob.Masch.
Uberscher, Otto, Fk.Ob.Gfr.

WRECK-SITE

The wreck sits in a 1m scour and is orientated in an east-north-east to west-south-west direction. It lies on a seabed of sand and gravel, in a general depth of 28m (91.8ft), being the lowest astronomical depth. The boat is upright and intact, with the conning tower still in place and a directional finding aerial mounted just to the fore of the conning tower. The conning tower hatch is open and the wreck lies with a 45-degree tilt to starboard. Some parts of the external casing have disintegrated, revealing the pressure hull beneath, and soft corals have established themselves on some of the external casing. There is no mention in the report of the propellers or torpedo tubes.

UC 2, SM IMPERIAL U-BOAT

DATE OF LOSS: 2 July 1916
DEPTH: 22m
REFERENCE: 52 26'.611 N, 001 49'.406 E
LOCATION: 3 nautical miles SE of Lowestoft

The destruction of First World War mine-laying U-boat UC 2 is perhaps more remarkable for the aftermath than for the actual sinking.

Type: UCI coastal mine-laying boat *Builders*: AG Vulcan, Hamburg for Kaiserliche Deutsche Marine *Ordered*: 23 November 1914, within the batch of UC 1–UC 10 *Keel laid*: as Yard No.46 *Launched*: 12 May 1915 *Commissioned*: by Oberleutnant zur See Karl Mey on 17 May 1915

TECHNICAL SPECIFICATIONS

Hull: Single *Surface displacement*: 168 tons *U/Dt*: 183 tons *LBDH*: 33.99m x 3.15m x 3.04m x 6.30m *Machinery*: 1 x 90ps Daimler diesel *Props*: 1 bronze *S/Sp*: 6.20 knots *Op/R*: 780 nautical miles at 5 knots *Sub/R*: 50 nautical miles at 4 knots *U/Power*: 1 x 175ps electric motor giving 5.22 knots *Batteries*: Lead/acid/accumulators *Fuel/Cap*: 3 tons *Torpedo tubes*: None *Torpedoes*: None *Guns*: 1 machine gun *Mine chutes*: 6 x 100cm (39.37in) *Mines*: 12 x UC 120 *Diving*: Max-op-depth 50m (164ft) and 33–36 seconds to crash-dive *Complement*: 1 officer and 13 ratings

Oblt.z.S. Karl Mey was the boat's only commander.

(1) On 24 June 1915, UC 2 departed Hamburg and sailed to Zeebrugge, where she arrived on 25 June and was formally transferred to the Flandern U-Flottille, joining the sixteen other boats. The base had just become operational on 29 March 1915, under the command of the veteran, Kplt. Bertenbach. During the early months of the First World War surface warships had laid most of the minefields off the English east coast.

FINAL VOYAGE

(2) Loaded with his full complement of twelve mines, Karl Mey departed Zeebrugge with UC 2 on the night of 29 June 1915; his mission was to lay mines off Lowestoft. Mey sailed to his designated area at his maximum speed of 6 knots on the surface and laid one small minefield off Great Yarmouth. At 14.50 on 2 July 1915, the 512-ton British coaster SS *Cottingham* was travelling at 8½ knots and was en-route from Calais to Leith when she struck an underwater object while passing through the Stanford Channel, approaching Yarmouth Roads. The master of the steamship Captain Colin Mitchell reported the incident to a patrol vessel, describing a violent blow felt on the starboard quarter, followed by another on the port side, then near the bow. At Leith the steamer was examined and all that was found was a 'very slight graze and scratches'. Captain Mitchell also claimed to have also seen a mass of bubbles rise up, 'as though a strong blast of air had come from below, and with a powerful smell of gas and then I saw some oil on the water'. The captain was so convinced that his ship had struck a submarine that minesweepers were ordered to the site. The minesweeper's wires fouled an obstruction, so indicator nets were laid immediately and then they waited. At 21.40 a massive underwater explosion occurred in the vicinity of the obstruction. Under Cdr G.N. Ballard of HMS *Halcyon*, divers were sent down from both HMS *Halcyon* and *Dryad*. The divers reported that the wreck of a new German mine-laying submarine had been found lying in just 57ft, but diving was made difficult due to strong currents and soup-like visibility. They claimed that the boat had seven mine-chutes, with mines in the three foremost and none in the other four. This type of U-boat only had six chutes and carried two mines in each chute, but the divers were unaware of this at the time, plus poor conditions may have contributed to the confused observation.

On 11 July Lowestoft reported that the U-boat had detonated one of her own mines. Divers found 47ft of the bow and amidships section, including the conning tower, but the stern end was missing. The rounded bow had no torpedo tubes and there were two plates measuring 2ft long by 14in wide, one on each side of the hull. From the stem on the starboard side extended a large hole, and plates here were somewhat warped and the edges rather jagged. In the boat's upper casing 12ft forward of the conning tower, the metal had been ripped open, leaving a 3ft-deep cut, apparently caused by the steamer slicing into it. The 'lost' stern section of the U-boat was found in the latter part of July and from it a diver retrieved some mis-shapen pieces of an accumulator. More dives produced bits of the sinker of another exploded mine, with a bit of the mooring still attached. Fragments of the wireless aerial, several stanchions, stays and pieces of wire were also salvaged in the operations. Several live mines were discovered and the patrols blew two of them up. However, three mines, with sinkers complete, were recovered and the first one raised was forwarded to *Vernon* for examination. The sinkers were reported as: 'a most complicated and ingenious mechanism…fitted with rollers to enable it to be dropped or pushed out of the tube' and these required further investigation by the Admiralty. A diver managed to get as far as 12ft into the stern section by 8 August and found mess tins and fragments of clothing; he also retrieved bits of accumulators from the batteries.

It was suggested by A.A. Ellison, the captain-in-charge at Lowestoft, that by passing wires through the mine chutes it would be possible to raise the fore section and acquire more information about the mine-laying system, but lifting never happened. However, a very distorted portion of outer skin, 25ft long and 9ft across, with several brass tallies, was lifted. There is no record of documents being found. On 13 July Admiral Oliver approved the ending of diving and the destruction of the remains of the U-boat. A.A. Ellison received an Admiralty telegram on 17 July, instructing him to blow the wreck up with guncotton, rather than an explosive sweep. Ellison was in favour of saving the wreck, writing a letter on 8 August suggesting to Admiral W.R. Hall that it would not be difficult to raise the fore part. Hall's reply was swift, 'Altho' there may be advantages in raising the wreck, there are also grave disadvantages – and I think the latter are more important'. On 24 August Ellison reported that 49lb of guncotton had been exploded in two mine tubes and the conning tower, plus two of the mines, had also detonated. What remained was reported as 'now a shattered wreck'.

Reports given to the Admiralty by the divers about the submarine did prove very positive though, because it led to alterations in the design of the six 'E' Class boats still under construction; E24, E34, E41, E45, E46 and E51. Mine chutes replaced the beam torpedo tubes situated in the saddle tanks and the boats carried twenty mines.

It was not until some time later that the wreck was identified as Oblt.z.S. Karl Mey's little submarine UC 2.

Confusion still reigns today as to what actually happened to UC 2. She was first accidentally struck in three places by the steamer *Cottingham* and the hull split open; that alone could have caused her to sink. The bodies of the fifteen crew, including that of Oblt. z.S. Karl Mey, were found in the flooded stern section, which seems to suggest that they at least had time to evacuate the bow before it flooded.

Then, during their sweep with nets, the minesweepers had forced one of her mines up against the stern casing, blasting a big hole in the boat. The submarine was blown up and it was confirmed that her own mine had destroyed the boat and her crew. It is also feasible that when she sank to the bottom, she settled against one of her own mines, which then detonated as a result of sweepers moving her around.

On 18 July Admiral Hall awarded *Cottingham* £500 for destroying the U-boat, but that was before he had learned it was sunk by an explosion and not ramming. Hall later reduced the amount to £200 and added: '…it would be well when giving the award to demand secrecy as to the locality.' NARA: T-1022, Roll 81, PG61885

UC 2 sank no vessels during her short career.

THE MEN WHO DIED IN UC 2
Bock, Ob.Hzr
Bruhn, Btn.Mt
Clausen, Ob.Stn.Mt
Drebelow, F.T.Ober Gast der Reserve
Federmann, Ob.Mts. der Reserve
Kade, Mn.Ing.Asp.
Kastner, Masch.Mt
Lemcke, Ob.Masch.Mt
Mey, Oblt.z.S.
Pahnke, Ob.Btn.Mt
Rath, Hzr
Scharnberg, Ob.Btn.Mt der Reserve
Spauke, Mts.
Stieper, Masch.Mt
Wolter, Masch.Anw.

WRECK-SITE

All that is left of the wreck these days are some broken battered plates and a small section of the boat, which is mostly buried. Otherwise very little of it remains to be seen.

C16, HM SUBMARINE

DATE OF LOSS: 16 April 1917
LOCATION: Sunk off Harwich and raised

Type: 'C' Class British coastal patrol boat of Group I   *Pennant No.*: I.46   *Builders*: Vickers Yard, Barrow-in-Furness for Royal Navy   *Ordered*: for 1906–1907 programme (C12–C18)   *Keel laid*: as Yard No.355 on 14 December 1906   *Launched*: 19 March 1908   *Completed*: 5 June 1908

TECHNICAL SPECIFICATIONS

Hull: Single   *Surface displacement*: 290 tons   *U/Dt*: 320 tons   *LBD*: 43.88m x 4.11m x 3.50m   *Machinery*: 1 x 600hp 16-cylinder Vickers petrol engine   *Props*: 1 bronze x 3-blade 1.70m (5ft-7in) diameter   *S/Sp*: 12 knots   *Op/R*: 740 nautical miles at 12 knots, or 1,000 nautical miles at 8.7 knots and 10-day endurance   *Sub/R*: 16 nautical miles at 8 knots   *U/Power*: 1 x 200hp electric motors giving 7½ knots max. and 7 knots service speed   *Batteries*: Exide accumulators of 66 tons (20 per cent of submerged displacement)   *Fuel/Cap*: 15½ tons   *Armament*: 2 x 45.72cm bow torpedo tubes   *Torpedoes*: 4 x 45.72cm (18in)   *Guns*: None   *Diving*: Max-op-depth 30.48m (100ft)   *Complement*: 2 officers and 14 ratings   *Cost to build*: £47,000

C16 was present when B2 was accidentally rammed (see Chapter Four). On 16 April 1917, C16 (Lt Harold Boase – aged twenty-five) was engaged in a series of routine exercises 7 miles off Harwich. Included in this 8th Flotilla exercise was C25 and the destroyer *Melampus* (Lt-Cdr Bignell).

FINAL VOYAGE

It was a fine, clear day. Each submarine was required to make a dummy attack at periscope depth on the destroyer. C25 made her attack then surfaced. The men on the destroyer's bridge (including Lt Arthur Forbes, soon to die in H5) looked on with interest as C16 made her attack. At 09.47 her periscope was spotted 25 yards off the port bow, closing fast on a course that if maintained, would bring C16 across the bows of the destroyer (upon later reflection, Lt Forbes believed that the submarine was rising and facing away from the destroyer). *Melampus* immediately went full astern; her helm put to hard a starboard. It was to no avail. The impact was felt as a slight bump near the destroyer's stern. Lt-Cdr Bignell:

> C16's periscope was seen 2 points on the bow about 25 yards away as if crossing ahead and her conning tower struck *Melampus* right aft. She never came to the surface and a large amount of air came up for half an hour.

Lt-Cdr Bignell buoyed the position of the water disturbance. News of the calamity was radioed to Harwich. The position given was ¾ mile north of the Rough Wreck Light Vessel. *Melampus* remained in the area for some time looking for survivors. The depth

HM S/M C16. (Author's collection)

was after all only 45ft (13.7m). *Melampus* was forced to return to harbour due to damage sustained, but she left a minesweeper to watch for survivors. At 16.10 the submarine was located by sweep. It is sad to relate that no survivors were recovered. The reader might like to compare this incident with the L24 disaster.

When C16 was raised, her wreck provided graphic evidence as to what had taken place. It was clear from damage on both *Melampus* and C16 that the submarine had struck the starboard bow of the destroyer. The conning tower and periscope were both bent to port. The fore hydroplanes were set at a 15-degree rise, but the aft planes conversely were at a 10-degree dive. It was observed that the fore hatch was open and unclipped. A lead weight had slipped under the seating, preventing its closure. The full implications of this discovery were only to be understood later.

Not only had the crew survived for some time; they had also made saving the boat a higher priority than preserving their own lives. The salvage men were able to reconstruct what had happened within the boat. C16 had sunk as a result of the weight of water flooding into the conning tower rather than damage to the pressure hull. The impact had distorted the inner conning tower hatch causing a steady flow of water to leak into the submarine. The leak had been controlled by stuffing clothes into the coaming. The pumps had also been used until the ingress of water forced the crew to abandon the machinery and turn to hand pumps instead. Damaged air pipes prevented the crew from blowing the boat to the surface but it was observed that No.1 tank had been blown in order to edge the bows closer. The gauge was found to read 16ft. When the body of First Lieutenant Anderson was found in the starboard torpedo tube, Lt Boase's plan became clear. He had opted to fire 1st-Lt Anderson out of the tube in the desperate hope that his release might contribute vital information to the rescue effort. The courage required for a man to allow himself to be fired from a flooded torpedo tube defies language and imagination, but this course of action was inspired by German escapes. This time, however, the attempt had failed. The salvage men discovered the following message in a watertight bag tied to 1st-Lt Sam Anderson's wrist:

'WE ARE IN 16 FEET OF WATER. THE WAY TO GET US OUT IS TO LIFT THE BOWS
BY THE SPECTACLE AND HAUL US OUT OF THE BOAT THROUGH THE TUBES.
H.BOASE'

By 16.30 growing carbon dioxide levels forced Lieutenant Boase to change tack. He
marshalled his crew in the fore-ends under the hatch. The inner door of one of the
torpedo tubes was carefully opened to flood the boat and the torpedo chamber door was
clipped to seal off the compartment – a flooded boat does not necessarily doom the crew.
Providing the survivors can maintain their sensibilities while flooding takes place, once the
water reaches a certain level within the sealed compartment, pressure will automatically
equalise. It is theoretically possible to open the hatch and ascend to the surface – indeed
many have succeeded, as various stories in this book demonstrate. However, fate played
the cruellest of tricks on the crew of C16. A jammed fender prevented the hatch from
opening more than 10in. Worse still, the lead weight attached to the fender slipped,
preventing the hatch from closing back on its seating. The compressed air escaped. The
airlock was broken and the North Sea flooded into the tiny submarine, drowning all on
board.

C16 was present when B2 was accidentally rammed. Lt Boase and his nine crew are
buried in the Submarine Enclosure in the RN plot at the Church of St Mary, Shotley,
Suffolk, where there is an attractive memorial (bodies said to be washed up from a
German submarine are also buried here in Shotley).
ADM 137/3709 – ADM137/3251 – ADM 137/ 3657

Petty Officer Winstanley of HM S/M C16.
(RN Submarine Museum)

HM S/M E54. (Author's collection)

HM S/M E41. (RN Submarine Museum)

THE MEN WHO DIED IN C16

Anderson, Samuel, Mate
Boase, Harold, Lieutenant
Brooks, John, Artificer First
Burton, Ernest, Leading Seaman
Clarke, Frederick John, Leading Stoker
Clemmett, Phillip George, Stoker First
Cope, George Frederick, Leading Seaman
Cowls, Frederick John, Artificer Fourth
Down, James, Petty Officer Stoker
Fitzgerald, John Jeremiah, Signalman
Freestone, Francis, Leading Stoker
Gaunt, John, Petty Officer
Hill, James, Able Seaman (lost 28 March 1915)
Howie, John Henry, Able Seaman
Humphreys, Alfred Stanley, Able Seaman
Linton, Andrew, Stoker First
Puddington, Arthur, Able Seaman

Note: Able Seaman J. Hill (Buoy Jumper) was lost overboard on 28 March 1915. He was the 'Buoy Jumper' who, as the boat came into moor onto the buoy, jumped over with rope to tie up. However, AB Hill missed, or slipped, and was lost while the boat was at Jarrow-on-Tyne.

WRECK-SITE
The submarine was raised.

HM S/M E4, showing unusual four-gun armament. (RN Submarine Museum)

E4 AND E41, HM SUBMARINES

DATE OF LOSS: 15 August 1916
LOCATION: Sunk off Harwich following a collision
HM Submarines E4 and E41 were both 'E' Class overseas
patrol submarines with some slightly different specifications.

E4, HM SUBMARINE

Type: 'E' Class British overseas submarine of Group I (E1–E6) **Pennant No.:** 84 **Builders:** Vickers Armstrong Ltd, Barrow-in-Furness for Royal Navy **Ordered:** for 1910–1911 programme **Keel laid:** as Yard No.416 on 16 May 1911 **Launched:** 5 February 1912 **Completed:** 4 January 1913

TECHNICAL SPECIFICATIONS

Hull: Admiralty saddle-tank-type **Surface displacement:** 655 tons **U/Dt:** 795 tons **LBD:** 53.64m x 6.95m x 3.65m **Machinery:** 2 x 800bhp Vickers Admiralty 8-cylinder diesels **Props:** 2 bronze x 3-blade of 1.60m (5¼ft) diameter **S/Sp:** 15 knots, (14 knots when hydroplane guards lowered) **Op/R:** 3,000 nautical miles at 10 knots or 1,500 nautical miles at full power **U/Power:** 2 x 420hp electric motors giving 9 knots **Batteries:** 2 x 112-cell Exide accumulators **Sub/R:** 65 nautical miles at 5 knots or 10 nautical miles at 9 knots and full-speed duration of 1 hour and 10 minutes **Armament:** 4 x 45.72cm torpedo tubes (1 bow, 2 beam and 1 stern) **Torpedoes:** 8 x 45.72cm (18in) **Guns:** 1 x 4-pounder (1.81kg) deck gun **Diving:** Max-op-depth 30.48m (100ft) **Complement:** 30 (Batteries manufactured by Mercury were tried on this first group)

At the outbreak of the First World War the pennant numbers changed to the name of the boat. Reference: BR3043

Early gun armament in the First World War was a bit *ad hoc* and boats were fitted with what was available. Hence gun armament varied, depending on what the boats were being used for at the time. Photographic evidence shows that during one period, E4 was equipped with four deck guns, two forward and two facing aft. Some boats, including E4 and E6, were fitted with extra guns to use against Zeppelins. However, submarines were susceptible to damage and underwater drag also increased when guns were fitted, so eventually the anti-Zeppelin activity was left to the flyers. The gun specifications given in technical data usually are the type and configuration used during the majority of time that the boat was armed, depending on duties and location. Early 'E' Class boats were unarmed until hostilities broke out. A similar thing happened at the outbreak of the Second World War, with some 'U' Class boats being retro-fitted with leftover First World War guns.

The Harwich based E4 (Lt-Cdr Ernest Leir) was operating in the Heligoland Bight when D5 made her failed torpedo attack upon *Rostock*. E4 is said to have returned with valuable intelligence. On 28 August, in the course of 'The Battle of the Heligoland Bight', E4 rescued ten men from one of HMS *Defender*'s whalers. The men had been attempting to save German sailors when *Defender* was menaced by a more powerful adversary. The ship was forced to abandon its rescue party. Fortunately Leir was at hand and E4 rescued *Defender*'s men plus three German sailors seized as 'samples'. During the first autumn of the First World War, E4 carried out several patrols in the Heligoland Bight. Leir was particularly keen on attacking U-boats in their own back yard. U 23 narrowly escaped one of E4's torpedoes. Edwards, in *We Dive at Dawn*, relates how Leir stern-chased an unknown U-boat deep

HM S/M E41 and E42 at Harwich. (RN Submarine Museum)

into German territorial waters in the hope that it would 'stand and fight'. Throughout the pursuit, Leir bombarded the U-boat with provocative signals such as 'How many women and children have you killed today then?' Ernest Leir, 'The Arch thief', was one of the great characters of the Submarine Service. He is believed to have been one of the first to fly the Jolly Roger pennant at Harwich, not least because the art of piracy came naturally to him (see Volume 3). Julian Tenison replaced Leir as skipper of E4 in early 1916. E4 was attacked and nearly bombed by a German seaplane. Tenison's swift presence of mind saved the boat. As the seaplane was about to drop its bomb, Tenison began waving in a friendly gesture. The pilot hesitated momentarily, fearing he was about to bomb a U-boat. The plane overshot E4. The gesture bought E4 just enough time to reach a safe depth.

E41, HM SUBMARINE

Type: 'E' Class British overseas submarine of Group III (E19–E56) *Pennant No.:* E41 *Builders:* Cammell Laird, Birkenhead, for Royal Navy *Ordered:* for 1914 Emergency War programme *Keel laid:* 15 February 1915 *Launched:* 26 July 1915 *Completed:* February 1916

TECHNICAL SPECIFICATIONS

Hull: Admiralty saddle-tank-type *Surface displacement:* 667 tons *U/Dt:* 807 tons *LBD:* 55.17m x 6.86m x 3.81m *Machinery:* 2 x 800bhp Vickers Admiralty 8-cylinder diesels *Props:* 2 bronze *S/Sp:* 15¼ knots *Op/R:* 3,225 nautical miles at 10 knots *Sub/R:* 85 nautical miles at 5 knots *U/Power:* 2 x 420hp electric motors giving 9¾ knots *Batteries:* 2 x 112-cell Exide accumulators *Fuel/Cap:* 41.67 tons in 8 tanks and 5.28 tons of 'lubricating oil' in 2 tanks *Armament:* 3 x 45.72cm torpedo tubes, (2 bow, 1 stern tube and 2 beam (mine chutes) *Torpedoes:* 10 x 45.72cm (18in) *Mines:* 20 *Guns:* 1 x 5.44kg quick-firing (12-pounder) and 1 x 0.91kg (2-pounder) pom-pom *Complement:* 3 officers and 27 ratings *Diving:* Max-designed depth 60.96m (200ft)

Note: E40 struck bottom at 53 fathoms (318ft or 96.92m) and survived – a testimony to the builder's workmanship at Palmers on the Tyne.

The 'E' Class boats were the first British type of submarine with beam tubes and sub-division by watertight bulkheads. E41 was also one of another five 'E' Class submarines (E24, E34, E45, E46 and E51) still under construction when RN divers discovered the mine-laying capability of the Imperial U-boat UC 2, which was sunk off Lowestoft. The information led to the two beam torpedo tubes being exchanged for mine chutes situated in the saddle tanks, and these boats would carry twenty mines.

E41 carried out a number of pioneering and dangerous mine-laying missions in the approaches to the Heligoland Bight, notably mine-laying off the island of Vlieland on 12 July. In late July 1916 the boat was laying in heavy weather when a series of heavy explosions were heard astern at regular intervals. British Elia mines were not very reliable and were known to explode prematurely. Naturally the prevailing instinct was to lay the cargo and return home but the laying mechanism chose that moment to jam. E41 was forced to return to Harwich in severe weather conditions with four highly unstable mines onboard.

FINAL VOYAGE

On 15 August 1916 the 9th Flotilla carried out a series of North Sea exercises, E41 (Lt Alfred Winser) was travelling at 12 knots when E4's periscope appeared on a collision course 50 yards off her starboard bow. E41 stopped her engines, but not before E4 (Lt-Cdr Julian Tenison) had collided with her forward of the bridge. Captain sent the following account to Admiralty:

> E41 carried out the first run successfully, while E31 and E4 attacked her. As E16 had been delayed, E41 was ordered to carry out the second run while the same two submarines attacked. When E41, who was steering 100 degrees at 12k was about 1600 yards E by N of the Cork Sand Buoy, the periscope of E4 suddenly appeared 3 points on the starboard bow, 50 yards away, apparently steering about 320 degrees and sailing fast.

Sub Lt. T Voysey was in the control room of E41:

> I first became aware that there was something wrong when the telegraph rang 'Stop Both'. Shortly afterwards I felt a slight bump followed by a strange noise... I shouted to close the fore bulkhead door. As I shouted I noticed that the water was coming in at the fore-end of the battery, starboard side abreast the bunk. Water was flooding in rapidly so I gave the order, 'Everyone up' and had the order passed along to the engine room. I then stood at the foot of the conning tower while the hands were going up...about four more men came up then the boat appeared to dive below the surface. The water came in very fast through the upper conning tower hatch. After the hatch closed it was noted the air pressure in the boat was rising and this pressure eventually blew open the hatch and escaping air carried Sub Lt Money and myself with it.

Stoker PO Brown:

> Something was heard to come into contact with the bottom of the boat for'rard and it hit twice in quick succession. The engine telegraph rang 'Out Clutches'. I took out the port clutch and closed the muffler valve. I then heard the report that the boat was making water. I proceeded for'rard to ascertain the position of the leak and came to the conclusion she was holed low down. My first instinct was to close the conning tower hatch. At this point the CERA asked if all hands were out of the engine room, I replied that I would go aft and find out...I found a man going for'rard so I ordered him to keep his head and his lifebelt on and to wait his turn at the foot of the conning tower. Finding there was no one else aft returned for'rard, I put on a life belt and closed the valve on the air trunk through the engine room bulkhead.

The men on the bridge and casing had no idea that E41 was sinking by the bow. Indeed when he saw the men evacuating the boat, Lt Winser ordered them back, smartly. However, when it was reported that the water was gurgling over the battery boards, Lt Winser relented:

> I then allowed the men to continue coming up and called down the voice-pipe to bring up life-belts. I ordered the signalman to report that we were sinking. The next moment the water was above the conning tower

HMS *Firedrake* (Cdr Tillard), which had been monitoring the exercise, took less than two minutes to reach the scene of the collision.

Of the twenty men who escaped from the submarine, eighteen were picked up. Not everyone had received notice to abandon ship. Three men were left behind, including Petty Officer William Brown in the engine room. Two of the men were running forward to the control room when the sinking submarine struck the seabed. As the boat flooded they found themselves in an airlock beneath the control tower. The men, an ERA and a stoker, decided to take their chances and swam upwards past the ladder towards the diminishing bright patch marking the open conning tower hatch. They successfully reached the surface, much to the amazement of the survivors shivering on *Firedrake*'s deck.

PO Brown, still trapped below, said:

> The control room was partly flooded and in darkness Chlorine gas began to come through. I closed the engine room door and started to unscrew the clips of the torpedo hatch above me. At this juncture the engine room was in complete darkness with the exception of the port pilot lamp, which was evidently burning through 'earth'. The water was slowly rising in the engine room through the voice pipes which I had left open to relieve the pressure on the bulkhead door.

PO Brown now set about disconnecting the torpedo hatch from its gearing and removing the clips – a Herculean task for one man. Brown had no option but to wait until there was sufficient pressure within the submarine to ease the hatch open. It should be borne in mind at this point that PO Brown was alone in a sunken submarine, with ice-cold water up to his waist. He was working in total darkness apart from the guttering flash of numerous shorting fuses and retching under the effect of chlorine gas fumes. Lesser men might have buckled against such immense odds. Fortunately William Brown was made of sterner stuff. Brown required no blueprint to find his way around an 'E' Class submarine; he could, quite literally, find his way in the dark.

> The heat at this time was excessive so I decided to rest awhile. I tried flooding the stern tube first, but I could open neither the stern cap nor the rear door. As I made my way for'rard again, I received several nasty shocks from the switchboards. All my attempts to flood the boat failed until I turned to open the muffler valve and the test cocks on the group-exhaust valves, followed by the engine room bulkhead scuttles. That did the trick so I climbed up on top of one of the engines under the hatch.
>
> Chlorine gas came in as well as water. I tried three times to lift the hatch but each time could open it only half way, and each time air rushed out through it and the hatch fell down...I then decided to flood the boat rapidly through the deadlight, until the water came up level with the hatch coaming. I was then able to open the hatch and rise to the surface.

By this time, PO Brown was standing with ice-cold water up to his jaw-line before the hatch would open. One and a half hours after E41 sank, PO Brown popped up on the surface to be rescued.

There were no survivors from the thirty-three strong crew of HMS E4. Both submarines were located and salvaged within the next two months, E41 returning to the 9th Flotilla at Harwich. One of the E41 survivors, ERA Bullock, actually volunteered to return to the boat. Indeed E41 was responsible for laying a productive defensive minefield in these very waters in April 1918. The tradition of salvaging sunken submarines prior to re-commissioning is worth bearing in mind with regard to the *Thetis* controversy of 1939. E4 had saved the crew of HMS *Defender* together with three German survivors on 28 August 1914.

THE MEN WHO DIED IN E41

Ashby, Christopher John, Petty Officer
Beail, Albert Victor, Able Seaman
Calvo, George, Stoker.1st
Daniels, Charles Ceal, Stoker.1st
Evans, Jack, Stoker.1st
Frener, Walter, Leading Stoker
Garland, John, Leading Stoker
Gaunt, Frederick Henry, Able Seaman
Grant, William Alexander, Leading Seaman
Gribble, Frederick, Stoker.1st
Klemp, Charles Thomas, Lieutenant RNR
Moncton, Sidney, Engine Room Artificer.4th
Roach, George Frederick, Able Seaman
Saywell, Herbert Nelson, E.R. Artificer.3rd
Stewart, Alfred George, Able Seaman
Wells, John, Stoker.1st
(Herbert Nelson Saywell is buried in Ostende, Belgium)

THE MEN WHO DIED IN E4

Bacon, Cyril, Stoker.1st
Bacon , James, Stoker.1st
Bagwell, Andrew, Able Seaman
Baker, Henry Tyneside, Engine Room Artificer.1st
Baldock, Alfred Henry, Leading Seaman
Bennett, George Henry, Stoker.1st
Broad, Alfred Henry, Able Seaman
Carpenter, Henry George, Leading Seaman
Cooley, Frank Edward, Able Seaman
Denison, John, Boy Telegraphist (24 December 1899)
Dudley, Charles Henry, Leading Stoker
Dundee-Hooper, Stewart Briscoe, Lieutenant
Fenwick, William Thackray, Able Seaman
Gadsby, William Wallace, Petty Officer Stoker
Gibson, John William, Leading Stoker
Halls, William Charles Edward, Stoker.1st
Hewlett, Harry, Leading Stoker.
Hunter, William, Lieutenant RNR
Hodgson, Ronald William, E.R.Artificer.4th
Jolliffe, Francis Henry, Leading Seaman
Matthews, Frank Richardson, Leading Seaman
Millard, Jocelyn Alfred, E.R.Artificer.3rd
Nichols, Frederick Noel, Able Seaman

Preskett, Harry, Leading Seaman
Repper, Charles, Petty Officer
Smith, Leonard William, Leading Telegraphist
Salisbury, James Henry, Petty Officer
Snow, Sidney, Stoker.1st
Tenison, Julian T., Lieutenant Commander
Tovey, Maurice William, Signalman
Ward, John James, Stoker.1st
Warwick, John Coster, E.R. Artificer.3rd

Some of these men rest alongside the crew of C16 in the Submarine Enclosure at St Mary's Church at Shotley, Suffolk.

ADM 1/8466/210 – ADM 1/8460/26

E6, HM SUBMARINE

DATE OF LOSS: 26 December 1915
DEPTH: 18m
REFERENCE: 51 49'.781 N, 001 37'.893 E
LOCATION: Near Sunk Light Vessel off Harwich

Type: 'E' Class British overseas submarine of Group I (E1–E6)   *Pennant No.*: I.86   *Builders*: Vickers-Armstrong Ltd, Barrow-in-Furness for Royal Navy   *Ordered*: for 1910–1911 programme   *Keel laid*: as Yard No.418 on 12 September 1911   *Launched*: 12 November 1912   *Completed*: 15 October 1913   *Commissioned*: at Portsmouth 8th Submarine Flotilla by Lt-Cdr C.P. Talbot, on 17 October 1913

TECHNICAL SPECIFICATIONS
Hull: Admiralty saddle-tank type   *Surface displacement*: 655 tons   *U/Dt*: 795 tons   *LBD*: 53.64m x 6.95m x 3.65m   *Machinery*: 2 x 800bhp Vickers Admiralty 8-cylinder diesels   *Props*: bronze x 3-blade of 1.60m (5¼ft) diameter   *S/Sp*: 15 knots, (14 knots when hydroplane guards lowered)   *p/R*: 3,000 nautical miles at 10 knots or 1,500 nautical miles at full power   *U/Power*: 2 x 420hp electric motors gave 9 knots   *Batteries*: 2 x 112-cell Exide accumulators   *Sub/R*: 65 autical miles at 5 knots or 10 nautical miles at 9 knots and full speed duration of 1 hour and 10 minutes   *Armament*: 4 x 45.72cm torpedo tubes (1 bow, 2 beam and 1 stern)   *Torpedoes*: 8 x 45.72cm (18in)   *Guns*: 1 x 4-pounder (1.81kg) deck gun   *Diving*: Max-op-depth 30.48m (100ft)   *Complement*: 30 (Batteries manufactured by Mercury were tried on this first group). Reference: BR3043

During anti-Zeppelins operations, E6 was temporarily fitted with two 12-pounder deck guns situated just aft of the conning tower

HM S/M E6 was part of the 8th Submarine Flotilla based at Harwich. The boat had an eventful career. Within hours of the declaration of war, E6 (Lt-Cdr Talbot) was patrolling within the Heligoland Bight, having been towed to her station by destroyers *Amethyst* and *Ariel*. In late August 1914 the boat acted as a live bait trap in the Battle of the Heligoland Bight. At 11.45 on 28 August 1914, Talbot was about to torpedo an enemy cruiser when a White Ensign was spotted just in time. E6 mistook HMS *Lowestoft* for an enemy cruiser and fired a torpedo at her, but fortunately it missed. On 25 September 1914 a German

HM S/M E6.

mine fouled the hydroplane mechanism off Norderney. On the return journey, a Zeppelin attacked the boat. On 20 October 1915, when under the command of Lt Byron, E6 attacked SMS *Danzig*; two explosions were heard, but the German warship survived, undamaged.

FINAL VOYAGE

By late 1915 the British Admiralty had decided that German U-boats would have to reach the North Sea via Horns Reef. On Christmas Day 1915, thirty-year-old Lt-Cdr W. J. Foster in HM Submarine E6 was ordered to proceed to the area of Horns Reef to intercept any U-boats passing that way. Foster left Harwich in E6 on 26 December and his patrol was due to last approximately six days, weather permitting. The area around Harwich had previously been mined and earlier that same morning the requisitioned armed trawler *Resono* (Admiralty No.1042) had detonated a mine and been lost with all hands in that same vicinity. A patrolling torpedo boat had seen E6 leaving and warned Lt-Cdr Foster that he was heading into danger, but it appears either the advice was not passed on, or Lt-Cdr Foster ignored the warning and continued on course. The crew of the torpedo boat watched as E6 detonated a mine and disappeared in a ball of smoke, leaving only some oil and flotsam on the surface. In all, thirty-eight lives were lost.

The Kaiser's Imperial U-boat UC 5 had laid the minefield earlier and was also responsible for the field that sank the British destroyer HMS *Lightning* off Kentish Knock on 30 June 1915.

But nemesis was waiting in the wings for UC 5 (see page 206) also.

THE MEN WHO DIED IN E6

Adams, Harry, Chief Stoker
Barry, John, Able Seaman
Bellingham, Harold William, Stoker.1st
Bowerman, George Joseph Hastings, Tele.
Burnett, George Logan, Chief E.R.Artificer.2nd

Cobb, Richard George, Able Seaman
Coltart, William, Petty Officer.1st
Coyles, George, Stoker
Davies, Albert, Petty Officer Stoker
Desborough, William George, Leading Seaman
Foster, William John, Lieutenant Commander
Gledhill, Alfred, Lieutenant
Hall, Clarence Trigg, Telegraphist
Hammond, Stephen Harris, Able Seaman
Horwood, William George, Stoker
Jackman, Arthur James, Able SeamanJones, James Edward, Stoker.1st
Kipp, Alf Charles, Leading Seaman
Leany, William, Able Seaman
Marrington, Arthur, Petty Officer
Norton, William Frederick, Leading Signalman
Phillott, Charles George Rodney, Lieutenant
Potts, Leonard Guy, Able Seaman
Rolland, James, Engine Room Artificer.4th
Slater, Ernest, Leading Stoker
Stevens, Ernest Edward, Chief E.R. Artificer
Stewart, Robert, Engine Room Artificer.3rd
Taylor, John, Leading Seaman
Tuck, Francis Victor, Stoker.1st
Wallis, William Guy, Stoker.1st
Watts, John James, Leading Stoker
Weatherston, Thomas, Engine Room Artificer
(Petty Officer Coltart, a Royal Navy diver, had earlier assisted in the salvage of A8.)

WRECK-SITE

What is believed to be the wreck of E6 lies a couple of miles from the Sunk Light Vessel. Divers report a large hole where the brass conning tower should be, and the bows are blown completely apart, with other bits of it partially buried under the sand.

UC 9, SM IMPERIAL U-BOAT

DATE OF LOSS: 20 October 1915
DEPTH: Unknown
REFERENCE: 51° 47' N, 01° 37' E (approx.)
LOCATION: Near Long Sands Light and Kentish Knock

Type: UC I coastal mine-laying boat *Builders*: AG Vulcan, Hamburg for Kaiserliche Deutsche Marine *Ordered*: 23 November 1914, within the batch of UC 1–UC 10 *Keel laid*: as Yard No.53 *Launched*: 11 July 1915 *Commissioned*: by Oberleutnant zur See Paul Schürmann on 15 July 1915

TECHNICAL SPECIFICATIONS

Hull: Single *Surface displacement*: 168 tons *U/Dt*: 183 tons *LBDH*: 33.99m x 3.15m x 3.04m x 6.30m *Machinery*: 1 x 90ps Daimler diesel *Props*: 1 bronze *S/Sp*: 6.20 knots *Op/R*: 780 nautical miles at 5 knots *Sub/R*: 50 nautical miles at 4 knots *U/Power*: 1 x

175ps electric motor giving 5.22 knots **Batteries**: Lead/acid/accumulators **Fuel/Cap**: 3 tons *Torpedo tubes*: None **Torpedoes**: None **Guns**: 1 machine gun and rifles *Mine chutes*: 6 x 100cm (39.37in) **Mines**: 12 x UC 120 **Diving**: Max-op-depth 50m (164ft) and 33–36 seconds to crash-dive **Complement**: 1 officer and 13 ratings

UC 9 was assigned to the U-Schule (training flotilla) from the commissioning until 23 September 1915 when she formally transferred to Flandern U-Flottille at Zeebrugge with Oblt.z.S. Paul Schürmann, the CO from 15 July 1915.

UC 9 made two patrols, the first being the transfer to Flanders and the second an operational patrol, but no Allied vessels were sunk.

FINAL VOYAGE
(2) UC 9 departed Zeebrugge on 20 October 1915 with a mission to lay mines off the Long Sands Light Vessel, but the boat failed to return to Flanders. It is possible that UC 9 detonated a British-laid mine or maybe one of her own that detonated prematurely. On 12 November 1915 the body of the chief engineer, Marine Ingenieur Asp Hans Neuhaus, was washed ashore on the Long Sands. Either his body floated out through a hole in the shattered hull, or at least some of the unfortunate crew had attempted a doomed escape, without the benefit of any Dräger equipment.

NARA: T-1022, Roll 63, PG61909

THE MEN WHO DIED IN UC 9
Behrend, Ob.Mts.d.S.I
Bohne, Ob.Masch.Mt
Duve, Btn.Mt.d.Res
Eckhoff, Ob.Mts.
Jork, Hzr
Käsler, Mts.
Keitel, Ob.F.T.Gast
Neuhaus, Mn.Ing.Asp
Outzen, Ob.Mts.
Peters, Btn.Mt.d.Res
Preuss, Masch.Anw
Schürmann, Oblt.z.S
Siekmann, Hzr
Soltau, Masch.Mt
Weller, Mts.
Willandsen, Masch.Mt

WRECK-SITE
The position of the wreck still remains a mystery.

UB 16, SM IMPERIAL U-BOAT

DATE OF LOSS: 10 May 1918
DEPTH: 31m
REFERENCE: 52 06'.630 N, 02 01'.290 E
LOCATION: 14 nautical miles ESE from Aldeburgh

Type: UB I coastal torpedo attack boat *Builders*: A.G. Weser at Bremen for Kaiserliche Deutsche Marine *Ordered*: 25 November 1914, within the batch of UB 16–UB 17 *Keel laid*: as Yard No.230 on 21 February 1915 *Launched*: 26 April 1915 *Commissioned*: by Oberleutnant zur See Hans Valentiner on 12 May 1915

TECHNICAL SPECIFICATIONS

Hull: Single *Surface displacement*: 127 tons *U/Dt*: 141 tons *LBDH*: 27.88m x 3.15m x 3.03m x 7.30m *Machinery*: 1 x 60ps Körting diesel *Props*: 2 bronze *S/Sp*: 7.45 knots *Op/R*: 1,500 nautical miles at 5 knots *Sub/R*: 45 nautical miles at 4 knots *U/Power*: 1 x 120ps electric motor giving 6.24 knots *Batteries*: Lead/acid/accumulators *Fuel/Cap*: 3 tons *Armament*: 2 bow 45cm-torpedo tubes *Guns*: 1 machine gun and rifles *Torpedoes*: 2 x 45cm (17.72in) *Diving*: Max-op-depth 50m (164ft) and 22–33 seconds to crash-dive *Mines*: Later, converted to carry 8 mines in bow section *Complement*: 1 officer and 13 ratings

UB 16 was assigned to the Flandern Flotilla on 1 June 1915. Oblt.z.S. Hans Valentiner served with the boat from 12 May 1915 to 4 April 1916. Valentiner was born on 17 June 1888 and was lost with UB 56 on 19 December 1917. UB 16 made a total of eighty-seven short patrols with ten commanders.

On 12 June 1915, Valentiner torpedoed and sunk the steamer *Leuctra* (SS Leuctra Co. Ltd, St John, N.B). She was carrying linseed from Rosario to Hull. On 26 June, a torpedo from UB 16 struck the SS *Tunisiana* (Furness, Withy & Co. Ltd, London), which was on passage from Montreal for Hull; the ship drifted onto Barnard Sands and became a total loss.

Eleven of her crew of eighteen, and one passenger, were killed when Valentiner torpedoed and sunk the SS *Mangara* (SS Mangara Co. Ltd, Glasgow), which was transporting 2,400 tons of iron ore from Bilbao to Hartlepool. The explosion took place under the No.4 hatch, cabin and poop deck at 11.50 on 28 July. An attempt was made to lower the lifeboats, but she sank within forty-five seconds and the crew found themselves in the sea. The steamer *Croxdale*, which rescued the master, pilot and three crewmen, sighted the U-boat's periscope. The SS *Canto* also tried to assist, but was lucky to get away when UB 16's periscope was sighted just 40 yards away, and a torpedo that had just been fired missed her stern end by just a few feet. UB 16 actually chased the *Canto*, which escaped, but then returned to the scene and rescued three men in a lifeboat and landed them at Yarmouth. Following a torpedo strike, the SS *Perth* (Ince Shipping Co. Ltd) also went down, while in ballast, travelling from Fécamp to Hull. A seaman on watch duty saw the U-boat surface and fire the torpedo that shattered the ship's fore part, where the chief engineer and five of the crew were killed. Captain McDonald and the surviving seven men escaped in the ship's boat; a pilot boat picked them up and took them to Great Yarmouth, having been adrift for seven hours.

Oblt.z.S. Paul Hundius assumed command on 5 April 1916. He was later promoted to Kapitänleutnant and was awarded the *Pour le Mérite* on 18 August 1918, while serving on UB 103. Without any warning, Hundius torpedoed the SS *Robert Adamson* (James Westoll, Sunderland), which sank without loss of life while en-route from Dundee to Le Havre with a cargo of pit props on 10 April 1916. A torpedo from the submerged and unseen UB 16 sunk the SS *Tragantle* (Hain Steamship Co. Ltd, St Ives), carrying 4,900 tons of wheat from Galveston, Texas, via Norfolk to Hull on 22 April. At the time of the attack – 22.45 – Captain F. Cundy sent out a distress message, which brought patrol vessels to assist in the rescue, and the crew of twenty-seven were landed at Lowestoft. The Norwegian steamer *John Wilson* (Dampskipsselskapet Aktieselskapet John Wilson, Stavanger) was captured, torpedoed and sunk, en-route from Rotterdam to London with foodstuffs on 2 August.

HM S/M E34. (Author's collection)

The Norwegian coaster *Velox* (Gjerdsjo & Bakkevig, Haugesund) was stopped by UB 16 and scuttled with explosive charges on 24 August, while voyaging from Newport to Genoa. Captain Larsen and his crew were picked up by Dutch fishing vessels

Oblt.z.S. Ernst Müller Schwarz assumed command of the boat on 30 August 1916 and served until 19 January 1917.

Oblt.z.S. Hans Edward Niemer became commander from 20 January 1917, until 17 March 1917.

Oblt.z.S. Hugo Thelmann took over command from 18 March 1917 until 22 April 1917, but during his short command, damaged the big Norwegian steamer *Kongsli* with a torpedo, which was sailing from Portland (Me) to Rotterdam with grain; she beached at the Hook of Holland and re-floated. However, on 18 August 1917 the ship was on passage from St Nazaire for Hampton Roads in ballast, when she was sunk by a torpedo.

Oblt.z.S. Wilhelm Rhein was CO from 23 April to 25 August 1917. Rhein torpedoed and sunk the British destroyer HMS *Recruit* (built by W. Doxford & Co.) off Noord Hinder Light Vessel on 9 August 1917; she was carrying a complement of about 100 at the time.

Oblt.z.S. Günter Bachmann was CO from 26 August 1917 until 24 December, followed by Oblt.z.S. Alfred Krameyer from 25 December 1917 to 19 February 1918 (Alfred Krameyer was lost with the entire crew of UC 79, on his next command).

Oblt.z.S. Rudolf Stier assumed command on 20 February 1918 until 21 April 1918. Stier torpedoed and sank the British SS *Lisette* (Yorkshire Coal & Steam Shipping Co. Ltd, Goole) on 13 March 1918 and one man was lost; she was voyaging from Goole to Honfleur with coal. A small fishing boat was also sunk the following day.

Oblt.z.S. Vicco von der Lühe assumed command from 22 April 1918 and made two patrols with UB 16. Vicco von der Lühe was born on 9 June 1890, was crewman from April 1908 and served as W/O on T-Boats V154 an S50. He joined U-boat school in December 1917 and was appointed as CO of SM UB 16 in April 1918.

Following the British attempt to blockade Zeebrugge harbour entrance, UB 16 was the first German submarine out of Zeebrugge, but she would never return.

FINAL VOYAGE

(87) On 6 May 1918, UB 16 sailed from Zeebrugge for operations in the Lowestoft–Southwold area. Lt R.I. Pulleyne RN, the commander of British submarine E34, was in an area where he was told he might encounter other British submarines on 10 May 1918. Lt Pulleyne – the sole survivor of HM S/M B2 in 1912 (See Chapter Four) – was returning to Harwich submerged, following a mine-laying operation, when he caught sight of a submarine in the distance. The unidentified submarine was bows-on. After carefully studying its profile through his periscope, he firmly identified it as a German U-boat and fired two torpedoes at it. E34 log – Lt Richard I. Pulleyne 10 May 1918:

18.50 –   Observed hostile S/M dived to attack

19.00 –   Flooded tubes

19.15 –   Fired both torpedoes. Target hit amidships and sank

19.20 –   Surface. Picked up survivor. Captain in wreckage and oil. 52.6 1/2 N 1.59 E. Name Otto van der Luhe

22.00 –   Secured alongside Maidstone

Right: HM S/M E34 in dock. (Crown copyright)

Below: Crew of HM S/M E34. (RN Submarine Museum)

Von der Luhe (28) was uncooperative. He would not speak to any other than self. He
  would not eat our food either.
I engaged him in conversation as brother submariner and he proved reluctant to talk.
  From what I gathered he had been on the bridge with the conning tower hatch open.
  With him on bridge were a PO and two seamen. They spotted a column of smoke
  on the horizon and pursued it. The lookout warned of a submarine. Von der Luhe
  spotted the conning tower of E34 and wake of two torpedoes. There was it seems a
  secondary explosion which wrecked the boat V.d.L was hurled into the water and we
  picked him up

ADM 173/1498 - NARA: T-1022, Roll 65, PG61753

While sweepers were searching the area the following day, Commander Guybon
Chesney Castell Damant was at Portsmouth waiting for explosives when orders arrived:
'Stand by to proceed with party to Harwich, for examination only, depth 13 fathoms,
question of *Moonfleet* being sent being decided'. (*Moonfleet* was a 145-ton salvage tug
used for diving purposes.) In no time at all, *Moonfleet* arrived with Damant's 'U-boat
Flying Squad', then the sweepers found something after about a week. Unfortunately
the wire slipped off, and when Damant went down in soup-like visibility, all he found
was some piping and a piece of plate. His observation was that after being hit by the
torpedo, the submarine appeared to have disintegrated. Oblt.z.S. Otto von der Lühe
was the sole survivor.

THE MEN WHO DIED IN UB 16

Bongert, Masch.Mt
Engelke, Mts
Gross, Hzr
Haase, Mts
Hofmann, F.T.
Jenk, Masch.Mt
Klockgether, Masch.Mt
Koch, Masch.
Köhler, Ob.Mts.d.Res
Kroll, Mts
Kuckhahn, Mts.
Lang, Ob.Mts.
Pohlmann, Mts.
Schmidt, Ob.Hzr
Schneider, Masch.Mt
Wagner, Hzr

Oblt.z.S. Otto von der Lühe sadly died of influenza at Keighley POW camp on 1 March
1919. He is now buried in Cannock Chase, Block 14 (Grave 202).

UB 16 was quite a successful boat, as she sank twenty-five vessels, totalling 18,825 tons:

AREA	VESSEL'S NAME	FLAG	TONS	D	M	YEAR	LOCATION
North Sea	*Boy Horace* (fish boat)	GBR	69	3	6	1915	50 miles SE of Lowestoft
North sea	*E&C* (fishing boat)	GBR	60	3	6	1915	40 miles ESE of Lowestoft
North Sea	*Economy* (fishing boat)	GBR	56	3	6	1915	50 miles SE of Lowestoft
North Sea	*Leuctra*	GBR	3027	12	6	1915	1½ miles SSE of Shipwash Light Vessel

North Sea	*Tunisiana*	GBR	4220	23	6	1915	Sunk off Lowestoft
North Sea	*Westward Ho* (f/v)	GBR	47	27	7	1915	25 miles SE of Lowestoft
North Sea	*Mangara*	GBR	1821	28	7	1915	¼ mile E of Sizewell Buoy, Aldeburgh
North Sea	*Emblem* (fishing boat)	GBR	50	7	9	1915	44 miles ESE of Lowestoft
North Sea	*Victorous* (fishing boat)	GBR	43	7	9	1915	44 miles ESE of Lowestoft
North Sea	*Boy Ernie* (fishing boat)	GBR	47	10	9	1915	58 miles E of Cromer
North Sea	*Nimrod* (fishing boat)	GBR	51	10	9	1915	45 miles ESE of Lowestoft
North Sea	*Evelyn* (fishing boat)	GBR	55	18	1	1916	34 miles ESE of Lowestoft
North Sea	*Foam Crest* (fishing boat)	GBR	46	18	1	1916	25–30 miles SE of Lowestoft
North Sea	*Sunshine* (fishing boat)	GBR	52	19	1	1916	27 miles SE of Lowestoft
North Sea	*Springflower* f/v	GBR	59	6	3	1916	28 miles E of Lowestoft
North Sea	*Young Harry* (f/v)	GBR	43	6	3	1916	35 miles E of Lowestoft
North Sea	*Perth*	GBR	653	1	4	1916	1 mile ESE of Cross Sand Light Vessel Yarmouth
North Sea	*Elziena Helena* (sail/v)	NLD	131	3	4	1916	Damaged 60 miles NW of Scheveningen
North Sea	*Robert Adamson*	GBR	2992	10	4	1916	3 miles NNE of Shipwash Light Vessel
North Sea	*Tregantle*	GBR	3091	22	4	1916	1½ miles ESE of Corton Light Vessel
North Sea	*John Wilson*	NOR	797	2	8	1916	20 miles W of Maas Light Vessel
North Sea	*Velox*	NOR	312	24	8	1916	11 miles WNW of Maas Light Vessel
North Sea	*Arie* (motor vessel)	NLD	107	20	4	1917	Sunk 16 miles off Egmond
North Sea	*Kongsli*	NOR	5822	20	4	1917	Damaged 18 miles W of Ymunden
North Sea	*Recruit* (HMS)	GBR	1075	9	8	1917	Sunk off Noord Hinder Light Vessel
North Sea	*Lisette*	GBR	899	13	3	1918	8 miles NNE of Shipwash Light Vessel
North Sea	*Ruth* (fishing boat)	GBR	44	14	4	1918	1½ miles ESE of Grose Sand Buoy

WRECK-SITE

The survey vessel never located this wreck, but a diver's report says it is totally collapsed, well broken up, partially buried and rather dispersed, with just a few steel plates and bits of debris left. It lies on a seabed of sand and shingle, in a general depth of 31m, being the lowest astronomical depth, and tidal streams are quite brisk.

It is sad to relate that the crew of E34 had just a couple of months to live. The boat was lost off the Netherlands on or around 20 July 1918. Lt Richard I. Pulleyne's body was washed ashore some time later. Lt Pulleyne (twenty-eight years old), the holder of both the DSO and a DSC, is buried in Noordwijk, near Den Haag.

E37, HM SUBMARINE

DATE OF LOSS: 30 November 1916
DEPTH: Unknown
REFERENCE: 52° 05' N
LOCATION: ENE of Harwich

Type: 'E' Class British overseas submarine of Group III (E19–E56)   *Pennant No.:* E37
Builders: Fairfield Shipyard, Govan for Royal Navy   *Ordered:* for 1914 Emergency War programme   *Keel laid:* December 1914   *Launched:* on 2 September 1915   *Commissioned:* by Lt-Cdr Robert Fellows Chisholm on 17 March 1916

TECHNICAL SPECIFICATIONS

Hull: Admiralty saddle-tank design **Surface displacement**: 667 tons **U/Dt**: 807 tons **LBD**: 55.17m x 6.86m x 3.81m **Machinery**: 2 x 800bhp Vickers Admiralty 8-cylinder diesels **Props**: 2 bronze **S/Sp**: 15¼ knots **Op/R**: 3,225 nautical miles at 10 knots **Sub/R**: 85 nautical miles at 5 knots **U/Power**: 2 x 420hp electric motors giving 9¾ knots **Batteries**: 2 x 112-cell Exide accumulators **Fuel/Cap**: 41.67 tons in 8 tanks and 5.28 tons of 'lubricating oil' in 2 tanks **Armament**: 5 x 45.72cm torpedo tubes, (2 bow, 2 beam and 1 stern tube) **Torpedoes**: 10 x 45.72cm (18in) **Mines**: None **Guns**: 1 x 5.44 kg (12-pounder) quick-firing deck gun and possibly 1 x 0.91kg (2-pounder) pom-pom **Diving**: Max-op-depth 60.96m (200ft) **Complement**: 3 officers and 27 ratings

The 'E' Class boats were all of Admiralty saddle tank design and were the first British type of submarines with beam tubes and sub-division by watertight bulkheads.

Lieutenant-Commander Robert Fellows Chisholm joined the submarine service in the early months of 1911 and went on to command HM S/M B3 on 13 May 1913. He remained in command right up to being appointed commander of E37 on 10 February 1016 and was her one and only commanding officer. The boat was based at Harwich and served with the Eighth Flotilla.

FINAL VOYAGE

After the First World War had ended it was discovered that the Imperial German U-boat UC 4 had laid three minefields off Orford Ness, each with a dozen mines. The first, Field-203, was laid on 24 November, followed by Field-208 on 8 December and Field-221 on 27 December.

The mines claimed the requisitioned minesweeping trawler *Burnley* (Admiralty No.3277) on 25 November and the trawler *Trevani* on 3 December and possibly even E30 (believed lost in the Heligoland Bight).

On the night of 30 November, the two British submarines E54, under the command of Lt-Cdr Robert Raikes, and E37, under Lt-Cdr Chisholm, were both outward bound on war patrols from Harwich. HM S/M E37, with Chisholm and his crew of thirty, failed to return. However, at 23.00, Commander Raikes's boat was hit by a violent shock wave while at latitude 52° 5' N and close to the war channel. At the time Raikes thought his boat had struck some submerged wreckage but, on reflection, it was presumed that this might have been E37 detonating one of the scattered mines. E37 may also have been lost through an accident or a mine in some other minefield.

THE MEN WHO DIED IN E37

Adams, John, Leading Seaman
Alexander, James, Engine Room Artificer
Archer, William, Petty Officer
Barrenger, Herbert, Engine Room Artificer
Chapman, William, Stoker
Chisholm, Robert, Lieutenant Commander
Cowlard, Frederick, Able Seaman
Edcombe, Herbert, Leading Seaman
Ellender, Ernest, Stoker
Emery, Henry, Able Seaman
Gran, Ernest, Able Seaman
Greaves, Edward, Able Seaman
Havery, Ralph, Chief Engine Room Artificer
Headly, Alfred, Lieutenant
Hoodless, Joseph, Signalman

Horlock, Phillip, Lieutenant
Hourston, David, Engine Room Artificer
Jenks, C., Leading Seaman
Matthews, Joseph, Leading Stoker
May, Henry, Stoker
Mellor, Horace, Able Seaman
Mockridge, William, Stoker
Mutton, Thomas, Leading Seaman
Parr, Charles, Leading Stoker
Powell, Eckford T., Telegraphist
Powell, Tom, Stoker
Sadler, Richard, Stoker
Salter, E., Stoker
Urquart, William, Petty Officer
Woodger, George, Stoker Petty Officer

WRECK-SITE
To date the wreck of HM S/M E37 has never been located.

E30, HM SUBMARINE

DATE OF LOSS: Wednesday, 22 November 1916
DEPTH: Unknown
REFERENCE: Unknown
LOCATION: North Sea

Type: 'E' Class British overseas submarine of Group III (E19–E56) *Pennant No.*: E30
Builders: Sir W.G. Armstrong Whitworth & Co. Ltd at Newcastle-upon-Tyne for Royal
Navy *Ordered*: for 1914 Emergency War programme *Keel laid*: December 1914
Launched: 29 June 1915 *Completed*: November 1915

TECHNICAL SPECIFICATIONS
Hull: Admiralty saddle-tank type *Surface displacement*: 662 tons *U/Dt*: 807 tons *LBD*:
55.17m x 6.86m x 3.81m *Machinery*: 2 x 800bhp Vickers Admiralty 8-cylinder diesels
Props: 2 bronze *S/Sp*: 15¼ knots *Op/R*: 3,225 nautical miles at 10 knots *Sub/R*: 85
nautical miles at 5 knots *U/Power*: 2 x 420hp electric motors gave 9¾ knots *Batteries*:
2 x 112-cell (224 total) Exide accumulators *Fuel/Cap*: 45 tons normally, 50 tons max.
Armament: 5 x 45.72cm torpedo tubes, (2 bow, 2 beam and 1 stern tube) *Torpedoes*:
10 x 45.72cm (18in) *Guns*: 1 x 5.44kg (12-pounder) quick-firing deck gun and possibly
1 x 0.91kg (2-pounder) pom-pom *Diving*: Max-op-depth 60.96m (200ft) *Complement*:
3 officers and 27 ratings

HM S/M E30 only had the one commanding officer – Lt-Cdr Geoffrey Nepean Biggs
– who had been in command from 31 August 1915, standing by while she was completed.
Lt-Cdr Biggs' other commands included B6, C32, A1 and C16, which he had commanded
between 20 November 1913 and 16 August 1915. Public Records Office information at
Kew shows that Lt-Cdr Biggs was born in Cardiff and lived in London Road. During his
service Lt-Cdr Biggs was awarded 'Order of the Rising Sun 4cl' (Japan).

HM S/M E30 at sea off East Anglia. (RN Submarine Museum)

On 'completion' (15 November 1915) she went to what was the 8th Flotilla, HMS *Maidstone*, at Harwich to work up, and was then transferred to the 11th Flotilla, HMS *Titania*, at Blyth on its formation in December 1915 (probably 8 December). Her duties were North Sea patrols off Norway, operating against the iron ore trade between Germany and Sweden.

On 7 April 1916 the submarine was operating off the Naze, Norway, when she suffered a battery explosion, which killed four men. Log of E30 – 7 April 1916:

Tuesday 7th April 1916
No's 1, 2 & 3 batteries exploded. P.O. Larcombe, L/S Bonnamy. AB Howard & Sto. Smith killed. Hands trying artificial respiration on deceased men with no effect'.

Log of HMS *Titania*:

Tuesday 11th April 1916 – at Blyth.
0800 –   Funeral Party landed to convey Leading Seaman Bonnamy's body to Railway Station (the other three men were buried at Blyth).
P.M.–   Landed Funeral Party, Lieut. Laidlaw in charge, to bury 3 Submarine Ratings. Funeral Party returned on board.

(Ship's Log details, courtesy of Dennis Feary)

The crew of E30 paid for a magnificent memorial to be erected in the Beach Cemetery at Blyth. The monument takes the form of a large broken stone mast and it contains a wealth of carved naval imagery, cables, anchors, a life buoy and, right in the centre, a carving of a submarine. On the monument are the following words:

Sacred to the Memory of:

They that go down to the sea in ships and occupy their business in great waters. These men see the works of the Lord and his wonders in the deep

Robert Barcombe PO tel 32
Edward Howard 28
John Smith Sto 24
Who were killed at sea. HM S/M E30 April 7th 1916

While patrolling in the Kattegat on 18 May 1916, E30 was credited with sinking the 762-ton German steamship *Trave* with gunfire in position 56° 21' N, 12° 32' E; Captain L. Grundt and her crew of fifteen were all lost. There was some confusion regarding this ship because, after many weeks of research, the only vessel the authors could find was a well documented passenger/cargo ship of 4,969 tons owned by Norddeutscher Lloyd, Bremen, and built by Fairfield at Govan in 1886. For almost twenty-three years, she had plied the route between Bremerhaven, Southampton and New York, carrying many thousands of passengers to the 'New World', albeit most of them immigrants. However that ship was scrapped in 1909. It was only through the perseverance of Dennis Feary that details of the other *Trave* that HM S/M E30 had sunk came to light.

She was a 613-ton steamer built by Ramage & Ferguson at Leith (BN.1) and launched as the *Shamrock* in February 1878. Her dimensions were 55.32m by length, an 8.19m beam and a 4.9m draught. She was powered by a single triple expansion engine that used one boiler (450 PS), manufactured by Hawthorn & Co. at Leith. J. Crawford, Grangemouth in Ireland were the original owners. Shamrock Steamship Co. of Larne became the owners in 1889, (T. Jack, manager) registered at Grangemouth in Ireland. In 1892 G. Bazeley & Sons, Penzance, England, purchased the ship. Nevall & Co. at Bristol rebuilt the machinery in 1893. On 20 May 1897, W. Minlos at Lubeck, Germany purchased her and renamed her *W.M. Limnos*, but the ship was London-registered. In May 1898 she was rebuilt to 762 tons at Lubeck. On 23 February 1904, she underwent another rebuild at Koch. On 13 April 1907 she was sold to Haseatic Steam Co. at Lubeck and, on 18 April 1907, renamed *Trave*. On 11 February 1916 she was sold to H. F. Bertling at Lubeck, who was the owner at the time of loss.

E30 remained at Blyth until the flotillas were re-organised in mid-1916 and these changes, which began in June, were complete by 20 August 1916, by which time HM S/M E30 was with the 9th Flotilla, HMS *Maidstone*, at Harwich.

FINAL VOYAGE

With Lt-Cdr Biggs in command, E30 left Harwich on 15 November 1916 for a patrol between positions 54°N and 53° 25' N and between 3° 30' E to 4°E, but she failed to return. The boat and her crew were never seen again. It is possible that she detonated a mine off Heligoland Bight, but the most likely place of loss would have been in a scattered minefield off Orford Ness. After the First World War it was found that the Imperial German U-boat UC 4 had laid the following three minefields off Orford Ness and Aldeburgh areas, each with a dozen mines:

Field-203 was laid on 24 November 1916 from 23.45 to 23.52, twelve mines at irregular intervals. Begin: Orford Ness at 262° 2.4 nautical miles. End: Orford Ness at 262° 3.2 nautical miles.

Field-208 was laid on 8 December 1916 from 22.37 to 22.46, twelve mines at irregular intervals. Begin: Orford Ness at 279° 6½ nautical miles. End: Orford Ness at 270° 5½ nautical miles.

The memorial to E30 crewmen at Blyth Beach Cemetery. (Ron Young)

Field-221 was laid on 27 December 1916 from 20.23 to 20.33, twelve mines at irregular intervals. Begin: Orford Ness at 270° 3 nautical miles. End: Orford Ness at 285° 3.8 nautical miles.

The first of these minefields was discovered on 25 November 1916 when the minesweeping trawler *Burnley* detonated one of them and sank. Then, on 3 December, the minesweeper HMT *Trevani* also sank after striking one of the mines. It is also highly likely that the British submarine E37, commanded by Lt-Cdr R.F. Chisholm, was lost in the first laid minefield on 30 November 1916. From October 1916 to July 1918, UC 4 laid a total of fifty-eight mine barrages, the majority in the Orford Ness and Shipwash Light Vessel and Aldborough Napes area. However, UC 11 also laid numerous minefields in the Shipwash and Sunk Light Vessel areas, from late 1916 through to June 1918, so any British boat that went missing could in theory have been lost in any of these.
ADM 173/1382 – ADM 53/63209

THE MEN WHO DIED IN E30
Biggs, Geoffrey Nepean, Lieutenant Commander
Farwell, Ralf Bay, Lieutenant
Bentley, Henry James, Leading Stoker
Bowley, Ernest William, Able Seaman
Bucks, William Henry, Petty Officer
Combes, William George, Petty Officer
Crocker, Sidney, Stoker. 1st
Fleming, Alfred Robert, P.O. French Med Militaire

Hand, Alfred Henry, Able Seaman
Haywood, Thomas Alfred, Petty Officer Stoker
Hedge, Bertie, Stoker.1st
Henderson, James, Engine Room Artificer.1st
Hurlock, Henry, Leading Seaman
Johnston, John, Stoker.1st
Jones, John Richard, Telegraphist
Langridge, Joseph Golden, Able Seaman
Leonard, William Charles, Leading Signalman
May, James, Chief Engine Room Artificer.2nd
Meats, Steven Arnold, Lieutenant R.N.R
Morris, Joseph William, Stoker.1st
Potter, William, Leading Seaman
Jones, John, Telegraphist
Presswell, John William, Leading Seaman
Reeves, Henry Chubs, Able Seaman
Rennison, Thomas Forster, Stoker.1st
Ridges, Arthur, Able Seaman
Roberts, Albert Charles, Engine R. Artificer.4th
Snowdon, Alfred William, Stoker.1st
Stevens, Harvey, Stoker.1st
Travers, Richard, Engine Room Artificer.3rd
Volze, Frederick Charles Hedges, Able Seaman
Wellfare, Thomas William, Leading Stoker

A memorial to Stoker Harvey Stevens of E30 can be seen in St Peter and Vincula's Church, Tibberton.

WRECK-SITE
The wreck of HM S/M E30 and her crew has never been located to date (2006).

UC 11, SM IMPERIAL U-BOAT

DATE OF LOSS: 26 June 1918
DEPTH: 25m
REFERENCE: 51 55'.00 N, 01 41'.00 E
LOCATION: 2.83 nautical miles SE of Shipwash
and 13½ nautical miles E of Landguard Point

Type: UC I coastal mine-laying boat **Builders**: A.G. Weser, Bremen for Kaiserliche Deutsche Marine **Ordered**: 23 November 1914, within the batch of UC 11–UC 15 **Keel laid**: as Yard No.225 on 26 January 1915 **Launched**: 11 April 1915 **Commissioned**: by Oberleutnant zur See Walter Gottfried Schmidt on 23 April 1915

TECHNICAL SPECIFICATIONS
Hull: Single **Surface displacement**: 168 tons **U/Dt**: 182 tons **LBDH**: 33.99m x 3.15m x 3.04m x 6.30m **Machinery**: 1 x 80ps Benz diesel **Props**: 1 bronze **S/Sp**: 6.49 knots **Op/R**: 910 nautical miles at 5 knots **Sub/R**: 50 nautical miles at 4 knots **U/Power**: 1 x 175ps electric motor gave 5.67 knots **Batteries**: Lead/acid/accumulators **Fuel/Cap**:

3 tons **Torpedo tubes**: None **Torpedoes**: None **Guns**: 1 machine gun and rifles **Mine chutes**: 6 x 100cm (39.37in) vertically inclined **Mines**: 12 x UC 120 **Diving**: Max-op-depth 50m (164ft) and 23 seconds to crash-dive **Complement**: 1 officer and 13 ratings

UC 11 was assigned to the Flandern U-Flottille from 26 May 1915 to 17 October 1915. From 17 October 1915 to 11 August 1916 she served with the U-Schule training Flottille. On 11 August 1916 the boat formally transferred to the Flandern/Flandern 1.U-Flottille.

UC 11 had eleven different commanding officers and she made eighty-three short two- or three-day patrols. From late 1916, UC 11 laid numerous minefields in the Shipwash and Sunk Light Vessel areas, right through to June 1918. Mines laid by the boat sank and damaged at least twenty-eight vessels, the larger ones being mentioned, but the total number of people killed is unknown.

Oblt.z.S. Walter Gottfried Schmidt was her first CO and remained with her until 11 August 1916. A mine laid the day before by UC 11 sank the SS *Erna Boldt* (The Admiralty) on 9 June 1915. She was an ex-German vessel (August Cords, Rostock) seized in London in August 1914, and was taking coal from the Tyne to London. Also on 9 June, the steamship *Lady Salisbury* (Gresham SS Co. Ltd) detonated a mine and foundered while transporting coal from Hartlepool to London and three seamen were lost.

Two Thornycroft-built RN torpedo boats, *Greenfly* (*No. 10*) and *Moth* (*No. 11*) were also lost to the mines on 10 June and then a steam trawler on 15 June.

Oblt.z.S. Reinhold Saltzwedel assumed command and served on her for just over a week, from 12 August to 20 August 1916.

Oblt.z.S. Max Schmitz commanded UC 11 from 21 August 1916 until 1 December 1916.

A mine laid on 22 September 1916 sank the British steamer *Huguenot* (Huguenot SS Co. Ltd, Newcastle) on 20 October, while on passage from London to the Tyne in ballast. She was commanded by Captain C.W. Stevens. Six men, including the master, were killed when the SS *Framfield* (Woodfield Steam Shipping Co. Ltd, London) struck a mine on 24 October while transporting iron ore from Port Kelah, Algeria, to the Tees. The mine had been laid on 22 September. The RN trawler *Lord Roberts* sank off Shipwash on 26 October. She was requisitioned in November 1914 and converted as Admiralty minesweeper No.545. On 21 November, the Dutch SS *Helena* (Naaml. Venn. A.C. Lensen's Stoomv. Mij. Terneuzen) struck a mine laid on 15 November and sank, while travelling in ballast from Rotterdam to New York. On 28 November the RN trawler *Lord Airedale* was lost to a mine off the Sunk Light Vessel; she was requisitioned in February 1915 and converted as Admiralty minesweeper No.847.

Oblt.z.S. Benno von Dittfurth took over command on 2 December 1916 and remained CO until 29 June 1917. Mines laid by Von Dittfurth sank the SS *Forth* (Carron & Co., Falkirk) on 9 December 1916. She was taking a general cargo from London to Leith.

The SS *Harlington* (Peninsular & Oriental Steam Navigation Co. Ltd, London) also sank that day, and seven men were killed, while transporting coal from the Tyne to London; the mine had been laid the previous day. Also on that day, two men were lost when the SS *Harlyn* (Harrison's (London) Ltd, London) struck a mine laid the previous day, while transporting coal from the Tyne to London.

The Danish SS *Michail Ontchoukoff* (Aktieselskab Dansk Russiske Dampskibselsk, Copenhagen) went down off the Sunk Light Vessel on 17 December; she detonated a mine laid the previous day while en-route from Rosario, Argentina, to Aarhus, Denmark, with 3,640 tons of maize. The British steamer *Zoroaster* (Turner, Brightman & Co.,

London) sank on 29 December after detonating a mine laid by UC 11 two days earlier. She was sailing from the Tyne for St Nazaire with coal. Three men were lost.

The steamer *Foreland* (Shipping & Coal Co. Ltd, London) sank while en-route from Blyth to Devonport with coal; the mine had been laid on 10 February. Five souls were given up to the sea when the steamer *Marie Leonhardt* (The Admiralty) detonated a mine on 14 February 1917, while transporting coal to London from Hartlepool. The RN trawler *Agile* sank after striking one of the mines on 27 April 1917; she was requisitioned in December 1914 and converted to Admiralty minesweeper No.697.

Oblt.z.S. Georg Niemyer took charge for three weeks from 30 June until 19 July 1917.

Oblt.z.S. Benno von Dittfurth then served as commander for a second time, from 20 July until 5 August 1917.

Oblt.z.S. Karl Dobbstein commanded the boat from 6 August to 16 November 1917.

Dobbstein was CO when the steamship *Wearside* (The Hartlepools Seatonia SS Co. Ltd, West Hartlepool) struck a mine and sank on 25 October 1917, while on passage from Newcastle for Genoa. The mine had been laid on 30 October. Two days later the RN trawler *Strymon* also sank off Shipwash Light Vessel after detonating one of those mines. She was requisitioned in 1915 and converted to minesweeper Admiralty No.1842.

Oblt.z.S. Ferdinand Schwartz assumed command from 17 November 1917. On 24 November the SS *French Rose* (R. Hughes & Co., Liverpool) was in ballast, on passage from Treport for Goole, when she detonated a mine that had been laid the day before, and sank. The next day, one crewman was lost when the ex-German steamer *Ostpreussen* (The Admiralty) struck a mine laid by UC 11 off Shipwash Light Vessel on 13 October. The ship was en-route from Sunderland to London with coal. On 27 October, while transporting coal from Hull, the steamship *Groeswen* (W. & C.T. Jones SS Co. Ltd, Cardiff) detonated one of her mines, laid on 23 October, and sank off the Sunk Light Vessel.

The RN trawler *John E. Lewis* was lost to a mine off Harwich on 16 January; she was requisitioned in August 1914 and converted as Admiralty minesweeper No.321.

Oblt.z.S. Reinhold Thomsen took over command from 11 February 1918 until 4 April 1918.

Thomsen was CO when HMS *Kale* (built by Hawthorn Leslie in 1904), a Royal Navy destroyer of 545 tons, struck one of UC 11's mines off Harwich and sank. She carried a complement of seventy crewmen. (No more vessels were lost to the mines after *Kale*.)

Oblt.z.S. Werner Lange, who was born on 18 July 1893, assumed command on 5 April 1918 and remained CO until 16 June 1918. Lange lived until 19 November 1965.

The last commander of UC 11 was Oblt.z.S. Kurt Utke, who took over on 17 June 1918 until she was lost a few days later.

FINAL VOYAGE

(Patrol 83) UC 11 sailed from Zeebrugge on 24 June 1918 to lay mines near the Sunk Light Vessel. On 26 June the boat was proceeding submerged at 15m, about 1½ miles north-east of the Sunk Light Vessel, when a violent explosion occurred. Water very quickly flooded into the boat and her crew were unable to blow the tanks to bring her to surface. During the 1930s Utke gave this account, later reproduced in *Der Signaal*:

> We had been diving for some time off Harwich and so I thought it was time for a look-see to enable the navigator to take a fix. It was early afternoon and I was keen to explore the swept channel a little further. As we rose to periscope depth there was an explosion and our boat was shaken like a rag doll in the jaws of a terrier. Everything went crashing around, the lights went out, metal screamed. I guessed we had struck a mine. Down, Down we went. Hansen was chanting the

rosary; others were resigned to death like the good U-boatman ought to be. Water was pouring into the boat, but my commands were useless now. Men cried out as the water covered their heads. I was proud to call them my crew. Faithful Hoffmann fought to the last gasp, I could not see him, but I heard him cry, 'To the very end sir'. I called to one of the sailors to help me release the hatch. As he tried to make his way over to me he became snared on an obstruction and the torrent dashed him against the pipes. I lifted the clips and 'Whoosh'; I was blown out of my dying boat. I too resigned myself to death. I thought of my parents, my dog and all the things I would never live to do. I thought my lungs would burst long before I ever reached the surface. Suddenly I was there, on the surface, alone.

He swam around for half an hour and the Sunk Lightship lifeboat picked him up after witnessing the explosion. Utke, the sole survivor, then in vain tried to pass himself off as the boat's engineering officer.

Two days later, RN divers were sent down and found the submarine with a huge break, 20ft aft of the conning tower. The wreck was also lying on her port side and all of the mines were still in place. The director of Naval Intelligence approved Lt-Cdr Guybon Chesney Castell Damant's suggestion of opening the conning tower up with explosives, even though there was nothing to ascertain. A charge of 100lb of TNT was detonated inside the conning tower, but access to the hull was still blocked and none of the mines exploded. After a second charge was set off, however, very large explosions occurred as a number of the mines detonated. Large quantities of debris and important documents then floated to the surface, all of which was salved.

A bit of a twist to this story was that Utke later claimed that his boat had been lost in a German minefield, yet it had almost certainly been a mine laid by UC 11 on an earlier operation! The Admiralty even alleged that the mines had been left there on purpose, rather in the same manner that UC 44 was lured to her doom on German mines (Volume 2).

<u>ADM 116/1634</u> – <u>NARA: T-1022, Roll 44, PG61914</u>

THE MEN WHO DIED IN UC 11
Behrens, Masch.d.Res
Finkler, Hzr
Gerstmann, Ob.Mts.
Hamm, Mts.
Henniges, Masch.
Hofmann, Ob.Masch.Mt
Holm, Mts
Josellis, Ob.Hzr
Klare, Hzr
Kunath, Mts.
Melzer, Masch.Mt
Möller, Ob.Hzr
Sauerhering, Btn.Mt
Siebert, Mts.
Stade, Stm.d.Res
Thinius, F.T.
Wellhäuser, Ob.Mts.
Zachäus, Masch.Mt
Zieger, Ob.Mts

UC 11 was a very successful U-boat in that she sank twenty-nine vessels totalling 38,556 tons. The following is a list of known vessels damaged or sunk by UC 11.

AREA	VESSEL'S NAME	FLAG	TONS	D	M	YEAR	LOCATION
North Sea	Mohawk (HMS)	GBR	865	1	6	1915	Mined and damaged S entrance to Downs
North Sea	Erna Bolt	GBR	1731	9	6	1915	Mined ½ mile ENE Sunk Light Vessel
North Sea	Lady Salisbury	GBR	1446	9	6	1915	Mined 1 mile N of Sunk Light Vessel, Thames
North Sea	Greenfly (HMS torpedo boot)	GBR	255	10	6	1915	Mined off Sunk L/v and Shipwash South Buoy
North Sea	Moth (HMS torpedo boot)	GBR	255	10	6	1915	Mined off Sunk L/v and Shipwash South Buoy
North Sea	Argyll (trawler)	GBR	280	15	6	1915	Mined 12 miles ESE of Harwich
North Sea	Huguenot	GBR	1032	20	10	1916	Mined 4 miles NE ½ E Sunk Light Vessel
North Sea	Framfield	GBR	2510	24	10	1916	Mined 3 miles NE of Sunk Light Vessel
North Sea	Lord Roberts (RN trawler)	GBR	293	26	10	1916	Mined off Shipwash
North Sea	Helena	NLD	1798	21	11	1916	Mined 5 miles SE of Cross Sand Light V
North Sea	Lord Airdale (RN trawler)	GBR	215	28	11	1916	Mined near Sunk Light Vessel
North Sea	Forth	GBR	1159	9	12	1916	Mined 4 miles SW of Shipwash Light Vessel
North Sea	Harlington	GBR	1034	9	12	1916	Mined 4 miles SW of Shipwash Light Vessel
North Sea	Harlyn	GBR	1794	9	12	1916	Mined 3–4 miles NE ¼ E of Shipwash Light vessel
North Sea	Michail Ontchoukoff	DAN	2118	17	12	1916	Mined 1½ –2 miles N ¾ E of Sunk Light vessel
North Sea	Zoroaster	GBR	3642	29	12	1916	Mined 1¼ miles ENE of Sunk Light Vessel
North Sea	Cape Colony (fishing boat)	GBR	82	8	1	1917	Mined and sunk off Harwich
North Sea	Foreland	GBR	1960	12	2	1917	Mined 6 miles S ¾ W of Shipwash Light vessel
North Sea	Marie Leonhardt	GBR	1466	14	2	1917	Mined at mouth of River Thames
North Sea	Agile (RN trawler)	GBR	246	27	4	1917	Mined off Sunk Light Vessel
North Sea	Hastfen (drifter)	GBR	77	24	9	1917	Mined S of Shipwash Sand (barr.473)
North Sea	Wearside	GBR	3560	25	10	1917	Mined 3 miles WSW Sunk Light Vessel
North Sea	Strymon (RN trawler)	GBR	198	27	10	1917	Mined off Shipwash Light Vessel
North Sea	French Rose	GBR	465	24	11	1917	Mined 2 miles SSW of Shipwash Light Vessel
North Sea	Ostpreusson	GBR	1755	25	11	1917	Mined 1½ miles E of Shipwash Light Vessel
North Sea	Groeswen	GBR	3570	27	11	1917	Mined 3 miles NE ½ E of Sunk Light Vessel
North Sea	John E. Lewis (RN trawler)	GBR	253	16	1	1918	Mined off Cork Light Vessel (Harwich)
North Sea	Kale (HMS)	GBR	545	27	3	1918	Mined N of Harwich

WRECK-SITE

The wreck was not located in the survey, but this is quite understandable because it is reported as having been blown in two by the initial mine blast.

C33, HM SUBMARINE

DATE OF LOSS: 4 August 1915
DEPTH: Unknown
REFERENCE: Unknown
LOCATION: North Sea

Type: 'C' Class British coastal patrol boat of Group II (C31–C38) *Pennant No.:* I.63
Builders: HM Dockyard, Chatham for Royal Navy *Ordered:* for 1908–1909 programme
Keel laid: 29 March 1909 *Launched:* 10 May 1910 *Commissioned:* by Lt Godfrey Herbert DSO on 13 August 1910

TECHNICAL SPECIFICATIONS

Hull: Single *Surface displacement:* 290 tons *U/Dt:* 321 tons *LBD:* 43.28m x 4.11m x 3.51m *Machinery:* 1 x 600hp Vickers 16-cylinder petrol engine *Props:* 1 bronze x 3 blade of 1.70m (5ft 7in) *S/Sp:* 11½ knots *Op/R:* 740 nautical miles at 12 knots, or 910 nautical miles at 8 knots and 10-day endurance *Sub/R:* 16 nautical miles at 8 knots *U/Power:* 1 x 200bhp electric motor giving 8 knots *Batteries:* Exide lead/acid of 68½ tons (20 per cent of boat's submerged displacement) *Fuel/Cap:* 15½ tons *Armament:* 2 x 45.72cm bow torpedo tubes *Torpedoes:* 4 x 45.72cm (18in) *Guns:* None *Diving:* Max-op-depth 30.48m (100ft) *Complement:* 3 officers and 13-ratings. *Cost to build:* £47,000 (More details of 'C' Class on C34)

Lt Godfrey Herbert DSO was appointed CO on 1 August 1910, just before she was completed on 13 August (Godfrey Herbert might be classed as one of the 'luckier' submarine officers). He was first lieutenant of A4 in October 1905 when Martin Nasmith was CO and underwater signalling experiments took place. Herbert later commanded D5 when she struck a mine and sank; only five crew members escaped and he was one of them. The next boat was E22, which he left the day before it was lost. However, to round it all off, he was the commanding officer of K13 when she sank while on trials in Gareloch.

Lt Gerald Ernest Berkeley Carter assumed command of C33 from 30 November 1911. His previous command was HM S/M A2 from 2 December 1910 to 30 November 1911.

FINAL VOYAGE

Encouraged by the success of C24 and C27, Lt Carter was ordered to carry out a two-day operation off East Anglia in company with the requisitioned decoy trawler HMT *Malta* (Admiralty No.700). C33 is known to have remained on station for two days before slipping tow at 20.15 on 4 August 1915 in order to return to port. Shortly before 21.50 Carter transmitted 'Have nothing to communicate'. Despite an intensive search by HMS *Firedrake* and other Harwich destroyers which had been dispatched at dawn on 5 August, C33 and her crew of seventeen were never seen again. *Fireglow* did, however, rescue survivors from four sunken fishing boats during the search. German sources make no claim for destroying C33, so a British mine is the most likely candidate.

THE MEN WHO DIED IN C33:

Alexander, Alfred, PO and Coxswain
Bennett, Ernest Granville, Signalman
Bishop, Arthur Godfrey, Gunner and Third Officer
Black, Henry Percival, Leading Seaman
Buchanan, Colin James, Sub-Lt RNR, First Lieutenant
Carter, Gerald Ernest Berkeley, Lieutenant RN, CO
Clarke, William Clarke, Able Seaman
Duncan, William Charles, E.R. Artificer.2nd
Green, Leonard Green, Able Seaman
Heath, G., Stoker Petty Officer
Hill, Albert William, Able Seaman
Hocking, Godfrey William, Leading Seaman
Hunt, Alfred, Engine Room Artificer.3rd
Lashbrook, William Thomas, Leading Stoker
Saunders, Edward Service, Stoker.1st
Wharton, Clarence John, Able Seaman
Windebank, William David, Leading Stoker

WRECK-SITE

To date the wreck of C33 has never been found.

UC 5, SM IMPERIAL U-BOAT

DATE OF LOSS: 27 April 1916
REFERENCE: Broken up

Type: UCI coastal mine-laying boat *Builders*: AG Vulcan, Hamburg for Kaiserliche Deutsche Marine *Ordered*: 23 November 1914, within the batch of UC 1–UC 10 *Keel laid*: as Yard No.49 *Launched*: 13 June 1915 *Commissioned*: by Oberleutnant zur see Herbert Pustkuchen on 19 June 1915

TECHNICAL SPECIFICATIONS

Hull: Single *Surface displacement*: 168 tons *U/Dt*: 183 tons *LBDH*: 33.99m x 3.15m x 3.04m x 6.30m *Machinery*: 1 x 90ps Daimler diesel *Props*: 1 bronze *S/Sp*: 6.20 knots *Op/R*: 780 nautical miles at 5 knots *Sub/R*: 50 nautical miles at 4 knots *U/Power*: 1 x 175ps electric motor giving 5.22 knots *Batteries*: Lead/acid/accumulators *Fuel/Cap*: 3 tons *Torpedo tubes*: None *Torpedoes*: None *Guns*: 1 machine gun and rifles *Mine chutes*: 6 x 100cm (39.37in) vertically inclined *Mines*: 12 x UC 120 *Diving*: Max-op-depth 50m (164ft) and 33–36 seconds to crash-dive *Complement*: 1 officer and 13 ratings

UC 5 was formally assigned to the Flandern U-Flottille with Herbert Pustkuchen her commander from the commissioning. UC 5 made a total of twenty-nine short patrols with two commanders.

The mines that Pustkuchen laid with UC 5 damaged or sunk twenty-two vessels, including a 380-ton warship and ten steamships. On 6 August 1915 the RN trawler *Leandros* sank after striking a mine; she was launched as *Leander*, but requisitioned in August 1914 and converted to Admiralty minesweeper No.18, then renamed *Leandros*, in February 1915.

The SS *Summerfield* (Zillah Shipping & Carrying Co. Ltd, Liverpool) sank on 13 August 1915, after detonating a mine laid the previous day, while en-route from Yarmouth in Norfolk to Douglas, Isle of Man, with coal and wooden huts. A violent explosion that rocked the ship caused her to heel over to starboard at 07.53. The lifeboats had been made ready and swung out when leaving Great Yarmouth and one of them cleared the ship before she sank, but three people drowned: the mate and his wife (a stewardess), and the chief engineer. Captain G.P. Hardley and an ordinary seaman were injured; the seven survivors were landed at Lowestoft. The people that drowned were:

Griffiths, Owen, Chief Engineer
Summerfield, Ann, Stewardess
Summerfield, Thomas, Mate

The Swedish steamer *Sverige* (E. Brodin), which was taking wood pulp from Sundswall, Sweden, to London, also sank in the Stanford Channel on 13 August 1915, the mine having been laid by UC 5 the previous day. Three days later she was beached close-by, but became a total loss.

The SS *William Dawson* sank off Boulogne on 21 August, while transporting coal from Boston (Lincs) to Dunkerque.

The SS *Honiton* (Tatem Steam Navigation Co. Ltd, Cardiff) was transporting linseed and maize from Buenos Aires to Hull when she detonated a mine laid on 27 August. She was beached at Shoeburyness and declared a total loss.

The French SS *St Chamond* struck a mine and was left damaged while on en-route from Rouen for Newcastle in ballast on 3 September 1915. She was towed into Harwich for repairs. However, on 29 April 1918, the ship was torpedoed and sunk off St Ives Head, while transporting general cargo from Glasgow to St Nazaire.

The SS *Monarch* (HM Post-Master – Telegraph Dept.) struck a mine and sank off Folkestone on 8 September 1915. She was a cable ship on passage from Santander to Newport and carrying a crew of seventy-three and a cargo of iron ore. Several patrol vessels rescued most of her crew, but the following three men were killed:

Ayers, N., Cable Hand
Johnson, G.W., Storekeeper
Seago, H., Cable Hand (Extra)

The SS *Brighton Queen* (The Admiralty) sank on 6 October after striking one of the mines that had been laid on 3 October, while employed as an auxiliary minesweeper off Nieport, near Ostend.

The British SS *Enfield* was mined and damaged on 4 October 1915, while en-route from Newcastle to St Nazaire with a cargo of coal. She was beached at Hythe, but re-floated.

The steamer *Newcastle* (Newcastle SS Co. Ltd, Newcastle) was on passage from Port Louis, Mauritius, to London with 4,987 tons of general cargo when she detonated a mine off Folkestone on 10 October 1915. The mine, which had been laid on 16 September, exploded aft directly beneath the cabin and blew off the propeller. On 6 August the ship had left Mauritius with a cargo consisting mostly of sugar and rum, plus one stowaway. The crew of twenty-seven and the stowaway abandoned ship in the boats and the trawler *Othello* landed them at Dover.

On 23 October, the bows of the SS *Ilaro* (African S.S. Co. Ltd, London) detonated a mine off Dungeness, while en-route from Forcados, West Africa, to Hull with maize and kernels. The mine had been laid by UC 5 on 18 October 1915. The engine was stopped and twenty-nine of the crew safely abandoned ship in two lifeboats. However, the chief engineer, Stephen Robert Blair (forty-six years old), unfortunately fell overboard and drowned. A patrol vessel picked up the men but stayed near the ship, which remained afloat. The following morning, despite a raging inferno in No.1 hold and the fact that the forepeak bulkhead had disappeared, the master and crew went back on board. Two Dover tugs arrived at the scene at 11.00 and towed the ship stern first to Deal Roads, where they beached her near Sandown Castle. The fire spread to No.2 hold and at 05.00 on 25 October, the master ordered his crew to abandon ship, only a few hundred tons of her cargo being saved.

On 19 October 1915, the RN trawler *Erin II* sank from a mine off the Nab Light Vessel and seven lives were lost. She had been launched as *Erin*, but requisitioned in September 1914 and converted to minesweeper No.381, then renamed *Erin II* in February 1915.

The SS *Anglia* (London & North Western Railway Co., Dublin) was off Folkestone on 17 November 1915 when a mine detonated on the port side, just forward of the bridge at 12.30. The force of the explosion blew Captain Manning from his position on the bridge onto the deck below, but he still managed to order out the boats, and fifty people got away in the first one. The ship was employed on Government Service as an auxiliary hospital ship and the mine had been laid earlier that day. On board, other than her crew and other medical staff, there were 4 military officers, 1 nurse, 13 wounded officers and 372 wounded other ranks. The ship quickly took on a heavy list and sank in ten minutes, taking with her, 4 military officers, 1 nurse and 129 soldiers and crewmen. The scene was witnessed by the steam collier *Lusitania* (John Hall Jnr. & Co. Ltd, London), 3 miles distant, which raced to the scene to assist. Two boats were launched and they found lots of people floating in the water, many of them wounded soldiers lying on cots. While picking up survivors, the *Lusitania* (Captain J.R. Rees) also struck a mine at 12.45, just after the *Anglia* had sunk. The tug *Undaunted* picked up one of her crewmen, while HMS *Hazard* rescued the remaining survivors and landed them at Dover; seven of her crew of thirteen were lost.

On 19 November 1915 the RN trawler *Falmouth III* detonated a mine and sank; she had been launched as *Falmouth*, but requisitioned in August 1914 and converted to Admiralty minesweeper No.152. In April 1915 she was renamed *Falmouth III*.

The last vessel to sink from mines laid by Pustkuchen, actually the same day, was the steamer *Dotterel* (Cork Steam Ship Co. Ltd, Cork), which was en-route from Manchester and Liverpool to Dunkerque with a general cargo. The master was amongst the survivors, but the following five men were killed:

Casey, Patrick, 73, Able Seaman from Ireland
Hughes, Peter, 59, Fireman from Ireland
Van Wingerden, P., 47, Fireman from Loosduien, Holland
Williams, William, Able Seaman from Anglesey
Van Cleef, C.J., 34, Able Seaman of Rotterdam, Holland

Oberleutnant zur See Ulrich Mohrbutter assumed command on 19 December 1915. All thirty-eight of her crew were lost when mines planted by UC 5, sank the British submarine E6, which detonated a mine and disappeared in a ball of smoke on 26 December 1915, leaving only some oil and flotsam on the surface. Thirty-three men were lost. That same day, the RN trawler *Resono* detonated a mine and sank; she was requisitioned in January 1915 and converted to Admiralty minesweeper No.1042.

The steamer *Algerian* (Ellerman Lines Ltd, Liverpool) struck a contact mine that had been laid by UC 5 on 19 October 1915. She was coming from Cowes, Isle of Wight, to

Avonmouth in ballast and sank on 12 January 1916. The mine detonated on her starboard side, abreast of No.2 hatch, and distress flares were fired, bringing three RN drifters and the Trinity House steamer *Warden* to the scene. The latter began towing the ship to Southampton, but the watertight bulkhead collapsed near Cowes, and at 14.30 she sank. Captain Leader was her master, and she was carrying a crew of fifty-three, all of whom were saved.

On 13 January, the RN trawler *Albion II* was lost to a mine off St Catherine's Point. She had been launched as *Albion*, but requisitioned in August 1914, and in February 1915 renamed *Albion II*, Admiralty No.139.

On 1 February the *Prinses Juliana* (N.V. Stoomv. Mij. Zeeland, Vlissingen), a Dutch steamer, struck a mine off the Sunk Light Vessel that had been laid on 31 January. She was travelling from Vlissingen, Netherlands, to Tilbury with passengers and was beached near Felixstowe. However the ship broke in two and sank on 29 March, being a total loss.

Nine men, including the master, were drowned (all hands) on 20 February 1916, when the steam coaster *Dingle* (Dale Coasters Ltd, Sunderland) struck a mine that had been laid by UC 5 on 9 February and sank en-route from Sunderland to Caen with coal.

The crew of twenty-nine were killed (all hands) on the Dutch tanker *La Flandre* (American Petroleum Co., Rotterdam) when she sank on 21 February 1916 after detonating a mine that had been laid by UC 5 the previous day off Galloper Light Vessel. She was on passage from New York to Rotterdam with petroleum oil.

The steamer *Tummel* (E.P. Hutchinson, Hull) was lost with nine crewmen on 24 February 1916. She was transporting coal from Grimsby to Treport when she struck a mine laid on 9 February.

On 26 March 1916 the French SS *Hebe* (Soc. Navale Caennaise, Caen) was in ballast, sailing from Caen, France, to Newcastle, when it sank after detonating a mine that had been laid on 4 March.

Under Skipper H. Jameson, the Hull steam trawler *Khartoum* (Hull Steam Fishing & Ice Co. Ltd) detonated a mine on 26 March. The mine had been laid on 24 March. The vessel was used as a company carrier, transporting 'boxing fleet' catches of fish to London Billingsgate Fish Market and sank 5 miles off Longsands Light Vessel with all nine hands, including:

Borkwood, Thomas William, 32, Second Engineer
Fowler, F., 26, Fireman
Fuller, William Henry, 32, First Engineer
Jickells, Joseph, 39, Able Seaman
Lindo, Fred, 37, Able Seaman
Richardson, Joe, 29, Able Seaman
Smith, Walter Cornelius, 35, Steward
Toogood, Charles, 49, Boatswain (Bosun)
Watkinson, James Robert, 41, Second Hand

The SS *Harriet* (Aktieselskab Dampskibsselskab Selsk. Heimdal, Copenhagen), a 1,392-ton Danish steamer, struck a mine that had been laid by UC 5 on 16 March 1916 and sank on 27 March, while voyaging from Oran, Algeria, for Leith with a cargo of esparto-grass.

UC 5 and Ulrich Mohrbutter's last mine victim was the SS *Alacrity* (Harris Bros & Co., Swansea), which was on passage from Le Havre for Seaham Harbour in ballast. The following thirteen crewmen went down with her, including the master:

Brilis, N., 45, Able Seaman from Greece
Burnett, Sydney, 28, Chief Engineer
Dickinson, Joseph, 43, Master from Dublin
Elder, John George, 35, Steward
Kandratoo, Paul, 30, Donkeyman from Russia
Le Huquet, W., 42, Able Seaman from Jersey
Newton, W., 29, Ordinary Seaman.
Nore, George, 29, Second Engineer from Ghent, Belgium.
Owen, Edward, 48, Fireman
Paterson, S., Able Seaman
Perdookis, G., 34, Able Seaman from Chios, Greece
Spears, William, 28, Boatswain (Bosun)
Walters, Frank Edward, Mate

UC 5 made a total of twenty-nine short two- and three-day patrols and sank twenty-nine vessels.

If Ulrich Mohrbutter was a superstitious person he would have been having serious bouts of panic on the boat's twenty-ninth patrol, because it would appear that someone or something was telling him not to leave Zeebrugge in the little mine-laying boat.

FINAL VOYAGE

(29) UC 5 departed Zeebrugge with Mohrbutter on 24 April 1916 with instructions to lay a field of twelve mines, 1 nautical mile east of the Shipwash Light Vessel. However, Allied patrol movement, including entire destroyer groups around the North Hinder Light Vessel area, forced the little boat back into Zeebrugge. Mohrbutter made another attempt to leave that same evening, but the presence of luminous sea phosphorescence from the bow waves blinded the lookouts. Mohrbutter thought the shimmering movements of his boat would attract British patrols, so once again he returned to port. At 08.00 on 26 April UC 5 'finally' departed Flanders. The submarine proceeded via the Thornton Ridge and the North Hinder prior to shaping a course for the Galloper Buoy. There was a light east wind but a sea-fret hampered visibility. That evening the boat edged along the Galloper sands, trimmed down to avoid being seen. Ulrich Mohrbutter was, of course, an expert on this part of the coast, its tricky tides and its lightships. Maritime traffic forced UC 5 to submerge but on surfacing five or so hours later at 22.15 on 27 April, the submarine ran aground on the Shipwash Shoal, against an ebb tide. The engines rang 'Full Speed', but it was to no avail. The current forced the boat further into the sandbank until the boat was forced over on its port side. The little submarine was stuck fast off an enemy coast. The skipper radioed for help, but the Harwich forces reached her first. The log of HMS *Firedrake* tells the rest:

13.00 –	Sighted German submarine aground on Shipwash. Closed, lowered whaler and took off crew – one officer and 17 men
18.20 –	Secured to Melampus at Parkeston
19.00 –	Discharged prisoners

Scuttling charges failed to explode.

ADM 53/41752 - *Firedrake* 28 September – 28 November 1917

NARA: T-1022, Roll 84, PG 61899

The following is a list of vessels sunk or damaged by UC 5:

North Sea	Leandros (RN trawler)	GBR	276	6	8	1915	Mined at north entrance Knock Deep
North Sea	Amethyst (trawler)	GBR	57	13	8	1915	Mined 7-miles ESE of Lowestoft
North Sea	Summerfield	GBR	687	13	8	1915	Mined 2-miles E of Lowestoft
North Sea	Sverige	SWE	1602	13	8	1915	Mined 1½ miles SE of Lowestoft
English Channel	William Dawson	GBR	284	21	8	1915	Mined 1 mile from Boulogne
North Sea	Honiton	GBR	4914	30	8	1915	Mined ½ mile E Long Sand L/v and beached
North Sea	St Chamond	FRA	2866	3	9	1915	Mined and damaged 5 miles E of Longsand L/v
English Channel	Monarch	GBR	1122	8	9	1915	Mined 2½ miles S of Folkestone
English Channel	Tord	SWE	1313	19	9	1915	Mined and damaged 3 miles SW Folkestone
English Channel	Enfield	GBR	2124	4	10	1915	Mined and damaged 2½ miles W by S of Folkestone
English Channel	Brighton Queen	GBR	553	6	10	1915	Mined off Nieuport
English Channel	Newcastle	GBR	3403	10	10	1915	Mined 4 miles SW of Folkestone Pier
North Sea	Frons Oliviae (drifter)	GBR	98	12	10	1915	Mined off Elbow Buoy
English Channel	Erin II (RN trawler)	GBR	181	19	10	1915	Mined off the Nab Light Vessel
English Channel	Star of Buchan (drifter)	GBR	81	20	10	1915	Mined off the Nab Light Vessel
English Channel	Grappler (tug)	GBR	102	22	10	1915	Mined off the Nab Light Vessel
English Channel	Ilaro	GBR	2799	23	10	1915	Mined 4 miles E of Dungeness
English Channel	Velox (HMS)	GBR	380	25	10	1915	Mined off Nab Light Vessel
English Channel	Anglia	GBR	1862	17	11	1915	Mined 1 mile E of Folkestone
English Channel	Lusitania	GBR	1834	17	11	1915	Mined 1 mile E Folkestone Gate
English Channel	Falmouth III (RN trawler)	GBR	198	19	11	1915	Mined off Dover
English Channel	Dotterel	GBR	1596	29	11	1915	Mined 4¾ miles N by E of Boulogne Pier
English Channel	E6 (HM Sub.)	GBR	725	26	12	1915	Mined SE of Sunk Light Vessel
English Channel	Resono	GBR	230	26	12	1915	Mined near Sunk Light Vessel
English Channel	Algerian	GBR	3815	12	1	1916	Mined 2½ miles SW of Needles L/h, Isle of Wight
English Channel	Albion II (RN trawler)	GBR	240	13	1	1916	Mined off St Catherine's Point
North Sea	Prinses Juliana	NLD	2885	1	2	1916	Mined 1 mile SW of Sunk Light Vessel
North Sea	Dingle	GBR	593	20	2	1916	Mined 10 miles S by W of Kentish Knock L/v
North Sea	La Flandre	NLD	2047	21	2	1916	Mined near Galloper Light Vessel
North Sea	Tummel	GBR	531	24	2	1916	Mined 7 miles S of Kentish Knock Light vessel
North Sea	Hebe	FRA	1386	26	3	1916	Mined 6 miles E of the Sunk Light Vessel
North Sea	Khartoum (fishing boat)	GBR	303	26	3	1916	Mined 5 miles NE by E of Longsands L/v
North Sea	Harriet	DAN	1392	27	3	1916	Mined 5 miles E of the Sunk Light Vessel
North Sea	Alacrity	GBR	1080	31	3	1916	Mined off Lowestoft

Right: Gun crew of 18-pounder, anti-submarine trawler. (Author's collection)

Below: British First World War commander at periscope.

WRECK-SITE

The Royal Navy brought UC 5 back to port and put it on display around the UK. It also gave the British a lead on how to use submarines as minelayers. The boat was eventually broken up.

CHAPTER FOUR

KENT AND THE SOUTH EAST

INTRODUCTION

There is a greater concentration of wrecked U-boats off the Kent coast than any other section of coast covered by this book. By 1918 the Folkestone–Gris Nez line, the nearest point of Continental Europe, was known as the 'Submarine Graveyard'.

The Dover Straits marked the gateway to the Channel and the Channel offered the quickest route to the western approaches. This route promised a time saving of six out of the twenty-five days normally allotted to a North Sea boat and a saving of eight days out of the fourteen-day patrol given to the Flanders submarines. However, as the long toll of U-boat wrecks testifies, it would develop into the most sophisticated sea defence in existence. By the summer of 1918 any U-boat ordered to run the Dover Straits faced what was tantamount to a suicide mission. The submarine wrecks can be found in two groups, one roughly north of the Varne following the South Foreland/Ruytingen Bank line and the other to the south of the Varne, marking the position of the legendary Folkestone–Gris Nez Barrage. The evolution of this defence is worth following in detail.

The Admiralty understood the strategic importance of the Dover Straits and sought to seal off the Channel at this, its narrowest point. In April 1915 a series of nets worked by drifters ran between Folkestone and the Colbart Ridge, thence to Cap Gris Nez. This defence was reinforced by a minefield stretching from the North Goodwins to Ruytingen but many of the Elia and Service Type mines proved defective. In fact British mines became prized as souvenirs by the German Imperial Navy and decorated many Wilhelmshaven wardrooms.

Gates marked by lightships were left within the net barrage to enable maritime traffic to make the crossing, but the Flanders-based U-boats hardly needed to make use of them. A favourite U-boat ploy was to bottom out just north of the Ruytingen Bank and then wait until the tide turned westwards or night fell. If possible the boats would search out a flashing buoy in order to make a navigational fix prior to making the Channel run. The tide would carry them over the nets with little difficulty. There is evidence that the U-boats were able to run the Straits at night on the surface with consummate ease until late 1917. U 8 was therefore rather unfortunate to become ensnared in nets near the Varne Shoal and become the first victim of the famous Dover Patrol. In September 1916 a net mine barrage was laid between the Goodwins and the Outer Ruytingen (then to the French coast), but this proved to be no more successful in deterring the U-boats.

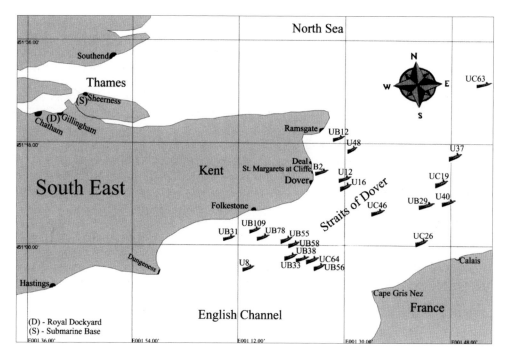

A map of the South East coast. (Ron Young)

In November 1917 Vice Admiral Bacon (Senior Naval Officer 6th Flotilla) ordered the creation of an awesome sea defence, a task completed by Admiral Keyes. From 21 November 1917 the Folkestone–Gris Nez deep mine barrage was laid and it was gradually improved throughout the war. A total of 39,000 H.4 and H.2 mines (based on a German design) were laid in a ladder pattern, at depths of 25, 22, 18 and 12m. The main minefield was augmented by constant patrols, anti-submarine nets, searchlights, magnesium flares and ultimately by the Bragg Loop system. The defence worked on the principle that a submarine might, with great difficulty, navigate its way above the deep minefield on the surface, but, in the likely event of it being suddenly forced to dive, there was every probability that a mine would be triggered. By the summer of 1918, the Folkestone–Gris Nez Barrage posed a near impenetrable barrier to U-boat activities. It became known as the 'U-boat graveyard' and the concentration of submarine wrecks in this small sector bears graphic testimony to the minefield's effectiveness. The minefield claimed veteran and novice crew alike. UB 56, the first victim, UB 109 and UB 55 happily yielded survivors. Many U-boat wrecks litter French waters but here, we are (largely) concerned with submarine wrecks in British territorial waters. Oddly enough, the remains of a couple of surrendered First World War U-boats can still be found in the Medway, where they were left to rot during the 1920s. One lies under deep mud in the Gillingham Reach, while the other lies off Sheerness.

The British learned from experience, and during the Second World War the Channel was once again mined. The minefield consisted of two lines of shallow mines and three lines of 3,000 deep mines between the Goodwins and West Dyck Bank (commenced 11 September), augmented by a series of 5,000 deep mines along the Folkestone–Gris Nez line, was planned in minute detail before the war. The loss of U 16, U 12 and U 40 in October 1939 revived bad memories for the Kriegsmarine and, following the loss of

U 16, U-boat commanders were ordered to avoid the Channel, although there was a flurry of mining sorties in the winter of 1940. Of course by the summer of 1940 this barring of the Channel was of little consequence, due to the availability of French Atlantic ports. An outburst of U-boat activity in the Channel following 'D-Day' will be dealt with in the following volumes.

The outer harbour was built in 1909 to shelter British battleships of the Grand Fleet. In the First World War, Dover Harbour was home to the famous 6th Destroyer Flotilla, known as the 'Dover Patrol', charged with policing the Channel. Not far away at St Margaret's at Cliffe, stands their memorial, erected by public subscription in 1921. The inscription reads: 'To the Grace of God and in everlasting memory of the Dover Patrol 1914–1918', and below, 'In memory of the officers and men of the Royal Navy and Merchant Navy who gave their lives in ships sailing upon the waters of the Dover Strait 1939-1945'.

There is an identical memorial on Cap Gris Nez on the French side of the Channel. What is not so well known is that, until 1917, the 4th Submarine Flotilla (HMS *Arrogant*) comprised of 'C' boats was also stationed in the harbour on coastal protection duties. Two British submarines were lost off Kent: B2 in 1912 off the South Foreland and *Truculent* in the Thames Estuary in 1950. Both sank following peacetime collisions.

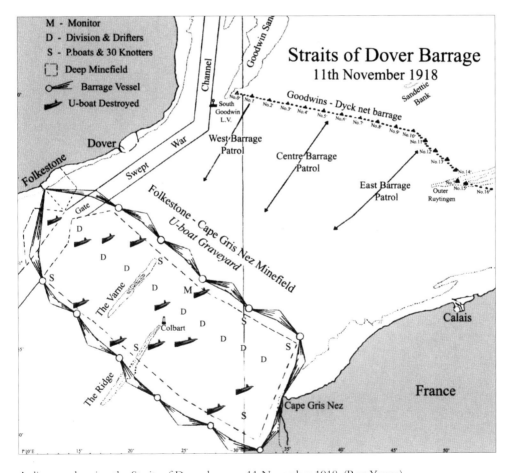

A diagram showing the Straits of Dover barrage, 11 November 1918. (Ron Young)

In 1926 work began on the construction of a memorial to fallen submariners of the First World War. It was finished in 1930 and stands at Möltenort. The bronze memorial plaques at the shrine are inscribed with the names of all 28,728 U-boat men, including those lost with their boats, and 1,275 men who died from other causes.

Submarine depot ship HMS *Arrogant* at Dover. (Author's collection)

War has cast a long shadow over Dover, Britain's premier cross-Channel port for over 2,000 years – that same fortress Dover immortalised by a combination of Dunkirk, the Battle of Britain, and the songs of Vera Lynn. Reminders of Dover's key wartime role abound. On the cliffs, in the Western Defences and in the subterranean passages of the mighty castle, the sense of momentous events having unfolded here is tangible. Dover was not protected from aircraft and long-range artillery, which continued to pulverise the town until the end of the Second World War. This part of the Channel coast lived up to its reputation as 'Hell Fire Corner'. Those interested in learning more about Dover's stirring wartime role should follow up a trip to the castle with a visit to the Dover Museum in Market Square, with its maritime history displays. The Deal Maritime and Local History Museum, at 22 St George's Road, should not be missed.

The celebrated chalk cliffs dominate the coast from Deal to Dover and beyond. The remainder of this coastal strip is flat, punctuated by groynes to prevent erosion. Since Napoleonic times the nature of the coast has rendered it vulnerable to invasion. Some 5 miles off the coast of East Kent lie the dreaded Goodwin Sands. There are actually two sandbanks, North and South Goodwins, separated by the Kellet Gut. Between the Goodwins and the shore, the anchorages of the North and South Downs enticed German submarines, but the Goodwins could dispose of a U-boat as easily as they could destroy any ship. The submarine U 48 will always be associated with the Goodwins, not least for her incredible tendency to reappear then return to the deep every few decades. Sometimes the submarine associations are not obvious. The village of Seal adopted HMS *Seal* during the Second World War. A memorial tablet in the Kentish Yeoman pub perpetuates this association.

North Kent is marshy around the Thames and Medway and it is here that two First World War U-boats can still be found, or at least what little remains of them. Apparently, after the First World War, several of the surrendered U-boats were purchased by scrap dealers in the Medway towns. Two of the boats (one of which is referred to as UB 122) were purchased by a scrap dealer at Strood (name unknown). The valuable and superb diesel engines were removed at Strood and the intention was to sell the hulks for scrap. However the metal market was in serious depression and the two submarines were proving to be an economical liability. After a while the hulks were towed down-river and abandoned in the ooze, at a place called Bees Ness marshes. Here they were unlikely to be a nuisance. Later a petroleum products firm called 'Barry Wiggens', set up on firm ground close-by and built a jetty extending out into deeper water. The company has gone now but the jetty remains, though it is not in use today. The U-boat remains are submerged at high tide, but have been visited very often and stripped of all useful items for souvenirs. They are also gradually sinking into the ooze. Thirty years ago they were recognisable at low water but not now.

Further east, cliffs rise around the North Foreland peninsula. The Thames Estuary and the great naval bases of Chatham and Sheerness, sited to guard the centre of power and commerce, dominate this stretch of coast. Sheerness was itself briefly a submarine base: the 5th Submarine Flotilla was based here in the first year of the First World War attached to the depot ship HMS *Thames*. The submarines included: C1, C2, C3, C4 and C5. In the spring of 1917 HMS *Arrogant* took up residence with C15, C17, C18, C19, C21, C22, C28 and C30 operating on coastal patrol duties in February, thereafter the strength was gradually reduced. Of course North Kent means Chatham, and a visit to the magnificent Historic Dockyards is essential.

Chatham, home of the Royal Dockyard was formerly one of the major centres of submarine production; both *Umpire* and *Swordfish* (Volume 2) were built here. Submarine HMS *Ocelot* provides a chilling insight into the Cold War operations but readers of this book may be attracted to HMS *Cavalier*. Launched in 1944, *Cavalier* saw service with the 6th Destroyer Flotilla. She is the sole remaining British destroyer of the Second World War and the focus of a projected 'Destroyer Memorial'. It should be noted that sixty-seven British destroyers were lost in the First World War with a further 143 sunk in the Second World War. Some of these were lost with all hands. It is a privilege to stand upon *Cavalier*'s bridge and reflect upon the proud history of these warships. Her cramped compartments are redolent with atmosphere, from the spartan crew space to the 'Ops Room', where your over-ripe imagination hears the cry 'Instantaneous Echo Sir!' The operations room was the very nerve centre of the ship. Here, information from ASDIC, lookout, radar and intelligence was evaluated by the commanding officer, then acted upon with split-second timing. Decisions were made here that would have implications for both hunter and quarry. Did the destroyer men hate their U-boat counterparts? Here are the forthright views of one destroyer veteran:

Top: Bragg Loop, anti-submarine mines exploding in the Dover Straits. (Crown copyright)

Above: Old HMS *Thames* submarine depot ship.

Left: Chatham naval memorial. (CWGC)

We hated U-boats. We all knew what they could do and we knew what they would do to us given half a chance. I'd help to fish too many burned up blokes out of the oggin to be in any doubt. Tom Laverick, my oppo on the gun had lost a brother on Barham. When the depth charges exploded he would jeer at our unseen enemy, 'get a load of that you dirty effing bastards'. Once, our group got a U-boat following a hunt, which went on for hours. The sub fought hard for his life, twisting and turning. After the 'can opener', the evidence was there for all to see and the sea gulls were having a feast. Some of our crew were yelling in triumph but others, like me stared in numbed silence. Tom, who had earlier cheered on the submarine's destruction, turned to me and quietly remarked, 'Oh, those poor, poor buggers!' and I heard him mutter a prayer for their souls.

Yes, I hated U-boats, but what did I think of U-boat men? When all is said and done, we were doing our job and they were just doing theirs — with about as much choice as we had — that's to say sweet eff all.

Robbie Robinson DSM★

Nearby stands St George's Centre, formerly the Royal Naval Barracks garrison church of HMS *Pembroke* until it closed with the dockyard in 1984. The walls are studded with all manner of naval memorials. A memorial window is dedicated to the men who died in H47 (See Volume 2). Another memorial remembers the men who lost their lives in the HMS *Truculent* disaster, an event made all the more poignant because many of those present had emerged unscathed from the recent war only to perish in the Thames on a cold January night in 1950.

TRUCULENT, HM SUBMARINE

DATE OF LOSS: 12 January 1950
SCRAPPED: 8 May 1950

Type: 'T' Class large British patrol submarine of Group III *Pennant No.*: P.315, ex-P.92 *Builders*: Vickers Armstrong, Barrow-on-Furness for Royal Navy *Ordered*: for 1940 programme *Keel laid*: as Yard No.815 on 4 December 1940 *Launched*: 12 September 1942 *Completed*: 31 December 1942 (in July 1941 the boat was renumbered and she was renamed in January 1943)

TECHNICAL SPECIFICATIONS

Hull: Double *Surface displacement*: 1,090 tons *U/Dt*: 1,319 tons *LBDH*: 83.85m x 8,09m x 4.34m x 7.46m *Machinery*: 2 x 6-cylinder Admiralty-pattern diesels supplied by Vickers that developed 2,500bhp *Props*: 2 bronze *S/Sp*: 15¼ knots *Op/R*: 11,000 nautical miles at 10 knots *Sub/R*: 80 nautical miles at 4 knots *U/Power*: 2 x Laurence Scott electric motors that developed 1,450hp and gave 8¾ knots *Batteries*: Exide lead/acid/accululators *Fuel/Cap*: 129–132 tons normal, or 230 tons max *Armament*: 8 bow and 3 stern 50.04cm torpedo tubes *Torpedoes*: 17 x 50.04cm (19.7in) *Guns*: 1 x 10.16cm (4in/40) QF Mk XII gun, 1 x 20mm (0.78in) Oerlikon and 3 x 7.69mm (0.303in) Vickers machine guns *Mines*: 12 x Mk II (in place of torpedoes) *Diving*: Max-op-depth 91.44m (300ft) *Complement*: 63–68

During her career, the boat had five 'main' commanders, but others took over for short periods. Lt Robert Love Alexander was the boat's first commander and was promoted to Lt-Com during his time as CO with her.

Lt-Cdr Stephen Lynch Maydon commanded up to August 1944.
Lt Edmund Charles Croswell assumed command in November 1944.
Lt John Chaloner Ogle took over in February 1946.
Lt Andrew Thomas Chalmers took command in July 1948.
Lt Charles Phillip Bowers assumed command in June 1949.

HISTORY

Truculent served in the three main theatres of war and lived up to her name.

(1) Between 15 February and 11 March 1943, she acted as cover for convoys JW.53 and RA.53 off Altafjord, Norway.
(2) She patrolled off Lofoten Islands between 20 March and 9 April 1943.
(3) From 30 April to 21 May 1943, she patrolled north of Iceland to attack and report enemy main units.

Eight of *Truculent*'s survivors. From left to right: ERA Mossman, Tel. Almond, AB Cheriton, ERA Stickland, ERA Buckingham, Sto. Mech. Kendall, LEM Hillier, PO Cook Fry. (Crown copyright)

(4) From 2–17 June 1943, she patrolled north-east of the Faroe Islands. On the morning of 4 June and in position 64° 28' N, 03° 09'W, *Truculent* torpedoed the Kriegmarine U-boat, U 308 (Oblt. Karl Mühlenpfordt), which sank with all forty-four hands.

(5) Between 10 and 23 July 1943 she patrolled the Atlantic area of the Azores.

(6) From 15–26 August 1943, a patrol was made in the Bay of Biscay.

(7) In September and October 1943, *Truculent* took part in Operation Source and towed X6 for the raid on the German battleship *Tirpitz*, at Kåfjord, Norway. X6 was one of the midget submarines previously commanded by Lt R.L. Alexander DSO RN.

(8) On 19 November 1943 she sailed from the UK and arrived in Gibraltar on 28 November.

(9) On 23 January 1944 she arrived at Trincomalee, Ceylon (Sri Lanka).

(10) Between 8 February and 7 March 1944 *Truculent* patrolled off Sabang (North Sumatra), Salang Island and One Fathom Bank. Off Sabang on 14 February, a small merchant vessel was attacked with four torpedoes, but all missed their target. Off Sabang in the eatly morning of 15 February, she attacked a large merchant vessel with four torpedoes; an explosion was heard later, but *Truculent* was forced to dive deep because of

aircraft – there is no record of the ship being hit. Later that day *Truculent* surfaced and attacked a small coaster with the deck gun before artillery fire from the land forced her to break off the attack. The vessel is believed to have sunk as it was reported last seen settling in the water, but this cannot be confirmed.

(11) From 18 March to 9 April 1944, she patrolled the Malacca Strait and on 28 March sank Japanese SS *Yasushima Maru* by torpedo. Then, on 1 April, a small steamer was sunk using the deck gun.

(12) The boat landed a reconnaissance force on Simalur Island, off the west coast of Sumatra, where Special Operation Sugarloaf II was carried out between 2 and 18 May. *Truculent* arrived back at Trincomalee, Ceylon, on 23 May.

(13) Patrolled in the southern Malacca Straits between 12 June and 5 July 1944. From 21 June to 23 June, Special Operation Retaliate I was carried out. On 24 June, a minefield was laid off Klang Strait. On 26 June *Truculent* was in the Malacca Straits and landed a Dutch Naval Intelligence Officer on the east coast of Sumatra. That afternoon a Japanese convoy, consisting of a freighter followed by a troop transport, two tankers and protected by two corvettes, came into sight. Lt-Cdr Lynch Maydon attacked with torpedoes and sank the transport SS *Harukiki Maru* (known as *Harugiku Maru* by the Japanese) in the Straits of Malacca, unfortunately also killing an unknown number of Allied POWs in the process. Five small junks were also sunk on this patrol by ramming or explosive charges, after first seeing the crews to safety.

(14) On 29 July 1944 the boat sailed from Trincomalee to Malta, where she arrived on 25 August.

(15) From 9–18 September she made passage from Gibraltar to the Clyde, with convoy MKS.60.

(16) *Truculent* left Dundee on 29 November 1944 for a refit at Philadelphia, where she arrived on 23 December 1944.

(17) *Truculent* left New London, Connecticut, 12 July 1945 and arrived at the Clyde on 24 July.

Those who knew *Truculent* describe her as a good boat.

Truculent was my favourite boat during my modest 13 years in submarines, even more so than my two wartime boats. She was a very happy submarine with Andy Chalmers as her skipper, Dickie Mason as her droll First Lieutenant, Lt Davis and Sub-Lt Ellis and Lt (E) J.E. Stevenson were the other officers. Her coxswain was that redoubtable arch-survivor Gordon Selby who had the reputation amongst us sailors and stokers of knowing everyone's official number off by heart. Between 1948 and 1949 we spent a happy time trolling in and out of Portland harbour day running and life was good. When we took the boat to Chatham we were heartbroken, most of us, to find out we had been drafted to HMS *Alliance*. With her fine lines, to me at least, *Truculent* had a certain feminine quality about her and leaving her was like leaving the arms of some charming girl and hearing of her loss was for me quite shattering

Gus Britton MBE ex-Sig. HM S/M *Truculent*.

FINAL VOYAGE

On 12 January 1950 *Truculent* (Lt C.P. Bowers) was on passage from the Nore exercise area (51° 35' 30 N, 01° 56' 00 E) to Sheerness, in company with HMS *Cowdray*, the submarine having recently undergone a refit in Chatham. Apart from her crew of sixty-one, she carried an additional eighteen shipyard specialists. *Truculent* was scheduled to sail to Scotland for further trials. She was due to depart Sheerness the next morning.

The surfaced submarine entered the Thames estuary, first through Princes Channel, and then proceeded between Red Sand Shoal and Shivering Sands Fort on course 280 degrees, speed 9 knots. The steaming lights of various ships denoted that maritime traffic was heavy that night. Upon entering Oaze Deep, her course was altered to 261 degrees to pass between South Oaze and the X4 marker-buoy, while escort HMS *Cowdray* returned to Chatham. It was dark with a slight sea fret, but visibility was about 2 miles. Present on the bridge were Lieutenants Bowers, Humphrey-Baker, Engineering Officer Lt Stevenson, Sub-Lt Frew Leading Seaman Headley, and Able Seaman Powell.

Shortly before 19.00 a mysterious triangle of green light, accompanied by two red lights, was spotted off the port bow by the officer on watch, Lt Humphrey-Baker (navigating officer), and reported to the skipper. L/S Fred Headley was at his station in the control room when he received a request from the bridge:

> An order came from the bridge to fetch the Manual of Seamanship. I was a bit surprised, as I had never known anyone to ask for it in the past. Nobody down below had a clue what it looked like. After rummaging through the wardroom and the chart cabinet, I eventually found it. It was very heavy and I had to hump it up the ladder onto the bridge.
>
> I handed the book to Sub-Lt Frew and watched him as he leafed through the pages, pointing out something to the captain.

The ship identification book was handed to Lt Humphrey-Baker and both officers concluded that ahead lay a stationary ship on the northern fringe of the channel. The presence of the Oaze Deep Shoal prevented a turn to starboard in the procedural fashion, but altering course to port (across the channel) seemed the most reasonable step to avoid either a collision, or running aground. Lt Bowers did not reduce speed, nor did he order the use of sound warnings. Unfortunately the ship was far closer than the lights had suggested, because no sooner did the submarine's bow swing to port than *Divina* emerged from the gloom on a collision course. Bowers gave the order. 'HARD A PORT HELM – STOP ENGINES – FULL ASTERN TOGETHER.' Lt Humphrey-Baker:

> We altered course 10 degrees to port while checking the chart to make sure there was sufficient room for our draught of 1ft. While doing this I heard the order 'Stop together'. I immediately jumped the telegraphs, which were behind me and put both to 'STOP'. I then looked round and saw the *Divina* on our starboard bow, at a distance of under a cable. The next order was 'Astern together' and 'Starboard thirty'. The next order was, 'SHUT ALL WATERTIGHT DOORS!'

The 643-ton tanker *Divina*, commanded by Capt. Karl Hommerberg, was travelling between Purfleet and Ipswich with a cargo of petroleum. The red light on her foremast signified she was carrying a volatile cargo, though this had no meaning outside the area controlled by the Port of London Authority. The impact caused the tanker to shudder, but for the submarine the screech of rending metal signified a mortal blow.

Bowers ordered the men on the bridge to go below. AB Powell reached the control room but before the rest could enter the hatch *Truculent* rolled over to port, spilling the men on her bridge into the Thames. Meanwhile Leading Seaman Headley found himself in a tricky situation:

> I was climbing back down the conning tower when I heard the captain issue a stream of urgent orders. He did not raise his voice but I realised we must be in trouble. There was an almighty crash and I found myself pinned against the conning tower as the boat keeled over with an almighty

lurch. The conning tower was flooding fast. Somehow I managed to squirm around the periscope standards. I remembered the drill and tried to breathe out as hard as I could. Moments later I found myself on the surface swimming aimlessly in the dark

Truculent righted herself then began to sink by the bows. Sub-Lt Frew dropped through the conning tower hatch only to stare in horror as the lower hatch was shut and clipped before he could reach it. ERA Buckingham (who closed it from within the control room) had been oblivious to his presence. The upper hatch now closed on his arm and he was dragged down with the submarine, trapped between the two hatches in the rapidly flooding conning tower. As the water rose and pressure equalised, Sub-Lt Frew was able to open the upper hatch and float to the surface holding a broken arm. Regaining his senses on the surface, he swam towards a channel light-buoy and was soon joined by the others, who had been hurled from the bridge. Two had lifebelts thrown down from the stern of *Divina*. Karl Hommerberg, master of *Divina*:

> Both the pilot and myself were on the bridge. A green light could be seen with a white one above it, at about 15 degrees to 20 degrees on the port bow. While occupied in turning to starboard at about 19.04, Divina collided with the approaching vessel, which sank almost immediately. The impact shook us from stem to stern. We saw men in the water and my crew rushed to get them out.

In fact the five men, including Lt Bowers, somehow survived in the wintry Thames estuary for forty-five minutes before the Dutch freighter *Almdijk* picked them up. For much of this time Lt Humphrey-Baker supported the failing Sub-Lt Frew. It took half an hour before they had recovered sufficiently to blurt out their story to the Dutch sailors. At 20.14 *Almdijk* sent the following signal:

> SOS HM SUBMARINE TRUCULENT SUNK NW RED SANDS TOWER BETWEEN X4 BUOY AND EAST PILES BUOY. HAVE PICKED UP FIVE SURVIVORS. BELIEVE SUBMARINE HAS BEEN IN COLLISION WITH SWEDISH DIVINA. ALL SHIPS PLEASE KEEP A LOOKOUT.

What had become of the rest of the crew who went down with the boat? Immediately the bow of *Divina* cleaved through *Truculent*, ten men died within minutes as the Thames flooded into the fore-ends. The surviving sixty-four men retreated through the control room and into the engine room beyond. Raymond Fry was one of them:

> Because of the extra numbers on board I was detailed to arrange supper earlier than usual. After everyone had been fed I took my own meal along to the mess. My supper companion was Frank Myatt. We were just about to begin when there was a heavy jolt on the starboard side, for'rard. We didn't take much notice. The next thing the lights went out and the water was up to our ankles. Truculent gave a list to port and went into a bow down angle. The First Lieutenant was giving the orders 'Collision Stations, all hands in the control room! Shut Bulkhead doors'!
>
> With Frank and others I got into the control room and tried to shut the bulkhead doors between us and the wardroom. We couldn't, so we entered the engine room.

Ernie Buckingham was for'rard in the ERA's mess:

> I felt the crash, stumbled to my senses and yelled 'Collision Stations!' Men were coming back from the fore-ends soaking wet and covered with oil. Water was gushing into the boat over the bulkhead door coaming. Then I realised, 'Oh hell, the batteries'. I set about trying to isolate Number One battery but already the circuits were shorting. I got down on my hands and knees

and somehow managed to pull the fuses just before the lights went out. I heard someone shout 'Leave that Buck'. I didn't fancy being left on my own so I headed off into the control room. Would you believe it, the hatches were wide open. Seawater was cascading in so I tried to shut the hatch using the long lever. I heaved it down but the hatch was blocked by an obstruction (only later did I learn that this was Sub-Lt Frew's arm…)

What follows is an extract from the official report:

After the collision had occurred and the submarine started to sink, one of the survivors, stoker mechanic Kendall closed the watertight door between the engine room and the after end. During the sinking the First Lieutenant Hindes ordered all men to lay aft. Both fore and after engine room bulkheads were closed. The engine room being overcrowded, the First Lieutenant ordered some men to pass into the after end. Some difficulty was encountered in opening the bulkhead door owing to there being a greater pressure in the engine room. When there were 25–30 men in each compartment the door was again shut. During this time water was steadily leaking into the engine room via the snort induction.

ERA Stickland:

I was in the ERA's mess when the engines stopped… as I made my way out with the CERA to see what was wrong there was a massive crash and we took a heavy list to port. I ran to the blowing panel. I blew no 4 port tank and took the list off but by that time we were going down by the bows and I blew No.1 Ballast tank

ERA's Stickland and Mossman remained at their post at the blowing panel until the boat settled on the bottom at 19.03. At last Ernie Buckingham had succeeded in shutting and clipping the lower hatch. These three men now set about saving their own lives. Ernie Buckingham:

I dragged one of the seamen with me as I groped through the pitch blackness to the engine room bulkhead which was by now shut against us. I hammered and hollered and after my assurance that it was safe, they opened up and in we went

Lt Hindes had ordered everyone aft. The crew wasted no time in attempting to shut the forward bulkhead doors, which would have had to be closed against the steep bow-down angle of the boat. Instead, the survivors sheltered behind the forward engine room bulkhead. Having taken this decision, Hindes now pondered his next move.

DSEA escape was certainly feasible, but the submarine was in 46ft (14m) of water on an even keel and in a pilotage area frequented by heavy traffic., First Lieutenant Hindes faced a dilemma. Should he order his men to attempt an escape immediately, or should he order them to wait until he knew for certain that rescue vessels were overhead? Young submariners of Lt Hindes' generation had been seared by the *Thetis* tragedy, when delay had cost the lives of an entire crew, too befuddled by carbon dioxide poisoning to escape, even when rescue vessels were standing by. The loss of *Untamed* had merely reinforced the conclusion that delay was fatal. Also in common with *Thetis*, *Truculent* was carrying eighteen additional dockyard personnel, none of them familiar with DSEA. Lt Hindes correctly calculated that there would be insufficient air on the submarine to sustain life until dawn; therefore, escape would have to be made in darkness, whatever happened. Besides, it was impossible to guess when the authorities would transmit a 'Subsunk' signal – and the crew did not have time on their side.

Lt Hindes made his fateful decision: he announced the crew would mount an escape bid within the hour. The escapees would just have to take their chances on the surface. Preparations for immediate escape were made in both compartments, the after end in the charge of Lt Hindes and the engine room escape made under Chief ERA Francis Hine, a submarine veteran of seventeen years experience. The Twill trunks were rigged and flooding commenced between 19.15 and 19.30. In the meantime the indicator buoy was released. Although twenty-six DSEA sets were known to be in the engine room and after ends, only eighteen sets were available for the escape. It was decided to give non-swimmers the priority. By 20.20 the men in both compartments were ready for escape. Raymond Fry:

> One young stoker, Kendall, couldn't swim and my chum Coxwain George Eldridge just calmly took his set off and passed it to the lad, 'There you go son, I can manage without'. Kendall survived; Eldridge was drowned. We then started to flood the compartment so that we could open the hatch. As we stood there we could hear a ship passing over us. You can imagine how it bucked our spirits. We all thought it was a case of getting out then getting picked up. I went up the canvas trunk, used the escape procedure and took off three of the clips and loosened the fourth according to the book. I went back down and waited, then up the trunk again to take off the fourth clip, back down and wait. By this time the water was up to our middles with the surface covered in bilge oil. (See pages 12 and 228)

Ernie Buckingham:

> What was I thinking of as we flooded up? I thought 'this can't be real, it can't be happening. It's got to be a nightmare'. The water was horribly fascinating as the thick oily tide gradually rose. We had spent all our working lives keeping that boat spotless, keeping brightwork shiny. I felt this terrible sinking feeling in the pit of my stomach. Then I realised that it was my birthday and I started laughing at how ludicrous it was.

The official report describes the escape from the engine room:

> The engine room was flooded through the DSEA valve, both main engine muffler valves and the snort muffler valve. The water rose slowly taking 45 minutes to flood the compartment. When the compartment was flooded PO Fry was ordered to open the vent on the escape hatch in order to flood the twill trunk. Fry, who was using a DSEA set, returned to the compartment after opening the vent. He then went over the escape drill with the others who had sets. He was sent into the twill trunk again to report whether all was clear.

Raymond Fry:

> The next move was for me to go up and open the valve in the hatch to release the air trapped in the trunk. For this I needed an escape set. Tel Almond gave me his, asking me to look after him when he got to the surface. I went up, opened the valve then returned to the engine room…then I went up again, giving my bag a good fill up with oxygen, got my head to the hatch and pushed it. The hatch opened fairly easily. Up I went. Moments later I broke surface.

Chief Engine Room Artificer Hine dipped under the Twill trunk and confirmed that it was open and clear. He then returned to the compartment and sent the men out. Those men without DSEA sets were sent first. CERA Hine calmed the natural anxiety of the escapees with the words, 'Cheer up lads. The hatch is open, Cookem Fry's gone up first to get our supper ready.'

Twill trunk on submarine, probably a 'T' Class boat. (Crown copyright)

One by one the men clambered under the Twill trunk and set off for the surface, each encouraged by a word from the irrepressible CERA. Nothing could prepare them for the bone-chilling Thames and the ordeal ahead however. The last men left were Francis Hines and ERA Ernie Buckingham, both war veterans, both fatalists in outlook. Buckingham had been involved in countless wartime scrapes in *Ursula* while 'Sam' Hine had ended up in a POW camp following the depth charging of *Saracen*. Both fully realised that the odds were stacked against them. Ernie Buckingham:

I slipped off my warm engine and waded towards the twill trunk. Those seconds in the icy water nearly froze me and I wondered what it would be like above. It was useless to put on my goggles, as they were black with oil. I adjusted my set, took one last look at a very brave man and we exchanged 'thumbs up'. I felt bloody awful.

The after ends escape bid did not go so smoothly. The DSEA flood valve was opened but the water trickled in at such a slow rate that Lt Hindes resorted to opening the weed trap, compressed air and signal gun-valves to help the flooding along. It took thirty minutes for the compartment to be flooded sufficiently for Lt Hindes to attempt to unclip the hatch. First he took the precaution of ordering Leading Electrical Mechanic Hillier to keep tight hold of his legs as the clips were removed. Like 'Cookem' Fry before him, Lt Hindes underestimated the pressure. The hatch flew open and the First Lieutenant was ejected from the hatch by the force of an air bubble. Lt Hindes was swept away and never to be seen again. Such resourcefulness deserved a better fate. There was no rush. The turbulence died down and the water rose sufficiently to form a seal around the Twill trunk. The remaining men left in an orderly fashion, some with DSEA sets, others without. Chief Stoker Mechanic Neighbour was the last man out of the after ends; sadly he did not survive to tell the tale.

One by one the men bobbed to the surface. Unfortunately though, there was no vessel waiting to rescue them, only a dark night and an ebb tide. Fighting hard against the numbing cold, they attempted to group together for as long as they could, but gradually they weakened. The merciless tide pulled them away from the lights and further out to sea. Sixteen of the eighteen dockyard workers died. After a while the cold took its toll among the veteran submariners too. Ernie Buckingham found himself alongside his mentor, CERA Hines: 'We rose to the surface almost together and swam together for a while. Then we drifted apart. I did not see him again.'

Raymond Fry:

> On the surface it was dark and very cold. After an hour – which seemed like a year – I began to lose feeling in my legs and kept trying to keep my feet out of the water. My thoughts were, 'I went all through the war without even getting my feet wet and then this happens'. The next half hour went by and I was praying to Christ to save me. After that I just gave up hope. It was so cold and dark I was thinking 'Lets just get it over quick', when a light appeared. I was thrown a lifebelt and helped into a boat. It was one of the boats from the Swedish steamer, the *Divina*.

The log of *Divina* again:

> As nothing could be seen or heard the lifeboat was taken in after one hour. The *Divina* crossed backwards and forwards and at 21.00 hours a cry for help was heard. The lifeboat was launched and four men were picked up.

Raymond Fry was unable to talk. He was laid in the galley and plied with hot coffee. The Swedish crew gently laid the four survivors on bunks, then at 23.00 the Margate lifeboat came alongside to transfer the submariners to HMS *Cowdray* where, in the words of 'Cookem' Fry;

> The wardroom had been cleared, beds and blankets put out. Hot rum, coffee and cocoa for all of us, cigs and food. To cap it all, a hot bath cleaned out later by a sub-lieutenant!
>
> At 04.30 next morning I was asked to go and identify four bodies that had been picked up. The first was Frank Myatt who I had been eating supper with barely ten hours before.

Divers from HMS *Reclaim* spent hours tapping on the hull, more in hope than expectation. Sixty-four men had died.

Divina picked ten men up in total, including: Stevens, Griffiths, Buckingham, Hillier, Almond, Stickland, Kendall and Cheriton. A further five were rescued by *Almdjik*, but that was all. There were fifteen survivors from a total of seventy-nine. Despite the casualties caused by the flooding following the collision, it was on the surface that the crew of HM S/M *Truculent* had died, in the dark waters of the Thames estuary. What had been arguably the most successful submarine escape in British naval history had turned into one of the worst peacetime disasters.

One hour and fourteen minutes had elapsed before *Almdjik* sent her message to the authorities – about the same time that the first DSEA escape from *Truculent* took place. Had *Divina* or *Almdjik* sent signals when the collision occurred, then lifeboats could have been at the scene in advance of the DSEA escapes. However, some time elapsed before the survivors were able to tell the crew of *Almdjik* what had happened. No blame should be apportioned to them in retrospect.

On 26 January the Swedish maritime authorities held an inquest designed merely to ascertain what had happened. Within a week a more substantial inquest was held at Royal Naval Hospital Gillingham over the bodies of seven of the victims. The coroner did not report any evidence of gross criminal negligence but instead found much to commend in the behaviour of the men trapped on the submarine. It is worth noting that a few days later on 7 February posthumous Albert medals were awarded to Lieutenant J.F. Hindes and Chief Engine Room Artificer F.W. Hine for their exemplary behaviour. In addition, there was a British Empire Medal for survivor Raymond 'Cookem' Fry, whose *sang-froid* had done much to maintain morale during the tense time spent waiting to escape.

Those men who survived the initial collision all succeeded in escaping from the submarine. In this sense the value of the DSEA set as a means of escape was proven, but it is not the full story. The post-mortem reports revealed that at least seven men had died from ruptured lungs. There seems little doubt that this was because the escapers were unable to regulate the speed of their ascent to the surface. Several were known to have dispensed with the DSEA apron in fear of becoming snagged in the ascent. On the surface many had died from exposure or drowning. In the final analysis, both the *Truculent* and *Umpire* disasters (see Chapter Three) demonstrated that the DSEA set provided a viable means of escaping from a sunken submarine. However, in common with the crews of *Swordfish*, *Umpire*, and who knows how many other submarines before them, the *Truculent* escapees discovered the drawback of the system. If help is not immediately at hand on the surface, survivors will surely drift away and drown or die of exposure. What was needed was a means of escape that could also provide protection on the surface until rescue was at hand. The new immersion suits might have saved the crew but these were not yet on general distribution. The lasting legacy of the *Truculent* disaster was that the immersion suit was made standard issue to the British Submarine Service, replacing DSEA as the principle means of submarine escape for the Royal Navy (although the Royal Navy was still using DSEA as late as 1954). In addition, an all-round white steaming light was introduced to the bows of British submarines, known as a 'Truculent Light'. One final result of the *Truculent* disaster was the erection of a 100ft-high escape tower at Fort Blockhouse.

The decision to escape at once was made in the firm belief that, since the submarine had been in collision with a surface ship and the ships' propellers were heard overhead, there would be at least one and probably more vessels ready to pick up survivors. In this the crew were cruelly mistaken. The Admiralty Board of Enquiry held on 9 February 1950 under Rear Admiral Hughes-Hallett concluded that Lt Hindes should have waited.

HMS *Truculent* rescue attempt ships. (Crown copyright)

> ...Had those in charge more knowledge of the deterioration of the air, they might well have delayed the escape until the arrival of the naval searching forces and it is probable that there would have been more survivors picked up.

The *Thetis* experience suggested otherwise and it must be doubted whether the man who wrote these words had ever been trapped in a flooding submarine with the air running out. At any rate Lt Bowers was cleared of the grave charge of negligently losing his ship. However, he shouldered part of the blame for hazarding his vessel. The Admiralty maintained that instead of altering course across the channel on sighting *Divina*'s lights, Lt Bowers should have maintained his original course, reduced speed and used sound warnings. *Divina* was at fault for failing to show correct lights, failing to turn to starboard earlier, not reducing speed and not making sound signals. Rightly or wrongly, Bowers was severely reprimanded.

As for *Truculent*, she was brought to the surface on 14 March 1950 – ironically by two German lifting vessels seized earlier as a war prize. The submarine was beached at Cheney Spit near Sheerness. There is a most harrowing account in the RN Submarine Museum from DSEA Coxwain Hedley Woodley who led the party charged with 'evacuating' the boat. The histological laboratory handed Woodley a lamp and a mouse (to warn of gas). The bodies of the men who had died in the boat were carefully removed. This was always a ghastly business, but in this case it was made worse by the refusal of the commanding officer to allow the evacuation volunteers any rum. Coxwain Woodley entered the fore-ends and made a surprising discovery:

> There was much debris, hammocks, cases, kitbags and, of course bodies. I went forward, slipping and sliding in the silt. In places there was up to 6in of water. The deck boards had been strewn everywhere... I was amazed that the tube space doors remained open. I think that there would have been no loss of life if these had been shut, which they should have been. It was a standing order that the fore-ends doors were to be shut and clipped and reported to the control room on leaving harbour.

Sixteen of the dead were buried in the delightful Woodlands Cemetery in Gillingham, where the Medway Towns branch of the Submariners' Association hold a moving annual ceremony. On 8 May 1950, the 'beautiful' *Truculent* was towed to the breakers yard. There is an interesting postscript: the early 1950s saw a spate of British submarine films, notably

'Morning Departure', starring John Mills and Richard Attenborough (1950, Roy Ward Baker) inspired by the Kenneth Woollard play of the same name. Although based (very) loosely upon the *Thetis* disaster, the film was criticised in some quarters as an attempt to cash in on the *Truculent* catastrophe. This criticism was very unfair, as the film had been made before the disaster took place.

As ever, we must pose the question, could the loss of life have been prevented? In taking the decision to order an immediate escape, Lt Hindes did not have the luxury of hindsight and it is difficult to argue against the view that his course of action was sound, based upon the information available to him at the time. The last word belongs with survivor Ernie Buckingham:

> You could say that we did the hard bit by escaping in the first place. It's a pity that there was no kind hand waiting to pick us up. Nobody to blame…just sheer bad luck really.

THE CREW OF *TRUCULENT* WHO DIED

Brookes, Ernest, Stoker Mechanic
Campbell, Eric, Stoker Mechanic
Child, John G., Steward
Daw, A., Stoker Mechanic
Denny, John Hughes, EM
Dighton, Warren E., Able Seaman
Donnelly, Patrick
Dorn, Alfred, Stoker Mechanic
Dring, Gordon R., Leading Seaman
Eldridge, George Thomas, Petty Officer
Ellis, F.G., Stoker Mechanic
Farman, N., Lieutenant
Firbank, W.J., Leading Seaman
Fox, F.R., Leading Seaman
Frost, R.A., Engine Room Artificer
Gutridge, Maurice Fredrick, Able Seaman
Harrison, George W. J., Able Seaman
Head, Percival Arthur Thomas, DSM L/Sn
Helliwell, Ronald Walter, Stoker Mechanic
Higgins, Leonard C., Leading Telegraphist
Hindes, Frederick Joseph, Lieutenant AM
Hine, Francis, Able Seaman
Johnson, Robert, Leading Signalman
Johnston, Mervyn Baptist MiD, P.O. Stoker
Jones, H.G., Stoker Mechanic
Likely, M.J., Stoker Mechanic
Mackenzie, G.E., Steward
Manley, Jack T., E Art
McIntyre, John Figg, Chief Elec.
Murphy, Michael, Able Seaman
Myatt, Francis, Petty Officer
Neighbour, Russell A., CPO Stoker Mechanic
Noon, Kenneth Charles, Able Seaman
Oliver, William A., Able Seaaman
Phillips, Edward C. Lampia, PO Telegraphist
Phillips, Terence P., E.R. Artificer.3rd

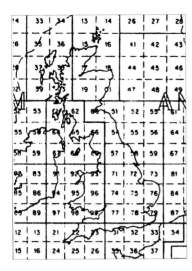

Above: Divina's bows. (Crown copyright)

Left: U-boat grid.

Powell, Dennis N., Able Seaman
Prouse, Kenneth, Able Seaman
Purkiss, Brian Sydney, Leading Seaman
Read, John Lynton, Leading Seaman
Robinson, Peter, Stoker Mechanic
Richardson, Thomas, Stoker
Smith, Anthony, Stoker Mechanic
Swire, William, Able Seaman
Taylor, Clifford, Stoker Mechanic
Woods, Edward N., Stoker Mechanic

THE CHATHAM ROYAL DOCKYARD PERSONNEL WHO DIED
Alexander, Ernest William, 36, Shipfitter
Austin, Edward William, 46, Electrician
Bailey, Philip John, 26, Electrician
Barnden, William Edward, 32, Electrician
Edwards, Kenneth King, 25, Shipfitter
Gutteridge, George, 56, Electrician
Hancock, Donald Arthur, 28, Constructor
Harling, Robert William, 25, Engine-fitter
Holmes, Arthur Andrew Thomas, 26, Shipfitter
Jenner, Albert Edward, 46, Electrician
McLaughlin, James, 59, Shipwright
Melville, John Frank, 27, Draughtsman
Mills, Norman Albert, 22, Draughtsman
Potts, Charles Walter Sedgewick, 40, Shipfitter
Strickland, Robert Henry, 35, Engine-fitter
Tester, Herbert George, 33, Electrician

The above information was taken from the *Chatham, Rochester & Gillingham News*, 29 January 1950.

ADM 1/22713 – ADM 116/5739 – ADM 116/6156 – ADM 199/1868 (Patrol reports)

The Downs of east Kent have always provided a welcome anchorage, albeit one in the shadow of the dreaded Goodwin Sands.

Little UB 12 was one of many U-boats sent to mine the Downs. Like so many other boats, she failed to return and was destined to be officially stamped '*Verschollen*' (missing), somewhere off the Kent coast. However, in more recent times, sport divers have found and identified a wreck off Flanders that was revealed to be SM UB 12.

UC 6, SM IMPERIAL U-BOAT

DATE OF LOSS: 27 September 1917
DEPTH: 22m
REFERENCE: 51 30'.102 N, 001 34'.695 E
LOCATION: 8.83 nautical miles NNE of
North Foreland, Broadstairs

Type: UCI coastal mine-laying boat **Builders**: AG Vulcan, Hamburg for Kaiserliche Deutsche Marine **Ordered**: 23 November 1914, within the batch of UC 1–UC 10 **Keel laid**: as Yard No.50 **Launched**: 20 June 1915 **Commissioned**: by Kapitänleutnant Matthias Graf von Schmettow on 24 June 1915

TECHNICAL SPECIFICATIONS

Hull: Single **Surface displacement**: 168 tons **U/Dt**: 183 tons **LBDH**: 33.99m x 3.15m x 3.04m x 6.30m **Machinery**: 1 x 90ps Daimler diesel **Props**: 1 bronze **S/Sp**: 6.20 knots **Op/R**: 780 nautical miles at 5 knots **Sub/R**: 50 nautical miles at 4 knots **U/Power**: 1 x 175ps electric motor giving 5.22 knots **Batteries**: Lead/acid/accumulators **Fuel/Cap**: 3 tons **Torpedo tubes**: None **Torpedoes**: None **Guns**: 1 machine gun and rifles **Mine chutes**: 6 x 100cm (39.37in) vertically inclined **Mines**: 12 x UC 120 **Diving**: Max-op-depth 50m (164ft) and 33–36 seconds to crash-dive **Complement**: 1 officer and 13 ratings

UC 6 was formally assigned to the Flandern Flottille on 31 July 1915. The boat made eighty-nine patrols of two or three days' duration, with the following commanders:

Kplt Matthias Graf von Schmettow from 24 June 1915 until 4 May 1916.
Kplt Otto Ehrentraut from 5 May 1916 to 5 September 1916.
Kplt Paul Günther from 6 September 1916 to 4 November 1916.
Oblt.z.S. Werner von Zerboni di Sposetti served from 5 November 1916 to 30 April 1917.
Oblt.z.S. Werner Löwe from 1 May 1917 to 1 September 1917.
Oblt.z.S. Gottfried Reichenbach from 2 September 1917.

Mines laid by UC 6 sank at least fifty-four known vessels, which included eighteen Royal Navy trawlers and drifters; only one other vessel, a lighter, was sunk using explosives. Mines also damaged seven steamships. The following vessels were amongst those sunk or damaged: the Royal Navy steam trawler *Worsley* (The Admiralty) had been requisitioned in 1915 and converted to a minesweeper (Port Reg. Gy. 814) when she was sunk by a mine off Aldeburgh on 14 August 1915. The mine had been laid by UC 6 the previous day. On 16 August the RN trawler *Japan* sank after detonating a mine off the Shipwash. She had been requisitioned in August 1915 as Admiralty minesweeper No.42.

The Swedish built SS *Disa* (Rederi A/B Disa, Gefle) foundered on 25 August 1915, after detonating a mine laid by UC 6 on the 13 August. The steamer was on passage from London for Hernösand, Sweden, with salt cake.

The steam RN trawler *Dane* was requisitioned in April 1915 and converted to Admiralty Armed Patrol Vessel No.1446; she struck a mine and sank off Aldeburgh on 28 August.

Two firemen, William George Brown (forty-six years old) and William Moore (thirty-six years old), were lost with the steamer *Sir William Stephenson* (Tyne-Tees Steam Shipping Co. Ltd, Newcastle), which struck a mine that had been laid by UC 6 on 21 August off Cockle Light Vessel at the entrance to Yarmouth. The ship was en-route from the Tyne to London with a general cargo and was taken in tow, but sank in Yarmouth Roads on 29 August 1915.

South of Deal on 16 September 1915, the SS *Africa* (Bennett SS Co. Ltd, Goole) detonated a mine laid by UC 6 the previous day and was forced to beach close inshore in 12ft of water; she was transporting four hospital railway carriages from London to Boulogne and two crewmen were lost. The wreck blocked the launch of North Deal lifeboat, so it had to be dispersed with explosives by Trinity House.

The *Lydian* was a steam trawler requisitioned in August 1915 and converted to Admiralty Armed Patrol Vessel No.162. Unfortunately on 18 September, it struck a mine and sank off South Foreland.

The SS *San Zeferino* (Eagle Oil Transport Co. Ltd, London) was on passage from Puerto Mexico for Sheerness with fuel oil when she struck a mine off the South Goodwin Light Vessel on 18 September 1915. She was beached, but re-floated in the October. (The ship was torpedoed and left damaged in St George's Channel by UC 33 on 26 September 1917, and three men were killed.)

Travelling in ballast and en-route from London for Hartlepool, the SS *Horden* (Burnett SS Co. Ltd, Newcastle) struck a mine laid by UC 6 on 13 August 1915. The mine detonated in the aft part of the ship at 12.40 on 20 September 1915, blowing the hatch covers into the air and shrouding the vessel in choking smoke. It immediately began to settle and the stern was actually submerged within one minute. A ship's boat was lowered and some of the crew of seventeen clambered into them, while others either jumped into the sea or rushed up forward. This stayed afloat for ten more minutes. As the ship sank one of the other boats floated off and men in the sea climbed into it. *Bob Read*, a Royal Navy patrol boat, rescued those on the fore section, and the steamer *Alice* saved those in the two boats. A second explosion occurred 50 yards away on the port side, soon after the first one. All the men were transferred to the *Bob Read* and taken to Lowestoft.

On 23 September 1915, Fireman Peter Martin Den Ouden was lost when the SS *Groningen* (General Steam Navigation Co. Ltd, London) went down off the Sunk Head Buoy, after detonating a mine laid by UC 6 on 8 September. She was on passage from Harlingen, Texas, for London with general cargo.

Near the South Goodwin Light Vessel, the *Nigretia* (Beaver Shipping Co. Ltd, Bristol) was damaged by a mine and beached on the Shingles Bank on 27 September 1915, but she re-floated later. *Nigretia* was taking coal from Hull to Rouen.

Another vessel damaged was the *Aleppo* (T. Wilson, Sons & Co. Ltd, Hull) off Sunk Head Buoy on 18 October 1915. The ship was bound for Hull from Alexandria, Egypt, with grain and general cargo; she beached, but re-floated.

The Norwegian steamer *Salerno* (Dampskipsselskapet Aktieselskapet Otto Thoresens Linie, Christiania) struck a mine laid by UC 6 on 12 October 1915. She was transporting general cargo, mail, and passengers, from Aaborg and the Tyne for Santos and foundered off the Sunk Head Buoy on 18 October.

The *Monitoria* (Ericsson Shipping Co. Ltd, Newcastle) was carrying coal from the Humber to London when it struck a mine on 21 October 1915 and foundered. UC 6 had laid the mine on 12 October.

Aries was a 268-ton vessel built in 1880 and hired by the Admiralty as an Armed Patrol Yacht on 12 September 1914. Sadly she struck a mine and sank off Leathercoat on 31 October 1915.

The Norwegian steamer *Eidsiva* (Adolph Halvorsen, Bergen) was travelling from South Shields to Rouen with coal when she struck a mine near South Goodwin Light Vessel. The ship then headed for the shelter of Dover, but sank offshore on 31 October 1915; UC 6 had laid the mine earlier that day.

On 31 October 1915, *Othello II* sank after detonating a mine, and only one man survived; she was a steam trawler that had been requisitioned in March 1915 as Admiralty trawler No.1193.

The *Toward* (Clyde Shipping Co. Ltd, Glasgow) foundered on 31 October 1915 after striking a mine laid by UC 6 earlier that day. The ship was travelling at 11 knots on passage from London for Belfast with general cargo when a detonation occurred in front of the bridge and under the No.2 hold at 09.45. The ship instantly caught fire and began to go down by the head, so Captain McTavish hurriedly ordered the engine stopped and the lifeboats lowered. Five men leaped overboard, but the rest of the twenty-one crewmen scrambled into the boats and cleared the ship. All of the men, including those in the sea, were rescued by patrol boats and landed at Dover at 17.00.

The 311-ton steam coaster *Moorside* (Catcheside SS Co. Ltd, Newcastle) was transporting coal from Leith to France when she detonated a mine off Boulogne on 12 November 1915. UC 6 had laid the mine on 8 November.

Five crewmen were lost when the SS *Nigel* (George Gibson & Co. Ltd, Leith) foundered off Boulogne after striking a mine on 12 November 1915. She was en-route from Newhaven to Boulogne with Government stores. UC 6 had laid the mine on 8 November.

FOUR OF THE MEN WHO DIED

Brown, Frank, 38, Greaser
Champion, Frank Edward, Fireman
Russel, William, 58, Fireman
Treasurer, William Bruce, 45, Chief Engineer

Transporting coal from Leith to Dunkerque, the SS *Traquair* (George Gibson & Co. Ltd, Leith) foundered off Dover on 12 January 1916 after detonating a mine that had been laid by UC 6 on 30 December 1915. The mine exploded at 10.45 between the engine room and No.3 hold, which blew the hatches and some of the cargo 90ft into the air. The ship then began to settle and list so heavily to starboard, almost instantaneously, that only the starboard boats could be lowered. The steamer sank in five minutes, but all of the crew of twenty, including Captain Telford, were rescued by the patrol boat *Strathyre* and landed at Dover at 11.30.

Seventeen crewmen were lost when the SS *Leicester* (Great Central Railway, Grimsby) detonated a mine at 10.30 on 12 February 1915, the mine having been laid by UC 6 on 10 February. The ship was bound from Portsmouth to Cromarty, Scotland, with 600 tons of general cargo; Captain S. Barley and six crewmen were rescued by trawlers and landed at Dover.

THE MEN WHO PERISHED

Barker, Fred, 42, Fireman
Brumund, Gerhard Frederick William, 41, Cook
Charlton, Robert, 44, First Engineer
Cosman, Ernest, 41, Second Engineer
Cumblidge, John Henry, Steward
Dale, Alfred, 50, Able Seaman

Edmonds, George Edward, 58, Able Seaman
Goodey, Edward, 32, Fireman
Hague, Ernest, 39, Second Mate
Harrington, George Herbert, 26, Able Seaman
Hollingworth, Arthur, 22, Donkeyman
Hudson, Albert, 52, Donkeyman
Larson, Charles Baden, 15, Mess Room Boy
Parker, Arthur, 43, Fireman
Shepherd, Edward, 31, Fireman
Smith, Harry Clarke, 53, Fireman
Wringe, Arthur George, 51, Fireman

The steam trawler *Carlton* was requisitioned in December 1915 as Admiralty minesweeper No.1965, but she struck a mine laid by UC 6 off Folkestone and sank on 21 February 1915.

The French *Trignac* (Soc. Anon. des Chargeurs de l'Ouest, Nantes), commanded by Captain H. Caudal, was in ballast and en-route from Nantes to Newcastle-upon-Tyne when she sank, 25 miles off Spurn Point on 24 February 1916. UC 6 had probably laid the mine on 7 December 1915.

The liner *Maloja I* (Peninsular & Oriental Steam Navigation Co. Ltd, Belfast), the company's largest ship, left Tilbury sometime after noon on Saturday 26 February 1916 under the command of Cdr Charles Edward Irving RNR. She was bound for Bombay with 456 persons on board – 121 of them passengers – and a general cargo. (She could carry 450 first class passengers, 220 second class passengers and 400 crew.) *Maloja I* was sister ship to the SS *Medina*, both built by Harland & Wolff. *Maloja* was quite a luxurious vessel, boasting a first class music room, complete with a baby grand piano. It was located on an open gallery over the dining saloon and had long tables, furnished with rows of fixed, but revolving, chairs. The ship anchored up for the night at the mouth of the Thames, as vessels were not allowed to pass through the Dover Straits after dark. She was given permission to weigh anchor at 08.00. A south-westerly gale had been blowing all night, which had hampered the minesweepers in completing their work clearing the Channel. The sweepers were still working at about 10.25 on 27 February when *Maloja I* struck a mine aft, 2 miles south-west of Dover, the mine having been laid by UC 6 earlier that day. The explosion destroyed many of the lifeboats and debris was thrown high into the air. The engines were put in reverse to slow the ship's forward movement and allow the boats to be lowered, but the engine room flooded and the engines could not be stopped. People rushed to the lifeboats, but those on the port side were up against the ship's side and a few capsized as they were being lowered. The big ship continued to go astern, while gradually building up speed to almost 9 knots. She stayed on an even keel for about five minutes, but then began listing at about 75 degrees which prevented any remaining boats from being lowered. Then the decks were awash. Twenty minutes after the detonation the ship foundered, taking 155 people down with her, many of them Lascar seamen. Lots of small craft set out to lend assistance and they rescued many of those still in the sea.

The steamer *Empress of Fort William* (ex-*Mount Stephen*), commanded by Captain W.D. Shepherd, approached from astern and stopped. The crew attempted to aid the stricken liner and were preparing to lower the boats when she too detonated a mine laid by UC 6 earlier that day. The *Empress of Fort William* (Canada Steamship Lines Ltd, Montreal) also sank, but without the loss of any of her twenty crewmen. She was carrying coal from South Shields to Dunkerque.

The 304-ton requisitioned Cochrane-built steam trawler *Angelus* had been converted to Admiralty minesweeper No.1629 when she detonated a mine and sank on 28 February, the mine having been laid by UC 6 the previous day.

The RN steam trawler *Weigelia* was requisitioned in August 1914 as Admiralty minesweeper No.153, but she struck a mine and sunk off Dover on 18 February 1916.

Likewise, the RN steam trawler *Flicker*, which had been requisitioned in November 1914 as Admiralty minesweeper No.412, sank off Dover after detonating a mine on 4 March 1916.

The 212-ton RN steam trawler *Carona* was on Admiralty Service off Ramsgate when she detonated a mine and sank on 23 March 1916.

Fourteen crewmen including the master, the first, second and third mates were lost with the SS *Sea Serpent* (Leach & Co. Ltd, London) on 23 March 1916, the four survivors being landed at Dover. She was on passage from Birkenhead for Dunkerque with a cargo of corrugated galvanized sheets/bar/rod and tube. UC 6 had laid the mine earlier that same day.

THE MEN WHO PERISHED

Anderson, George James, 24, Fireman
Barrow, Frederick William, 16, Mess Room Boy
Bontempi, Primus Jacobus, 33, Fireman
Douglas, Alfred Edward, 48, Fireman
Hamon, Alfred De Gruchy, 48, Second Mate
Hill, J., Chief Engineer
Nurcombe, Robert, Able Seaman
Philps, W., 49, Master
Priest, Harry Adams, 41, Chief Officer
Sheldrick, George William, 36, Able Seaman
Sheldrick, William Charles, 27, Able Seaman
Springett, Ernest Mills, 41, Able Seaman
Stothard, James John, 24, Donkeyman
Warans, Nelson Napier, 25, Fireman

Off Folkestone, the Danish SS *Christianssund* (Det Forenede Dampskipsselskapet Selsk., Copenhagen), sank after striking a mine on 24 March 1916, while transporting a general cargo including cork, wood, salt and tobacco from Falmouth to Copenhagen, the master being G. Indresen. The mine had been laid the previous day by UC 6.

The steamer *Saint Cecilia* (Hogarth Shipping Co. Ltd, Ardrossan) foundered on 26 March 1916. The mine that sank her was laid earlier that day and she was carrying general cargo from Portland, Maine, to London.

While voyaging from Almeria to the Tees with 4,880 tons of iron ore and general cargo, the *Lavinia Westoll* (Westol Line, Sunderland), struck a mine at 13.40 on 28 March 1916. UC 6 had laid the mine on 26 March. The explosion occurred at the forward part of the ship and then, moments later, a second detonation was felt aft and she began to sink. The crew abandoned ship at 14.20 and the small steamer *Wave Queen*, which was just 440 yards away, rescued all the crew of twenty-seven and landed them at Grimsby at 11.00. No one saw what time the ship sank, due to falling snow and sleet.

The British steamer *Halcyon* (General Steam Navigation Co. Ltd, London) foundered on 7 April 1916 after striking a mine laid by UC 6 that same day. She was en-route from Bordeaux to London with general cargo.

Greaser William Carlson (thirty-two years old) and Fourth Engineering Officer Gordon Millett Sara (twenty-two years old) were both lost with the SS *Shenandoah* (Furness, Withy & Co. Ltd, London) on 14 April 1916, after she struck a mine and sank while travelling from St John, New Brunswick, and Halifax, Nova Scotia, to London with general cargo. UC 6 had laid the mine on 7 April.

The steamer *Batavier V* (William H. Müller & Co.'s Algemeene Scheepv. Mij., Rotterdam), a Dutch ship, foundered after striking a mine on 16 May 1916. She was conveying passengers and a general cargo, including 7,000 bales of rice, coffee, piece goods, fourteen cases of gold and £5,000 in Stirling-coins-specie-plate, from London to Rotterdam. UC 6 had laid that mine on 5 May.

The 646-ton coaster *Excellenz Mehnert* (O.G. Gjessen m. fl., Skudeneshavn) sank on 1 June 1916 after striking a mine laid by UC 6 on 20 May. The ship was transporting wood pulp from Drammen, south-east Norway, to Gravesend, England.

Kaphreda was an RN steam trawler requisitioned in August 1914 and converted to Admiralty minesweeper No.364, but she struck a mine and sank near Corton Light Vessel on 8 June 1916.

Otis Tarda (Hudig & Pieters Algemene Scheepvaat Maatschappij, Rotterdam), a Dutch coaster, was carrying general cargo from Rotterdam to Goole when she detonated a mine and sank on 21 June 1916. The mine had been laid by UC 6 the previous day.

On 23 June 1916, seven men were lost with the steamer *Burma* (Bennett SS Co. Ltd, Goole), which detonated a mine laid by UC 6 on 20 June. The coaster was en-route from London to Goole in ballast.

SIX OF THE MEN WHO DIED
Champion, Robert John, 31, Fireman
Duffill, Thomas William, 29, Fireman
Gillyon, James Walter, 48, Able Seaman
Jackson, Herbert, 34, Fireman
Shay, John, 48, Chief Engineer
Turner, Albert Levy, 36, Able Seaman

The Dutch SS *Wallstroom* (N.V. Hollandsche Stoomboot Mij., Amsterdam) was commanded by Captain P. Kalishoek and transporting a general cargo from Swansea to Amsterdam when she struck a mine and sank north-east of Shipwash Light Vessel on 27 June 1916, the mine having been laid the previous day.

The *Hirose* (ex-Dutch *Onze*), a steam trawler requisitioned in June 1916 as Admiralty armed trawler No.3280, was sadly lost to a mine off Aldeburgh Napes on 29 June 1916.

Also lost near the Shipwash due to a mine on 7 July 1916, was the SS *Gannet* (General Steam Navigation Co. Ltd, London) with eight crewmen. She was hauling general cargo from Rotterdam to London. Captain F.G. Cole was amongst the survivors.

THE MEN WHO PERISHED
Burton, Albert Edward, 26, Able Seaman
Burton, Charles Edgar, 26, Able Seaman
Knegt, J., 40, Fireman
Persy, L., 25, Fireman
Smith, Joseph Robert, 44, Carpenter
Stead, George Henry, 41, Donkeyman
Wiles, William Robert, 27, Cook Steward
Wyburd, Albert Vernon, Able Seaman

The SS *Kara* (London & Paris SS Co. Ltd, London) was lost to a mine on 10 July 1916, which had been laid by UC 6 earlier that day. The steamer was in ballast on passage from Rouen for South Shields. The ship was proceeding in convoy when a violent detonation occurred on her port side, amidships at 19.00. The starboard side appeared to bulge outward and both ends of the ship lifted right up. Captain E.G. Badcock ordered the crew of twenty-two into the lifeboats and a tug towed the ship to Corton Sands, where it was beached, but became a total wreck. The Lowestoft lifeboat towed the men in their own boats back to Lowestoft.

Donkeyman William Buchanan (sixty-five years old) was lost with the SS *Mascotte* (George Gibson & Co. Ltd, Leith) on 3 October 1916 due to a mine, while journeying from Rotterdam to Leith with 500 tons of general cargo. A violent detonation occurred on the starboard side at 08.25, directly beneath the engine room. Twenty-one crewmen and one passenger (probably a DEMS gunner) took to the boats as the vessel immediately began to settle. Unfortunately a donkeyman had been killed in the explosion and his body was underwater in the engine room – the chief engineer had reported this to Captain W.A. Miller. The men cleared the ship and watched it sink at 08.40; they were all then picked up by a patrol boat and taken to Gorleston.

Six crewmen were lost (all hands) when the *Lonada* (Port of London Authority, London) detonated a mine and foundered off Shipwash Light Vessel on 29 December 1916. Originally mud hopper No.22 and refitted for cargo service, the vessel was en-route from the Tyne to London with coal. UC 6 laid the mine on 27 December.

THE MEN WHO DIED
Guilmant, Norman Reginald, 24, Able Seaman
Nessworthy, George Thatthew, 29, Third Engineer
Scott, John Joseph, 34, Second Engineer
Spalding, John, 39, Fireman and Donkeyman
Tracey, George William, 44, Steward
Willing, James Robinson, 49, Chief Officer

The Ascot Class Royal Navy steam-powered paddle minesweeper *Ludlow* sank on 29 December 1916 after detonating a mine laid by UC 6. She carried a complement of seventy-two.

The 7,025-ton *Ashtabula* (Anglo-American Oil Co. Ltd, Newcastle) was badly damaged on 22 February 1917 by a mine laid by UC 6 near Elbow Buoy. The ship was bound from Port Arthur, Texas, to London.

On 31 March the hired RN drifter *Forward III* sank detonating a mine laid by UC 6 off the Shipwash.

The SS *Lumina* (Lumina SS Co. Ltd, Liverpool) was also damaged near Elbow Buoy on 19 April 1917 and put back into Gravesend. She was en-route from Thames Haven to Cardiff without a cargo.

The 1,968-ton steamer *Waterville* (New Line SS Co. Ltd, Leith) was damaged in the same area on 12 May 1917, while transporting coke from Dunston-on-Tyne to Havre. She beached at Deal and re-floated later.

The Norwegian steamer *Roald Amundsen* (Aktieselskapet Laboremus, Christiania) was badly damaged while voyaging from London to Philadelphia, USA, after detonating a mine near Tongue Light Vessel on 16 June 1917. The ship (which was in ballast), beached on Mucking Flats and was re-floated on 21 June.

While transporting coal from the Tyne to Rouen, the 2,086-ton Danish SS *Dorte Jensen* (Dampskibsselskabet Hamlet Aktieselskabet, Copenhagen) sank near Tongue Sand Light Vessel after detonating a mine at position 51° 29' N, 01° 23' E on 18 June 1917.

FINAL VOYAGE
On 27 September 1917, and on her eighty-ninth patrol, UC 6 departed Zeebrugge, with Oblt.z.S. Gottfried Reichenbach, for a mine-laying mission off Kentish Knock, but they never returned. According to two British sources, British seaplane 8676 was attributed to the destruction of UC 6 on 28 September 1917, at the south-west corner of Thorton Ridge. However, when the boat left Zeebrugge on 27 September Oblt.z.S. Reichenbach

had been unaware that the British had laid explosive nets off Kentish Knock that same day. It was also later that day that patrols reported powerful explosions in the area of the nets, at position 51° 30' N, 01° 34' E.

Sport divers have just recently (2005) found the last resting place of UC 6 and her crew of sixteen. The wreck lies in the exact position where the explosions occurred, all those years ago.

THE MEN WHO DIED IN UC 6

Binz, Ob.Masch.Mt
Brase, Hzr
Brückner, Ob.Masch.Mt
Detloff, Ob.Mts
Gorke, Ob.Masch.Mt.d.Res
Jepsen, Ob.Btn.Mt
Kraft, Ob.Hzr
Kunkel, Masch.Anwärter
Lehmann, Masch.Mt
Nabrotzki, Mts.
Nachtigal, Masch.Ob.Anwärter
Reichenbach, Gottfried, Oblt.z.S.
Schubert, Mts.
Schwarz, Mts.
Wunderlich, Stm.

UC 6 is known to have either damaged or sunk the following vessels and possibly more:

AREA	VESSEL'S NAME	FLAG	TONS	D	M	YEAR	LOCATION
North Sea	Worsley (RN trawler)	GBR	309	14	8	1915	Mined off Aldeburgh
North Sea	Japan (RN trawler)	GBR	205	16	8	1915	Mined off the Shipwash Light Vessel
English Channel	Disa	SWE	788	25	8	1915	Mined 5–6 miles N by E of Shipwash L/v
North Sea	Dane (RN trawler)	GBR	265	28	8	1915	Mined off Aldeburgh
North Sea	Sir William Stephenson	GBR	1540	29	8	1915	Mined at the entrance to Yarmouth
English Channel	Africa	GBR	1038	16	9	1915	Mined 2½ miles S of Deal
English Channel	Lydian (RN trawler)	GBR	244	18	9	1915	Mined off South Foreland
English Channel	San Zeferino	GBR	6430	18	9	1915	Mined and damaged 2 miles NNW of S. Goodwin L/V
North Sea	Horden	GBR	1434	20	9	1915	Mined ½ mile E of Aldeburgh Napes buoy
North Sea	Groningen	GBR	988	23	9	1915	Mined 1½ miles N by E of Sunk Head Buoy
English Channel	Great Heart (RN drifter)	GBR	78	24	9	1915	Mined E of South Goodwin Light Vessel
English Channel	Nigretia	GBR	3187	27	9	1915	Mined and damaged near S Goodwin L/v
North Sea	Aleppo	GBR	3870	18	10	1915	Mined and damaged 1½ miles E of Sunk Head Buoy
North Sea	Salerno	NOR	2431	18	10	1915	Mined 2 miles ESE of Sunk Head Buoy

North Sea	*Monitoria*	GBR	1904	21	10	1915	Mined at mouth of River Thames 51 °47'N 01° 31' E
English Channel	*Aries* (RN trawler)	GBR	268	31	10	1915	Mined off Leathercoat
English Channel	*Eidsiva*	NOR	1092	31	10	1915	Mined 2 miles SW of South Foreland
English Channel	*Othello II* (RN trawler)	GBR	206	31	10	1915	Mined off Leathercoat
English Channel	*Toward*	GBR	1245	31	10	1915	Mined off South Foreland
North Sea	*Friargate*	GBR	264	3	11	1915	Mined 4 miles E of Oxfordness
English Channel	*Moorside*	GBR	311	12	11	1915	Mined off Boulogne
English Channel	*Nigel*	GBR	1392	12	11	1915	Mined off Boulogne
English Channel	*Traquair*	GBR	1067	12	1	1916	Mined 1 mile SW of Admiralty Pier, Dover
English Channel	*Leicester*	GBR	1002	12	2	1916	Mined 2½ miles SE by E of Folkestone Pier
English Channel	*Carlton* (RN trawler)	GBR	267	21	2	1916	Mined off Folkestone
North Sea	*Trignac*	FRA	2375	24	2	1916	Mined about 7 miles W of Outer Dowsing L/v
English Channel	*Empress of Fort William*	GBR	2181	27	2	1916	Mined 2 miles S of Dover Pier
English Channel	*Maloja*	GBR	12431	27	2	1916	Mined 2 miles SW of Dover Pier
English Channel	*Anjelus* (RN trawler)	GBR	304	28	2	1916	Mined off Dover
English Channel	*Weigelia* (RN trawler)	GBR	262	28	2	1916	Mined off Dover
English Channel	*Flicker* (RN trawler)	GBR	192	4	3	1916	Mined off Dover
English Channel	*Corona* (RN trawler)	GBR	212	23	3	1916	Mined near Ramsgate
English Channel	*Sea Serpent*	GBR	902	23	3	1916	Mined off Folkestone Pier
English Channel	*Christianssund*	DAN	1017	24	3	1916	Mined 3 miles SW of Folkstone
English Channel	*Saint Cecilia*	GBR	4411	26	3	1916	Mined 4 miles off Folkestone
North Sea	*Lavinia Westoll*	GBR	3131	28	3	1916	Mined 33 miles SE by S Spurn Light Vessel
English Channel	*Halcyon*	GBR	1319	7	4	1916	Mined 3½ miles SW by S of Folkestone Pier
English Channel	*Shenandoah*	GBR	3886	14	4	1916	Mined 1½ miles W of Folkestone Gate
English Channel	*Estafette* (RN trawler)	FRA	267	21	4	1916	Mined Dunkerque Roads
English Channel	*Saint Corentin* (RN trawler)	FRA	216	29	4	1916	Mined 900m off Dunkerque harbour
North Sea	*Batavier V*	NLD	1562	16	5	1916	Mined ½ mile E of North Buoy, Inner Gabbard
North Sea	*Volharding* (lighter)	BEL	1000	25	5	1916	Sunk by explosives N of Noord Hinder Light vessel
North Sea	*Excellenz Mehnert*	NOR	646	1	6	1916	Mined 5 miles SSW of Winterton
North Sea	*Kaphreda* (RN trawler)	GBR	245	8	6	1916	Mined near Gorton Light Vessel
English Channel	*Saint Jaques* (trawler)	FRA	72	19	6	1916	Mined off Le Havre
North Sea	*Otis Tarda*	NLD	759	21	6	1916	Mined 52° 39' N, 02° 10'E
North Sea	*Burma*	GBR	724	23	6	1916	Mined 15 miles E of Harwich
North Sea	*Waalstroom*	NLD	1441	27	6	1916	Mined 4 miles NE of Shipwash Light V

North Sea	*Hirose* (RN trawler)	GBR	275	29	6	1916	Mined off Aldeburgh Napes
North Sea	*Gannet*	GBR	1127	7	7	1916	Mined 5 miles ENE of Shipwash Light vessel
North Sea	*Kara*	GBR	2338	10	7	1916	Mined near Pakefield Gate Buoy
North Sea	*Mascotte*	GBR	1097	3	9	1916	Mined 6–5 miles SE of Southwold 52° 15'N 01° 50' E
English Channel	*Girl Eva* (drifter)	GBR	76	30	9	1916	Mined near Elbrow Buoy
North Sea	*Lonada* (ex-P.L.A. Hopper.22)	GBR	1286	29	12	1916	Mined 5 miles N by E ½ E Shipwash Light vessel
North Sea	*Ludlow* (RN paddle M/S)	GBR	810	29	12	1916	Mined off Shipwash Light Vessel
English Channel	*Ashtabula*	GBR	7025	22	2	1917	Mined and damaged near Elbow Buoy
North Sea	*Forward III* (RN drifter)	GBR	89	31	3	1917	Mined S of Shipwash L/V (barr.260)
English Channel	*Lumina*	GBR	5856	19	4	1917	Mined and damaged about 3m N of Elbow Buoy
English Channel	*Waterville*	GBR	1968	12	5	1917	Mined and damaged near Elbow Buoy
North Sea	*Roald Amundsen*	NOR	4390	16	6	1917	Mined and damaged 3 miles W of Tongue L/v
North Sea	*Dorte Jensen*	DAN	2086	18	6	1917	Mined near Tongue Sand Light Vessel

WRECK-SITE

The wreck is orientated in a north–north-east to south–south-west (055/235-degrees) direction. It lies on a seabed of silty sand, in a general depth of 22m, being the lowest astronomical depth. Although it has not been officially identified, the wreck is that of a small mine-laying U-boat, and is almost certainly that of UC 6. The front two mine tubes are empty, but tubes three and four still have mines in them with the horns sticking out! Forward of the first tube the bow is missing. There is no access into the interior of the submarine at this point because the mine tube blocks the way. There is a small conning tower and hatch lying immediately behind where the conning tower should be. Only a few feet behind this part, the stern section of the submarine, including the rudder(s) and propeller(s), are buried in a sand-wave.

Another set of coordinates has the wreck at position: 51 30'.700 N 001 34'.660 E, in 23m, at the lowest astronomical depth.

UC 63, SM IMPERIAL U-BOAT

DATE OF LOSS: 1 November 1917
DEPTH: 32m
REFERENCE: 51 23'.013 N, 002 00'.162 E
HISTORICAL POSITION: 51° 23'N 02° 00'E
LOCATION: 20.76 nautical miles E of North Foreland

Type: UCII coastal mine-laying boat   ***Builders***: AG Weser, Bremen for Kaiserliche Deutsche Marine   ***Ordered***: 12 January 1916, within the batch of UC 61–UC 64   ***Keel***

laid: as Yard No.261 on 3 April 1916 **Launched:** 6 January 1917 **Commissioned:** by Oblt. z.S. Karsten von Heydebreck on 30 January 1917

TECHNICAL SPECIFICATIONS

Hull: Double **Surface displacement:** 422 tons **U/Dt:** 504 tons **LBDH:** 51.85m x 5.22m x 3.68m x 7.46m **Machinery:** 2 x 250ps MAN diesels **Props:** 2 bronze **S/Sp:** 11.9 knots **Op/R:** 8,000 nautical miles at 7 knots **Sub/R:** 59 nautical miles at 4 knots **U/Power:** 2 x 230ps electric motors giving 7.2 knots **Batteries:** Lead/acid/accumulators **Fuel/Cap:** 43 tons **Armament:** 2 external 50.04cm torpedo tubes at the bow, one either side of the mine chutes and 1 stern internal tube **Torpedoes:** 7 x 50.04cm (19.7in) maximum **Guns:** 1 x 88mm (3.46in) forward deck gun **Ammo:** 133 rounds of 88mm **Mine tubes:** 6 **Mines:** 18 x UC 200 **Diving:** Max-op-depth 50m (164ft) and 33 seconds to crash-dive **Complement:** 3 officers and 23 ratings

Torpedo load as designed: 4 – a torpedo in each tube plus a reload for the stern tube. Storing an additional torpedo in pieces internally for the stern tube later augmented this, although this was optional. Two extra torpedoes (total) for the external bow tubes could be carried as well – these were lashed to the deck. So up to a total of seven torpedoes were carried, although not all boats sailed with that many.

UC 63 was formally assigned to the Flandern Flottille on 27 April 1917, with Oblt.z.S. Karsten von Heydebreck, the commander from 30 January 1917. In just nine months, von Heydebreck sank thirty-six Allied vessels, totalling 36,404 tons.

(1) UC 63 left Bremen on 25 April 1917 and transferred to Flanders, arriving on 27 April 1917; a Dutch fishing vessel was also sunk en-route.

(2) On 3 May 1917 UC 63 sailed from Flanders to patrol in the Hoofden and off English east coast. One Dutch sailing vessel was sunk on the outbound voyage and the boat arrived back in port 11 May.

(3) Between 11 and 16 June 1917 the U-boat made a fruitless patrol in the Hoofden.

(4) Leaving Flanders on 23 June 1917 UC 63 operated off the English east coast. On 27 June the coaster SS *Longbenton* (Harries Bros & Co., Swansea) was carrying 1,200 tons of coal from Newcastle for Devonport and steaming at 7½ knots when UC 63 torpedoed her at 20.00. The track of the weapon was observed moments before it detonated level on the No.2 hold and the ship went down by the head in two minutes. However, the entire crew of fourteen managed to abandon ship in the boats; the steamship *Hogarth* (Hall, Russell & Co.) picked them up (*Hogarth* was herself torpedoed and sunk by UB 107 on 7 June 1918).

The Danish SS *Markersdall* (Aktieselskabet Dampskibsselskabet Rødby Havn, Rødby Havn) was also lost after a torpedo attack by UC 63, while transporting 2,500 tons of coal from Dunston-on-Tyne to Rouen.

Using explosives or gunfire, UC 63 also sank ten small fishing boats during the patrol and arrived at Zeebrugge on 2 July 1917.

(5) UC 63 made an unsuccessful sortie to the English east coast between 21 and 27 July 1917.

(6) On 31 July 1917 UC 63 left Flanders and sailed to the English east coast for mine-laying operations. The SS *Empress* (Amaryllis Shipping Co. Ltd) detonated one of the mines at 05.00 on 31 July and sank with the loss of five of her crewmen. She was on Italian Government Service and en-route from the Tyne to Southend-on-Sea with 3,760 tons of coal. The mixed cosmopolitan crew abandoned ship in the boats, but one boat was smashed while being lowered and another capsized, drowning five of its occupants. The rest of the crew, which consisted of two Swedes, one Russian, three Norwegians, one Portuguese, one Spaniard, a Dane, one Dutchman, fourteen Britons and two Argentineans,

were picked up by a patrol-vessel and landed at Grimsby. The *Empress* sank at 05.30, taking the confidential papers down.

FOUR OF THE MEN WHO DIED
Anderson, Peter, 47, Able Seaman
Husby, Olaf, 49, Boatswain (Bosun)
Parker, Thomas, 25, Fireman and Trimmer
Van Klanders, Peter, 26, Fireman

On 6 August, the *Fane* (Aktieselskapet Dampskipsselskapet, Fane), a Norwegian steamer, detonated a mine and sank, while in ballast and on passage from Rouen for Sunderland. The master was Captain J.S. Pedersen and the mine had been laid earlier that day. On 7 August, the Italian steamer *Onestá* (Fratelli Beraldo, Genoa) was torpedoed and sunk while under the command of Captain P. Costa. She was voyaging from Newcastle to Genoa with coal.

A torpedo fired from UC 63 damaged the SS *Zamora* on 6 August 1917, while she was en-route from Arkhangelsk, Russia, to London with timber. She beached in the river Humber and re-floated later. Three small vessels were also captured and sunk by explosives or gunfire. The U-boat returned to Flanders on 9 August 1917

(7) Von Heydebreck left Flanders on 11 August 1917 and took UC 63 to the Humber estuary for operations. During the war-cruise, von Heydebreck sunk the Italian steamer *Constanza* (Gustavo Palazio, Genoa) with a torpedo. The ship was en-route from the Tyne to Leghorn, Italy, with coal. UC 63 damaged the Norwegian SS *Luna* (Det Bergenske Dampskibsselskab, Bergen), which was bound for London from Trondheim with deals and batten-boards. The steamer beached at Grimsby and re-floated later. Gunfire also sank three small vessels; two of them were small Royal Navy Q-ships. UC 63 arrived at Flanders on 16 August 1917.

(8) UC 63 sailed from Zeebrugge on 13 September 1917 for operations against Allied shipping around the Bay of Biscay. During the patrol von Heydebreck sank three French steamers, an RN trawler and two sailing vessels. The French SS *Italia* (French owner unknown, previous owner: Cia. Argentina de Nav., Ltda., Buenos Aires) (ex-*Hans*) was captured and scuttled with explosives in the Bay of Biscay by UC 63 on 22 September 1917. One of the sailing vessels was the full-rigged ship *Europe* (Ant. Dom. Bordes. & Fils). She was sunk by a torpedo and foundered en-route from Sydney to Europe. The 255-ton RN trawler *James Seckar* (Admiralty No.3526) was allegedly sunk by UC 63, 19 miles off Santana with all hands on 25 September. The SS *Dinorah* (French Government, Bordeaux) of 4,208 tons was torpedoed, shelled and sunk, while on passage from Cardiff to the French Mediterranean with coal. UC 63 returned to Flanders on 29 September 1917.

FINAL VOYAGE
(9) UC 63 was carrying a crew of twenty-six when she left Flanders on 18 October 1917, the mission being to lay mines and attack Allied shipping as far as the Bay of Biscay. On 23 October, the Danish steamer *Ulfsborg* (Aktieselskabet Dampskibsselskabet Selsk. af 1896, Copenhagen) detonated a mine that was laid by UC 63 and sank in position 46° 03' N, 01° 43' E, while on voyage from Bilbao to Newport, Monmouth, with a cargo of iron ore.

The SS *Baron Garioch* (Kelvin Shipping Co. Ltd, Ardrossan) was torpedoed and sunk on 28 October and two crewmen were lost with the ship, which was in ballast and bound from Calais to Liverpool. Next day the French steamship *Marne* (Mory & Cie., Le Havre) was shelled and sunk while travelling from Rouen to Cardiff.

On 1 November 1917 the U-boat had completed her mission and was on the return leg of the voyage. Her crew would have been pleased to be on their way home – perhaps they were too relaxed. At any rate there was an emphatic dereliction of duty in terms of lookout procedure, given that the boat was well inside enemy territory. Ubootsmansmaat Fritz Marsal:

> I was on the bridge. The boat was being steered from the control room With me on the bridge was the officer on watch, looking to port I was watching starboard while a rating was sweeping astern. I recall it was such a bright moonlit night and very cold. The officer on watch decided he wanted some coffee so he sent the rating below to get some.

The men on watch did not realise that they were being stalked. The British submarine E52, commanded by Lt P. Phillips had been assigned for anti-U-boat patrols operating out of Dover Harbour as part of a revamp ordered by Rear Admiral Keyes. As previously described, U-boats tended to frequent known navigational aids such as buoys and lightships in order to take a fix prior to running the barrage at high water. For this reason, the British submarines allocated to these patrols usually carried flashing lights on their conning towers, aimed at luring U-boats to their doom. Unfortunately the 'C' boats usually allocated this task had a pathetically slow turning speed, but E52 had no such problems.

E52 had left her temporary base in Dover Harbour at 16.30 on 'All-Hallows-Eve'. The patrol had been without incident until 01.12 when lookouts of E52's bridge watched as a second submarine, UC 63, glided out of the murk, a mere 1,200 yards off the port bow. Although clouds now hid the moon, it was astonishing that the German lookouts did not spot the British boat. But as Fritz Marsal relates, they were otherwise occupied:

> The engineer officer joined us and began talking to the officer on watch. The officer on watch must have been distracted because when I glanced to port I saw another surfaced submarine, turning to bring her bow tubes to bear. The officer on watch immediately gave the warning and our helm was turned.

Phillips closed to 200 yards before firing two torpedoes. A column of water 100ft high followed the detonation. The concussion waves shook E52 so much that one of her loaded torpedoes was discharged from the beam tube. Ubootsmansmaat Fritz Marsal takes up the story:

> I am not sure what happened next, but UC 63 had just started to turn when I was hurled against some hard object. I was held under the water and being dragged deeper. I had to kick myself free, but eventually I reached the surface. Not far away the war pilot was flapping around, drowning. His heavy boots were full of water and they dragged him down.

Out of the crew of twenty-six, only Marsal survived. Interestingly, Marsal had previously served on destroyers and had seen action at both the Dogger Bank and the Scarborough raid of 1914.

Marsal later described how UC 63 had managed to pass across the Dover/Calais net barrage on the surface. When the boat was 18 miles off Dover, the exact radio bearings position was established at 01.00. UC 63 was attacked and sunk by E52 fourteen minutes later. Marsal suffered a split chin and had several teeth knocked out by the torpedo impact, but he expressed gratitude for the kindness of his treatment on-board E52.

Even after UC 63 was lost, mines she had laid sank three more steamships: the Norwegian *Lyra* (Aktieselskapet Laly, Christiania) foundered off Spurn Light Vessel, while sailing from Skien for Rouen with a cargo of ammonium nitrate and aluminium; the mine had been laid on 24 November.

The steam tanker *Oriflamme* (Oriflamme SS Co. Ltd, London) was transporting benzine from New York to Le Havre and Rouen when she detonated a mine at 05.45 on 25 November. A distress rocket was fired, but it unfortunately ignited benzine fuel-vapour (possibly released by the exploding mine). The thirty-nine crewmen and one passenger thought it wise to abandon ship in the boats, but one man could not be found. Tugs towed the ship into Sandown Bay and the absent crewman was found on board, but unconscious. The *Oriflamme* capsized when she drifted ashore and was sunk by gunfire from RN torpedo-boat-destroyers.

Two men were also killed on the armed SS *Brigitta* (Colonial Coal and Shipping Co. Ltd, London), while carrying coal to Dieppe from Barry. The mine had been laid on 15 December. ADM 137/3898 – ADM 137/3318 – ADM 137/3813 – NARA: T1022 Roll 108, PG61984

THE MEN WHO DIED IN UC 63

Auserodt, Ob.Masch.Mt
Beck, Albrecht, Masch.Mt
Beck, Rudolf, Masch.Mt.de.Reserve
Bergmann, Masch.Mt
Binder, Hzr
Brandt, Lt.z.S.de Reserve
Danker, Mn.Ing.Asp
Dittmeyer, Masch.Anw
Duda, Ob.Hzr
Düsing, Ob.Mts.
Dähne, F.T.Ober Anw
Fix, Ob.Masch.Mt
Ginz, Ob.Btn.Mt der Reserve
Glatzel, Stm. der Reserve
Gottschall, Masch.Mt
Grunert, Hzr
Heydebreck, von Karsten, Oblt.z.S.
Kirschte, Mts.
Mandelkow, F.T.
Obst, Hzr
Pilawa, Hzr
Prigge, Ob.Mts.
Ptak, Hzr
Restorff, Masch.Mt
Sonntag, Mts.
Trosse, Mts.

The following is a list of the known vessels sunk or damaged by UC 63:

AREA	VESSEL'S NAME	FLAG	TONS	D	M	YEAR	LOCATION
North Sea	*Amsteldijk* (fishing-vessel)	NLD	186	26	4	1917	Sunk near the Haaks Light Vessel
North Sea	*Gruno* (sailing-vessel)	NLD	171	10	5	1917	8 miles SSW of Noord Hinder Light vessel
North Sea	*Frigate Bird*	GBR	20	26	6	1917	Sunk off Flamborough Head
North Sea	*Longbenton*	GBR	924	27	6	1917	12 miles S by W of Flamborough Head.

North Sea	*Elsie* (fishing-vessel)	GBR	20	28	6	1917	10 miles NE of Spurn Point
North Sea	*Frances* (fishing-vessel)	GBR	20	28	6	1917	10 miles NE of Spurn Point
North Sea	*Glenelg* (fishing-vessel)	GBR	32	28	6	1917	18 miles off Spurn Point
North Sea	*Harbinger*	GBR	39	28	6	1917	18 miles off Spurn Point
North Sea	*Rose of June* (fishing-vessel)	GBR	20	28	6	1917	10 miles NE of Spurn Point
North Sea	*William and Betsy* (fish-boat)	GBR	21	28	6	1917	10 miles NE of Spurn Point
North Sea	*Markersdall*	DAN	1640	30	6	1917	Sunk 12 miles S of Flamborough Head
North Sea	*Advance* (trawler)	GBR	44	1	7	1917	5 miles SE of South Ower's Buoy
North Sea	*Gleam* (trawler)	GBR	54	1	7	1917	3½ miles ENE of South Ower's Buoy
North Sea	*Radiance* (trawler)	GBR	57	1	7	1917	3 miles S by W of North Lemon Buoy
North Sea	*Empress*	GBR	2914	31	7	1917	Mined 4½ miles E by S Withernsea L/h
North Sea	*Young Bert* (fishing-vessel)	GBR	59	2	8	1917	Sunk off the Humber
North Sea	*Alfred* (sailing-vessel)	FRA	107	6	8	1917	Sunk off the Inner Bank, Dunkerque (?)
North Sea	*Fane*	NOR	1119	6	8	1917	Mined 2½ miles E Inner Dowsing L/v
North Sea	*Zamora*	GBR	3639	6	8	1917	Damaged 2 miles NW Inner Dowsing L/v
North Sea	*Onestá*	ITA	2732	7	8	1917	Sunk near the Inner Dowsing Light Vessel
North Sea	*Marie Jesus Protegez Nous* (s/v)	FRA	46	8	8	1917	Sunk off Lowestoft
North Sea	*Coastanza*	ITA	2545	14	8	1917	3½ miles SE by ESE of Inner Dowsing L/v
North Sea	*Luna*	NOR	959	14	8	1917	Damaged 16–18 miles N of Humber L/v
North Sea	*Ethel and Millie* (Q-ship)	GBR	58	15	8	1917	Sunk off the Humber
North Sea	*G&E* (Q-ship)	GBR	61	15	8	1917	Sunk off the Humber
North Sea	*G.Y.541* (mot)	GBR	25	15	8	1917	Sunk off the Humber
Bay of Biscay	*Italia*	FRA	627	22	9	1917	Sunk in the Bay of Biscay
E/Channel	*Perseverence* (sailing-vessel)	GBR	118	23	9	1917	14 miles NW of St Valery en Caux
Bay of Biscay	*Europe* (sailing-vessel)	FRA	2839	24	9	1917	Sunk in the Bay of Biscay
E/Channel	*James Seckar* (RN trawler)	GBR	255	25	9	1917	19 miles off Santana
E/Channel	*Dinorah*	FRA	4208	25	9	1917	19 miles off Santana
E/Channel	*Baron Garioch*	GBR	1831	28	10	1917	5 miles SE of Anvil Point.
E/Channel	*Marne*	FRA	979	29	10	1917	Sunk in the English Channel
North Sea	*Lyra*	NOR	1141	4	11	1917	Mined NE of the Humber
E/Channel	*Oriflamme*	GBR	3764	25	11	1917	Mined 9 miles S of the Nab L/v
E/Channel	*Brigitta*	GBR	2084	4	12	1917	Mined 6 miles SW of Nab Tower L/h
Bay of Biscay	*Ulfsborg*	DEN	2055	23	10	1917	Mined in Bay of Biscay

Courage is the very warp and weft of the material in this book. An aside to this story concerns two armed Lowestoft fishing boats acting as decoy vessels: *Boy Alfred*, alias *Ethel & Millie* (Skipper Charles William Manning) and *I'll Try*, alias *Nelson* (Skipper Thomas Crisp). Admiralty ordered periodic name changes in order to safeguard identity. The two small craft were manned by a mixture of Royal Navy and Royal Naval Reserve men – the latter normally being fishermen by trade. Moreover, the crews were experienced. Following an encounter with a U-boat on 1 February 1917, Crisp had been awarded a DSC. On this particular day, *Nelson*'s cosmopolitan crew included a naval gunner, L/S Percy Ross, and Pte George Cox of the RMLI.

On 15 August 1917 both *Ethel & Millie* and *Nelson* were fishing on the Jim Howe Bank, off the Humber, some distance away from each other when the crew of *Nelson* spotted a U-boat approaching fast from the north-west.

By 14.45 *Nelson* had shot her net and Skipper Thomas Crisp was below packing fish. When Crisp came on deck he spotted a U-boat closing fast. It was UC 63. Crisp gave the order 'Clear for Action'. The submarine opened fire. One shot landed 100 yards off the port bow. Already the U-boat had the range. The 13-pounder gun was manned and the fishing smack's engines were started. The U-boat easily outranged the smack. The fourth U-boat shell penetrated *Nelson*'s bow just below the waterline. Crisp turned *Nelson* about in response when the seventh shell tore through Thomas Crisp, the deck, and the hull. The sea was pouring into the fishing smack and it should have been all over, but the skipper's son took charge of the tiller while the crew continued to fire the 13-pounder. All this time the partially disembowelled Thomas Crisp urged his men on: 'It's all right. Just do your best!' The crew of *Nelson* maintained their fire until the angle of elevation became too great. Skipper Crisp dictated a carrier pigeon message to his son. It read: '*Nelson* being attacked by a submarine. Jim Howe Bank. Skipper killed, send assistance at once.'

Red Cock, the pigeon, carried this message back to Lowestoft. Only five rounds of ammunition remained on the rapidly foundering smack. Thomas Crisp ordered his son to throw the confidential books over the side and abandon ship. As his son attempted to move him into the lifeboat, the old man gasped, 'Tom, I'm done. Throw me overboard'. This his son could not do. The despairing crew had no option but to pull away, leaving their dying skipper on deck smiling, dying. Then *Nelson* sank. The U-boat withdrew, but as it did so, the crew of *Nelson* witnessed the survivors of *Ethel & Millie* lined up on the casing when the U-boat disappeared eastwards. Following a two-day-long ordeal, Harwich minesweepers eventually picked up the crew.

However a very dark shadow hangs over this tale when describing the fate of *Ethel & Millie*. The crew of *Ethel & Millie* apparently put up a fight with their 6-pounder gun, but their position was hopeless. Their ammunition exhausted, they had little option but to surrender.

As the crew of *Nelson* rowed away from their sinking vessel, they watched the crew of *Ethel & Millie* rowing towards the U-boat, refusing all exhortations to join them. Tom Crisp Jnr made the following observation: 'We saw the submarine's crew line the E&M's crew up on the boat's fore deck. The Germans then tied the lifeboat astern. Shortly afterwards they disappeared over the horizon'.

Skipper Thomas Crisp was awarded a posthumous Victoria Cross and his son the DSM. There is a memorial to Skipper Crisp in the Church of St Margaret, Lowestoft. Mystery surrounds the ultimate fate of the *Ethel & Millie* crew.

WRECK-SITE

To date (2006) the U-boat has never been located, but by calculating the distance and times, it should lie some 10 miles closer to Dover than the co-ordinates given as 53° 23' N, 02° 0' E. There is actually a wreck very close-by to the position suggested, and it lies on a seabed of sand and shingle, in a general depth of 32m, being the lowest astronomical depth. The wreck sits in a scour and stands about 4m high amidships, which could possibly be this submarine.

Of the estimated 2,500 vessels destroyed on the infamous Goodwin Sands, there is no tale more extraordinary than that of U 48, a First World War U-boat, which cannot resist returning to haunt the coast of Kent...

U 48, SM IMPERIAL U-BOAT

DATE OF LOSS: 24 November 1917
DEPTH: 2m
REFERENCE: 51 17'.351 N, 001 31'.529 E
LOCATION: 4.77 nautical miles SE from Ramsgate

Type: U 43 Mittel-U torpedo attack boat   *Builders:* Kaiserliche Werft, Danzig for Kaiserliche Deutsche Marine   *Ordered:* 4 August 1914, within the batch of U 46–U 50 *Keel laid:* as Yard No.26   *Launched:* 3 October 1915   *Commissioned:* by Kapitänleutnant Berndt Buß on 22 April 1916

TECHNICAL SPECIFICATIONS

Hull: Double   *Surface displacement:* 725 tons   *U/Dt:* 940 tons   *LBDH:* 65m x 6.20m x 3.7m x 8.70m   *Machinery:* 2 x 1,000ps Maschinefabrik-Augsburg-Nürnberg (MAN) diesels   *Props:* 2 bronze   *S/Sp:* 15.2 knots   *Op/R:* 11,400 nautical miles at 8 knots *Sub/R:* 51 nautical miles at 5 knots   *U/Power:* 2 x 600ps electric motors giving 9.7 knots   *Batteries:* Lead/acid/accumulators.   *Fuel/Cap:* 56 + 74 tons   *Armament:* 4 bow and 2 stern 50.04cm torpedo tubes   *Torpedoes:* 8 x 50.04cm (19.7in)   *Guns:* 1 x 105mm (4.13in) deck gun forward and 1 x 88mm (3.46in) gun 5m aft of conning tower *Ammo:* 276 rounds   *Diving:* Max-op-depth 50m (164ft) and 55 seconds to crash-dive *Complement:* 4 officers and 32 ratings

U 48 was formally assigned to the III.U-Flottille at Wilhelmshaven on 8 June 1916, with Kplt. Berndt Buß as CO from the commissioning until 9 March 1917. Berndt Buß made the following five patrols with the boat:

(1) U 48 left Wilmhelmshaven on 4 August 1916 for a training run into the North Sea. During the voyage Berndt Buß captured the 2,123-ton Norwegian steamer *Pendennis* on 6 August and took her back to port, where U 48 arrived on 8 August.

(2) U 48 left Wilhelmshaven on 18 August to take part in North Sea operations. Admiral Scheer had the idea of bombarding Sunderland and trapping the Grand Fleet during the night of 18 and 19 August 1916. U-boats were positioned in a line to the north-east of Blyth and more positioned off Flamborough Head, the Swarte Bank, off Terschelling and Heligoland, while eight Zeppelins acted as fleet scouts over the North Sea. However, British submarines had left their bases at Scapa Flow, Cromarty and the Firth of Forth and headed out into the North Sea. One of the boats, HM S/M E23, attacked the German battleship *Westfalen* with a torpedo and left her badly crippled. U 48 returned to Heligoland on 19 August, but saw no action. The U-boat was now fitted with an 88mm deck gun.

(3) U 48 sailed from Germany on 19 September 1916 and made a successful patrol in the Arctic Ocean. The SS *Lotusmere* (Irismere Steam Shipping Co. Ltd) was captured and sunk by torpedo while on a voyage from Barry to Arkhangelsk, Russia, with coal. On 4 October, the Norwegian SS *Brink* (Aktieselskapet Blink, Tønsberg) was captured, torpedoed and sunk, while transporting lumber from Onega, Russia to Hull.

To the north of North Cape, the Russian steamship *Suchan* (Russian Volunteer Fleet Association) was captured by U 48 on 6 October 1916 and sent to Germany with a prize crew; the ship was returned to her owners and later that year, sold to Hamburg-Amerika Line, Hamburg, and renamed *Spezia*. The Swedish SS *Tuva* (Otto Banck, Helsingborg) was captured, torpedoed and sunk at position 71° 00' N, 23° 00' E on 7 October 1916, while voyaging from Arkhangelsk, Russia, to Hull with timber. U 48 arrived back in Germany on 16 October 1916.

(4) Leaving Heligoland on 27 December 1916, Kplt. Buß took U 48 into the North Sea, around the Orkney and Shetland Isles to the south coast of Ireland and the Bay of Biscay. During this voyage Buß sank the following ten steamships and one sailing vessel:

The Russian SS *Tuskar* (Russian Ministry of Commerce & Industry) was travelling from Arkhangelsk, Russia, to London with hides and skins, but was captured by U 48 and scuttled with explosives on 29 December 1916.

On 6 January 1917, the iron-hulled SS *Alphonse Conseil* (Sociéte les Affrêteurs Réunis), a French steamer and ex-British *Port of Alicante*, was torpedoed and sunk with all hands in the Bay of Biscay, 180 miles off La Coruna, while en-route from Nantes to an unknown destination. The French SS *Ville du Havre* (Cie. Havraise Péninsulaire de Nav. à Vapeur, Havre) was torpedoed and sunk that same day, while in ballast en-route from Saigon, French-Indo China, to Dunkerque. The SS *Borgholm* (Aktieselskapet Borgå, Christiania), a Norwegian steamer, was captured in the Atlantic and scuttled with explosives, while conveying coal from Newport, Monmouth, to Gibraltar. Later that day, the Greek steamship *Evangelos* (Ambatielos Brothers, Argostoli) was captured, then shelled and sunk while carrying wine and esparto grass from Algiers to Dunkerque. The Norwegian SS *Tholma* (Aktieselskapet Borchs Rederi, Drammen) was captured on 8 January 1917 at position, 43° 23' N, 11° 01' W and, on 10 January, she was scuttled with explosives, 90 miles north-west of Cape Finisterre. She was voyaging with coal from Cardiff to Genoa, Italy. In the Bay of Biscay, the 183-ton French sailing vessel *Emeraude* was destroyed by gunfire, while en-route from Lisbon to Paimpol in Brittany. The SS *Vestfold* (Clausen's Rederi Aktieselskapet, Haugesund), another Norwegian steamship, was captured and scuttled with explosives, while en-route from Hull to Sète with coal. The French SS *Sidney* (Joseph Lasry, Marseille) was shelled and sunk en-route from Cardiff to Bône, Algeria (now Annaba). Voyaging in ballast from Spezia to Barry, the Norwegian steamer *Esperanca* (Aktieselskapet South Atlantic, Tønsberg) had been fitted out as a whale-factory-ship during 1915, but was then converted back for cargo service. On 15 January 1917, she was captured by U 48 at position 43° 03' N, 10° 12' W and scuttled with explosives the next day, 165 miles north of Cape Finisterre. She was en-route from La Spezia, Italy, to Cardiff, in ballast.

The SS *Nailsea Court* (Morgan & Cadogan Ltd, Hull (Cardiff)) was transporting iron ore to Barrow from Bougiein Northern Algeria when a torpedo destroyed her, 32 miles west of the Skelligs.

U 48 returned to Wilmhelshaven on 26 January 1917, travelling via the west coast of Ireland and the Shetland Isles. On return to port, the 88mm deck gun was replaced with a new one of 105mm.

(5) Leaving Wilmhelmshaven on 28 February 1917, U 48 sailed for operations in the English Channel, going via the Dover Straits. During this patrol, four steamers and three sailing vessels were destroyed. Three crewmen were lost with the steamer *Connaught* (City of Dublin Steam Packet Co. Ltd, Dublin). She was torpedoed while voyaging from Le Havre for Southampton.

The SS *Antonio* (Egypt & Levant SS Co. Ltd, London) sank with eleven men including the master, Captain J. Burman, while transporting hay from Barry to Cherbourg (the British official list indicates the *Antonio* was mined, but German sources indicate it was shelled after the torpedo missed).

On 9 March the SS *East Point* (Norfolk & North American Steam Shipping Co. Ltd, Liverpool) was hauling a general cargo from London to Philadelphia, USA, when a torpedo, fired by U 48, slammed into her and exploded. However, before the the steamer sank, she rammed the boat. Berndt Buß and the Steersman were both killed when the conning tower was crushed. The U-boat quickly sank to the bottom in 70m. Damage to the boat was extensive, but IOW Hinrich II Hermann Hashagne managed to raise her to the surface. The following day Hashagne took U 48 back to Germany, travelling via the Shetland Isles, and arrived at Heligoland on 16 March. On 17 March 1917, Kplt. Karl Edeling assumed command.

U 48 ghost ship surfaces in 1973. (Courtesy Mirrorpix)

(6) Edeling departed Emden base with U 48 on 6 May 1917 for operation off the Isles of Scilly, going via the North Sea, around the Orkney Isles, down the Irish west and south coasts.

U 48 sank three steamers with torpedoes: the SS *San Onofre* (Eagle Oil Transport Co. Ltd, London) sank on 12 May while transporting fuel oil from Puerto Mexico, Mexico to Queenstown, Ireland. At 14.38 on 11 May, the crew of the tanker spotted the wake of a torpedo heading towards them from quite a distance, but the ship successfully manoeuvred to avoid it. Five minutes later the U-boat, which was U 48, was sighted 4 miles astern. While the gun crew kept the U-boat at bay, the master dispatched a radio message requesting assistance. The submarine began firing, and chased the ship until 16.15, but failed to make up any distance between them. A British warship arrived on the scene at 18.25 and searched the area until 19.40 when it returned to the tanker and instructed Captain Osbon to make towards the Skelligs. The *San Onofre* was proceeding on the suggested bearing under escort when a torpedo detonated in the engine room at 05.20, killing one man. The ship sank in ten minutes. The forty-eight survivors got away in the boats and were landed at Queenstown, Ireland, after being taken on board the escort.

The SS *Jessmore* (Johnston Line Ltd) was proceeding to Manchester with a general cargo from Baltimore when she sank off Fastnet Rock on 13 May. The French steamer *Meuse* (Cie. de Nav. D'Orbigny, La Rochelle), was sunk on 14 May, while transporting general cargo from New York to Le Havre.

Scuttling charges or gunfire accounted for three large sailing vessels during the patrol: the Russian *Margareta* was en-route from Beaumont to Liverpool with timber; another Russian vessel, the *Lynton,* was on passage from Pensacola, Florida, for the Clyde when she sank on 21 May. Later that day, the Norwegian *Madura* was sunk while voyaging from Gulfport, on the Mississippi Sound, to Cardiff with timber. U 48 arrived back at Emden on 29 May 1917, travelling via the Shetland Isles.

(7) Departing Emden on 1 July 1917, U 48 patrolled the area at the west end of the English Channel and 150 miles off the Cornish coast, south-west of Ushant. Klaus Edeling sank three steamships and one trawler during the war-cruise. The SS *Gibel Yedid* (M.H. Bland & Co. Ltd, Gibraltar) was captured and scuttled by explosive charges, en-route from Newport, Monmouth, to Gibraltar with general cargo. Six crewmen were lost with the SS *Exford* (Tatem Steam Navigation Co. Ltd, Cardiff) when a torpedo sank her, while she was taking steel and oats from New York to Cherbourg. A crewman was lost with the SS *Torcello* (Ellerman's Wilson Line Ltd, Hull), which was torpedoed and sunk en-route from Palermo and Oran to Hull with general cargo. U 48 returned home via Shetland and arrived at Wilhelmshaven on 24 July 1917.

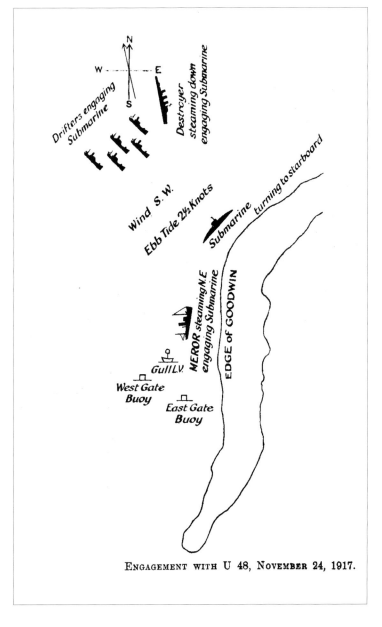

ENGAGEMENT WITH U 48, NOVEMBER 24, 1917.

A chart showing U 48 trapped on Goodwins.

(8) On 20 August Edeling left Heligoland with U 48 and journeyed around the Shetland Isles to his patrol area off the Irish coast. Edeling sank three steamships and a large Danish sailing vessel on his last war-cruise. First to go down was the SS *Westbury* (Alexander Shipping Co. Ltd, Glasgow), when a torpedo struck her on 31 August. She was steaming from Barry to Halifax, Nova Scotia, with coal.

A torpedo from U 48 hit the 13,714-ton steamship *Minnehaha* (Atlantic Transport Co. Ltd, Belfast) and she sank off Fastnet, with the loss of forty-three people, the master being amongst the survivors. The ship was transporting a general cargo from London to New York.

On 9 September, the Danish sailing ship *Elsa* (K.S. Petersen) was captured and sunk off Kinsale, while transporting coal to France. The last victim to succumb to a torpedo on the war-cruise was the steamer *Rollesby* (Sir R. Ropner & Co. Ltd, West Hartlepool), 80 miles off Muckle Flugga on 15 September 1917. She was carrying coal from Cardiff to Arkhangelsk, Russia. U 48 returned home via Shetland and arrived at Wilhelmshaven on 19 September 1917.

FINAL VOYAGE

(9) U 48 sailed for the Irish Sea from Ems/Wilhelmshaven on 21 November 1917. Kplt. Karl Edeling chose the dangerous Channel passage rather than the time-consuming journey around northern Britain. On the afternoon of 23 November U 48 bottomed out prior to running through the Straits, but she was observed by a British seaplane which then responded with a bomb. The submarine was not damaged. When the moon had finally set at 19.30 she rose to the surface, 'conned-down', and followed a course designed to reach Buoy 2A, east of the dreaded Goodwins. Here things went disastrously wrong. The gyrocompass failed at this critical juncture and the westerly current drove U 48 ever-closer to the barrage nets. At 04.30 the inevitable happened and she snagged the nets. Frantic efforts were made to free the screws and Edeling decided to proceed on the submarine's motors. The U-boat grounded on a sandbank, 2 miles north-east of the Gull Light Vessel. High water passed and soon the boat was gently rocked by the ebbing tide. What follows is an extract from the interrogation report of an unnamed U 48 officer, almost certainly that of Oblt. Friedrich Maertens:

> We knew we were in a serious situation and U 48 would not budge no matter what we did. We pumped out some 60 tons of oil and non-essential water from the tanks. We threw most of our ammunition over and finally fired our torpedoes. It was all to no avail because we were still hard aground. We took the precaution of destroying our confidential books. It would take a miracle to save us now so I was put in charge of rigging the charges.

Log of HMS *Gipsy* – 24 Nov 1917 – Lt-Cdr F. Robinson RNR (6th DF)

> While on Downs patrol at 06.40 I sighted an object on my starboard beam bearing S 60E, 1 mile distant. Twilight had just begun. The object disappeared and my suspicions were aroused... Action Stations was called and proceeded at full speed towards the submarine. I now observed 4–5 drifters south west of the submarine firing on her and although the submarine was returning fire, they closed on her in a bold manner deserving of praise.
>
> The drifters were *Present Help*, *Majesty*, *Paramount*, *Feasible* and *Acceptable*. Skipper Edward Hemp at the wheel of *Paramount* first spotted the U-boat at 06.55.
>
> We at once steered straight for the submarine putting the red rocket up and hoisting the green flag. We opened fire with our six pounder and maxim guns. The submarine opened fire at the same time as we did. One of his shells blew our searchlight off its mounting. We got within 30 yards of him when we touched the Goodwins. We blasted him all right and our fourth shot blew his aft gun to hell.

Edward Hemp RNR

Loading torpedoes on a
Second World War U-boat.

Meanwhile, on U 48 an unnamed officer looked on in dismay at the vessels bearing down on the boat and said:

U 48 opened fire with our gun, but still the little ships came on. Our gunnery was not so good. – One shell hit our gun, killing the gun captain and wounding the gun-layer.

As Cdr Robinson relates, *Gipsy* now chimed in with her forward gun:

I commenced firing with my twelve pounder. The first two shots were overs, the fourth straddled the submarine, but the rest all struck her. I watched her crew jump for their lives as she burst into flames for'rard. I now ceased firing at 07.20. Two violent explosions followed, both attributed to Gipsy's shell.

It seems probable that the explosion was partly due to the ignition of the scuttling charges rigged earlier. A shell splinter in his temple mortally wounded Edeling. The most controversial episode occurred when the auxiliary patrol ships aimed machine gun fire at the German sailors floundering in the water. According to Cdr Robinson this action was taken in the tragically mistaken belief that the red cork location buoys thrown over the side were German bombs. Robinson is on record as stating that the auxiliary patrol personnel had been a 'little over zealous' and difficult to control at times. It is possible that their 'enthusiasm' got the better of them when they noticed that the Imperial Battle flag (flying over the stricken submarine in a final gesture of defiance) had not been struck. The evidence points to a very unpleasant episode but were the men of U 48 mistakenly killed in the heat and fury of battle or were they murdered in cold blood as German survivors maintained? Readers must make their own minds up as to whether or not this incident constituted a British atrocity.

The official British report states that twenty-two survivors were rescued, including one officer, Maertens. (German sources contend twenty-one were lost and seventeen survived).

Despite the rather unsavoury ending to this encounter, the drifter skippers were allowed to claim the traditional £1,000 bounty. Locked in the embrace of the Goodwin Sands she may have been, but Kent had not seen the last of U 48. ADM 137/3327 – ADM 137/38/98 – ADM 137/3 – NARA: T-1022, Roll 18, PG61604

THE MEN WHO DIED IN U 48

Bergmann, Stm
Betz, Ob.Hzr
Burgwardt, Oblt.z.S. der Reserve
Busz, Bernd, Kplt
Drews, Ob.Hzr der Reserve
Edeling, Karl, Kplt

Henning, ObBtn.Mt
Kienitz, Hzr
Kummer, Ob. Masch. Anw
Löhndorf, Ob.Mts.
Matzke, F.T.Maat
Menzel, Ob.Masch.Anw
Michler, Mts.
Pagels, Ob.Btn.Mt
Reinhardt, Mts.
Rosemann, Ob.Stm.
Schühle, Hzr
Seidenfaden, Ob.Masch.Mt
Wachter, Hzr
Wolf, Btn.Mt
Wölk, Ob.Hzr

Vessels sunk or damaged by U 48:

AREA	VESSEL'S NAME	FLAG	TONS	D	M	YEAR	LOCATION
North Sea	Pendennis	GBR	2123	6	7	1916	North Sea – taken as prize of war
Arctic	Lotusmere	GBR	3911	2	10	1916	48m NNE Teriberski Lighthouse
Arctic	Brink	NOR	1647	4	10	1916	50 miles NE of Vardo
Arctic	Suchan	RUS	3781	6	10	1916	Captured per KTB translation
Arctic	Tuva	SWE	2270	6	10	1916	70 miles N of North Cape
North Sea	Tuskar	RUS	3042	29	12	1916	60 miles E of Kirkwall
Bay of Biscay	Alphonse Conseil	FRA	1591	6	1	1917	Biscay Bay, no details
Bay of Biscay	Ville du Havre	FRA	5026	6	1	1917	Sunk N of Cape Finisterre
Atlantic	Borgholm	NOR	1715	7	1	1917	75 miles off Finisterre 4319N 1107W
Atlantic	Evangelos	GRE	3773	7	1	1917	Sunk off Finisterre
Atlantic	Tholma	NOR	1896	10	1	1917	90 miles NE of Cape Finisterre
Bay of Biscay	Emeraude (sailing vessel)	FRA	183	12	1	1917	Sunk off the Spanish coast
Bay of Biscay	Vestfold	NOR	1883	12	1	1917	SSW of 43° 46' N, 11° 49'W
Bay of Biscay	Sydney	FRA	2736	14	1	1917	In the Bay of Biscay
Atlantic	Esperanca	NOR	4428	16	1	1917	220 miles WSW of Ushant
Atlantic	Nailsea Court	GBR	3295	19	1	1917	32 miles W of the Skelligs
English Channel	Connaught	GBR	2632	3	3	1917	29 miles S by W ½ W Owers Light Vessel
English Channel	Adelaide (sailing vessel)	GBR	180	4	3	1917	Damaged 42 miles NNW of Cherburg
English Channel	The Macbain (sailing vessel)	GBR	291	4	3	1917	20 miles SSW of Portland Bill
English Channel	Antonio	GBR	2652	7	3	1917	Sunk 7 miles off Dartmouth
English Channel	Abeja (sailing vessel)	GBR	174	9	3	1917	20m SSW Start Pt 4953N 0342W
English Channel	East Point	GBR	5234	9	3	1917	9m E by S ½ S of Eddystone Lighthouse
Atlantic	Guerveur (barque)	FRA	2596	12	3	1917	84 miles of Tory Island
Atlantic	San Onofre	GBR	9717	12	5	1917	7 miles W of Bolus Head, Co Kerry
Atlantic	Jessmore	GBR	3911	13	5	1917	180 miles WNW of Fastnet
Atlantic	Meuse	FRA	4075	15	5	1917	52 00' N, 15 46'W
Atlantic	Margareta (sailing vessel)	RUS	1873	17	5	1917	Off Castletown (Bere)
Atlantic	Lynton (sailing vessel)	RUS	2531	21	5	1917	50 miles SW of Queenstown

Atlantic	*Madura* (sailing vessel)	NOR	1096	21	5	1917	50 miles SW of Queenstown
English Channel	*Giben Yedid*	GBR	949	13	7	1917	150 miles W ¾ N of Ushant
Atlantic	*Exford*	GBR	4503	14	7	1917	180 miles W bS ½ S Ushant
Atlantic	*Torcello*	GBR	2929	15	7	1917	160 miles SW by W of Bishop Rock
Atlantic	*Asama* (trawler)	GBR	284	16	7	1917	190 miles due W of Lundy Island
Atlantic	*Westbury*	GBR	3097	31	8	1917	8 miles SSE of Fastnet
Atlantic	*Minnehaha*	GBR	13403	7	9	1917	12 miles SE Fastnet
Atlantic	*Elsa* (sailing vessel)	DAN	1236	9	9	1917	Sunk 6 miles off Kinsale
North Sea	*Rollesby*	GBR	3955	15	9	1917	Sunk 80 miles ENE of Muckle Flugga

WRECK-SITE

U 48 keeps coming back! The boat emerges from the Goodwins every few decades. The wreck put in an appearance in 1921 and 1939 and was last seen in the summer of 1973. The *Daily Mirror* carried the photo on 6 June 1973 under the headline 'A War Ghost Returns'. The *East Kent Times* for the same day carried the story and picture on its front page. The wreck lies in the Goodwin Knoll, in a general depth of 2m, being the lowest astronomical depth. The propeller was reported as still being attached and live shells are scattered in the sand. There is also extensive damage at the bow section with lots of holes in the deck casing and the boat's conning tower is missing. However the wreck is now well under the sand, so perhaps this particular wartime ghost really has been finally laid to rest. Or has it? The East Kent Museum Service has relics of U 48 and the Dover Patrol Service.

U 37, SM IMPERIAL U-BOAT

DATE OF LOSS: April 1915
DEPTH: 38m
REFERENCE: 51 14'.312 N, 001 52'.155 E
LOCATION: 17.34 nautical miles ENE of
Deal, on N side of Sandettie Bank

Type: U 31 coastal torpedo attack boat *Builders*: Germaniawerft, Kiel for Kaiserliche Deutsche Marine *Ordered*: 12 June1912, within the batch of U 37–U 41 *Keel laid*: as Yard No.197 on 2 January 1913 *Launched*: 25 August 1914 *Commissioned*: by Kapitänleutnant Erich Wilche on 9 December 1914

TECHNICAL SPECIFICATIONS

Hull: Double *Surface displacement*: 685 tons *U/Dt*: 878 tons *LBDH*: 64.70m x 6.32m x 3.56m x 7.68m *Machinery*: 2 x 925ps GW 6-cylinder diesels *Props*: 2 bronze *S/Sp*: 16.4 knots *Op/R*: 8,790 nautical miles at 8 knots *Sub/R*: 80 nautical miles at 5 knots *U/Power*: 2 x 600ps electric motors giving 9.7 knots *Batteries*: Lead/acid/accumulators *Fuel/Cap*: 55 + 56 tons *Armament*: 2 bow and 2 stern 50.04cm torpedo tubes *Torpedoes*: 6 x 50.04cm (19.7in) *Guns*: None *Mines*: None *Diving*: Max-op-depth 50m (164ft) and 50 seconds to crash-dive *Complement*: 4 officers and 31 ratings

U 37 was formally assigned to II.U-Halbflottille at Heligoland from December 1914, with Erich Wilche as the commander.

FIRST AND FINAL VOYAGE

(1) U 37 left Heligoland on 16 March 1915 for operations against Allied vessels in the English Channel, it being the boat's first patrol. At around 16.30 on Wednesday 31 March 1915, Wilche torpedoed and sank the French steamer *Emma* (Worms et Cie.) off Beachy Head. The 1,617-ton ship, which was in ballast on passage from Dunkerque for Bordeaux, sank in three minutes, when the missile detonated on the port side, just abaft the engine room. Out of her crew of twenty-one, only two men were saved from the sea when a British destroyer picked them up one and a half hours later. In the same area next day (1 April), Wilche torpedoed and sank the British steamer *Seven Seas* (Leach & Co. Ltd, London), which was in ballast and on passage from London for Liverpool. Nine men were drowned, including:

Glover, John Alfred, 63, First Mate
Barnes, A.E., Master
Barnes, Leonard, 19, Able Seaman
Cameron, A., Able Seaman
Haseman, Michael Richard, 54, Able Seaman
Hawkes, Henry George, 51, Second Mate
Jaffa, P.H., 38, Chief Engineer
Wiseman, Charkes William, 70, Steward

Having about completed the patrol, U 37 would have been returning home when she most probably detonated a mine near the Sandettie Bank.

The boat and her crew of thirty-two were never heard from again.

NARA: T-1022, Roll 16, PG61582

THE MEN WHO DIED IN U 37

Behrens, Ob.Btn.Mt
Bosse, Masch.Mt
Buda, Masch.Mt der Reserve
Christensen, Mts.
Ertl, Mts.
Firnhaber, Lt.z.S.
Fröbel, Lt.z.S.
Helfenrath, Mts.
Hellwig, Ob.Masch.Mt
Jürgens, Oblt.z.S.
Kaske, Masch.Anw
Leschhorn, Hzr
Malchow, Masch.Mt
Meyer, Masch.Anw
Möller, F.T.Gast
Naber, Ob.Mts.
Neumann, Hzr
Nöller, Masch.Anw
Opitz, F.T.Gast
Paulich, Mts.
Putze, Masch.Mt der Reserve
Reinhard, Btn.Mt
Riecken, Ob.Stm.Mt

Rissmüller, U–Maschinist
Schmidt, Hzr
Seebach, Mn.Ing.
Sehrendt, Hzr
Steinbüschel, Ob.Hzr der Reserve
Tietzel, Ob.Hzr
Wilcke, Kplt
Woltersstedt, Masch.Mt der Reserve
Ziggel, Mts.

WRECK-SITE

The wreck of a large First World War German submarine near the Sandettie Bank was among the U-boats dived and described by the Belgian diver Tomas Termote. Additional archival research by Michael Lowrey has confirmed Termote's suspicion that the wreck is that of U 37. It is orientated in a north–north-east to south, south–west (020/200 degrees) direction and lies on a seabed of sand, pebbles and shingle, in a general depth of 38m, being the lowest astronomical depth. The wreck is intact and almost upright, with the internal bulkheads visible and two hatches at the stern both open. It stands 4.4m high around the small intact conning tower, but most of the plating on the saddle tanks is missing. The area around the boat is quite flat, but there is a large isolated sand-wave positioned about 200m to the north of the wreck. This wreck is also a war grave.

UC 19, SM IMPERIAL U-BOAT

DATE OF LOSS: 6 December 1916 (probably)
DEPTH: 32m
REFERENCE: 51° 10.06' N, 01° 43.47' E
LOCATION: 13.26 nautical miles ENE from South Foreland
and 1.2 nautical miles NW from Sandettie Buoy

Type: UCII coastal mine-laying boat *Builders:* Blohm & Voss, Hamburg for Kaiserliche Deutsche Marine *Ordered:* 29 August 1915, within the batch of SM UC 16–UC 24 *Keel laid:* as Yard No.269 *Launched:* 15 March 1916 *Commissioned:* by Oberleutnant zur See Alfred Nitzsche on 21 August 1916.

TECHNICAL SPECIFICATIONS

Hull: Double *Surface displacement:* 417 tons *U/Dt:* 493 tons *LBDH:* 49.35m x 5.22m x 3.68m x 7.46m *Machinery:* 2 x 250ps MAN diesels *Props:* 2 bronze *S/Sp:* 11.6 knots *Op/R:* 9,430 nautical miles at 7 knots *Sub/R:* 55 nautical miles at 4 knots *U/Power:* 2 x 230ps electric motors giving 7 knots *Batteries:* Lead/acid/accumulators *Fuel/Cap:* 14 + 15 tons *Armament:* 2 bow and 1 x stern 50.04cm torpedo tubes *Torpedoes:* 7 x 50.04cm (19.7in) *Guns:* 1 x 88mm (3.46in) forward deck gun *Ammo:* 133 rounds of 88mm *Mine tubes:* 6 *Mines:* 18 x UC 200 *Diving:* Mmax-op-depth 50m (164ft) and 48 seconds to crash-dive *Complement:* 3 officers and 23 ratings.

UC 19 was formally assigned to Flandern U-Flottille on 9 November 1916, with Oblt. z.S. Alfred Nitzsche the commander from 22 August 1916.

(1) Sailing from Hamburg on 8 November 1916, UC 19 transferred to Zeebrugge, where she arrived on 9 November.

(2) Departing Zeebrugge on 15 November 1916, UC 19 sailed to the English east coast to lay mines and attack Allied shipping. UC 19 is known to have sunk the RN trawler *Dhoon* with a mine after she returned to Zeebrugge on 21 November. *Dhoon* was requisitioned in September 1916 and converted to Admiralty armed patrol vessel No.2959, but it sank near the Newarp Light Vessel on 24 November.

FINAL VOYAGE

(3) On 27 November 1916, UC 19 sailed from Zeebrugge to lay mines between Boulogne and Le Havre and attack Allied shipping. All that is known for certain is UB 29 had also accompanied UC 19 out of Flanders, but that nothing further was heard from either boat from 5 December 1916. Neither of them returned.

It is believed, however, that UC 19 torpedoed and sunk the SS *Briardene* (Colchester SS Co. Ltd) on 1 December 1916. She had left New York on 11 November, for a voyage to London with 2,600 tons of general cargo. She was making 8½ knots on a zigzag course when an Imperial German U-boat surfaced on her starboard bow and fired two shells at her. The master ordered the engine stopped, but when a third shell was fired, the crew abandoned ship in the boats. The U-boat, which was believed to have been UC 19, moved over to the boats and seized the ship's papers from the master. It then towed the lifeboats back to the *Briardene* and the German crew placed explosives charges on board, before leaving the scene. The steamer's crew, consisting of twelve British, two Spanish, three Chilians, three Russian Finns, two Argentinians, one Mexican, one Puerto Rican, two Peruvians and one Norwegian, were rescued by the SS *Luna* and taken to Falmouth.

Mines laid by the boat also accounted for the destruction of at least two large steamships on 9 and 11 January 1917 respectively: the Swedish *Fernebo* (Ångbåts A/B Ferm, Göteborg) was on passage from Gelfe for London with timber when she detonated a mine laid on 17 November and Johan Adolf Andersson, an engine man was killed; the Norwegian *Ole Bull* (C. Mathisen, Bergen) sank after striking a contact mine laid by UC 19 on 17 November 1916. The steamer was voyaging from Hartlepool to Rouen with coal.

Survivor accounts point to UC 19 having being sighted, but there is no positive evidence to confirm this. In addition, the destroyer HMS *Lewellen* attempted to ram a U-boat, reportedly UC 19, off Calais on 4 December 1916. Following an unsuccessful attempt, she then dropped depth charges. Next day, a large oil slick was found and it was still bubbling up four days later. However this location is well to the west of UC 19's confirmed positions.

At the western end of the Channel on 6 December, the armed merchantman *John Sanderson* engaged a U-boat in a gun battle at position 49° 13' N, 6°40' W, south of the Isles of Scilly.

UC 19 had been ordered to patrol in that locality and it was previously suggested that it may have been the boat in question.

The third part of the puzzle now emerges. On the afternoon of 6 December, when a look-out on the destroyer HMS *Ariel* caught sight of a diving submarine, some 1½ miles away. *Ariel* dropped a single depth charge over the position. The explosive paravanes were then lowered to a depth of 30ft (9m) and swept over the U-boat's estimated track. The starboard paravane fired and the resulting explosion brought oil and debris to the surface. Log of Ariel – Wed 6 December 1916 – Lt-Cdr C. Blackman:

14.03 – Sighted conning tower of enemy submarine to starboard. Full speed.

14.16 – Dropped dc. Speed as requisite for sweeping. Start Dynamonitor firing

Ariel's paravane report had four options: (1) Possibly slight damage (2) Probably serious damaged (3) Probably sunk, or (4) Known sunk. The paravane report of *Ariel* makes no reference to a 'kill' however, and the evidence is less than convincing. Finally, as if to muddy the waters even further, the destroyer *Landrail* carried out an apparently successful attack on a U-boat on 13 December south-east of the Goodwin Sands. Initially, Admiralty intelligence thought that the victim of this attack was UC 19 (see UB 29 for details).

In the post-war period Arno Spindler attempted to assemble a sketch of the destruction of UC 19 from a confused mosaic of sightings and attacks. As UB 29 was known to have survived beyond the 6 December attack, Spindler concluded that the U-boat attacked by *Ariel* was probably UC 19 and this attribution has been accepted as fact ever since. However, denied British primary sources, Spindler overlooked the very real doubts surrounding the success of the *Ariel* attack. Explosive sweeps were believed to have destroyed five submarines during the First World War but recent analysis has tended the question all these claims. It is worth recording that this was not the only time the Jutland veteran HMS *Ariel* was involved in a U-boat incident (see Volume 3).

Having discussed this issue with Michael Lowrey, the First World War U-boat expert, the authors are convinced that *HMS Ariel* may have attacked, but not actually destroyed, UC 19 in the encounter. Until and unless further evidence emerges, the boat must be regarded as lost, cause unknown. However, a battered wreck off Calais may provide a tantalising clue.
ADM 53/34079 – NARA T-1022, Roll 46, PG61924

THE MEN WHO DIED IN *UC 19*

Adebar, Mts.
Belger, Ob.Masch.Mt
Gammelin, Mts.
Gehrt, Masch.Mt
Gülstorff, Btn.Mt
Heiden, Obe.Mts.
Kaiser, Hzr
Kittel, Hzr
Krüger, Mn.Ing.
Kühnert, Hzr
Lindner, Hzr
Luhrenberg, F.T.Obergast
Mellin, Masch.Mt

Meyer, Lt.z.S. der Reserve
Müller, Ob.Mts.
Nietzshe, Oblt.z.S.
Pietsch, Btn.Mt
Rückwart, Masch.Mt
Scheffner, Ob.Hzr
Schiefer, Hzr
Sönksen, Stm.
Vorck, Mts.
Wegener, Hzr
Wolter, Rasmus, Masch.Mt
Zander, Masch.Mt

UC 19 sank a minimum of four vessels by torpedo and mines:

AREA	VESSEL'S NAME	FLAG	TONS	D	M	YEAR	LOCATION
North Sea	*Dhoon* (RN Trawler)	GBR	275	24	11	1916	Mined and sunk near Newarp Light Vessel
English Channel	*Briardene*	GBR	2701	1	12	1916	12½ miles SE by S of Bishop Rock
North Sea	*Fernebo*	SWE	1440	9	1	1917	Mined 3 miles NE of Gromer
North Sea	*Ole Bull*	NOR	1835	11	1	1917	Mined in North Sea

According to Arno Spindler, the following nine vessels could have been sunk by either UC 19 or UB 29, but most probably the last two, the sailing vessels *Maria* and *Ans*, were sunk by UB 29:

AREA	VESSEL'S NAME	FLAG	TONS	D	M	YEAR	LOCATION
English Channel	*Heinrich* (sailing boat)	GBR	125	30	11	1916	Approx. 29 miles SE by S of Start Point
English Channel	*Bossi*	NOR	1462	1	12	1916	33 miles WSW of The Lizard

English Channel	Rene Montrieux (s/v)	FRA	234	1	12	1916	Sunk off Ushant at 48° 37' N, 05° 10'W
English Channel	Hitterøy	NOR	1260	2	12	1916	26 miles SW of Bishop Rock
English Channel	Giustizia	ITA	1168	3	12	1916	Sunk off Scilly Isles at 49° 17' N, 07° 18'W
English Channel	Julian Benito	SPA	1075	4	12	1916	40 miles S6°W of St. Agnes, Scilly Isles
English Channel	Fede	ITA	1987	5	12	1916	35 miles W of Bishop Rock
English Channel	Ans (or Anita) (sail boat)	RUS	362	6	12	1916	15 miles SW of Bishop Rock
English Channel	Marie (sailing vessel)	DAN	325	6	12	1916	10 miles W of Bishop Rock

The 125-ton *Heinrich*, a British sailing vessel, was travelling from London to St Malo with pitch when she was sent to the bottom.

The Norwegian steamer *Bossi* (Skibs Aktieselskapet Adalante, Christiania) was en-route from Bordeaux to Barry with pit props when she was captured and sunk with explosive charges, 33 miles off the Lizard.

The voyage of the 234-ton French sailing vessel *Rene Montrieux*, which was destroyed on 1 December, is not known. The next day the SS *Hitterøy* (Dampskipsselskapet Aktieselskapet Øy II, Christiania), a 1,260-ton Norwegian ship, was captured and scuttled 25 miles off Bishop Rock while en-route from Glasgow for Civitavecchia, Italy, with coal.

The Italian steamship *Giustizia* (Vito Cassisa fu V., Trapani), which was transporting cork from Lisbon to Glasgow on 3 December, was shelled and sunk near the Isles of Scilly.

The 1,075-ton Spanish steamer *Julian Benito* was sunk off the Scilly Isles on 4 December 1916, while on passage from the Tyne for St Vincent (CV).

The 1,987-ton Italian steamship *Fede* (Comm. Tomaso Astarita, Naples), transporting chestnuts from Naples and Huelva to Barry, was sunk on 5 December 1916.

Two sailing vessels were sunk on 6 December: the 362-ton Russian *Ans* was travelling from Preston to Nantes and the 325-ton Danish *Marie*, transporting pitch from Liverpool to Tonnay Charente, France were both sunk off Bishop Rock.

WRECK-SITE

No submarine wreck has been found in the area where *Ariel* made her attack. At the time of writing, a UC-boat has been located off Calais and this may well turn out to be UC 19. It is feasible that UC 19 survived *Ariel*'s paravane only to be sunk by a British destroyer when nearly home (see UB 29).

SM UB 29, IMPERIAL GERMAN U-BOAT

DATE OF LOSS: 13 December 1916
DEPTH: 35m
REFERENCE: 51 20'.900 N, 002 06'.437 E
LOCATION: 19.2 nautical miles NNW of Dunkurque
and 24.8 nautical miles W of North Foreland

Type: UB II coastal torpedo attack boat   *Builders*: A.G. Weser, Bremen for Imperial German Navy   *Ordered*: 30 April 1915, within the batch of SM UB 24–UB 29   *Keel laid*: as Yard No.243 on 15 July 1915   *Launched*: 10 February 1916   *Commissioned*: by Kapitänleutnant Herbert Pustkuchen on 18 January 1916.

TECHNICAL SPECIFICATIONS

Hull: Single *Surface displacement*: 265 tons *U/Dt*: 291 tons *LBDH*: 36.13m x 4.36m x 3.70m x 7.34m *Machinery*: 2 x 142ps Daimler diesels *Props*: 2 bronze *S/Sp*: 8.9 knots *Op/R*: 7,200 nautical miles at 5 knots *Sub/R*: 45 nautical miles at 5 knots *U/Power*: 2 x 140ps electric motors giving 5.72 knots *Batteries*: Lead/acid/accumulators *Fuel/ Cap*: 22 + 6 tons *Armament*: 2 bow 50.04cm torpedo tubes *Torpedoes*: 4 x 50.04cm (19.7in) *Guns*: 1 x 88mm (3.46in) forward deck gun *Mines*: None *Ammo*: 120 rounds of 88mm *Diving*: Max-op-depth 50m (164ft) and 22 seconds to crash-dive *Complement*: 2 officers and 21 ratings

UB 29 was assigned to the Training Flottille on 8 March 1916 with Kplt. Herbert Pustkuchen the CO from the commissioning until 2 November 1916. Pustkuchen sunk or damaged thirty-one vessels with UB 29, including sixteen steamships. They include the French *Nominoe* (Soc.Anon. des Chargeurs de l'Quest) lying at anchor off Lowestoft on 19 March 1916; she was in ballast, going from Rouen to Newcastle. The *Langeli*, (Aktieselskapet Dampskipsselskapet Langeli), a Norwegian ship, was anchored 5 miles off Corton lightship when she was torpedoed by UB 29 on 20 March. However, the ship up-anchored and steamed a further 10½ miles before she succumbed to the damage and sank off the north end of Middle Cross Sand; she was on her maiden voyage, en-route from Rouen to Blyth in ballast.

The Danish *Skodsborg* (Aktieselskabet Dampskibsselskabet Selsk. af 1896, Copenhagen) was torpedoed and sunk 5 miles off Corton Light Vessel, while voyaging from New Orleans to Helsingborg, Sweden, with cottonseed cake (oilcake). The British steamer *Salybia* (Scutton, Sons & Co., London) was sunk with a torpedo on 24 March. She was carrying general cargo from Trinidad to London.

At this time during the First World War, submarine commanders had instructions not to attack passenger ships and that all vessels making for Channel ports could be regarded as passenger transports. However, Pustkuchen caused the German Government great embarrassment when, on 24 March 1916, UB 29 hit the French cross-Channel packet *Sussex* (Chemins de Fer de l'État Français, Dieppe), with a torpedo. She was on her way from Folkestone to Dieppe and the projectile was fired at 4,000 yards range. It actually struck the ship's bow, killing over fifty men, women and children. The ship stayed afloat and was towed back to Boulogne, where salvage experts found fragments of a German torpedo embedded in the shattered section. Berlin first denied responsibility for the attack, but when the evidence was produced, they finally admitted it was a U-boat that caused it. The *Sussex* was heavily damaged in the incident, but was repaired and returned to service as a minesweeper under French Naval requisition. In 1921 she was renamed *Aghia Sophia* when sold to D. Demetriades of Constantinopole and broken up around 1922.

The SS *Vesuvio* (General Steam Navigation Co. Ltd) was bound from Messina for London with a general cargo, including ammunition, and had left Sicily on 22 March. The skipper had just reported in at Beachy Head on 6 April when a massive detonation occurred, level with the bridge on the port side. Seven of her crew were lost, including the second officer, a donkeyman, at least one sailor and the mess-room boy, who were all killed outright; three crewmen were also injured, one of them seriously. The area all around the engine room was completely demolished and the ship, which immediately began to settle, sank in ten minutes. At 11.30, HM patrol vessel No.25 rescued fifteen survivors and landed them at Newhaven.

A torpedo also accounted for the 4,574-ton SS *Braunton* (Tatem Steam Navigation Co. Ltd, Cardiff) on 7 April; she was bound from Boulogne to Newport, Monmouth, with Government stores, including empty steel shell heads and brass cases.

On 24 April the Norwegian ship *Berkelstroom* (N.V. Hollandsche Stoomboot Mij., Amsterdam) was on passage from Amsterdam for London with general cargo when Pustkuchen captured and scuttled it with explosives. A torpedo fired by UB 29 in the Lowestoft area also damaged HMS *Penelope* later that day. The Norwegian steamer *Gotthard* (Aktieselskapet Uto) was captured and scuttled with explosives in the English Channel on 3 September. She was bound from Middlesbrough to Rouen with pig iron and ammonium sulphate. The *Jeanne* (Aktieselskapet Dampskipsselskapet Selsk. Heimdal, Copenhagen) followed her to the bottom when she was captured and torpedoed north-east of the Casquets on 5 September. She was a Danish vessel en-route from Oran, Algeria, to Leith with esparto grass. The British *Torridge* (Tatem Steam Navigation Co. Ltd, Cardiff) was captured by Pustkuchen on 6 September and sunk by explosives, while sailing from Genoa, Italy, to the Tyne in ballast.

At around 10.30 on 21 October, the Norwegian collier *Fart III* (Aktieselskapet 'Fart', N.M. Nielsen, Kristiania) was shelled and sunk off the French coast, while en-route from Llanelly in Wales to Tréport with coal. Two British motor torpedo boats (MTBs) rescued the whole crew including Captain Johan Peter Eriksen from Kragerø, Norway, at about 16.00 and landed them at Newhaven. On 22 October, the Greek steamer *Georges M. Embiricos* (S.G. Embiricos, Andros) was captured, then shelled and sunk south-east of the Lizard, while voyaging from Buenos Aires to Brixham with maize. The *Anna Curine* (J.A. Knudsen, Haugesund), a Norwegian steamship was captured and sunk with explosive charges, while voyaging from Glasgow to Nantes with coal. On 14 October the SS *Sidmouth* (Griffiths Lewis Steam Navigation Co. Ltd, Cardiff) was taking coal from Cardiff to Spezia, Italy, when she was captured, then torpedoed and sunk off Wolf Rock.

Oblt.z.S. Erich Platsch assumed command of UB 29 on 3 November 1916. Platsch sank thirteen vessels, including nine steamships, before his career and life came to an abrupt end.

Two 1,085-ton Dutch steamers, the *Batavier VI* and *Midsland* were captured by Platsch off the Hoofden in November 1916 and taken back to Germany as prizes-of-war. The *Midsland* (N.V. Scheepvaart en Steenkolen Mij., Rotterdam) was en-route from Rotterdam to Newcastle and was condemned by the prize court (she was scuttled at Zeebrugge on 17 October 1918, but refloated by Belgian salvors in the spring of 1919; in 1920 she was owned by Soc. Navale Charbonnière, Antwerp). During the first week in December 1916, five steamers of varying nationalities, and three sailing vessels, were also sunk: the SS *Bossi* (Skibs Aktieselskapet Adalante, Christiania), a Norwegian ship, was en-route from Bordeaux for Barry with pit props when she was captured and scuttled with explosives, 33 miles off the Lizard; the SS *Hitteroy* (Dampskipsselskapet Aktieselskapet Øy II, Christiania), another Norwegian ship, was on passage from Glasgow for Civitavecchia in Italy with coal, when she was captured and scuttled with explosives by UB 29 (or possibly UC 19) on 2 December; the Italian steamer *Giustizia* (Vito Cassisa fu V., Trapani) was shelled and sunk near the Isles of Scilly on 3 December (probably by UB 29 or maybe UC 19), while transporting cork from Lisbon to Glasgow.

The Spanish steamer *Julian Benito* sank after a torpedo attack off the Scilly Isles, while on passage from the Tyne for St Vincent (CV). The Italian steamship *Fede* (Comm. Tomaso Astarita, Naples) was transporting chestnuts from Naples and Huelva, Spain, to Barry when she was sunk 33 miles off Bishop Rock. Also sunk off Bishop Rock were two sailing vessels. The first was captured by Platsch on 6 December: The Russian *Ans*, travelling from Preston to Nantes. The second was the Danish *Marié*, transporting 168 standards of pit props from Holmstad to West Hartlepool.

The number of casualties from all these ships is unknown.

FINAL VOYAGE

(17) As has been previously mentioned under the UC 19 entry, UB 29 is known to have left Zeebrugge in company with UC 19 for the Channel on 27 November 1916. Both were stamped as 'verschollen'. Controversy continues to surround their destruction as a result of claim and counterclaim for their sinking. British naval intelligence believed that the attack made by HMS *Ariel* (described under the UC 19 entry) had destroyed UB 29, and on 14 July 1917 a prize court awarded the crew of HMS *Ariel* £115 for the boat's destruction.

However, UB 29 is known to have operated beyond that point in time. The day after she was reported sunk, UB 29 captured, torpedoed and sunk the Norwegian *Meteor*, 40 miles west of the Scilly Isles. The *Meteor* (Det Bergenske Dampskibsselskab, Bergen) was on passage from Philadelphia, Pennsylvania, for London with general cargo. Although crewmen on the steamer identified the U-boat's markings, painted on the side of the bow, it may have been mistaken for UC 19.

On 7 December 1916, some 40 miles off the Isles of Scilly, UB 29 attacked the Belgian steamship *Keltier* (Antwerpsche Zeevaart Mij., Antwerp) with a defective torpedo. *Keltier* was still left damaged and taken in tow to Falmouth, then beached on the east side of the harbour entrance on 12 December. She later re-floated. Incidentally, almost two years later on 29 September 1918 and under a different owner, the *Keltier* (Lloyd Royal Belge, Soc. Anon., Antwerp) departed Milford Haven for New York and left the convoy on 1 October at position 46° 16' N, 09° 52' W. She was believed to have detonated a mine and was never seen again.)

HMS *Ariel* could not have sunk UB 29 but an attack made by the destroyer HMS *Landrail* in the early hours of 13 December cannot be so easily dismissed. The incident began with the sighting of the conning tower of a U-boat during a routine patrol south of the Goodwin Sands. The boat dived instantly, but the Dover Patrol destroyer *Landrail* raced to the spot. Her log provides terse detail. Log of *HMS Landrail* – Wednesday 13 December 1916:

> 0152 Sighted enemy submarine diving in 51.7 40N, 1.45 10E
> Expended 2 depth charges – oil and debris on surface. Collected sample.

If *Landrail* did destroy a submarine, this would make the unfortunate boat the first depth charge victim. Maritime historians agree that viable depth charges were not produced until January 1916 when the British Type 'D' depth charge (slowly) entered into service. The Type 'D' contained a 300lb TNT charge. A hydrostatic pistol could be pre-set to explode the depth charge at either 40 or 80ft. Each destroyer carried just two to four depth charges. They were released from chutes carried at the stern. Wartime experiments suggested that the Type 'D' would destroy a submarine if it exploded within 70ft (21m) and cause various degrees of damage out to 140ft (42m). In fact post-war analysis demonstrated that a Type 'D' charge would have to explode within 14ft (4m) of a submarine to achieve a kill. An explosion within 28ft might well disable a U-boat and force her to the surface. A detonation at a distance of 60ft would probably frighten the crew and shatter a few light bulbs but the submarine would survive the experience. It was soon found that Type 'D's were suitable only for fast fleet destroyers. There was an excellent chance that a 300lb charge exploding under the stern of a slow moving armed trawler would blow the vessel in half. Smaller vessels, such as drifters, trawlers and launches, were armed with the 120lb Type D. At the time of its introduction, it was thought that the Type D was effective up to 90ft (58m). Post-war this was revised down to 10–15ft. In other words if the most modern, highly trained RN warships and their crews could only achieve mediocre results from depth charge experiments replicating wartime conditions, an auxiliary patrol vessel would have to score a direct hit for its depth charge to be remotely effective. In the light of this information, some of the unsupported claims made by the indifferently trained and poorly equipped auxiliary patrol crews must be treated with judicious scepticism.

Spindler considered both the *Ariel* and the later *Landrail* attacks and concluded that *Landrail* must have destroyed UB 29, yet it is clear that conclusive evidence for a sinking is missing from the log. Could the crew of HMS *Landrail* really have been lucky or skilled enough to achieve a direct hit for the expense of just two Type 'D' depth charges? And if so, which boat was the victim, UC 19 or UB 29? ADM 137/3201 – NARA T-1022, Roll 55, PG 61776

THE MEN WHO DIED IN UB 29

Asch, Ob.Mts.

Birk, Btn.Mt

Breuer, Ob.Hzr

Denzel, Oblt.z.S. der Reserve

Freyer, Ob.Masch.Mt

Gockel, Mts.

Jonas, Mts.

Köhn, Masch.Mt

Loewe, Hzr

Ostermeier, Mts

Pfeiffer, Mn.Ing.Asp.

Platsch, Oblt.z.S.

Prang, Hzr

Riesinger, Signalgast

Schabrick, Hzr

Schielein, Hzr

Schmidt, Masch.Mt

Schukat, Masch.Mt

Schwan, F.T.

Steffen, Hzr

Wiedenfeld, Ob.Masch.Mt

Winter, Btn.Mt

UB 29 made seventeen war patrols and sank, damaged or captured the following vessels:

AREA	VESSEL'S NAME	FLAG	TONS	D	M	YEAR	LOCATION
North Sea	*Nominoe*	FRA	3155	19	3	1916	Sunk at anchor off Lowestoft
North Sea	*Langeli*	NOR	1565	20	3	1916	5 miles SSE of Corton Light Vessel
North Sea	*Skodsborg*	DAN	1697	20	3	1916	5 miles SSE of Corton Light Vessel
English Channel	*Salybia*	GBR	3352	24	3	1916	4 miles SW by W of Dungeness
English Channel	*Sussex*	GBR	1353	24	3	1916	Seriously damaged off Dieppe
English Channel	*Vesuvio*	GBR	1391	6	4	1916	6 miles E of Owers Light Vessel
English Channel	*Braunton*	GBR	4575	7	4	1916	4½ miles S by W of Beachy Head
English Channel	*Marguerite*	FRA	42	7	4	1916	Between Owers L/v and Beachy Head
North Sea	*Berkelstroom*	NLD	736	24	4	1916	16 miles ENE of N. Buoy, Outer Gabbard
North Sea	*Penelope* (HMS)	GBR	3750	25	4	1916	Damaged in Lowestoft area
North Sea	*Boy Percy* (fishing vessel)	GBR	46	17	5	1916	Sunk off Southwold
North Sea	*Boy Sam* (fishing vessel)	GBR	46	17	5	1916	Sunk off Southwold
North Sea	*Wanderer* (fishing vessel)	GBR	47	17	5	1916	Sunk off Southwold
North Sea	*Loch Lomond* (fishing vessel)	GBR	42	7	8	1916	18 miles E of Lowestoft
English Channel	*Gotthard*	NOR	1636	3	9	1916	45 miles WSW of Beachy Head
English Channel	*Notre Dame des Victoires* (f/v)	FRA	161	3	9	1916	Sunk in the English Channel
English Channel	*Jeanne*	DAN	1191	5	9	1916	16 miles NE of Casquets
English Channel	*Torridge*	GBR	5036	6	9	1916	40 miles SSE of Start Point
English Channel	*Yvonne* (sailing vessel)	FRA	163	6	9	1916	Sunk off English south coast
English Channel	*Alice* (sailing vessel)	FRA	119	7	9	1916	30 miles N of Ushant
English Channel	*Consolation* (fishing vessel)	GBR	47	9	9	1916	15 miles SSE of Start Point
English Channel	*Dorado* (fishing vessel)	GBR	36	9	9	1916	20 miles SSE of Start Point
English Channel	*Favourite* (fishing vessel)	GBR	38	9	9	1916	20 miles SE of Start Point
English Channel	*Muriel Franklin* (fish vessel)	GBR	29	9	9	1916	20 miles SE of Start Point
English Channel	*Fart III*	NOR	232	21	10	1916	25 miles off French coast- Beachy Head

English Channel	*Grit* (fishing vessel)	GBR 147	21 10 1916	25 miles S of Beachy Head
English Channel	*Princess May* (sailing vessel)	GBR 104	21 10 1916	25 miles S of Beachy Head
English Channel	*Georges M. Embiricos*	GRE 3636	21 10 1916	18 miles SE of Lizard 49° 50'N 04° 40'W
English Channel	*Anna Curine*	NOR 1147	24 10 1916	30 miles SSW Longships Light Vessel
English Channel	*Sidmouth*	GBR 4045	24 10 1916	22 miles S of Wolf Rock
English Channel	*St Charles* (sailing vessel)	FRA 521	28 10 1916	Sunk off Ushant 48° 37' N, 05° 10'W
North Sea	*Batavier VI*	NLD 1085	12 11 1916	Captured off the Hoofden
North Sea	*Midsland*	NLD 1085	15 11 1916	Captured off the Hoofden
English Channel	*Heinrich* (sailing vessel)	GBR 125	30 11 1916	Sunk about 29 miles SE by S of Start Point
English Channel	*Bossi*	NOR 1462	1 12 1916	33 miles WSW of Lizard
English Channel	*Rene Montrieux* (sail vessel)	FRA 234	1 12 1916	Sunk off Ushant 48° 37' N, 05 °10'W
English Channel	*Hitterøy*	NOR 1260	2 12 1916	26 miles SW of Bishop Rock
English Channel	*Giustizia*	ITA 1168	3 12 1916	Sunk off Scilly 49° 17' N, 07° 18'W
English Channel	*Julian Benito*	SPA 1075	4 12 1916	About 40 miles S6°W of St Agnes (Scilly Isles)
English Channel	*Fede*	ITA 1987	5 12 1916	About 35 miles W of Bishop Rock
English Channel	*Ans* (sailing vessel)	RUS 362	6 12 1916	15 miles SW of Bishop Rock
English Channel	*Marie* (sailing vessel)	DAN 325	6 12 1916	10 miles W of Bishop Rock
Atlantic	*Keltier*	BEL 2360	7 12 1916	40 miles W of Scilly Island
English Channel	*Meteor*	NOR 4217	7 12 1916	40 miles W ½ S of Scilly Isles

WRECK-SITE

At the time of writing, no UB wreck has been found in the vicinity of the attack made by *Landrail*. Interestingly, a mined UB II wreck discovered off the Belgian coast could possibly be either UB 29 or UB 32. Ammunition found by divers dates to the week before UB 29 sailed and the minefield in question was laid in early 1916. How ironic that a highly successful boat such as UB 29 had survived the perils of the English Channel, only to strike a mine on her own metaphoric doorstep?

Local Ramsgate archaeologist and diver Bob Peacock has discovered the remains of a UC-boat 13 nautical miles off South Foreland, which is listed in Innes McCartney's book *Lost Patrols* to be at position 51° 10.06' N, 01° 43.47' E. It is quite possible that this is the wreck of UC 19, although no positive identification has taken place to date (2006).

U 12, KRIEGSMARINE U-BOAT

DATE OF LOSS: 8 October 1939
DEPTH: Unknown
REFERENCE: 51° 10' N, 01° 30' E, (approx. historic position)
LOCATION: English Channel, near Dover

Type: IIB coastal torpedo patrol boat *Builders:* F. Krupp Germaniawerft AG, Kiel-Gaarden for Kriegsmarine *Ordered:* 20 July 1934, within the batch of U 7–U 12 *Keel laid:* as Yard No.546 on 20 May 1935 **Launched:** 11 September 1935 **Commissioned:** by Kapitänleutnant Werner von Schmidt on 30 September 1935 **Feldpost No.:** M 17 865

TECHNICAL SPECIFICATIONS

Surface displacement: 279 tons **U/Dt:** 329 tons **LBD:** 42.7m x 4.1m x 3.8m x 8.60m **Machinery:** 2 x 6-cylinder 350ps 4-stroke diesel by Motoren-Werke-Mannheim (MWM) **S/Sp:** 13 knots **Props:** 2 bronze **U/Power:** 2 x 180ps SSW electric motors giving 7 knots *Battery:* 1 x 62-cell lead/acid by Accumulatoren-Fabrik-Aktiengesellschaft in Berlin **Op/R:** 1,800 nautical miles at 12 knots, or 3,900 nautical miles at 8 knots **Sub/R:** 43 nautical miles at 4 knots *Fuel/cap:* 21 tons **Armament:** 3 bow torpedo tubes (no stern) **Torpedoes:** 5 **Guns:** 1 x 20mm (0.79in) AA Flak **Ammo:** 220 rounds 20mm AA **Mines:** only carried on special order and in exchange for torpedoes **Diving:** Max-op-depth 100.40m (330ft) and 30 seconds to crash-dive (apparently this type of boat was later restricted to 45m (150ft)) **Complement:** about 25

Werner von Schmidt was born in Görlitz on 17 April 1906 and commenced his naval career in 1926. Schmidt began his service as first watch officer on-board the U-boat depot ship *Isar* between December 1934 and September 1935. He was promoted to Korvettenkapitän on 1 April 1941.

U 12 was assigned to 3.U-Flottille '*Weddigen*' in Kiel as *Ausbildungsboot* (training boat) from her commissioning until 30 September 1937, with Kplt. Werner von Schmidt the commander. Dönitz, who commanded the flotilla, commissioned '*Weddigen*' U-Flottille on 25 September 1935 (the flottille was named after the famous First World War German submarine ace, Otto Weddigen).

In 1936, Werner von Schmidt took the boat down to 341ft (103.93m) on a training exercise, but an internal angle-bar joint failed, the hull suddenly cracked and water flooded in to a dangerous level. U 12 was saved and her hull was reinforced, along with all the others. The OKM however, restricted all these boats ('ducks') to 45m (147.63ft) diving depth. From then on, Kplt. Hans Pauckstadt assumed command of U 12 in December 1936 and was CO until 1 October 1937 (Hans Pauckstadt was born in Grimnitz on 27 September 1906 and commenced his naval career in 1926; he was promoted to Fregattenkapitän on 1 April 1944).

U 12 was formally assigned to 3.U-Flottille '*Lohs*', also at Kiel for frontline service on 1 October 1937 and Kplt. Dietrich von der Ropp assumed command of the boat. Von der Ropp was born in 27 July 1909 at Mitau, Lithuania and commenced his naval career in 1929. He began his submarine service as watch officer on board U 11 between 1935 and 1936 and was promoted to Kapitänleutnant on 1 August 1938.

(1) On 25 August 1939 U 12 sailed from Wilmhelmshaven for a patrol off the English east coast. At the outbreak of the Second World War on 3 September 1939, five U-boats, including U 12, formed a north-east to south-west patrol line south-west of Norway, on the Great Fisher Bank in the North Sea. She sank no ships and returned to Wilhelmshaven on 9 September 1939.

FINAL VOYAGE

(2) On 22/23 September 1939, Adm. Dönitz ordered von der Ropp to the English Channel, with a view to attacking France-bound Allied troopships. Dönitz did not believe that the British had mined the Channel, based on previous reconnaissance by other small IIB boats, or 'ducks' as they were commonly known. In fact, between 11 and 17 September, the Allies had actually placed 3,000 anchored and floating mines between Dover and Cap Gris Nez. They were also preparing to add another 3,636 deep-laid anti-submarine mines into the barrier in the form of a Bragg Loop system.

U 12 made no report after departing Wilhelmshaven and was lost, with all twenty-seven hands. The assumption has always been that she was mined off Dover on or about 8 September. Certainly U 12 was posted as overdue on 20 October. Kplt. von der Ropp's body was washed ashore near Dunkerque on 29 October 1939. He was later buried in Bourdon, near Amiens, block 16, row 10, plot 377.

NARA: T-1022, Roll 2831, PG30009/1-4

THE MEN WHO DIED IN U 12

Bölke, Emil–Gustav, St.Bt.Sm.
Breiter, Hermann, Mt
Eckersberger, Alfred, Ob.Gfr.
Ehlert, Harry, Gfr.
Fischer, Otto, St.Ob.Strm.
Fredriksson, Werner, Ob.Mt
Hähnel, Henry, Ob.Gfr.
Heymühle, Willi, Gfr.
Horn, Werner, Ob.Gfr.
Kohlisch, Ernst, Ob.Gfr.
Kresse, Walter, Ob.Gfr.
Lerch, Otto, Ob.Gfr.
Mayr, Michael, Mt
Meyer, Hans, Mt
Pein, Klaus, Oblt
Reng, Joh, St.Masch.
Ropp, von der Dietrich, Kapitänleutnant
Schellenberger, Franz, Mt
Schmid, Franz, Ob.Gfr.
Schymik, Ewald, Mt
Söte, Ludwig, Mt
Stolte, Bruno, Ob.Gfr.
Thöllden, Hans, Mn.Ob.Ing.
Westphal, Hermann, Ob.Gfr.
Wittke, Friedrich, Ob.Gfr.
Zeidler, Georg, Mt
Zschemisch, Erhard, Ob.Gfr.

WRECK-SITE

At the time of writing the wreck of U 12 has not been located.

U 16, KRIEGSMARINE U-BOAT

DATE OF LOSS: 25 October 1939
DEPTH: 26m
REFERENCE: 5I 09'.084 N, 01 28'.202 E
LOCATION: 3 miles NNW off Dover

Type: IIB coastal torpedo patrol boat **Builders:** Deutsche Werft AG, Kiel-Gaarden for Kriegsmarine **Ordered:** 2 February 1935, within the batch U 13–U 16 **Keel laid:** as Yard No.251 on 5 August 1935 **Launched:** 28 April 1936 **Commissioned:** by Kapitänleutnant Heinz Beduhn on 16 May 1936 *Feldpost No.:* M 13 014

TECHNICAL SPECIFICATIONS

Surface displacement: 279 tons **U/Dt:** 329 tons *LBD:* 42.7m x 4.1m x 3.8m x 8.60m
Machinery: 2 x 6-cylinder 350ps 4-stroke diesel by Motoren-Werke-Mannheim (MWM)
S/Sp: 13 knots **Props:** 2 bronze **U/Power:** 2 x 180ps SSW electric motors giving 7
knots *Battery:* 1 x 62-cell lead/acid by Accumulatoren-Fabrik-Aktiengesellschaft, Berlin
(AFA) **Op/R:** 1,800 nautical miles at 12 knots, or 3,900 nautical miles at 8 knots **Sub/R:**
43 nautical miles at 4 knots *Fuel/cap:* 21 tons **Armament:** 3 bow torpedo tubes (no stern
tube) *Torpedoes:* 5 *Gun:* 1 x 20mm (0.79in) AA Flak *Ammo:* 220 rounds of 20mm AA
Mines: only carried on special order and in exchange for torpedoes **Diving:** Max-op-
depth 100m (330ft) and 30-second crash-dive (this type was later allegedly restricted to
45m (150ft) **Complement:** about 25

Heinz Beduhn was born on 11 August 1907 in Berlin and commenced his naval career in
1926. He carried out U-boat training between November 1935 and April 1936. Beduhn
was promoted to Korvettenkapitän on his death on 1 July 1943.

U 16 was assigned to 3.U-Flottille 'Weddigen', at Kiel as Ausbildungsboot from
May 1936 to October 1937. Kplt. Beduhn was CO from 1 May 1936 to 29 September
1937.

Kplt. Hannes Weingärtner assumed command on 30 September 1937 and U 16 formally
transferred to 3.U-Flottille 'Lohs', also at Kiel, in October 1937. Hannes Weingärtner was
born at Innesbruck, Austria on 11 July 1908 and commenced his naval career in 1928.
He commanded U 4 between 17 August 1935 and 29 September 1937. On 1 June 1942
Weingärtner was promoted to Korvettenkapitän.

(1) On 2 September 1939 U 16 left Wilhelmshaven with Weingärtner for a mine-laying
operation off the English north-east coast. Mines were laid in Tees Bay off Hartlepool on
5 September, but there is no record of any vessels being lost to these. The boat returned
to Kiel on 8 September.

(2) On 13 September 1939, U 16 left Kiel and patrolled off the Norwegian coast
near Skudesnes. At 00.30 (Continental time) on 28 September, Weingärtner stopped
the 3,378-ton Swedish steamer *Nyland* (Angfartgs AB Tirfing), 45 miles south-west of
Stavanger. She was on passage from Stavanger for Amsterdam and Antwerp with iron ore.
Her master went on board U 16 and stated that his ship's papers had fallen overboard. A
boarding party from the U-boat, with the chief engineer in charge, boarded the steamer
at 04.30. However, at 07.05 an approaching aircraft forced the U-boat to crash-dive. The
boat resurfaced at 07.15 and the boarding party returned to U 16 at 07.20. Weingärtner
ordered the crew to evacuate the ship before he torpedoed it at 08.25 (Continental time).
Just five minutes later, Weingärtner had to crash-dive again because of an aircraft. U 16
returned to Kiel on 5 October.

Kplt. Horst Wellner became the CO on 12 October 1939. He was born on 30 August
1908 in Zwickau, Saxony and commenced his naval career in 1929. Wellner served on U
10 as watch officer in 1936 and was promoted to Kapitänleutnant on 1 October 1938. U
16 made the final war patrol with Wellner.

FINAL VOYAGE

(3) U 16 departed Kiel on 18 October 1939 for a mine-laying operation off the English
south-east coast. Mines laid off Dungeness on 22 October sank the requisitioned 56-ton
French Navy cordier (trawler) *Sainte Claire*, (ex-*Bon Pasteur*) during the early morning of
20 November, 10 miles south-east of Folkestone. All eleven crewmen were lost, including
the owner Mr J.B. Pannequin of Boulogne.

U 16 was near the Goodwin Sands and returning to Kiel on 24 October, when
the St Margaret's Bay Indicator Loop detected what appeared to be a submarine. The

Corvette HMS *Puffin*. (Author's collection)

station faced a dilemma, because the British submarine *Porpoise* was known to be in the immediate area. Should they wait to confirm identity, or should they throw the switches and risk destroying a British submarine? Report of St Margarets Bay Indicator Loop Station 24 October 1939 12.30:

> 24th Oct St Margaret's Bay Indicator Loop Station sighted HMS *Scimtar* escorting S/M *Porpoise* towards direction of Number 1 Loop. Shortly afterwards the complete signature of a typical submarine form was detected passing up Channel, ie West to East. Dover Castle confirmed this contact. This was passed by W/T to *Puffin* on patrol to the north of Number 1 Loop

Report of Corvette HMS *Puffin* (L52) 24 Oct. 1939 – Lt-Com Hon. J. Waldegrave:

> At 12.30 a crossing was reported on No 1 Loop. At 1341 *Puffin* obtained a contact at 900 yards, 327 degrees from South Goodwin Light Vessel and contact was maintained for the next 17 minutes. The echo was sharp and clearly defined with doppler effect. An attack was carried out at 1409 with a single DC at 51 09 40N 1 28 54E in 11 fathoms produced no visible results. Contact was maintained for two hours. Shortly after 1600 the target began to move more rapidly. An attack was made at 51 00 40N 1 29 12E at 16.25. Cayton Wyke (FY 191 - Skipper D. Noble) attacked at 1657. Some oil appeared on the surface. At 17.15 ordered to return to harbour and at 1728 passed a long oil slick in position 51 08 40N 1 25 00E
> 1748 Secured to No 23 Buoy.

On 23 November the body of a German naval officer was recovered and he was carrying papers referring to U 16. Bodies washed up on the Kent coast on 26 and 27 October wore Dräger apparatus marked 'U 14'.

The wreck was located and entered the next day. Admiralty divers noted a large hole in the pressure hull forward of the conning tower. Further efforts at salvage failed, although useful information was recovered. Nineteen dead submariners were either recovered by the Royal Navy, or washed ashore elsewhere. The loss of this boat was the cause of much analysis by Fdu West. In late October it was feared, wrongly, that German radio codes had been compromised, leading to the destruction of U 16.

THE MEN WHO DIED IN U 16
Baumbach, Erich, Mt
Bieker, Hermann, Gfr.
Branke, Walter, Mt
Dielforter, Karl, Ob.Mt.
Eickmann, Anton, Mt
Fett, Paul, Ob.Gfr.
Hanf, Paul, Ob.Gfr.
Keil, Hans, Ob.Gfr.
Kramer, Rolf, Ob.Gfr.
Kretschmer, Fritz, Mt
Kuhn, Heinrich-Johann, Ob.Stm.
Linke, Hans, Mn.Ob.Ing.
Mahnke, Friedolin, Stb.Gfr.
Materna, Hubert, Btn
Noske, Heinz, Ob.Gfr.
Schneider, Hugo, Mt
Schneidmüller, Rudolf, Mt
Schreiber, Rudolf, Gfr.
Schuchna, Otto, Mt
Sobek, Siegfried, Gfr.
Tischer, Heinz, Gfr.
Tomiczek, Georg, Ob.Gfr.
Trott, Christian, Ob.Gfr.
Tryanowski, Ernst, Ob.Gfr.
Wagner, Alfred, Ob.Gfr.
Woschke, Heinz-Joachim, Oblt.z.S.
Wust, Hans, Stb.Masch.

CREWMEN BURIED AT CANNOCK CHASE:
Paul Hanf: Block 1 Row 12 Plot 481
Hans Keil: Block 1 Row 12 Plot 485
Rolf Krämer: Block 1 Row 12 Plot 484
Friedhelm Mahnke: Block 1 Row 12 plot 482
Heinz Noske: Block 1 Row 12 Plot 486
Rodolf Schneidmuller

Other bodies which were washed ashore and found are buried in cemeteries in France and the Netherlands. HMT *Cayton Wyke* was herself torpedoed by an E-boat on 8 July 1940. ADM 199/126 – ADM 53/110119 – ADM 199/2032-33 – ADM 53/56297 NARA: T-1022, Roll 3027, PG30013/1-6, PG30903

WRECK-SITE
The wreck sits in a 4m scour, on a seabed of sand and stones, in a general depth of 26m. It is in reasonable condition, with the only damage being to the 'under-hull' area at the stern section, where it appears to have been blown open by a depth charge and a large hole forward of the conning tower. However, the conning tower was never actually seen. A rifle, which was later found to be a British 1939 Lee Enfiield, was also recovered from within the hull by local divers.

B2, HM SUBMARINE

DATE OF LOSS: 4 October 1912
DEPTH: 29m
REFERENCE: 51 07'.151 N, 001 27'.597 E
LOCATION: 5.93 nautical miles E of Dover piers

Type: 'B' Class coastal patrol submarine *Ordered:* for 1904–1905 programme (B2–B11) *Keel laid:* as Yard No.230 *Pennant No.:* I-22 *Builders:* Vickers Yard, Barrow-in-Furness for Royal Navy *Launched:* 19 August 1905 *Commissioned:* 9 December 1905 (commanding officers were not nominated for individual boats, only to a depot ship 'for command of submarine attached')

TECHNICAL SPECIFICATIONS

Hull: Single *Surface displacement:* 287 tons *U/Dt:* 316 tons *LBD:* 43.34m x 3.84m x 3.40m *Machinery:* 1 x horizontal 600hp Vickers 16-cylinder petrol engine *Props:* 1 bronze x 3 blade of 1.70m (5ft 7in) *S/Sp:* 12 knots *Op/R:* 740 nautical miles at 12 knots, or 1,000 nautical miles at 8.7 knots and 10 days endurance *U/Power:* 1 x 225ehp triple armature electric motor operated on 100 volts and rated for 1,500 amps *Sub/R:* Designed endurance range and 280rpm: 50 nautical miles and 4½ knots, service endurance range and 280rpm: 22 nautical miles at 6½ knots *Batteries:* 159-cell lead/acid manufactured by Chloride, max. 143 volts, max. 500 amps giving duration at full speed of 3 hours and 45 minutes Batteries weighed 65.55 tons *Fuel/Cap:* 15½ tons *Armament:* 2 x 45.72cm (18in) bow torpedo tube, angled slightly downwards *Torpedoes:* 14 x 45.72cm (18in), two for re-loading *Diving:* Max-test pressure depth 30.48m (100ft) and 15.24m (50ft) normal *Complement:* 15 (2 officers and 13 ratings) Reference: BR3043

The loss of B2 was another of those submarine accidents which plagued the Submarine Service prior to the First World War. Present at the time was Richard Pulleyne, who we have already met in Chapter Three, when in command of E34.

The boats' total cost was £47,000 per unit. In addition to the ones fitted aft, the 'B' Class were the first British submarines to be equipped with a second set of hydroplanes, which were fitted on the forward side of the conning tower. However, at a later stage in development on the 'B' Class they were moved further forward to the bows. The inside of the submarines had very little accommodation space and there was no ventilation at all for the crew's living area. In other words, the boats were very uncomfortable to spend any time on.

On commissioning, B2 was attached to HMS *Thames* and later in 1906 to HMS *Mercury* at Portsmouth. In October 1906 she was attached to HMS *Forth* at Devonport. In 1910 the Royal Navy had seven flotillas of submarines, which were then called 'sections' and B2 was still at Devonport in 'Section 1'. By 1912 the name 'section' was changed to flotilla. Many of the 'B' Class boats, including B2 remained in home waters for training purposes, coastal defence duty and especially the Dover Strait, until 1912. However, B6, B7 and B8 went to Gibraltar, while B9, B10 and B11 were based at Malta.

Officers commanding B2 were: Lt George Campbell-Street, from 13 May 1907 to 10 June 1909 (Lt Street later died at the Battle of Jutland); Lt Thomas Frederick Parker Calvert from 16 January 1909 until 26 October 1911; Lt Percy Borough O'Brien from then until he was lost with the boat on 4 October 1912.

FINAL VOYAGE

HMS B2, then commanded by Lt P.B. O'Brien, was one of several submarines sent to Dover to take part in Channel exercises during the overtures to the First World War.

HMS B2. (Author's collection)

HMS *Thames* depot ship and her children. (Author's collection)

On 4 October 1912 the tiny submarine was surfaced some 4 miles north-east of Dover, probably charging batteries. It was a calm, clear night and dawn had not yet broken. It appears that lookouts on board the 23,000-ton Hamburg-Amerika liner SS *Amerika*, on passage from Hamburg for Southampton, failed to see the low profile of HMS B2 until it was too late. The bows of SS *Amerika* sliced into B2 just forward of the conning tower and the little submarine sank at once. Lt Richard Pulleyne, who was on the bridge with a petty officer, was the only survivor. The boat was badly holed near the conning tower and sank immediately. Pulleyne was sucked down, but as the boat struck bottom, the impact released him. His oilskins contained air, enabling Pulleyne to tread water for nearly thirty minutes, until he was rescued.

On arrival at Southampton the crew of SS *Amerika* began to talk to the press.

Lt Richard Pulleyne of B2 later became commander of the 'E' Class boat E34 (see Chapter Three). Interestingly, in 1917 the boats B6, B7, B8, B9 and B11 were converted to surface patrol boats in Malta. The conning tower was replaced by a wheelhouse and the hull-area forward of the conning tower was raised to form a platform to facilitate a 12-pounder QF gun (quick firing gun). The electric motor was then removed and finally the 'B' in the boat's name was replaced with 'S', so they became S6, S7, S8, S9 and S11.

THE MEN WHO DIED IN B2

Andrews, Richard Sydney, Able Seaman
Barratt, Sidney Charles, Able Seaman
Bryant. James Arthur, Stoker
Douglas, Alexander, Petty Officer Stoker
House, Walter Charles, Able Seaman
Keast, Herbert, Leading Seaman
Lancey, William Barrow, Leading Seaman
Ledo, William, Leading Seaman
Lee, Eneas, Able Seaman
Millar, William Crawford, Engine R. Artificer
O'Brien, Percy Borough, Lieutenant
Reid, William, Engine Room Artificer
Rivers, Walter Charles, Petty Officer
Russell, Frank, Leading Stoker
Sherrell, William Henry, Able Seaman

A plaque to Eneas Lee, inscribed 'a brave lad and a good son', can be seen in Ilminster. A memorial to W.B. Lancey can be found at Marlborough, Kingsbridge in Devon.

WRECK-SITE

The wreck is orientated in a south–south-east to north–north-west (150/330 degrees) direction and lies on a seabed of sand, in a general depth of 29m, being the lowest astronomical depth. The bow and stern are well uncovered, as is the solid brass conning tower. Just forward of the tower is filled with sand, the conning tower hatch is easy to open and close, but the control room is sanded up. There are no trawl nets on the wreck and it is very clean, with not much marine growth.

The submarine looks just as if it was sitting on a sandy beach and some children have tried to bury it forward of the conning tower. The conning tower points upwards at a 60-degree angle with the hatch open. There is also a lot of scattered debris away from the wreck. (Report given by Andy Nye of Taurus Diving at Dover.)

U 40, KRIEGSMARINE U-BOAT

DATE OF LOSS: 13 October 1939
DEPTH: 31m
REFERENCE: 51 07'5 N, 01 48.00 E
LOCATION: 18.22 nautical miles E from Dover Harbour

Type: IXA ocean-going boat *Builders*: Deutsche Schiff-und Maschinenbau AG (A.G. Weser), Bremen, for Kriegsmarine *Ordered*: 29 July 1936, within the batch of U 37–U 40

Keel laid: as Yard No.945 on 29 July 1936 *Launched:* 9 November 1938 *Commissioned:* by Kapitänleutnant Werner von Schmidt on 11 February 1939 *Feldpost No.:* M 19 297

TECHNICAL SPECIFICATIONS

Surface displacement: 1,032 tons *U/Dt:* 1,153 tons *LBD:* 76½m x 6½m x 4.7m x 9.4m *Machinery:* 2 x 2,200ps Maschinefabrik-Augsburg-Nürnberg (MAN) diesels *S/Sp:* 18.2 knots *Props:* 2 bronze *U/Power:* 2 x 500ps SSW electric motors giving 7.7 knots *Battery:* Lead/acid by Accumulatoren-Fabrik-Aktiengesellschaft, Berlin *Op/R:* 8,100 nautical miles at 12 knots, or 11,350 nautical miles at 10 knots *Sub/R:* 65 nautical miles at 4 knots *Fuel/ cap:* 154 tons *Armament:* 6 x below waterline torpedo tubes (4 bow and 2 stern) *Torpedoes:* 22 *Gun:* 1 x 105mm (4.13in) deck gun and 1 x 37mm and 1 x 20mm AA Flak *Ammo:* 110 rounds of 105mm and 220 rounds of 37mm *Mines:* Only carried on special order and in exchange for torpedoes *Diving:* Max-op-depth 100m (330ft) and 35 seconds to crash-dive *Complement:* about 48. These boats had one periscope in the control room, plus two in the tower and the hydroplanes and rudder systems were the same as VIIC boats.

U 40 was assigned to the Germany-based 6.U-Flottille 'Hundius' at Wilhelmshaven on 11 February 1939, with Werner von Schmidt her first CO.

(1) U 40 departed Wilmhelmshaven on 19 August 1939 and sailed for operations to the west of Gibraltar, where von Schmidt attacked a convoy on 5 September. In preparation for Atlantic operations, the boat was recalled on 7 September and arrived back at Wilmhelmshaven on 18 September.

Kplt Wolfgang Barten assumed command of U 40 on 21 September 1939 and was lost on his first patrol. Barten was born on 18 August 1909 at Minden, Westphalia and commenced his naval career in 1931. He began his submarine service as watch officer on board U 29 between 1936 and 1937, and was promoted to Korvettenkapitän on 1 October 1939.

FINAL VOYAGE

(2) On 10 October 1939 U 40 left Wilmhelmshaven and sailed at full speed on the surface for the south-west coast of Ireland. There, U 40 joined up with five other U-boats – U 45, U 46, U 48, U 37 and U 42 – as well as three VIIBs and three IXs from two different Flottilles, with the senior officer being Kplt. Werner Hartmann of 'Hundius' Flottille and commander of U 37. The six boats would then proceed to a position off the west coast of Portugal, where they would jointly attack convoys and shipping, being the first controlled 'wolfpack' operation of the Second World War. However, Dönitz, in his wisdom, wrongly believed at the time that the English Channel had not been mined and had ordered thirty-year-old Wolfgang Barten to take the direct route with U 40 through the Channel. The decision was made so U 40 should catch up with the other boats that had set off five days earlier via the safer route around the north of Scotland.

At 03.00 on the morning of 13 October and three and a half hours after high water, U 40 detonated a mine in the Dover/Cap Gris Nez minefield. Almost at once, the control room and fore section flooded and the best part of her crew were killed. U 40 quickly went down to the bottom, where she lay in 35m with a severe list to starboard. Nine men had survived in the rear compartments as a result of the watertight door in the stern room being sealed in time. After gathering his senses, twenty-one-year-old Otto Winkler, the 'senior' man of those left, organised an escape from the after-deck hatch. Some biscuits were eaten as the men calmed themselves down and then Dräger escape apparatus was strapped on before the compartment was flooded. The deck hatch had a skirt for escape purposes and, as pressure inside the boat equalised with the water pressure outside, the hatch flew open. Otto Winkler was the last one out of the stricken boat, as the nine men floated toward the surface. In a statement later, he described how, after reaching the surface, he saw the eight other crewmen swimming around in a group. All the men were wearing their Dräger escape apparatus, labelled 'U 40', but one man drowned on reaching the surface.

It was still very dark, with a new moon, but in the distance Winkler believed he could see a lighthouse and struck out towards it. The seawater was freezing cold and Winkler began feeling faint. Then, he said, he must have passed out. The next thing he knew was later that morning when the two British destroyers HMS *Brazen* and *Boreas* arrived, nine hours after U 40 had sunk, and picked him up at 09.15 at No.6 Buoy (14). Two other men were also found alive and five bodies recovered, the men having succumbed to hypothermia before being rescued. Nothing else was ever seen of the other thirty-nine.

The crew of HMS *Boreas* also recovered an emergency telephone-equipped buoy the next day. On it was a brass plate, inscribed: 'U-boat 40 is sunk here. Do not raise buoy. Telegraph the situation to the nearest German naval command'. It had probably been ripped off the U-boat during the explosion. Winkler and the other two survivors became prisoners of war. The British were amazed that the Germans had not removed the U-boat's name from the emergency equipment to hide her identity.

A comment was made about the U-boat skipper in the monthly Anti-Submarine Report of October 1939, which read: 'Barten had not profited from the experience of his predecessors in the 1914–18 war, who would only transit the Straits at high water so that the mines would be at their maximum dip.' Unaware of the loss of U 40, the other boats in the pack proceeded as planned to the Western Approaches, where two British destroyers also sank one of the other big IX boats, U 42.

THE MEN WHO DIED IN U 40

Alex, Helmut, Mt
Barten, Wolfgang, Kplt
Briesenick, Willi, Ob.Gfr.
Conrad, Heinz, Ob.Gfr.
Czapski, Albert, Mt
Decker, Gustav, Mt
Ferl, Rudolf, Ob.Gfr.
Geldner, Robert, Ob.Gfr.
Hawelsky, Helmut, Mt
Jäger, Walter, Ob.Gfr.
Kasparek, Wilhelm, Ob.Gfr.
Kemper, Wilhelm, Ob.Gfr.
Koppler, Bernhard, Ob.Gfr.
Kraus, Berthold, Ob.Gfr.
Kruse, Adolf, Ob.Stm.
Kulitzscher, Kurt-Heinz, Ob.Gfr.
Ledebur, Gunter, Gfr.
Lork, Robert, Ob.Gfr.
Luchs, Otto, Mt
Mai, Willi, Gfr.
Maus, Wilhelm, Ob.Masch.
Mayer, Karl, Stb.Btn.
Medritzki, Walter, Ob.Gfr.
Meier, Heinrich, Ob.Gfr.
Meschenmoser, Friedrich, Oblt.
Meyer, Karl, Stb.Btn.
Miltenberger, Helmut, Mt

Moll, Karl-August, Oblt
Pfeifer, Helmut, Mt
Piehl, Gerhard, Mt
Schuster, Horst, Ob.Gfr.
Thomas, Friedrich, Ob.Gfr.
Threike, Heinrich, Mt
Trinoga, Siegfried, Mt
Vollmer, Friedrich-Hermann, Kl.Ing.
Wack, Siegfried, Ob.Gfr.
Wegener, Kurt, 'Lt.Marine-artillery, Sonderfýfrer'
Wendel, Kurt, Ob.Gfr.
Wendte, Adalbert, Ob.Gfr.
Wolfrum, Hans, Ob.Gfr.
Wollersheim, Hubert, Kplt.Ing.
Zaun, Franz, Dr

MEN TAKEN PRISONER
Weber, Karl-Heinz
Winkler, Otto
Vogt, Philip

ADM 53/107841 – ADM 199/2032-33 NARA: T-1022, Roll 3115-6, PG30038/1-3

WRECK-SITE
The wreck lies on an undulating seabed of sand and shingle, in a general depth of 31m (101.7ft), being the lowest astronomical depth. It is upright, lists over to starboard and is generally in excellent condition, except for the bow section forward to the hydroplanes, which is badly damaged. The boat's propellers are also still in place and, at the time of writing, the after hatch, where the crewmen made their escape, remains open.

UC 46, SM IMPERIAL U-BOAT

DATE OF LOSS: 8 February 1917
DEPTH: 34m
REFERENCE: 51 06.86 N, 01 37.15 E
ALSO: 51 06'.902 N, 001 37'.081 E
LOCATION: 10.88 nautical miles E from Dover piers

Type: UCII coastal mine-laying boat *Builders*: A.G. Weser, Bremen for Kaiserliche Deutsche Marine *Ordered*: 20 November 1915, within the batch of UC 46–UC 48 *Keel laid*: as Yard No.256 on 1 February 1916 *Launched*: 8 August 1916 *Commissioned*: by Oberleutnant zur See Friedrich (Fritz) Moecke on 15 September 1916

TECHNICAL SPECIFICATIONS
Hull: Double *Surface displacement*: 420 tons *U/Dt*: 480 tons *LBDH*: 51.85m x 5.22m x 3.68m x 7.46m *Machinery*: 2 x 250ps MAN diesels *Props*: 2 bronze *S/Sp*: 11.7 knots *Op/R*: 7,280 nautical miles at 7 knots *Sub/R*: 54 nautical miles at 4 knots *U/Power*: 2 x 230ps electric motors giving 6.9 knots *Batteries*: Lead/acid/accumulators *Fuel/Cap*: 41 + 14½ tons *Armament*: 2 external 50.04cm torpedo tubes at the bow, one either side

of the mine chutes and 1 stern internal tube **Torpedoes**: 7 x 50.04cm (19.7in) maximum **Guns**: 1 x 88mm (3.46in) forward deck gun **Ammo**: 133 rounds of 88mm **Mine tubes**: 6 **Mines**: 18 x UC 200 **Diving**: Max-op-depth 50m (164ft) and 33 seconds to crash-dive **Complement**: 3 officers and 23 ratings

Torpedo load as designed: 4 – a torpedo in each tube plus a reload for the stern tube. Storing an additional torpedo in pieces internally for the stern tube later augmented this, although this was optional. Two extra torpedoes (total) for the external bow tubes could be carried as well – these were lashed to the deck. So up to a total of seven torpedoes were carried, although not all boats sailed with that many.

UC 46 was formally assigned to Flandern U-Flottille on 29 November 1916, with Oblt.z.S. Fritz Moecke the commander from 15 September 1916.

(1) After a short training period and sea trials, UC 46 left Bremen on 27 November 1916 and transferred to Flanders base at Zeebrugge, where she arrived on 29 November.

(2) On 4 December 1916 UC 46 departed Zeebrugge and sailed to the English east coast to lay mines. Three weeks later, one of those mines laid on 8 December sank the Norwegian steamer *Modig* (Aktieselskapet Ivar An. Christensens Rederi, Christiania) off Flamborough Head; she was under the command of Captain O.J. Vaarli and, carrying a 2,400-ton cargo of coal from the Tyne for Rouen (the ship had previously been captured and taken to Swinemunde, then released back into Norwegian service again). UC 46 returned to Zeebrugge on 9 December.

(3) Departing Flanders base on 16 December, UC 46 sailed to the Bristol Channel and laid mines. The SS *William Middleton* (James Westoll, Sunderland) was attacked and damaged off Lundy Isle, while sailing in ballast from Boulogne to Dublin. The ship was beached at Tenby, re-floated and taken to Port Talbot (on 28 September 1917, the ship was damaged by another mine). During the patrol, the steamer *Paul Paix* (Lennard's Carrying Co. Ltd, Middlesbrough) was also damaged by a mine off Swansea and three other small boats were sunk. On the return voyage home, Moecke captured and scuttled the Greek steamer *Sappho* (C. Hadjipateras & N&C Pateras, Piraeus) with explosive charges. It was travelling from Alexandria in Egypt to Hull with cottonseed. Two days later, the Swedish SS *Goosebridge* (Ångfartygs AB Goosebridge, Helsingborg) was stopped by UC 46, whereby all of the crew abandoned ship in the lifeboats and the vessel was sunk with explosive charges about 10 nautical miles west-north-west of Ushant. She was en-route from Port Talbot to St Nazaire with 2,400 tons of coal. UB 46 arrived back at Zeebrugge on 3 January 1917.

FINAL VOYAGE

(4) On 25 January 1917, UC 46 sailed out from Flanders with Moecke for a mine-laying operation in the English Channel. The Dutch steamer *Gamma* (N.V. Vrachtvaart Mij. Bothnia, Amsterdam), taking linseed cake from New York to Amsterdam was captured, then torpedoed and sunk near Land's End on 1 February, then Moecke sunk a sailing vessel on 2 February and another one on 4 February. The 12,097-ton SS *Argyllshire* (Scottish Shire Line Ltd, Glasgow) was en-route from London to Barry on 5 February, when a torpedo damaged her off Start Point. She put into Plymouth for repairs.

A mine laid in the Irish Sea, off Neil's Point, also destroyed the RN trawler *Longset* on 6 February. She had been requisitioned in May 1915 as Admiralty armed patrol vessel No.1503.

UC 46 had completed her mission and in the early hours on 8 February, was on the return leg of her voyage to Zeebrugge. Moecke brought his boat to the surface in bright moonlight east of the Goodwin Sands. He was probably hoping to avoid the mines, which would be at their maximum dip at high water, but he must have been oblivious to the fact that a British destroyer was close by. Log of HMS *Liberty* – 8 February 1917 – Lt-Cdr P. King:

Above and below: HMS *Liberty.* (Author's collection)

03.10   Rammed and sunk enemy S/M 4 miles WSW of no 7A buoy

03.20   Proceeded to Dover at 12knots. Making water forward heavily. Marked submarine position with dan buoy

06.30   Tug secured alongside

8.00   Hands employed in painting ship

Notes at the bottom of the log section mention how four depth charges were drawn from stores that night to replenish charges dropped on the enemy submarine.

HMS *Liberty* was patrolling on a WSW course towards 7A Buoy of Dover Barrage (see sketch on page 217 for position). She changed course at 02.50 to ENE, when, half a mile from No.7A, a large U-boat was seen to break surface at right angles to the destroyer a short distance off the starboard bow. Visibility was reasonably good, which points to a major failure on the parts of both the officer on periscope watch and the hydrophone operator. *Liberty* fired one round, but it fell short and blinded the men on the bridge with the flash. Lt-Cdr King decided to ram. Travelling at 24 knots, *Liberty* sliced through the U-boat some 2ft forward of the conning tower and the boat rolled on its beam end. As the destroyer backed off, UC 46 disappeared beneath the surface.

Lt-Cdr King then ordered four depth charges dropped over the U-boat, which finished her off. All of the crew of twenty-three were lost. UC 46 was credited to HMS *Liberty* and her captain awarded a DSO. ADM 53/46627 – NARA: T-1022, Roll 48, PG61959

THE MEN WHO DIED IN UC 46

Beissele, Hzr
Berger, Masch.Mt der Reserve
Brachmann, Mts.
Drees, Ob.Masch.Mt
Hagen, Masch.Mt
Halscheidt, Hzr
Heitmann, Mts.
Haas, Hzr
Kessler, Mts.
Kramer, Mn.Ing. Ober Asp
Kränzlein, Masch.Mt der Reserve
Köhler, Hzr
Lembke, Stm.
May, Masch.Mt der Reserve
Meier, Hzr
Moecke, Friedrich, Oblt.z.S.
Neumeier, Btn.
Proske, F.T.Maat
Schuppe, Lt.z.S. der Reserve
Sest, Masch.Mt
Thalmann, Ob.Mts.
Weinmann, Mts.
Zoeke, Hzr

The following are vessels damaged or sunk by UC 46:

AREA	VESSEL'S NAME	FLAG	TONS	D	M	YEAR	LOCATION
North Sea	*Modig*	NOR	1704	21	12	1916	Mined 15 miles SE by S 3/4 S of Flam.Head
Irish Sea	*William Middleton*	GBR	2543	23	12	1916	Damaged 4 miles NNW of Lundy Island
Irish Sea	*Paul Paix*	GBR	4196	24	12	1916	Mined and damaged off Swansea
Irish Sea	*Agnes* (sailing boat)	GBR	99	26	12	1916	15 miles SW by W St Ann's Head
Irish Sea	*Neptune* (fish boat)	BEL	199	26	12	1916	Sunk near the Smalls
Irish Sea	*Saint Louis* (s/v)	FRA	184	26	12	1916	Sunk about 3½ miles S of Mumbles Hd
English Channel	*Sappho*	GRE	2087	30	12	1916	25 miles of N Ile Vierge, Brittany coast
English Channel	*Goosebridge*	SWE	1928	1	1	1917	Scuttled off Ile de Sein 48 33' N, 05 25' W
Atlantic	*Gamma*	NLD	2115	1	2	1917	Sunk near Land's End

English Channel	Isle of Arran (s/v)	GBR	1918	2	2	1917	Sunk in Western Channel 5015' N, 0705'W
English Channel	Marthe (sailing boat)	FRA	154	4	2	1917	Sunk 15–18 miles S of Scilly Isles
English Channel	Argyllshire	GBR	12097	5	2	1917	Damaged 2¾ miles from Start Point
Irish Sea	Longset (HMT)	GBR	275	6	2	1917	Mined off Nell's Point

WRECK-SITE

The wreck, most probably that of UC 46, lies on a seabed of fine sand, black shells, mud, shingle and weed, in a general depth of 34m, being the lowest astronomical depth. It lies with the bows to the north-west, is reasonably intact, and is lying on its port side. The deck gun is allegedly still mounted, but the outer casing is badly corroded and trawl nets cover much of the wreck. Soft corals are well established and shoals of fish can usually be found hovering just above it.

UC 26, SM IMPERIAL U-BOAT

DATE OF LOSS: 9 May 1917
DEPTH: 35m
REFERENCE: 51 01'.702 N, 001 41'.188 E
ALSO: 51 01.70 N, 01 41.32 E
LOCATION: 15 nautical miles SE of Dover

Type: UCII coastal mine-laying boat   *Builders:* AG Vulcan, Hamburg for Kaiserliche Deutsche Marine   *Ordered:* 29 August 1915, within the batch of UC 25–UC 33   *Keel laid:* as Yard No.65   *Launched:* 22 June 1916   *Commissioned:* by Oberleutnant zur See Matthias Graf von Schmettow on 18 July 1916

TECHNICAL SPECIFICATIONS

Hull: Double   *Surface displacement:* 400 tons   *U/Dt:* 480 tons   *LBDH:* 49.45m x 5.22m x 3.68m x 7.46m   *Machinery:* 2 x 250ps MAN diesels   *Props:* 2 bronze   *S/Sp:* 11.6 knots   *Op/R:* 9,260 nautical miles at 7 knots   *Sub/R:* 55 nautical miles at 4 knots   *U/Power:* 2 x 230ps electric motors giving 6.6 knots   *Batteries:* Lead/acid/acculators   *Fuel/Cap:* 41 + 14 tons   *Armament:* 2 external 50.04cm torpedo tubes at the bow, one either side of the mine chutes and 1 stern internal tube   *Torpedoes:* 7 x 50.04cm (19.7in) maximum   *Guns:* 1 x 88mm (3.46in) forward deck gun   *Ammo:* 133 rounds of 88mm   *Mine tubes:* 6   *Mines:* 18 x UC 200   *Diving:* Max-op-depth 50m (164ft) and 33 seconds to crash-dive   *Complement:* 3 officers and 23 ratings

Torpedo load as designed: 4 – a torpedo in each tube plus a reload for the stern tube. Storing an additional torpedo in pieces internally for the stern tube later augmented this, although this was optional. Two extra torpedoes (total) for the external bow tubes could be carried as well – these were lashed to the deck. So up to a total of seven torpedoes were carried, although not all boats sailed with that many.

UC 26 was formally assigned to Flandern U-Flottille on 12 September 1916 for the duration of her service, with Oblt.z.S. Matthias Graf von Schmettow as the boat's only commander. UC 26 made the following nine patrols:

(1) On 11 September 1916 she departed Germany and transferred to Flanders, arriving the following day.

(2) UC 26 sailed from Zeebrugge on 17 September 1916 for mine-laying operations off the English east coast. On 23 September and 50 miles off Spurn Head, one of the mines damaged the Swedish steamer *Princsessan Ingeborg* (Rederiaktiebolaget Nordstjärnan, Stockholm) at position 53° 10' N, 01° 13' E; the ship was on passage with a general cargo from London for the Tyne, but she made it back to Grimsby Roads without assistance. UC 26 returned to Flanders on 22 September.

(3) On 28 September 1916 the U-boat left Flanders to lay mines and attack Allied shipping along the French Channel coast and western English Channel. A sailing vessel was sunk on 30 September and then a contact mine laid by UC 26 the previous day was detonated by the SS *Maywood* (Maywood SS Co. Ltd, Cardiff) on 30 September; she was bound from Newport, Monmouth to Le Havre with coal and coke. On 1 October a small sailing vessel was sunk and then the SS *Vanellus* (Cork Steam Ship Co. Ltd, Cork) struck a mine laid on 29 September and foundered. The steamer was on passage from Portishead for Rouen with coal and the following three men were killed in the explosion:

Crespin, Charles William Victor, 34, Fireman
Jarrett, Alfred Edward, 32, Second Cook
Tapping, Charles Bertram, 37, Boatswain (Bosun)

On 3 October 1916 the Norwegian steamer *Ada* (Aktieselskapet Dampskipsselskapet Ada, Kragerø) was captured and sunk with explosive charges off Wolf Rock, while journeying from Bilbao to Glasgow with iron ore.

The Norwegian SS *Risholm* (Skibs Aktieselskapet Grimstad, Grimstad) was also transporting coal when she was captured and sunk by gunfire, while en-route from Blyth to Bordeaux. The SS *Isle of Hastings* (Alexander Shipping Co. Ltd, Newcastle) was transporting tinned meat from Fray Bentos, Uruguay, to London when she was captured and scuttled with explosives on 5 October, 10 miles off Ouessant. The U-boat returned to base on 9 October, but the Finnish steamer *Mercator* (Helsingfors Rederi A/B, Helsingfors), voyaging from Dunkerque to the Bristol Channel, detonated a mine laid on 29 September and sank with all hands on 13 October.

(4) UC 26 sailed from Zeebrugge on 24 October 1916 and returned for operations in the English Channel, along the French coast. Mines laid by the boat on 26 October, sank the French naval trawler *Blanc Nez* on 27 October. The SS *Galeka* (Union Castle Mail SS Co. Ltd, Southampton) sank on 28 October and nineteen people were lost on her. She had been requisitioned by the British Government and employed as a hospital ship. The vessel was beached at Cape la Hague, but was written off as a constructive total loss. On 30 October, the French naval trawler *Saint Hubert* struck a mine and sank. UC 26 arrived back in Flanders on 1 November.

(5) On 13 November 1916 Von Schmettow departed Flanders for operations off the French Channel coast and the western English Channel. A Royal Navy trawler, three sailing vessels and six steamships were sunk and two steamers left damaged during this sortie. The SS *St Leonards* was voyaging from Philadelphia for Havre with grain when she detonated a mine, but she reached port safely. On 16 November the RN trawler *Anthony Hope* struck a mine and sank; she had been requisitioned in April 1916 and converted to Admiralty minesweeper No.1380. The Norwegian SS *Joachim Brinch Lund* (Dampskipsselskapet Aktieselskapet Joachim Brinch Lund, Bergen) was captured and on 16 November 1916, scuttled with explosives during her voyage from Santander, Spain, to Sunderland with iron ore.

The Portuguese steamer *San Nicolao* (Portuguese Government – Transportes Maritimos do Estado, Lisbon) was bound from Lisbon to Havre on 17 November, when she was captured and scuttled with explosives, about 30 miles north of Sept Iles at position 49° 20' N, 03° 48' W. The SS *Monmouth* (Canadian Pacific Railway Ocean Lines, Liverpool) was left damaged after detonating a mine, during her voyage from Newport News, south-east Virginia, to Cherbourg. She beached near Cherbourg harbour, but re-floated.

The Norwegian ship *Finn* (Aktieselskapet Ivar An. Christensens Rederi, Christiania) was en-route from Newcastle for Genoa, Italy, with coal and coke when Von Schmettow captured and scuttled her with explosives on 19 November. A torpedo destroyed the SS *Brierton* (Brierton Shipping Co. Ltd, West Hartlepool), hauling grain from Karachi, India, to Manchester. Under the command of Captain P. Th. Bang, the Danish steamship *Dansted* (Dampskibsselskabet 'Roedby Havn', Roedby) was captured, 40 miles off Ushant. After inspecting the ship's papers the sixteen crewmen were ordered to abandon ship in the boats, while four of the U-boat's crew placed explosive charge, on board, one at the main hatch, one in the engineroom and two at the after hatch. The *Dansted* then exploded and sank. Soon after, the Greek steamer *Thetis* was stopped and, after being searched, was ordered to wait and pick up the crew of the *Dansted*, which had been underway from Barry to St Nazaire with a full cargo of coal for the French company Cie de Charbon & Briquettes.

The Norwegian SS *Trym* (Aktieselskapet Trym, Tønsberg) was bound from Partington in Manchester to La Rochelle with coal when Von Schmettow captured and sunk her on 22 November with explosives.

While voyaging from New York to Le Have with a general cargo, the British steamship *Strathalbyn* (Strathalbyn SS Co. Ltd, Glasgow) was destroyed by a mine on 10 December 1916. The mine had been laid by UC 26 on 20 November. UC 26 returned to Zeebrugge on 27 November 1916.

(6) UC 26 left port on 2 January 1917 and laid mines off the Humber Estuary. The mines sank two Norwegian steamships off the Inner Dowsing Light Vessel on 28 January. The Russian steamer *Egret* (West Russian SS Co. Ltd, St Petersburg/Petrograd RU 480) struck a floating contact mine and sank on 28 January in position 53° 16' N, 00° 35' E, 5 miles south-west of the Inner Dowsing Light Vessel. She was journeying from Archangelsk, Russia, to London with timber; the mine had possibly been laid by UC 26 the previous day. *Egret* was the ex-*Cynthiana*, built at West Hartlepool by W. Gray & Co. Ltd in 1905. She was commanded by Captain R. Joshwich and was on British Government Service, under the Russian flag and insured by the British Government's War Risk scheme.

The *Argo* (H.M. Wrangell & Co. Aktieselskapet) was transporting 650 tons of coal from Hull to Rouen when she struck a mine. The crew abandoned ship and the vessel drifted for a while with the tide before settling on the seabed with her mast still 4½m above the surface. Later that same day, the Norwegian *Heimland I* (Aktieselskapet Dampskipsselskapet Heimland, Askerøen), commanded by Captain J.B. Johnsen, was carrying 700 tons of coal from Newcastle to St Nazaire when she sank after detonating a contact mine laid the previous day. UC 26 returned to Flanders on 19 January 1917.

(7) Leaving Zeebrugge on 2 February 1917, Von Schmettow laid mines off the French coast and along the English Channel. However, on the night of 6 February, an attempt to ram UC 26 was made by the 1,559-ton paddle steamer RMS *Mona's Queen 2* (Isle of Man Steam Packet Co.). The ship was on charter to the Admiralty, acting as a troopship. She was ferrying about 1,000 soldiers from Southampton to France when a German U-boat was spotted. Despite a torpedo being fired at her, she made full speed and struck the U-boat's conning tower with her port paddles. The steamer's paddle required major refurbishment due to this incident, but UC 26 was able to reach Flanders on 8 February. That same day, the French naval trawler *Noelle* detonated one of the mines and sank.

(8) From 7 April 1917 Von Schmettow laid mines and patrolled the English Channel and west coast of France with UC 26. The 613-ton RN patrol boat HMS P26 detonated a mine and sank on 10 April and then, later that day, seventy-nine people died when the SS *Salta* (The Admiralty, London, operated by Union-Castle Mail SS Co. Ltd) detonated a mine and sank. The mine had been laid the previous day. She was employed as a hospital ship in Government

Service, voyaging from Southampton to Le Havre with hospital stores. The RN trawler *Amy* struck a mine and sank off Le Havre on 11 April. She had been requisitioned in August 1914 as Admiralty minesweeper No.334. On 11 April, the SS *Duchess of Cornwall* (Duchess of Cornwall SS Co. Ltd, Falmouth) was torpedoed off Cape Barfleur by von Schmettow, while en-route from London to Le Havre and she sank with all hands, including:

Bascombe, Arthur Stanley, 31, Second Engineer
Carter, C., 59, Sailor
Davies, Rees, 31, Third Engineer
Goodley, Victor George Vine, 16, Mess Room Steward
Harris, John, 61, Fireman and Trimmer
Hoolocombe, William, 47, First Engineer
Irvine, William, 49, Master
Lelean, James, 53, Chief Officer
Lumley, Robert, 39, Able Seaman
Mallet, T.M., 23, Second Mate
Mills, Charles Thomas, 43, Able Seaman
McDonald, Jass, 32, Fireman & Trimmer
Pearce, Arthur, 47, Ship's Cook
Petersen, E., 36, Able Seaman from Russia
Smith, A., 59, Fireman and Trimmer
Smith, Robert Scott, 35, Boatswain (Bosun)
Sullivan Philip, 49, Donkeyman
Taylor, Albert Edward, 15, Ordinary Seaman
Trott, W., 16, Ordinary Seaman
Van Noey, Augustine Antonio Antonette, 27, Steward from Belgium
Van Rossen, T., 56, Sailor from Belgium
Webb, W.A., 44, Fireman and Trimmer

A small sailing boat was next to be sunk, then the Spanish SS *Tom* (Cia. Naviera Bachi, Bilbao) on 14 April, which was transporting iron ore from Bilbao to Cardiff and went down with all hands following a torpedo hit. Two more small sailing boats were sunk before UC 26 returned to Flanders on 20 April. On 26 April 1917, von Schmettow was promoted to Kapitänleutnant.

FINAL VOYAGE

(9) On 30 April 1917, UC 26 left her base at Flanders to lay mines off the French coast at Le Havre, Ouisterham and Cherbourg and patrol the English Channel off France. On 2 May, von Schmettow torpedoed and sunk the Norwegian steamer *Certo* (Dampskipsselskapet Aktieselskapet Certo, Haugesund), 10 miles off Le Havre. She was voyaging from Newcastle to Le Havre with coal. The British destroyer HMS *Derwent* (built by Hawthorn, Leslie & Co.) detonated a mine and sank on 2 May. Her official complement was seventy. The British steamer *Ussa* (J. Holt & Co. Ltd, Liverpool) was carrying hay and wagons from Manchester to Cherbourg when she foundered after detonating a mine on 3 May. The mine had been laid earlier that day. Von Schmettow sank the small sailing boat *Iris* on 8 May and was off Calais by dawn on 9 May. UC 26 was returning to Zeebrugge and von Schmettow attempted to run through the Dover Barrage on the surface. HMS *Milne* (Cdr Campbell) was patrolling off Buoy 7A, near the position where UC 46 had been destroyed. *Milne*'s log states that, at 23.50 on 9 May 1917, a surfaced submarine was sighted three points on *Milne*'s port bow, heading in an easterly direction. Log of HMS *Milne* – 9 May 1917 – Cdr V Campbell (21 DF):

Above: HMS *Milne*, which rammed U 26.

Left: HMS P58 at Dover. (Author's collection)

1150 Submarine spotted
12.20 S Rammed S/M midships. Cut straight through. Explosion occurred as fore and aft parts fell away and C/T passed. Dropped dc Moderate bow damage. Other ships commenced dc attack

HMS *Miranda* picked up Lt.z.S. Petersen and Machinestenmaat Acksal. UC 26 was attempting to return to base when *Milne* pounced. British naval intelligence extracted this account of the sinking from Lt Petersen:

> The boat was slow in diving. The conning tower hatch was closed and the boat had submerged to the base of the conning tower when she was struck just before this point. She at once sank and struck bottom with a considerable bump at 46m. Shortly afterwards the sound of depth charges was heard.
>
> Water came in at the starboard side directly after the boat was rammed. No excessive amount of gas was noted, probably due to the accumulators being swamped. There was a certain amount of confusion, but discipline held. The light gradually went out. An attempt was made to blow the tanks with compressed air and the man at the depth guage reported that the boat was rising, but this must have been broken as the boat stayed put. The tanks had not been closed in time.
>
> Water rose steadily and we divided the crew into two groups, one in the control room and the other gathered under the engine room hatch. The first attempt to open the hatches failed, as the pressure outside was too great.
>
> The Captain declared 'Its no good boys. Three cheers for the Emperor!'
>
> Meanwhile the cox'n had the idea of turning on the compressed air in the after torpedo room. The water soon ceased to rise. The pressure inside equalised then became greater than that outside. We were able to open the hatches.
>
> The first men shot to the surface and probably died at once. Our captain was not the last man to leave and I did not see him on the surface. I was dressed in heavy oilskins and boots. As a result I came to the surface slowly and with my lungs bursting. (Acksal put on a horseshoe lifebelt and also surfaced slowly.) I would say that 10 mins had elapsed between the ramming and the first men reaching the surface.

Of the eight men who escaped the boat, only two survived. The rest either drowned or died of an embolism.

After this, two other destroyers dropped depth charges over the position. The destroyer was left with a badly crumpled stem with pieces of the submarine's casing embedded in her forecastle. The Germans later claimed that the British had deliberately left the other men in the sea to drown.

Oblt.z.S. Mathias Graf von Schmettow had previously commissioned UC 6 on 24 June 1915, which he commanded until 5 May 1916. While UC 26 was under repair following a ramming attempt by a steamer on her seventh patrol, von Schmettow, being too valuable to sit around for two months, took command of UB 10, from

13 February to 3 March 1917 for one patrol off the Noord Hinder Light Vessel from 23 to 28 February 1917. However, from 19 February until 20 March 1917, he was given command of UB 23 and went on one patrol in the Hoofden with her from 10 to 11 March 1917. This meant that von Schmettow was actually CO of three boats at once over this period – UC 26, UB 10 and UB 23 – but the patrols on these three didn't produce any 'kills' (note that UC 26 was the second UCII boat, by a day to UC 16, to arrive in Flanders. Obviously, as the honour suggests, von Schmettow was very highly regarded and a well-respected U-boat officer).

Von Schmettow sank over 100,000 tons of Allied shipping, a total higher than several Flanders-based commanders that were awarded the *Pour Le Mérite*. Had Mathias Graf von Schmettow dived more quickly in the encounter with HMS *Milne* and survived in UC 26, he would undoubtedly have won the *Orden Pour Le Mérite* (Order of the Blue Max). ADM 137/3897 – ADM 53/46627 – NARA: T-1022, Roll 71, PG 61834

THE MEN WHO DIED IN UC 26

Arpke, Stm. der Reserve
Bauer, Mts.
Bonke, Mts.
Botz, Btn.
Brussatis, Lt.z.S.
Eickhoff, Ob.Hzr
Fischer, ObMasch.Mt
Fritsche, Mts.
Grefe, Ob.Mts.
Hadass, Ob.Mts.
Hoffmann, Hzr
Härtel, F.T.
Kraemer, Ob.Masch.Mt
Kreis, Masch.Mt
Köthe, Masch.Mt
Liersch, Ob.Btn.Mt der Reserve
Linke, Mn.Ing.Asp.
Loges, Masch.Mt
Nickelsen, Hzr
Pleger, Mts.
Pösch, Masch.Anw.
Schmettow, Graf von Matthias Kapitänleutnant
Schmidt, Hzr
Schneider, Hzr
Silbernage, l Hzr
Weber, Hzr

The following is a list of known vessels, either sunk or damaged by UC 26:

AREA	VESSEL'S NAME	FLAG	TONS	D	M	YEAR	LOCATION
North Sea	*Princessan Ingeborg*	SWE	3670	23	9	1916	Mined and damaged 50m SE by E of Spurn Head
E/Channel	*Maywood*	GBR	1188	30	9	1916	Mined 1 mile W of Whistle Buoy, Le Havre Roads

E/Channel	Vanellus	GBR	1797	1	10	1916	Mined in Le Havre Roads
E/Channel	Villebois Mareuil (s/v)	FRA	32	1	10	1916	20 miles SSE of Wolf Rock
E/Channel	William George (s/v)	GBR	151	30	9	1916	10 miles NNE of Cap la Hague
E/Channel	Ada	NOR	1111	3	10	1916	15 miles S ½ W of Wolf Rock
E/Channel	Risholm	NOR	2650	5	10	1916	12 miles WSW of Ushant
E/Channel	Isle of Hastings	GBR	1575	5	10	1916	10 miles S by W of Ushant
E/Channel	Mercator	FIN	2827	13	10	1916	Mined Off Boulogne
E/Channel	Blanc Nez (Naval Trawler)	FRA	247	27	10	1916	Mined in Straits of Dover SE of buoy de Baas
E/Channel	Galeka	GBR	6772	28	10	1916	Mined 5 miles NW of Cap de la Hague
E/Channel	Saint Hubert (Naval Trawler)	FRA	216	3	11	1916	Mined 1 miles NW of entrance to Cherbourg Harbour
E/Channel	St Leonards	GBR	4574	15	11	1916	Mined and damaged 400m ESE of Whistling Buoy
E/Channel	Anthony Hope (RN Trawler)	GBR	288	16	11	1916	M-? ½ mile N of Whistle Buoy, Cherbourg Roads
E/Channel	Joachim Brinch Lund	NOR	1603	16	11	1916	60 miles ENE of Ushant
E/Channel	San Nicolao	POR	2697	16	11	1916	15 miles SW of Casquets Rocks
E/Channel	Monmouth	GBR	4078	17	11	1916	Mined and damaged at Cherboufg
E/Channel	Finn	NOR	3806	19	11	1916	40 miles W by S of Portland Bill
E/Channel	Cap Lihou (sailing vessel)	FRA	252	21	11	1916	20 miles NE of Sept. Isles
E/Channel	Brierton	GBR	3255	22	11	1916	32 miles SW of Ushant
E/Channel	Dansted	DAN	1492	22	11	1916	40 miles E by S of Ushant
Atlantic	Trym	NOR	1801	22	11	1916	About 9 miles WNW of Armen Rock
E/Channel	Alfred de Courcy (s/v)	FRA	164	25	11	1916	Sunk off Ushant
E/Channel	Malvina (sailing vessel)	FRA	112	25	11	1916	15 miles off Ushant
E/Channel	Strathalbyn	GBR	4331	10	12	1916	Mined 2 miles NE of Cherbourg
North Sea	Argo	NOR	1261	28	1	1917	Mined 1½ miles SE of Inner Dowsing Light-vessel
North Sea	Heimland I	NOR	505	28	1	1917	Mined 2 miles off Inner Dowsing Light Vessel
E/Channel	Noelle (Naval Trawler)	FRA	277	6	2	1917	Mined About 5 miles from Le Havre
E/Channel	P26 (HMS Patrol boat)	GBR	613	10	4	1917	Mined Off Le Havre
E/Channel	Salta	GBR	7284	10	4	1917	Mined Off Le Havre, ½ mile N of Whistle buoy
E/Channel	Amy (RN Trawler)	GBR	270	11	4	1917	Mined Off Le Havre
E/Channel	Duchess of Cornwall	GBR	1706	11	4	1917	5 miles N of Cape Barfleur
Bay of Biscay	Gambetta (sailing vessel)	FRA	39	13	4	1917	Sunk off Isle d'Yeu
Bay of Biscay	Tom	SPA	2413	14	4	1917	Sunk about 12 miles from coast off Hourtin
E/Channel	Surcouf (sailing vessel)	FRA	195	18	4	1917	Sunk off Ile Vierge, Brittany
E/Channel	Senator Dantziger (s/v)	GBR	164	19	4	1917	15 miles S of Newhaven
E/Channel	Derwent (HMS)	GBR	555	2	5	1917	Mined Off Le Havre
E/Channel	Ussa	GBR	2066	3	5	1917	Mined 2½ miles NW of Western Fort, Cherbourg
E/Channel	Iris (sailing vessel)	GBR	75	8	5	1917	Sunk in the English Channel
North Sea	Egret	RUS	4055	28	1	1917	Mined 5 miles SW of Inner Dowsing L/v
E/Channel	Certo	NOR	1629	2	5	1917	10 miles W by N ¾ N of Le Havre

WRECK-SITE

The wreck lies on a seabed of rock, stone and sand, in a general depth of 35m (114.8ft), being the lowest astronomical depth. It is well broken, with the outer casing badly corroded and the conning tower broken off. Both hatches are open and the propellers are still in place, which identified the boat in September 2003. The wreck-site is also a war grave.

Now for that great concentration of submarine wrecks south of the Varne associated with the Folkestone–Gris Nez Barrage. UB 109 lies close inshore, near the site of the 'Folkestone Gate'.

UB 109, SM IMPERIAL U-BOAT

DATE OF LOSS: 29 August 1918
DEPTH: 29m
REFERENCE: 51 03'.723 N, 001 14.134 E
LOCATION: 1.87 nautical miles SE of Folkestone harbour

Type: UB III coastal torpedo attack boat *Builders*: Blohm & Voss, Hamburg for Kaiserliche Deutsche Marine *Ordered*: 23 September 1916, within the batch of UB 103–UB 117 *Keel laid*: as Yard No.315 *Launched*: 7 July 1917 *Commissioned*: by Oberleutnant zur See Kurt Ramien, on 31 December 1917

TECHNICAL SPECIFICATIONS

Hull: Double *Surface displacement*: 519 tons *U/Dt*: 649 tons *LBDH*: 55.30m x 5.80m x 3.60m x 8¼m *Machinery*: 2 x 550ps MAN /Vulcan diesels *Props*: 2 bronze *S/Sp*: 13.3 knots *Op/R*: 7,420 nautical miles at 6 knots *Sub/R*: 55 nautical miles at 4 knots *U/Power*: 2 x 394ps electric motors gave 7½ knots *Batteries*: AFA lead/acid/acculators *Fuel/Cap*: 35 + 36 tons *Armament*: 4 bow and 1 stern 50.04cm torpedo tubes *Torpedoes*: 10 x 50.04cm (19.7in) *Guns*: 1 x 105mm (4.13in) forward deck gun *Ammo*: 160 rounds of 105mm *Mines*: None *Diving*: Max-op-depth 50m (164ft) and 30 seconds to crash-dive *Complement*: 3 officers and 31 ratings

UB 109 was assigned to Flander I.U-Flottille on 30 March 1918 with Oblt.z.S. Kurt Ramien the boat's only CO. Ramien made the following three patrols with UB 109:

(1) UB 109 left Hamburg on 25 March 1918 and transferred to Flanders base at Zeebrugge, where they arrived on 30 March.

(2) Leaving Flanders on 6 April 1918, UB 109 made a war patrol in the English Channel and Irish Sea. Ramien torpedoed the French SS *President Leroy-Lallier* (Cie. des Bateaux à Vapeur du Nord) and six of her crew were lost when she sank on 9 April. Next day, the SS *Henley* (Britain SS Co. Ltd, London) was torpedoed and sunk 25 miles off the Lizard, while transporting coal from Barry to St Nazaire, and six men were drowned, including:

Baker, Evan Dare, 19, Third Engineer
Bell, James, 39, Fireman and Trimmer
Baptista, Antar, 44, Fireman and Trimmer
Murphy, James, 58, Sailor

The sailing vessel *Wilson* was sent to the bottom while carrying flint-stone from Dieppe to Runcorn. The SS *Runswick* (St Just SS Co. Ltd, London) was also hit by torpedo

3 miles north of Trevose Head on 18 April, while under charter to the Italian Government and sailing from Newport, Monmouth, with coal. The projectile discharged on the port side in the No.4 hold at 12.30 and she was taken in tow by patrol vessels, the crew of twenty-three having abandoned ship in the boats. The tow hawsers broke loose twice and the ship finally drifted ashore on the Outer Quies Rocks, where it broke up. Patrol vessels picked up the crew and landed them at Penzance. UB 109 arrived home on 25 April. (By 1918 technology was transforming the undersea war in the Allies' favour. The sophisticated Folkestone–Gris Nez Barrage successfully closed off most of the Channel to U-boats. The only route west out of the Channel was via the 'Folkestone gap', a narrow swept seaway between the barrage and the coast. By the summer of 1918 the options for U-boat skippers running the Channel were disappearing fast. They would soon evaporate altogether.)

FINAL VOYAGE

(3) On her last patrol, UB 109 left her base at Zeebrugge for a war-cruise at 01.00 on 27 July 1918. The voyage took UB 109 around the Azores to check out convoy routes. Having completed her task by 16 August 1918, UB 109 began the homeward voyage and headed back. On 17 August 1918 Ramien attacked the British steamship *Zinal* (Turner, Brightman & Co., London) with a torpedo, which sunk 360 miles north-north-east of the Azores. The ship was carrying a general cargo from Barry to Campana, Argentina, and two crewmen were lost.

While approaching Guernsey on the surface, aircraft bombed the boat, but no damage was caused. UB 109 succeeded in sinking two more vessels with torpedoes. The 1,183-ton French steamer *Pontet Canet* (Worms & Co.), sank with six crewmen, while on passage from Havre for Nantes. The Swedish steamer SS *Helge* (Aktieb H. Unér) was torpedoed and sunk on 26 August, while transporting cement from London to Brest. Eleven men and two women died:

Axel Edvard Svensson-Lif
Bror Zackeus Svensson
Emil Johannes Johnsson
Ernst Johan Nordahl
Hulda Johanna Andersson
Johanna Charlotta Thorén
Karl Anders Svensson
Karl Sigfrid Andersson
Karl Wilhelm Eriksson
Nils Fredrik Birger Gisslén
Nils Ragnar Svensson
Olof August Sigfrid Mickelsson
Paul Andreas Kaald

Leaving the September Iles area between Cherbourg and Brest, Oblt.z.S. Kurt Ramien headed for the Blankenberghe buoy and lay on the seabed off Blight Bank for the rest of that day, prior to attempting his run through the Channel. The next section of his patrol took him to Buoy 15 in the Dover barrage, but the 109-ton RN drifter *Monarda* located UB 109 and, as she dived, four depth charges were dropped. Two more RN drifters arrived and a further five depth charges were released. UB 109 came to the surface when the aft hydroplane motors short-circuited, but the crew all rushed forward, which forced her bow down and she settled on the bottom. Ramien heard explosions coming from above and thought they were mines, but in fact they came from the depth charges.

By 02.00 on 29 August 1918 UB 109 arrived off Dungeness. Ramien was intending to return through the 'Folkestone gap' but, instead, changed his mind, and went outside of the steamship channel. In the course of Ramien's patrol, the Allies had set about closing this gap with the aid of the 'Bragg Loop'. A Bragg Loop was, in effect, a series of cables arranged in loops on the seabed. Whenever a steel vessel passed over one of the loops, the needle on a shore-based galvanometer registered its presence. An operator monitoring the U-boat's progress through hydrophones was able to selectively detonate the minefield (the Flanders Flotilla had actually learned of this new field, but had no way of alerting UB 109 as Ramien had removed the long-distance aerials because they interfered with trim).

The impact of the explosion shattered the boat's hull and sent violent pressure waves through the boat, followed by water pouring in through the massive fractures (in the stern). There was panic inside the boat as lights went out and men stumbled around. Oblt.z.S. Kurt Ramien said later in his report that he heard men shouting out loud and then everything seemed to go quiet. Having been hurled into the periscope-well by the impact, Ramien explained that he was stunned and tried to pull his senses together. After what seemed an eternity, Ramien managed to crawl into the conning tower. He found the helmsman and navigator still conscious and tried to speak to them, but the deafening hissing noises, caused by the release of compressed air, rendered it impossible to hear what anyone was saying. The boat was filling fast and, as it flooded up to the conning tower, Ramien was forced to clamber up the ladder to the hatch, while the navigator stood on the ladder-rung just below him. Ramien claimed that as he tried to open the hatch the pressure suddenly blew it open, forcing both men through the opening. The two thrashing men became jammed together in the hatch for half a minute until they were able to free themselves. The force of air then pushed the skipper out and upwards and he said as he rose up amid bubbles he felt his lungs were running out of air, but the air flowed out naturally, in large amounts. When he reached the surface, the radioman, helmsman and navigator bobbed up behind him. Ramien was amazed to find another five men on the surface. Immediately after the explosion, the torpedo-men had opened the forward hatch and just by chance these five men were propelled through it. A stoker had been actually carried down the full length of the boat's compartments by a surging torrent of water, prior to being propelled out the forward hatch. Ramien disposed of his boots and heavy leather coat and had been treading water for about forty-five minutes when a British armed trawler arrived and picked eight of them up. About twenty men had escaped through the conning tower and forward hatches when the boat dropped to the bottom, but just nine men actually surfaced and one had succumbed to either injuries, or to the sea by the time the trawler arrived.

By 10.30 next morning the wreck was buoyed and two of Cdr Damant's regular divers, Leading Seaman Ernie Blackford and Able Seaman Tom Clear, descended to the wreck in record time two hours after she sank, according to one source. They later reported that the boat was lying in 14 fathoms and had a 30-degree list to starboard. The fore and conning tower hatches were open and there was no buoyancy left. When entering the forward hatch, the water inside the wreck was found to be still rather hot, due to sulphuric battery acid mixing with the seawater and the short time it had taken for them to reach it. 'Some twenty feet abaft the conning tower the damage begins and from there aft the vessel is a shapeless wreck', said the report. The fore section was found to be quite intact, with a large mirror in the skipper's wardroom not even cracked. To reach their objective, the divers had to clear away floating debris, bedding and bodies from the men's quarters first and negotiate five narrow apertures before getting through the bulkhead into the forepart and officer's quarters. It took the men until the afternoon to clear away all the obstacles, then some personal material was sent to the Admiralty.

There was no need for explosives, which was the norm. Diving was made more difficult, however, due to inclement weather, which allowed them to work on one tide only. On 30 and 31 August the divers successfully recovered lots of valuable material. On 1 September, even though the divers could only work one tide, they had pushed their way past the control room and entered a watertight cabinet containing more valuable material.

Bad weather put a halt to the diving until 4 September when the two men were able to complete their search, but spring tides ceased any more salvage work on the outside.

Information recovered by Ernie Blackford and Tom Clear included UB 109's entire stock of charts and new amendments, plus a chart overlay of the boat's last patrol, which had taken her from the Channel to the Azores in the mid–Atlantic, then south of Gibraltar, up along the coast of Spain and France and back into the English Channel, where she was lost. According to <u>ADM 116/1634</u>, Dusty Miller also worked on this wreck. <u>ADM 137/3060</u> – <u>ADM 137/4698</u>

THE MEN WHO DIED IN UB 109
Angerstein, Mt
Bohn, Mts.
Dade, Mts.
Diehl, Hzr
Dood, Masch.Mt
Draht, Masch.d.Seew.I
Dribbusch, Masch.Mt
Edelmann, Masch.Mt
Geiler, Ob.Hzr
Gepp, Mts.
Grothmann, Masch.Mt
Hinnemann, Mts.
Höfle, Ob.Hzr
Jacobsen, Mts.
Jäger, F.T.
Keidel, Hzr
Koch, Ob.Btn.Mt der Reserve
Kronenberg, Hzr
Krug, Ob.Masch.Mt
Luhmann, Ob.Hzr
Reinhold, Mts.
Schilling, Ob.Mts.
Schubert, von, Lt.z.S.
Schulz, Masch.Mt
Sonnabend, Mts.
Voss, Mn.Ing. der Reserve
Westkamp, Ob.Hzr
Winterhoff, Masch.Mt

The following is a list of vessels either sunk or damaged by UB 109:

AREA	VESSEL'S NAME	FLAG	TONS	D	M	YEAR	LOCATION
English Channel	*President Leroy-Lallier*	FRA	1320	9	4	1918	Sunk off Brest 4850N 0513W
English Channel	*Henley*	GBR	3249	10	4	1918	25 miles WSW of the Lizard
English Channel	*Wilson*	GBR	110	13	4	1918	10 miles NW of the Smalls

English Channel	*Runswick*	GBR	3060	18	4	1918	3 miles N of Trevose Head
English Channel	*Zinal*	GBR	4037	19	8	1918	360 miles NNE of Terceira, Az
English Channel	*Pontet Canet*	FRA	1183	25	8	1918	12 miles NNW of Heaux de Br
English Channel	*Helge*	SWE	1133	26	8	1918	Sunk off September Iles (coast convoy)

WRECK-SITE

The wreck of UB 109 lies on a seabed of sand, shell and shingle, in a general depth of 29m, being the lowest astronomical depth. It is broken open and lying in two halves, with the engine area smashed up, but very intact from just aft of the conning tower to the bow. The hatches are open, offering glimpses down into the dark interior. The prism is still present in the periscope standard, while the deadeyes in the conning tower are very impressive as they reflect in the torchlight. The conning tower hatch where the captain and navigator escaped is said to be incredibly small, but you can see down the height of the tower, until you get to the sand-filled hull. It is heavily silted in places but, surprisingly, the large-bore 105mm deck gun is still in place and points menacingly off the starboard bow. The torpedo loading hatch forward of the gun is open – evidence of the escape attempt.

The 'jackstaff' socket on the bow also remains intact. The wreck is absolutely smothered in rope, fishing line and netting, and some of this tends to float around and could easily wrap itself around an unwary diver. The wreck provides a home for a large variety of wrasse and crabs and is encrusted with life of all kinds. The propellers, one of which was stamped UB 109 and the other UB 104, have both been removed. It has been suggested that the propellers identified the boat, although the Admiralty are also aware of the position. The wreck-site is a war grave.

A short distance to the south lies the wreck of UB 31. If attempting to run the Folkestone–Griz Barrage at night was near impossible, during daylight it was positively suicidal.

UB 31, SM IMPERIAL U-BOAT

DATE OF LOSS: 2 May 1918
DEPTH: 24m
REFERENCE: 51 02'.068 N, 01 10'.227 E
LOCATION: 2.77 nautical miles SSW from Folkestone harbour

Type: UB II coastal torpedo attack boat **Builders:** Blohm & Voss, Hamburg for Kaiserliche Deutsche Marine **Ordered:** 22 July 1915, within the batch of UB 30–UB 41 **Keel laid:** as Yard No.255 **Launched:** 16 November 1915 **Delivered:** 18 March 1916 **Commissioned:** by Oblt.z.S. Karl Vesper on 24 March 1916

TECHNICAL SPECIFICATIONS

Hull: Single, saddle tank design **Surface displacement:** 274 tons **U/Dt:** 303 tons **LBDH:** 36.90m x 4.37m x 3.70m x 7.34m **Machinery:** 2 x 142ps Benz diesels **Props:** 2 bronze **S/Sp:** 9.06 knots **Op/R:** 8,150 nautical miles at 5 knots **Sub/R:** 45 nautical miles at 5 knots **U/Power:** 2 x 140ps electric motors giving 5.71 knots **Batteries:** AFA lead/acid/accumulators **Fuel/Cap:** 21 + 7 tons **Armament:** 2 bow 50.04cm torpedo tubes **Torpedoes:** 4 x 50.04cm (19.7in) **Guns:** 1 x 88mm (3.46in) forward deck gun **Ammo:** 120 rounds of 3.46mm **Mines:** None **Diving:** Max-op-depth 50m (164ft) and 30 seconds to crash-dive **Complement:** 2 officers and 21 ratings

Oblt.z.S. Karl Vesper assumed command on 18 March 1916 and UB 31 was formally assigned to the Baltic U-Flottille at Libau on 16 May 1916. UB 31 made the following three Baltic Sea patrols with Vesper, but no ships were sunk:

    (1) From 20–27 May 1916.
    (2) From 18–25 June 1916.
    (3) From 29 June to 6 July 1916.

Oblt.z.S. Thomas Bieber assumed command of the boat on 12 August 1916 and sank or damaged thirty vessels during his time with UB 31. The first four patrols in the Baltic Sea however, were unsuccessful:

    (4) From 11–20 September 1916.
    (5) From 30 September to 7 October 1916.
    (6) From 14–20 October 1916.
    (7) From 2–10 November 1916.
    (8) UB 31 departed Libau with Bieber on 20 February 1917 and transferred to Flandern U-Flottille with three other boats – UB 20, UB 32 and UB 36 – arriving at Flanders on 24 February.
    (9) Still under Bieber, UB 31 made an uneventful patrol off the coast of Antwerp between 1 and 5 March 1917.
    (10) Departing Flanders on 12 March 1917, UB 31 patrolled the area off the Schowen Bank and, after an uneventful voyage, returned to base on 18 March.
    (11) Leaving Flanders on 4 April, UB 31 patrolled the Hoofden and the Dutch and Belgian coasts, where Bieber torpedoed and sunk his first victim with UB 31: the 1,866-ton SS *Kittiwake* (Cork SS Co. Ltd, Cork). Seven men were lost with the ship, which was on passage from Liverpool for Rotterdam with general cargo. UB 31 returned to Flanders on 12 April.
    (12) UB 31 made a fruitless war-cruise in the Hoofden area between 15 and 18 April 1917.
    (13) UB 31 sailed from base on 22 April 1917 for the boat's thirteenth and luckiest patrol. On 28 April 1917, the 12,358-ton liner SS *Medina* (Peninsular & Oriental Steam Navigation Co. Ltd, Greenock) was off Start Point on the last lap of her voyage when a torpedo fired from UB 31 exploded in the starboard engine room, killing the fourth engineer (Mr Palmer) and five foreign firemen. The *Medina* (Captain H.S. Bradshaw) was carrying general cargo and passengers from Sydney, Australia, and various Indian ports for London, via Plymouth. The engines stopped and, as the liner began to sink, wireless messages were sent out and passengers and crew took to the boats. Fortunately, most of her passengers had disembarked at Plymouth, where she had departed earlier that day. At 19.15 and, forty-five minutes after being hit, the ship sank to the bottom. Destroyers and motor launches towed the lifeboats to Dartmouth and Brixham. UB 31 jubilantly arrived back in port on 3 May 1917.
    (14) Leaving the Flanders on 14 May 1917, UB 31 made a sortie along the English Channel where, south-west of the Lizard on 21 May, the steamer *City of Corinth* (Ellerman Lines Ltd, Liverpool) was struck by a torpedo, while en-route from Singapore to London with 8,500 tons of general cargo. The ship was travelling at 12½ knots when a massive explosion occurred in the No.2 hold at 15.40. The engine was stopped and a radio message dispatched requesting assistance. Meanwhile, the Chinese and Lascar seamen, amongst her crew of sixty-eight, were put in four boats. The master received a reply reporting that help was on its way, but he also decided to try and reach port, and restarted the engine. Little progress had been made and with water flooding the ship, the engineers were ordered up on deck. Then, suddenly, a second torpedo from UB 31 detonated amidships and she began settling fast. The U-boat's periscope was sighted and shells fired, but at 16.20, and four minutes after the second hit, the ship sank. A patrol vessel landed the crew at Falmouth. UB 31 returned to Flanders on 25 May.

(15) Bieber left port with the boat on 7 June 1917 and patrolled the English Channel, where the SS *Teesdale* (Sir Robert Ropner, West Hartlepool), en-route from Hartlepool to Gibraltar with a consignment of coal, was damaged by a torpedo. The ship was towed to Plymouth, where she arrived on 16 June. Temporary repairs were made to the damaged hull and she was re-floated some weeks later and sailed for the river Tees for docking and repairs. However, on 2 August, the *Teesdale* was 3 miles north of Saltburn Pier at position 54° 39' N, 00° 59' W when she foundered and was lost, presumably due to the damage inflicted by the torpedo earlier. Two of her crew of twenty-three were lost. Soon after hitting the *Teesdale*, Oblt.z.S. Bieber fired a torpedo, while submerged, at the SS *Stanhope* (English Steamship Co. Ltd, Middlesbrough) and twenty-two of her crew of twenty-six were lost. The master and three seamen clung to floating debris for one and a half hours before a patrol boat rescued them and took them to Portsmouth. The ship had been making 8½ knots and transporting steel rails from Barrow to Dunkerque when the projectile exploded at 00.45. The men that perished included:

Andersen, Patrick, 54, Fireman and Trimmer (Sweden)
Ashworth, James Taylor, 28, Third Engineer
Carter, Richard Gatenby, 19, Sailor
Chanioty, Photis, 21, Fireman and Trimmer (Greece)
Clark, George, 21, Ordinary Seaman
Evers, F., 48, Ship's Cook (Belgium)
Joannan, M., 19, Fireman and Trimmer (Cyprus)
Middleton, Thomas, 41, First Engineer
Midri, M., 34, Fireman and Trimmer (Riga, Russia)
Morrell, Arthur, 29, Second Engineer
Morris, Frederick George, 32, Carpenter
Nelson, G.J., 26, Donkeyman (Russia)
Petty, Robert Percy, 22, Mess Room Steward
Rochardson, Ernest Branch, 50, Boatswain (Bosun)
Richardson, John Robinson, 41, Mate
Snowdon, Robert Steele, 17, Sailor
Sousa, Nicholas, 41, Fireman and Trimmer (Portugal)
Trenchard, Eli, 31, Steward
Weatherill, James, 39, Able Seaman

On 19 June 1917 UB 31 arrived back at Flanders.

(16) UB 31 left Flanders on 2 July 1917 for operations against Allied ships in the English Channel. Bieber sank two sailing vessels and badly damged the SS *Adriane Christine*. The ship was en-route from Manchester to Cherbourg with Government stores and was beached at Salcombe, but re-floated. Two steamships were also torpedoed and sunk. The *Bellucia* (Bellucia SS Co. Ltd, Glasgow) was hit on 7 July, while bound from Montreal for London with bagged wheat and flour, and four men were lost. The ship was towed into shallow water off Cadgwith where she sank and fell over on the port side. However, most of the cargo was saved after salvage men cut holes through the starboard side, which was still above water. The men who died were:

Bell, Robert Stanley, 26, Third Engineer
Kidney, Dennis, 33, Fireman and Trimmer
O'Leary, Eugene, 31, Fireman and Trimmer
Pepprell, John Edwin, 29, Chief Steward

The *Brunhilda* (Capel & Co. (Newcastle and Hull) Ltd, West Hartlepool) was the next to sink on 7 July, while delivering 3,500 tons of aluminium earth (bauxite) and esparto grass to Sunderland from San Rafael, California. The torpedo from the submerged and unseen UB 31 detonated in the after part of No.2 hold at 01.50 and she immediately started to settle. However, as water reached the esparto grass it slowed the sinking process and allowed the crew of twenty-three more time to lower the boats. The ship disappeared beneath the surface at 02.20 and a drifter rescued the crew and took them to Plymouth. The U-boat returned to Flanders on 13 July.

(17) Between 28 July and 11 August 1917, UB 31 patrolled the English Channel where she sank two sailing vessels and damaged the French steamship *Algerie*, travelling from Calais to Cardiff in ballast; the ship was towed to Portland Roads.

Torpedoes fired by UB 31 sank two more steamers: fourteen men were lost with the SS *Laertes* (Ocean Steam Ship Co. Ltd, Liverpool) on 1 August, which was bound from Southampton to Montreal in ballast. The wake of the torpedo was sighted just before it detonated in the No.5 hold at 10.50, but about one minute later a second explosion occurred, which was thought to have been another torpedo strike. The crew abandoned ship in lifeboats, rafts and even floating wreckage just before it sank at 10.52. Forty-one men were rescued by a patrol boat, then transferred to HMS Bittern and taken to Plymouth. The men who died were:

Avard, H., 37, Storekeeper
Broomfield, George Henry, 20, Able Seaman
Burns, G., 19, Wireless Operator
Clasby, Stephen Charles, 34, Fireman
Edmonds, W., 26, Fireman
Goldsmith, Frederick William, 27, Fireman
Hooper, Frank George, 20, Fireman
Maidment, Albert, 18, Greaser
Medley, W., 27, Greaser
McLane, Thomas, 26, Able Seaman (St Lucia)
Proudly, Richard Charles, 18, Fireman
Rose, Leonard Augustine Conway, 27, Able Seaman
Tilling, Percival Arthur, 39, Ship's Cook
Williams, Harry Sidney, 29, Fireman

The SS *Newlyn* (Newcastle SS Co. Ltd, Newcastle) sank on 2 August, en-route from the Tyne to Genoa, Italy, with 6,000 tons of coal and coke. UB 31 was unseen when Bieber torpedoed the ship without warning, instantly killing a donkeyman and two firemen when the engine room exploded. The generator was also destroyed, so the wireless was rendered useless. The crew abandoned ship at 09.26, but when it stayed afloat, the master returned to it. Three patrol boats and a tug took the vessel in tow but, an hour and a half after the torpedo strike, the ship sank at 10.42. Another man was lost, but out of her crew of thirty-six, patrol boats rescued thirty-two and landed them at Plymouth. The three men who died were:

Brown, James Ramsey, 53, Fireman
Collins, Bernard, 41, Fireman
Young, Jacob, 32, Donkeyman

UB 31 arrived back in port on 11 August 1917.

(18) Leaving Flanders on 30 August 1917, UB 31 cruised the English Channel. Bieber captured and sunk the 49-ton sailing boat *Elizabeth* with scuttling charges on 8 September. She was transporting coal from Newport to Cherbourg. The following day the Norwegian steamer *Pluton* (Aktieselskapet Sørlandske Lloyd, Christiania) was torpedoed and sunk 6 miles off Start Point; she was on passage from Port Talbot for Rouen with patent fuel. The U-boat returned to Flanders on 12 September 1917.

(19) On 15 October 1917, UB 31 departed Flanders for an English Channel war-cruise. The following two large steamers were sunk with torpedoes: the Waikawa (Union SS. Co. of New Zealand Ltd, London) was in ballast and had left Le Havre for Barry on 18 October, but was struck by the projectile on 19 October and she sank at 09.35. The crew of fifty-one abandoned ship in the lifeboats and patrol vessels landed them at Dartmouth. When the Colorado (Ellerman's Wilson Line Ltd, Hull) was sunk on 20 October, four men were lost with the ship, which was carrying 8,000 tons of coal and coke from Hull to Alexandria, Egypt. A single torpedo struck her on the port side level with the engine room at 09.30, instantly killing one donkeyman and a fireman, the ship having sunk at 10.10. A patrol vessel picked up the forty-one survivors after they had abandoned ship; they were landed at Dartmouth. The men that died were:

Milne, W.J., First Engineer
Ingberg, Adolf, 42, Donleyman (Stockholm, Sweden)
Rojahn, Carl, 43, Fireman and Trimmer (Oslo, Norway)
Stretton, John Henry, 21, Fourth Engineer Officer

The SS *Lepanto* (Ellerman's Wilson Line Ltd, Hull) was damaged while en-route from Middlesbrough to New York (the ship was also damaged by a torpedo on 15 March). UB 31 returned to Zeebrugge on 25 March.

(20) The U-boat left port on 10 November 1917 and patrolled in the English Channel, where she sank the steamer *Farn* (The Shipping Controller, London) with torpedoes. It was en-route from London to Salonica, Greece, with 4,500 tons of general cargo. At 14.45 on 19 November she was hit in the aft part of No.4 hold on the starboard quarter and the crew of thirty-four abandoned ship in the lifeboats and landed at Dartmouth, the ship having sunk at 15.15 (previously owned by Fargrove Steam Navigation Co. Ltd, London, the *Farn* was captured by the German surface warship SMS *Karlsruhe* on 5 October 1914 and 140 miles from St Paul Rocks. She was used as tender and sent to San Juan, Puerto Rica, where she was interned on 12 January 1915, then released to the British Government by an American prize court in February 1917). UB 31 arrived back at Flanders on 21 November 1917.

(21) After leaving harbour on 8 December 1917, UB 31 returned to the English Channel, where one small sailing boat was sunk and the SS *Sachem* was damaged with a torpedo; the ship had left London and was towed into Plymouth for repairs.

On 18 December Bieber torpedoed and sunk the SS *Riversdale* (R.C. Thompson, Sunderland) and one man was lost. She had left the Tyne on passage for Savona with 4,000 tons of coal, but at 13.15 on 18 December, a torpedo slammed into her port side. The master beached her close to Prawle Point, where the bulkheads were strengthened and salvage experts patched up the big hole caused by the torpedo. Then compressors were installed on the deck to pressurise the hull. Tugs then re-floated her, but before she'd gone half a mile, she sank upright to the bottom and a donkeyman was drowned. The twenty-seven survivors landed at Salcombe.

Three more steamers were destroyed by torpedoes on 20 December. On 13 December, the SS *Warsaw* (Leith, Hull & Hamburg Steam Packet Co., Leith) sailed from St Malo in ballast for Liverpool with a crew of twenty but, at 02.00 on 20 December, she was hit by a torpedo. The chief officer arrived on deck to discover many of the crew had been killed, including the captain, and the survivors were trying to launch a lifeboat. However, the ship then went down very quickly and capsized the lifeboat. Five survivors eventually righted the boat and clambered into it. UB 31 then went alongside the lifeboat and Bieber callously ordered the men to stop shouting. Unfortunately two of the men had died of exposure before a Royal Navy vessel rescued them. Those who died included:

Dalby, Robert, 17, Assistant Steward
Gibson, Alan, 41, First Engineer
Gray, William Frederick, 50, Steward
Hawick, Andrew Hugh, 50, Second Mate
Iwasi, Tsunataro, 24, Seaman (Japan)
Le Karimi, 32, Fireman (Bombay, India)
Murakami, Shrichi, 27, Seaman (Japan)
Tajima, Matsuzo, 25, Seaman (Japan)
Uchida, Schachi, 49, Seaman (Japan)
Valentine, John, 49, Master
Wilson, Duncan Charles, 33, Cook

The SS *Eveline* (Pyman, Bell & Co. Ltd, Newcastle) sailed from Barry on 16 December, for a passage to Rouen with 4,000 tons of coal and general cargo, but at 04.00 a torpedo discharged in the after part of the reserve coalbunker of the engine room. The crew of twenty-eight abandoned ship, without loss, immediately, and were rescued by a patrol boat and taken to Dartmouth. The ship sank at 04.50.

The *Alice Marie* (Rodney SS Co. Ltd, Newcastle) was voyaging from Newcastle to Rochefort with 2,950 tons of coal when a torpedo detonated in the engine room at 23.55. The crew of twenty-six immediately abandoned ship in two boats, but Bieber questioned them, as to the whereabouts of her captain and mate. The steamer's crew declared that they had both been killed. After watching the ship disappear beneath the surface at 00.10, the boats were allowed to leave and they landed safely at Dartmouth later that day. UB 31 put back into Zeebrugge on 22 December.

(22) On Bieber's last patrol with UB 31, he sank three steamships by torpedo between 15 and 27 January 1918: the 2,358-ton *Greatham* (Coombes, Marshall & Co. Ltd, Middlesbrough) was sunk on 22 January, while transporting a 3,100-ton cargo of coal and a crew of twenty-six from Grimsby to Blaye. The torpedo exploded in the rear part of the No.2 hold at 13.55 and only one boat, a motor launch, was left serviceable. The crew abandoned ship in the launch, when the ship sank at 14.25. At first, a fireman died in the boat from his injuries, then it filled up and sank, drowning the chief engineer, the wireless operator, the boatswain, cook, one seaman and another fireman. Patrol boats rescued the remaining nineteen men and landed them at Dartmouth. Those that perished included:

Austin, Alexander, 21, Sailor
Carter, Albert, 44, Ship's Cook
Peggs, Arthur Clifford Sydney, 18, Wireless Operator
Readman, Herbert Isaac, 35, Boatswain (Bosun)
South, Frank Arthur, 47, First Mate

The 2,958-ton Spanish *Victor de Chavarri* (Altos Hornos de Vizcaya, Bilbao) was also torpedoed and sunk off Berry Head on 22 January, while en-route from Newcastle for Bilbao with coal. On 24 January, Bieber once again remained submerged and unseen, when the Norwegian *Elsa* (Aktieselskapet Den Norske Afrika og Australielinje, Tønsberg) was hit with a torpedo and sunk, while carrying a general cargo, including coffee, tea, rice, coal and coke from Newport, Monmouth, to Christiania (Oslo) in Norway. The crew landed at Dartmouth later that day. UB 31 returned to Flanders on 27 January.

Oblt.z.S. der Reserve Wilhelm Braun, assumed command of UB 31 on 1 February 1918 (Oblt.z.S. Thomas Bieber and his crew were lost with UB 104 that September).

Wilhelm Braun made the last three patrols in UB 31:

(23) Leaving Flanders on 24 February 1918, UB 31 made a sortie off the Hoofden and the English east coast where, south-west of Swartebank Light Vessel, the Dutch *Heenvliet* (N.V. Nationale Stoomv. Mij., Rotterdam) was sunk, with the loss of seven of her crew. She was en-route from Rotterdam to Leith with general cargo. UB 31 returned to Flanders on 6 March 1918.

(24) On 18 March 1918, UB 31 sailed from Zeebrugge for the English Channel. During the war-cruise, Braun damaged the SS *Boorara* (Australian Commonwealth requisition, London). The ship was on passage from Southampton for the Tyne with general cargo and was towed into the Tyne for repairs. UB 31 arrived back at Zeebrugge on 1 April.

FINAL VOYAGE

(25) SM UB 31 left her Flanders base for a war patrol on 16 April 1918 for operations in the English Channel and Wilhelm Braun successfully negotiated the dangerous stretch of water in the Dover Strait. On 23 April the little sailing boat *Frances*, transporting coal from Swansea to St Brieuc, was disposed of. The next day, Braun captured and sunk the 42-ton French sailing boat *Joseph*. However, Braun's luck ran out at 08.05 on 2 May when the Royal Navy drifter *Lord Leitrim*, sighted her periscope between the Varne and Folkestone. The submarine was said to be travelling east-north-east. The sighting was reported to the Admiralty and the *Lord Leitrim* dropped a depth charge over the site, bringing oil and air bubbles to the surface. Two more Royal Navy drifters then joined the hunt, with new technology in the form of the airship *SSZ29* guiding in the little warships. HM drifter *Ocean Roamer* (directed by airship *SSZ29*) probably delivered the *coup de grace* when she dropped a depth charge, which in turn triggered a mine, that destroyed both submarine and crew. Oil bubbled to the surface. A Dan bouy was used to mark the position and oil was still observed at 10.00. Cdr Guybon Chesney Castell Damant's 'U-boat Flying Squad' was then sent to the scene in August 1918 and confirmed the identity of UB 31.
NARA: T-1022, Roll 56, PG 61780

THE MEN WHO DIED IN UB 31

Becken, Masch.Mt
Beinder, Ob.Hzr
Braun, Oblt.z.S. der Reserve
Fuls, Ob.Mts.
Göntgen, Hzr
Hoffmann, Mts.
Hoppe, Mts.
Jacob, Ob.Masch.Mt
Kühne, Masch.
Mahler, Ob.Mts.
Matthes, Hzr
Müller, Kark Masch.Mt
Müller, Albert Mts. Olschory, F.T.
Prass, Lt.z.S. der Reserve
Rössler, Hzr
Schlör, Ob.Btn.Mt

Schminke, F.T.
Schwentke, Mts.
Ströbel, Ob.Btn.Mt
Thalmann, Ob.Mts.
Weidemann, Masch.Mt
Weiss, Mt
Winkler, Maschi.Mt
Wodrich, Masch.Mt
Woest, Hzr

The following is a list of vessels either damaged or sunk by UB 31:

AREA	VESSEL'S NAME	FLAG	TONS	D	M	YEAR	LOCATION
North Sea	Kittiwake	GBR	1866	9	4	1917	25 miles NW Maas Light Vessel
English Channel	Medina	GBR	12358	28	4	1917	3 miles ENE Start Point
English Channel	City of Corinth	GBR	5870	21	5	1917	12 miles SW Lizard
English Channel	Teesdale	GBR	2470	15	6	1917	Damaged 2m off Bolt Head
English Channel	Stanhope	GBR	2828	17	6	1917	7 miles WSW of Start Point
English Channel	Ocean Swell (s/v)	GBR	195	5	7	1917	15m SE of Start Point
English Channel	Adriane Christine	GBR	3550	6	7	1917	Damaged off Start Point
English Channel	Bellucia	GBR	4368	7	7	1917	2 miles SSE of the Lizard
English Channel	Hildegard (sail vessel)	USA	622	10	7	1917	10 miles SE of Start Point
English Channel	Brunhilda	GBR	2296	11	7	1917	7 miles S of Start Point
English Channel	Alcyone (sailing boat)	GBR	149	1	8	1917	45 miles NNW of Roches Downes
English Channel	Laertes	GBR	4541	1	8	1917	1¼ miles SSW of Prawle Point
English Channel	Newlyn	GBR	4019	2	8	1917	2 miles S of Prawle Point
English Channel	Renee Marthe (s/v)	FRA	50	3	8	1917	Sunk W of Start Point
English Channel	Algerie	FRA	3386	8	8	1917	Damaged 2 miles SW of Portland Bill
English Channel	Elizabeth (sail vessel)	GBR	49	8	9	1917	12 miles ESE of Start Point
English Channel	Pluton	NOR	1449	9	9	1917	Approx. 6 miles ESE of Start Point
English Channel	Waikawa	GBR	5666	19	10	1917	4 miles ENE of Start Point
English Channel	Colorado	GBR	7652	20	10	1917	1½ miles E of Start Point
English Channel	Lepanto	GBR	6389	23	10	1917	Damaged 3–4 miles off Dartmouth
English Channel	Farn	GBR	4393	19	11	1917	5 miles ENE of Start Point
English Channel	Britannic (sailing boat)	GBR	92	13	12	1917	12 miles NNW of Les Hanois lighthouse
English Channel	Sachem	GBR	5354	14	12	1917	Damaged off Start Point-reached Plymouth
English Channel	Riversdale	GBR	2805	18	12	1917	1 mile S of Prawle Point
English Channel	Alice Marie	GBR	2210	20	12	1917	6 miles ENE of Start Point
English Channel	Eveline	GBR	2605	20	12	1917	9½ miles S ½ W of Berry Head
English Channel	Warsaw	GBR	608	20	12	1917	4 miles ESE of Start Point
English Channel	Greatham	GBR	2358	22	1	1918	3 miles SE of Dartmouth
English Channel	Victor de Chavarri	SPA	2958	22	1	1918	Sunk west section of Channel
English Channel	Elsa	NOR	3581	24	1	1918	5 miles ESE of Dartmouth Harbour
English Channel	Heenvliet	NLD	492	28	2	1918	15 miles SW of Swartebank Light Vessel
English Channel	Boorara	GBR	6570	20	3	1918	Damaged 2½ miles S 25 E of Beachy Head
English Channel	Frances (sailing boat)	GBR	56	23	4	1918	6 miles S of the Lizard
English Channel	Joseph (sailing boat)	FRA	42	25	4	1918	Sunk N of Cherbourg

WRECK-SITE

The wreck lies on a seabed of sand, mud and shell, in a general depth of 24m, being the lowest astronomical depth. The boat is intact and lying on her port side, with the conning tower still in place, but there is a massive hole in the fore section. The wreck is carpeted with colourful anemones and shoals of fish swarm around it.

UB 78, SM IMPERIAL U-BOAT

DATE OF LOSS: 19 April 1918
DEPTH: 23m
REFERENCE: 51 01'.020 N, 001 16'.481 E
LOCATION: 4.91 nautical miles SSE of Folkestone harbour

Type: UB III coastal torpedo attack boat *Builders*: Blohm & Voss, Hamburg for Kaiserliche Deutsche Marine *Ordered*: 23 September 1916, within the batch of UB 75–UB 79 *Keel laid*: as Yard No.307 *Launched*: 2 June 1917 *Commissioned*: by Oberleutnant zur See Woldemar Petri on 20 October 1917 *Combat-ready*: 2 January 1918

TECHNICAL SPECIFICATIONS

Hull: Double *Surface displacement*: 516 tons *U/Dt*: 648 tons *LBDH*: 55.30m x 5.80m x 3.68m x 8¼m *Machinery*: 2 x 550ps MAN diesels *Props*: 2 bronze *S/Sp*: 13.6 knots *Op/R*: 8,680 nautical miles at 6 knots *Sub/R*: 55 nautical miles at 4 knots *U/Power*: 394ps electric motors giving 7.8 knots *Batteries*: Lead/acid/accumulators *Fuel/Cap*: 34 + 39 tons *Armament*: 4 bow and 1 stern 50.04cm torpedo tubes *Torpedoes*: 10 x 50.04cm (19.7in) *Guns*: 1 x 105mm (4.13in) forward deck gun *Ammo*: 160 rounds of 105mm *Mines*: None *Diving*: Max-op-depth 50m (164ft) and 30 seconds to crash-dive *Complement*: 3 officers and 31 ratings

The boat was originally assigned to the Germany-based V.U-Flottille at Bremerhaven on 2 January 1918, with Oblt.z.S. Woldemar Petri the commander from 20 October 1917. Petri made just one operational patrol with the boat:

(1) UB 78 left Bremerhaven on 12 January 1918 for a war-cruise in the northern section of the North Sea and returned to Germany on 20 January.

Oblt.z.S. Ulrich Pilzecker assumed command of the boat on 16 February and made two patrols:

(2) On 16 February 1918, Pilzecker left Germany and transferred the boat to Flanders, where they arrived on 18 February and formally joined the Flandern I.U-Flottille.

(3) UB 78 departed Flanders on 25 February, for operations off the English east coast, but no ships were sunk. UB 78 returned to base on 2 March.

Oblt.z.S. Arthur Stoßberg assumed command on 18 March 1918 (Pilzecker took command of the newly commissioned UB 113, but was lost with her in September). Stoßberg made two patrols with UB 78 and was lost on the second.

(4) UB 78 sailed from Flanders on 16 March 1918 and patrolled the English and Scottish east coast. While just north of the river Tyne, Stoßberg remained submerged and unseen when he torpedoed the steamship *Polleon* (The Shipping Controller, London) and four men were lost when she sank; the ship was en-route from Blyth to the Tyne with coal. The men who died were:

Amans, Gustav Albion, 49, Able Seaman
Anderson, Carl Erik, 56, Able Seaman

Kasaki, Y., 25, Able Seaman
Larsen, Kudvig Mattias, 57, Able Seaman

On 25 March, the hired Admiralty drifter *Border Lads* was engaged in protecting a convoy that was assembling about 2 miles off the entrance to the river Tyne, when she suffered a large explosion at 11.25, broke up, and sank rapidly, with the loss of four men (it was uncertain at the time whether a mine or torpedo had been responsible, but a subsequent search failed to find any mines, and it was presumed the vessel had been hit by a torpedo, most probably fired at long range at the merchant convoy by Arthur Stoßberg, in UB 78).

The following day, the SS *British Star*, which was travelling from North Shields in ballast, was left badly damaged from a torpedo hit, but she turned back and reached the Tyne safely. On 28 March, UB 78 arrived back at Flanders.

FINAL VOYAGE
(5) On his second patrol in UB 78 and the boat's fifth, Oblt.z.S. Stoßberg departed Zeebrugge on 18 April 1918 for a war patrol in the English Channel and the Western Approaches, but the boat never returned.

TRADITIONAL LOSS THEORY
Shortly after midnight on 9 May 1918, a lookout aboard the troop transport and cross-channel steamship *Queen Alexandra* sighted a U-boat in mid-Channel. The approximate position of the sighting was 49° 50' N, 01° 40' W, and the U-boat was in the process of diving. *Queen Alexandra*, which was loaded with troops, was completing her voyage across the Channel to Cherbourg. The ship turned and, just as the U-boat's conning tower rim was awash, she rammed it at 20 knots. The escort of *Queen Alexandra*, HMS P35, heard the collision and dropped a depth charge and a marker buoy. At 04.00 that morning, P35 returned to the area and found a stretch of oil, debris and battery acid 7 miles long. On examination in dry dock later, the stem, rudder and screws of *Queen Alexandra* were shown to be have been bent and damaged in the collision.

ALTERNATIVE LOSS THEORY BY MICHAEL LOWREY AND THE AUTHORS
If we accept that the UB 78 was mined off Dover, what are we to make of this attack?

It seems certain that a U-boat was, in fact, rammed. If it wasn't sunk, then it must have at least suffered severe damage. But no U-boat limped home after being rammed on that date. The solution, we conclude, is that *Queen Alexandra* in fact rammed and sank UC 78.

UC 78 had sailed on 2 May 1918 and her loss was often attributed to a mine explosion, followed by a depth charge attack off Dover on the same day. This claim is examined in detail by Robert M. Grant in *U-Boat Intelligence* and rejected. Grant notes that UC 78 had only sailed five hours before the explosions observed off Gris Nez, and the boat could not have arrived there within the time available. UC 17 was the boat off Gris Nez and was attacked and/or heard mine explosions!

UC 78 laid mines off Boulogne on 4 May, and off Newhaven on 8 May 1918. The causes of loss, listed by the British for UB 78 as 'ramming', and UC 78 as 'mined' on 2 May, were both generated during the First World War. For UB 78 for example, the 9 May date is listed in the 1919 edition of *Jane's Fighting Ships* and is based upon an obviously incomplete knowledge of German operations.

We suggest therefore, that after laying the last of her mines off Newhaven, UC 78 then turned toward mid-Channel, where the *Queen Alexandra* rammed her. The date is consistent with a standard UCII patrol duration of up to three weeks or so. There is no other U-boat that could have been the victim of this attack and there is also no other credible cause of loss for UC 78. NARA: T-1022, Roll 80, PG61838

THE MEN WHO DIED IN UB 78

Bauer, Hzr
Bloss, Mts.
Borgmann, Hzr
Brandenburg, Lt.z.S.
Böhler, Hzr
Dengler, Hzr
Doerfert, Ob.Btn.Mt
Ducke, F.T.
Feyertag, Ob.Masch.Mt
Hale, Mts.
Heimbech, Hzr
Helmer, Ob.Mts.
Herchenröder, Masch.Mt
Knöfler, F.T.Ober Gast
Koch, Hzr
Kressmann, Masch.Mt
Kundschaft, Mts.
Kübler, Btn.Mt
Künnert, Ob.Masch.Anw
Morgenstern, Mts.
Nahrstedt, Hzr
Nix, Hzr
Przibylla, Masch.Mt
Reckmann, Masch.Anw
Rusp, Mts.
Schramm, Masch.Mt
Schultz, Mn.Ing.Asp.
Schück, Mts.
Specht, Masch.Mt der Reserve
Steen, Masch.Mt
Stosberg, Oblt.z.S.
Strotmann, Mts.
Weinreich, Mts.
Wolf, Mts.
Zikoll, Mts.

The following is a list of the vessels either sunk or damaged by UB 78:

AREA	VESSEL'S NAME	FLAG	TONS	D	M	YEAR	LOCATION
North Sea	*Polleon*	GBR	1155	22	3	1918	3 miles ENE entrance river Tyne
North Sea	*Border Lads*	GBR	86	25	3	1918	Sunk in the river Tyne area
North Sea	*British Star*	GBR	6888	26	3	1918	Damaged 1 ½ miles E of river Tyne

WRECK-SITE

The wreck of UB 78 lies on a seabed of sand, shell and shingle, in a general depth of 23m, being the lowest astronomical depth. It was reported as being intact and upright but the casing is deteriorating badly, with most of the 'interesting items' having been removed, including the two propellers, which originally identified the submarine. There is also a large gash forward of the conning tower.

UB 55, SM IMPERIAL U-BOAT

DATE OF LOSS: 24 April 1918
DEPTH: 30m
REFERENCE: 51 01'.308 N, 001 19'.817 E
LOCATION: 6.20 nautical miles SE from Folkestone
and 2½ nautical miles N of The Varne Bank

Type: UB III coastal torpedo attack boat *Builders*: A.G. Weser, Bremen for Kaiserliche Deutsche Marine *Ordered*: 20 May 1916, within the batch of UB 54–UB 59 *Keel laid*: as Yard No.267 on 5 September 1916 *Launched*: 20 April 1917 *Commissioned*: by Kapitänleutnant Ralph Wenninger on 1 July 1917

TECHNICAL SPECIFICATIONS
Hull: Double *Surface displacement*: 516 tons *U/Dt*: 646 tons *LBDH*: 55.85m x 5.80m x 3.68m x 8¼m *Machinery*: 550ps Körting diesels *Props*: 2 bronze *S/Sp*: 13.4 knots *Op/R*: 9,020 nautical miles at 9 knots *Sub/R*: 55 nautical miles at 4 knots *U/Power*: 394ps electric motors giving 7.8 knots *Batteries*: Lead/acid/accumulators *Fuel/Cap*: 36 + 39 tons *Armament*: 4 bow and 1 stern 50.04cm torpedo tubes *Torpedoes*: 10 x 50.04cm (19.7in) *Guns*: 1 x 105mm (4.13in) forward deck gun *Ammo*: 160 rounds of 105mm *Mines*: None *Diving*: Max-op-depth 50m (164ft) and 30 seconds to crash-dive *Complement*: 3 officers and 31 ratings

UB 55 was formally assigned to the Flandern U-Flottille on 30 August 1917, with Kplt. Ralph Wenninger the CO from 1 July 1917. Wenninger, who was born on 22 April 1890, was awarded the *Pour le Mérite* (Blue Max) on 30 March 1918 and died on 18 March 1945. Wenninger made the following patrols with the boat:

(1) UB 55 left Bremen on 27 August 1917 and transferred to Flanders, where she arrived on 30 August.

(2) On 15 October 1917, UB 55 left Zeebrugge for a war-cruise in the English Channel, but Wenninger aborted the voyage because of machinery problems and arrived back in port on 18 October.

(3) On 27 October 1917, UB 55 sailed from Flanders for operations against Allied shipping in the English Channel. A torpedo from UB 55 damaged the SS *Clan Cumming* (The Clan Line Steamers Ltd), voyaging from Baltimore, Maryland, to Brest with copper, steel and timber. The ship was towed to Falmouth Harbour, then beached and re-floated after repairs. UB 55 arrived back at Zeebrugge on 8 November.

(4) Wenninger departed Flanders on 4 December 1917 and took UB 55 to the Bay of Biscay and the west coast of Portugal for operations. Five small boats were captured and destroyed and the following two steamships were torpedoed and sunk on the patrol: the Norwegian *Corinto* (Aktieselskapet Dampskipsselskapet Corinto, Bergen), on passage from Swansea to Brest with steel bars was captured, then shelled and sunk on 8 December; the SS *Foylemore* (Johnston Line Ltd) was sunk on 16 December, en-route from Calais to Manchester in ballast. UB 55 returned to Flanders on 21 December.

(5) Leaving Flanders on 17 January 1918, UB 55 sailed to the English Channel for operations. A torpedo sunk the SS *Eastlands* (Wilson Shipping Co. Ltd, West Hartlepool), while she was on passage from Bordeaux for Dunkerque with Government stores. One man drowned, five trawlers and one small Q-ship were also sunk. The SS *Manhattan*, voyaging from New York to London with horses and general cargo, was forced to put into Falmouth for repairs after being hit by a torpedo off the Lizard. UB 55 arrived in port on 2 February 1918.

(6) Departing Flanders on 11 March 1918, UB 55 patrolled the English Channel. A torpedo from UB 55 sank the US steamer *A.A. Raven* (American Transportation Co.) off Wolf Rock on 14 March. She was sailing from Barry and was lost with seven men killed and six others injured. Wenninger also torpedoed and sank the SS *Begonia* (Stag Line Ltd, North Shields) on 21 March, 44 miles off Wolf Rock. The ship was on passage from the Tyne and Plymouth for Salonica in Greece with Admiralty stores. Fortunately, no one was killed when UB 55 torpedoed and sank the US steamer *Chattahoochee* (US Shipping Board) on 23 March, which was voyaging from London for St Nazaire with cement and motor lorries. The SS *Madam Midas* (T.G. Beatley & Son, Grangemouth (London)) was torpedoed and sunk in the Bay of Biscay on 23 March, while transporting coal from Cardiff to La Roche. The Spanish SS *Mar Bàltaco* (Cia. Maritima del Nervion, Bilbao) was en-route from Port Talbot to Bilbao, but sank after a torpedo hit on 23 March. The Norwegian steamer *Venborg* (Aktieselskapet Venborg, Haugesund) was captured on 23 March and scuttled with explosive charges while transporting coal from Port Talbot to Lorient. Wenninger captured and sank the 89-ton French sailing boat *Fileur*, before UB 55 arrived at Flanders on 24 March.

FINAL VOYAGE

(7) With a crew of forty-two, including seven trainees and commanded by Ralph Wenninger, UB 55 left Zeebrugge on 21 April 1918. The U-boat was the last to sail before the celebrated British raid on Zeebrugge and Ostend. On 24 April Wenninger attempted to pass through the Dover Strait, while travelling on the surface. At 04.00 on 24 April, UB 55 had just finished charging her batteries on the surface off the Varne buoy. In addition to the hazards posed by the flares and searchlights of the Folkestone Barrage, a patrol was observed heading towards the submarine and Wenninger had no option but to dive; he then proceeded submerged at 39ft (11.8m). Kplt. Ralph Wenninger:

> Just as the boat was levelling out I heard a scraping noise. I believed that we had snagged mine net. Seconds before the motors stopped, the mine exploded on the starboard side at the junction between the engine room and the aft torpedo room. Flooding was immediate and overpowering. Trim was lost and there was nothing I could do to restore it because of the flooding in the stern. I sent some of the control room personnel to the fore-ends in order to achieve some semblance of trim.

Engineer Dietrich attempted to shut the watertight door between the engine room and the torpedo compartment, but the situation was hopeless:

> The force of water was too great and we were knocked off our feet. It was hopeless. Every time we closed the door the water forced it open again. I turned instead to blowing the tanks, but this too was useless because the PS air was leaking and starboard ballast tanks were too badly holed. I resolved instead to keep the boat on an even keel in order that an escape might be organised. All this time the boat was sinking ever deeper. The engine room was totally flooded and the bulkhead between the engine room and the control room leaked. As the boat levelled, icy water came rushing through the control room via the ventilation ducts and voice pipes.

UB 55 slammed into the seabed at 83ft (24m). The lights went out immediately and the survivors (eight in the control room and twelve in the fore-ends) were forced to rely on the meagre light provided by a handful of torches. With the rising water, intense air pressure caused unendurable headaches. Breathing became painful and, worse still, chlorine gas was detected. Kplt. Ralph Wenninger again:

The men in the fore-ends closed the door leading to the warrant officers' quarters, but all attempts to open the torpedo hatch failed. One of the torpedo men blew the compressed air flasks of the torpedoes in order to try and counterbalance the external water pressure on the hatch, but this too failed.

Wenninger ordered the flooding of the remaining compartments. The situation may have seemed hopeless but, thanks to Dietrich and his staff, the submarine had bottomed out on an even keel and the hatches were clear. Once pressure had equalised the hatches might be opened. Not all shared Wenninger's optimism – many of the submariners resigned themselves to death. Surviving ratings described how two of their boat-mates committed suicide by placing wadding into their mouth and nostrils, prior to hurling themselves into the flooded parts of the boat. Attempts to commit suicide using handguns failed because the ammunition was waterlogged. One and a half hours elapsed before the freezing water rose to a depth of 3ft within the submarine, allowing pressure to equalise. Now the hatches could be opened, yet the skipper was all too aware that only four Dräger escape sets were available. Ascent to the surface would have to be made without oxygen. Wenninger divided his crew into two groups – six (including Wenninger and Dietrich) huddled beneath the conning tower hatch, while twelve men gathered under the torpedo-loading hatch. Clips were removed from the conning tower hatch. The hatches flew open, powering the terrified sailors to the surface in a couple of vast air bubbles.

Wenninger estimated that twenty men reached the surface, but he could not be certain, because it was pitch black. The rest of the crew drowned either on their way to the surface or as UB 55 flooded. Tragically several men who successfully made the ascent died because the sudden change in pressure caused their lungs to burst. Dräger sets also ruptured. Survivors had to contend with exposure and Caisson's Disease – the dreaded 'bends'. They died one by one until out of a crew of thirty-two ratings and three officers, only Wenninger, Dietrich, Roenspiess and three ratings survived to be dragged aboard *Mate* in a semi-conscious state.

The armed drifter *Mate* was on patrol between number 12 buoy and the Varne Shoal on 24 April, when suddenly at 04.00 there was an explosion. Oil, wood and assorted wreckage bobbed to the surface. A terrible screaming was heard. At 04.30 bubbles were still rising. The position was buoyed and *Mate* returned to search again at first light. At 05.15 three men were plucked from the sea and three more Germans were hauled out by the 275-ton RN trawler *Seaflower* (Admiralty No.1, ex-*Osprey*). The armed and hired Admiralty drifter *Ivy* also picked up a body. The wretched state of the Germans shocked the British sailors who thought them unlikely to survive. Two were vomiting a mixture of blood and oil, while others could not stop screaming. One cried for his mother. All had been deafened and traumatised by their experiences. In the days that followed the survivors were identified as Wenninger, Engineer Officer Dietrich, two petty officers and two ratings. Slowly the Admiralty interrogators pieced together the harrowing story of UB 55's last mission.

Roenspiess died of internal injuries, while the heroic Dietrich succumbed to influenza in the officers' POW camp at Skipton, Yorkshire. He was later buried in Cannock Chase, Block 14, Grave 257.

UB 55 was dived by Royal Navy divers on 14 August 1918, who brought up documents that identified the wreck.
ADM 137/3872-4 – ADM 137/3060 – NARA: T1022 Roll 68 PG1815 – ADM 137/3874 – ADM 137/3916

THE MEN WHO DIED IN UB 55

Brendel, Hzr
Dietrich, Mn.Ing.
Dohndorf, F.T.Ober Gast
Dollmann, Oblt.z.S.
Elbers, Hzr
Flurbacher, Masch.Mt
Gunkel, Mts.
Hirschfelder, Ob.Hzr
Lembeck, Ob.Hzr
Matag, Mts.
Müller, Hzr
Niemand, Ob.Stm.
Petzel, Ob.Mts.
Pfannkuche, Mts.
Preikszas, Ob.Mts.
Pätau, Masch.Mt der Reserve
Rickertsen, Mts.
Roenspies, Masch.
Rogotzki, Ob.Masch.Anw
Schmucker, Mts.
Schüler, Ob.Hzr
Schönfelder, F.T.Gast
Seemann, Ob.Masch.Mt
Simson, Mts.
Stephan, Hzr
Strauss, Mt der Reserve
Suffa, Mts.
Weiss, Hzr
Wellmann, Ob.Masch.Mt
Wolff, Ob.Hzr
Wollenberg, Masch.Mt
Zeltmann, Ob.Mts.

The following is a list of vessels damaged or sunk by UB 55:

AREA	VESSEL'S NAME	FLAG	TONS	D	M	YEAR	LOCATION
English Channel	*Clan Cumming*	GBR	4808	5	11	1917	Damaged 20 miles SW of Lizard
English Channel	*Proba* (sailing vessel)	GBR	105	7	12	1917	3 miles SE Cape Lizard
English Channel	*Corinto*	NOR	999	8	12	1917	26 miles NNE of Ushant
Atlantic	*Argus* (fishing vessel)	POR	100	11	12	1917	Sunk off Leixoes harbour
Atlantic	*Ligeiro* (fish vessel)	POR	25	11	12	1917	Sunk off Leixoes harbour
Atlantic	*Portuegesa* (s/v)	POR	107	11	12	1917	Sunk off Leixoes Harbour
Atlantic	*Virgeira* (fish vessel)	POR	25	11	12	1917	Sunk off Leixoes Harbour
English Channel	*Foylemore*	GBR	3831	16	12	1917	22 miles E ½ S Lizard
English Channel	*Eastlands*	GBR	3113	25	1	1918	13 miles NW of Ile Vierge
English Channel	*Manhattan*	GBR	8001	26	1	1918	Damaged about 50 miles off Lizard
English Channel	*Addax* (fish vessel)	GBR	40	29	1	1918	Sunk near Start Pont 50 21' N, 03 18'W
English Channel	*General Leman* f/v	GBR	45	29	1	1918	14 miles SE of Beachy Head
English Channel	*Ibex* (fishing vessel)	GBR	40	29	1	1918	14 miles ESE Of Berry Head

English Channel	Perrington (s/v)	GBR	90	29	1	1918	Approx. 20 miles E of Berry Head
English Channel	Perseverance (f/v)	GBR	40	29	1	1918	14 miles SE of Berry Head 50 21' N, 03 10'W
English Channel	Wellholme	GBR	113	30	1	1918	Sunk SW of Portland
English Channel	A.A. Raven	USA	2459	14	3	1918	16 miles SSW of Wolf Rock
English Channel	Begonia	GBR	2929	21	3	1918	44 miles SSW of Wolf Rock
English Channel	Chattahoochee	USA	8007	23	3	1918	28 miles S of Penzance
English Channel	Madame Midas	GBR	1203	23	3	1918	38 miles S by W ¾ W of Lizard
English Channel	Mar Baltico	SPA	2042	23	3	1918	Sunk in the Lizard area
English Channel	Venborg	NOR	1065	23	3	1918	25 miles N of Ushant 48 55' N, 05 02'W
English Channel	Fileur (sail vessel)	FRA	73	24	3	1918	40 miles NW of Ile de Bas

WRECK-SITE

The wreck lies on a firm seabed of sand, shell and shingle, in a general depth of 30m (98.4ft), being the lowest astronomical depth. It is upright and lists slightly to port but, overall, the U-boat is in quite reasonable condition. The conning tower and periscope housing are still in place, but the periscopes are bent back towards the stern. There is quite a lot of damage to the hull casing with lots of small holes and a large hole on the port side forward of the conning tower, about midway between the bow and conning tower. Unfortunately the deck gun is missing. The bow section is very badly damaged and there seems to be either a torpedo, or just a tube, showing at the bow, but visibility was poor at the time of the report. The stern part appears to have been blown off recently because it was reported that at least one of the boat's propellers was still in place.

U 8, SM IMPERIAL U-BOAT

DATE OF LOSS: 4 March 1915
DEPTH: 32m
REFERENCE: 50 56'.006 N, 001 15'.402 E
LOCATION: 9 miles SSE of Folkestone and 1¼ miles
WSW of the South Varne Bank buoy

U 8 was the first U-boat lost in the Channel. She was also the most photographed as Allied propagandists milked her surrender to the full. Photographs of the little petrol-driven submarine were despatched all over the English-speaking world.

Type: U 5 coastal torpedo attack boat **Builders:** Germaniawerft, Kiel for Kaiserliche Deutsche Marine **Ordered:** 8 April 1908, within the batch of U 5–U 8 **Keel laid:** as Yard No.150 on 19 May 1909 **Launched:** 14 March 1911 **Commissioned:** by Kapitänleutnant Wilhelm Friedrich Starke on 18 June 1911

TECHNICAL SPECIFICATIONS

Hull: Double **Surface displacement:** 505 tons **U/Dt:** 636 tons **LBDH:** 57.38m x 5.6m x 3.55m x 7.28m **Machinery:** 4 x 225ps Körting paraffin (kerosene)-fuelled engines **Props:** 2 bronze **S/Sp:** 13.4 knots **Op/R:** 3,300 nautical miles at 9 knots, or 1,900 nautical miles at 13 knots **Sub/R:** 80 nautical miles at 5 knots **U/Power:** 2 x 520ps electric motors giving 10.2 knots **Batteries:** Lead/acid/accumulators **Fuel/Cap:** 52 tons **Armament:** 2 bow and 2 stern 45cm (17.72in) torpedo tubes **Torpedoes:** 6 x 45cm (17.72in) **Guns:**

SM U 8 in port. (Author's collection)

Designed with none, but by end of 1914, one reverse facing 105mm (4.13in) deck cannon **Ammo**: 300 rounds of 105mm **Mines**: None **Diving**: Max-op-depth 50m (164ft) and 65 seconds to crash-dive **Complement**: 4 officer and 25 ratings

Kplt Wilhelm Friedrich Starke was the commander from the commissioning until 1 August 1914. U 8 was formally assigned to I.U-Flottille at Brunsbüttel on 1 August 1914 and Kplt Konrad Gansser took over the command from Starke. Gansser, who was born on 13 March 1882, made one patrol in the boat and left her on 31 August 1914.

(1) U 8 sailed from Germany on 6 August 1914 for a short uneventful cruise in the North Sea and returned to port on 11 August.
Kplt. Alfred Stoß assumed command on 1 September 1914.

(2) On 16 September 1914, U 8 sailed for a three-day patrol in the North Sea and returned to port on 19 September.

(3) Stoß left Brunsbüttel with U 8 on 9 October 1914 and operated in the Dover area before returning to base on 14 October.

(4) U 8 departed her base on 17 November 1914 and sailed for an uneventful war-cruise around the Isles of Shetland and Orkney, before arriving back in Germany on 26 November.

(5) Between 26 and 30 December 1914, U 8 acted as Vorpostenboot (Outpost boat).

(6) Leaving her German base on 15 January 1915, U 8 operated off the Frisien Islands and returned to harbour on 20 January.

(7) On 13 February 1915, Stoß left Germany with U 8 and sailed to Ostend in Flanders, where they arrived on 14 February.

(8) U 8 left port on 21 February 1915 and sailed for operations in the area around Beachy Head, in the eastern section of the English Channel. On 23 February Stoß sank two British steamers with torpedoes. The *Branksome Chine* (Branksome Chine SS Co. Ltd, Cardiff), which was on passage from Grimsby Roads for Portsmouth with coal, went down 6 miles off Beachy Head. The *Oakby* (Sir R. Ropner & Co. Ltd, West Hartlepool) was hit 4 miles from Royal Sovereign Light Vessel, while travelling in ballast from London to Barry Roads. Next day (24 February) Stoß attacked another four British steamers. The *Harpalion* (J.&C. Harrison Ltd, London) was in ballast and en-route from London to Cape Henry, Virginia, in ballast, when a torpedo damaged her, 6½ miles west of the Royal Sovereign Light Vessel on 24 February. The ship carried on towards Cape d'Antifer, but then sank in mid-Channel on 26 February, about 40 miles off Le Havre and three crewmen were drowned. The *Rio Parana* (London-American Maritime Trading Co. Ltd, London) was transporting coal from the Tyne to Portoferraio in Italy when she sank 4 miles off Beachy Head. Stoß's final victim, the 1,166-ton *Western Coast* (Powel, Bacon & Hough Lines Ltd, Liverpool), was transporting general cargo from London to Liverpool on 25 February, when a torpedo sent her to the bottom, 8 miles off Beachy Head. U 8 put into Ostend on 26 February 1915.

FINAL VOYAGE

(9) Accompanied by U 20 (Kplt. Schwieger), U 8 departed Ostend on 4 March 1915, en-route for the English Channel. Alfred Stoß had orders to sink as many enemy vessels as possible in the shortest possible time and return to Ostend, re-arm and refuel his boat for the next operation. When the two boats reached the minefield off Ruytingen Bank they both parted company and U 8 crossed the minefield while travelling on the surface. However, Stoß almost immediately found himself encountering a new, second minefield and an extraordinarily thick and unexpected one, plus fog had developed, reducing visibility. Under the circumstances, Stoß decided to remain on the surface for as long as it was possible, in order to obtain an accurate fix on his position before entering the Strait of Dover. Surface

HMS *Viking* spotted the conned-down U 8 north-east of Varne Buoy. (Crown copyright)

visibility, however, deteriorated even further, so he decided to dive to the bottom and lie on the seabed, close to South Foreland. The rocky bottom and the very strong current caused the boat major problems and controlling it proved an almost impossible task. In the end, Stoß decided to surface, but keep the electric motors running. He also trimmed down to make the boat ready to dive instantly and proceeded on a westerly course.

U 8 had the misfortune to run into an indicator net barrage as she was passing westwards through the Straits on 4 March 1915. In calm, slightly foggy seas HMS *Viking* spotted a 'conned down' submarine 5 miles north-east of the Varne buoy at 12.10. The destroyer opened fire, forcing the U-boat to dive. At 12.30 the RN drifter *Ma Freen* investigated net indicators moving eastwards at a speed of 4 knots, apparently of their own accord. Captain Johnson in command of the Dover destroyers was alerted and the hunt was on. By 13.30 the 6th Flotilla destroyers *Maori* and *Viking* were hot on the trail of U 8.

Kplt. Stoß realised the serious predicament U 8 was now in, because there was a minefield behind him and the entrance to the dangerous Dover Strait was ahead. There was also a problem with the tides, in view of the fact that it was about to turn and flow in the opposite and a westerly direction in one hour. This would have prevented the boat from making any submerged headway against it.

Stoß's options were fast running out; he couldn't lie on the rocky bottom, especially with the strong currents running, and if he showed his periscope, it would be instantly seen by the destroyer flotilla. For safety's sake he decided not to use the periscope again and took U 8 down to 20m. He turned westerly and continued on the new course for fifteen minutes, before turning east, south-east over a distance of about 4½ miles. The U-boat skipper then set a new course that would bring him abeam of Dungeness. In his statement later, Stoß said the crew heard the sounds of high-speed propellers, as several destroyers passed directly overhead and, at 15.30, a distant explosion was heard.

A spate of periscope sightings marked the submarine's journey through the Channel. At 15.55 *Mohawk*, *Nubian*, *Cossack*, *Ghurka*, *Ure* and *Syren* joined the hunt.

The destroyers towed explosive sweeps set to detonate on impact at 50ft (15m). The log of destroyer HMS *Ghurka* describes what happened next:

HMS *Ghurka*, fell victim to a mine off Dungeness and sank with great loss of life on 8 February 1917. (Courtesy of the Imperial War Museum)

16.16   Commenced sweeping.
16.57   German submarine came to surface stern first 45-degree angle and then gradually righted. Crew appeared waving white flag. Opened fire with starboard foremost gun.
Submarine crew taken off my *Nubian* and *Maori*.
17.12   Submarine sank.

Kplt. Stoß:

At 16.30 I heard a distant explosion. Ob Sauerland relieved Lt. Morgenroth on the diving planes and reported they were not responding. Sauerland thought that we must have fouled a net. I heard a faint, but clearly audible noise that sounded alarming. I went forward to the fore-ends to listen. At 1645 a terrible explosion, accompanied by a brilliant flash caught U 8. The lights went out and only the emergency lights in the forward and after sections of the boat came on. All control room lights were destroyed. Water poured in through rents in the conning tower and flooded the control room. A fire broke out behind the starboard switch panel and water poured through the main induction valve, cascading down on the electric motors.

An attempt was made to couple the port electric motor to both shafts, but this resulted only in smoke and the stench of burning rubber. The motors just stopped. Ob Sauerland reported that the boat was starting to sink. The fire in the control room was spreading and the heavy flooding was forcing the bow down. We quickly went from 25° down angle to 50° and then 60° and the boat started sinking rapidly. Things started breaking loose and Ob Sauerland ordered the crew to move to the stern to counter weight aft. The batteries mixed with seawater and produced chlorine gas.

Ingenieur Pelz ordered the tanks blown with compressed air and U 8 surfaced stern first, still 45° down by the bow. We broke surface with only the conning tower and after deck above the surface. Two British destroyers immediately opened fire, scoring two hits on the conning tower, wounding Ob Ryman. I ordered the crew to abandon ship through the conning tower hatch while Ob Sauerland, Ingenieur Pelz and I scuttled the boat. The flooding valves were still open and I ordered Pelz to shut off the compressed air. At the same time I opened the main induction valve. By the time we emerged from the conning tower, boats from the British destroyers were taking the crew off the stern as U 8 settled deeper. Moments later U 8 sank beneath the surface.

ADM 53/42680 – ADM 137/3912 – NARA:T1022 Roll 23 PG61507

Four officers and twenty-five ratings were taken into captivity. That evening Kplt. Alfred Stoß and his officers were invited to dinner with the British officers in the depot ship HMS *Arrogant* and, after a few rounds of cheerful drinks, amazingly (and if it is true), they were persuaded to sing the 'Hymn of Hate' against Britain. Ironically HMS *Ghurka* fell victim to a mine off Dungeness and sank with great loss of life on 8 February 1917. Equally intriguing is the suggestion that HMS *Viking* actually spotted U 20 at 12.10. It will be recalled that it was the sinking of *Lusitania* by U 20 that was instrumental in bringing the USA into the First World War. Would the course of history have been changed had the destroyers latched onto Schweiger's U 20 rather than U 8?

Vessels sunk by U 8:

AREA	VESSEL'S NAME	FLAG	TONS	D	M	YEAR	LOCATION
English Channel	*Branksome Chine*	GBR	2026	23	2	1915	6 miles E by S ¾ S of Beachy Head
English Channel	*Oakby*	GBR	1976	23	2	1915	4 miles E by N of Royal Sovereign Light Vessel
English Channel	*Harpalion*	GBR	5867	24	2	1915	6½ miles W of Royal Sovereign Light Vessel
English Channel	*Rio Parana*	GBR	4015	24	2	1915	4 miles SE of Beachy Head
English Channel	*Western Coast*	GBR	1165	24	2	1915	8 miles SE by E ½ of E Beachy Head

WRECK-SITE
The wreck is orientated in a north-east to south-west direction and lies on a seabed of sand and shell, in a general depth of 32m (105ft), being the lowest astronomical depth. The wreck is reported as intact and upright, but with a fair amount of damage to the casing. It is also rumoured that collapsible columns on her deck identified her.

UB 38, SM IMPERIAL U-BOAT

DATE OF LOSS: 8 February 1918
DEPTH: 28m
REFERENCE: 50 57'.849 N, 001 21'.631 E
LOCATION: 9.40 nautical miles SSE of Folkestone
and 0.90 nautical miles ESE of The Varne

Type: UB II coastal torpedo attack boat **Builders**: Blohm & Voss, Hamburg for Kaiserliche Deutsche Marine **Ordered**: 22 July 1915, within the batch of UB 30–UB 41 **Keel laid**: as Yard No 262 **Launched**: 1 April 1916 **Commissioned**: by Kapitänleutnant Erwin Waßner on 18 July 1916

TECHNICAL SPECIFICATIONS
Hull: Single, saddle tank design **Surface displacement**: 274 tons **U/Dt**: 303 tons **LBDH**: 36.90m x 4.37m x 3.70m x 7.34m **Machinery**: 2 x 135ps Körting diesels **Props**: 2 bronze **S/Sp**: 9.06 knots **Op/R**: 7,030 nautical miles at 5 knots **Sub/R**: 45 nautical miles at 5 knots **U/Power**: 2 x 140ps electric motors giving 5.71 knots **Batteries**: AFA lead/ acid/accumulators **Fuel/Cap**: 21 + 7 tons **Armament**: 2 bow 50.04cm torpedo tubes **Torpedoes**: 4 x 50.04cm (19.7in) **Guns**: 1 x 88mm (3.46in) forward deck gun **Ammo**: 120 rounds of 88mm **Mines**: None **Diving**: Max-op-depth 50m (164ft) and 30 seconds to crash-dive **Complement**: 2 officers and 21 ratings

UB 38 was in service by 8 September 1916 and was assigned to Flandern Flottille on 11 September 1916, where she remained throughout her career (Flanders commanders usually stayed in the Flanders base and very rarely transferred out to take over boats based in the German ports). UB 38's first commander, Kapitänleutnant Erwin Waßner, assumed command on 10 September 1916 and went on to win the *Orden Pour Le Mérite* (Order of the Blue Max). Waßner made the following seven patrols with UB 38:

(1) Her first patrol was the transfer from Hamburg to Flanders base.

(2) On 15 September 1916, UB 38 departed Flanders for an uneventful patrol along the Dutch coast, before returning to harbour on 21 September.

(3) UB 38 left Flanders on 28 September 1916 for a war patrol in the English Channel. Waßner sank nine French and Norwegian vessels during the patrol, including six steamers: the *Irma* (E. Marcesche & Cie., Mortagne (Lorient)), was captured, then shelled and sunk while voyaging from Newport to Montagne with coal; on 1 October the French *Cap Mazagan* (F Richard et Bertho, Bordeaux) was captured and sunk en-route from Port Talbot for Tonnay Cherente. The *Le Blavet* (Soc. Bois et Charbons F. le Brise, Lorient) bound from Cardiff for Lorient was shelled and sunk, and the Norwegian ship *Mallin* (Aktieselskapet 'Skutefjord', Stavanger) travelling from Newport, Monmouth, to St Nazaire with general cargo and steel plates was captured and scuttled with explosives on 1 October. The Norwegian steamer *Cederic* (Aktieselskapet Det Selmerske Rederi, Trondheim) was en-route from Bordeaux to Barry with pit props when she was captured, then torpedoed and sunk off Wolf Rock on 5 October. While carrying coal and general cargo, the SS *Rosenwold* (Aktieselskapet Rosenvold, Kristiansand) was captured, then shelled and sunk on 5 October, while en-route from Manchester for La Pallice. On 8 October 1916 UB 38 arrived back at Flanders.

(4 & 5) Both these patrols were off the Flanders coast, but no ships were sunk.

(6) From 2 to 7 November 1916, Waßner made a fruitless patrol along the English Channel.

(7) UB 38 left Zeebrugge on 12 November 1916 for operations along the English Channel. Eight vessels were demolished on this patrol, including one French Navy patrol vessel and four steamers. The SS *Caterham* (Caterham SS Co. Ltd, Glasgow) was in ballast on passage from Rouen for Newcastle when she was captured, 15 miles off Beachy Head. The U-boat was first sighted off the starboard side, about an hour before it opened fire with its deck gun at 07.30 on 13 November. After the second shell, the master stopped the engine and the crew abandoned ship in the boats. However, the German crew used one of the boats to board the steamer and placed explosives on her, below decks. UB 38 then made off, while firing four shells into the hull, the *Caterham* sinking at 08.00. The crew of twenty-one were rescued by a Royal Navy destroyer and landed at Dover.

On 13 November the SS *Bernicia* (Leith, Hull & Hamburg Steam Packet Co. Ltd, Leith) was shelled by UB 38 at 09.10 and the master stopped his vessel. The German crew then went on board and ransacked the ship for provisions, brass and tools before placing explosive scuttling charges on board. After questioning the master, the U-boat made off towards an unidentified sailing vessel, allowing the twenty crewmen from *Bernicia* to row away in their lifeboats. The steamer had been voyaging in ballast from Rouen to London.

The SS *Polpedn* (Farrar, Groves & Co. Ltd, London – Crown Nominees) was bound from Dunkerque to Ayr in ballast when Waßner torpedoed and sunk her without warning at 03.30 on 11 November. Her crew of twenty got clear away in one of the boats, the other having been shattered by the explosion. The U-boat, which was observed for a few seconds prior to the detonation, then dived and was not seen again. A patrol vessel rescued the survivors off St Catherine's and took them to Portsmouth. Originally the Norwegian *Thor* (Joh. E. v. d. Ohe, Bergen), she was intercepted by HMS *Berwick* on 9 September 1914 at position 10° 30' N, 57° 00' W, east of Trinidad, en-route from New York to supply the 4,900-ton German light cruiser SMS *Karlsruhe* (Captain Kohler) with 2,000 tons of coal; a British prize court condemned the action. At 18.30 on 4 November 1914 a major internal explosion blew the bow off the *Karlsruhe* and, within half an hour, she had sank, 129 survivors being picked up by the supply ships *Rio Negro* and *Indrani-Hoffnung*; the cause of the explosion was thought to have been an ammunition accident.

The Norwegian SS *Ullvang* (Dampskipsselskapet Aktieselskapet Ullvang, Haugesund) was carrying general cargo, including military stores, from Liverpool to Técamp when she was captured on 14 November and scuttled with explosives. UB 38 returned to Flanders on 16 November.

Oblt.z.S. Wilhelm Ambereger assumed command on 19 November 1916, while Erwin Waßner took control of the brand new minelayer, UC 69. Amberger made the following eleven patrols with UB 38:

(8) UB 38 patrolled the Hoofden between 20 November and 5 December 1916, but no ships were sunk.

(9) Departing Zeebrugge on 11 December 1916, UB 38 sailed for operations in the English Channel and sank five vessels, including two steamships. Sixteen men, including the master (all hands) went down off Beachy Head with the SS *Coath* (George Baseley & Sons Ltd, Penzance); she was outbound from Le Havre when a torpedo from UB 38 struck her. The 2,084-ton Spanish SS *Ason* (Cia. Montañesa de Nav., Santander) was first captured on 17 December and then sunk by a torpedo 27 miles off the Scilly Isles. She was en-route from Santander to Ardrossan with copper ore. UB 38 returned to base on 22 December 1916.

(10) UB 38 left Zeebrugge on 11 January 1917 and Ambereger sank four vessels, including the following two steamships: the Spanish *Manuel* (Echevarietta y Larrinaga, Bilbao) was on passage from Bilbao for Glasgow with copper ore when she was captured off Ushant on 16 January and sunk; the Norwegian *ASP* (Aktieselskapet Vesterhav, Kristiansand) was captured on 18 January and scuttled with explosive charges, while transporting coal from Barry Docks, South Wales, to Faqal in the Azores. UB 38 returned to Flanders on 24 January.

(11) Amberger captured and scuttled the Norwegian steamer *Dalmata* (Aktieselskapet Dalmata, Drammen) with explosive charges, 25 miles north-west of Bishop's Rock, while on a patrol as far as the Irish coast between 8 and 22 February 1917; the ship was carrying a general cargo from New York to Havre.

(12) UB 38 made a sortie along the English Channel from 8–24 April 1917 and sunk two fishing boats.

(13) Leaving Flanders on 25 April 1917, UB 38 operated in the English Channel and sank six vessels, including three steamers. At 06.00 on 1 May, two submarines were sighted by the crew of the *Lady Wood* (William France, Fenwick & Co. Ltd, London), one about 1 mile ahead, and the other the same distance astern. The submarine astern, UB 38, began shelling the steamer, so the engine was stopped and the crew of twenty-four abandoned ship in the boats. The enemy crew boarded the ship and placed explosive scuttling charges below decks. The Germans were still on board when a British warship was sighted and they hastily left the ship with the senior German officer firing his revolver into the deck, in order to hurry the master along, who was collecting some clothes. After the enemy sailors had returned to the U-boat, the *Lady Wood*'s crew was allowed to get away in the boats, but not before the Germans had taken the ship's chronometer and sextant from them. A patrol vessel picked the men up and landed them at St Mary's on the Isles of Scilly. The steamer sank at 06.45; she had been transporting 2,700 tons of copper ore from Port Nolloth, South Africa, to Swansea.

The *Aghios Nikolas* (Nicolas Valmas, Syra), a Greek steamer, was stopped and scuttled with demolition charges on 4 May, while travelling from Oran, Algeria to Boulogne. On that same day the Greek steamship *Assos* (G. Yannouloto Frères, Piraeus) was also destroyed while voyaging from Colombo, Ceylon, to Dunkerque. UB 38 returned to Ostend on 7 May.

(14) UB 8 departed Flanders on 22 May 1917 and sank two sailing ships in the English Channel off Portland, but was forced home early with machinery problems, arriving at Ostend on 29 May 1917. On 5 June 1917 Allied warships damaged the U-boat, during the bombardment of Ostend.

(15) Following major repairs, UB 38 sailed from port on 4 August 1917 and began patrolling the English Channel. However, an oil leak forced Amberger to return to harbour on 6 August.

(16) UB 38 departed Flanders on 14 August 1917 for operations in the English Channel. The turret-hulled ship SS *Claverley* (Sutherland SS Co. Ltd, Newcastle) was torpedoed and sunk on 20 August, with the loss of ten crewmen, while voyaging from the Tyne for Genoa, Italy, with coal (two of those lost were: fifteen-year-old apprentice George Lloyd Kent and Third Engineer Herman Carl Schier, aged twenty-five).

The British steamer *D.H. Dwyer* (Forwarders Ltd, Sunderland (Kingston, Ontario)) was in ballast and on passage from Rouen for Newport, when Ambereger sank her with a torpedo on 26 August. UB 38 arrived back at Flanders on 28 August.

(17) Having left Zeebrugge on 9 September 1917, UB 38 operated along the English Channel. Amberger sank a British sailing vessel taking flints from Dieppe to Liverpool and then, four days later, he torpedoed the French steamship *Aline Montreuil* (Montreuil & Cie., Rouen), which sank en-route from Rouen to Swansea. UB 38 arrived back at Flanders on 23 September.

(18) Amberger left Flanders in UB 38 on 11 October 1917 and patrolled the English Channel. While transporting coal and coke from the Tyne to Falmouth, a torpedo from UB 38 damaged the British SS *Teespool* (Pool Shipping Co. Ltd, West Hartlepool) on 19 October. She was beached at Dartmouth and re-floated.

Twenty-one crewmen, including the master, were lost the next day (20 October), when the SS *Algarve* (The Shipping Controller) was torpedoed without warning. She was in ballast voyaging from Rouen to Swansea. The projectile discharged against No.3 hold on the port side at 03.50 and the ship sank immediately. However, the crew clambered into the port lifeboat, but just as it reached the water, the ship rolled over on top of them, taking the boat and three men down with it, although those men came back up and clung to floating wreckage. A patrol boat arrived on the scene at 08.40 and landed the three men at Weymouth. Sadly, all the rest of their colleagues had drowned.

THE MEN WHO DIED

Ah Ling, Fireman
Ah Wong, Fireman
Ah Yi, Fireman
Alegy, R., Sailor
Bell, John Henry, 52, Second Engineer
Bralo, F., Sailor
Brooks, Edward, 44, First Mate
Chu Ng, Cook
Davison Sidney Ford, 45, First Engineer
Holt, John Mountjoy, 22, Third Engineer
Kow Leong, Fireman
Kow Long, Fireman
Lewis, Patrick George, 44 Master
Ng Hoi, Fireman
Romas, R., Sailor
Tan Ah Kim, Fireman
Tucker, John Henry, 33, Second Mate
Wong C., Steward
Wong Wah, Steward

Some time after this last attack, UB 38 was badly damaged by shellfire from an unidentified merchantship and was forced to return to Flanders for major repairs, where she arrived on 24 October 1917. Oblt.z.S. Waldemar von Fischer assumed command on 6 December 1917 (in July 1918, Wilhelm Amberger and his crew disappeared with UB 108, possibly in the Folkestone–Gris Nez Barrage).

(19) Patrolling in the Hoofden and off the English east coast was Waldemar's first operational area after leaving Flanders on 8 December, but no ships were sunk. The boat returned to port on 19 December. Oblt.z.S. Günther Bachmann became the new commander on 25 December 1917.

(20) UB 38 patrolled the English east coast from 1–15 January 1918. Bachmann torpedoed the SS *Birtley* (Burnett SS Co. Ltd, Newcastle) and eighteen crewmen (all hands), including Captain Henry Valentine Adams, went down with her near Flamborough Head. The steamer had left Dunkerque in ballast on 1 January for passage to the Tyne and reported into Yarmouth Roads on 3 January. The following morning she sailed at daylight. The French steamer *Outreau* was just 200 yards away from a steamship off Flamborough Head that blew up and sank at 23.45, according to the French master and a pilot. German records released after the war revealed that the vessel in question was the SS *Birtley*, which was sunk by a torpedo from UB 38.

ELEVEN OF THOSE MEN WHO DIED
Adams, Henry Valentine, 46, Master
Carmichael, William, 63, First Engineer
Carroll, James Godfrey, 44, Steward
Crocker, James, 34, Able Seaman
Edwards, Arthur Rowe, 23, Able Seaman
Hails, Matthew Errington, 49, Second Engineer
Jones, William Francis, 49, First Mate
Maaronen, A., 25, Able Seaman
McGregor, M., Second Hand
Petersen, Peter, 37, Boatswain (Bosun)
Robson, Albert, 24, Second Mate

Bachmann also damaged the SS *Caledonia* with a torpedo off Whitby; she was taking coal from Methil to Rotterdam, but managed to reach her destination. On 15 January, UB 38 arrived back in port.

FINAL VOYAGE
(21) On 29 January 1918, UB 38 departed Zeebrugge at 02.00 for operations in the English Channel. Bachmann had almost completed his patrol by 8 February to the west of the Folkestone–Gris Nez deep-mine barrage and was homeward bound. At 12.30 that day, he exchanged recognition signals with the outward-bound UB 33.

At around 21.25 that evening, HM drifter *Gowan II* had sighted a U-boat on the surface (half a mile NW of No.15 Buoy) at the northern end of Le Colbart sandbank, which was almost certainly UB 38. Realising his boat had been sighted, Bachmann immediately submerged, but *Gowan II* had already radioed for assistance and, within twenty minutes, a number of other Royal Navy vessels, including a destroyer, joined in the hunt. As the ships swept the sea, three massive underwater explosions suddenly rocked the British warships at 22.45 and large quantities of debris and oil rose to the surface. Nothing more was ever heard from Günther Bachmann and his crew of twenty-seven. It was believed that in trying to escape from the patrol vessels, the U-boat had unknowingly dived into the great minefield. For destruction of the U-boat, the Royal Navy boats reaped the £1,000 bounty offered by Admiralty. However, in this case the money was donated to the Mayor of Dover's Fund. RN divers later located the wreck. Once again the Folkestone Barrage had triumphed. <u>NARA: T-1022, Roll 61, PG61796</u>

THE MEN WHO DIED IN UB 38

Bachmann, Oblt.z.S.
Brecht, Stm. der Reserve
Böhme, Masch.Mt
Döbberitz, Mts.
Eber, Hzr
Eckhardt, Hzr
Engfer, Ob.Masch.Anw
Haeseler, Ob.Masch.Mt
Horn, Masch.Anw
Hornig, F.T.Ober Gast
Joneck, Masch.Mt
Knaack, Mts.
Koch, Mts.
Lamarche, Mts. der Reserve
Leiderer, Mts.
Lindenmann, Ob.Mts.
Luderer, Masch.
Markmann, Mt
Maart, Mts.
Rumpf, Ob.Hzr
Röhrbein, Masch.Mt
Schönfelder, Masch. der Reserve
Specht, Ob.Hzr
Stachowitz, Hzr
Steffens, Mts.
Weglau, Oblt.z.S.
Züge, Mts. der Reserve

The following is a list of the known vessels sunk or damaged by UB 38:

AREA	VESSEL'S NAME	FLAG	TONS	D	M	YEAR	LOCATION
E/Channel	Irma	FRA	844	30	9	1916	Sunk west end of Channel
E/Channel	Cap Mazagan	FRA	760	1	10	1916	Sunk west end of Channel
E/Channel	Le Blavet	FRA	1010	1	10	1916	Sunk west end of Channel
E/Channel	Mallin	NOR	479	1	10	1916	Sunk west end of Channel
E/Channel	Musette (sailing vessel)	FRA	245	1	10	1916	44 miles NW of Ushant
E/Channel	La Fraternite (sail vessel)	FRA	477	3	10	1916	Sunk off the Scilly Isles
E/Channel	Cantatrice (sailing vessel)	FRA	109	4	10	1916	12 miles S of Wolf Rock
Atlantic	Cederic	NOR	1128	5	10	1916	18 miles SSW of Wolf Rock
E/Channel	Rosenvold	NOR	749	5	10	1916	15 miles S of Wolf Rock
E/Channel	Bernicia	GBR	957	13	11	1916	20 miles SSE of Beachy Head
E/Channel	Caterham	GBR	1777	13	11	1916	15 miles SSE of Beachy Head
E/Channel	Riquette (sailing vessel)	FRA	164	13	11	1916	Sunk N of Dieppe
E/Channel	St Nicholas (sailing vessel)	FRA	261	13	11	1916	Sunk N of Dieppe

E/Channel	Dominee (patrol vessel)	FRA	327	14	11	1916	Sunk E of Cap Barfleur
E/Channel	Polpedn	GBR	1510	14	11	1916	20 miles S of Littlehampton
E/Channel	Prof. Jalaguier (sail vessel)	FRA	223	14	11	1916	Sunk in Isle of Wight area
E/Channel	Ullvang	NOR	639	14	11	1916	Sunk N of Cap Antifer
E/Channel	Coath	GBR	975	12	12	1916	3 miles SW of Eastbourne
E/Channel	Conrad (sailing vessel)	GBR	975	12	12	1916	Sunk in Mid Channel at 50° 05' N, 00° 40'W
E/Channel	Ason	SPA	2084	15	12	1916	Sunk near the Bristol Channel
E/Channel	Naiad (sailing vessel)	GBR	1907	15	12	1916	25 miles SE of Bishop Rock
E/Channel	Ocean (sailing vessel)	FRA	339	19	12	1916	40 miles WNW of Ushant
E/Channel	Independent (sailing vessel)	FRA	153	15	1	1917	Sunk N of Ushant
E/Channel	Manuel	SPA	2419	16	1	1917	Sunk NW of Ushant
E/Channel	Asp	NOR	1759	18	1	1917	45 miles NW of the Scilly Isles
E/Channel	Lilian H. (sailing vessel)	GBR	467	19	1	1917	Sunk near Old Head of Kinsale
Irish Sea	Dalmata	NOR	1773	11	2	1917	25 miles NW of Bishop Rock
E/Channel	Precedent (fishing vessel)	GBR	36	11	4	1917	12 miles ESE of Berry Head
E/Channel	Maria (fishing vessel)	GBR	175	13	4	1917	Sunk near Portland Bill
E/Channel	King Oskar II (sail vessel)	NOR	842	26	4	1917	Sunk in the Seine Estuary
E/Channel	Jessie (sailing vessel)	GBR	108	27	4	1917	7 miles W of Portland Bill
E/Channel	Lady Wood	GBR	2314	1	5	1917	15 miles SW of Wolf Rock
E/Channel	Aghios Nikolas	GRE	2231	4	5	1917	Sunk in Seine Estuary
E/Channel	Assos	GRE	2840	4	5	1917	Sunk in Seine Estuary
E/Channel	Joseph (sailing vessel)	GBR	205	4	5	1917	20 miles off NW of Caen
E/Channel	Gudrun (barque)	NOR	1472	23	5	1917	Sunk in Portland area
E/Channel	Thyra (sailing vessel)	DEN	285	23	5	1917	Sunk in Portland area
E/Channel	Claverley	GBR	3829	20	8	1917	4 miles SE of the Eddystone Lighthouse
E/Channel	W.H. Dwyer	GBR	1770	26	8	1917	15 miles E by N of Berry Head
E/Channel	Dependence (sailing vessel)	GBR	120	15	9	1917	Sunk west end of the Channel
E/Channel	Aline Montreuil	FRA	1624	19	9	1917	Sunk in the Cap Barfleur area
E/Channel	Teespool	GBR	4577	19	10	1917	Damaged in the Dartmouth area
E/Channel	Algarve	GBR	1274	20	10	1917	15 miles WSW of Portland Bill
North Sea	Birtley	GBR	1438	5	1	1918	8 miles N of Flamborough Head
North Sea	Caledonia	NLD	863	13	1	1918	Damaged in the Whitby area

WRECK-SITE

The wreck lies on a seabed of sand, shells, lose sediment and shingle, in a general depth of 28m, being the lowest astronomical depth. It is reasonably intact and lies well over to the port side, with the conning tower still in place, but the stern end has been blown off. The wreck is covered in soft corals and attracts shoals of fish.

UB 58, SM IMPERIAL U-BOAT

DATE OF LOSS: 10 March 1918
DEPTH: 22m
REFERENCE: 51 00.11 N, 01 18.58 E
LOCATION: 6.36 nautical miles SSW of Folkestone

Type: UB III coastal torpedo attack boat *Builders:* A.G. Weser, Bremen for Kaiserliche Deutsche Marine *Ordered:* 20 May 1916, within the batch of UB 54–UB 59 *Keel laid:* as Yard No.270 on 13 September 1916 *Launched:* 22 June 1917 *Commissioned:* by Oberleutnant zur See Werner Fürbringer on 10 August 1917

TECHNICAL SPECIFICATIONS

Hull: Double *Surface displacement:* 516 tons *U/Dt:* 646 tons *LBDH:* 55.85m x 5.80m x 3.68m x 8¼m *Machinery:* 2 x 550ps Körting diesels *Props:* 2 bronze *S/Sp:* 13.4 knots *Op/R:* 9,020 nautical miles at 9 knots *Sub/R:* 55 nautical miles at 4 knots *U/Power:* 2 x 394ps electric motors giving 7.8 knots *Batteries:* AFA lead/acid/accumulators *Fuel/Cap:* 36 + 39 tons *Armament:* 4 bow and 1 stern 50.04cm torpedo tubes *Torpedoes:* 10 x 50.04cm (19.7in) *Guns:* 1 x 88mm (3.46in) forward deck gun *Ammo:* 160 rounds of 88mm *Mines:* None *Diving:* Max-op-depth 50m (164ft) and 30 seconds to crash-dive *Complement:* 3 officers and 31 ratings

On 15 October 1917, UB 58 was formally assigned to Flandern I.U-Flottille with Fürbringer the commander from 10 August 1917. He was later promoted to Kapitänleutnant while in command of this boat and made the following five patrols:

(1) UB 58 left Kiel on 10 October 1917 and transferred to Zeebrugge, where she arrived on 15 October. However, the enterprising skipper sank two sailing vessels on 13 October during the transfer: the 257-ton Norwegian *Bethel*, voyaging Holmestrand to West Hartlepool with pit props, and the 830-ton Swedish barque *Esmeralda*, which was transporting pit props from Holmestrand to the Tyne.

(2) On 28 October 1917 UB 58 left port and sailed into the English Channel, but technical problems forced Fürbringer back to Zeebrugge on 31 October.

(3) After departing Flanders on 4 November, UB 58 patrolled the English Channel as far as the Atlantic Ocean. Fürbringer sank one 116-ton sailing boat before returning to harbour on 23 November.

(4) December 1917 was more lucrative for Fürbringer when UB 58 patrolled the English Channel between the 12 and 28 December and sank three steamships. The French *Saint Andre* (Soc. Navale de l'Ouest, Le Havre) was lost when voyaging from Rouen to Algiers with empty casks on 19 December. On 22 December, a torpedo struck the *Clan Cameron* (Cayzer, Irvine & Co., Glasgow) on the starboard side at 11.30 and the explosion occurred in No.3 deep tank. The ship was transporting tea and jute from Chittagong to London and Dundee. The master ordered the stern gun fired to warn other shipping of the danger, but the commotion also brought a tug out to assist. At 13.00, the crew abandoned ship, while the tug stood by until other vessels arrived to help with the tow. However, a second torpedo was fired and detonated in the engine room, sinking the ship soon after. The tug landed the crew at Plymouth. The Norwegian *Start* (Aktieselskapet 'Start', Skien) was bound from Swansea to Rouen with coal, when Fürbringer torpedoed and sunk her soon after the *Clan Cameron*.

(5) Leaving Zeebrugge on 17 January 1918, the skipper made his last patrol in UB 58 along the English Channel. He returned to Flanders on 2 February 1918 after sinking two small British sailing boats.

After that patrol, Werner Fürbringer was given overdue medical leave and admitted to hospital in an exhausted state. However, the skipper resented leaving his boat, and his prevailing sense of foreboding was to prove all too correct. In *FIPS*, the book he wrote after the war, Fürbringer declared that inwardly, from the moment he read the first letter, he knew that UB 58 would not return from the patrol. Three weeks later U-Flottille wrote to tell him that UB 58 was missing, believed lost with all hands. Reading the letter, Fürbringer stated that he felt 'part of him die'.

Oblt.z.S. Werner Löwe, having previously been skipper of UC 6 and UC 79, assumed command of UB 58 on 8 February 1918 and took the boat on its final patrol.

FINAL VOYAGE

(6) UB 58 departed Zeebrugge for operations in the English Channel on 8 March 1918, but two days later it detonated a mine off Folkestone, near the Varne Light Vessel. At 04.00 in the morning of 10 March the boat was moving through the Dover Strait on the surface, but was forced to dive when a patrol vessel lit a flare and illuminated the line of RN drifters. Unfortunately for the crew of thirty, UB 58 had dived straight into the minefield. Log of P24 – 10 March 1918:

04.00   Raced to the scene of a triple explosion.
16.00   Underwater explosion heard in vicinity of Varne LV.
18.18   Sighted large oil patch 1.4 miles NE of Varne LV. Searched vicinity. Proceeded to Folkestone.

Searchlights revealed nothing, but the following debris was fished out: loaves of bread, insulation material, wood and large quantities of oil. Over the course of the day, mixed oil and debris floated to the surface. Among numerous German language items recovered was a report detailing the boat's acceptance trials in October 1917.

Divers from the salvage tug *Moonfleet* examined the U-boat wreck near the No.13 Buoy on 9 August. They found the fore section, right up to the 105mm deck gun, had been blown off. The inside of the boat, which was searched the following day, was also found to be totally smashed to pieces, with parts of human bodies, bedding and rotten clothing, all mixed up together. The deck gun and its mounting was raised on 12 August. Also on the same day and fairly close to UB 58, the divers found another 'old' U-boat, full of sand.
ADM 53/56297 P24 10 March 1918 – NARA: T-1022, Roll 68, PG61818

THE MEN WHO DIED IN UB 58

Baumgart, Ob.Hzr
Buschbeck, Masch.Mt
Böhme, Masch.Mt
Christoph, F.T.Gast
Cron, Mts.
Egler, Ob.Mts.
Eurich, Ob.Masch. der Reserve
Fenner, Masch.Mt
Flüss, Ob.Mts.
Freudenberg, Mn.Ing. der Reserve
Gaubitz, Hzr
Haussleiter, Lt.z.S.
Heide, Btn.Mt
Krocker, Ob.Mts.
Kurmis, Mts.
Löwe, Oblt.z.S.
Michaelis, Hzr
Misch, Ob.Masch.Anw
Müller, Hzr
Oertel, F.T.Gast
Otto, Hans Masch.Anw
Otto, Dietrrich Mts.

Pieper, Masch. der Reserve
Roggelin, Masch.
Schneiderheinze, Masch.Mt
Schössler, Mts.
Skotzki, Ob.Mts.
Steinecke, Ob.Hzr
Theide, Ob.Mts.
Ulatowski, Mts.
Wegener, Hzr
Wessel, Masch.Mt
Wieneck, Masch.Anw
Willmer, Ob.Mts.
Zotz, Hzr

The following is a list of known vessels damaged or sunk by UB 58:

AREA	VESSEL'S NAME	FLAG	TONS	D	M	YEAR	LOCATION
North Sea	*Bethel* (sailing vessel)	NOR	257	13	10	1917	Sunk N of the Dogger Bank 56 08' N, 00 58' E
North Sea	*Esmeralda* (barque)	SWE	830	13	10	1917	Sunk N of the Dogger Bank
English Channel	*Minnie Coles* (sail vessel)	GBR	116	19	11	1917	30 miles WNW of Les Hanois Lighthouse
English Channel	*Saint Andre*	FRA	2457	19	12	1917	9 miles SW of Eddystone
English Channel	*Clan Cameron*	GBR	3595	22	12	1917	23 miles SW by S ½ S Portland Bill
English Channel	*Start*	NOR	728	22	12	1917	Sunk in position 50 31' N, 02 04'W
English Channel	*Lousie Bell* (sail vessel)	GBR	118	26	1	1918	15 miles N of Cherbourg 49 53' N, 01 44'W
English Channel	*W.H.L.* (sailing vessel)	GBR	97	28	1	1918	8 miles SSE of Portland Bill

WRECK-SITE

The wreck of UB 58, which has been identified by the name on the propellers, lies on a seabed of sand and shingle, in a general depth of 22m (72.1ft), being the lowest astronomical depth. The U-boat is in reasonable condition generally, but the bow section where the mine exploded is badly broken up, and what can be seen of the inside is very silted up. Tidal streams in the vicinity are quite brisk.

UB 33, SM IMPERIAL U-BOAT

DATE OF LOSS: 11 April 1918
DEPTH: 27m
REFERENCE: 50 56'.021 N, 001 17'.980 E
LOCATION: 9¾ nautical miles SSE of Folkestone
and 0.10 miles WSW of the Varne Bank

Type: UB II coastal torpedo attack boat **Builders:** Blohm & Voss, Hamburg for Kaiserliche Deutsche Marine **Ordered:** 22 July 1915, within the batch of UB 30–UB 41 **Keel laid:** as Yard No.257 **Launched:** 5 December 1916 **Commissioned:** by Oblt.z.S. Herbert Lefholz on 20 April 1916

TECHNICAL SPECIFICATIONS

Hull: Single, saddle tank design **Surface displacement**: 274 tons **U/Dt**: 303 tons **LBDH**: 36.90m x 4.37m x 3.70m x 7.34m **Machinery**: 2 x 135ps Benz diesels **Props**: 2 bronze **S/Sp**: 9.06 knots **Op/R**: 8,150 nautical miles at 5 knots **Sub/R**: 45 nautical miles at 5 knots **U/Power**: 2 x 140ps electric motors giving 5.71 knots **Batteries**: AFA lead/acid/accumulators **Fuel/Cap**: 21 + 7 tons **Armament**: 2 bow 50.04cm torpedo tubes **Torpedoes**: 4 x 50.04cm (19.7in) **Guns**: 1 x 88mm (3.46in) forward deck gun **Ammo**: 120 rounds of 88mm **Mines**: None **Diving**: Max-op-depth 50m (164ft) and 30 seconds to crash-dive **Complement**: 2 officers and 21 ratings

UB 33 was formally assigned to the Baltic U-Flottille at Libau (Liepãja in present day Latvia) on 22 June 1916 until 24 October 1917, with Oblt.z.S. Herbert Lefholz the commander from 22 April 1916. The boat's first nine patrols were in the Baltic Sea and were of no great significance.

Oblt.z.S. Waldemar von Fischer took command on 1 February 1917 until 21 March, followed by Oblt.z.S. Karl Ruprecht on 22 March 1917.

While on her tenth patrol during May and June 1917, UB 33 searched in the Skagerrak and Kattegat for merchant vessels.

ObLt.z.S. Fritz Gregor assumed command of the boat on 17 September 1917 and UB 33 and Gregor formally transferred to Flandern U-Flottille on 24 October 1917. Gregor remained with the boat until her demise.

The eleventh patrol was off the English east coast from 12 October until 24 October 1917 and that was followed by two short and quick tours in the Hoofden area.

(14) On 22 December 1917, UB 33 made a sortie in the Hoofden and off the English east coast. Gregor badly damaged the British steamer *Genesse* off Flamborough Head. The ship was on passage from the Tyne for London with coal and it put into Hartlepool for repairs. UB 33 returned to Flanders on 4 January 1918.

(15) Departing Zeebrugge on 7 February 1918, UB 33 hunted along the English Channel and returned to Flanders on 23 February. During the trip Gregor sank nine small boats with gunfire and explosive charges. The steamer *Northville* (The Lowlands Stm. Shipping Co. Ltd, South Shields (Newcastle)) was also sunk with a torpedo on 17 February, while voyaging from Newport, Monmouth, to Dieppe with 3,400 tons of coal. The torpedo detonated aft on the starboard side at 10.20. All the crew of twenty-six got safely away in the boats and were rescued by the steam tug *Dencode* and landed at Brixham. The ship sank at 10.28, taking the confidential papers down with it.

A torpedo also damaged the SS *Pikepool* (Pool Shipping Co. Ltd, West Hartlepool), voyaging from Rouen to Barry Roads in ballast. The ship was then towed to Portland.

(16) On 13 March 1918, UB 33 left the harbour and sailed to Lyme Bay and that area of the English Channel. Fritz Gregor sank the Norwegian barque *Carla*, which was in ballast on passage from Havre for New York. A small sailing boat was also sunk before UB 33 returned to Flanders on 18 March.

(17) On 31 March, UB 33 was due to leave on a patrol, but the trip was aborted because of mechanical problems.

FINAL VOYAGE

(18) UB 33 resumed her patrols on 6 April 1918 and left Zeebrugge for operations in the English Channel. The Norwegian steam coaster *Nyasaland* (Aktieselskapet 'Nyasaland', Tonsberg) was transporting coal from Cardiff to Le Havre when Gregor captured, then shelled and sunk it off Berry Head on 8 April. Late in the afternoon on 10 April, the 613-ton White (Cowes)-built patrol boat HMS P59 sighted a U-boat carrying a sail in position 50° 19'30 N, 00° 32' W, which was probably UB 33 (if it was, she must have

been experiencing some engine problems). However, as P59 approached, the U-boat dived and four depth charges from the patrol boat followed it down. The submarine broke surface and then went down again, so three more depth charges were dropped. As oil and bubbles rose to the surface, P59 and HMS P16 sent more depth charges after the boat, but she must have escaped. The following day Fritz Gregor must have decided to return to Flanders early, due to the damage, but UB 33 detonated a mine and sank in the Dover Strait. HM drifter *Ocean Roamer* witnessed the explosion at 18.00 between Le Colbart and the Varne, when a huge thick column of smoke and seawater shot into the air. *Ocean Roamer* was able to pick up a bucketful of oil, plus some wood covered in an acid-proof composition that had risen to the surface. By nightfall oil was still bubbling up and the drifter marked the spot with a buoy. The position was said to be not quite in the minefield, but perhaps a submarine had fouled a mine cable and later ran into the mine. Divers who were sent to investigate the wreck could not locate her, because the RN drifter had not given an accurate position where the explosion had occurred. Almost two weeks after the explosion, sweepers succeeded in locating the wreck and on 6 May divers identified it as a submarine. The Admiralty then approached Lt-Cdr Damant, who had already used explosive charges while seaching for gold on the 14,892-ton White Star Liner *Laurentic,* after she detonated a mine and sank in Lough Swilly. Damant reached Dover on 21 May and went down with Cdr Cooper and a party from the 145-ton Admiralty salvage tug *Moonfleet.*

The aft section of wreck was found to be extensively damaged and lying on her starboard beam-ends. The hull plating had been crushed over about 180 sq. ft. On opening the hatch, the body of her commander, Oblt.z.S. F. Gregor, was found to be blocking the confined space. This may be evidence that some of the crew survived the initial detonation only to perish in a failed escape attempt, as the boat was flooded up. On the seabed, a spherical mine with the number '832' painted on it and obviously British, was touching the damaged part of the wreck. It also had at least five projecting horns and one that was doubled over. Ironically the divers found an eye painted on the UB's bow, an image used by German fishermen to bring good luck.

Four days later, Damant exploded 45lb of TNT inside the conning tower and, the following day, blew his way into the control room. RN diver Dusty Miller finally broke through beyond the control room and recovered a steel waterproof chest containing UB 33's valuable confidential codebooks, signals, ciphers and related documents, including the new call-signs from 12 April onward. The finds were valuable enough to warrant immediate despatch to London by Cdr Cooper. That July, the head of the Salvage Section recommended that Dusty Miller receive a decoration for his achievement and he was presented with a medal the following year. All of the submarine's crew were lost with the boat, but it has been stated that Gregor's body was later buried on land; the authors have been unable to locate his place of rest, however.

ADM 137/2100 – ADM 116/1634 – NARA: T-1022, Roll 59, PG61786

THE MEN WHO DIED IN UB 33

Beckendorf, Ob.Stm. der Reserve
Beyer, Masch.Mt
Bierhals, Mt
Bleichert, Masch.
Boldt, Ob.Mts.
Brendemühl, Hzr
Dillwitz, Mt der Reserve
Fritzen, Mts.

Funke, Hzr
Gregor, Oblt.z.S.
Heinke, F.T.Gast
Heuer, Masch.Mt
Junker, Ob.Masch.Mt
Lipp, Masch.Mt
Molly, Mts.
Maass, Lt.z.S.
Paulien, Mts.
Peter, Mts.
Rose, Masch.Anw
Schnoov, Ob.Mts.
Schumann, F.T.Ober Gast
Schönhofer, Hzr
Sommer, Masch.Mt
Suwe, Ob.Btn.Mt
Tränkner, Masch.Mt
Utecht, Masch.Anw
Vanselow, Lt.z.S.
Zacharias, Ob.Hzr

The following is a list of vessels captured, damaged or sunk by UB 33:

AREA	VESSEL'S NAME	FLAG	TONS	D	M	YEAR	LOCATION
North Sea	Gertie (Taken as prize of war)	SWE	257	24	5	1917	Captured in Skagerrak and Kattegat
North Sea	Gotha (Taken as prize of war)	SWE	720	24	5	1917	Captured in Skagerrak and Kattegat
North Sea	Krager (Taken as prize of war)	NOR	550	24	5	1917	Captured in Skagerrak and Kattegat
North Sea	Genesse	GBR	2830	1	1	1918	Damaged off Flamborough Head
E/Channel	Kia Ora (barge)	GBR	77	8	2	1918	20 miles WNW of Dieppe
E/Channel	Pikepool	GBR	3683	16	2	1918	Damaged in Start Point area
E/Channel	Commander (sailing vessel)	GBR	47	17	2	1918	Sunk in Lyme Bay
E/Channel	Northville	GBR	2472	17	2	1918	3½ miles ESE of Berry Head
E/Channel	Commandant Baratier (s/v)	FRA	324	19	2	1918	Sunk in the Lizard area
E/Channel	Snow Drop (fishing vessel)	GBR	40	20	2	1918	8 miles SW of Eddystone lighthouse
E/Channel	Idalia (fishing vessel)	GBR	23	21	2	1918	Sunk in Lyme Bay
E/Channel	Irex (fishing vessel)	GBR	16	21	2	1918	Sunk in Lyme Bay
E/Channel	Leonora (fishing vessel)	GBR	26	21	2	1918	Sunk in Lyme Bay
E/Channel	Onyx (fishing vessel)	GBR	38	21	2	1918	Sunk in Lyme Bay
E/Channel	Rosebud (fishing vessel)	GBR	44	21	2	1918	Sunk in Lyme Bay
E/Channel	Carla (barque)	NOR	1668	14	3	1918	Sunk S of the Isle of Wight
E/Channel	Sparkling Foam (sail vessel)	GBR	199	15	3	1918	9 miles S of Beer Head, Lyme Bay
E/Channel	Nyasaland	NOR	383	8	4	1918	Sunk off Berry Head

WRECK-SITE

The wreck lies on a seabed of sand, mud and shingle, in a general depth of 27m (88.5ft), being the lowest astronomical depth. It is very broken up aft, partially buried, lying on its starboard beam, with the conning tower broken off and lying on the seabed. The conning tower hatch cover is open and a large section of the lower casing is crushed in, with masses of jagged metal. A large shoal of fish usually swarms over the top of the wreck. Tidal streams are fairly brisk.

UB 56, SM IMPERIAL U-BOAT

DATE OF LOSS: 19 December 1917
DEPTH: 28m
REFERENCE: 50 56'.800 N, 01 23'.861 E
LOCATION: 10.79 nautical miles SE of Folkestone
harbour and 2.39 nautical miles from The Varne

Distinguished submarine commander and society gambler 'Lala' Lafrenz unintentionally provided Admiralty with information on U-boat evasion techniques – information that would ultimately assist in the creation of the virtually submarine – proof Folkestone Barrage. The crew of UB 56 were among the first to discover the new realities of running the Channel.

Type: UB III coastal torpedo attack boat **Builders:** A.G. Weser, Bremen for Kaiserliche Deutsche Marine **Ordered:** 20 May 1916, within the batch of UB 54–UB 59 **Keel laid:** as Yard No.268 on 5 September 1916 **Launched:** 11 May 1917 **Commissioned:** by Oberleutnant zur see Hans Valentiner on 19 July 1917

TECHNICAL SPECIFICATIONS

Hull: Double **Surface displacement:** 516 tons **U/Dt:** 646 tons **LBDH:** 55.85m x 5.80m x 3.68m x 8¼m **Machinery:** 2 x 550ps Körting diesels **Props:** 2 bronze **S/Sp:** 13.4 knots **Op/R:** 9,020 nautical miles at 9 knots **Sub/R:** 55 nautical miles at 4 knots **U/Power:** 394ps electric motors giving 7.8 knots **Batteries:** Lead/acid **Fuel/Cap:** 36 + 39 tons **Armament:** 4 bow and 1 stern 50.04cm torpedo tubes **Torpedoes:** 10 x 50.04cm (19.7in) **Guns:** 1 x 88mm (3.46in) forward deck gun **Ammo:** 160 rounds of 88mm **Mines:** None **Diving:** Max-op-depth 50m (164ft) and 30 seconds to crash-dive **Complement:** 3 officers and 31 ratings

UB 56 was formally assigned to the Flandern I.U-Flottille on 10 December 1917 with Oblt.z.S. Hans Valentiner the commander from 19 July 1917. Valentiner was born on 17 June 1888 and was a long-serving Flanders officer, having previously commanded UB 16 in 1915. He made four patrols with UB 56 and was lost on the last one:

(1) Valentiner left the shipyard at Bremen with UB 56 on 2 September 1917 and transferred her to the Flanders base, where they arrived on 10 September.

(2) On 4 October 1917, UB 56 departed Flanders for an uneventful patrol in the English Channel, then returned to Zeebrugge on 31 October 1917.

(3) Leaving Flanders on 10 November 1917 UB 56 sailed into the English Channel for operations against Allied shipping and Valentiner sank four steamships: on 13 November the *Atlas* (The Shipping Controller, London) was struck by a torpedo just abaft the bridge at 02.05, while en-route from Warkworth in Northumberland for Rouen with coal. The crew of twenty abandoned ship in the boats and watched the vessel sink at 02.15 and then a patrol boat took them to Newhaven.

Also on 13 November, the SS *Axwell* (Broomhill Collieries Ltd, West Hartlepool (Newcastle)) was voyaging from Warkworth to Rouen with coal when she collided with a U-boat (UB 56) at 04.55, which was seen to move off. The steamer tried to attract attention by circling around, in order to bring a patrol boat to the area, but at 05.15 her portside amidships erupted in a massive explosion, which killed twenty-six-year-old James William Scott, the second engineer, and Fireman John Lambros. The surviving crew of eighteen abandoned ship in the boats and a patrol boat landed them at Portsmouth. The *Axwell* was taken in tow, but foundered with the confidential papers.

The Spanish SS *Lalen Mendi* (Cia. Naviera Sota y Aznar, Bilbao), which was lost on 17 November, believed with all hands, while transporting 3,110 tons of coal from Middlesbrough to Bilbao and Barcelona.

The French steamer *Maine* (Chemins de Fer de l'État Français, Dieppe) was torpedoed on 21 November and was lost with all hands, en-route from Newhaven with coal.

A torpedo fired from UB 56 also damaged the SS *David Lloyd George* (Williams & Mordey Ltd, Cardiff), which was bound from Havre to New York with rabbit skins, flints and dyestuff. The ship was beached at Dartmouth Harbour and re-floated after repairs. UB 56 arrived back at Flanders harbour on 26 November.

FINAL VOYAGE

(4) On 18 December 1917, Valentiner left Flanders with orders to sink Allied ships in the English Channel (unfortunately for him, he commanded the first U-boat to be lost in the Folkestone–Gris Nez minefield. 'Lala' Lafrenz had been duped into revealing the U-boat evasion tactics and the Admiralty had put the intelligence to very good use). UB 56 was still outward bound on the night of 19/20 December 1917 and Valentiner's intention was to cross the defences under the cover of darkness. However, light provided by a multitude of searchlights, forced the skipper to dive between the Le Colbart Ridge and Cap Gris Nez.

The 335-ton 'C' Class destroyer HMS *Gipsy* observed a powerful explosion in the Folkestone–Gris Nez deep-mine barrage soon afterwards. Shouts were then heard coming from the water (it will be recalled that *Gipsy* had played a major role in the destruction of U 48 in the previous month). At least two people were seen struggling in the sea, but by the time *Gipsy* arrived at the scene, only one man was still afloat. He was taken on board the ship, but was found to be unconscious and died a short time later. His clothes identified him as Machinistmaat Max Bleek, a crewman of UB 56 (another source claims that, before he died, Max Bleek was able to confirm the identity of the submarine as UB 56). Log of *Gipsy* 19 December 1918 – Lt-Cdr F. Robinson RNR:

Dec 19 1917
1142 Heard very heavy explosion on port bow
12.10 Voices heard in water in vicinity of explosion
12.12 Saw men in water
12.15 Lowered dinghy and proceeded to rescue. One survivor taken in
01.15 Prisoner Bleeker expired. Buried at sea

All of the thirty-seven crew, including Oblt.z.S. Hans Valentiner, perished when UB 56 was lost.

When Cdr Guybon C. C. Damant's 'U-boat Flying Squad' divers went to examine the wreck of UB 56 on 12 August 1918, they identified it as being the one close to the scene of the mine explosion. They found the U-boat's hull had a significant amount of sand inside it and the stern section was also very badly damaged.

The total of U-boats lost to this 'new' illuminated Folkestone–Gris Nez minefield rose to more than ten in the months to follow, among which, were: UB 56, UB 31, UB 33, UB 38, UB 55, UB 58, UB 78 and UB 109.
ADM 53/42739 – NARA: T-1022, Roll 68, PG61816

THE MEN WHO DIED IN UB 56

Andrae, Oblt.z.S.
Binz, F.T.
Birkhan, Masch.

Bleeck, Masch.Mt
Born, Hzr
Brackhahn, Ob.Mts.
Bretschneider, Hzr
Dirschauer, Mts.
Dross, Ob.Hzr
Groote, Hzr
Gross, Ob.Btn.Mt
Gumser, Btn.Mt
Hartmann, Masch.Anw
Kleinstäuber, Ob.Hzr
Kolp, Stm. der Reserve
Kwistkowsky, Mts.
Laeh, Mts.
Lathe, Ob.Masch.Anw
Lehner, Hzr
Mainz, Masch.Mt der Reserve
Mergler, Ob.Mts.
Mühlmann, F.T.Obergast
Müller, Georg, Masch.Mt
Müller, Otto, Masch.Mt
Praschma, Ob.Masch.Mt der Reserve
Pypetz, Mts.
Rosell, Hzr
Schnabel, Ob.Hzr
Schneider, Ob.Masch.Mt
Schönbeck, Hzr
Steinbrecht, Mn.Ing.
Stemp, Hzr
Tischler, Ob.Mts.
Valentiner, Hans, Oblt.z.S.
Wilde, Btn.Mt der Reserve
Wrangowski, Mts.
Zimmermann, Btn.

The following is a list of vessels damaged and sunk by UB 56:

AREA	VESSEL'S NAME	FLAG	TONS	D	M	YEAR	LOCATION
English Channel	Atlas	GBR	989	13	11	1917	5 miles SE of Owers Light Vessel
English Channel	Axwell	GBR	1442	13	11	1917	3 miles WSW of Owers Light Vessel
English Channel	David Lloyd George	GBR	4764	17	11	1917	Damaged in position 50° 13' N, 03° 36'W
English Channel	Lalen Mendi	SPA	2183	17	11	1917	Approx. 5 miles SE of Beachy Head
English Channel	Maine	FRA	773	21	11	1917	30 miles off Newhaven

WRECK-SITE

The wreck lies on a seabed of shingle and silty sand, in a general depth of 28m (91.8ft), being the lowest astronomical depth. It is partially buried, reasonably intact, with the conning tower leaning over. The conning tower hatch is open, revealing the inside of the hull to be quite full of sand.

The stern section and both the propellers are missing and there is a large hole forward of the conning tower. One of the propellers is actually on display at Herne Bay Angling. The casing has a number of well-established soft corals growing on it. This wreck is also a war grave.

UC 64, SM IMPERIAL U-BOAT

DATE OF LOSS: 20 June 1918
DEPTH: 35m
REFERENCE: 50 58'.730 N, 001 23'.506 E
LOCATION: 8.70 nautical miles SSE of Dover
and 1¼ nautical miles ESE of the Varne Bank

Type: UCII coastal mine-laying boat *Builders:* A.G. Weser, Bremen for Kaiserliche Deutsche Marine *Ordered:* 12 January 1916, within the batch of UC 61–UC 64 *Keel laid:* as Yard No.262 on 3 April 1916 *Launched:* 23 January 1917 *Commissioned:* by Oberleutnant zur See Ernst Müller-Schwarz on 22 February 1917

TECHNICAL SPECIFICATIONS
Hull: Double *Surface displacement:* 422 tons *U/Dt:* 504 tons *LBDH:* 51.85m x 5.22m x 3.68m x 7.46m *Machinery:* 2 x 250ps MAN diesels *Props:* 2 bronze *S/Sp:* 11.9 knots *Op/R:* 8,000 nautical miles at 7 knots *Sub/R:* 55 nautical miles at 4 knots *U/Power:* 2 x 230ps electric motors giving 7.2 knots *Batteries:* Lead/acid/accumulators *Fuel/Cap:* 43 tons *Armament:* 2 external 50.04cm torpedo tubes at the bow, one either side of the mine chutes and 1 stern internal tube *Torpedoes:* 7 x 50.04cm (19.7in) maximum *Guns:* 1 x 88mm (3.46in) forward deck gun *Ammo:* 133 rounds of 88mm *Mine tubes:* 6 *Mines:* 18 x UC 200 *Diving:* Max-op-depth 50m (164ft) and 33 seconds to crash-dive *Complement:* 3 officers and 23 ratings

Torpedo load as designed: 4 – a torpedo in each tube plus a reload for the stern tube. Storing an additional torpedo in pieces internally for the stern tube later augmented this, although this was optional. Two extra torpedoes (total) for the external bow tubes could be carried as well – these were lashed to the deck. So up to a total of seven torpedoes were carried, although not all boats sailed with that many.

UC 64 was formally assigned to the Flandern/Flandern II.U-Flottille on 13 May 1917 with Oblt.z.S. Ernst Müller-Schwartz the CO from 22 February until 12 September 1917, during which time he sank six small vessels on five patrols:

(1) On 11 May 1917 UC 64 left Bremen and transferred to the Flanders base at Zeebrugge, arriving there on 13 May.

(2) On 18 May 1917, Müller-Schartz left Flanders and patrolled in the Hoofden with UC 64; one Dutch sailing vessel was sunk and another damaged before the boat returned to port on 24 May.

(3) UC 64 sailed from Flanders on 19 June 1917 to patrol in the Hoofden area again. Two sailing vessels were sunk and, on 24 June, the 306-ton Dutch coaster *Telegraaf XVIIINV* (Vrachtvaartondern. Telegraaf XVIII, Rotterdam) was captured, then shelled and sunk 36 miles off the Hook of Holland, at position 52° 18' N, 03° 10' E. She was bound from Rotterdam for London with general cargo. The U-boat returned to harbour on 25 June.

(4) Between 8 and 17 July 1917, UC 64 patrolled in the Hoofden again and one small Dutch motor vessel was destroyed.

Left: Bell from the *Ville de Valenciennes.*

Below: A Paravane. A device equipped with sharep teeth and towed alongside a ship to cut mooring cables of submerged mines.

(5) Leaving Flanders on 6 August 1917, UC 64 laid mines at the western end of the English Channel. A French trawler was lost when it detonated one of the mines on 17 August and the U-boat returned to port on 19 August. Oblt.z.S. Erich Hecht assumed command on 13 September 1917 and served until 22 February 1918. Hecht made the following five patrols with UC 64:

(6) On 15 September, UC 64 left Flanders and patrolled along the English east coast. Hecht sank the Dutch steam trawler *Eendracht VII* on 16 September. The following two French steamers sunk with torpedoes: the SS *Paraciers* (Soc. Anon. des Aciéries de Paris et d'Outreau, Boulogne), on passage from Newcastle for Boulogne with coal, was lost on 17 September. The SS *Ville de Valenciennes* (Cie. des Bateaux à Vapeur du Nord, Dunkerque) sank with all hands on 22 September, en-route from the Tyne to Bordeaux with coal (divers at Bridlington in Yorkshire recently identified the wreck of this ship). UB 64 arrived back at Zeebrugge on 24 September.

(7) Between 11 and 22 October 1917, Hecht patrolled the English Channel and the Cornish coast, where he laid mines and sank two steamships. The Norwegian *Altair* (Aktieselskapet Altair) foundered following a torpedo attack on 18 October, while en-route from Rouen for Cardiff in ballast. Later that day, the SS *Sten* (The Shipping Controller, London) was carrying 1,000 tons of coal from Barry to St Malo when a torpedo detonated level with the No.2 hatch on the starboard side at 14.10 and she sank almost at once. Only one boat got away with eight men in it, including the chief mate who took charge. However, they also managed to save an able seaman and the second mate; an attempt was made to save the master too, but without success. After thirty minutes, a patrol boat arrived and shelled the U-boat, which cleared off. The survivors were picked up at 15.30 and taken to St Ives. Nine men were lost.

THE MEN WHO DIED

Arthur, Robert Beckwith, 32, First Engineer
Brown, John, 26, Fireman
Daniels, Joseph, 46, Fireman
Dawson, Benjamin, Master
Dechares, M., 37, Donkeyman
Gill, George, 24, Sailor
Oaktree, Frederick, 22, Able Seaman
Owens, Evan, 19, Sailor
Wilhelmsson, Axel, 21, Sailor

On 16 November, the French boat *Jules Verne* also sank after detonating one of the mines.

(8) The English and Bristol Channel was the next patrol area, from 22 November to 5 December 1917. The French steamship *Ville de Thann* (Groupement Industriel de Charbons & de Transports) was sunk by torpedo, while in ballast and en-route from Havre to Newport, Monmouth. A torpedo dispatched by UC 64 damaged the SS *Manchester Mariner* (Manchester Liners Ltd, Manchester), voyaging from Leith with coal on 4 December. A mine laid by UC 64 on 16 October detonated under the No.1 hold of the SS *Volnay* (Volnay SS Co. Ltd, Glasgow) at 00.45 on 14 December, 2 miles off the Manacles Buoy. Tugs assisted the vessel towards Porthallow, but it sank offshore. The ship had been on passage from Montreal for Plymouth with an Admiralty cargo, including luxury goods, such as perfume and tinned meat, plus fruit, flour and other foodstuff. However, the lower part of the holds also held fixed ammunition.

(9) Hecht returned to patrol the English and Bristol Channel from 18–29 December 1917. The SS *Trevelyan* (Hain SS Co. Ltd, St Ives) was torpedoed and damaged on 19 December, while steaming in ballast from Rouen to Barry Roads. She was beached, but declared a constructive total loss. However, the wreck was sold and repaired and in 1919 put back into service as the *Esperia* by Soc. di Nav. Sicilia, Palermo. In 1921, Soc. Anon. di Nav. Orientale, Palermo owned her until 1924, when she was broken up at Genoa, in the second quarter.

Also on 19 December, the Norwegian SS *Borgsten* (Aktieselskapet Borgå, Christiania) was torpedoed and sunk while voyaging in ballast from Rouen to Newport, Monmouth.

The large Norwegian barque *Manicia* was damaged by gunfire on 23 December while en-route from Southampton to Delaware Breakwater. She was towed to St Mary's harbour, in the Scilly Isles. UC 64 arrived back in port on 29 December.

(10) Hecht's last patrol with the boat was in the English Channel, from 5–30 January 1918. Hecht sank two small boats and the mines that were laid damaged the steamship *Queen Margaret* (Dunlop SS Co. Ltd, Glasgow). The ship was sailing from Halifax, Nova Scotia, to Boulogne with general cargo and was towed to Southampton. UC 64 arrived at Zeebrugge on 30 January 1918.

Oblt.z.S. Ferdinand Schwartz then assumed command on 23 February 1918, while Hecht took over the command of UB 54 and was lost with the entire crew on her next patrol.

Ferdinand Schwartz made five patrols with UC 64:

(11) UC 64 left Zeebrugge on 7 March 1918 and patrolled the English east coast but no ships were sunk, and she returned to Flanders on 14 March.

(12) Schwartz left harbour with UC 64 on 24 March 1918 for operations off the English east coast. Four fishing boats were sunk and the requisitioned and armed steam coaster *Vianna* (The Admiralty, London) was torpedoed on the port side of No.2 hold by the submerged and unseen UC 64 at 09.20 on 31 March. The vessel sank in minutes, taking four of her crew down, including the mate. She was on passage from the Tyne for

Ipswich with 360 tons of coal. The surviving crew of eleven were rescued by a patrol boat after fifteen minutes and taken to the river Tyne. The men who died were:

Brackenbury, Walter, 51, First Mate
Dunton, Herbert George, 36, Able Seaman
Howell, Joseph James, 49, Donkeyman
Rusher, Charles Bonnes, 42, Able Seaman

UC 64 arrived back at Zeebrugge on 3 April 1918.

(13) On 18 April 1918, UC 64 returned to the English east coast for mine-laying operations and sank three steamships: the SS *Laurium* (Thordis Shipping Co. Ltd, London) sank on 23 April after striking a mine laid on 21 April; she was carrying coal from Hull to Rouen, and one man was drowned. Off Bridlington, the Swedish SS *Sota* (Angfartygs Aktiebolaget 'Thule', Göteborg) was torpedoed on 25 April; she was quickly taken in tow, but all efforts made to beach her were in vain when she filled up and sank in shallow water near Barmston. Her crew were taken off before the vessel went down and most of the cargo was successfully salvaged. Unfortunately, however, a twenty-six-year-old stoker, Gustaf Adolf Jansson, was killed by the explosion. The *Sota* (Captain S.B. Thorbjornsson) was voyaging from Göteborg, Sweden, to London with an unspecified general cargo, which included wood, paper and iron and a crew of eighteen, including two women.

On 26 April 1918, the *Llwyngwair* was torpedoed and sunk while in ballast and on passage from Dunkerque for Newcastle-upon-Tyne. The missile detonated amidships at 00.10 and killed eight of her crew of eighteen. The SS *Abbas* had already sighted the U-boat on the surface and shelled it, forcing the boat to submerge, but it came too late to save the *Llwyngwair*, which went down to the bottom soon after the engagement. The *Abbas* picked up the remaining ten survivors and landed them at Sunderland.

FIVE OF THE MEN WHO DIED
Bergstrom, Otto, 23, Boatswain (Bosun)
Harris, John George Edward, 26, Second Engineer
Shepherd, William John, 38, Steward
Whorlow, Alfred John, 28, Second Mate
Williams, Joseph Alexded, 34, First Engineer

UC 64 returned to port on 29 April.

(14) UC 64 sailed out from Zeebrugge on 16 May and patrolled the English and Bristol Channels where Schwatz sank his last vessel off Trevose Head on 23 May. The Norwegian SS *Meffold* (Dampskipsselskapet Aktieselskapet Bois, Skien) was hit with a torpedo at 01.00 and sank soon after, while en-route from Newport, Monmouth, to Rouen, with coal. The master and seven crewmen left in a boat and landed at Newquay, while the rest came ashore at Mother Ivey's Bay. The U-boat arrived back in Flanders on 31 May 1918.

FINAL VOYAGE
(15) On her last patrol with Ferdinand Schwartz, UC 64 left Zeebrugge at 21.20 for the coast Bordeaux-Gironde area of Brittany on 18 June 1918. Soon after she sailed, U-boat Command radioed and asked Schwartz if he was in possession of the Channel conditions report of UB 80. After that, nothing more was ever heard of the boat. UB 64 appeared to have detonated a mine in the Dover Strait between Colbart and the Varne on 20 June 1918.

Badly damaged, the U-boat seemed to have survived and was still moving. However, the Royal Navy's veteran anti-submarine drifter, *Ocean Roamer*, which was on watch duty at the barrage between Buoys Nos 15 and 16, reported the explosion at 04.15 and witnessed a shadowy submerged object moving north-eastwards, with streams of oil and air rising to the surface. Another drifter *Loyal Friend*, then joined in the hunt and they depth-charged the U-boat, probably finishing her off in the process because, for seven hours, more oil and air rose to the surface. Lost with UC 64 was the entire crew of thirty, including commander Oblt.z.S. Ferdinand Schwartz.

After completing their work on UC 11, Cdr Guybon Chesney Castell Damant's 'U-boat Flying Squad' left Harwich and arrived at Dover on 3 July. Diving on the wreck began two days later and revealed a minelayer complete with a full cargo of un-discharged mines in all six chutes. Unarmed torpedoes were secured close to the two deck tubes. Damant also reported finding a '22-pounder' gun forward of the conning tower. The hull had been camouflaged and Damant noted that the bottom coating of paint appeared 'brand-new and a glossy black colour, or dark red'. He described how the hatch at the conning tower was partially raised, but unyielding; although on reflection the closed hatches fore and aft could possibly be opened. He believed that the boat was too dangerous to search for any documents, in view of instability of the mine cargo, combined with the danger posed by a British mine, gently lolling along on the seabed nearby. Damant went on to describe how the bottom of the U-boat between the conning tower and the mine-chambers was crushed-in up to 10ft, leaving the fore-ends packed solid with detritus from the accumulator. Within this grim assortment of twisted metal and debris lay crushed, decomposing bodies, still in their hammocks. The floor of the control room was so driven upwards by the mine explosion that entry to the radio room was impossible. Cdr Damant said it would have taken weeks of dangerous hand-clearance to remove the blocking debris. Explosives offered the only solution. Conditions within the boat beggared description and, not surprisingly, the Salvage Department vetoed this idea because of the extreme dangers involved. There was a delay in opening the conning tower hatch, because of inclement weather conditions, but on 16 July, Damant used small explosive charges to blow off the hatch and enlarge the passage into the control room. On 1 August, the divers uncovered some personal articles, which were despatched to Naval Intelligence for identification purposes. Finally, a wallet found in the pocket of a corpse identified the boat as UC 64.

NARA: T-1022, Roll 108. PG61985

THE MEN WHO DIED IN UC 64

Andres, Ob.Masch.Mt
Andrzejak, Hzr
Bathe, Masch.Mt
Günther, F.T.Ober Gast
Hannemann, Ob.Hzr
Hasse, Masch.Mt
Hirsch, Masch.Mt
Hitschfeld, Masch.Anw
Holzner, Mts.
Hormes, F.T.
Jander, Mts. der Reserve
Klein, Ob.Masch.Mt
Liebelt, Mts.
Lässler, Mn.Ob.Ing.Asp
Minkus, Hzr

Müller, Ob.Mts.
Pfenningstorf, Ob.Hzr
Rebehn, Masch.Mt
Richardt, Masch.Mt
Schillow, Mts.
Schneider, Mts.
Schreiber, Ob.Mts.
Schubert, Ob.Hzr
Schwartz, Oblt.z.S.
Seeger, Lt.z.S. der Reserve
Simon, Ob.Mt
Sörensen, Mts.
Valk, Hzr
Witt, Mts.
Ziegenfuss, Masch.Mt

Between them, the three commanders of UC 64 sank twenty-seven vessels, totalling 25,038 tons.

The following is a list of the known vessels believed sunk or damaged by UC 64:

AREA	VESSEL'S NAME	FLAG	TONS	D	M	YEAR	LOCATION
E/Channel	Telegraaf XVIIIN.V	NLD	306	24	6	1917	36 miles WSW Hook of Holland
North Sea	Voorwaarts (sailing-vessel)	NLD	114	20	5	1917	Damaged near Terschelling
North Sea	Alberdina (sailing-vessel)	NLD	100	23	5	1917	25 miles NW of Maas Light Vessel
North Sea	Hendrika (sailing-vessel)	NLD	109	21	6	1917	Sunk off Callentsvog
North Sea	Telegraaf XVIII (sailing-vessel)	NLD	306	24	6	1917	26 miles W of the Hook of Holland
North Sea	Timor (motor-vessel)	NLD	135	16	7	1917	Sunk off Noord Hinder Light Vessel
E/Channel	Esperance (trawler)	FRA	130	17	8	1917	Mined off Dieppe
North Sea	Eendracht VII (fishing vessel)	NLD	251	16	9	1917	8 miles off Yonuiden
North Sea	Paraciers	FRA	2542	17	9	1917	8 miles E of Spurn Head
North Sea	Ville de Valenciennes	FRA	1910	22	9	1917	About 5 miles SSE of Flamborough Head.
Irish Sea	Altair	NOR	1674	18	10	1917	8 miles NE ¾ N of Newquay
E/Channel	Sten	GBR	928	18	10	1917	5 miles N of the Godrevy Lighthouse
E/Channel	Jules Verne (sailing-vessel)	FRA	157	16	11	1917	Mined off Dieppe
E/Channel	Ville de Thann	FRA	1416	27	11	1917	Sunk off Falmouth
E/Channel	Manchester Mariner	GBR	4106	4	12	1917	Damaged 7–8 miles E of Manacles
E/Channel	Volnay	GBR	4610	14	12	1917	Mined 2 miles E by S of Manacles Rocks
E/Channel	Trevelyan	GBR	3066	19	12	1917	Damaged 20 miles N of Cap Barfleur
E/Channel	Borgsten	NOR	1718	19	12	1917	30 miles S ½ W of Barfleur
E/Channel	Manicia (barque)	NOR	1868	23	12	1917	Damaged 7–10 miles S of Scilly Isles
E/Channel	Queen Margaret	GBR	4972	20	1	1918	Mined. & damaged 1 mile E of the Nab L/v
E/Channel	May (trawler)	GBR	24	26	1	1918	18 miles ESW of Berry Head

E/Channel	Rob Roy (sailing-vessel)	GBR	112	26	1	1918	20 miles SW of St Catherine's Point
North Sea	Botha (fishing-vessel)	GBR	17	28	3	1918	3 miles E of Whitby
North Sea	Honora (fishing-vessel)	GBR	29	28	3	1918	6 miles ENE of Whitby
North Sea	Brotherly Love (fish-vessel)	GBR	19	28	3	1918	6 miles NE by E of Whitby
North Sea	Noel (fishing-vessel)	GBR	21	28	3	1918	6 miles NE by E of Whitby
North Sea	Vianna	GBR	401	31	3	1918	4 miles E of Seaham Harbour
North Sea	Laurium	GBR	582	23	4	1918	Mined 15 miles E of Skegness
North Sea	Sote	SWE	1379	25	4	1918	3½ miles S of Bridlington Harbour
North Sea	Llwyngwair	GBR	1304	26	4	1918	5 miles SSE of Seaham Harbour
E/Channel	Meffold	NOR	720	23	5	1918	7 miles WSW of Trevose Head

WRECK-SITE

The wreck lies on a seabed of sand, shell, loose sediment and shingle, in a general depth of 35m (114.8ft), being the lowest astronomical depth. The bottom of the wreck is partially buried and the conning tower lies to one side. Much of the hull casing is very badly damaged, especially the midships and fore-ends, but the stern is reasonably intact. Tidal streams are quite severe. This wreck-site is, of course, a war grave.

CHAPTER FIVE

SILENT WARRIORS

Friends are good on the day of battle.
(Translation of wording on Cannock Chase German Cemetery Memorial)

Over 150 submarine wrecks lie in British coastal waters and divers now visit some of these vessels on a regular basis. Depths previously unachievable with compressed air have now become the norm, with technical divers using mixed-gas and re-breather technology. Deep diving has also brought a wealth of 'new' shipwrecks into the fold, including those of long-lost submarines, many dating back to the First World War. It is now widely accepted by maritime historians of the calibre of Dr Axel Niestlé and Michael Lowrey that responsible divers can make an immense contribution to our knowledge of the fates of these submarines and their crews. Divers alone can provide that last tantalising piece of the jigsaw, the description of the wreck. Not only can the diver work with maritime experts to identify the submarine, he can also help bring peace of mind and solace to relatives, as moving cases in this book demonstrate. Many more submarine wrecks await discovery. However, divers should be warned that entering the very confined space within a submarine, even supposing it is not a war grave, would be a very foolhardy and dangerous thing to do and, secondly, except during times of conflict, divers have no reason whatsoever to enter the wreck of a submarine, even for the purpose of identification. Many of these wrecks are war graves. They are sacred ground and that demands respect. Submariners crewed these boats and in all too many cases, submariners crew them still.

In the early 1990s the U-boat Comrades Association unveiled a stone in the Memorial Garden behind the celebrated U-boot Archive in Altenbruch, near Cuxhaven. The stone reads simply: 'DEN TOTEN DER MEERE'.

In 1993 the Merseyside Branch of the Submarine Old Comrades Association reciprocated by erecting another memorial in the Altenbruch Garden, this time in English: 'MEN WHO SERVED THE SEA WERE NOT ENEMIES BUT OPPONENTS'.

Submariners like having the last word. Two Second World War submariners shall have it here. One happens to be German, the other British, but their sentiments transcend both nationality and milieu:

They were all good lads brimming with life and fun. Rolling around that hostile sea, how we would anticipate our next run ashore. The next one was always going to be the best yet. Were we scared? You bet we were. You see you have to have been there to know what it was like. I was proud to be a submariner and I always will be. I missed the last trip through illness. The boat just disappeared. Another statistic. Yes they were a fine bunch! The faces come flooding back to me, sometimes with names, more often these days, without. But after sixty years I still think about those boys every day.

Above: Depth charge exploding. (Author's collection)

Left: Passing Type 11B at sea.

I look back on my days in boats with a mixture of affection and abject terror. I think often of my mates who were like brothers to me. I remember my friends in training class, all killed except for me and one other. There can never come a time like the days we spent in boats nor the comradeship, fear and endurance we knew then. I think, perhaps, men are not like that now.

APPENDIX

TECHNICAL DETAILS OF THE VIIC AND VIIC/41 U-BOATS

DIMENSIONS

The VIIC boat became the 'workhorse' submarine of the Kriegsmarine during the Second World War. The official tonnage of the original design as per 22 March 1941 was 761.89 tons on the surface and 864.69 tons submerged. However the figure may change to a very small degree with later modifications. Usually 769 tons and 871 tons, are given as the standard official figures throughout the war. Boats from different yards may also have varied to a certain degree due to small design variations. The overall general dimensions measured 67.1m in length overall, 6.22m in beam, 4.8m in draught and 9.60m in height around the conning tower.

MACHINERY

Two diesel/oil engines powered the two propellers, originally designed in bronze, but a shortage of non-ferrous metals led to the use of steel propellers during the war. Boats already ordered before the war were fitted either with engines manufactured by Maschinefabrik–Augsburg–Nürnberg (MAN) or by the Germaniawerft (GW). After the start of the war, other companies or yards manufactured these two diesels types under licence. Front line experience soon showed the more rigid GW construction, being superior and new constructions were gradually fitted with GW-type diesels only. Both types were fitted with *Gebläse* (super-chargers) and developed 1400ps each at 475 revolutions per minute continuous power, or 495 revolutions maximum power for thirty minutes developed 1600ps, which give a maximum surface speed of 17 knots. The boat had a calculated operational range of 9,700 nautical miles at 10 knots, or 6,500 nautical miles at 12 knots and carried a maximum fuel/oil capacity of 113 tons.

For running submerged, two 62-cell lead/acid batter/accumulators usually manufactured by Accumulatoren-Fabrik-Aktiengesellschaft (AFA) powered the two electric motors that developed 375ps at 295 revolutions and gave her a maximum speed of 7.6 knots. The four electric motors manufacturers were:

AEG (Allgemeine Elektricittäts-Gesellschaft)
BBC (Brown, Boveri & Cie.)
GL u. Co. (Garbe, Lohmeyer & Co.)
SSW (Siemens-Schuckert-Werke)

These companies all produced more or less very similar designed motors and sometimes under licence (GL). Using battery power the boat had a calculated operational range underwater of 80-n.miles at a steady 4-knots.

ARMAMENT

TORPEDOES

The VIIC boat was designed with five torpedo tubes, four at the bow and one at the stern.

Initially fourteen torpedoes were carried until summer 1943, with two of them in the upper-deck reserve containers. These were later then removed to save weight and because it became too dangerous to reload them in North Atlantic waters. In 1944 the number was reduced to ten to increase living conditions in the bow room when the boats stayed submerged for long times.

From autumn 1944 onward, on boats operating in the Atlantic, or British coastal waters, the ten torpedoes usually consisted of five T5 and five LuT, often stowed as follows:
T5 one in forward tube, three in forward bilges and one in aft tube. Five LuT stowed: three in forward tube, one in forward bilges and one in the aft bilges.

MINES

Mines were only carried on special order and in exchange for torpedoes – not in addition.

The figures for mines offered in reference books are theoretical numbers and have nothing to do with operational realities.

There were three different types of U-boat mines, which were called *Torpedominen* and these were delivered through the torpedo tubes:
TMA – moored floating mines, designed for, but never actually used on U-boats.
TMB – small ground mines with various fuses and an explosive charge of 1,276lb (578.7kg).
TMC – large ground mines with an explosive charge of 2,200lbs (997.9kg).
The exchange ratios of mines/torpedo were:
One torpedo – three TMB
One torpedo – two TMC

GUNS

Initially, the VIIC gun specifications consisted of: one 88mm (3.46in) deck gun, plus 220 rounds and one 20mm (0.79in) AA Flak gun, plus 4,380 rounds of ammunition. On Atlantic boats the deck gun was removed in summer 1943. The single gun bandstand aft of the bridge (model 0) was modified in early 1943, by adding a second, lower bandstand with another single 20mm gun (this was then called conning tower modification II). The Type I modification (two 13.2mm twin machinegun mounts on upper bandstand, single 20mm on lower bandstand) was abandoned when tests showed that the machine guns were not powerful enough. From May 1943, modification IV was introduced, showing at first two single 20mm mounts on the widened upper bandstand and a quadruple 20mm mount on the enlarged, lower bandstand. After 20mm twin mounts became available in July 1943, twin mounts replaced the single mounts. From October 1943 onward, the 37mm mount replaced the quadruple mounts. This represented the final variation of the Type IV conning tower modification. Later in the war 37mm twin mounts were tested experimentally on a few boats, but the snort had already reduced the threat from aircraft, by then. This was a summary of standard AA-modifications on Atlantic boats.

Other experimental modifications were carried on some boats, however, but they never became a standard form. Modifications were done to all front-line or working-up boats regardless of their date of commission and boats were continuously up-graded to the latest version, during yard layovers.

DIVING DEPTHS

The operational diving depth of a VIIC boat was 100m (328ft), with a maximum depth 165m (541.33ft) and a crush depth of 200m (656ft). A crash-dive to 20m took 30-seconds on average.

The VIIC/41 boat was almost the same in all respects as the VIIC, but was designed with a stronger pressure hull, which gave the boat an operational diving depth of 120m (394ft) and a crush depth of 250m (820ft).

COMPLEMENT

Both VIIC and VIIC/41 boats carried between 44 and 52 crewmen. With increased AA-armament in 1943/44, the crews reached the highest figures. Following the introduction of the Schnorchel the crews were often reduced to 46–50 crewmen.

Each Type VII U-boat carried thirty-six *unteroffiziere* and ratings, generally two *unteroffiziere* to every three ratings. Apart from the officers, the crew of a U-boat was divided between technical personnel and seamen. The technical division comprised of specialist personnel; diesel machinists, electricians, radio operators and torpedo mechanics. There were four senior NCOs.

SOURCES OF INFORMATION

SOURCES OF GENERAL INFORMATION AND OFFICIAL HISTORIES:

A Precarious Existence, R. Mackay, Periscope Publishing
Allied Submarine Attacks of World War Two, J. Rowher, Greenhill Books
Amazing Adventure, E. Keble Chatterton, Hurst & Blackett
Axis Successes of World War Two, Jürgen Rohwer, Greenhill Books
Beating the U-boats, E. Keble Chatterton, Hurst & Blackett
Beneath the Waves, A.S. Evans, William Kimber
Blue Guide to Scotland
Britain's Maritime Memorials and Mementoes, D. Saunders, Patrick Stephens
British and Commonwealth Merchant Ship Losses to Axis Submarines 1939–1945, Alan J. Tennent, Sutton Publishing
British Merchant Ships sunk by U-Boats in the 1914–1918 War, A.J. Tennent, Starling Press
British Submarines of WWI, Paul Kemp
By Guess and by God, W. Carr, Hutchinson
Convoy, J. Winton, Hutchinson
Damned Un-English Machines, Jack Hool & Keith Nutter, Tempus Publishing
Der Krieg sur Zee: Der Handelskrieg mit U-booten, Konteradmiral Arno Spindler, 5 Volumes, Mittler & Son
Dictionary of Disasters at Sea During the Age of Steam, Charles Hocking FLA, Lloyd's Register of Shipping
Die Deutschen Kriegsschiffe, Erich Groner, 2 Volumes, Lehmanns Verlag
Dive Kent, Dive Sussex, Dive Hampshire & the Isle of Wight, Dive South Devon, – all by Kendall McDonald, Underwater World Publications
Encyclopaedia of British Submarines, Paul Akermann, Periscope Publishing
Endless Story, 'Taffrail', Hodder & Stoughton
Far Distant Ships, J. Schull
Few Survived, E. Gray
Fighting the U-boats, E. Keble Chatterton, Hurst & Blackett
Find and Destroy, Dwight R. Messimer, Naval Institute Press
FIPS – Legendary U-boat Commander, G. Brooks, Leo Cooper
German U-Boat Commanders of World War II, Rainer Busch & Hans-Joachim Röll, Greenhill Books, Naval Institute Press
German U-Boat losses during World War II, Dr Axel Niestlé, Greenhill Books
History of the Great War: Naval Operations Corbett and Newbolt, 5 Volumes, Longmans
Hitler's U-boat War – the Hunted, Clay Blair, Weidenfield and Nicholson

Hitlers U-Boat War – the Hunters, Clay Blair, Weidenfield and Nicholson
HM U-Boat, J. Drummond, Wyndham
HMS Dolphin, Keith Hall, Tempus Publishing
Hull Down, Sir Bertram Hayes, Cassell
Jane's Fighting Ships of World War I, Jane's Publishing
Jane's Fighting Ships of World War II, Jane's Publishing
Liverpool and the Battle of the Atlantic 1939–45, Paul Kemp, Maritime Books
Lloyd's War Losses, The First World War, Lloyd's of London
Lloyd's War Losses, The Second World War, 2 Volumes, Lloyd's of London
Lost Patrols, Innes McCartney, Periscope Publishing
Memoirs of a Swedish Seafaring Family, Eva Ternström-Lidbetter-Sessions, Ebor Press
Mines, Minelayers and Minelaying, Capt. J.S. Cowie, OUP, 1949
Mit dem Einhorn Gegen Engelland, Franz J. Fröwls
Neither Sharks nor Wolves, T. Mulligan, Naval Institute Press
One Man Band, B. Bryant
Q Ships and their Story, E. Keble Chatterton, Conway Press
Records of Armstrong Whitworth, Tyne Wear Archive
Records of Messrs Cammell Laird, Birkenhead
Records of Messrs Vickers, Barrow
Royal Dockyards, P Macdougall, Shire
Royal Navy Trawlers Part 1, Gerald Toghill, Maritime Books
Shipwreck Index of the British Isles, 5 Volumes, Richard & Bridget Larn, Lloyd's Register
    Shipbuilders of Hull & Beverley 1883–1963, Cook, Welton & Gemmell, Hutton Press
Shipwrecks of North East Norfolk, Stephen Holt, Ayer Tikus
Shipwrecks of North Norfolk, Stephen Holt, Ayer Tikus
Shipwrecks of the East Coast, 2 Volumes, Ron Young, Tempus Publishing
Shipwrecks of the Forth, Robert Baird, Nekton
Shipwrecks of the Isle of Man, Adrian Corkhill, Tempus Publishing
Shipwrecks of the North East Coast (2 Volumes), Ron Young, Tempus Publishing
Shipwrecks of the North of Scotland, Robert Baird, Birlinn
Shipwrecks of the West of Scotland, Robert Baird, Nekton
Shore Establishments of the Royal Navy, Lt. Cdr. Warlow, Maritime Books
Staff History; Submarine Operations: Home Waters
Submarines, War Beneath the Waves, Robert Hutchinson, Janes
Subsunk, W. Shelford, Harrap
Swept Channels, 'Taffrail,' Hodder & Stoughton
The 'K' Boats, D. Everitt, Airlife Publishing
The Admiralty Regrets, Warren and Benson
The Auxiliary Patrol, E. Keble Chatterton, Lauriat & Co.
The Battle of the East Coast, J.P. Foynes
The Clyde Submarine Base, Keith Hall, Tempus Publishing
The Codebreakers of Room 40, Admiral Sir William James
The Dover Patrol, 2 Volumes, Admiral Sir R. Bacon, Hutchinson
The German Submarine War 1914–1918, R. Gibson and M. Prendergast, Periscope Publishing
The Illustrated Guide to Britain, Automobile Association
The Isle of May, J. Allen
The Log of a U-boat Commander Ernst Hashagen, Putnam
The Saint & the Sparrow, Richard W. Skinner, Historic Military Press
The Shipbuilder
The Sinking of U 309, Richard W. Skinner, Historic Military Press
The Tin Openers, Kendall McDonald, Historic Military Press

The U-BOAT – Evolution and Technical History, Eberhard Rössler, Cassell & Co.

The U-boat Commanders Handbook, Thomas reprint

The U-Boat Offensive 1914–1945, V.E. Tarrant, Arms & Armour

The U-Boat War in the Atlantic, G. Hessler

The World's Merchant Fleets 1939, Rodger Jordan, Naval Institute Press

Thetis, Secrets and Scandal, D. Roberts, Avid

This Dangerous Menace, A. Jeffrey, Mainstream

This Present Emergency, A. Jeffrey, Mainstream

This Time of Crisis, A. Jeffrey, Mainstream

Type VII U-boats, R. Stern, Naval Institute Press

U 995 -Das Boot von Laboe, E. Wetzel, Motorbuch Verlag

U-297, Richard W. Skinner, Historic Military Press

U-Boat bases and Bunkers, G. Williamson, Osprey

U-boat Crews 1914–45, G. Williamson, Osprey

U-boats of the Kaiser's Navy, G. Williamson, Osprey

U-Boat Fact File, Peter Sharpe, Midland Publishing

U-boat Hunters, R. Grant, Periscope Publishing

U-boat Intelligence, R. Grant, Periscope Publishing

U-Boat Operations of the Second World War, 2-Volumes, Kenneth Wynn, Chatham Publishing

U-boats Destroyed, R. Grant, Periscope Publishing

U-BOATS, The Illustrated History of the Raiders of the Deep, David Miller, Pegasus Publishing

Verschollen, Dwight R. Messimer, Naval Institute Press

Watchdogs of the Deep, Jones

We Dive at Dawn, Lt. Cdr. K. Edwards, Rich & Cowan

The Paravane Adventure, Cornford

WEBSITES USED:

http://www.ubootwaffe.net

http://www.warsailors.com

http://www.uboat.net

http://www.yorkshire-divers.co.uk/forums/

http://www.diverforum.co.uk

http://members.iinet.net.au/~eadej/homepage.html

http://www.multimap.com/index/NO1.htm

http://users.hunterlink.net.au/~maampo/militaer/glenn/marine/kaiserliche_marine_1914.htm

http://www.u-boot-net.de/

http://www.british-merchant-navy.co.uk/U-BOATS.htm

http://www.britsub.net/

http://web.ukonline.co.uk/chalcraft/sm/page6.html

http://www.dropbears.com/w/ww1subs/index.htm

http://www.usmm.org/ww1merchant.html

http://users.pandora.be/tree/wreck/wrecksite/wrecksite.html

http://www.gwpda.org/naval/sml00003.htm

http://www.dropbears.com/w/ww1subs/jclass.htm

http://www.rnsubmus.co.uk/losses.htm

http://www.cwgc.org/

http://www.gwpda.org/naval/n0000000.htm

http://www.royal-naval-reserve.co.uk/

http://www.cronab.demon.co.uk/wss.htm

http://www.harry-tates.org.uk/

http://www.world-war.co.uk/index.php3
http://www.hazegray.org/
http://www.feldgrau.com/
http://www.combinedfleet.com/ss.htm
http://www.usmm.org/ww1merchant.html
http://www.voy.com/65298/
http://www.irishwrecksonline.net/
http://www.numa.net/expeditions/north_sea_and_english_channel_hunt.html
http://ubootwaffe.net/quadrant.cgi
http://www.periscopepublishing.com/images/Deadlight%20gallery%20pages/
    OD%20exhibition.
http://tmg110.tripod.com/3reich1.htm
http://www.deutsche-marinesoldaten.de/lebenslaeufe/liste-ritterkreuztraeger-t-z.htm
http://www.deepimage.co.uk/wrecks/vandal/vandal_pages/vandal-mainpage.htm
http://www.ukdiving.co.uk/
http://www.2worldwar2.com/knights-cross.htm
www.ronyoung.co.uk
www.ubootkameradschaft-kiel.org
www.uboat-memorial.org

INDEX

The Battle of the Atlantic

MARC MILNER

'Makes a powerful case, and is likely to keep historians arguing for many years
to come' THE INDEPENDENT

'A masterly survey of one of the longest and most complex struggles of World War Two...
well illustrated and written, which never forsakes the personal stories of the conflict in its
grander sweep' MILITARY ILLUSTRATED

World War Two was only a few hours old when the Battle of the Atlantic, the longest
campaign of the conflict and the most complex submarine war in history, began with the
sinking of the unarmed passenger liner Athenia by the German submarine U30.
Based on mastery of the latest research and written from a mid-Atlantic rather than the
traditional Anglo-centric perspective, Marc Milner's history focuses on the confrontation
between opposing forces and the attacks on Allied shipping that lay at the heart of the
six-year struggle. Against the backdrop of the battle for the Atlantic lifeline, he charts the
fascinating development of U-boats and the techniques used by the Allies to suppress and
destroy these 'stealth' weapons.

0 7524 3332 6

RMS Lusitania – The Ship and her Record

ERIC SAUDER

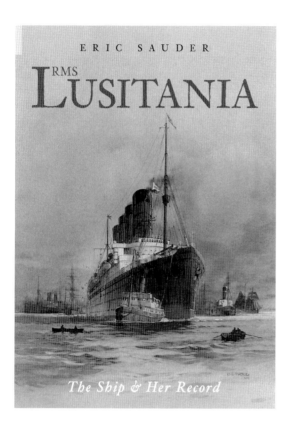

RMS *Lusitania* sank in May 1915 as the result of a torpedo from the U-20. 1,198 people died that day, as she sank in less than twenty minutes off the coast of Ireland. Built in 1907, she had a successful career spanning nearly eight years before that fateful day. Famous for her sinking, she was the fastest ship in the world when built, and was the first of the superliners.

For the first time, Eric Sauder looks at her as a ship, and not just at her sinking. She was the first true 'Ship of State'; subsidised by the British Government, she had luxurious interiors, double-deck restaurants, glorious public rooms and sumptuous cabins. The cream of the world's high society travelled aboard her.

This illustrated history looks at Lusitania in her true context as the finest ship afloat for eight years. Eric Sauder is the foremost expert on the history of the Cunard Line's RMS *Lusitania*. He has dived on her wreck and was with Dr Robert Ballard on expeditions to the wreck sites of *Lusitania*, *Titanic* and *Britannic*.

0 7524 3417 9

Cammell Laird – Volume Two: The Naval Ships

IAN COLLARD

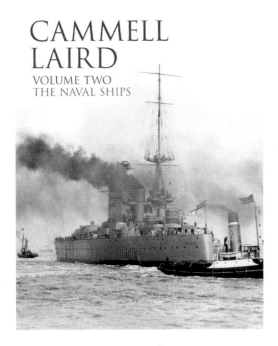

IAN COLLARD

CAMMELL
LAIRD
VOLUME TWO
THE NAVAL SHIPS

Since its founding as an engine manufacturer in the 1820s, Cammell Laird has had connections with both British and foreign navies. The Birkenhead shipbuilding yard has built many ships for the Royal Navy, including submarines, destroyers, dreadnoughts, aircraft carriers and cruisers.

Once an employer of thousands, the yard is now empty of the noise of welders, riveters, joiners, engineers and the myriad other skilled tradesmen needed to build a ship. But its history remains – one that reads like a roll of honour for the British Navy; *Ark Royal*, *Audacious*, *Birkenhead*, *Chester*, *Hardy*, *Hogue*, *Thetis*, to name a few.

Illustrated with many previously unpublished images, this will prove to be the definitive book on the most famous of the Cammell Laird-built navy vessels.

As well as British Navy ships, this book includes a varied selection of foreign naval vessels from the Confederate blockade runner *Alabama* to many ships and submarines built for navies around the world.

Ian Collard lives in the Wirral and has written many books on Mersey shipping. He is a regular contributor to *Ships Monthly* magazine.

0 7524 3874 3